changing approaches to the psychotherapies

changing approaches to the psychotherapies

Edited by

Henry H. Grayson, Ph.D.

and

Clemens Loew, Ph.D.

National Institute for the Psychotherapies, New York

S P Books Division of
SPECTRUM PUBLICATIONS, INC.
New York

Distributed by Halsted Press
A Division of John Wiley & Sons

New York   Toronto   London   Sydney

Copyright © 1978 Spectrum Publications, Inc.

SPECTRUM PUBLICATIONS, INC.
175-20 Wexford Terrace, Jamaica, N.Y. 11432

Library of Congress Cataloging in Publication Data

Main entry under title:

Changing approaches to the psychotherapies.

   Includes index.
   1. Psychotherapy. I. Grayson, Henry, 1935-
II. Loew, Clemens A., 1937-   [DNLM: 1. Psycho-
therapy. WM420 C456]
RC480.C46   616.8′914   77-24270
ISBN 0-89335-026-5

Distributed solely by the Halsted Press Division of John Wiley & Sons, Inc., New York, New York.   ISBN 0-470-99177-1

79-2637

Contributors

RICHARD G. ABELL, M.D., Ph.D.
Transactional Analysis Institute of New
   York and Connecticut
William Alanson White Psychoanalytic
   Institute
New York, New York

TERESA BERNADEZ-BONESATTI, M.D.
College of Human Medicine
Michigan State University
East Lansing, Michigan

RICHARD M. CARLTON, M.D.
Psychiatric Services
National Institute for the Psychotherapies
Counseling and Human Development
   Center
New York, New York

RUTH C. COHN, M.A.
National Psychological Association
Postgraduate Center for Mental Health
Workshop Institute for Living-Learning
New York, New York

HELEN E. DURKIN, Ph.D.
Postgraduate Center for Mental Health
New York, New York

NINA FIELDSTEEL, Ph.D.
Postgraduate Center for Mental Health
New York, New York

MARY ANN H. FURDA
American Psychological Association
New School for Social Research
New York, New York

JOSEF ERNEST GARAI, Ph.D., A.T.R.
Department of Art Therapy and
   Psychology
Pratt Institute
Brooklyn, New York

CARL GOLDBERG, Ph.D.
Department of Psychiatry
George Washington University Medical
   School
Silver Springs, Maryland

ROBERT L. GOULDING, M.D.
Western Institute for Group and Family
   Therapy
Watsonville, California

BARBARA K. HOGAN, Ph.D.
Sexual Treatment and Education Program
The New York Hospital - Cornell Univer-
   sity Medical Center
Payne Whitney Psychiatric Clinic
Human Sexuality Program
Department of Psychiatry
The Mount Sinai School of Medicine
New York, New York

MICHAEL KRIEGSFELD, Ph.D.
Gestalt Psychotherapy Associates, N.Y.C.
Residential Training Seminars
National Institute for the Psychotherapies
New York, New York

RICHARD LASKY, Ph.D.
Department of Clinical Psychology
City University of New York
Postgraduate Center for Mental Health
New York Center for Psychoanalytic
    Training
American Institute for Psychotherapy
    and Psychoanalysis
New York, New York

MAURY NEUHAUS, Ph.D.
National Institute for the Psychotherapies
Morton Prince Center for Hypnotherapy
International Graduate University
Westside Pediatric Group

ILANA RUBENFELD
N.Y.U. School of Continuing Education
Eastern Institute for Gestalt Therapy and
    Esalen
New York, New York

JOHN J. O'HEARNE, Ph.D.
Department of Psychiatry
University of Missouri School of Medicine
Kansas City, Missouri

IVAN WENTWORTH-ROHR, Ph.D.
Behavior Therapy - Biofeedback Service
St. Vincent's Hospital and Medical Center
Pace University
New York, New York

SHELDON D. ROSE, Ph.D.
University of Wisconsin
Madison, Wissonsin

STEVEN P. SCHINKE, Ph.D.
University of Washington
Seattle, Washington

Preface

For many years there were only a limited number of psychotherapeutic approaches which were widely used — psychoanalysis, behavior therapy and sometimes these combined with hypnosis. In the last two decades numerous schools of psychotherapy have emerged on the scene: client-centered therapy, gestalt therapy, bioenergetic analysis, transactional analysis, assertiveness training, just to mention some of the more prominent ones. In addition, there are a number of systems which serve as adjuncts to psychotherapy or are combined with other forms of psychotherapy: structural integration therapy (Rolfing), the Alexander technique, sensory or body awareness, art therapy, dance therapy, and biofeedback.

The advent of so many schools of psychotherapy has produced both chaos and a stimulus for innovative thinking for professionals and laymen alike. In addition, it has created a dilemma, not only for the practicing psychotherapists and their patients, but also for those who are training psychotherapists. Fewer people are adherents of the orthodoxy of two decades ago, though a small number do remain even today. Increasing numbers of professionals and lay persons are recognizing that different forms of therapy seem to be more effective for certain people and not for others. It is also becoming apparent that different combinations or sequences of psychotherapy are effective with different people at different times.

What are the implications then for the practitioners and the trainers of psychotherapists — not to mention the problems for the trainees? How does one keep abreast of all these new developments? Does one have to learn them all? Does it even fit one's personality to practice them all even if one should learn all the therapeutic approaches? What are the limitations if one does not know the various possible treatment approaches? And what are the limitations of one who does?

Perhaps the following analogy will shed some light on the issue:

Mr. G. goes to a physician with a complaint. Since the physician is a surgeon, he recommends an operation at the earliest possible date. Wanting to get a second opinion, having been warned to do so by *Moneysworth,* Mr. G. consulted with an internist. He prescribed massive doses of a "high powered" drug, saying that surgery certainly was not indicated. Wanting to get one further opinion, Mr. G. decided to consult with a naturopathic physician and nutritionist. This doctor advised that neither surgery nor strong medication was indicated. On the other hand, a change of diet and particular vitamins are his recommendations to restore Mr. G's health.

We wonder if the same is true in psychotherapy. The age of specialization brings with it liabilities as well as assets.

Perhaps one solution to the problem is to train psychotherapists in a variety of modalities from the beginning. In this way, the therapist does not become a gestaltist, a psychoanalyst or a behaviorist. He or she may become all of these and more. The clinician can then be one who has a wide armamentarium of therapeutic approaches available to him and can work, not only according to what best fits his personality, but also consider the therapy needs of his or her patients in a more comprehensive way.

The purpose of this volume is to bring together some of the recent creative changes in the field of psychotherapy. It includes new theoretical and technical developments within old systems as well as newer systems. In addition, one section deals with the integrative approach to therapy, where several modes may be used together, thereby comprising a new system in itself.

Since there is a growing awareness of the need for more efficient psychotherapeutic services, it is hoped that this volume will stimulate thinking and research in the field of psychotherapy.

Contents

AFFECTIVE AND EXISTENTIAL APPLICATION

BODY RELATED APPROACHES

INTEGRATIVE THERAPEUTIC APPROACHES

changing approaches to the psychotherapies

Theoretical and Technical Developments

There is a growing social and economic need to provide patients with optimal and efficient therapeutic services. Equally important is a scientific necessity for theoretical and technical organization to fulfill these clinical requirements. Part I encompasses a variety of conceptual and practical models developed to provide optimal methods for change. Regardless of whether the papers represent a new approach, modification of a traditional school, or focus on a particular methodology, they represent attempts to expand established paradigms and explore new directions.

Assertive Training

SHELDON ROSE and STEVEN SCHINKE

Carole B., 29 years old and divorced, meets with her therapist for the first time. She reports that she has recently experienced a series of interpersonal and career failures and often feels quite depressed. The therapist continues the interview:

Therapist: Could you tell me something about these recent failures you've been experiencing which led to your depression?

Ms. B.: I don't know where to begin. My whole life is falling apart. I can't do anything right . . . my job, men . . . everything has gone sour.

Therapist: Please go on. I'd like to know exactly what things have "gone sour," and when this all started to happen.

Ms. B.: I don't know. I guess everything has come down on me in the past couple of months. To be perfectly honest, life is pretty rotten. Just when I thought I had it made—everything was going to be great—bam! The bottom falls out. What's the use?

Therapist: I'm sorry. I guess I don't quite understand; what do you mean, "just when things were going to be great"?

Ms. B.: I mean my marriage. I mean getting out of it. You see, I had this rotten marriage. No, it wasn't rotten, It was terrible! And I got out of it—not without a lot of trouble—but I finally felt like I was out. Free. I thought, "Wow, I can start all over. Fresh. Do everything like I've always wanted." Well that lasted for about two weeks, maybe a month. Now I see that things haven't changed. My job is still a hassle. Men are still a problem. I'm still lonely, unhappy . . . and confused.

The therapist continues to press for details of the etiology and chronology of the patient's depression. A consistent pattern quickly emerges. The patient reports a lifelong struggle of trying to live up to high expectations set by significant people in her life. These people, specifically male friends and superiors at work, invariably make demands Ms. B. cannot possibly meet. Ms. B. then fails, by her own standards and by the evaluation of others, thus confirming her worthlessness. She gives a recent example of this pattern.

> *Therapist:* We seem to be narrowing your range of troublesome relationships to those with men and supervisors at work. Perhaps you could describe a recent incident in which you "failed" to meet someone's expectations.
> *Ms. B.:* Well, at my job, in addition to all my other responsibilities, I edit a personnel newsletter that comes out once monthly. You know, who gets transferred where, who's new, promotions, marriages, babies, anything. I hate it. Anyway, two months ago, my boss asked me if I could start laying out two issues a month if I were given the material. He said all of my other issues looked great and he knew I would do a fine job. Well, *I* knew I couldn't do two issues a month; even if I could, I didn't want to. It's a time-consuming, boring job. Well, I said, "Sure." Now I find I just can't do it. I'm working nights and weekends and I still can't put out two issues a month. Everyone is asking me about the stupid newsletter; they're giving me pages of material, and I'm swamped. Everything is coming out late and people are really starting to get mad at me—including my boss. If I don't get out of that newsletter, I'll have a nervous breakdown. I've got so much to do, but I can't seem to get anything done. I wish everyone would drop dead or the office would blow up, or something! I'm beginning to hate those people.

The ability to engage in clear, honest, and effective communication represents a necessary social skill for all members of our interactive and gregarious society. Deficits in these social skills can cause interpersonal difficulties and anxiety. Most of these difficulties and accompanying anxieties are viewed as routine attendants in a world full of surprises and stresses. Many people establish isolated and narrow interactive patterns in order to avoid such uncomfortable social interactive situations. Others learn to rely on friends, relatives, and co-workers to help them minimize unfamiliar social situations and unpleasant interactions. A growing number of people with social-skills deficits, however, are coming to the attention of the psychotherapeutic community.

Patients with inadequate or personally unsatisfying social skills rarely request therapy or counseling in this general area. In our experience, these persons present a range of complaints such as depression, social isolation, marital and sexual problems, heavy drinking, specific fears, or pervasive anxiety. Often, patients do not

complain of the inability to express themselves or engage in social interactive behaviors, but rather of the anxiety accompanying such behaviors. If the therapist
is able to identify a deficit of certain social skills and/or anxiety associated with the
performance of social skills, assertive training is probably in order. Another glimpse
at Ms. B. demonstrates one possible explanation of the assertive-training procedure.

> *Therapist:* From what you've been telling me, I gather that you are often able to
> predict, well in advance, that you cannot succeed at some tasks—at least in the
> time constraints you are given.
>
> *Ms. B.:* Right. I know if I can do something for someone and when it can be
> done. But I am only human. I can't do everything immediately.
>
> *Therapist:* Would it also be fair to say that you would not have to do some of
> these things if you declined them?
>
> *Ms. B.:* Sure. That's what everybody else does. They say, "I'm too busy," or
> "Are you crazy, I can't have that done in two days!"
>
> *Therapist:* How does this sound? I would like to help you learn to tell the people
> at your job, male friends, everyone you relate to, what you *really* feel. To tell
> them what you can and cannot do, what you *want* to do, and what you would
> like *them* to do. How about it?
>
> *Ms. B.:* I'll try, but it will take a miracle for me to do those things.

Assertive training refers to a therapeutic procedure aimed at increasing the
patient's ability to engage in socially appropriate and satisfying behaviors. The
goals of therapy usually include new social-skill acquisition and a reduction of
anxiety when certain interpersonal skills are performed. The assertive-training
procedure is primarily based on an assumption that maladaptive behaviors and
feelings will decrease as a result of an increase in adaptive and rewarding social
skills.

While a major criterion of assertive behavior is an individual patient's subjective
satisfaction with her/his social interactions, it is important to discriminate among
nonassertive, aggressive, and assertive behaviors. Alberti and Emmons (1) suggest
that a nonassertive response to a given stimulus situation often requires that individual actors deny themselves and are inhibited from expressing true feelings. The
nonassertive response may result in pain and anxiety, and seldom helps individuals
to achieve their own personal goals. At the other extreme, aggressive responses
usually accomplish the desired goals, but at other people's expense. Although
aggressive behavior is often immediately rewarding and expressive, it usually hurts
others and may ultimately result in negative consequences. Appropriately assertive
behavior, however, is self-enhancing and honest. Assertive responses usually achieve
individual goals and are accompanied by good feelings about self and others.

A second case example from our clinical practice may illustrate the nonassertive,
assertive, and aggressive continuum. In a recent group therapy session, a 23-year-
old male expressed frustration and anxiety over his interactions with a friend. It
seems that the friend frequently borrowed money from the patient, but was

habitually negligent in paying it back. The patient valued his friend, but often felt angry and hurt since he saw himself being "used." These feelings resulted in a depreciation of the patient's own self-worth and increased ruminations about his friend's cavalier behavior. The patient therefore found himself moving toward a confrontation with his friend where he would accuse the friend of being irresponsible and demand a return of the outstanding money. While the patient thought that he would probably be repaid the money using this aggressive approach, he also realistically feared that this aggression would result in termination of the friendship. Assertive training helped this patient to openly discuss the dilemma with his friend, appropriately ask for a return of the borrowed money, and maintain, if not enrich, the friendship.

BACKGROUND AND THEORETICAL FOUNDATIONS

The foundations of assertive training were developed long before the technique gained its present popularity. Salter's *Conditioned Reflex Therapy* (93), originally published in 1949, was the first work to give a rationale and set of procedures for the acquisition of assertive (Salter's term was *excitatory*) behaviors. In this early work, Salter outlines excitatory exercises and provides a number of case examples stressing the importance of assertive behaviors. Moreno (74, 75) and Kelly (55) are two theorists who also made early contributions to present-day assertive-training techniques. Moreno is the founder of psychodrama, the staged performance of the real-life attitudes and conflicts of participating patients. In contrast, Kelly's fixed-role therapy involves giving patients instructions to act out the behaviors of an individual who is free of the anxieties and behavioral deficits troubling the patient. The work of these three authors set the stage for more recent theorists.

The writings of Wolpe (110, 111, 112, 113) have probably had the greatest influence on assertive-training techniques as currently practiced. Wolpe's *Psychotherapy by Reciprocal Inhibition* (110), published on the heels of Dollard and Miller's (17) learning interpretation of psychodynamic theory and Skinner's (99) ultrabehavioristic *Science and Human Behavior,* closely tied together the theory of systematic desensitization and assertive training. Wolpe pioneered the concept of the situational specificity of assertive behavior, and was quite concerned with the interpersonal consequences (especially the negative consequences) of assertive acts.

Although both Wolpe and Salter provided excellent pioneer work in the area of assertive training, the empirical support for many of their specific assumptions has yet to be generated. The psychophysiological evidence that Wolpe (110, 111, 112, 118) presents for the phenomenon of anxiety reduction as a result of muscle relaxation does not totally support the notion of anxiety reduction as a result of assertive training. Salter's (93) therapeutically useful exercises are also based on a weak theoretical position. One of his major premises (that nonassertiveness reflects a conditioned state of psychological inhibition) is based on a small number of now outmoded Pavlovian conceptions. A second assumption of Salter's, the wide range of trait generalization, has not been supported by empirical investigations of the generalization of assertive training.

The dearth of satisfactory theoretical explanations for assertive-training results certainly does not detract from the burgeoning body of anecdotal and experimental literature supporting the effectiveness of this therapeutic procedure. The following literature review presents a representative sample of the myriad case reports and research studies currently available on assertive training.

SUPPORTING LITERATURE

Anecdotal Evidence

The efficacy of assertive-training procedures published as case histories begins with the reports of Salter and Wolpe, the two main theoreticians of this method. In *Conditioned Reflex Therapy* (93), Salter surveys 57 persons who employed his excitatory exercises. Without a great deal of documentation, Salter claims success with a variety of problems, including fear of the dark and public speaking, homosexuality, and alcoholism. Wolpe (110) describes an anxious salesman, a dependent woman, and a male stutterer who complained of emotional outbursts. All three were treated successfully with assertive training, with positive follow-up data reported for the second and third cases at two and one half years posttreatment.

Stevenson (101) reports on 21 patients treated with assertiveness training, 12 remaining much improved at a one-year follow-up. Stevenson and Wolpe (102) present detailed case histories on an assertive-training intervention with two homosexuals and one pedophile. All three patients reported that their deviant sexual behaviors had been replaced by heterosexual behaviors by the termination of therapy. Wolpe and Lazarus (113) delineate case histories of two males who were experiencing difficulty with their jobs. Assertive training resulted in self-reported improvement for both of these cases.

Cautela (8) relates the treatment of three cases of pervasive anxiety with assertive training as well as other modes of treatment. The author states that all three patients showed marked and lasting improvement after training. Rimm (86) describes the use of assertive-training procedures to terminate chronic crying in a hospitalized male. Lazarus and Serber (61) present two case histories in which assertive training was found to be effective after systematic desensitization had failed.

Hosford (47) describes the treatment of a sixth-grade girl fearful of classroom speaking. Success for the assertive-training procedure was partially based on a posttreatment incident in which the girl volunteered to give an oral classroom presentation. Varenhorst (105) reports on a similar case involving a junior high school student unable to participate in an art class prior to assertive training.

Additional case-history evidence for the effectiveness of assertive training is given by Edwards (20) treating a homosexual pedophilia; MacPherson (65) working with a woman experiencing relationship problems with her husband and mother; and Nydegger (76) treating hallucinatory and delusional responses. Patterson (78) successfully used assertive training in conjunction with time-out to reduce the crying and dependency behaviors of a nine-year-old child. Ross, Ross, and Evans (92) report the successful treatment of a six-year-old, socially withdrawn preschooler with similar assertive-training procedures. That explosive rage can be successfully modified by assertive training is indicated by Foy, Eisler, and Pinkston (30). They describe abatement of the rage response and improvement of prosocial behaviors in a 56-year-old patient. Frederikson, Jenkins, Foy, and Eisler (31) report similar beneficial results with two psychiatric inpatients who displayed abusive verbal outbursts prior to assertive training. Unobtrusive data gathered on the ward indicated a generalization of training to other socially appropriate responses.

Assertive Training with Homogeneous Populations and Problem Areas

Assertive-training procedures have been empirically validated as representing an effective therapy for the treatment of a variety of clinical populations and problems. One of the most interesting and logical experimental applications of this procedure has been in the area of dating. Melnick (71), in an early adaptation of various assertive-training procedures, found that dating behavior could be increased through a variety of techniques including participant modeling and behavioral feedback. Although the author does not label his techniques "assertive training," he draws parallels between his procedures and those developed by researchers in the area of assertive training. Additional assertive-training components used with nondaters include graded tasks with self-reinforcement (84) and arranged interactions with members of the opposite sex (9, 10, 66). Recent research findings reported by a number of investigators have contributed further evidence to the demonstrated effectiveness of assertive training with dating behaviors.

Studies by Curran (13) and Curran and Gilbert (14) show the effectiveness of assertive training and systematic desensitization procedures in teaching various aspects of dating responses. Both studies found the assertive-training groups to have more actual dating skills than the systematic desensitization groups. A six-month follow-up of the latter study (14) found the assertive-training subjects to be significantly more skilled on an assessment of interpersonal dating responses. Twentyman and McFall (103) randomly assigned 31 "shy" males, who reported no more than one date in the month prior to the study, to either an assertive-training group or an assessment-only control group. Subjects who received the assertive-training procedure showed less anxiety and were more skilled at role-played dating interactions at a posttreatment assessment period than control subjects. Behavioral diaries kept by the subjects revealed more interactions with women for the assertive-training subjects at a six-month followup.

Dating has been further explored by McGovern, Arkowitz, and Gilmore (70), who compared three different assertive-training programs for college men with dating inhibitions. All three assertive-training groups showed significant gains over a waiting-list control group on a variety of outcome measures. An interesting finding of this study was that a discussion-only training group did as well as two groups receiving a more action-oriented training program. Finally, a study by MacDonald et al. (64) examined the relative effectiveness of four group training conditions: behavior-assertion training, behavior-assertion training with client contact between sessions, attention-placebo, and a test-retest control condition. A role-play dating-interaction rating scheme revealed significant improvements for both of the assertive-training groups when compared to the two control groups.

The enhancement of marital interactions represents another area where assertive training has demonstrated effectiveness. Eisler, Miller, Hersen, and Alford (23) present an interesting marital-interaction study of three dysfunctional married couples with passive-avoidant husbands. By use of an innovative observation and measurement procedure, the couples were individually videotaped while discussing their marital difficulties both before and after the husband received brief, but intensive assertive training. The content of these pretherapy tapes was then used to develop three separate training regimens for the husbands. One husband received assertive training using unstructured scenes related to pretreatment marital interaction. A second husband received assertive training based on structured interpersonal situations unrelated to his marital interaction. In the third case, the husband was trained on structured scenes related to specific areas of his marital conflicts. Other than being directed to talk with their husbands as if they were at home, the wives received no specific instructions to change their behavior. In all three cases, posttherapy tests revealed substantial improvement in the husbands' assertiveness on a number of measures. In two of the three cases, increased assertiveness produced marked changes in the couple's marital interactions. Similar improvements in marital interactions due to assertive training are reported by Fensterheim (26). Miller and Elkin (72) and Miller and Hersen (73) report the successful treatment of alcoholism, within the marital dyad, by use of assertive-training procedures.

Many additional experiments and case histories published in recent years document the clinical efficacy of assertive training in treating a range of populations and presenting problems. Successful procedures in the assertive training of women, as a special population, have been reported by Brockway (7), Jakubowski-Spector (48), and Richey (85). Shoemaker and Paulson (98) describe a successful assertive-training procedure used with mothers lacking effective communication skills. The modification of sexual deviancy served as the target behavior for a study by Laws and Serber (57). Weinman, Gelbart, Wallace, and Post (108) record a study in which schizophrenics were found to significantly improve their behavior with the induction of assertive training. Hersen, Turner, Edelstein, and Pinkston (46) identify similar results with a single schizophrenic who was also given phenothiazines. Hersen and Bellack (42) cite an assertive-training procedure used with two chronic schizophrenics with the effectiveness demonstrated in a multiple-baseline evaluation format. Edelstein and Eisler (19) describe a similar multiple-baseline design in which a schizophrenic male significantly increased appropriately assertive responses. Serber and Nelson (97), however, report a systematic desensitization and assertive-training program which was found to be ineffective with schizophrenics.

Speech-anxious middle-school students served as the client population for a study by Johnson, Tyler, Thompson, and Jones (49) comparing systematic desensitization and assertive training. Posttherapy evaluation of these two programs indicated that both groups improved as a result of training with no differences between them. Rimm, Hill, Brown, and Stuart (87) report on an experimental design in which 13 subjects with difficulty in controlling their tempers were assigned to either an assertive-training group or an attention-placebo control group. After eight hours of assertive training, the experimental group showed significant improvement over the controls on two objective and two self-report measures. A number of social-skill problems identified as problematic by college students have been treated by Friedman (33), Galassi, Kostka, and Galassi (35), and McFall and Twentyman (69). Psychiatric inpatient populations have also been successfully given assertive training by Goldsmith and McFall(38), Hersen and Bellack (43), Hersen, Eisler, and Miller (44), and Percell, Berwick , and Beigel (79).

AN ASSERTIVE-TRAINING PROGRAM

The previous literature clearly shows the wide application and efficacy of a variety of interventive programs conducted under the rubric of assertive training. Most of these programs are an amalgam of several therapeutic techniques, carefully chosen and individually validated. In this section, we describe an assertive training program we have used with anecdotal and empirical success for the past five years (90, 95, 96). This program consists of four nonexclusive phases of treatment: conceptual structuring of therapy, assessment, intervention, and the transfer and maintenance of behavior change. We discuss each of these phases in detail with special emphasis on intervention and application. We also mention the unique characteristics of assertive training in groups.

Conceptual Structuring

Prior to or as part of assessment, the patient is given a theoretical overview of the basic assumptions underlying assertive training. This conceptual structuring is usually initiated by a didactic overview of a number of assumptions unique to the procedure. We use a fairly standard explanation of the conceptual structure, regardless of where it occurs in the chronology of therapy.

Specific explanations of the social-learning and assertive-training approach vary, of course, with the sophistication of the patients or group members. All conceptual overviews, however, contain elements of the following four assumptions:

1. The social-learning approach views ineffective coping patterns as learned responses which can be unlearned (or retaught) within the therapeutic environment (4, 104).
2. A patient's maladaptive and unsatisfactory behavior is no one's fault: blame, moral recrimination, and/or confrontation with anxiety-eliciting situations are of no inherent benefit (112).
3. Problematic situations constitute a normal part of life, and will continue to occur even after a successful therapeutic regimen (18).
4. All people, by virtue of being human, have a right to assert themselves in a self-satisfying and honest manner (1).

In summary, presentation of conceptual prerequisites to assertive training helps the patient begin viewing her/his own behavior from an objective and positive perspective. These assumptions are discussed with the patient, and the patient's reactions to them are noted as part of assessment.

Although conceptual restructuring is presented early in therapy, this introduction is often insufficient to dispel many of the self-depreciatory notions patients often bring to therapy. These distorted ideas are often diluted by the process of behavioral change itself. If not, cognitive-change procedures may be indicated. In any case, such misconceptions must be identified in the assessment phase.

Assessment

Assessment is the process of collecting information for the purpose of determining targets of change and intervention strategy. Assertive training, like any therapeutic regimen, is deemed appropriate only after a careful assessment. The most common targets for assertive training are refusing inappropriate or unfair demands or requests, expressing feeling to others, responding to the expression of feeling by others, making reasonable demands or requests, participating in group discussion, carrying out interviews, using appropriate affect, and controlling aggressive responses. Most targets are behavioral deficits; i.e., behaviors the patient needs to perform, but for which she/he lacks the skills to perform, at least in a given situation. To decide whether assertive training is necessary, the therapist must first determine whether an interpersonal-skill deficit exists. Second, the therapist must specifically define the type of situation with which the patient has difficulty. Third, the therapist must identify the patient's present strategies for dealing with these situations and their relative effectiveness. Fourth, the therapist should determine the level of anxiety associated with the patient's approach to dealing with problematic situations. As patients identify problematic situations, they are asked to rate their anxiety under those conditions and their satisfaction with the interaction.

In addition, it is necessary to examine concomitant problems associated with interpersonal-skill deficits. These deficits may be directly or indirectly related to a wide variety of other complaints with which the patient may come to therapy. For example, in the previous section we related how various authors treated pervasive anxiety, crying, dependency, dating inhibitions, marital-interaction problems, parenting problems, sexual deviancies, speech anxiety, and temper control with assertive training. In each of these cases, the target behavior was a specific interpersonal-skill deficit which seemed to be associated with the more general problem. The result of acquiring interpersonal skills and the ability to deal with interpersonal situations reduced the incidence of the more general problem.

In assessment it is also imperative that the therapist examine the consequences of the desired strategy with the patient. Wolpe (112), for this reason, recommends that the therapist should *"Never instigate an assertive act that is likely to have punishing consequences"* (p. 87). One usually assumes that assertive behavior will result in change in other people's responses, which will more closely conform to the patient's wishes. In some cases, however, the behavior may result in loss of a relationship or job, or even in bodily harm. Often it is difficult to ascertain what the external consequences of the behavior may be. Once these consequences are analyzed and the patient is fully aware of them, a plan can be evolved to increase assertive responses in specific situations.

A number of procedures for assessment are used in therapy. In the case of Carole B., the therapist initially used careful nondirective interviewing. Gradually the therapist requested considerably more specificity in the patient's responses until it was clear which new responses were required and what the parameters of the specific desired responses were.

Most therapists do not depend solely on interviewing. Often behavior checklists are mailed or given to the patient and completed prior to or at the first interview. Available checklists include the Rathus Assertiveness Schedule (83), the Assertion Inventory (36), and the College Self-Expression Test (34). An advantage of checklists is that they elicit responses to a wide variety of situations in a very short time period. Furthermore, the lists can then be used by the therapist as an interviewing guide. They may also be used as a measurement for indicating change. In our experience (95), however, patients seem to improve on such checklists even in a placebo-control therapy. As a result, these instruments do not appear to be highly discriminating for research purposes. Moreover, most have been validated on college populations, and not with the more diverse clinical populations encountered in therapy.

Some therapists use other trait or personality measures in assessing assertiveness problems (see, for example, the Situation Reaction Inventory of General Trait Anxiousness [24]; the Willoughby Personality Inventory [111]; the Eysenck Personality Inventory [25]). We have not, however, found these to be sensitive in determining relevant situations or providing adequate measures of change due to assertive training.

A common assessment tool used in assertive training is a diary in which the patient is instructed to record each stressful or demanding interpersonal situation that would potentially require an assertive response. The patient is asked to record the situation, what occurred, the anxiety level (on a scale of 0-100), and how satisfied she/he was with the response. Examples of such entries are the following:

> 5/3: My sister called. She wanted me to stop by the library on the way home from work and pick up some books for her. I wanted to go bowling with a friend, but agreed, even though her husband could have done it just as easily. (Anxiety level–60) (Satisfaction–0)

> 5/4: At the bowling alley, a young woman spoke to me. I was so nervous, I couldn't look at her. I wanted to continue the conversation but I left as quickly as I could. (Anxiety level–80) (satisfaction–0)

Not all patients can immediately use a diary. Most can be taught how to look for situations and then how to describe them. A few seem to have continuous difficulty finding appropriate entries.

Another instrument used in the assessment of assertive responses is the behavior role-play test. In this test the patient is presented with a number of situations and is expected to respond as if she/he were actually in each of these situations. For example:

> You loaned your friend 100 dollars which he promised to pay back last month. He has avoided you the past several weeks and doesn't answer his phone. One day you see him in the drugstore. He seems to pretend he doesn't see you. You say . . .

The response may be recorded on audio- or videotape for later rating and/or comparison. The respondent is asked to record the anxiety level experienced when imagining her/himself in the given situation and the degree of satisfaction felt with the response. When the resources are available, a confederate can act opposite the patient during an *in vivo* role-play situation. Our role-play tests follow guidelines suggested by Goldfried and D'Zurilla (37) for generating relevant situations and responses, and evaluating the relative appropriateness of each set of responses.

In evaluating patients' responses, the most important criterion is the effectiveness of the response in dealing with the given situation. In addition, such criteria as voice quality and volume, fluency, eye contact, degree of relaxation, firmness in voice, appropriate use of gestures, appropriate expression of feelings, empathic statements, and timing have been used. Patients are trained in the use of these criteria as a means of self-evaluation.

It is possible to obtain independent raters' observations on the tape responses and to share these observations with the patient as part of assessment. If patterns exist, they become the focus of treatment. Often, however, the problem is purely situational: that is, an inability to deal with a specific situation.

A number of role-play tests have been developed, but almost all utilize a single response for experimental purposes. (One exception is a role-play test developed by Galassi and Galassi [34], which uses a multiple response by significant others who alternate responses with the subject.) Schinke and Rose (95) report on the application of a behavioral role-play test to a diverse clinical population. A role-play test to estimate assertiveness of the elderly in nursing homes is cited by Berger (6). DeLange (15) has developed a role-play test specifically for women. Freedman (32) has a similar test for delinquents. Psychiatric inpatient Vietnam veterans provided the target population for a behavioral role-play test constructed by Clark (11). In all of these studies, the role-play tests were sufficiently sensitive to distinguish the group trained with assertiveness procedures from a placebo-control group. Developing such a test for research purposes is a time-consuming and costly process. Some practitioners have used the above-mentioned tests as a means of assessing the patient's initial capacity for dealing with interpersonal situations, and for evaluating outcomes. As more researchers evaluate assertive-training programs, role-play tests for other populations will become available.

Assessment represents an ongoing component in assertive training. As new situations emerge, they are discussed and role-played. New problem areas result in the development of new assertive responses. Assessment is therefore inextricably linked with intervention.

Intervention

The following excerpt from a second interview with Carole B. demonstrates the major procedures used in assertive training. The problem in this session involves Ms. B.'s inability to refuse her employer's unreasonable requests. This is the first of a series of situations on which the therapist and Ms. B. have agreed to work.

> *Therapist:* Last week we identified several situations you were having difficulty with. The most pressing was the problem with your boss. Could you go over that again?
>
> *Ms. B.:* I really have a good job, so I don't want to complain. The other day my boss even told me what a good job I was doing. That was fine, but then he asked me if I wanted to continue editing the personnel newsletter every two weeks. I'm already working overtime just to keep up with my regular work, and don't get any more pay for it. But he was so insistent, I just couldn't say no.
>
> *Therapist:* What did you say?
>
> *Ms. B.:* I said that if it was really important, I'd be glad to do it.
>
> *Therapist:* Were you really glad to do it?
>
> *Ms. B.:* No! It isn't fair.
>
> *Therapist:* How did you feel about saying you would do it?

Ms. B.: I felt sick, absolutely sick . . . and hypocritical too. That night I got terribly depressed again.

Therapist: What would you have liked to have said? Something that you wouldn't be depressed about.

Ms. B.: I don't know exactly, but somehow I would have liked to have refused without being offensive.

Therapist: So your goal would have been to say something that gives the clear message that you have enough to do. How about saying something like, "I'm glad you complimented me, and that you appreciate my work, but I can't continue to do my work well with the additional edition. So I just can't take it on?

Ms. B.: Yes, I'd like to say something like that.

Therapist: But do you think you have a right to say it . . . to refuse?

Ms. B.: Yes, I do!

Therapist: I agree, but is there any risk involved? You're the only one that can really judge that.

Ms. B.: None at all. I do my job well. He can't replace me. He just lost one person. I won't even lose my raise.

Therapist: Are you perhaps worried that he won't like you?

Ms. B.: No, I really don't care. In fact, I think he'd respect me more. Besides everyone else tells him when they've got too much to do.

Therapist: From my experience with others, my guess is that he'd respect you more too. So as far as you can tell there is really no concrete reason why you don't respond the way you want to.

Ms. B.: None!

Therapist: Then there isn't any reason why we can't teach you to deal more effectively with this and similar situations. Let's begin by your summarizing in your own words how I suggested you respond to your boss.

Ms. B.: I'll try [she paraphases the words, hesitatingly and flatly].

Therapist: That's a good beginning. Now I wonder if you couldn't say it a little louder and with more emphasis and firmness in your voice like this. [The therapist repeats sentences with greater emphasis.] Does that fit?

Ms. B.: Yes, I'd like that better. I think I can do it.

Therapist: Would you like to try it again?

Ms. B.: [Repeats the sentence with more affect.]

Therapist: Good, you sound firmer, and more convincing. If you speak just a little louder and perhaps with a little more eye contact, I think we're in business. Now let's try it once more. Only this time I'll pretend I'm the boss. We'll try to make the situation as similar as possible to the real situation. Have you ever role-played before?

Ms. B.: Yes, once long ago, I sort of liked it.

Therapist: Good, because that is what we will be doing. Now tell me how your boss talks.

Ms. B.: Well, he speaks quickly . . . and curtly and, well, he doesn't look at you. He always sounds a little bit like he is angry. Like this [gives imitation].

Therapist: That is helpful. Now describe the situation to me, so I get the feel of it.

Ms. B.: [Describes the situation.]

Therapist: OK. I've got the idea . . . let me start. [As employer] Well, Carole, I'm very impressed with the work you've been doing. We all are.

Ms. B.: Thank you [smiles].

Therapist: [As employer] We like the little personnel newsletter so much that we want you to continue putting out two issues a month. Can you keep it up? I hope you can.

Ms. B.: [Meekly] In addition to my other work?

Therapist: [As employer] I'm sure you can handle it; you're so competent.

Ms. B.: [Flustered] Well, gee, I don't know. I guess . . .

Therapist: [As employer] Think how much everyone appreciates the little news-letter, and how much they appreciate your putting it together.

Ms. B.: I'd rather not do it twice a month. Once a month is even hard. Isn't that really enough?

Therapist: [As therapist] That's a good start. The important thing is that you said no, even under pressure. Is there anything else you would like to have done differently?

Ms. B.: I got confused when he flattered me. I should have been firmer.

Therapist: I agree. Perhaps you could also lose your smile. Your eye contact was good. Let's go back to "You are so competent." What might you say?

Ms. B.: [In role] I'm afraid I have far too much to do. I can only do the news-letter once monthly and keep up with my other work. I would really like to have some help on it and eventually turn it over to someone else.

Therapist: [As employer] Oh come now; I'm sure you can crank it out more often than that, all by yourself. You're so good at everything you do.

Ms. B.: [Serious expression] Thank you, Mr. K., but I only have limited time available. As you know, I'm already working overtime without pay. I can't keep up this newsletter and do my own work too. Which comes first? In my opinion I should finish my own work and do the newsletter once a month, with help.

Therapist: [As therapist] Very good. I especially like the new way you gave your opinion. Eye contact was still good, you dropped the smile, your voice was firm. How did you feel about it?

Ms. B.: Really good. I could hardly believe it was me saying it.

Therapist: By the way, do I sound like your boss?

Ms. B.: I'll say! I was beginning to get annoyed with you.

Therapist: OK. Let's do it again from the beginning. You're really getting it down.

[They repeat the role-play]

Therapist: Much better. It flowed and seemed quite natural. How do you feel about that one?

Ms. B.: If I could do it that way with my boss I'd be delighted.

Therapist: You're getting real good. The more practice you get, the easier it will be to do it with your boss. Even though you're doing great, let's do it one more time, and this time I'll really put on the pressure.

During this process of goal setting, the therapist provided suggestions to the patient. In the above example, we observe that the therapist first elicited what the patient would like to do or say. He then demonstrated or *modeled* how the patient could perform the situation in a role-play. He gradually eased the patient into a *behavioral rehearsal,* using small steps or shaping. He provided the patient with *feedback* on what she did well and made some suggestions as to what she might do better. The patient repeated the rehearsal with some *coaching* or verbal instructions by the therapist. Throughout the interview the therapist made use of *social reinforcement* for effective performance, good ideas, and attempts at new activities. Note that the therapist provided the patient with ample opportunity for success. Final rehearsals prepare the patient for a *home assignment,* which will include performing the rehearsed behavior in an actual situation, recording the performance in a diary, and self-administering reinforcement for completing the assignment.

Most of the major procedures in this approach have a solid empirical foundation. In the remainder of this section we shall define, illustrate, and, by use of the experimental literature, validate these techniques.

Behavior rehearsal is the most important procedure in the assertive-training package. It involves the patient performing those behaviors agreed upon as effective in a problematic situation. Once the patient has either seen a modeling demonstration or has discussed what she/he would like to do in a role-play, she/he rehearses the desired behavior. Usually the first rehearsal is brief. The patient may voice only one response to one statement by the antagonist. As the patient successfully negotiates the relatively easy role-play, successively more difficult rehearsals are developed, as observed in the case of Carole B.

In order to provide variation in the rehearsal process and to increase the difficulty, the therapist often introduces unfamiliar persons as protagonists. Therapists have used their receptionists, student volunteers, and former patients in the roles of significant others.

Based on the assumption that frequent practice is likely to lead to success, patients are given the assignment to rehearse the desired behaviors at home, if possible, with cooperative friends or relatives. If no significant others are available, the therapist asks the patient to audiotape her/his homework role-plays while performing in front of a mirror. These practice sessions are then reported on at the following interview. An initial study of behavior rehearsal by Lazarus (58) compared four 30-minute sessions of behavior rehearsal with two other approaches: advice giving and reflection-interpretation. Results showed behavior rehearsal produced greater improvements in the management of interpersonal difficulties than those produced by the other two methods. Lazarus, the only therapist for all of his groups, evaluated the success of the groups based on specific criteria of improvement. Lazarus acknowledges that the possibility of experimenter bias severely limits any conclusions drawn from this study. A series of studies by McFall and his colleagues (67, 68, 69) demonstrate that behavior rehearsal is capable of producing significant increases in refusals to unreasonable requests.

The most common form of *modeling* occurs when the therapist role-plays the patient as a means of demonstrating the appropriate affect and other nonverbal cues and words to be used in the situation. Prior to modeling, the therapist elicits what the patient would like to say. In the modeling demonstration, the therapist incorporates as many of the patient's ideas as possible. There is some danger that the therapist's modeling may be so far removed from the patient's skill level that she/he is likely to be discouraged by comparison. We often provide the patient with brief modeling segments, and gradually increase the level of difficulty presented in the modeling situation.

Some therapists have introduced former patients or other persons similar to the given patient as models. Since these models are more similar to the patient, it is more likely that they will be imitated (4). One must be careful with outside persons as models, however: if not prepared in advance, they may model the wrong behavior. Occasionally patients are given assignments to observe real-life models. They are instructed to find someone whom they admire and watch what that person does in critical interpersonal situations. The patient then discusses with the therapist what she/he observed.

Eisler, Hersen, and Miller (22) have demonstrated that modeling can augment behavior rehearsal in the acquisition of complex social responses. Expanding the studies of McFall et al., these investigators compared a modeling and rehearsal group, a rehearsal-only group, and a test-retest group. They found that rehearsal only did not contribute significantly to change on several verbal and nonverbal measures of assertiveness. However, the modeling and rehearsal groups, when compared with two control groups, improved on five of eight components of assertiveness.

In a similar study, Hersen et al. (45) compared four groups: modeling and instruction, instruction only, rehearsal only, and test-retest control. The results support Eisler et al. (22) in indicating that a combination of modeling and instructions was equal or superior to modeling or instructions alone. It is interesting to note that the rehearsal-only group did not differ from the test-retest group. A study by Friedman (33) indicates that both modeling plus role-playing and modeling alone can contribute to changes on a behavioral-assertion measure among non-assertive college students. Eisler and Hersen (21) suggest that it often becomes necessary for the therapist to model appropriate behavior when the client becomes excessively anxious or when she/he does not possess requisite interactional skills. The techniques of covert modeling, in which clients imagine a model engaged in a behavior they wish to develop, and model reinforcement have been demonstrated as effective assertive-training components by Kazdin in a series of studies (51, 52, 53).

Coaching, or verbal instructions, involve explicit therapist descriptions of what constitutes an appropriate assertive response in a given situation. As we have seen in the case of Carole B., the therapist coached her throughout therapy. However, before coaching, he also explored her own suggestions for change. Coaching is usually diminished as the patient shows increased competence and independence. Research on the treatment contributions of verbal instructions is limited, but the available evidence supports its usefulness in assertive training. Hersen et al. (45), in their investigation of the components contributing to effective assertive training, found a highly significant treatment effect for verbal instructions when assessed by both a situational-behavior self-report and a behavioral role-play assertion task. Whalen (109) investigated the effects of modeling versus instructions on self-disclosure. Similarly, Green and Marlatt (40) found instructions and modeling resulted in greater self-disclosure by college students than either instructions or modeling alone. Edelstein and Eisler (19) confirm this phenomenon in a report on the treatment of a schizophrenic patient. They found that while modeling alone increased affect, modeling combined with instructions and feedback increased eye contact, gestures, affect, and overall assertiveness.

Feedback is provided by the therapist as to her/his specific impressions of the patient's performance. Feedback can facilitate response acquisition both by providing an external perspective on social behavior and by its reinforcement effects. Feedback is usually given in terms of specific criteria such as effectiveness, firmness of voice, voice volume, eye contact, and expression of feeling. As in verbal instruction, patients are gradually taught to provide their own feedback.

A number of investigators suggest the therapeutic potential of response feedback (3, 5, 8, 113). McFall and Marston (68), comparing assertive training with and without audiotaped feedback of rehearsed behaviors, offer some limited support to this suggestion; subjects receiving feedback had a nonsignificant tendency to show more improvement on self-report and behavior role-play measures than did subjects receiving no performance feedback. A study by McFall and Lillesand (67) however, found a significant trend in the opposite direction, Melnick (71), in a study evaluating the effects of response feedback, compared six groups of nondating college men. Results showed modeling alone, participant modeling, participant modeling plus video feedback, and participant modeling plus video feedback with systematic verbal reinforcement resulted in significantly more improvement on self-report measures when compared with the no-treatment and placebo-control groups. When groups receiving feedback and those receiving no feedback were compared, feedback was found to lead to greater improvement on the simulated dating-interaction test. In a study comparing three group-training techniques for teaching Vietnam veterans social skills, Clark (11) found a behavior-rehearsal group to show more improvement than either a role-play feedback group or a didactic-instruction group.

Social reinforcement of rehearsed responses represents an important source of therapeutic intervention. In the case of Carole B., the therapist praised her endeavors as a means of shaping desirable performance. In addition, the therapist used nonverbal cues such as smiles, nods of approval, and body posture. Fensterheim (26) and Lazarus (59) describe the effective use of response reinforcement during assertive training. Yalom (115) points out that group psychotherapy relies on the use of subtle social reinforcers. Certainly, the effectiveness of verbal and nonverbal social reinforcement in changing behavior has been well documented (4, 5, 16, 50). Two studies by Wagner (106, 107) show that the expression of anger during role-playing is responsive to reinforcement.

Home assignments involve a number of specified and negotiated tasks to be performed between sessions. These assignments may include keeping a diary, performing a rehearsed behavior in the natural environment, contacting the therapist, joining a social organization, observing someone who has the skills the patient is attempting to develop, and reading about assertive training in popular manuals or journals. The purpose of assignments is to transfer the learning taking place in the session to the outside world. Thus assignments represent an essential step in the therapy process. Tasks are usually quite simple in the early sessions, becoming more difficult as therapy progresses. Social reinforcement is then made contingent on the completion of the negotiated tasks. A few therapists have reported the use of fee refunds, informal talk time, or added therapy as reinforcement for the completion of behavioral assignments. Tokens are often used to mediate concrete reinforcement for task completion. To our knowledge, the single component of home assignments has not been empirically validated.

Assertive Training in Groups

The small group represents an effective and facilitative setting for training in assertive skills (95). The group can serve as a protected laboratory to practice skills that must eventually be performed in the community. It provides members with a variety of social situations and potential roles for each to play. Moreover, in role-play, modeling, and rehearsal, participants offer each other an assortment of antagonists and protagonists. Group members have opportunities to assert themselves as leaders, therapeutic partners, or consultants to other participants.

Several studies have partially demonstrated the effectiveness of assertive training in groups. Shoemaker and Paulson (98) show that mothers participating in such a program exhibited significant increases in assertive behaviors and decreases in aggressive ones. Similar results were obtained for their husbands, who had only indirectly participated in the program. Moreover, parents' ratings of their children also improved. Two studies by Rathus compare group assertive training with either discussion (81) or placebo therapy (82), and a no-treatment control. Both studies found that assertion subjects reported greater gains on the Rathus Assertiveness Schedule. Only subjects in the latter study, however, were judged by independent raters as superior an overall assertiveness. Conclusions drawn from these studies are limited because Rathus used college students from his own classes and served as the therapist for all of his groups. Hedquist and Weinhold (41) compared a behavior-rehearsal group, involving role-play, modeling, and coaching, with a group involving only modeling followed by subjects' attempts to carry out an assigned task in their natural environments. Both of the behavioral groups proved superior to a group-discussion control on self-reported assertive verbal responses at the end of therapy. There were no significant differences, however, at a two-week follow-up. Sarason (94) treated three groups of juvenile offenders in an experimental assertive-training procedure. One group received group behavioral rehearsal; the second only described problematic behaviors; and a third group served as no-treat-

ment controls. Posttherapy results showed significant improvements for the assertive-training group on staff ratings, ratings of review boards, and attitudinal measures.

Rimm, Keyson, and Hunziker (88) assigned a small number of adult males,
institutionalized for antisocial and aggressive behavior, to either an assertive-training or attention-placebo group. Objective ratings of the subjects' appropriate assertive behavior revealed significantly greater improvements for the assertive-training
group than the controls. Subjective and follow-up observations supported these
improvements. Lomont, Gilner, Spector, and Skinner (63) compared results of
therapy for hospitalized patients through group assertive training and group insight
therapy. Assertively trained patients showed significant changes on various sub-
scales of the Minnesota Multiphasic Personality Inventory and the Leary Interpersonal Checklist, whereas the insight groups showed no such changes.

Wright (114), in a study of college discussion-group participation, conducted
treatment in groups, and performed assessment in simulated group discussions
and actual college group-discussion sections. Although behavioral-training effects were
found in a simulated group discussion, they apparently did not transfer to the
"real" discussion section. Fensterheim (27) describes a "mini-group" model in
which three bachelors were given assertive-training skills to combat social isolation.
Since the program did not employ an experimental design, the results are used to illustrate the efficacy of small assertive-training groups as an ancillary treatment procedure. Two previously cited studies by McGovern et al. (70) and MacDonald et al.
(64) found group assertive training to be an effective procedure for the treatment
of dating responses. Rose (90) reports on the successful group treatment of clients
from five different social-service agencies. Schinke and Rose (96) give empirical
documentation that assertive training in groups with social-agency clients is more
effective than group discussion. The package described in these two studies is used
as the basis for the group-training model described in this section.

Assessment in groups is similar to assessment in individual training with interviewing carried out by all group members. This provides the patients with training
and practice in interviewing and assessment. It also gives them an opportunity to
observe and try out leadership skills. Just as in individual therapy, the major procedures used in group treatment are rehearsal, modeling, coaching, feedback,
reinforcement, and home assignments. In addition, groups also use group feedback,
group goal planning, the buddy system, member-to-member coaching, and procedures for building cohesion and resolving group problems.

Behavioral rehearsal in groups involves members serving as adversaries, significant others, and coaches. One technique, borrowed from psychodrama, involves a
role-player with a problematic situation, an antagonist, and a coach sitting behind
the role-player. When the role-player seems to be in difficulty, the coach gives
the verbal and nonverbal cues needed to maintain interaction. This technique is
especially useful when the role-player has difficulty in generating spontaneous and
appropriate responses.

Covert rehearsal in groups can supplement overt rehearsal. The advantages of covert rehearsal are that it can be used with the entire group at the same time, it permits a large number of trials in a short period, it protects the highly anxious patient from the stress of being observed, and it is a procedure that can be readily practiced at home. After explaining the basic steps and rationale of the covert rehearsal, the therapist describes a common problem situation. Members are asked to imagine how they would respond. After a brief discussion of their imagined responses, the therapist makes several suggestions. Members are then asked once again to imagine their response, this time incorporating the most suitable suggestions from other group members and leaders. McFall and Lillesand (67) provide experimental support for the effectiveness of this procedure with a college-student population.

Modeling in groups is enhanced by the presence of other members. In fact, every rehearsal represents a potential model for other members. In addition, models may be brought into the group because of special competence. In a dating group, one member invited a friend who dated frequently, and the other group members were delighted with the ideas he gave them. Home assignments are also similar to those given to the individual patient. One difference is that performance of the assignment is sometimes monitored by other group members, by telephone or in person, between group sessions. In fact, the contacting of one group member by another may be a home assignment.

A number of procedures are uniquely characteristic of group assertive training. We shall describe the procedures we have found to be most helpful.

Group goal planning involves establishing a set of explicit goals and an agenda for each meeting to provide a framework for maintaining a task orientation. Initially the therapist designs the goals. As the patients learn the criteria for goal determination, they increasingly take responsibility for goal formulation. The criteria for the establishment of goals for each meeting are: (1) the session goals should be related to the long-range goals of the group; (2) they can reasonably be achieved before the next meeting; (3) the criteria for the goals' achievement are explicated; and (4) the goals have implications for most of the group members. One group, for example, established the following goals for the third meeting:

> By the end of this session:
>
> (a) All members will have interacted at least four times with each other member.
> (b) All members will develop a homework assignment and decide on a buddy to monitor that assignment.
> (c) All members will have rehearsed at least one situation and be provided with feedback from the group.

Once session goals have been established, agenda items are developed to facilitate their attainment. Unfinished items are usually relegated to a subsequent meeting. The attainment of group goals is often used as an estimate of productivity.

Cohesion-increasing procedures are especially relevant to group therapy. Two purposes of increasing cohesion are to keep group members in treatment, and to increase the reinforcement strength of the therapist and the group. There is also some evidence that cohesion is related to group effectiveness (54). Many come to an assertive-training group to learn how to socialize with others in informal ways. Interaction that is too task-oriented may limit the group's attractiveness for these members. A number of procedures are used to stimulate group cohesion. First, since most group members give role-playing a high rating, this technique is used in the first sessions. In addition, members interview each other in subgroups as a way to learn names and get acquainted. Cohesion also appears to be increased when the therapist clearly identifies the advantages of group therapy. Since active participation by all persons seems to be related to attraction, everyone is encouraged to speak at the first meeting. Too much pressure to speak, however, may drive away unusually taciturn or anxious patients. The records of attendance and promptness at a given session are used to assess the group cohesion of that session. In addition, patients are asked, at the end of every session, how helpful they found the group.

Group feedback is one of the most important procedures in group assertive training. In individual therapy the major source of support is the therapist. In groups, however, suggestions, advice, corrections, reinforcement, support, information, and expression of understanding can come from the members as well as the therapist. Each member has a particular expertise: the therapist is expert in the training program; the members are experts of their own experiences, whether or not they are similar to each other. The therapist must often elicit and even shape comments from the members, usually following a behavioral rehearsal or modeling role-play. As we mentioned earlier, members are trained by the therapist to provide group feedback in two ways. First, the therapist provides her/his own comments as a model, fading these and allowing others to give feedback. Second, the therapist provides the members with a list of criteria for use in evaluating fellow members' performance. Once trained in giving feedback, members can often come up with suggestions well beyond the limited range of any one therapist. As the group evolves, the therapist's role shifts to protecting patients from too heavy criticism, and to ensuring that members receive sufficient reinforcement from each other. If too much criticism or not enough reinforcement occur, or if group goals are not reached, the group may develop problems interfering with the attainment of individual treatment goals.

Group problem resolution is of obvious importance since a high level of group functioning is essential for individual members to derive maximum benefit. Because the group impinges on the treatment of each patient, group or interactive patterns sometimes have to be modified. For example, some persons are rarely able to give help or feedback to others or ask for help themselves. Occasionally, members tend to communicate with the therapist rather than with each other. Often, there is a tendency for therapists to perform all of the leadership functions, which should be more broadly distributed. In other groups the degree of mutual reinforcement among members may be so low that the therapist's intervention is required. Simply pointing out the problem and discussing its relation to the attainment of treatment goals may be sufficient intervention. In other situations, social reinforcement of the desired responses by the therapist and/or by the members may resolve the interaction impediment.

The buddy system, as described by Fo and O'Donnell (29) and Rose (90), is used to facilitate monitoring the performance of extra-group behavior. Patients select partners with whom they exchange either telephone calls or visits between sessions. During these contacts, they discuss the difficulties they are having with the assignments and ways of resolving these difficulties. This is used to train patients in the self-therapy behaviors they will need when the group has terminated. To provide members with different types of partners, buddies in most groups are shifted once during the treatment period. For many, the buddy system serves as a first opportunity for experimenting in successful extra-group interaction.

Transfer and Maintenance of Assertive Behaviors

It is not sufficient for patients to learn and perform assertive responses within the therapy setting. These behaviors must be maintained after treatment ends if the individual is to continue functioning satisfactorily. Moreover, the behaviors must be transferred from performance in the therapy situation to the outside world. Most assertive training programs, therefore, employ procedures that aim at both maintenance and transfer of the assertive behaviors. These procedures have been derived primarily from principles extrapolated from research on cognitive learning (see, for example, Goldstein, Heller, and Sechrest [39] and Rose [89, 91]).

The major transfer and generalization principles used in a basic assertive-training program include: (1) gradually increasing the similarity between therapy and extra-therapy situations; (2) increasing the degree of unpredictability in therapy; (3) gradually increasing the degree of patient responsibility for her/his own therapy; (4) increasing extra-therapy incentives; (5) encouraging overlearning of the original subtasks; (6) conceptualizing learning; and (7) preparing the patient for an unsympathetic environment. Similarity between therapy and the outside world is enhanced by increasing the difficulty of the role-playing. Some therapists also introduce outsiders into therapy to play antagonist roles. We have moved the therapy into cafes, bars, and other locations stressful to the patient, as a means of more nearly simulating the real world.

The unpredictability of therapy may be increased by a guest therapist or former patient initiating role-plays. Patient responsibility is increased by the therapist reducing the structure of therapy. Role-plays are designed by patients in later sessions; patients evaluate their own performance with criteria learned in earlier sessions. In group treatment, patients assume direct leadership functions for the group. In some cases, former patients are asked to assist as models and as co-therapist for new groups. Patients are taught to identify and deal with group problems themselves. By the end of therapy, patients should be able to provide their own assertion therapy when necessary.

Extra-therapy incentives are increased when members are encouraged to join nontherapeutic groups. The patient is taught how to approach and enter these groups as part of the therapy regimen. Repeated rehearsals are used in order to encourage overlearning of the specific subtasks. Covert rehearsal provides an opportunity for numerous repetitions, either in therapy or at home, or even preceding the overt responses in the problematic situation. Conceptualization of learning is obtained by early and repeated presentation of the assertive-training paradigm. As patients learn to deal with highly specific situations, the therapist reviews the basic theory and ideology underlying their achievements. Patients are prepared for an unsympathetic environment by being trained in difficult situations in which assertive skills may bring adverse consequences. They learn to deal with friends and relatives who may not appreciate their new responses to familiar situations. They are also taught how to administer their own reinforcement, obviating the need to rely on others for benefits of being appropriately assertive. When assertive training is done with couples or with children, both parties learn how to cope with the changes in others. Unfortunately, training of significant others can rarely be developed due to the exigencies of coordination and cooperation.

The concept of maintenance and generalization of change have undergone considerable empirical study in recent years. The experimental reports, however, present mixed conclusions in support of these two phenomena.

A series of studies examining the transfer of training have been done by McFall with his colleagues and doctoral students (11, 38, 67, 68, 69). In the earliest of these studies, McFall and Marston (68) developed an innovative real-life posttreatment assessment procedure in which subjects were telephoned by an experimental confederate posing as a magazine salesperson. Although several measures of sales resistance were rated by the caller, and later by independent judges from audio recordings, only one of the telephone measures achieved significance. This measure, representing the relative point in the call when resistance was first noted, discriminated between the combined experimental groups and a no-treatment control group.

McFall and Lillesand (67) employed a telephone follow-up assertion test, which failed to find significant evidence of generalization in any of three assertive-training groups. Results, however, showed a trend toward behavioral-rehearsal subjects' more frequently refusing the caller's request, and some evidence for generalization of treatment effects was obtained on untrained situations in a behavioral role-play assessment task. McFall and Twentyman (69) employed a posttreatment telephone assessment in which an experimental confederate asked to borrow the subject's lecture notes. The call was constructed so that subjects were confronted with a series of seven increasingly unreasonable requests. Assertive-training subjects refused the requests at a significantly earlier point than did control subjects.

A study by Goldsmith and McFall (38) was specifically designed to assess generalization of treatment effects in a sample of psychiatric inpatients, who were trained in interpersonal skills for relating to strangers. An inventory of problem situations was constructed, some of these situations were used in training, and all of the situations were used for assessment purposes. Both the inventory of situational self-reported behavior and a role-played task showed significant treatment effects for assertive-training subjects on untrained, as well as trained, problem situations. In addition to these indications of treatment generalization, the researchers found further evidence during a "real-life" interaction with a "stranger." Assertive-training subjects completed a significantly greater number of the assigned interaction tasks, were rated significantly higher on two of three scales by the "stranger" confederate, and rated themselves as significantly more comfortable and competent in the interaction than did subjects in either of the two control groups.

Clark's study (11) measured the generalization of treatment effects by post-testing for changes on trained and untrained demand situations. Results indicated nonsignificant trends toward generalization of treatment in an assertive-training group. Follow-up data also offered suggestive, albeit nonsignificant, evidence for transfer of training to real-life situations. Hersen, Eisler, and Miller (44) evaluated the generalization of assertive training to untrained situations by comparing five treatment conditions: test-retest, practice-control, practice-control with generalization instructions, modeling and instructions, and modeling plus instruction with generalization instructions. Results showed that the modeling and instructions groups effected the greatest changes on seven of the eight training-scene components, but on only five of the eight components for the generalization scenes. No differences were found between either of the two practice-control groups and the test-retest group. Transfer of training effects was minimal on an independent *in vivo* test. Schinke and Rose (96) found that subjects given assertive training performed more assertively than placebo-control subjects on novel untrained-stimulus role-plays, and maintained their assertiveness at a three-month follow-up. Self-report paper and pencil tests did not substantiate the behavioral differences between the two groups.

In many of these experiments the test used to ascertain maintenance and transfer of behavior was a highly specific stimulus situation to which the patient was expected to respond assertively. Failure to obtain strong differences may have been due to a small or idiosyncratic sample. A broad spectrum of situations would provide better answers. Nevertheless, the findings suggest that limited maintenance does indeed occur, even in short-term programs. It is clear, however, that the clinician must consciously strive to maximize the maintenance and transfer of learning from assertive training.

Format for Assertive Training

This section addresses organizational variables of assertive training, including length of treatment, length and frequency of sessions, size of groups, number of therapists, place of therapy, and composition of the group. These parameters are based primarily on our experience and will no doubt vary with individual clinicians.

Most groups last from six to 12 sessions. In our experience, more sessions result in repetition and a high drop-out rate. While meetings are usually held once weekly, it is often useful to meet twice a week in the early stages of treatment and less frequently in the later phases. This provides an opportunity for early changes to occur and then a gradual fading of therapist and group support. Marathon sessions may also be possible, although none to our knowledge have been evaluated.

The number of sessions in individual therapy is entirely dependent on the amount of time it takes to achieve mutually agreed-upon goals. In some cases, one session with follow-up phone calls has been sufficient. Usually, however, three to five sessions have proven sufficient for most problems solely concerned with a deficit in assertiveness. In more complex cases, of which an assertive deficit is only one aspect, many more sessions may be required.

Group sessions vary in length from one and a half to three hours. Our preference is for two hours, since this provides sufficient time for each person to carry out at least one rehearsal, but is not so long as to become boring or fatiguing. Individual assertive-training sessions vary in length from 15 minutes to two hours. The main criterion is whether a minimum of one situation has been successfully dealt with during each session.

Groups vary in size from four to 12 patients. In our experience, one therapist should not handle more than six patients, in order to individualize treatment and provide ample opportunity for all members to role-play. If the group is too small (four or less), the interaction tends to be therapist-dominated. Two therapists are often used in assertive-training groups, although one is sufficient. Co-therapists are almost never used in individual therapy, although additional persons may be introduced as models. As mentioned earlier, we have used former patients in this role, both in individual as well as group training, with favorable results.

The location of assertive training is not restricted to the clinic or office. Sessions may be held in churches, clubs, school buildings, or other nontherapeutic locations. This attracts patients who might not otherwise seek help. Special sessions may be held in bars, restaurants, or social clubs, especially if such places represent problematic situations for some individuals.

Most research studies have used subjects who were grouped on homogeneous demographic or presenting-problem variables. Such arrangements have facilitated the development of common treatment and evaluative procedures. Homogeneously composed groups also appear to be more attractive to patients than heterogeneous groups. In our clinical experience, however, groups of highly diverse individuals seem to be equally as effective as the more homogeneous groups. Mixed groups are usually easier to form, since waiting lists are shorter and new members can be added in early stages without significant interruption of group process. Heterogeneous groups offer the additional benefit of a wide range of life experiences from which to draw upon. Empirical studies validating these anecdotal judgments have yet to be generated.

SUMMARY AND CONCLUSIONS

Findings presented by numerous case reports and well-controlled assertive-training studies establish an effective and beneficial clinical procedure. A set of prescribed and replicable training techniques have been validated, and a diverse range of presenting problems and populations have been successfully treated. Therapeutic improvement as a result of these techniques has been manifested in broad-based evaluations of change—including self-report personality inventories and objective behavioral ratings.

The recent growth of case history and research literature documenting the effectiveness of assertive training is paralleled by publication of myriad clinical and lay manuals on this procedure (1, 2, 12, 28, 56, 60, 62, 77, 80, 100). Some of these manuals are intended for relatively skilled clinicians; others are addressed to the lay public with no previous clinical training; all maintain that assertive training can be incorporated into every person's life with profitable and satisfying results.

Clearly, assertive training is reaching its zenith of popularity as a psychotherapeutic panacea. An increasing number of clinics, social agencies, hospitals, and private therapists, of various theoretical orientations, are developing programs in assertive training. Many clinics specialize in this single methodology. Community colleges, churches, high schools, and social organizations are incorporating assertive-training programs into their community programs.

The very popularity of this procedure may lead to its major abuse: in many instances, untrained lay persons are conducting assertive-training sessions. The apparent simplicity of the techniques, as suggested by some of the popular manuals, obfuscates the highly developed discipline and technology reported in the professional literature. The clinician is well advised to carefully weigh the merits of assertive training as a therapy of choice for a given subset of patients, and should question whether she/he is capable of delivering such procedures.

This chapter has identified assessment techniques to facilitate the acceptance or rejection of assertive training as an appropiate and preferred intervention. We have also provided an empirical basis and clinical model for the practice of this therapy. The clinician is encouraged to further examine the research literature relevant to her/his practice before initiating any assertive-training techniques.

The impressive body of research on assertive training leaves specific areas in need of additional investigation. The assessment and evaluation of assertive deficits and skills is one such area. Current assessment methods, paper and pencil inventories and role-plays rated on behavioral and subjective dimensions, are a far cry from the "real world" of our patients. But the natural environment is an inhospitable place for a controlled and precise measurement of social behavior. Field observation has become especially difficult with recent legislation forbidding deceptive (unobtrusive) data-collection procedures. Another area requiring further study concerns the relative efficacy of various treatment techniques, or sets of techniques, with specific presenting problems and populations. Known and predictable interactions of patient, problem, and intervention would be an invaluable aid to case-management planning. Finally, we have yet to empirically compare group and individual training. Most investigators seem to have based the context of treatment on parameters of time and efficiency, rather than on process and outcome. These represent a few of the challenges faced by clinicians and researchers working with this rapidly growing training procedure.

REFERENCES

1. Alberti, R.E., and Emmons, M.L. *Your Perfect Right,* 2nd ed. San Luis Obispo, Cal.: Impact Press, 1974.
2. Alberti, R.E., and Emmons, M.L. *Stand Up, Speak Out, Talk Back.* New York: Pocket Books, 1975.
3. Bailey, J.G., and Sowder, W.T. Audiotape and videotape self-confrontation in psychotherapy. *Psychol. Bull.,* 74: 127-137, 1970.
4. Bandura, A. *Principles of Behavior Modification.* New York: Holt, Rinehart & Winston, 1969.
5. Bandura, A. Psychotherapy based upon modeling principles. In: *Handbook of Psychotherapy and Behavior Change,* ed. A.E. Bergin and S.L. Garfield. New York: Wiley, 1971.
6. Berger, R.M. Interpersonal skill training with institutionalized elderly patients. Unpublished doctoral dissertation, University of Wisconsin, Madison, 1976.
7. Brockway, B.S. Assertive training for professional women. *Social Work,* 21: 498-505, 1976.
8. Cautela, J.R. A behavior therapy approach to pervasive anxiety. *Behav. Res. Ther.* 4: 99-109, 1966.
9. Christensen, A., and Arkowitz, H. Preliminary report on practice dating and feedback as treatment for college dating problems. *J. Counsel. Psychol.,* 21: 92-95, 1974.
10. Christensen, A., Arkowitz, H., and Anderson, J. Practice dating as treatment for college dating inhibitions. *Behav. Res. Ther.,* 13: 321-331, 1975.
11. Clark, K.W. Evaluation of a group social skills training program with psychiatric inpatients: Training Vietnam era veterans. *Dissert. Abs. Internat.,* 35: 4642B, 1975.
12. Cotler, S.B., and Guerra, J. *Assertion Training.* Champaign, Ill.: Research Press, 1976.
13. Curran, J.P. Social skills training and systematic desensitization in reducing dating anxiety. *Behav. Res. Ther.,* 13: 65-68, 1975.
14. Curran, J.P., and Gilbert, F.S. A test of the relative effectiveness of a systematic desensitization program and an interpersonal skill training program with date anxious subjects. *Behav. Ther.,* 6: 510-521, 1975.
15. DeLange, J.M. Effectiveness of skill training and desensitization in increasing assertion in high and low anxiety women. Unpublished doctoral dissertation, University of Wisconsin, Madison, 1976.
16. Doering, M., Hamlin, R., Everstine, L., Eigenbrode, C., Chambers, G., Wolpin, M., and Lackner, F. The use of training to increase intensity of angry verbalization. *Psychol. Monogr.,* 76: No. 37 (Whole No. 556), 1962.
17. Dollard, J., and Miller, N.E. *Personality and Psychotherapy.* New York: McGraw-Hill, 1950.
18. D'Zurilla, T.J., and Goldfried, M.R. Problem solving and behavior modification. *J. Ab-*

norm. Psychol., 78: 107-126, 1971.

19. Edelstein, B.A., and Eisler, R.M. Effects of modeling and modeling with instructions and feedback on the behavioral components of social skills. *Behav. Ther.,* 7: 382-389, 1976.

20. Edwards, N.B. Case conference: Assertive training in a case of homosexual pedophillia. *J. Behav. Ther. Experiment. Psychiat.,* 3: 55-63, 1972.

21. Eisler, R.M., and Hersen, M. Behavioral techniques in family-oriented crisis intervention. *Arch. Gen. Psychol.,* 28: 111-116, 1973.

22. Eisler, R.M. Hersen, M., and Miller, P.M. Effects of modeling on components of assertive behavior. *J. Behav. Ther. Experiment. Psychiat.,* 4: 1-6, 1973.

23. Eisler, R.M., Miller, P.M., Hersen, M., and Alford, H. Effects of assertive training on marital interaction. *Arch. Gen. Psychiat.,* 30: 643-649, 1974.

24. Endler, N.S., and Okada, M. A multidimensional measure of trait anxiety: The S-R Inventory of General Trait Anxiousness. *J. Counsult. Clin. Psychol.,* 43: 319-329, 1975.

25. Eysenck, H.J., and Eysenck, S.B.G. *Manual for the Eysenck Personality Inventory.* San Diego, Cal.: Educational and Industrial Testing Service, 1968.

26. Fensterheim, H. Assertive methods and marital problems. In: *Advances in Behavior Therapy,* R.D. Rubin, H. Fensterheim, J.D. Henderson, and L.P. Ullman, eds. New York: Academic Press, 1972.

27. Fensterheim, H. Behavior therapy: Assertive training in groups. In: *Progress in Group and Family Therapy,* ed. C.J. Sager and H.S. Kaplan. New York: Brunner/Mazel, 1972.

28. Fensterheim, H., and Baer, J. *Don't Say Yes When You Want to Say No.* New York: Dell, 1975.

29. Fo, W.S.O., and O'Donnell, C.R. The buddy system: Relationship and contingency conditions in a community intervention program for youth with nonprofessionals as behavior change agents. *J. Consult. Clin. Psychol.,* 42: 163-169, 1974.

30. Foy, D.W., Eisler, R.M., and Pinkston, S. Modeled assertion in a case of explosive rages. *J. Behav. Ther. Experiment. Psychiat.,* 6: 135-137, 1975.

31. Frederiksen, L.W., Jenkins, J.O., Foy, D.W., and Eisler, R.M. Social-skills training to modify abusive verbal outbursts in adults. *J. Appl. Behav. Anal.,* 9: 117-125, 1976.

32. Freedman, B.K. An analysis of social-behavioral skill deficits in delinquent and non-delinquent boys. *Dissert. Abs. Internat.,* 35: 5110B-5111B, 1975.

33. Friedman, P.H. The effects of modeling and role-playing on assertive behavior. In: *Advances in Behavior Therapy,* ed. R.D. Rubin, H. Fensterheim, A.A. Lazarus, and C.M. Franks. New York: Academic Press, 1971.

34. Galassi, J.P., and Galassi, M.D. Validity of a measure of assertiveness. *J. Counsel. Psychol.,* 21: 248-250, 1974.

35. Galassi, J.P., Kostka, M.P., and Galassi, M.D. Assertive training: A one year follow-up. *J. Counsel. Psychol.,* 22: 451-452, 1975.

36. Gambrill, E.D., and Richey, C.A. An assertion inventory for use in assessment and research. *Behav. Ther.,* 6: 550-561, 1975.

37. Goldfried, M.R., and D'Zurilla, T.J. A behavioral-analytic model for assessing competence. In: *Current Topics in Clinical and Community Psychology,* Vol. 1, ed. C.D. Spielberger. New York: Academic Press, 1969.

38. Goldsmith, J., and McFall, R.M. Development and evaluation of an interpersonal skill training program for psychiatric inpatients. *J. Abnorm. Psychol.,* 84: 51-58, 1975.

39. Goldstein, A., Heller, K., and Sechrest, L. *Psychotherapy and the Psychology of Behavior Change.* New York: Wiley, 1966.

40. Green, A.H., and Marlatt, G.A. Effects of instructions and modeling upon affective and descriptive verbalization. *J. Abnorm. Psychol.,* 80: 189-196, 1972.

41. Hedquist, F.J., and Weinhold, B.K. Behavioral group counseling with socially anxious and unassertive college students. *J. Counsel. Psychol.,* 17: 237-242, 1970.

42. Hersen, M., and Bellack, A.S. A multiple baseline analysis of social-skills training in chronic schizophrenics. *J. Appl. Behav. Anal.,* 9: 239-245, 1976.
43. Hersen, M. and Bellack, A.S. Social skills training for chronic psychiatric patients: Rationale, research findings, and future directions, *Comprehen. Psychiat.,* 17: 559-580, 1976.
44. Hersen, M., Eisler, R.M. Miller, P.M. An experimental analysis of generalization in assertive training. *Behav. Res. Ther.,* 12: 295-310, 1974.
45. Hersen, M., Eisler, R.M., Miller, P.M., Johnson, M.B., and Pinkston, S.G. Effects of Practice, instructions, and modeling on components of assertive behavior. *Behav. Res. Ther.,* 11:443-451, 1973.
46. Hersen, M., Turner, S.M., Edelstein, B.A., and Pinkston, S.G. Effects of phenothiazines and social skills training in a withdrawn schizophrenic. *J. Clin. Psychol.,* 31: 588-594, 1975.
47. Hosford, R.E. Overcoming fear of speaking in a group. In: *Behavioral Counseling: Cases and Techniques,* ed. J.D. Krumboltz and C.E. Thoresen. New York: Holt, Rinehart & Winston, 1969.
48. Jakubowski-Spector, P. Facilitating the growth of women through assertive training. *Counsel. Psychol.,* 4: 75-86, 1973.
49. Johnson, T., Tyler, V., Thompson, R., and Jones, F. Systematic desensitization and assertive training in the treatment of speech anxiety in middle-school students. *Psychol. in Schools,* 8: 263-267, 1971.
50. Kanfer, F.H., and Phillips, J.S. *Learning Foundations of Behavior Therapy.* New York: Wiley, 1970.
51. Kazdin, A.E. Effects of ocvert modeling and reinforcement on assertive behavior. *J. Abnorm. Psychol.,* 83: 249-252, 1974.
52. Kazdin, A.E. Covert modeling, imagery assessment, and assertive behavior. *J. Consult. Clin. Psychol.,* 43: 716-724, 1975.
53. Kazdin, A.E. Effects of covert modeling, multiple models, and model reinforcement on assertive behavior. *Behav. Ther.,* 7: 211-222, 1976.
54. Kelley, H.H., and Shapiro, M.M. An experiment on conformity to group norms where conformity is detrimental to group achievement. *Amer. Sociol. Rev.,* 19: 667-677, 1954.
55. Kelly, G.A. *The Psychology of Learning Constructs.* New York: Norton, 1955.
56. Lange, A.J., and Jakubowski, P. *Responsible Assertive Behavior.* Champaign, Ill.: Research Press, 1976.
57. Laws, D.R., and Serber, M. Measurement and evaluation of assertive training with sexual offenders. In *The Crumbling Walls: Treatment and Counseling of Prisoners,* ed. R.E. Hosford and C.S. Moss. Champaign, Ill.: University of Illinois Press, 1975.
58. Lazarus, A.A. Behavior rehearsal vs. nondirective therapy vs. advice in effecting behavior change. *Behav. Res. Ther.,* 4: 209-212, 1966.
59. Lazarus, A.A. *Behavior Therapy and Beyond.* New York: McGraw-Hill, 1971.
60. Lazarus, A.A., and Fay, A. *I Can If I Want To.* New York: William Morrow, 1975.
61. Lazarus, A.A., and Serber, M. Is systematic desensitization being misapplied? *Psychol. Rep.,* 23: 215-218, 1968.
62. Liberman, R.P., King, L.W., DeRisi, W.J., and McCann, M. *Personal Effectiveness: Guiding People to Assert Themselves and Improve Their Social Skills.* Champaign, Ill.: Research Press, 1975.
63. Lomont, J.F., Gilner, F.H., Spector, N.J., and Skinner, K.K. Group assertive training and group insight therapies. *Psychol. Rep.,* 25: 463-470, 1969.
64. MacDonald, M.L., Lindquist, C.U., Kramer, J.A., McGrath, R.A., and Rhyne, L.D. social skills training: Behavior rehearsal in groups and dating skills. *J. Counsel. Psychol.,* 22: 224-230, 1975.

65. MacPherson, E.L.R. Selective operant conditioning and deconditioning of assertive modes of behavior. *J. Behav. Ther. Experiment. Psychiat.,* 3: 99-102, 1972.
66. Martinson, W.D., and Zerface, J.P. Comparison of individual counseling and a social program with nondaters. *J. Counsel. Psychol.,* 17: 36-40, 1970.
67. McFall, R.M., and Lillesand, D.B. Behavioral rehearsal with modeling and coaching in assertion training. *J. Abnorm. Psychol.,* 77: 313-323, 1971.
68. McFall, R.M., and Marston, A.R. An experimental investigation of behavior rehearsal in assertive training. *J. Abnorm. Psychol.,* 76: 295-303, 1970.
69. McFall, R.M., and Twentyman, C.T. Four experiments on the relative contributions of rehearsal, modeling, and coaching to assertion training. *J. Abnorm. Psychol.,* 81: 199-218, 1973.
70. McGovern, K.B., Arkowitz, H., and Gilmore, S.K. Evaluation of social skill training programs for college dating inhibitions. *J. Counsel. Psychol.,* 22: 505-512, 1975.
71. Melnick, J.A. Comparison of replication techniques in the modification of minimal dating behavior. *J. Abnorm. Psychol.,* 81: 51-59, 1973.
72. Miller, P.M., and Elkin, T. Marital assertiveness training in the treatment of alcoholism. Presented at the meeting of the Association for Advancement of Behavior Therapy, Miami, December, 1973.
73. Miller, P.M., and Hersen, M. Modification of marital interaction patterns between an alcoholic and his wife. Unpublished manuscript, University of Pittsburgh School of Medicine, 1976.
74. Moreno, J.L. *Psychodrama,* Vol. 1. New York: Beacon House, 1946.
75. Moreno, J.L. The discovery of the spontaneous man with special emphasis upon the technique of role reversal. *Group Psychother.,* 8: 103-139, 1955.
76. Nydegger, R.V. The elimination of hallucinatory and delusional behavior by verbal conditioning and assertive training. *J. Behav. Ther. Experiment. Psychiat.,* 3: 225-227, 1972.
77. Osborn, S.M., and Harris, G.G. *Assertive Training for Women.* Springfield, Ill.: Charles C Thomas, 1975.
78. Patterson, R.L. Time-out and assertive training for a dependent child. *Behav. Ther.* 3: 466-468, 1972.
79. Percell, L.P., Berwick, P.T., and Beigel, A. The effects of assertive training on self-concept and anxiety. *Arch. Gen. Psychiat.,* 31: 502-504, 1974.
80. Phelps, S., and Austin, N. *The Assertive Woman.* San Luis Obispo, Cal.: Impact Press, 1975.
81. Rathus, S.A. An experimental investigation of assertive training in a group setting. *J. Behav. Ther. Experiment. Psychiat.,* 3: 81-86, 1972.
82. Rathus, S.A. Instigation of assertive behavior through videotape-mediated models and directed practice. *Behav. Res. Ther.,* 11: 57-65, 1973.
83. Rathus, S.A. A 30-item schedule for assessing assertive behavior. *Behav. Ther.,* 4: 398-406, 1973.
84. Rehm, L.P., and Marston, A.R. Reduction of social anxiety through modification of self-reinforcement: An instigation therapy technique. *J. Consult. Clin. Psychol,* 32: 565-574, 1968.
85. Richey, C. Increased female assertiveness through self-reinforcement. Unpublished doctoral dissertation, University of California, Berkeley, 1974.
86. Rimm, D.C. Assertive training used in the treatment of chronic crying spells. *Behav. Res. Ther.,* 5: 373-374, 1967.
87. Rimm, D.C., Hill, G.A., Brown, N.N., and Stuart, J.E. Group-assertive training in treatment of expression of inappropriate anger. *Psychol. Rep.,* 34: 791-798, 1974.
88. Rimm, D.C., Keyson, M., and Hunziker, J. Group assertion training in the treatment of antisocial behavior. Unpublished manuscript, Arizona State University, 1971.

89. Rose, S.D. *Treating Children in Groups*. San Francisco: Jossey-Bass, 1972.
90. Rose, S.D. In pursuit of social competence. *Social Work*, 20: 33-39, 1975.
91. Rose, S.D. *Group Therapy: A Behavioral Approach*. Englewood Cliffs, N.J.: Prentice-Hall, 1977.
92. Ross, D., Ross, S., and Evans, D. The modification of extreme social withdrawal by modeling with guided participation. *J. Behav. Ther. Experiment. Psychiat.*, 2: 273-279, 1971.
93. Salter, A. *Conditioned Reflex Therapy*. New York: Capricorn, 1961. (Originally published, New York: Farrar, Straus, & Giroux, 1949.)
94. Sarason, I.G. Verbal Learning, modeling, and juvenile delinquency. *Amer. Psychol.*, 23: 254-266, 1968.
95. Schinke, S.P., and Rose, S.D. Assertive training in groups. In: *Group Therapy: A Behavioral Approach*, S.D. Rose. Englewood Cliffs, N.J.: Prentice-Hall, 1977.
96. Schinke, S.P., and Rose, S.D. Interpersonal skill training in groups. *J. Counsel. Psychol.*, 23: 442-448, 1976.
97. Serber, M., and Nelson, P. The ineffectiveness of systematic desensitization and assertive training in hospitalized schizophrenics. *J. Behav. Ther. Experiment. Psychiat.*, 2: 107-109, 1971.
98. Shoemaker, M.E., and Paulson, T.L. Group assertion training for mothers: A family intervention strategy. In: *Behavior Modification Approaches to Parenting* ed. E.J. Mash, L.C. Handy, and L.A. Hammerlynck, New York: Brunner/Mazel, 1976.
99. Skinner, B.F. *Science and Human Behavior*. New York: Macmillan, 1953.
100. Smith, M.J. *When I Say No, I Feel Guilty*. New York: Bantam Books, 1975.
101. Stevenson, I. Direct instigation of behavioral changes in psychotherapy. *Arch. Gen. Psychiat.*, 1: 99-107, 1959.
102. Stevenson, I., and Wolpe, J. Recovery from sexual deviations through overcoming of nonsexual neurotic responses. *Amer. J. Psychiat.*, 116: 737-742, 1960.
103. Twentyman, C.T., and McFall, R.M. Behavioral training of social skills in shy males. *J. Consult. Clin. Psychol.*, 43: 384-395, 1975.
104. Ullmann, L.P., and Krasner, L. *A Psychological Approach to Abnormal Behavior*. Englewood Cliffs, N.J.: Prentice-Hall, 1969.
105. Varenhorst, B.B. Helping a client speak up in class. In: *Behavioral Counseling: Cases and Techniques*, ed. J.E. Krumboltz and C.E. Thoresen. New York: Holt, Rinehart & Winston, 1969.
106. Wagner, M.K. Reinforcement of the expression of anger through role-playing. *Behav. Res. Ther.*, 6: 91-95, 1968.
107. Wagner, M.K. Comparative effectiveness of behavioral rehearsal and verbal reinforcement for effecting anger expressiveness. *Psychol. Rep.*, 22: 1079-1080, 1968.
108. Weinman, B., Gelbart, P., Wallace, M., and Post, M. Inducing assertive behavior in chronic schizophrenics: A comparison of socioenvironmental, desensitization, and relaxation therapies. *J. Consult. Clin. Psychol.*, 39: 246-252, 1972.
109. Whalen, C. Effects of a model and instructions on group verbal behaviors. *J. Consult. Clin. Psychol.*, 33: 509-521, 1969.
110. Wolpe, J. *Psychotherapy by Reciprocal Inhibition*. Stanford, Cal.: Stanford university Press, 1958.
111. Wolpe, J. *The Practice of Behavior Therapy*. New York: Pergamon, 1969.
112. Wolpe, J. *The Practice of Behavior Therapy*, 2nd ed. New York: Pergamon, 1973.
113. Wolpe, J., and Lazarus, A.A. *Behavior Therapy Techniques*. New York: Pergamon, 1966.
114. Wright, J.C. A comparison of systematic desensitization and social skill acquisition in the modification of a social fear. *Behav. Ther.*, 7: 205-210, 1976.
115. Yalom, I.D. *The Theory and Practice of Group Psychotherapy*. New York: Basic Books, 1970.

The Impact of Object Relations on Psychoanalysis: Theory and Treatment Techniques

RICHARD LASKY

Following on the heels of Jones' (20) and particularly Abraham's (1) fascinating studies of the determinants of early character organization, Melanie Klein (22) revolutionized psychoanalysis with her ground-breaking studies of the development of object relations and of character formation in early infancy. Previous studies of object relations had focused primarily on narcissism, and subsequently on the phallic development of superego introjects. Although Freud (8) paid attention to the oral period, his conception of the ego, and the developmental tasks of the infant, gave rise to a predominantly psychosexual theory of development. When clinical experience led him to an understanding of the nature of unconscious sexuality, he then placed primary emphasis on the development and resolution of the oedipal conflict. The emergence of oral and anal material in psychoanalytic therapy sessions led him to formulate a "psychosexual" theory, since most of these manifestations were understood by him as memory traces, or as remnants of infantile erotic activities which became hypercathected (superemphasized). Early development is seen more as a backdrop (a precursor, a preparation, or a waiting period) for the phallic phase with its organization and structuralization of the psyche.

Explanations of the oral and anal stages are often attempted from the phallic stage backward. In other words, the activities of these stages are seen as predominantly sexually oriented, especially when the phallic stage is used as a starting point. Oral erotism, anal erotism, primary and secondary masochism, sadism, memory, perception, motility, cognition, along with all other mental functions, are seen to have their roots in their abilities to satisfy the infant's instinctual needs. While it is true that Freud eventually postulated that ego instincts (related to self-preservative drives) would cause the infant to develop adaptations to the environment, his early assumptions concerning the motivating forces of oral and anal development are based on a pleasure-unpleasure model.

THE INSTINCTS AND THE EGO

One of Freud's main reasons for assuming that sexuality is the prime motivator in adaptation is that he postulates that there is no ego present at birth. Rather, he thinks there is only the capacity to develop an ego. He suggests that the infant has only an ego-percept, equivalent to perception and based on perception, which provides no defensive and adaptive mechanisms. The ego-percept, because of its relation to perception, causes the (eventual) ego to become reality-oriented, as its task develops along the lines of objective assessment of the inner and outer environment. In addition, because of its relation to the self-preservative instincts, Freud suggests that it causes the infant to retain memory traces of experiences that reduced tension, thus beginning cognitive development. For Freud, early in life the ego is limited to the most primitive functions and contents, with most of its tasks centering around reality perceptions and the development of survival techniques. For the most part, he does not ascribe major defensive functions to the ego early in infancy.

Parenthetically, it is worth noting that when psychoanalysts (whether Freud, Klein, or any other analyst) use the word *instinct,* they are not referring to the ethological concept of an instinct (the web a spider spins, or the nest a bird builds). By instinct, they merely mean the psychological (or mental) representative of the bodily process or processes. The mental activities of human beings are seen as derivatives of the attempts to decrease unpleasure, or increase pleasure, as bodily tensions vary.

THE KLEINIAN VIEWPOINT

When Klein entered the scene in the early 1930's, her first major change in Freud's theory was her extraordinary emphasis on the power and importance of the death instinct. For her, the death instinct is the mental experience of the body's tensions, frustrations, needs, and pressures, for various kinds of discharges (chemical as well as mechanical). Achievement or grafitication of these needs is experienced as sexually pleasurable (libido), whereas the tension occurring until the need is met is experienced as painful or unpleasurable (the death instinct, or aggression). Hence, the infant exists in a perpetual state of tension as different life processes need to be fulfilled.

The Paranoid-Schizoid Position

Klein suggests that the infant experiences the death instinct as a feeling of anxiety and persecution (based on the memory of the birth trauma). She believes the ego *to be present at birth* and postulates that is has immediate adaptive and defensive capabilities. For Klein, the ego's first task is to protect the infant from the persecutory anxiety of the death instinct. The ego does this by the use of splitting and projection. It makes an assumption that there is some sphere of existence outside the infant's rather encompassing boundaries (contrary to the Freudian view) that can act as a receptacle for the psyche's waste products, i.e., aggression and all other unpleasure-related affective and cognitive material. This split between the infant and an outside universe is complemented by an equivalent split between the pleasure-unpleasure experiences of the infant. Instead of experience being perceived as partly good and bad, or pleasurable and unpleasurable in an integrated way, Klein suggests that the infant isolates the positive and negative aspects of experience and perception so that all positive experience can occur without a sense of negative contamination. Things are either all good or all bad—nothing inbetween.

This is the splitting defense of the ego, present at birth, which enables the infant to protect *good* experiences from *bad* ones. Now we have an infant who has *absolutely good* and *absolutely bad* experiences, existing in an environment where there is *one's self* versus *everything else* (lumped together as "out there"). In order to rid the self of the bad experiences, the ego needs to project the *badness* outside the self into the *everything else* (an amorphous concept, at best). This enables the infant to be left with all the *goodness* as an integral part of the self, and to have the *badness* entirely externalized. In this fashion, the infant protects both the *good experience* and the *good self* from contaminating contact with *badness*.

This defense of projection, when used in conjunction with splitting, affords the infant protection from the overwhelming anxieties associated with aggression. The infant can maintain the fantasy of safety and perfection as long as these mechanisms are sufficiently active and effective. This implies essentially that the ego's first tasks are centered around a psychotic adjustment and not around reality testing and the secondary process, as Freud originally suggested. For Klein the concept of unconscious fantasy includes the idea that there is no objective perception that is uncolored by instinctual demands and necessities, blending together primary- and secondary-process activities in ways inconsistent with classical theory.

Freudians, represented particularly by the "New York School" of ego psychologists (Hartmann, Kris, Loewenstein, Rapaport, Gill, and others), have hypothesized that there are ego contents and ego functions present at birth. They differ radically from Klein in their belief that major ego functions (specifically perception, memory, and motility) are free from instinctual coloration. They suggest that these functions begin autonomously, and only traumatic conflictual conditions cause them to become instinctualized. Where Klein conceived that all ego functions stem from instinctual responsivity, modern Freudian analysts see major portions of the ego as having freedom from what is, in Klein's view, a psychotic core of predetermined, instinctually originated activity.

Klein refers to the first period of life as the paranoid-schizoid position. The main ego tasks are to split and project outward all unpleasure and bad experiences and maintain a happy inner environment free from anxiety. This is an ideal, however, that the infant cannot achieve because aggression (in the form of anxiety) impinges on his experience. Because of the paranoid-schizoid mechanisms, however, the child now experiences the threat as coming from the *outside* and not as a threatening part, or aspect, of the self. This becomes the basis for the infant's persecutory fears and causes the primitive ego to develop a new method of defense. Where, up until this point, only splitting and projection were at the infant's disposal, Klein suggests that the new development is the mechanism of projective identification. The infant needs to "defend" himself from the persecutory "external" environment, and continued splitting and projection are insufficient. Projective identification is similar to identification with the aggressor, but with the following major difference: the aggressor is not a "reality" but merely the projected aggression of the identifier, that is, the infant.

The following example may serve to clarify this. A hostile child projects his rage onto a parent who in reality is not enraged or even particularly aggressive. The child, through projection, believes that the parent is enraged and consequently sees the parent as being quite dangerous. The child feels overwhelmed with anxiety for his own safety in the presence of such a danger, the "persecutory" parent. He assumes that the parent's power is derived from rage, that is, pure aggression, and to defend himself begins to generate rage and aggression (a seeming act of identification) to balance the dangers "presented" by the parent. In this way, the force and potential of the aggressive impulses is reinternalized, and the child is able to experience this with safety. If projective identification did not occur, the danger is that the aggression would be self-directed. Where this mechanism has been employed, the child has the opportunity to experience the aggression as a facet of himself while keeping it outwardly directed. The fact that the parent never was enraged, aggressive, or particularly a source of danger is split off and discarded (repressed or projected outward depending on the child's developmental level). Projective identification takes place with libidinal impulse derivatives as well as with aggression (lest the above example lead one to assume that this ego function is designed only to respond to the death instinct).

Another example of projective identification would be in the case of a patient who comes into therapy with hostile impulses and then begins to experience the therapist as if the therapist were hostile toward him, the patient. This is a direct projection of the patient's hostility onto the therapist where the patient assumes that the rage comes not from himself, but from the therapist. If the patient were to say, in effect, "the only way to protect myself from this hostile therapist is to learn his hostile aggressive techniques and make them my own," this would be a form of projective identification, where the aggression and hostility is reinternalized, but directed outward rather than toward the self.

The Depressive Position

As the infant continues to develop, particularly along neurological lines, greater degrees of both perception and memory become possible. These attributes, along with actual experiences, eventually cause the infant's ego to develop additional skills which are somewhat more reality-related. Up until this point, the infant has had only two objects in his world—the *good breast* (good mothering experience) and the *bad breast* (bad mothering experience). Klein suggests that if severe deprivations in mothering occur, the infant's ability to grow (psychologically) will be impaired (resulting in any number of phase-specific fixations and/or retardations). We will assume, for our purposes, that our hypothetical infant exists in what Hartmann (17) called the "average expectable environment," where good-enough mothering is presumed to have existed. In this atmosphere, the infant ego's reality-testing ability will be enhanced.

In a more psychotic vein, however, the integration of the *good* and *bad breast,* that is, mothering experience, which has good and bad aspects (an object rather than a part-object), is pursued on a basis that bears only a small relation to reality. Through the mechanism of projective identification, a primitive integration of *good* and *bad* breasts, selves, and drives takes place. Although projective identification permits the infant to tolerate instinctual aggression, its negative consequence is that it prevents objects from remaining exclusive in their *goodness* or *badness.* The primitive ego, in attempting to both split and integrate experiences of self and objects, begins to become less and less able to protect *goodness* from *badness.* If the infant protects the vulnerable *"good self"* from aggression by conceiving of the *"bad persecutory object,"* which the good self then identifies with (for protection), then the *bad* (aggressive) *object* exists within the *good self*—and to some extent acts as a contamination, destroying the exclusivity of the *goodness.*

In a sense, Klein is describing an infant whose libidinal needs cause it to exist in a state of either absolute hunger, or complete satiation. Since the mother cannot conceivably meet the infant's feeding needs at the very instant they take place, the resulting frustrations (in waiting for the feeding) threaten to spoil the gratifications of feeding because of the aggression generated and reinforced by the waiting period. The infant splits this off, and projects it into the image of a *good gratifying breast* and a *bad persecutory breast.* Since this mechanism is not perfect and absolute, the good breast is contaminated by *badness* (in the infant's fantasy that *its greed is greater than the breast's capacity to be gratifying).* Further unmanageable aggression is experienced when the fantasy of the breast's inability to gratify causes the infant to experience greater hunger, as he imagines future deprivations. Continued projection of the rage helps a bit, but is not sufficient, as the baby imagines scooping out, sucking dry, and emptying the breast. The infant, using the model of oral incorporation of the milk (and sweating, spitting, defecating, urinating, and vomiting of the body's wastes on the side of badness), enhances projective identifications with the *good breast* to take in more *goodness* (and with the *bad breast* to rid himself of *badness).* In this fashion, each object is kept separate. However, that is the plan, but not the case. When the infant projectively identifies with the *bad breast,* then he is part *bad.* When he is in a projective identificatory merger with the *good breast,* part of the shared self is *bad,* thereby contaminating the *good breast* with the *bad breast's badness.* This then makes the *good breast* that much less *good,* and consequently less able to be totally gratifying. This "reality confirmation" of the *good breast's badness* drives the infant into a further rage, causing even more aggression to be directed to the *good breast* (and to be incorporated by the *good breast).* The infant, in a total rage at the *good breast's badness* (inability to be perfect forever and interminably) also experiences great envy at the *good breast's goodness* (that part of the *good breast* not yet given over to the *good self)* and now, in projective identification with the *bad breast,* wishes to destroy the *good breast* in retaliation. In fantasy, projective identification with the *good breast* is helpful, but insufficient in balancing projective identification with the *bad breast.* The infant is overwhelmed with rage and envy, and his ability to survive the experience (as aggression predominates) is diminished unless new mechanisms of defense are developed by the ego.

Klein suggests that guilt develops to interfere with envy, thereby safeguarding and protecting the *good breast.* She believes that as the infant begins to become aware of the impending destruction of the *good breast* from past assaults, present assaults, and the wish to make future assaults, the infant moves into a period of depression. In addition, the inability to keep the *self* free from contamination causes the infant to become further depressed as the self is also under the shadow of impending destruction. Since this is the result of an inner process of the aggressive instinct, and the ego's relation to it, she suggests that an inner process of the ego will be developed only where the environment (in reality) has been supportive. The reality supports of the environment are, according to Klein, the supporters not only of life, but also of libido and the ego's defenses. This strongly supported libido is what feeds the ego's ability to create further defenses against the destructive, aggressive process. The infant in this stage is in what Klein calls the depressive position.

The Reparative Position

In the depressive position, the child experiences both a sense of self and of objects which is contaminated, damaged, and ruined. The destruction of *good* objects by *bad* objects, the imposition of *badness* into *goodness,* as a result of the child's projections (in attempting to rid itself of his own aggression), and the wish to continue to contaminate *good* objects through envy (and through retaliation) all cause the child to remain in an untenable position. The depressive position is an overwhelmingly guilty position, and the child must find a way to resolve this position. If the depressive position were to continue for too long, guilt would continue to grow as a defense against envy, rage, and aggression and would eventually be turned inward so that the self would be destroyed by one's own guilt. The infant would suffer not only a retaliation that represented a punitive outside aggressor, but also a self-directed, self-initiated retaliation designed both to punish the *bad self* for having made an attack on *good objects* and to provide the *good objects* with continued protection against the retaliatory aggressive impulses of the *bad self.* In addition, this would provide *good objects* and *good selves* with protection against the inherent *badness* of *bad objects* and *bad selves.* Unfortunately, this would lead to a state of total self-directed aggression if it were not defended against by the production of other viable ego defenses.

Klein suggests that as perception occurs and integration continues to progress, and as the infant begins to develop other kinds of ego functions (alongside these purely defensive ones), the infant will be able to defend against guilt with the production of love. She implies that the infant will have to find a way to protect all of these *good* objects (including the *good self*) from the overwhelming aggression of guilt, and from the terror and apprehension of the fact that its past aggressions (and wished-for aggressions in the future) will damage all *good objects* and *good selves.* The infant therefore undertakes the task of first defending against *bad objects* and *bad* impulses with the production of guilt and, then, having once more to defend against all the self-directed rage. The infant engages in this activity by developing the feeling that if he can counterbalance all his aggressive projections of *badness,* then he would be balanced equally (if not more heavily weighted) in favor of *goodness.* What this requires is that the infant be willing to divest himself of some of his own *goodness* to replace lost *good* portions in *good objects* and fill them up so that they are not as susceptible to *badness* (which has been the cause of the original lost *goodness*). By giving to an object a part of the infant's own *goodness,* the infant is making a reparation for the past destruction of *good* portions of the object (and for future wishes to destroy *good* objects, as they hold within them the possibility of turning *bad*). In effect, the infant is making a reparation. The infant is attempting to undo the damage he has done, by giving off part of his self.

One frequently hears the expression that emulation is the highest form of compliment, and it is not unreasonable to speculate that it has its origins in this kind of activity. To some extent, this is a way of making objects *good* by turning them into part of the self. That is, the infant gives up part of his self, gives it to the object, and then doubly cathects the object, in a process of identification. However, to see this process only as taking the object into the self and creating, in effect, a double cathexis, which causes the object to be loved as a part of the self, is to some extent an oversimplification. While one can understand the reparative affective state that Klein is suggesting in this, which she calls the reparative period, it may be better understood by some of the more classical formulations of narcissism postulated by Freud.

LOVE AND OBJECTS

Freud indicates the development of love has a somewhat different origin than that suggested by Klein. Klein proposes that love, as described above, develops as a response to guilt and as an attempt to make reparation for having damaged objects (by injecting one's *badness* into them). She suggests that as envy and greed begin to predominate, guilt defends, with the eventual production of love. In contrast, Freud hypothesizes that this identification process occurs in the following fashion. Initially Freud believed that the first relationship of loving is indifference. He thought that there is no such thing as love, that there are no such thing as objects, that anything that exists in the outside world is considered hostile and alien, that in fact it is nothing more than a noxious impingement upon a primary state of pleasure (or a primary state including the lack of unpleasure). Freud suggests that where libido exists it is entirely narcissistic and directed only at the self, although he clearly indicates that there is no concept, at least no mental concept, of self present for the infant at this stage. Nonetheless, all libido is narcissistic and none is directed toward the outside world. Where the outside world becomes necessary for the infant, or where it impinges upon him so that he can no longer ignore it, it is experienced not merely as a nonexperience, but as an act of the alien and hostile experience, and the infant's first response to it after indifference is to reject it. The infant's response is not simply to reject it, but if the stimulus becomes insistent enough, to actively begin to hate it.

In this context, the development of object cathexes occur which are somewhat separate from narcissistic cathexes, but which are not yet sufficiently endowed with libido to be considered the development (even in a primary sense) of *object love.* The infant narcissistically attends to objects in the sense that he will respond to them when they are narcissistically gratifying, but beyond that the object really has no value for the infant. The infant uses the object to meet whatever inner wishes he has for the moment and then rejects the object as if it were nonexistent all along, quickly forgetting that the object existed even within the context of a narcissistic gratification. Over time, as memory traces continue, the infant begins to hold internally the object memory, or the trace of the object, and more object libido is given over from narcissistic libido so that longer and longer periods not only of attention, but now of memory as well, continue to occupy the infant with regard to an object.

In Freud's early model, memory is not an autonomous ego function. Therefore, in order for memory to exist, a certain amount of libido has to be maintained in a cathexis to the object even after the object is no longer in actual contact with the infant. In this hydraulic economic model, only a limited amount of libido can exist, which then has to be split in any number of ways in order for more than one cathexis to occur. One of the consequences of this activity is that some of the libido, which previously was narcissistic libido, now has to be used for object cathexes. The ego, and the sense of self, experiences this as a depletion. The withdrawal of libido from the ego and the subjective experience are felt as loss and depletion. For the infant loving, if loving in this very primary stage is equated with attention and object investment, is thus experienced as a loss.

So then, the infant, after the stage of simple indifference (which in effect is a nonact of loving), first experiences the act of loving not as a gratifying experience, but as something depleting. The infant cannot positively experience, for any length of time, consistent loving directed toward an object. He can't experience object love of object cathexes for too long before experiencing this as a depletion of the self. The infant's response to this is to try to withdraw whatever libido he gave up to the object and to redirect that libido back onto the self, making it once more narcissistic libido. This, in effect, is an attempt of the ego to force itself back upon the id as a primary love object, but Freud states that this is impossible for the infant for two reasons. First, it is impossible because there is a saturation point beyond which the ego itself is unable to tolerate narcissistic cathexis, and that the overflow must go somewhere (and hence must be directed outward for health to continue). Second, if this were to occur and to continue, it would require that the infant, in effect, became totally autistic and remain that way for the rest of his life. What Freud suggests is that the infant will once again direct cathexis out to an object, but this time will *identify* with the object, that is, make the object part of the self (either through early oral incorporative fantasies or other similar fantasies). The infant will draw the object into the self so that there is no difference between self and object. Therefore, since a merger now exists between the self and the object, the object has become part of the ego. In this way, a double cathexis has been directed at the object, that is, if it is part of the ego, then loving the object is also equivalent to loving one's self. If this is the case, then object cathexes and narcissistic cathexes exist side by side, directed at both object and self simultaneously, and this is what leads to the ultimate development, not of just object cathexis, but of actual object love. Although the ego initially tried to withdraw cathexes from objects and force itself back upon the id as the primary love object, it relinquishes that demand as the need to experience depletion of self is lessened by virtue of this double cathexis. In this way, the act of loving can occur without the simultaneous experience of deprivation, depletion, and loss.

CHARACTER AND THE DEFENSES

Returning now to Klein's theory, if one uses this initial Freudian concept to explain the decrease in aggressive impulse during the reparative period, one recognizes the importance of the development of envy which is then defended against by guilt, which is in turn defended against by reparation. One can also see that the object becomes not only integrated, but more genuinely loved. For Klein, this is the beginning of an *object love,* not simply designed to meet narcissistic wishes, but which will eventually develop into adult romantic love. Essentially the three "positions" Klein hypothesizes all children go through—the paranoid-schizoid, the depressive, and the reparative position—make up the bulk of character development. She suggests that very early in life, in fact within the first six or seven months of life, certainly no later than the first year of life, the essential character structure (including the infant's basic affective states) already exists and persists as the sequence is undergone.

More recent research findings in the area of perception, sensation, neurology, pediatrics, developmental psychology, and child psychology indicate that it is somewhat unlikely that Klein's chronology (the first stage occurring roughly within the first two months of life; the second stage, up until about the fifth month of life, and the third stage, between the sixth and eighth or tenth month of life) is accurate. However, the dynamics she suggests may be quite pertinent and it is precisely these dynamics that are the mainstay of most current object-relations theories. Whether one views the more traditional psychoanalytic concept of object-relations (which would include the combination of instinct theories with environmental theories), or whether one looks at the more exclusively environmental theories of object relations (such as those proposed by Fairbairn [4], Guntrip [11], or Laing [30], one sees that Klein's basic dynamic concepts are held to, even though the chronology is given up. It might be best for us to hold our ideas about chronology in abeyance while paying careful attention to the dynamic states Klein has proposed.

This has had a strong impact not only on psychoanalytic theory but on psychoanalytic treatment, as differing concepts of ego and id functions (and unconscious psychic structure) began to evolve, from the original psychoanalytic assumptions to the assumptions of the object-relations school. In addition, the ego-psychology approach placed great emphasis on development of the ego and the superego and these ideas tended to influence classical psychoanalysis in a direction even further divorced from the direction of object-relations theory.

For example, ego psychologists such as Hartmann, Kris, Loewenstein, Rapaport, and Gill believed that an ego is present at birth, which is not particularly different from Klein's view. However, they thought that a number of ego functions (particularly perception, memory, and motility) are autonomous, that is, they are not at the mercy of the instincts, and that these activities are innate properties all infants (unless there is a pathological genetic defect) have at their disposal. The object-relations school's view of the ego assumes that there are no autonomous ego functions and that all ego functions are instinctually colored and designed primarily to meet the demands of defense against psychotic anxiety. For the ego-psychology school, the initial ego functions are not based on their relation to psychotic anxiety, but are genetically there to help the child to relate accurately to reality. They enhance the child's developing abilities of cognition and secondary-process functioning.

To some extent, the object-relations school's assumptions about the early nature and quality of the ego are very close to Freud's first theory of anxiety. Freud suggests that the ego creates the conscious experience of anxiety simply as the mental representation of dammed-up and/or repressed sexual feelings, i.e., libido. He assumes that the way one would experience this, since one could not experience it as sexual feelings (because of repression), would simply be as anxiety. Klein proposes that aggressive rather than sexual feelings are at the origin of anxiety, and that in fact the ego's first task is to make one aware of anxiety and to cope with it. Freud, however, did develop a second theory of anxiety. This is his concept of "signal anxiety," which basically postulates that the ego, with its ability to test reality adequately, is able to send a signal to the individual when it experiences danger. It is really irrelevant whether the danger arises from internal or external sources; signal anxiety is the ego's way of stating that some danger will occur in order to alert the individual to take some kind of action (even if it is an action that ultimately turns into a more maladaptive response than originally planned for by the ego). This then suggests that for Freudians and the ego psychologists the ego is primarily attuned to reality and the secondary-process function of reality testing; whereas for members of the object-relations school the ego is the mainstay of what eventually develops into an essentially psychotic core of mental functioning.

One may also wish to consider the work of Fairbairn (4, 5, 6) and Guntrip (11, 12, 13), which is essentially nonanalytic in that it forgoes traditional concepts of drive theory. In their theories one finds even more drastic differences in the nature and construction of the ego. For Fairbairn, there is no such thing as an id, there is no libido, there are no repressed drives, there is no aggression (except as a response to frustration), and the only human instinct is the instinct to be object-seeking. This then turns the ego into nothing more than a structure designed to help the individual find objects he is "instinctively" seeking. The problem with this theory is its inability to clearly differentiate between an individual's natural inclinations to be object-*hungry* and his instinctual object-*seeking*. To suggest that the biological and physiological characteristics an individual brings to the developmental process are irrelevant seems to be somewhat specious; and to suggest that people are intuitively and instinctually object-*seeking* seems to be unsupported by any clear empirical research or clinical data. Certainly, many psychoanalytic object-relations theorists recognize that objects are important in the lives of individuals, and since all individuals (unless they have been pathologically affected) are object-*hungry*, they tend to have strong relations to objects which color what the original aims were regarding the objects. Frequently, objects become so hypercathected that they appear to be things which people are instinctually driven toward, but this is reason to separate the difference between *object hunger* and "instinctual" object-*seeking*, not to consolidate it. In any event, this view of the ego is even more radically different from the Freudian (or ego-psychology) view of the ego, and other major consequences accrue.

PSYCHOANALYSIS AND PSYCHOTHERAPY

Since the basic theory has been rather fully outlined, it seems useful to discuss the major differences that exist in therapy done by practitioners of psychoanalysis.[1] I shall contrast and compare the various schools on the following major topics: (1) the nature of transference, (2) the nature of the working alliance, (3) the timing and depth of interpretations and (4) the relation of regression to treatment. By looking at these four major constructs, we can get a better idea of where object-relations theory differs from traditional psychoanalytic theory, and also get a picture of what it is not simply complementary but enriching.

THE TRANSFERENCE

Regarding the nature of psychoanalytic treatment from the traditional point of view, an idea regarding the transference neurosis is that it is resolved exclusively via the use of verbal interpretations. The goal is the achievement of the reality principle, and interventions are designed to continuously aid in the further structuralization of the ego. The object-relations schools sees the transference neurosis as essentially a projection of the patient's varying infantile object relations onto the analyst and into the therapy. The assumption here is that the transference neurosis will be resolved through early interpretations of primitive psychotic anxiety, when the regressions (which occur in the projections of the infantile object relations) to pregenital and unconscious fantasy situations take place.

From the traditional psychoanalytic model, one can see that transference is conceived of as essentially a process of the *displacement* from the past into the present of an apperceptive mass which includes feelings, ideas, associations, affects, cognitions, opinions, beliefs, action tendencies, sensations, etc. Naturally this is an inap-

---

[1] For the purpose of the rest of this chapter, traditional psychoanalysis is meant to include the more recent findings of ego psychology, since in America ego psychology is included in what is referred to as the classical psychoanalytic position.

propriate activity as it is not based on reality, but rather on assumptions that derive from unconscious conflict.

From the object-relations viewpoint, the transference is a projective activity, rather than a displacement. Although object-relations theorists recognize the origins of current object relations in infantile object relations, they suggest that these infantile object relations are no different than one's current object relations (which are then projected into the treatment process onto the analyst and into the treatment itself). They work with projection, splitting, projective identification, and in their own countertransference with projective counteridentification, as a means of resolving what they see as essentially a projective process having its source of origin in the past. From the traditional psychoanalytic point of view, the transference can include projections along with many other defensive functions of the ego, but the projections and all the other ego activities take place in the context of a process of displacement.

For members of the object-relations school, transference (which is for them synonymous with the *transference neurosis*) is essentially characterological, in the sense that people carry their transference relationships with them all the time, and project transference relationships into virtually every activity (the degree to which transference relationships become symptomatic depends on the health or pathology of one's inner object relations). From a traditional psychoanalytic point of view, while analysts accept the idea that all situations carry with them transferential aspects, they do differentiate between generalized characterological transference and the transference neurosis. For traditional analysts, the transference neurosis is an artifact, that is, an artificial outcome of the psychoanalytic situation where transference demands and transference attitudes and displacements tend to become intensified. So much so, that essentially most symptoms and most of the blatant transference relationships outside of the analytic process seem to fall away and become magnified primarily within the context of the analytic process. One may say that the transference neurosis has developed when the patient has lodged most of his/her conflicts and interests in the analyst and the therapeutic setting, and most of the environmental concerns and symptoms which have occurred outside of the treatment setting have been displaced into the transference relationship (rather than remaining in externalized symptom formation). This is a major point of difference between members of the traditional psychoanalytic school and the object-relations school, since the object-relations school tends not to differentiate between the specific concept of the transference neurosis and characterological transference.

In addition, traditional analysts assume that there is a kind of transference which they refer to as a *floating* transference. This transference is the aspect of the transference relationship that exists from the time the patient initially comes to treatment until the time the patient has actually invested most of his/her transferential energies in the analyst and the analytic hour. As the intensity of this relationship builds, it is described as "floating" rather than characterological transference, or a transference neurosis. Because it has not become a special unique artifact of psychoanalysis as yet, it is not yet considered a transference neurosis.

As a result of this, most traditional analysts tend to focus on the role of the ego and on the defenses represented in the transference neurosis, in the context of the various instinctual conflicts. It is true that analysts recognize the importance of early object relations; however, these early object relations have no special or preferred focus and are not considered the issue of absolute and paramount importance, as they are by the object-relations school. For the most part, traditional analysts stress and emphasize attempts to participate in this resolution. Once these kinds of controls are achieved, they then suggest that the analyst can be seen with fewer transference distortions.

THE WORKING ALLIANCE

A basic assumption, which needs to be looked at in order to clarify this, is the nature of the differences in attitudes regarding the working alliance. From a traditional psychoanalytic point of view, when Freud conceived of that part of the relationship between the patient and the therapist that kept the patient connected to the treatment (during times of stress or negative transference), he made the assumption that the patient would need to rely on positive transference. Initially, before the concept of autonomous ego functions was developed, there was no strong assumption that ego functions would be relatively, or entirely, free of instinctual conflict. Freud felt the need to rely on a concept of positive transference, which in effect is nothing more than a simple balance (the development of negative transference versus the development of positive transference) so that at the very worst, in a moderately healthy patient, nothing more countertherapeutic than a stalemate develops. In more healthy patients, the positive transference overcomes the negative transference and keeps the patient in treatment.

With the evolution of ego psychology, and the assumption of autonomous ego functions, the nature of the working alliance tended to change, and traditional psychoanalysts began to consider that patients should not rely on a transference relationship for anything, nor should analysts stake their goals on transference relationships since transference relationships really did not have much to do with secondary process or with reality. They felt that the positive transference was just an idealized form of aperceptive displacement, instead of a negative form of aperceptive displacement, and should be replaced with the concept of autonomous ego functions (which would keep the patient tied into the analytic process when the going got rough). In effect, what this means is that in order to be analyzable, the patient needs to have an observing ego that he or she can maintain even during the most stressful parts of the analysis. For example, a patient in the midst of a very strong negative transference should be able to say something to the effect of: "It seems as if you are like my father," or "You remind me so much of my mother," without falling into the pitfalls of: "There is no difference between you and my father or you and my mother," or "You are so much alike that you are for all practical purposes the same." It became a criterion of analyzability that the patient to be able to hold onto that "as-if" quality, recognizing, if not technically at least implicitly, the transferential nature of his/her feelings.

Thus, what changed in the analytic position regarding the working alliance was that analysts no longer relied on idealized and positive relationships with their patients which were based on unconscious conflict, but on healthy, strong, adequate ego functions that would permit the patient to remain adult and realistic even during times when they were feeling rather infantile, helpless, and unrealistic. Additionally, it was assumed that the patient would have to be able to identify with the analyzing functions of the analyst, and not simply model him/herself after the analyst (as if the analyst were the only image worth following, as a child frequently follows in the footstpes of a parent). Part of the "growing-up" process is the potential ability to develop a depersonification of one's identifications, and this is a necessary prerequisite for analyzability in the traditional model.

Since this is based essentially on a concept of autonomous ego functions, which remain deinstinctualized except under severe trauma, and since the nature of the ego is so different depending on whether one is a traditional psychoanalyst or a follower of the object-relations school, the whole question not only of analyzability, but of the working alliance in general, is in conflict when one turns to the assumptions of the object-relations school. The object-relations school, not considering the ego to be autonomous, or to have autonomous functions, cannot require the maintenance of autonomous ego functions throughout the analytic process as a measure of analyzability. In fact, because their view is that the ego is essentially a reactive-respondent organ to the instincts, they don't really consider seriously the issue of the working alliance (based on a patient's ability to maintain a healthy relationship with the analyst even at the moments they are feeling most sick). They suggest that the working alliance is dependent only on the analyst's ability to reduce primitive persecutory anxiety, and that if the analyst, through proper interpretations, can reduce the patient's anxiety level, then the patient will feel less persecuted and be in more of an alliance with the analyst. In addition, if the patient is feeling less persecuted, then he/she will be required to engage in fewer pathological ego activities, and hence the healthy nonpathological aspects of the ego will be strengthened and the patient will be more tightly bound to the analyst. The outcome of these varying points of view regarding the working alliance indicates that traditional psychoanalysts tend to be very selective about those individuals they feel are analyzable (as opposed to those individuals who either need preliminary psychotherapy in preparation for psycholanalysis, or for whom psychoanalysis would never be useful), in opposition to object-relations theorists who feel that everyone is analyzable, and accept for analysis patients with character disorders, children, psychotics, and others who would not be acceptable to traditional analysts as analysands.

INTERPRETATION

The question of the way in which one interprets to the patient is radically different depending on one's point of view. Practitioners with an object-relations orientation tend to make early transference interpretations, and at times, rather deep interpretations (in the sense of interpreting deep uncounscious meaning in patient's action tendencies, actions, attitudes, beliefs, or any other kind of production, as well as the thoughts they suggest during the hour). Their approach is that patients are plagued in the development of adequate object relations by inadequate ways of dealing with primitive persecutory anxiety, and that frequently what patients will do is to bring to the treatment hour the very persecutory anxieties that prevent them in the present (and prevented them in the past), from developing adequate object relations. This interferes with the other tasks of the ego. What object-relations practitioners will do is to make interpretations of the unconscious content of the material, and the various ways in which it is acted out transferentially in the treatment with the analyst, based on the assumption that this will reduce primitive anxiety (as the patient is able to integrate material in such a way so as not to be doomed only to the use of projection, splitting, and projective identification to defend against persecutory anxiety). The assumption is that because these interpretations will be anxiety-reducing for the patient they will help the patient to develop more adequate object relations in the process.

From a more traditional psychoanalytic point of view, just the opposite is suggested: early transference interpretations and early interpretations of deep unconscious material will create more, rather than less anxiety in the patient. Traditional analytic practitioners tend to shy away from deep interpretations until late in treatment. This is based on the belief that conflict is unconscious and gets expressed in very displaced and transformed ways. Not only is the conflict unconscious, but even most of the defenses are unconscious. In additon, if they assume that they are working with generally healthy people who have made relatively successful gestures in the direction of deinstinctualizing ego functions, then there will be continuing pressure not to reinstinctualize ego functions (which would constitute a trauma), and people will resist the acquisition of this kind of "truth," even if presented on only a superficial and intellectualized level, let alone to the deepest "roots" of one's consciousness. Their assumption, then, is that people will tend to erect stronger defenses against the anxiety (which is realistic, rather than persecutory), as the ego is forced into a traumatic situation where many of its functions will be required to be reinstinctualized under the pressure of *premature* analytic insights. Therefore, the traditional analytic assumption is that although the accuracy of the interpretation may in fact be equivalently correct in both cases, it is not accuracy of interpretation, but timing of interpretation and readiness to tolerate interpretations—*without too much trauma to the ego,* that determines when and to what degree an interpretation is made. Generally, their feeling is that one can only work with material where conflict already has been mobilized, and is apparent (or preconscious) to the patient. One must first analyze resistances and defenses, and then, subsequently, one may be able to get into the very nature of impulsive wishes or of unconscious instinctual conflicts. Finally, one may work on resolving archaic intersystemic and instinctual difficulties. This leads us to consider and discuss the issue of the role of regression.

REGRESSION

Because object-relations theorists tend to see the transference relationship as a relationship existing both in the past and in the present simultaneously (by virtue of its being a present object relation left over from the past), they tend to understand a regression on the part of the patient as a deepening of the transference, and view the regression in the transference as essentially a cooperative activity on the part of the patient. They thus imply that regression is a deepening of the transference and an attempt by the patient to interact therapeutically with the therapist (so that the therapist will have greater access to making anxiety-reducing transference interpretations, which will then lead to better treatment-results). From the more traditional psychoanalytic point of view, regression is a further attempt by a patient to get the analyst to meet the various kinds of tranference wishes and provide the transference gratifications the patient may have in mind. As the patient is frustrated in his/her ability to get transference gratification, he/she will tend to use earlier and more infantile mechanisms of persuasion and tend to rely on more primitive defensive activities. The consequence of this is a regressive activity, which is seen not as a deepening of the transference in a constructive way, but rather as a resistance (since its motive is not to have insight, supremacy of the ego, structuralization of the ego, and genital primacy). This resistance is designed to force the therapist to meet the transference demands the patient feels are necessary. And so, even with regard to the role of regression in treatment, there are major differences between traditional psychoanalytic and object-relations points of view.

OTHER DIFFERENCES

Another important difference is that object-relations theorists have been relatively unconcerned with anal and phallic development, development during latency, adolescent development, or adult development. They have tended to specialize in the first year of life (the oral period), more or less to the exclusion of other phases of development. Where Klein has talked about the early development of the superego, which she places in the oral period (as basic aggression, and also as persecutory objects which are identified with and introjected), he talks about it in an "archaic" sense, and not as the heir to the oedipal conflict. She thus makes no dinstinction between superego contents, superego function, and the superego as a structure. Where she mentions the phallic period, she essentially talks about there being a kind of racially unconscious knowledge of the sexual activities so that in effect every suckling activity (where the breast is incorporated into the mouth) is also a phylogenetic (unconscious) activity concerning the incorporation of the penis into the mouth (and the incorporation of the penis into the vagina). It has been suggested, on the basis of some of these ideas, that Klein is somewhat of a biological mystic. Whether one wants to go that far or not, one can see that for all practical purposes a strong adherence to the object-relations point of view reduces much of psychological development to the limits only of the oral period. On the other hand, from a traditional psychoanalytic point of view, perhaps one might say that in classical analysis there has been too much emphasis on purely oedipal development.

CONCLUSIONS

One of the things that object-relations theory has done, which has been quite helpful for the traditional psychoanalytic position, is to refocus on the more primitive characterological developmental processes in the psyche that occur in early infancy. All in all, one might say that this is one of the most valuable contributions object-relations theory has made. In addition, when traditional analysts dealt with various kinds of projections in the transference, they viewed them not as projections which are part of the displacement process, but as forms of pathological ego functioning, or they saw them as projections of early object relations only insofar as they were representations or internalizations of ruthless superego introjects (which belonged originally with the parents and have now been displaced onto the analyst).

Object-relations theory has helped traditional psychoanalysis to incorporate into the treatment process a finer and more thoughtful understanding of the various ways in which splitting, projection, and projective identification can occur under the pressure of displacement in the transference neurosis. For the most part, one might be rather skeptical of some suggestions that object-relations theory makes about the nature of transference (not as a displacement, but as a projection). One might also be skeptical of the idea of regression as a healthy deepening of the transference. In a constructive way, one might be critical of the idea that there are no autonomous ego functions, or that there is no such thing specifically as a working alliance, which then suggests that everyone is analyzable. One might be better advised to adhere to the more traditional psychoanalytic model (both in terms of understanding and in terms of treatment). Thus, many of the conceptions of the object-relations position have become displacements of traditional psychoanalytic concepts and do not seem as useful as one might have hoped. On the other hand, there are a number of additions that serve not as displacements but as enrichments of psychoanalytic thinking and that tend to be rather helpful, particularly in elucidating many of the psychological dynamics concerning early infantile development and the basic relation of the infant to the object world. Perhaps *in cases where pathology is severe, and primitive and archaic ego functions are predominant,* the techniques of object-relations theory might prove most useful. Most certainly, a great deal of exploration and integration of object-relations theory into traditional psychoanalysis is called for in the future.

REFERENCES

1. Abraham, K. *Collected Papers.* London: Hogarth Press, 1927.
2. Balint, M. *Primary Love and Psychoanalytic Technique.* London: Hogarth Press, 1952.
3. Bowlby, J. *Attachment and Loss,* 2 vols. London: Hogart Press, 1969.
4. Fairbairn, W.R.D. A revised psychopathology of the psychoses and the psychoneuroses. *Internat. J. Psycho-Anal.,* 22: 250-279, 1941.
5. Fairbairn, W.R.D. *An Object-Relations Theory of Personality.* London: Tavistock, 1952.
6. Fairbairn, W.R.D. On the nature and aims of psychoanalytical treatment. *Internat. J. Psycho-Anal.,* 39: 374-385, 1958.
7. Freud, A. *The Ego and the Mechanisms of Defense.* London: Hogarth Press, 1936.
8. Freud, S. *Collected Papers on Psycho-Analysis; Standard Edition.* London: Hogarth Press, 1974.
9. Giovacchini, P. Transference, incorporation, and synthesis. *Internat. J. Psycho-Anal.,* 46: 287-296, 1965.
10. Greenacre, P. *Emotional Growth,* 2 vols. New York: International Universities Press, 1971.
11. Guntrip, H. *Personality Structure and Human Interaction.* New York: International Universities Press, 1961.
12. Guntrip, H. *Schizoid Phenomena, Object-Relations, and the Self.* New York: International Universities Press, 1968.
13. Guntrip, H. *Psycho-Analytic Theory, Therapy, and the Self.* New York: International Universities Press, 1972.
14. Hartmann, H. Psychoanalysis and developmental psychology. *The Psychoanalytic Study of the Child,* 5: 7-17.
15. Hartmann, H. The mutual influences in the development of the ego and the id. *The Psychoanalytic Study of the Child,* 7: 9-30. New York: International Universities Press, 1952.
16. Hartmann, H. *Essays on Ego Psychology.* New York: International Universities Press, 1964.
17. Hartmann, H. *Ego Psychology and the Problem of Adaptation.* New York: International Universities Press, 1961.
18. Hartmann, H., Kris, E., and Lowenstein, R.N. Comments on the formation of psychic structure. *The Psychoanalytic Study of the Child,* 2: 11-38. New York: International Universities Press, 1946.
19. Jacobson, E. *The Self and the Object World.* New York: International Universities Press, 1964.
20. Jones, E. *Papers on Psycho-Analysis.* London: Balliere, 1948.
21. Kernberg, O. A psychoanalytic classification of character pathology. *J. Amer. Psychoanal. Assn.,* 18: 800-822, 1970.
22. Klein, M. *Psycho-analysis of Children.* London: Hogarth Press, 1932.
23. Klein, M. *Developments in Psycho-Analysis.* London: Hogarth Press, 1952.
24. Klein, M. *Contributions to Psycho-Analysis.* London: Tavistock, 1957.

25. Klein, M. *Envy and Gratitude.* London: Tavistock, 1957.
26. Klein, M. *Narrative of a Child Analysis.* New York: Basic Books, 1961.
27. Klein, M., Heimann, P., and Money-Kyrle, R.E. (eds.). *New Directions in Psycho-Analysis.* London: Tavistock, 1955.
28. Klein, M., and Riviere, J. *Love, Hate, and Reparation.* London: Hogarth Press, 1937.
29. Kohut, H. *The Analysis of the Self.* New York: International Universities Press, 1971.
30. Laing, R.D. *The Divided Self.* London: Tavistock, 1960.
31. Loewenstein, R. Some remarks on defenses, autonomous ego, and psychoanalytic technique. *Internat. J. Psycho-Anal.,* 35: 188-193, 1954.
32. Loewenstein, R., Newman, L.M., Schur, N., and Solnit, A.J., eds. *Psychoanalysis—A General Psychology.* New York: International Universities Press, 1966.
33. Mahler, M., and Furer, M. *On Human Symbiosis and the Vicissitudes of Individuation.* New York: International Universities Press, 1968.
34. Mahler, M., Pine, F., and Bergman, A. *The Psychological Birth of the Human Infant.* New York: Basic Books, 1975.
35. Rapaport, D. *Collected Papers,* ed. M. Gill. New York: Basic Books, 1967.
36. Winnicott, D.W. *Collected Papers.* New York: International Universities Press, 1952.
37. Winnicott, D.W. *The Maturational Process and the Facilitating Environment.* New York: International Universities Press, 1965.

Women's Groups: A Feminist Perspective on the Treatment of Women

TERESA BERNARDEZ-BONESATTI

In recent years, the impact of the women's movement has made itself felt in a variety of ways. More women have become aware of cultural assumptions about their role-prescribed behaviors and of the conflict generated when they try to exercise a greater variety of options or grow more in line with their personal aspirations than with social expectations. Even women who dismiss or disagree with feminist claims express doubts and questions about their sexual and social role that agree with those raised by more militant women. The preponderance of psychic distress among women today is partially the result of contradictory expectations about how women should behave and what they should aspire to, caused by a shift in society's sets of goals for females.

As clear-cut documentation of discriminatory practices against females in education and work has begun to appear, it has been impossible to deny the evidence that the female sex is held back from achieving satisfaction, autonomy, and financial independence despite the idealization of women in the traditional role of wives and mothers.

Biased views of women are known to be held as well by mental health practitioners (5). "Normal" behavior for females includes characteristics that are not expected of a fully grown person. Clinicians accepting sex-role stereotypes tend to perpetuate them in treatment, particularly since unaware patients are not likely to question their biased assumptions. In my own clinical practice, I have noticed, like others (2, 6, 9), the increase in women's dissatisfaction and the regularity with which certain complaints are voiced. These complaints, appearing as "symptoms" to be treated by experts, can be regarded as veiled signs of anger and frustration at women's lot. They in fact fueled a rebirth of feminism, which in turn brought to the surface the aspirations and desires of women and gave them new options for their realization.

Although feminism has been narrowly defined as a movement to win equal rights for women, at its most encompassing it is a theory that attempts change in sociopolitical as well as cultural, economic, and psychological spheres. In its ideological framework, style, and process of accomplishing these changes, and even in its operational language, it departs and differentiates itself from masculine notions and styles that have for so long ruled the attitudes, behaviors, and aspirations of both sexes.

The women's movement in the United States has relied from the very beginning on the small group as the arena of exploration and discovery, as the supportive network in a hostile or indifferent environment, and as a creative political tool and agent of change. These "consciousness-rising" groups, at first exploratory in nature, born of a profound need to share unvalidated personal experiences, later grew to assert these experiences more and more, to destroy female myths, and to increase awareness of the social induction of incapacity and disease.

In contrast to masculine organizations, the women's movement departed strikingly from masculine modes of organizing and of raising the awareness of its potential members. In part because of the experience of women in male political organizations and the frustrations of women's aspirations in them (8), women were forced to analyze the factors responsible for perpetuating the very conditions of oppression and inequality those groups wanted to conquer. The traditional methods of raising the awareness of "oppressed" groups by ideological analysis and lecturing were abandoned in favor of a small group situation in which no one "knew more" than the others and there was no clear ideological agenda. Leaders came to be considered characteristic of a paternalistic mode, more central to issues of power and control than to social justice and the protection of human freedom. Women had learned this lesson in particular, for they had been taught to respect the authority of the expert and the person in power, to demonstrate their compliance with the most valued characteristics of their sex by submitting willingly to a serving position. The leaderless group was partly born of this profound distrust of leaders. It asserted that no one person had the expertise, wisdom, and insight that a group of persons could lend to the task and that domination began when others relinquished their power by delegating that much authority to a single person. This democratic sharing of opinions and skills conforms to a model that moves toward integration and noncompetitiveness and in which the central issue is the creative integration of the individuals and their particularities, needs, and skills.

Although the eventual task of the groups became clearer and changed during their evolution, the women were seizing a potentially very powerful agent of change: the small group. I shall try to delineate the characteristics of the small group used in consciousness raising, which met so well the multiple needs women have in their process of growth away from stereotyped assumptions of their role and behavior. These characteristics are preserved in the therapeutic groups that I propose are indicated in the treatment of women today. There are, however, some important differences which will be discussed in more detail. One of them, the existence of a therapist and her function in the group, merits special description because of its departure from more traditional views of therapeutic conduct.

The small group gratified the long-denied needs of affiliation of their members. Women in particular had become disenfranchised members of society because of their minor participation in social and political spheres. Even when working and participating in organizations, women felt apart. The depersonalization of organizations and institutions characteristic of industrial societies better fitted the socialized male. Either because males are socialized to encounter impersonal organizations or become dehumanized in the process of their interaction, they have adapted to sustain the deprivation women find hard to tolerate.

The small group provided responsiveness to and validation of "feminine" modes of experience. Women had found their intimate partners often lacking when it came to speaking of and understanding affective needs. Isolated from each other, women complained that men often ignored their requests for affection or berated their explicit show of emotional needs as "irrational," "hysterical," or "illogical." The masculine mystique made men uncomfortable with a language other than a logical, cognitive one oriented to problem solving. Women had frequently experienced their rejection as a sign that they were deficient in integrity and strength, intellectual ability, or health.

The small group served as a supportive network in the exploration of painful experiences and the transition to change out of traditional roles. Women had been socialized into being aware of and able to provide for the needs of others. This nurturant ability could now be placed at their service to permit facing disapproval in relation to behaviors society did not sanction.

The small group served as a therapeutic agent without imposing labels of inadequacy or illness or authorities that had to be recognized. The therapeutic effect of sharing experiences not validated before, of finding trusting and supportive companions, and of revising views about the self vis-à-vis the society's responsibility had the effect of decreasing the guilt women felt about "their" problems. The depressive aspects of their helplessness were reduced by a new analysis that permitted a different course of action. Although frightening and uncertain, the path was no longer obscure and without companions. Women began to rely again on their own perceptions, asserted their own needs, and discovered themselves capable of lucid, creative, and rational thinking.

The small group served as a training laboratory to experiment with and try out behaviors until then shrouded in mystery, shame, or fear. To speak loud, to be active, to speak with authority, to respond with anger without collapsing in tears could be attempted with sympathetic peers in similar straits. The more honest and objective the feedback received in the group, the more useful to situations outside the group in which support couldn't be mustered.

The small group served as the nucleus of a political organization at a level not dehumanized by ignorance of the personal values and feelings of its members. Action to alter the social milieu or the political process began in intimate association with peers struggling for each other and themselves and translating personal needs into personal and social change. The members knew each other and their own special needs and they made specific preparations for those with small children or those without money or without jobs. Meetings were arranged to take into account the necessity not to dissociate the political from the personal or the familiar, not to cause alienation or disaffection.

The group raised the social awareness of its members by confronting them with the reality of sex discrimination. It was impossible to continue to support notions of personal inadequacy when so many different members compared notes and found that their common denominator was cultural prejudice, social injustice, and paradoxical demands. From then on, a clearer analysis of one's experience began to be contrasted with a deciphering of contradictory social expectations that caused "illness" in women whenever they attempted to adapt to them. The further the exploration of one's personal experience with others went, the more obvious it became that certain "problems" were not personal but social, in the sense that their origin was in the social milieu and the "problem" became personal in attempting to adapt or respond to an injurious social demand.

The group permitted the integration of affective, bodily, and cognitive experience as well as personal, interpersonal, and social dimensions of a self and of a problem. Women have had the experience of leaving aside one aspect of their experience because society functioned in ways that were not regulated by women. Different members' styles as well as each member's varying experience could be utilized beneficially if patience and tolerance for difficulties could be exercised. The so-called irrationality of women (i.e., logical rules of behavior giving way to personal concern, impulses being considered just as much as thoughtful action, playfulness helping to bring perspective to excessive seriousness) could be allowed to exist and to sculpt the very process that was undertaken.

In finding the small leaderless group, the women's movement made an important attempt to reintegrate previously split spheres of experience. In this movement, members attempted sociopolitical analysis, while simultaneously remaining embedded in a matrix of personal experience and psychological exploration. The continuous dialogue between social awareness, on the one hand, and personal and psychological insight leading to personal change and social transformation, on the other, is a very valuable characteristic of these groups.

What can mental health professionals in general and group therapists in particular gain from feminist assumptions and from the experience of women in leaderless groups? For one, an intrapsychic interpersonal model is insufficient at the present time in the understanding of women's distress as well as in planning a therapeutic modality of most usefulness and efficiency for the person. The social context has to be considered in as much depth and as consistently as the patient's interpersonal or intrapsychic realms.

The polarization and arbitrary assignment of sex differences needs to be thoroughly examined to clarify their effects upon persons. One of the ways in which this can be done is in the context of same-sex groups to disentangle what is acquired as a result of compliance to masculine expectations from what appears to have more intrapersonal roots. The social factors responsible for keeping women from gaining freedom, status, better pay or better education, and the manner in which women adapt to them, should also be examined. Beyond more specific therapeutic changes in women, changes in the social milieu can be brought about if individuals are aware of these factors and their effects upon persons. In this regard, therapeutic groups have a natural advantage over individual forms of therapy.

RATIONALE FOR WOMEN'S GROUPS

The small group setting appears ideally suited to make explicit the common denominators of distress among women. What follows are a number of characteristics frequently found in women as a result of their socialization which reduce options and impede growth. The opportunities a small therapeutic group offers for their transformation are stated as well.

1. In accepting female stereotypes, women acquire a distaste for other women, mixed with distrust, contempt, and the tendency to expect envy and manipulativeness in other women. They are frequently unaware of how, in so believing, they have lowered their own self-regard. They have internalized views of their sex as inferior and contemptible.

2. Women tend to respond to expectations about their passivity, submissiveness, and compliance by acting accordingly, particularly in regard to persons in authority. They do not challenge "experts," they infrequently voice their criticism, and they tend to feel guilty if they do so. These assumptions can be made conscious and can be tested in interaction with other women. Since women are specially capable of nurturance and support, they can give it and receive it from others rather than attempt to live up to a selfless image of exclusive service to others. Women discover, sometimes with surprise, that other women demonstrate discriminating judgment,

honesty, and the capacity to share in effective problem solving when not inhibited by negative expectations.

The female therapist in the group helps to challenge those assumptions, to question the genuineness and appropriateness of such a posture, and to explore the roots of this behavior. The therapist is utilized to check female-authority models and to examine the members' strong feelings concerning the desire and fear to exercise leadership, the ubiquitous concerns that females share about "dominating" others, and the omnipotent fantasies of female power that lie underneath the helpless behavior of many females. The roots of female authority go back to a woman's mother and frequently to her first teachers. These models are therefore associated with infantile needs and behaviors, childlike submission and rebelliousness, and fantasies of great power. These feelings are likely to reoccur in groups and can be utilized to bring into perspective the archaic and inappropriate sources of fear that get transferred to the female therapist.

3. Women are trained to seek approval from males and to rule their behavior in accordance to masculine definitions of what is desirable or expected in a woman. Compliance to male expectations tends to generate increasing dependence on males, increasing resentment of their power, and decreasing ability to rely on the self for discriminating and perceiving accurately personal needs and expectations. The absence of males in the group forces women to rely on their own experience, their own perceptions, their own desires, to read them more discriminately, and to engage each other in the process of exploration. Since men are often women's intimate and sexual partners, the providers of financial and social security, and the most frequent sources of potential gratification, these steps are fraught with the perceived danger of losing an important relationship. Increasing awareness and increasing authoritativeness about the self lead to the natural desire for self-regualtion and self-control which threaten the woman's desire to depend and her partner's desire to control. Quiescent relations with intimate partners are likely to get energized or strained before they become more truly equalitarian. The attainment of true mutuality and responsibility for the self in an intimate relationship is achieved at various levels by different women and is highly dependent on the work the women do with each other in the "here-and-now" situation of their small group. Those who have been able to change in this regard in relation to their peers and the therapist show equal changes in their relations to intimate friends and spouses.

4. Women tend to relinquish leadership functions and denigrate their authority in areas designated as "masculine." The general tendency is to shy away from self-assertive, independent action, to voice and support with evidence critical judgments, to state without self-effacement their knowledge and skill, to be aggressive and direct in relation to others when desired. The prohibitions surrounding such behaviors have to do with cultural imperatives that tend to question the "femaleness" of the woman who does so. In a group without males, such functions cannot be assigned to them. Women have to exercise them and can explore their inhibitions and fears which become very obvious in the process. I have stated before (1) that

unconscious assumptions about the potential destructiveness of women are commonly held by both sexes. Such beliefs have the effect of triggering stringent restraints whenever aggressive impulses are close to expression in women. This powerful inhibition leads to the incapacity for appropriate expression of affect that has the slightest negative connotation as well as the dampening of appropriately aggressive and creative activity. it is only when such "aggressive" impulses are admitted to consciousness and can be expressed that an exploration of the destructive underlying assumptions holding them in check can be carried out. It is then possible to begin to resolve the conflicts created by such injunctions against "aggression" in women so that the desirable ability to state openly one's own needs, carry out creative actions, and protest successfully can be freed from hostilities and resentment accumulated in the process of indiscriminately shutting off aggressive impulses.

5. Women have acquired myths and misinformation regarding their sexual functioning, behavior, and experience. The chronic attempts to match male expectations and to adapt to men's needs have led women to develop standards of sexual behavior more in accord with men's desires, which handicaps the search for self-definition in this area and consequently confounds women in their attempt to resolve heterosexual conflicts. In an all-women group, discussion of sexual experience can take place more frankly than in mixed groups. The presence of other females who can validate similarities in experience or conflicts helps to clarify what is "expected" behavior and separate it from the woman's actual experience, desires, or fantasies. Contrasting views enrich the context of exploration and remove stereotypes about what is "female sexual experience." When the issues of competition for sexual adequacy or fear of being found sexually inadequate are dealt with, women find a women's group the ideal place for exploring sexual conflicts and airing doubts and concerns. The absence of men is an important factor in the freedom of women to share their own perceptions of their bodies and their sexual desires.

6. The femaleness of the group and its leadership permits a profound exploration of mother-daughter relationships. A continuous reassessment of identification patterns established early, of conflicts of a pregenital nature, of issues of separation and autonomy, and of the changing view of mother as a woman whose influence needs to be diminished, denied, challenged, or accepted permeates the group's sessions. Disappointment with mother for her inability to sustain her own self-esteem and reproaches for her dependence and submissiveness are commonly encountered among women. Mother is perceived as primarily responsible for her daughter's second place in the world and the contempt for her that her daughter feels leads to an identification with a devalued object and guilt over the angry attack. Women discover in the group the common social roots of much of their female behavior. A more compassionate view of one's own mother emerges, in which the woman identifies the social conditions that permeated the mother's circumstances and that prevented her development. This analysis is just as important as that in which the women clarify the nature of their complaints. Only then can

women move beyond mother's fate, strive for their own fulfillment, and restore the positive bonds with mother that are critical in reaching a well-anchored and satisfying sense of femaleness.

In a women's group all the elements that help in this process are available: other female models, peers in similar straits, a female authority figure upon whom to re-edit the past. Under present social conditions, women cannot use healthy men as identification figures. A male therapist is no model for a woman when in the social order the characteristics defining a grown person are labeled "masculine" and women are therefore under an injunction to reject such traits in themselves. In addition, the presence of a male authority in the group reproduces the situation encountered overwhelmingly in the social world: it is the man who confers status and well-being, not the woman who brings it upon herself.

7. Women tend to denigrate their belonging to the "second sex." The group encourages the development of a bond of loyalty and trust among the members which extends to other women. Since much of the socially encouraged competition for men is suspended in the group, rivalries are observed in their earlier determinants: the desire to be mother's ally or favorite. The closeness achieved among the women in the group after resolution of these rivalries is an important developmental stage. Comfortable and close relations with one's own sex usually precede the search for heterosexual object choice. In many instances, women are socially encouraged and seek premature heterosexual bonds when in fact they are fleeing from resolving conflicts over dependency and developing autonomy.

Homosexual fears manifested by women in the group appear to have early oral determinants. Regressive desires to merge with an all-giving mother take the form of homosexual fears and are more pronounced in women with a history of maternal deprivation. These conflictual wishes, if not uncovered, often prevent women from sharing intimacy and are partly responsible for women seeking sexual intercourse with men when the actual wish is to fulfill longings for nurturance and engulfment.

8. Women have had little encouragement and opportunity to behave assertively. The tendency to derogate aggressive action in women and to question their adequacy in their "feminine role" when they behave "aggressively" has the effect of inhibiting active strivings or producing covertly hostile behavior. It is impossible to elicit assertive behavior, free of revengeful and bitter feelings, if women are kept from voicing their resentment openly and from moving toward accomplishing what they need to. Being able to tolerate and give expression to anger can be explored in a group. This is just the beginning of a process of coming to terms with one's own needs, being able to stand up for them, respect and withstand the anger of others, and find ways to achieve satisfaction at nobody's expense. In a women's group this is one of the most arduous problems to resolve. Despite women's assumed freedom to voice anger at other women (greater than at men), the tendency to shy away, avoid, or internalize anger in self-punitive ways requires continuous attention. Fear of disapproval and isolation has to be overcome to develop the capacity to tolerate the temporary distance from others that expression of anger entails and the free-

dom that ensues when the anger can be dissipated and understood. Attempts to derogate or induce guilt in members who evoke angry feelings are explored and discouraged. It is not infrequent to see in women the tendency to regress to infantile behavior as a means to justify and yet disown angry feelings. This behavior is self-defeating since the person and her complaints can thus be dismissed as "childish" and in turn generate further resentment. Many women tend to cry when they are angry and to collapse into helplessness as a way to maintain the precarious balance between dependency needs and strivings for autonomy. In the group, women can readily observe the effect of tears on others, while at times being the object of such attempts, and discover the ultimate ineffectiveness of such behavior. Conscious acknowledgment of angry feelings and a more honest exposure of such impulses are encouraged, and while initially this produces considerable tension, the step toward resolution in the increase in one's capacity to see oneself through an angry interchange and the consequent effect on the group's ability to then concentrate on the immediate task free of tension operate to extinguish covert behaviors.

9. Women have been encouraged to follow "leaders," to be obedient and compliant, and to "serve" others. In the group, leadership functions rather than leaders are emphasized. The therapist is assigned the function of keeping the group working at the task of uncovering and resolving conflict and unveiling covert messages. The therapist discourages, by interpreting, the desire to rely on a leader for guidance, safety, and control. These functions have to be gradually taken up by members who discover their capacity and pleasure in exercising personal responsibility, their unique skills for problem solving, and the opportunity to profit from the special capacities of other members. Envious feelings, stemming from the belief that one lacks what others have and what one would wish, stand in the way of identifying with desirable characteristics in others. Envy is voiced more freely and openly in a group of women partially because it is assumed to be a female characteristic. Once active strivings are freed from conflict, women move toward desirable goals and encourage each other to actualize potentialities and achieve satisfaction.

THE ROLE OF THE THERAPIST

Psychotherapists are not neutral or objective members of their culture. Elsewhere (2) I have pointed out how therapists do not escape stereotypical beliefs about the sexes. In my view, a therapist ought to place herself in a position of critic of the social context and continually explore her own behavior and beliefs to free herself increasingly from social biases. Ideally, she is neither an agent of the social order nor a political proselitizer. In the groups I organize, my political ideas and activity are known to the members, but I do not use the sessions as a political forum. I regard one of the therapist's functions as making sure that the members' freedom of exploration, information, choice, and action are enhanced and protected.

The therapist is a member of the group with specific skills and experience that can be gained and incorporated by the group members. Once this task is done successfully, the therapist is obsolete as such, although she may be a valued and loved member of the group. It is in the lending of her skills to others and in helping others free themselves from her authority that the therapist's behavior is congruent with the aim of feminist change: women do not relinquish their own authority and responsibility; they are their own experts and labor on their own definitions. In keeping with this aim, the therapist encourages meetings in her absence. To that end, the therapist explores the members' fears that determine their avoiding meeting at those times, or inversely the retaliatory and counterdependent aspects of meeting while "doing away" with the feared authority.

The therapist, in addition, points out and encourages clarification of external sources of distress, social invectives, and contradictory expectations, whenever they become apparent to her. Women need to use discriminating judgment as to what is their problem and what is not.

The groups are organized so that they can continue to function therapeutically after the therapist terminates her contract with the group (9 months of two-hour weekly sessions in our case). The group-as-a-whole approach seems especially suited to this goal since it aims at the development of a cohesive and well-functioning unit, while striving toward the development of individual autonomy. In the beginning, the therapist's efforts are directed at the group process in the here and now with the goal of achieving a work group (3). At a later time, the clarification and resolution of group conflicts alternates with the exploration of the members' experience and their interpersonal activity. I function as a "group consultant" in the sense of keeping in touch with the group process and lending my skills to enhance the creative functioning of the group. My other important role is as an authority figure upon whom transference reactions toward maternal figures can be examined. My eventual goal is to emerge from the transferences as a "regular" member of the group.

The critical assessment of the therapist by the members is an important task in the group. Women especially need to exercise authority and discriminating judgment in evaluating others as well as themselves. In my groups, a preliminary period of eight to ten sessions is set at the beginning to explore and evaluate the experience and decide whether or not to stay in for the rest of the year. This step guarantees a greater degree of educated choice and makes for more responsible participation. Consistent with the attempt to demystify authority and promote egalitarian relations, the therapist herself shares her experience with the other members. It is important to keep in mind that the group members often have conflicting feelings about the therapist's role, wishing alternatively for dependence on an all-powerful figure and strict equality. The therapist integrates the specific function she has in the group with her own participation as a member. As a rule, her self-disclosures increase with time and the increasing autonomy of the members.

COMPOSITION OF THE GROUPS

Since it is felt that most women can profit from women's groups, the exceptions merit consideration. Aside from the usual contraindications of group therapy (i.e., individuals in crisis who require immediate help), it is best not to include in the group women with marital problems whose husbands are motivated to work with them. Marital or family therapy may be the treatment of choice. In the face of marital disharmony, the woman's participation in a woman's group without her partner's equal chance to grow and change is likely to lead to further alienation and conflict.

My groups have not included psychotic women. They appear to be most beneficial to women struggling with conflicts in sexual and personal identity, those who feel alienated from other women, and those searching for integration in family and work roles. Women who wish to be more active and assertive, or who struggle with vocational conflicts find the women's groups particularly helpful.

In our experience members' ages ranging from 20 to 50 years permit the elucidation of common conflicts at different stages of development, allow the possibility to explore mother-daughter conflicts within the group, and increase the chances of looking at generational differences in outlook and profiting from others' experience. Women much younger or older may need groups of their age peers to deal with the age-appropriate dilemmas most crucial to them.

It is desirable to mix women with different educational and occupational backgrounds: it is blatantly clear to women that common problems exist despite apparent differences in education and work. Housewives, professionals, students, and workers can break down class stereotypes and profit from each other's experience. Racial mixture is also desirable. Black and white women share more commonalities than black and white men. Racial divisions and mistrust give way to a recognition of common prejudice and common dilemmas. The presence of married, single, and divorced women and of those with a feminist or a more traditional orientation help to challenge stereotypical assumptions and behaviors on all sides and allow women to quarrel productively with orientations that are presumed to be antagonistic.

DISCUSSION

All-female groups led by a female therapist appear best suited to explore and resolve common problems of contemporary women: their isolation, their discontent with their sex and destiny, their tendency to self-derogation, and their problems in integrating social, personal, and family needs. These problems are the result of attempts on the part of women to adapt to social demands and definitions of their behavior that are not consonant with psychological growth, autonomy, and freedom (7).

Until social change takes place that makes possible equality between the sexes and the desirable flexibility in sexual roles, indications are that the awareness and resolution of socially induced conflict is best accomplished in a small group composed only of women and conducted with a feminist philosophy. Since we are in a period of social transition and turmoil regarding the roles of men and women, it is imperative that we prepare therapists for dealing with the social as well as the intrapsychic and interpersonal determinants of conflict in patients (13).

Leaderless groups organized by women themselves for self-help and for raising the awareness of their members should be encouraged and supported by professional therapists. Group psychotherapists may be best utilized by providing such groups with the skills of a small-group expert, as a consultant would. Particularly when problems centering around anger and competition get in the way of the continuous development of a leaderless group, such expertise could render opportune help. If leaderless groups could have this expertise available to them when needed, fewer therapeutic groups might be required.

When therapy groups are deemed necessary, it is important to keep in mind that they are conducted in a way that may enable the participants to continue to function without the therapist after a year's time. The therapist, in essence, attempts to prepare the members to use a leaderless group. A supportive network of her contemporaries is one of the most needed resources for women today.

REFERENCES

1. Bernardez-Bonesatti, T. Feminist and non-feminist outpatients compared. Presented at American Psychiatric Association Meeting, Detroit, 1974.
2. Bernardez-Bonesatti, T. Psychotherapists' biases towards women: Overt manifestations and unconscious determinants. Presented at American Psychiatric Association Meeting, Anaheim, Cal., 1975.
3. Bion, W.R. *Experiences in Groups.* New York; Ballantine Books, 1961.
4. Brodsky, A.M. The consciousness-raising group as a model for therapy with women. *Psychother.: Theory, Res. Pract.,* 10 (1), 1973.
5. Broverman, I.K., Broverman, D.M., Clarkson, F.E., Rosenkrantz, P.S., and Vogel, S.R. Sex role stereotypes and clinical judgments of mental health. *J. Consult. Clin. Psychol.* 34, 1970.
6. Chesler, P. Patient and patriarch: Women in the psychotherapeutic relationship. In: *Woman in Sexist Society.* New York: Basic Books, 1971.
7. Costa Eastman, P. Consciousness-raising as a resocialization process for women. *Smith Coll. Studies Soc. Work,* 43 (3), 1973.
8. Freeman, J. *The Politics of Women's Liberation.* New York: David McKay, 1975.
9. Gove, W.R., and Tudor, J.F. Adult sex roles and mental illness. *Amer. J. Sociol.,* 78, 1973.
10. Hymer, S., and Atkins, A. Relationship between attitudes toward women's liberation movement and mode of aggressive expression in women. Proceedings 31st Annual Convention, APA, 1973.

11. Kirsch, B. Consciousness-raising groups as therapy for women. In: *Women in Therapy.* New York: Brunner/Mazel, 1974.
12. Mintz, E.E. What do we owe today's woman? *Internat. J. Group Psychother.,* 24 (3), 1974.
13. Rice, J.D., and Rice, D.G. Implications of the women's liberation movement for psychotherapy. *Amer. J. Psychiat.,* 130 (2), 1973.

Art Therapy—Catalyst for Creative Expression and Personality Integration

JOSEF E. GARAI

Art, music, and dance are the three universal languages of mankind. Through the use of these expressive modalities, people from widely divergent countries, cultures, and ethnic backgrounds can experience a spontaneous climate of exchange of intimate feelings, moods, impressions, sensations, thoughts, and ideas. We perceive the world as a kaleidoscope of images, pictorial impressions, and dreamlike shifts, as if in all our thinking, planning, reminiscing, and meanderings of our mind our "inner eye" were watching a motion picture composed of stimulating and often confusing scenarios. There is a continuous interplay between our inner vision and our perception of external "reality" or our view of the world at large.

Symbolic communication based on pictorial, sculpted, musical, dance, and movement expressions serves as a powerful means of instantaneous resonance and recognition and therefore it forms a strange contrast to the multiplicity of confusing languages with their semantic ambiguities. This immediacy of spontaneous artistic expression of man's inner perception of his outer world provides us with deep insights into the lives of people in past civilizations, as when we admire the cave paintings of Lascaux or the hieroglyphs, the sacred carvings of symbols representing objects, events, and people in ancient Egypt. These early works of pictorial art formed the building stones for the alphabets of all languages. Since time immemorial, artistic expression has served as both the most immediate and the most permanent medium for the disclosure and communication of man's intimate feelings, desires, hopes, anxieties, frustrations, ambitions, goals, and the conflicts aroused by the interplay of these primordial forces in his inner experience and in his relations with his fellow men.

Modern technocratic societies tend to overemphasize the importance of verbal expression. Words can be used to disclose and reveal as well as to hide and conceal feelings, attitudes, ideas, and thoughts. They can soothe, heal, reassure, and encourage, but they can also hurt, reject, manipulate, and destroy. Networks of verbal communication are subject to the sending and receiving of ambiguous or "doublebind" messages. Therapeutic techniques based on verbal communication tend to reinforce an eloquent client's resistance to the development of insight into his or her compulsive repetition of destructive patterns of behavior. Spontaneous artistic creativity frequently breaks down the barriers of a person's defensive structure to reveal the underlying primary processes of the id. Repressed anger, frustrated sexual desires, and feelings of loneliness, isolation, and despair may surge forth in paintings, drawings, sculptures, collages, clay modelings, stone chiseling, weavings, sandplay, etc. The patient frequently interprets the symbolic meanings of these creative products under the sympathetic guidance of the art therapist and is enabled to move toward increased self-discovery and awareness of the roots of intrapsychic and interpersonal conflicts.

The cathartic effects of creative expression were exalted by the ancient Greeks, who regarded the presentation of tragedies as profound experiences mirroring man's titanic struggle with his inner demonic and idealistic projections and their relation to outer reality. Through processes of identification, both the actors and the audience were encouraged to immerse themselves in the deep feelings of the protagonists evoked by their attempts to resolve their conflicts. This empathetic identification was perceived as a means for the resolution of related conflicts experienced by the actors and the spectators themselves. The discharge of repressed and painful emotions served as a catharsis or purification leaving them "pure" or free again to divert their energies toward the pursuit of new goals. The release of deep emotional energies in art therapy has been described by some existential art therapists as providing a similar cathartic effect which in their estimate constitutes the essence of genuine therapy. But most therapists who are not strict existentialists or adherents of different theoretical frameworks would agree that catharsis merely leads to a temporary release of tension, whereas therapy as a long-term process of growth and change requires the working through of deep-seated intrapsychic and interpersonal conflicts in a therapeutic relationship of mutual trust based on an exploration and analytic techniques of interpretation of primary process material. This type of therapy leads to an increasing awareness of unconscious motivation, the gradual loosening of the defensive structure, and the strengthening of the ego. The different frameworks based on a variety of personality theories that art therapists have adopted will be further discussed.

A SHORT HISTORY OF THE DEVELOPMENT OF THE FIELD OF ART THERAPY

As Jolande Jacobi (18, 19) points out, since the beginning of the twentieth century psychiatric and psychological research has increasingly turned its attention to the creative expression of psychological problems. She mentions the meritorious preliminary work done by Nagy, Bertschinger, Fay, Kürbitz, and Hamilton in Hungary, Germany, and France between 1905 and 1918. They paved the way for the basic standard works of Prinzhorn (36), Morgenthaler (29), and Pfeifer (5) in the 1920's which served as the foundation for the introduction of diagnostic and interpretive techniques by a limited number of psychiatrists. Prinzhorn's book is still one of the most thorough and intelligently conceptualized works and provides a fascinating survey of the art of mental patients with whom Prinzhorn and his associates worked. Prinzhorn found astonishing similarities between some of the artwork of these patients and the work of artists in the genius range. With his vast erudition in the fields of art, archeology, anthropology, psychology, mythology, metaphysics, and creativity, he outlined the whole range of future developments and foreshadowed the contributions made by Jung (20, 21), Jacobi (18), Campbell (6), and Garai (13, 14).

Prinzhorn believes that the artistic creativity of mentally disturbed patients reveals their areas of most intense conflict, and that the art of children, earlier civilizations, and even scribbles and doodles reflect the basic kinetic rhythm of life, the deeper layers of the personality, and mankind's common heritage of emotional responsiveness. He states that the psychological basis of artistic creativity includes: (1) the metaphysical meaning of the artwork as reflected in the process of its creation, (2) the expressive urge and the schematic framework of its tendency to create, (3) the play urge or activity drive, (4) the decorative urge which attempts to enrich the environment, (5) the urge for order, i.e., the need to create order our of chaos, (6) the urge for pictorial expression stimulated by the need for imitation, (7) the urge for symbolic meaning, and (8) the urge for a perceptual image and creative completion. Any serious student of art therapy should read the English translation of Prinzhorn's standard work (37).

Jolande Jacobi reports that Carl Gustav Jung already integrated pictures as examples of symbolic communication of feelings in his first major publication in 1912 (20). James Kirsch (24) reminisces how Jung decided to embark on an intensive journey of self-exploration through a "descent into the unconscious" during a period of three and a half years between December 1913 and July 1917. He kept a diary of all his fantasies, dreams, imagery, and thoughts which eventually comprised 1,330 handwritten pages resembling the script pattern of thirteenth-century medieval manuscripts. During this period he also painted a great many pictures of images he had seen in his dreams and fantasies. He bought the pigments and made the paint himself. The most impressive paintings he put into a special book bound in red leather which he called the "Red Book." At the end of his life there were four volumes which included paintings from later periods of his life. Some of the paintings, like the one of Philemon, he repeated on the walls of his house in Böllingen. That painting is also reproduced in his book *Memories, Dreams, Reflections* (22).

Jung's conception of symbolic communication through painting was further influenced by Heinrigh Zimmer's famous book *Kunstform and Yoga* or *Artform and Yoga* (45). In this book Zimmer emphasized that the configuration of such pictures as the geometric yantra must be considered as the creation of a certain inner message with symbolic meanings. Similarly, Jung believed that the mandala can be symbolically used as the harmonious circle which integrates the four basic modalities of thinking, feeling, sensing, and intuiting to lead to individuation through the perfect integration of these four human faculties.

Jacobi, inspired by Jung's theories, became one of the leading pioneers in the field of art therapy in Europe. Her book *Vom Bilderreich der Seele* (The Inner Kingdom of Images) is undoubtedly the most comprehensive and intuitive basic art-therapy textbook written so far (18). Jacobi is greatly influenced by Jung's theoretical postulates of the collective unconscious as the reservoir of the "archetypes" and of the purposiveness of symbolic communication or activity directed toward the achievement of individuation, i.e., the development of a more inclusive sense of self, and the need for integration of contradictory personality characteristics and feeling states such as persona and shadow, animus and anima, and introversion and extraversion to attain a more harmonious individuation. Jacobi's analytical interpretations of patients' drawings and paintings reveal her extraordinary empathy into the universal images of archetypal quality, such as the Great Mother, the Witch, the Trickster, the Eternal Youth, which constitute symbolic expressions of the experiences of men throughout the ages. The inner perceptions of these experiences of outer and inner events appear in the form of tribal lore, myth, and fairy tales as well as in the comic books and plays of our time. They also emerge in the artwork of mental patients and normal people.

In the United States art therapy began to be introduced in some mental health settings in the early 1940's. The writings of Margaret Naumburg (30, 31, 32, 33) provided the impetus for further work in this field. Her theory follows traditional psychoanalytic Freudian principles. She claims that analytically oriented art therapy

> bases its methods on releasing the unconscious by means of spontaneous art expression; it has its roots in the transference relation between patient and therapist, and in the encouragement of free association. It is closely allied to psychoanalytic therapy ... Treatment depends on the development of the transference relation and on a continuous effort to obtain the patient's own interpretation of his symbolic designs ... The images produced are a form of communication between patient and therapist; they constitute symbolic speech.

She regards the introduction of art-therapy techniques such as painting and clay modeling into analytically oriented psychotherapy as a method accelerating the analytic process rather than as an independent therapeutic method in its own right. As such an adjunct technique, art therapy has the following four advantages over verbal therapy in her opinion: First, it permits direct expression of dreams, fantasies, and other inner experiences that occur as pictures rather than words. Second, pictured projections of unconscious material escape censorship more easily than do verbal expressions so that the therapeutic process is speeded up. Third, the productions are durable and unchanging; their content cannot be erased by forgetting and their authorship is hard to deny. Fourth, the resolution of the transference is made easier because the autonomy of the patient is encouraged by his growing ability to contribute to the interpretation of his own creations. He is enabled to gradually substitute a narcissistic cathexis to his own art for his dependence on the therapist (32).

Naumburg's conceptualization of artistic expression as a form of "symbolic speech" begs the issue because we have already pointed out that as a means of communication "speech" or verbal communication appears to be less direct and more dependent on specific conventions of structural components such as grammar, syntax, and conventions of semantic usage and meaning. The use of the term "symbolic communication" therefore would reflect the uniqueness of artistic expression more adequately without suggesting that it is merely a substitute for conventional speech rather than a specific modality of communication conveying symbolic meanings more directly and independently of the restrictive bondage of traditional speech.

Edith Kramer's (25) conception of art therapy emphasizes the importance of the creative experience for personality integration. She feels that the creative process has an inherent healing quality which can be utilized in art therapy. She states:

> Art is a means of widening the range of human experiences by creating equivalents for such experiences. It is an area wherein experiences can be chosen, varied, repeated at will. In the creative act conflict is re-experienced, resolved, and integrated ... The arts throughout history have helped man to reconcile the eternal conflict between the individual's instinctual urges and the demands of society ... The process of sublimation constitutes the best way to deal with a basic human dilemma, but the conflicting demands of superego and id cannot be permanently reconciled ... In the artistic product conflict is formed and contained but only partly neutralized. The artist's position epitomizes the precarious human situation: while his craft demands the greatest self-discipline and perseverence, he must maintain access to the primitive impulses and fantasies that constitute the raw material for his creative work.

> The art therapist makes creative experiences available to disturbed persons in the service of the total personality; he must use methods compatible with the inner laws of artistic creation ... His primary function is to assist the process of sublimation, an act of integration and synthesis which is performed by the ego, wherein the peculiar fusion between reality and fantasy, between the conscious and the unconscious, which we call art is reached [25, pp. 6-23].

She regards the art therapist as an adjunct to traditional analytic therapy. He or she is distinguished from the art teacher by greater emphasis on the process of artistic creation than on the product resulting from it and by his or her ability to offer acceptance and respond to the special needs of every patient. Kramer's distinction between art therapist and art teacher appears to be artificial. She seems to refer to traditional art-teaching practices which regarded the creative process as somehow abstracted from its creator. The genuinely concerned and empathetic art teacher has always intuitively incorporated the emphasis on the process of creative expression and the special individual needs of each student. More and more art education programs are moving toward the integration of art therapy techniques into their curricula because traditional methods of teaching art emphasizing methods and tools have proven ineffective as a result of their inability to reach the deeper layers of the unconscious to stimulate artistic expression.

Kramer attempts to integrate her considerable experience as a creative artist into her work as an art therapist and her success in her work stems from her ability to be in touch with her own creative energies. She knows that the creative person must never lose the connectedness with his or her spontaneous and childlike impulses, dreams, fantasies, and imagery. But the genuinely creative artist finds it difficult to go along with the Freudian concept of "sublimation," which postulates that creative expression is the result of repressed or frustrated aggressive or sexual energies or libido that are channeled into socially acceptable forms of behavior and expression. The concept of sublimation is insufficient to explain the vast scope of creative activities characteristic of most societies. Most art therapists tend to hold a theoretical position that acknowledges the creative drive as a separate instinct which is not necessarily dependent on sexual energy or libido as narrowly defined by Freud. We must either assume that there is a basic reservoir of energies or libido which can express itself in three or more qualitatively different forms, i.e., the sexual, creative, and aggressive domains. Or we may assume that man has an inherent creative disposition that stimulates his artistic and transformative expression in the world. Recent experiments with animals have clearly shown that curiosity appears to be an innate drive separate from sexual instincts.

In my own work, I have developed the humanistic approach to art therapy as a broad framework permitting the integration of a variety of recently emerging theoretical models in an effort to broaden and deepen the scope of interaction between inner experience and outer "reality" (13). This approach is based on three assumptions: First, the humanistic therapist does not regard people as "mentally ill" but rather as encountering specific problems in their efforts to cope with life as a result of intrapsychically or environmentally caused conflicts. Treatment must be directed toward the reinforcement of the will to live and the development of the ability to find meaning and identity in as fully a creative life style as possible. The second assumption implies that the inability to cope successfully with the vicissitudes of life or to find satisfactory avenues toward self-actualization, meaning, and identity is a common phenomenon affecting most people to a greater or lesser extent at different stages of their lives. The so-called identity crisis is not a one-stage phenomenon the adolescent goes through to reach "maturity;" identity crises may occur at each stage of life when a transition toward some new kind of life style is required. There are the identity crises of the three-year-olds, the six-years-olds, the preadolescents, the adolescents, the thirty-year change of life, the middle life, the early old age, and the middle old age, at least. The assumption that life is an ongoing process with the need for continuous growth, change and development forms the essence of such a psychodynamic humanistic approach. Instead of waiting to "cure" people when periods of tension and "identity crises" occur, the humanistic art therapist attempts to assist the client in his or her attempts to integrate the various "identity crises" into creative-expressive life styles and to prepare movement toward further experiences of change. This preventive mental health care is based on the promotion of those types of life experiences that enhance curiosity, excitement, self-expression, and intimacy.

The third assumption implies that self-actualization resulting from the adoption of life styles of genuine self-disclosure and honesty remains basically sterile unless the self-actualizing person is able to formulate a *self-transcendent* goal that makes life more meaningful by adding a "spiritual" dimension to it, as suggested by Frankl (7). This requires a conscious commitment to relate one's own self-actualizing needs to those of the community at large both through the attainment of genuine interpersonal intimacy and through increasing openness and honesty in relations with others in efforts to improve and expand the opportunities in the life space of the community. My three principles can be summarized as follows: (1) emphasis on life problem solving, (2) encouragement of self-actualization through creative expression, and (3) emphasis on relating self-actualization to intimacy and trust in interpersonal relations and the search for self-transcendent life goals.

In accordance with these basic philosophical considerations, patient and therapist embark together on a journey of exploration of inner images, fantasies, dreams, and archetypes. This adventure into the depths of the psyche enables both to crystallize blocked or unexplored facets of the inner experience to bring about increased awareness of deep feelings, anxieties, and hopes. Humanistic art therapy can become the royal road to the emergence of *creative man* who is no longer alienated from the inexhaustible wellsprings of his vital inner energies revealed in his dreams myths, fantasies, and intuitive imagery. As a result of modern technological "progress," man has become robotized, mechanized, and automatized. The global fear visualizes man as submerged in the ice-cold efficiency of the mass society. Humanistic art therapy can be the "secret weapon" directed against this Skinnerian society of "adjustment" through manipulation of "rewards" and "punishments," a society that has no use for man's inner experience and denies the existence of the "self." In a recent article (11) I outlined the concepts and methods that provide avenues for investigation of these little explored dimensions that determine the present and future of mankind. It appears paradoxical that man has been able and willing to extend his most intensive exploration into the outer spaces of planets and the solar system, while he has been unable or unwilling to explore the vast uncharted territories of his own "inner space."

My theory is greatly influenced by Otto Rank, whose book *Art and Artist* (38) takes the reader on a journey of discovery through the realms of creation and encourages a person to become an "artist-in-life" shaping his or her own existence. Rank believes that it is the depth of inner experiences that needs to be tapped to assist the individual to integrate their meanings into his or her whole life history so as to become the true "artist-in-life." In accordance with the theories of Shostrom (40) and Assagioli (2), the goal of humanistic art therapy consists in the development of the rhythmically balanced personality who can establish a rhythmical flow between the polarities of love and anger, weakness and strength, privacy and intimacy, cooperation and competition, dependency and independence, dominance and submission, hope and despair, and so on. The atmosphere the humanistic art therapist attempts to create reflects the total absence of moralistic judgmental attitudes suggesting that man must be either good or bad, strong or weak, loving or hating, and dependent or independent. It confirms the conviction that man can be both good and bad, strong and weak, loving and angry, and dependent and independent. Once man is aware of these conflicting polarities, he can give up perfectionistic standards of performance and behavior to proceed toward self-actualizing choices and commitments rather than self-desructive ones.

The Gestalt approach to art therapy is outlined by Janie Rhyne (39). Her theory is based on the existential approach developed by Fritz Perls (34). Gestalt techniques focus on awareness and self-responsibility related to the present. Rhyne describes the specific techniques she has developed to enable her clients to get in touch with their basic body needs, their needs for enjoyment and "centeredness," and their needs for spontaneity, honesty, and self-actualization. Margaret F. Keyes presents lively descriptions of her own efforts to integrate the basic principles of Gestalt, transactional, and Jungian analytic theories in her own work in the book *The Inward Journey* (23). She has also devised an ingenious method of making family sculptures out of clay which can be used as excellent diagnostic and therapeutic tools to achieve a deeper comprehension of patterns of family interaction and conflict in family art psychotherapy. Other art therapists have described various techniques of group art therapy which will be further discussed in a special section.

After a review of some techniques of art therapy, including those developed by Naumburg, Kramer, and other psychoanalytically oriented art therapists, while disregarding recent theoretical contributions and practical applications made by Garai, Keyes, and Rhyne, Elinor Ulman (42) attempts to provide a synthesis of current theoretical viewpoints. This synthesis is formulated by her as follows:

> Therapeutic procedures are those designed to assist favorable changes in personality or in living that will outlast the session itself. The motive power of art therapy comes from within the personality; it is a way of bringing order out of chaos—chaotic feelings and impulses within, the bewildering mass of impressions from

without. It is a means to discover both the self and the world, and to establish a relation between the two. In the complete creative process, inner and outer realities are fused into a new entity [42, pp. 12-13].

As a humanistic art therapist, I tend to agree that this definition provides the least common denominator for a general consensus about the definition of art therapy among the different theoretical frameworks. I would like to elaborate, however, on one aspect of art therapy which reflects the views of Winnicott (43) on the role of play as a stimulant for creative expression. I would therefore add the following definition to that presented by Ulman above:

> Art therapy provides a testing ground for the organic interplay between inner and outer realities which permits the fusion, confusion, diffusion, and effusion of creative energies in efforts to attain the type of fluid integration and balance permitting a person to experience his or her own life space and life time as spontaneously and reflectively as possible. Through self-actualization and self-transcendence, the person can move toward individuation and integration of the four basic human faculties of thinking, feeling, sensing, and intuiting.

PRACTICAL APPLICATIONS OF ART THERAPY TECHNIQUES

Art-therapy techniques are increasingly employed in a variety of mental health, educational, rehabilitative, and preventive health care settings with populations ranging from the mentally retarded to the highly gifted. A survey of the two quarterly journals, the *American Journal of Art Therapy* (41) and *Art Psychotherapy* (1), indicates that art therapy can be most effectively utilized with those patients who are unwilling or unable to respond to verbal methods of therapy. Autistic children, brain-damaged individuals with speech defects, deaf and blind persons, stutterers, mute or noncommunicative schizophrenics, depressed patients who refuse to talk, and patients suffering from partial or total amnesia have learned to communicate their feelings, conflicts, anxieties, and problems through drawings, clay modeling, collages, sculptures, weaving, etc. The spoken or graphically depicted stories they make up with regard to these pictures frequently reveal their genuine feelings of loneliness, abandonment, despair, and alienation, their inner sufferings caused by feelings of hurt and rejection from parents, siblings, spouses, and other significant persons, and their repressed longings for nurturance, love, recognition, and self-actualization.

Artistic expression uses a variety of techniques and materials such as drawing with crayons, pastels, or pencils; painting with oils, aquarels, luma paint, magic markers; making collages; modeling clay; sculpting with all kinds of stones; weaving; doing batik work; printmaking; beadstringing; fingerpainting; drawing or painting individual and group murals; using wiremesh, puppets, etc. The creative art therapist embarks upon a continuous journey of discovery of new avenues toward the integration of inner experience through utilization of the vast treasures of organic and inorganic materials provided by nature and man's genius in transforming these materials into new products and composite materials. One art therapist instituted a summer workshop which encouraged adolescents to work only with those materials that could be found in the ecological environment of the summer camp. They developed an inventory of over 300 types of such materials including moss, leaves, roots, mushrooms, decayed animal bones, and berries. They also tried to replace industrial materials such as foam rubber and found that a certain mixture of mushrooms with the resin of tree bark could be made into a much more resilient "foam rubber" than the commercially sold one.

The types of material and techniques utilized are, however, only incidental to the creative process, which is determined by the urge toward the expression of deep-seated feelings and energies. These alone determine the qualities of the material and the types of techniques most likely to channel the expression of inner experience into suitable outlets. Thus, for instance, modeling with soft plastelline clay may enable persons who are literally "out of touch" with their tender emotions and their needs to reach out and "touch" people, whose closeness they desire, to begin to stroke, caress, and mold the clay as if it were a symbolic representation of the person they want to get in touch with. There are exercises such as "getting in touch with yourself" using clay, marble, foam rubber, leather, flowers, shells, etc. Typical responses include: "I am getting in touch with my soft and tender self; feeling the clay I experience smoothness, softness, and yet some rough edges—just like my own tenderness emerges at times, while I have also rough spots and a hard core." To deepen the experience of inner space, the person keeps his or her eyes closed. Clay modeling can also be employed as a method of transcendental meditation in various ways.

To enumerate some of the innovative techniques introduced by art therapists and creativity specialists, the following short descriptions, based on the writings of Betensky (3), Garai (9, 11), Hammer (16), Harris and Joseph (17), Keyes (23), Lystad (27), Rhyne (39), and Winnicott (44), are presented:

Draw first your real self and then your ideal self.

Draw a cartoon or mold a sculpture about an animal family.

Create your own image in clay, shells, or collage as you are now, then as you would like it to be one day, then as your mother would like it to be, etc. Relate these images to those you have made of others.

Draw yourself crossing a river with strong rapids.

Draw a maze, then draw yourself in the maze, and then draw how you get out of the maze.

"Space yourself in" and "space yourself out" by drawing or depicting yourself with any medium related to your own inner space and then connect this inner space to your outer space or the outer world.

Draw or model with clay your occupational self as you see it now and as you see it five years from now.

Draw a dream or a daydream you had recently and make up a story about it (or write a poem about it).

Draw or fashion with clay your "devil, monster, ghost, shadow, or rejected self" and your "angel, god, immortal self, or perfect self" and make up a story about these two opposing sides of your personality.

Make a collage of your "fragmented self" followed by a collage of your "integrated self."

Draw your own mandala or "perfect circle," showing how you attempt to integrate your sensing, thinking, feeling, and intuiting faculties.

Depict in any way you want the most shocking (or the most exciting) event in your life and make up a story about it.

Draw or represent in any way desired two polarities such as death and rebirth, hope and despair, intimacy and privacy, dependency and independence, competition and cooperation, courage and fear, Superman and Mickey Mouse, etc., and make up a story around this conflict.

ART THERAPY IN INDIVIDUAL PRACTICE

Diagnostic Tools

A variety of fairly elementary diagnostic tests have been developed by art therapists. These appear to tap primary process material more directly than verbal procedures. Symbolic communication breaks down the habitual defensive structures through the ambiguity of the symbolic images and the possibility of different interpretations of their meanings. The client creates a product expressing inner feeling states which can then serve as the basis for the exploration of the meanings of the images and symbolic communication and their relevance to the client's own experience and life space. Through the processes of projection of the conflict onto other persons in the drawing or picture, the client can deal with it at first on an impersonal level and then be slowly guided toward the acceptance of the conflict as reflecting his or her own inner turmoil and anxieties. The symbolic communication permits initial distancing through projection, but this barrier can be much more easily removed when the client begins to realize that these projections reflect his or her own inner experiences.

The most widely used diagnostic tools include the Draw-A-Person (D-A-P) test by Machover (28), the House-Tree-Person (H-T-P) test by Buck (4), and the Kinetic-Family-Drawing (K-F-D) test by Burns and Kaufman (5). The client is requested to draw a person, then a house, then a tree, and, finally, a family doing something. The Post-Drawing-Interrogation (P-D-I) revolves around a number of questions related to the meanings of the drawings or their symbolic representations. The following examples illustrate the diagnostic application of these tests.

The results of the H-T-P test administered to Ilana are described elsewhere (10). Ilana is an eleven-year-old Puerto Rican girl with a slender body in constant motion, a pretty face, smiling and seductive eyes, and light skin. She is bright, attending the highest-level sixth-grade class. Other girls dislike her because of her "chasing or being chased by boys" as a result of her early sexual maturation. Ilana has one older brother, aged 18, and two younger brothers, aged ten and seven, but reports that her mother lost six other children. One boy died at age two just before her birth by "falling from the apartment window and going 'splat' on the sidewalk." Her father is said to dislike her because he claims she is too "dark" to be his own daughter since he is so "light." Ilana was born in New York and visited Puerto Rico, the birthplace of her parents, only once. Ilana thinks that all women talk too much and is afraid that she will be excessively talkative when she grows up. She feels that her father punishes her unjustly for whatever her brothers are doing because he thinks *they* can do no wrong. He threatens that he will send all the kids away when their mother dies.

Ilana's chromatic drawing of a house (Figure 1) depicts an empty house lacking warmth. It looks like a ghostlike face or a hooded, masked figure. It is paper-based, indicating insecurity. The watchdog is on the alert and the ladder is put in; she exclaims: "I'll put in the ladder in case I fall and break my leg." Then she draws the trees and points out where people have carved in the bark. The letters "I & N" are interpreted by her to mean "Ilana and Nobody" engraved sideways. The tree on the right side reflects a sad and tearful face' The house, in general, reinforces feelings of lack of warmth, loneliness, fear of anxiety-arousing fantasies, and impaired contact with the outside world, as indicated by the heavily shaded brown door with the black doorknob preventing access. The attempt to seek help appears frustrated. She carves a heart on the top of the trunk on the right side but it is very small, too high up to be clearly perceived, and counteracted by the outline of a grim face appearing in the crown of the tree. The sideway carving of "Ilana and Nobody" (I & N) reflects her feelings of utter hopelessness. She fears that her messages reach no one in the world who might ever help her.

Her chromatic tree drawing (Figure 2) represents a tree surrounded by a confused and agitated environment. It is tall and stretches way up into the sky as if to seek some kind of warmth and nurturance. Its height also indicates Ilana's need for intellectual achievement, which constitutes her only hope of ever gaining her mother's approval. A gaping hole around the age of four to six years points to some traumatic experience leaving her "scarred." The initials "I & N" (Ilana and Nobody) appear again on the top left of the bark of the trunk, expressing her feelings of abandonment and inability to secure nurturance. The small heart has literally "sunk to the bottom" and the absence of roots reinforces the impression of rootlessness and despair. This tree bears no fruit and the crown or fantasy area has become much more wildly swirling and confused. The tree shows that Ilana is a per-

Figure 1. Ilana's Drawing of a House.

son with ego strength and ambition who nevertheless feels a lack of support and recognition from her environment. She is constantly expecting to be attacked, and therefore assumes a posture of defensive alertness, while seeking escape in fantasies of seducing and being seduced by boys. She generally feels lonely, depressed, rejected, and misunderstood.

Ilana's drawing of a person (Figure 3) depicts a warm, cheerful, friendly, smiling, and happy-looking girl. She tries to please others and wants to be a "nice" girl. She has evidently invested great effort in making herself pretty with cosmetics and jewelry and sports a large but contrived smile. Her eyes try to be sparkling, although they do not quite manage to conceal their sadness. Her huge, oversized head indicates her emphasis on brightness and intellectual achievement. Her large hairdo expresses her need to be sexually appealing, but the carefully controlled outline and neatly arranged strands of hair point out her need to control her pubescent sexuality.

This person is said to be 16 years old, i.e., five years older than Ilana herself, revealing a wish to be a teenager rather than a preadolescent. Ilana drew her facial

Figure 2. Ilana's Drawing of a Tree.

Figure 3. Ilana's Drawing of a Girl.

features last, revealing that she hesitates to define herself and is unsure of her identity. The face shows defensiveness and an overconcern with wanting to make a good impression. Yet, despite the doll-like face, she feels that her face is the worst part of her. She is particularly disturbed by the poor shape of her nose, which may be due to her unwillingness to show aggression, anger, or a desire for dominance, and perhaps also, at her pubescence, a fear of her own sexual impulses as well as of male aggression, if the nose is regarded as a phallic symbol.

The eyes and ears fail to make contact with the environment. The mouth, an open smile, displays an artificial friendliness as well as strong, unfulfilled oral dependency needs. Her hair, which is profuse yet neatly controlled, indicates a conflict over sexual drives which is reinforced by the specifically emphasized crotch area, the tightly held-together legs, and the thick "Peace" belt that separates the sexual from the power area. The body is also separated from the head by a long neck and another "Peace" necklace, which again shows that intellect and feelings are not satisfactorily integrated.

The weak shoulders, thin trunk, and generally emaciated body, while stressing her emphasis on slenderness, also suggest feelings of powerlessness, weakness, and inadequacy. The short, rigid arms with their tiny, ineffectual hands reveal her inability to set goals and derive satisfaction from her environment. Her feet are receding and, in general, she appears helpless and impotent. The curving groundline implies strong maternal dependency needs. She overcompensates by trying to appear grown-up, self-assured, and sexually appealing in spite of strong conflicts aroused by feelings of inadequacy, loneliness, and depression. At present, she is almost entirely functioning in the role of the "pleasant, friendly, bright, young girl." But underneath she feels mechanical and robotlike.

Ilana's chromatic person drawing (Figure 4) represents a little boy trying to appear happy, although he strikes the viewer as rigid, immobile, helpless, and crippled in his crucified stance. While at camp, he can only watch others playing. He remains isolated from them and has no ears to hear or hands to touch to make contact with them. Ilana chose to draw a boy "because it's easier." She remarked, "He's ugly, man!" After she finished the face, she said, laughing, "I'm telling you the truth, he's *ugly!* If he asked girls out, they'd say 'U-hugh! Nope!' " She then drew the pink trunk and the blue shorts, saying that blue was "the wrong color for these hot pants." Drawing the legs in brown, she attempted to detail the knee area and exclaimed, "What *skanky* [skinny] legs man, they're skanky! I tried to draw the knee-bone but they look like braces!" This is an emasculated and ineffective boy, standing there helpless and forlorn, trying to hide his anger behind a facade of superficial friendliness. He may also represent her secret desire to emasculate or castrate her brothers whom she regards as her father's favorites, while she herself feels rejected by him.

From the analysis of these drawings, with the help of interpretations made by the client and the analyst, we can formulate the following diagnostic report:

Figure 4. Ilana's Drawing of a Boy.

1. Ilana suffers from feelings of depression and inadequacy. Her emerging sexual desires in the preadolescent stage lead to sexual confusion and "identity diffusion" with increasing retreat into fantasies.

2. She has experienced very early oral deprivation. Her needs for love, nurturance, and maternal dependency have largely been unmet. Feelings of loneliness, abandonment, and depression compel her to withdraw into fantasies. Her isolation is graphically expressed in the carving of the initials "I & N" in the bark of the tree. For her, the world consists of "Ilana and Nobody." She cannot ask her parents or siblings for love, recognition, or approval.

3. She is confused about her sexual identitiy. She rejects women as excessive talkers and men as ugly and ineffective weaklings. She has no clear idea of her own emerging sexual energies and is unable to ask her parents or teachers for guidance. Her current behavior appears seductive and narcissistically exhibitionistic, although she is afraid of men. She secretly identifies with the male role, which she considers as stronger than that of the female, despite her frequent denigrations of men.

4. As a result of feeling ugly and unaccepted, she has a low self-esteem, which she tries to bolster by emphasis on scholastic achievement. She still holds out some dim hope that she may gain her mother's love one day by her excellence in academic performance.

5. Deep fears of impairment and "castration anxieties" stem from her conviction that she has been rejected and stunted in her growth. She sees herself as the "mutilated cat" she drew spontaneously after completion of the H-T-P test. This cat has a strong desire for survival in a hostile environment despite the loss of her two legs.

6. She has learned to cope with an unfriendly world by keeping her anger and aggression tightly repressed. At the same time, she seeks to prepare escape routes to save herself from attacks threatening her survival. This is shown by the inclusion of escape ladders in her house drawings.

The sensitive art therapist may assist Ilana in the establishment of a more definite sense of sexual and personal identity and the formulation of meaningful life goals in accordance with her intellectual abilities. Ilana will then move toward increased expression of *all* her feelings, including anger, despair, aggression, and sexual desires, in an atmosphere of unconditional acceptance which is not based on standards to high-level performance. She needs to work with a sympathetic female art therapist first who is able to inspire trust through encouragement of frank self-disclosure. Ilana's basic ego strength can then be mobilized to resolve her sexual and personal identity confusion. Although Ilana feels that she is fighting a losing battle, her resources for survival are strong despite intense feelings of being cut off, stunted, and damaged. In her spontaneously drawn cartoon sequence after she finished the H-T-P- test, she appears to identify with the cat who lost two legs in an accident but refuses to yield to fate and survives defying the assaults of a hostile world. Ilana's basic ego strength is intact but her energies are available to her only for the purpose of sheer survival without joy.

Another diagnostic technique is theme-centered. The client is asked to draw or model with clay a situation relevant to his or her own life. In my seminar on "The Search for Identity and Meaning in Life" at the New School, I asked participants to draw pictures around the themes of "being trapped" and "getting out of the trap" and to write poems related to these pictures. The following drawing was made by Suzanna, who felt trapped in a prison of her own making (Figure 5). Her picture showing her face trapped in a vise formed by jagged steel edges is accompanied by this poem:

> GRAY GRAY GRAY my world is . . .
> The steel walls closing in
> cutting my flesh,
> denying me sleep or tranquility,
> isolating me from the blue sky
> and green grass and freedom . . .
> I am alone, manacled and bleeding . . .

Her drawing of ways to get out of the trap (Figure 6) reflects the face of a young woman looking straight out into the world with trust and openness. Suzanna, the 26-year-old woman who drew both pictures, had recently been released from a mental hospital. She added the following poem to her second drawing:

> I find the key to understanding
> that the terrible walls were only
> creations of my own mind—
> The more I see the real world,
> the less real my prison seems . . .
> I watch it crumble, disintegrate.
> It can't hurt me at all,
> I am free, I see the world,
> the blue sky surrounds me
> and I wave out my window.

Suzanna realizes that her "inner prison" or state of isolation is more confining than the walls of the hospital and she appears to be ready to relinquish this "prison."

Therapeutic Process

The following excerpts from case histories of clients in art therapy illustrate some of the basic therapeutic techniques and the psychodynamics involved. The first presentation is derived from my article "The Use of Painting to Resolve an Artist's Identity Conflicts" (12). Ken, a student of fine arts, entered psychotherapy at the age of 21 because he went into a psychotic episode as a result of the use of marijuana. He was a tall, well-built young man whose deep-seated, penetrating eyes

Figure 5. Suzanna's First Drawing.

Figure 6. Suzanna's Second Drawing.

usually had a suspicious expression. At the beginning of therapy, he was unable to complete his artwork for graduation, had broken up with his girlfriend, had quarreled with his mother, and was afraid of "going crazy." He was the only child of parents who divorced when he was five years old. He was still greatly attached to his overprotective, seductive, rejecting mother whose love he had sought to gain in his childhood by playing the "cute clown" and by intellectual precocity. He harbored deep feelings of resentment against his father who had remarried since and who had never acknowledged him as an artist. Ken suffered from severe depressive reactions combined with feelings of guilt and repressed anger. There were paranoid projections, hysterical symptoms, and various psychosomatic complaints. He vacillated between impulsive acting out and withdrawal into dreamlike states. He was diagnosed as an inadequate personality with passive-aggressive dependency strivings and sexual confusion.

In a series of paintings of self-portraits and the dreams he experienced, Ken was able to resolve his identity conflicts and move toward increasing self-actualization. The resolution of his oedipal dependency can be followed through a series of paintings. The first painting was made shortly after the onset of Ken's therapy. It depicts a dream scene (Figure 7). Ken described it as follows: "I am the black man in a crowd in the city . . . I am the gorilla in the red shirt . . . I'm really a 'dumb fuck' taking care of the queen. She is my mother with a crown on her head and an anxious look on her face . . . worried about being raped by the brute. On my head is a figure, half bird and half a woman . . . the bird is clawing my head. It's a symbol of my mother not letting go of me." This painting reveals the three archetypal maternal figures as "the queen mother, the witch mother, and the prostitute mother," with the latter lying prone at the right of the "gorilla" who has turned away from her toward the mother queen. Ken's oedipal conflict has resulted in ambivalent feelings toward women, as illustrated in this painting. He sees women as being simultaneously alluring seductresses, devouring and oppressive witches, and demanding queens. His black face, white arm, and red shirt reflect inner conflict between purity and sin, "goodness" and "badness," pleasure and pain, virginity and promiscuity, and depression and joy—themes that emerge in various guises in the works of most creative artists.

The discussion of this painting with a group of patients induced Ken to work feverishly on another canvas (Figure 8), which he could hardly get through the door of our office because of its huge size. It stunned the group into several minutes of surprised silence by its graphic depiction of sexual intercourse between two very different persons. Several members of the group said that they thought the painting depicted the realization of Ken's oedipal fantasy. Ken answered defensively that he had had in mind "intercourse between two lovers." But almost in the same breath, he admitted that the man seemed to be much younger than the woman and that the woman's face resembled that of his mother. After the group had given several interpretations, Ken said at the end of the session, "I guess I still want to get even with my mother . . . I don't know whether I should love her or hate her."

Figure 7. Ken's First Painting.

The interpretations made by the group members and the therapists were based in the main on the following impressions of the painting: Ken has intercourse with his mother. Her flaming red hair and sensuous lips entice him but she looks haughtily rejecting, diverting her gaze from him and closing her lips tightly, adopting the superior position. Instead of her nipples feeding him, he must support her right breast with his palm. Both dependency and sexual needs remain unfulfilled, since his position compels him to engage in cunnilingus rather than in actual sexual inter- course. Different parts of his back are again black, red, and white, reiterating the conflict between good and evil or passion and abstention expressed in the drawing

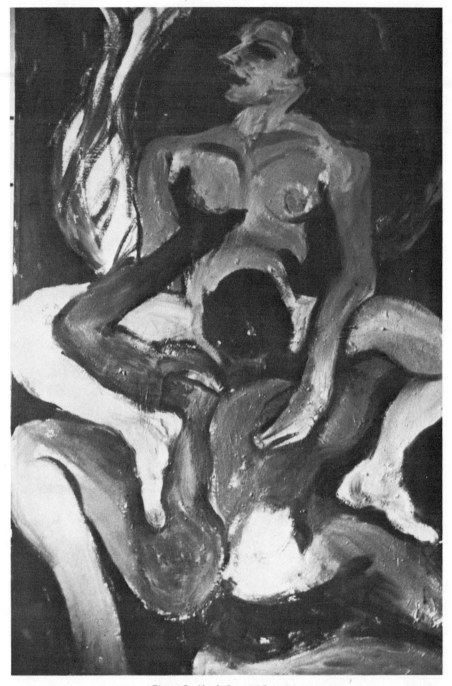

Figure 8. Ken's Second Painting.

of the gorilla surrounded by the archetypes of maternal women. This painting graphically depicts his unresolved oedipal conflict.

Three weeks after showing the intercourse painting to the group, Ken brought in a painting of a dream from which he remembered awakening in a state of joyful relief (Figure 9). This time he did not wait for the group to volunteer interpretations but went right ahead to explain it as follows: "My mother is finally dead, buried in the rock-tomb. Her head is cut off and she breathes her last gasp . . . The monkeys are glad and dancing around the grave. The green guy [bottom left] is me getting rid of my anger, and laughing. The blue fellow [bottom right] represents my more serious self that grieves about her death and wants to contemplate the newly won freedom." Two members of the group pointed to a yellowish penis on the "serious self," which showed a strong erection. Ken eventually acknowledged it and then explained that his mother's symbolic death permitted him to enjoy his sexuality and potency without further guilt feelings.

Ken's paintings illustrate the working through of unresolved problems of oedipal dependency and sexual confusion through the use of artistic creative expression.

The case history of Lester shows that a predelinquent boy with a negative self-image can move toward the incorporation of a positive self-image and the replacement of self- and other-destructive tendencies with self-affirmative and constructive goals. Lester, a thin, frail youth of Jamaican descent, was an adolescent of short stature who was always well-dressed, taking great pride in his appearance. His father and older brother had both died of overdoses of heroin and, as the sole remaining male sibling, he tended to assume the role of provider and protector for his mother and sister. Left without a positive role model, he tried to establish his masculine identity by getting involved in minor crime and "soft" drugs. One day he was apprehended by police as he and some companions attempted to dispose of furniture they had stolen from his school office, which they had also vandalized. Fred, a well-known art therapist, became interested in working with Lester, whose innate creativity and preference for art served as the foundation for a positive therapeutic relationship. The first two drawings were made by Lester on the day following his involvement in the burglary and his subsequent arrest.

The first drawing (Figure 10) presents several unrelated objects bound together by an encapsulating line resembling the amniotic sac of the newborn in the womb. It is symbolic of how Lester experienced himself in relation to other people and things in his life. Everything is separate and, at times, incomplete. Size and proportion are irrelevant as things don't really relate to each other—just as Lester is cut off and unrelated to the world.

The second drawing (Figure 11) displays a conspicuous absence of people in an unreal world. Objects are floating and not really connected to the ground or to other buildings. The "holes" between the buildings symbolize the "holes" in Lester's personality in accordance with the Gestalt theories of Fritz Perls (34). His world is one of unconnected buildings which do not house any human beings or signs of real life.

Figure 9. Ken's Third Painting.

Figure 10. Lester's First Drawing.

Figure 11. Lester's Second Drawing.

Lester's art therapist introduced polaroid photography as a means to reach Lester. The immediate feedback provided by the polaroid camera's quick processing mechanisms stimulated Lester's imagination and interest. He was able to see fast results and gain a sense of accomplishment once he mastered the technical procedures of taking and developing his "instant" pictures. Lester started out by taking photographs of inanimate objects—roaming the neighborhood to seek them out. He put his favorite pictures into a scrapbook. After a period of time, he began to take pictures of people. Then he entered a period when all he wanted to do was to take pictures of his art therapist and of himself. He took many pictures of Fred and asked to have pictures of himself taken in all kinds of serious and funny poses so that he could add them to his scrapbook. The best pictures were mounted by Fred and Lester on large display boards. Lester showed the displays to his teachers and classmates with great pride. Lester also imitated various poses of Fred. This polaroid period served as a means of pictorial identification, enabling Lester to gain a positive self-image reflected in the versatility and expressiveness of the poses assumed by him and his ability to "copy" the activities of his idealized image, i.e., his therapist, successfully. He felt encouraged to develop his own potential, taking his therapist as his role model.

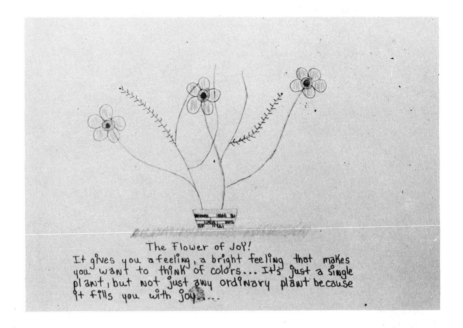

The Flower of Joy!
It gives you a feeling, a bright feeling that makes you want to think of colors... It's just a single plant, but not just any ordinary plant because it fills you with joy...

Figure 12. Lester's "Flower of Joy."

One day Lester told Fred that he wanted to work on a new project. He wanted to write a book including a collection of drawings and poetry. The following drawings reflect the progress made by Lester in the development of his identity and personality integration. Figure 12 represents the first drawing for his book. He is no longer encapsulated and alienated. He can now write and draw freely and express his feelings openly and directly. The "Flower of Joy" symbolizes his own more joyful self who is now extending all over the space and connected to the other two flowers which may symbolize the important people in his life. The accompanying poem suggests that Lester genuinely sees himself now as a "special individual" different from other individuals. He has attained "individuation" in the Jungian sense. Here is his poem:

The Flower of Joy

It gives you a feeling,
a bright feeling
that makes you want to
think of colors . . .
It's just a plant,
but not just any ordinary plant
because it fills you with joy . . .

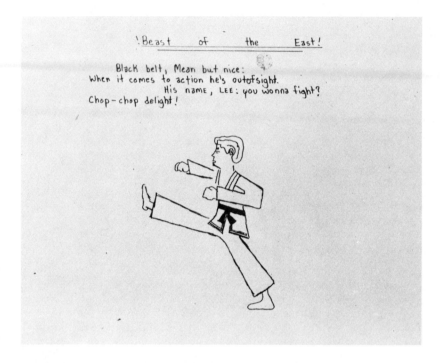

Figure 13. Lester's "Beast of the East."

Figure 13 represents Lester's first complete drawing of a human figure. He appears as the "Beast of the East," the courageous karate fighter with the black belt. He considers himself ready to tackle the world with his fighting skill and strength. The person reveals strength, power, and self-confident movement.

The next drawing (Figure 14) expresses Lester's perception of women as sad and helpless, though beautiful. This may reflect the impressions he has gained from his mother and sister who look to him for guidance and protection instead of offering him their support and nurturance. The smooth, fluid, and delicate drawing of the outline of the woman's body furnishes evidence that the acquisition of a positive self-image has promoted a more mature conception of the sexual role of the woman and her own struggle for identity and self-actualization. He is sensitive enough to empathize with the unhappiness of women who are deserted by the men they cherish. His mother and sister were deserted by his father and brother who destroyed their lives by excessive use of drugs. The accompanying poem vividly expresses these strong feelings of compassion.

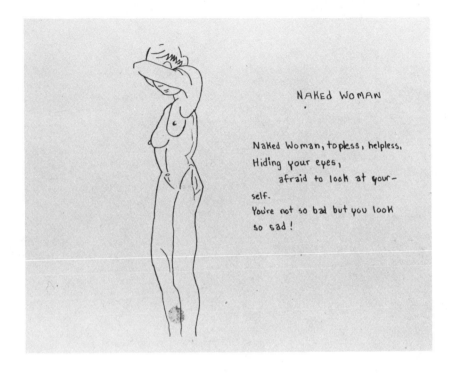

Figure 14. Lester's "Naked Woman."

Naked Woman

Naked woman, topless, helpless,
Hiding your eyes,
    afraid to look at your-
self.
You're not so bad but you look
so sad!

Lester's next drawing (Figure 15) is that of a large hand on which he outlines his characteristic personality traits. He now feels that he is in charge of his mastery over the environment, and the hand is symbolic of this competence and skill. It is a strong hand ready to tackle reality with an excellent grip. This hand enables Lester to apply it both as a means of self-defense and as an aid to others providing strength and protection to them. This is poignantly expressed in the poem inscribed on the back of the hand.

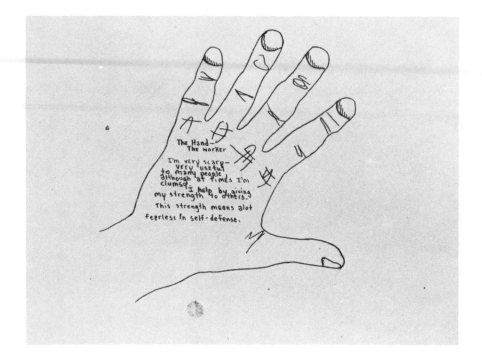

Figure 15. Lester's "The Hand."

The Hand
The Worker
I'm very scary
    very useful
to many people,
although at times I'm
clumsy
    I help by giving
my strength to others.
This strength means alot
fearless in self-defense.

In another drawing (Figure 16), Lester depicts a whole block of huge and strong buildings, which are all connected and well-designed, while a huge crane hovers over the housetops indicating that more construction is going on. This scene reveals Lester's continuing growth, development, and movement toward personality integration and forms a strong contrast to the initial drawing of a row of disconnected and unfinished, abandoned-looking houses (Figure 11). His poem underlining the

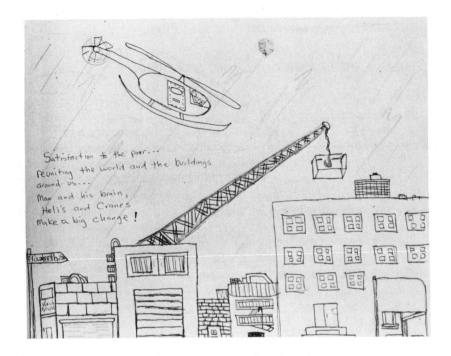

Figure 16. Lester's Drawing of Buildings.

flight of the huge helicopter describes the big change Lester has undergone since then.

> Satisfaction to the peer
> reuniting the world and the buildings
> around us . . .
>
> Man and his brain,
> Helis and Cranes
> Make a big change!

This well-integrated scene symbolizes Lester's progress toward integration of his own life with that of the community at large.

A few months later Lester graduated from the junior high school division of the center where he was working with the art therapist. On the day of his graduation, the young man, who only a few months ago had been on the verge of becoming a high school dropout and juvenile delinquent, approached Fred, his art therapist, proudly introducing his girlfriend to him and asking for permission to borrow a polaroid camera to record and remember that special day.[1]

THE THEORY AND PRACTICE OF GROUP ART THERAPY

The steady growth of the group art therapy movement in recent years stems from experiences of art therapists in working with exceedingly isolated individuals in medical settings. They discovered that several of the most withdrawn patients who refused to participate in any group activities manifested some interest in looking at other patients' artwork or in getting others to look at theirs. This spark of interest sometimes provided the impetus for the establishment of nonverbal communication which was later followed by verbal interchanges. Art therapists began to realize the potential of group art therapy and developed innovative structured and unstructured techniques of dynamic group art interaction. Most of these techniques reflect the theoretical viewpoints of their originators. But many art therapists utilize their own experiences to design new techniques and structure specific theoretical frameworks based on creative expressive needs. Limited space allows me to describe only a few of the most widely used methods.

Group Mural Art Therapy Techniques

This popular technique is characterized by a wide variety of styles, approaches, and philosophies. Groups range in size from four to 12 members with a preferred range of six to ten. Their nosological composition may be homogeneous or heterogeneous. Most therapists mount the mural panel on portable easels or blackboards on which they attach gray, white, or brown cardboard or smooth types of wood. Pastels are preferred, but the use of crayons, magic markers, felt-tipped pens, luma or liquid sumi paints, or even sprays has also been reported. Patients are usually arranged in a semicircle around the mural area. The free-drawing period encourages each patient to draw whatever he or she feels like. Fellow patients are free to comment, while the therapist takes the somewhat passive role of facilitator of group interaction. The "theme-choice" method allows the group members to move toward a group consensus about the subject matter they want to depict. Each patient is then encouraged to contribute some drawing to the group theme. A specific theme may also be suggested by the therapist, particularly when the situation requires the exploration of a certain conflict area in greater depth.

One technique based on the psychoanalytic model is described by Harris and Joseph in their book *Murals of the Mind* (17). They found that long-term patients

---

[1] The case history was contributed by Bob Wolf, Director of Art Therapy of the Henry Street School. He also took the photographs of Lester's drawings. The author owes a special debt of gratitude to him for his cooperation.

in a psychiatric hospital who participated in mural sessions for a period of one year were able to articulate previously inaccessible feelings. The authors claim that during the first six months the group evolved in a way closely resembling early ego development in young children. During the second six months, however, the group underwent a process of structural disintegration which the authors ascribe to a kind of "group schizophrenia" resulting from disruptive influences in the hospital milieu. The most interesting aspect of this study relates to their analysis of 50 group murals, which leads to the formulation of a tentative hypothesis that group murals follow a developmental sequence of stages defined as: (1) a reality-bound mural, (2) a mural stating the group's problem in a more or less disguised form, (3) a mural of anxiety, flight, and defense, (4) a mural depicting topographically the unconscious in relation to the conscious (with the underwater scene perhaps symbolizing the primary processes of the id, while the land area concerns the conscious or ego of the client), (5) a mural recombining the recent symbols in restitutive terms, and (6) a mural of resolution and return to reality. Such attempts at formulating relevant theories are commendable, although they need further research under controlled conditions to establish their validity and reliability.

The interpretation of the symbolic meanings expressed in group murals frequently provides deeper insights into intrapsychic and interpersonal conflict areas. In mural sessions, the group members are encouraged to share symbolic communication patterns resulting at times in instant intuitive recognition of feeling tones, moods, and conflicts. The following discussion centering around a group mural entitled *Freedom and Imprisonment* executed by eight patients in one of our workshops demonstrates the depth of symbolic communication achieved by them.

Harry, pointing to Susan's jail which has a slightly open window in the top area through which a little bird is trying to escape, says. ""You seem to be stuck in your jail. You are desperately trying to get out, but your wings seem to be clipped." Susan answers. "That's my life story. I'm always trying to get out of my mother's grip, but her jail has too heavy bars.... Nobody helps me to get out and I can't make it on my own." Then Susan begins to draw a green field with a wide open pasture where a huge butterfly with colorful wings buzzes over the grass and around Richard's horse, which has escaped from a ranch nearby. Richard then turns to Susan, saying. "You try to be like me.... I have just gotten out of the confines of my stable....you would like to be free like a butterfly to join me." Josephine, who has added a snail which is sticking only its feelers out of its shell toward some large blades of grass on Richard's ranch, chimes in, "Yeah, you innocent little birdie or butterfly ...You always have an excuse that you are buzzing around all the men by sheer accident. You are a supermanipulator!"

Five of the eight members of this group were able within a period of six to 17 months to resolve very difficult problems of overdependency by drawing and interpreting the meanings of such murals as *Freedom and Imprisonment, Dependency and Independence, Privacy and Intimacy, Togetherness and Loneliness, Hope and Despair,* and others. We have introduced a technique that alternates group mural sessions with sessions in which each group member creates an individual painting, clay model, or collage to be shown and discussed by the group members. This appears to accelerate the movement toward change and conflict resolution. Other useful methods include the drawing of dreams, which can be juxtaposed on a mural panel to lead to group discussion or the production of a joint dream mural. Dream states can be induced by placing a piece of soft plastelline clay into each member's hand and instructing him or her as follows: "Close your eyes and let yourself feel the clay, imagining it to be whatever you want it to be. Try to dream about touching the soft surface of the clay and permit your dream to take shape."

Group murals can also be made of collages incorporating shells, magazine cutouts, cloth patches, batik, pieces of wood or metal, leaves, plants, rocks, etc. Sandplay and fingerpaints have been successfully applied. Plastelline clay, particularly the nontoxic, colorful Swiss Caran d'Ache clay, can enable group members to portray bas-relief murals or topographical maps. Getting in touch with clay often means getting in touch with the deeper layers of one's feelings. One method requires the group members to share a large chunk of clay, sitting around in a circle with their eyes closed and working on a common theme. We had one group that produced such a marvelously lively assortment of animals in an African jungle that it won a prize at an art exhibition.

The benefits derived from group mural therapy can be summarized as (1) the free choice of a theme promotes self-confidence and autonomy strivings because the clients feel that they can make their own decisions and determine the topics they want to deal with, (2) clients tend to accept interpretations by other clients more readily than those made by therapists and they develop a climate of mutual trust and acceptance of differences in attitudes and moods, (3) the mural interaction enables the clients to develop specific roles such as leader, negotiator, initiator, rebel, conciliator, or goalsetter, while exposing themselves to the critical evaluation of other members as a test of reality in the development of skills in the enactment of relevant roles, (4) isolated clients who cannot communicate verbally learn to communicate symbolically through art expression and are subsequently able to move toward increased socialization patterns, (5) socially undesirable attitudes and taboo subjects can be more easily expressed symbolically, permitting conflicts created by sexual, aggressive, and antisocial desires to be revealed and eventually resolved, (6) the supportive attitudes of group members and the controls exerted by group consensus provide a larger and safe scope for the expression and working through of feelings of hostility, aggression, loneliness, and despair, (7) "sympathetic identification" with similar experiences of other group members promotes the resolution of intrapsychic and interpersonal conflicts in a supportive atmosphere, (8) mutual joy, elation, and surprise can be experienced as a result of the sharing of creative encounter when they stand back and look at the mural they created is a genuine incentive to further self-actualization through creative expression.

Specific Innovative Small Group Art Therapy Techniques

Our theoretical framework is derived from an integration of the basic postulates of Maslow's theories of self-actualization; Jung's concepts of the need for individuation through the integration of the four basic faculties of sensing, thinking, feeling, and intuiting; and Shostrom's definition of the rhythmic flow between polarities of feeling tones and moods that is the prerequisite for a balanced and self-actualizing life style. Unfortunately, our prescribed social and sexual roles usually require the repression of some vital feelings. Rigid sexual roles compel men to repress any feelings of weakness, tenderness, or indecision in order to project toughness and "masculine" determination. Women must repress any feelings or show of anger and aggression and any pride in their intelligence and intellectual achievements in order to conform to the stereotype of the "nice" woman who is not too smart. Couples can only show their needs for togetherness, while they must conceal their needs for privacy and separateness. A genuinely self-actualizing person must gain awareness of his or her conflicting needs to cope with inner experience and outer reality.

Specific exercises have been developed by art therapists to reveal states of disequilibrium between the polar emotions of love and anger, weakness and strength, tenderness and toughness, intimacy and privacy, sadness and joy, dependency and independence, competition and cooperation, introversion and extraversion, and others. One exercise I have designed attempts to guide participants to connect their "inner space" with their "outer space" (11). It requires four members of each group to share one sheet of paper, with each placing himself or herself at the exact corner of the sheet. The first instruction is: "Draw anything you like." Most people tend to respect each other's boundaries and it is quite remarkable how the amount of space each person claims for himself or herself in his or her drawing reflects his or her assertiveness in real life. Shy and timid persons usually stick closely to their corners and surround their drawings at times with thick fences or boundary lines. Expansive persons may take up so much space that they reach the center point of the sheet. The next instruction is: "Draw moving out of your corner toward the center." This reveals a person's readiness to move out of his or her space into someone else's space. The overaggressive person may move right into another person's space, sometimes obliterating the image drawn by that member. All kinds of entanglements may ensue and, as a result, the group members can analyze the symbolic meanings of their pictorial movements to gain more profound insights into their own needs for inner experience and its connection with external reality.

Other exercises include the drawing of a maze by the whole group. Each member is then requested to place himself or herself at some specific point in the maze. The final step is to draw a route showing how each member manages to get out of the maze. The discussion centering around the maze often reveals deep-seated feelings of being trapped in an untenable or unsatisfactory life situation and crystallizes ideas how to change this situation to find more satisfactory avenues and life styles. The exercise "Draw yourself crossing a river" frequently reveals problems of indecision centering around important goals. A variety of other techniques are described by Garai (9, 10, 11, 12, 13, 14), Keyes (23), and Rhyne (39).

Group Art Projective Techniques

Any artistic product is, in a certain sense, a projective technique because the creator cannot help introducing some of his or her most basic inner feeling states and moods into the artwork. This serves as a projection of one's personal experience and feelings. The previously mentioned projective techniques, including the D-A-P, the H-T-P, and the K-F–D tests, can be applied as diagnostic and therapeutic tools in group settings or family therapy. For instance, each group member may be required to draw a house, a tree, a person, a family doing something, etc., and then the other group members encouraged to comment on all the drawings. Further discussion ensues. This technique furnishes clues about the ways in which group members deal with their needs to make contact with other people and the defenses they enlist in avoiding closeness and interaction. Other projective techniques include: "Draw your most liked activity" followed by "Draw your most disliked activity." This may reveal conflicts centering around professional life goals. Art therapists are developing more and more projective tools of this type.

Gestalt Art Therapy Groups

Janie Rhyne describes various techniques utilizing Gestalt-Therapy principles in group experiences in her book *"The Gestalt Art Experience* (39). She calls her groups "Personal Growth Groups" where members are engaged in a search for identity and meaningful life goals through fulfillment of their creative potentials. She works in small groups of about ten persons with the leader acting as a participant in "free creative expression" in which members can work individually, in pairs, in small groups, or in the group as a whole, using any materials they see fit as a bridge for communication of inner experiences. They make noises when so desired, move about into various different spaces and environments, dance, make music, portray persons or animals, etc. This type of experience moves out of the realm of pictorial expression into the area of free expression of feelings through any available medium or modality.

Analyzing, interpreting, or explaining are discouraged since the emphasis is placed on the experience of the "here and now" in the existential sense. We have found that this type of experience can induce certain isolated and withdrawn patients to move toward some kind of cathartic expression of feelings, while less withdrawn individuals struggling with deeper problems may become more anxious as a result of anxiety that is aroused but not adequately worked through. The dogmatic insistence on the need to refrain from interpretation and analytic investigation of the experience detracts from the long-range effectiveness of this method. By the way, it appears that Janie Rhyne and other Gestalt practitioners are actually integrating diverse interpretations into their work despite their denials. We feel that the Gestalt approach can be extremely valuable, provided it is combined with depth analysis and the interpretation of the meanings of symbolic communication.

TECHNIQUES OF FAMILY ART THERAPY

Hanna Y. Kwiatkowska's work and research have laid the foundation for the increased application and recognition of family art therapy in recent years. In her work with schizophrenic and hysteric families, she developed a very effective technique of family evaluation based on an initial drawing of whatever comes to each family member's mind, followed by the drawing of an abstract family protrait. In her article on "Family Art Therapy and Family Art Evaluation" (26), she presents some striking examples of the diagnostic effectiveness of this method in the clarification of basic family problems and pathologies. Selma Garai and I have briefly described our approach in "Techniques of Family Art Therapy" (15).

The most valuable contributions of family art therapy consist in its effectiveness as a tool for the uncovering of primary process material, the breaking down of resistances in an atmosphere of minimal threat, and the promotion of more spontaneous and honest patterns of communication among family members based on the expression of genuine needs and feelings, rather than on expected role performance and projections. Repressed feelings related to aggressive, sexual, and competitive drives frequently emerge quite spontaneously in the symbolic expressions of the family members.

To illustrate these points, we are presenting several drawings made by members of the Gonzales family with whom Selma Garai worked for a period of 18 months (15). The family consists of Mrs. Gonzales, aged 29, and her children, Robert, aged 13, Fred, aged 8, and Francine, aged 7. Mrs. Gonzales had sought therapy because she experienced her son Robert as increasingly disobedient, rebellious, and unmanageable. She had been divorced a year before entering therapy from her husband who had practically deserted the family after the birth of the first child. She portrayed herself as the ideal mother who sacrifices her life for her children. Robert had become the family scapegoat. A moralistic atmosphere was created by her to ensure that the neighbors would get the impression that she was raising an ideal family. But the tensions mounted to such an extent that Robert voiced fears that his mother would kill him after she had repeatedly thrown dishes and tools at him and beaten him up during temper tantrums.

Mrs. Gonzales was an attractive woman who looked more like a teenager than a 29-year-old mother. This reinforced Robert's attraction to her, but constant prohibitions and reluctance to grant the children and particularly her preadolescent, rapidly growing son Robert any freedom from maternal supervision aroused feelings of strong frustration and resistance. The mother appeared certain that her antagonism toward Robert was shared by Fred and Francine. But in one family session the children focused their attention in a spontaneous play with animal and human puppets on the mother, portraying her as always saying no to any suggestion made by the children and as setting strict rules forbidding them to engage in any independent activities. Mrs. Gonzales realized that her policeman's role left little room to give positive support to her children.

Robert experienced an unresolved oedipal involvement with his mother. He had ambivalent feelings toward her. On one hand, he hated her for playing the role of the authoritarian disciplinarian who failed to provide sufficient stimulation and scope for his self-exploration and growth and who still compelled him to share a room with Fred. Robert had always been an excellent student in school, but he needed some more creative outlets for his surging energies. On the other hand, he was strongly attracted and had sexual fantasies of engaging in intercourse with his mother who looked more like his older sister.

In Figure 17 we see this conflict graphically expressed. Robert draws his mother as a huge prehistoric dinosaur that spews flames of death on him intended to "burn him up." Is it her anger or her love that burns Robert up? Dinosaurs are frequently drawn by adolescents as symbolic archetypal expressions of the upsurge of libido, i.e., sexual and aggressive desires of the id.

In Figure 18 Robert draws a picture around the theme of "family" in which his whole family is killed in an automobile accident. He himself, his dog, and his maternal grandfather, whose shopping bags are filled with presents for him, are the sole survivors. This grandfather was always regarded by Robert as the only genuinely supportive male in his family. His father is prostrated dead on a railroad crossing. Robert's goal is to seek wealth by getting gold from Fort Knox, a wishful dream to get out of the poverty necessitating the family's living on welfare. His dog is the only creature with access to the innermost layer of his triple-layered heart. He himself appears in the outer layer of this heart, running to join his companion.

The next drawing (Figure 19) was made in response to the request to depict his favorite activity. Robert portrays himself on a hunting and fishing expedition which enables him to catch a huge fish and shoot a big bird. He takes along his younger brother Fred. This is the first sign that he seeks to establish a closer relationship with his younger brother whom he used to fight, ridicule, or ignore. In contrast to the drawing of the automobile accident, which appears to be fragmented and scattered all over the sheet, this drawing is well-integrated and theme-centered. Such changes in the style and composition of drawings reflect progress toward personality integration and individuation.

The last drawing (Figure 20) shows the first scene drawn by eight-year-old Fred. It depicts him standing high up on a plateau overlooking the huge, multicolored, frightening, yet strangely alluring wide world in relation to which he feels infinitely

Figure 17. Robert's Drawing of His Mother.

small and helpless. He is overawed and confused but also curious and seeking guidance to overcome feelings of powerlessness. It is a statement asking his mother and siblings to help him cope with this frightening reality. Fred said that he was overlooking the city and felt lost, anxious, overwhelmed, and confused by its size.

As a result of family art therapy the Gonzales family members were able to establish a network of more honest and open, direct communication with one another. For the first time in her life, Mrs. Gonzales has begun to establish a relationship with a single man who takes her needs seriously into consideration and who relates with warmth and sensitivity to her children, who have begun to regard him as their "real" father because he loves to play and share activities together with them. She has enrolled in a community college and is developing definite vocational goals—wanting to become a registered nurse. She has moved into a larger apartment in which each child has a separate room. Robert has received permission to visit his friends in his old neighborhood to ease him through the period of transition until he makes enough new friends in his present environment. Family art therapy will be continued to assist the members to resolve their remaining problems.

Family art therapy is particularly effective when carried on by a conjoint male-female therapeutic team. As a conjoint wife-husband team, we have found family art therapy most fascinating because it provides continuous learning experiences

Figure 18. Robert's Drawing of His Family.

that enable each of us to empathize ever more readily and intuitively with the secrets of symbolic communication expressed through the creative act. There is no doubt that family art psychotherapy that combines artistic expression with analytic insights will modify the field of family therapy in various ways and help to focus attention on the subtle areas of hidden clues which can only be understood through the acquisition of a thorough knowledge of symbolic processes of communication.

TRAINING OPPORTUNITIES AND RESOURCES

Training opportunities in art therapy have been steadily expanding with a variety of Master's degree programs requiring intensive fieldwork (from 600-1200 hours) and relevant professional supervision. The October 1975 issue of the *American Journal of Art Therapy* presents a comprehensive list of graduate programs, clinical training programs, special programs, and ancillary undergraduate programs in the United States and overseas. The American Art Therapy Association has a total membership of about 500 and it has established criteria for registration of individual practitioners who are awarded the title of A.T.R. or registered art therapist. This is a purely intraprofessional attempt at limiting the field to practitioners who

Figure 19. Robert's Drawing of His Favorite Activity.

have received adequate clinical training and supervision. It is an initial step toward accreditation by responsible state mental health licensing or accrediting agencies. Applicants for admission to Master's degree programs must meet admission standards requiring either a Bachelor's degree in the fields of the fine or commercial or applied arts with a minimal preparation of four basic courses in psychology or a Bachelor's degree in psychology or the social sciences with a minimal preparation of four basic fine arts courses with studio experience. All applicants must submit a portfolio of slides selected from their best artwork. Most training programs are moving toward the development of Master's degree programs in the expressive-creative therapies, integrating art, dance, music, and poetry therapy.

The majority of art therapists in training today come from the ranks of students of the fine arts. Experienced trainers have found that there exists a certain intuitive, empathetic type of artist who utilizes these abilities of the right cerebral hemisphere so effectively in interpersonal relationships that he or she establishes immediate rapport with other persons on a nonverbal level. This empathy makes them ideal "born" therapists. They bring to the field of therapy those intuitive elements that "rational" therapeutic orientations based on cognitive processes and logic

Figure 20. Fred's Drawing of Himself.

causality frequently tend to minimize or rule out altogether. About 80 percent of all practicing art therapists in the United States are artists themselves and only ten percent come from the field of psychology, while the remaining ten percent come from a combiniation of art, psychology, and literature backgrounds. No matter what theoretical framework they prefer, they always contribute their own special artistic empathy derived from their deep connectedness with the creative process to reach the deeper layers of their clients' personality. More and more psychoanalysts introduce art therapy techniques into their own diagnostic and therapeutic practices.

The new field of *art psychotherapy* is composed of two converging streams: persons who started out as art therapists and acquired specialized analytic training during and after their studies in art therpay, and psychoanalysts who underwent training in art therapy either through self-study or participation in special training seminars and workshops. This cross-fertilization has led to an expansion of the scope of interdisciplinary theory, practice, and research in art and psychotherapy. The psychotherapist's curiosity about the deeper meaning of symbolic communication leads him or her to exploration of the field of art therapy in the same way as the theories of personality developed by Freud, Jung, Rank, Adler, Horney, Maslow, Rogers, and others induce the art therapist to familiarize himself or herself with the postulates of depth psychology. The recently published *Art Therapy: A Bibliography, January 1940-June 1973* by Gantt and Schmal (8) furnishes ample evidence of the growing body of theoretical and research literature in art therapy.

In the current decade the growth of art therapy as both an adjunctive and independent therapeutic modality has been unprecedented. Art therapists work with individuals, in groups, with couples, and with families in mental hospitals, community mental health centers, outpatient clinics, nursing homes, nursery schools, at all levels of the public and private school systems, in agencies for the mentally retarded, the physically handicapped, in prison and other correctional settings, and in agencies or institutions serving special populations such as alcoholics and drug addicts. They usually work as members of therapeutic teams together with psychiatrists, psychologists, clinical social workers, and other mental health professionals in the treatment of neurotic, psychotic, psychosomatic, character disorder, and other patient populations. The most recent developments converge toward an integration of a variety of expressive-creative modalities such as art, dance, movement, music, poetry, puppetry, photography, film, psychodrama, sociodrama, Gestalt, and transactional methods. Art therapists may have individual clients or groups of patients draw murals or pictures, while they listen to different musical or rhythmical selections or while they dance, move, or portray imaginary scenes and activities in response to these tunes or rhythms. They may write short poems or make up stories about their drawings, clay models, collages, dreams, and fantasies. They may use puppets, masks, or costumes to act out dreams, which they previously painted or drew, or engage in psychodramatic portrayals of their conflicts. Perhaps the most exciting aspect of art therapy consists in its attempts to open up the hidden treasures of our inner experience and symbolic images through scientific and observational investigation of their specific meanings in our life space. We are beginning to embark on this journey of discovery of man's inner space which we have neglected so long in our vain attempts to seek the solution of our most basic human problems in the exploration of the farthest reaches of outer planetary space.

CREATIVE-EXPRESSIVE THERAPIES AS CATALYSTS OF CHANGE

It is by no means an unrealistic vision to foresee a time when creative-expressive modalities of therapy will transform our institutions for the mentally ill and the physically disabled into places where the lethargy of depressed, alienated, and robotized patient populations will be replaced by the bustling activities of patient groups and individual clients painting, drawing, clay modeling, sculpting, dancing, rhythmically moving, playing musical instruments, putting on plays with puppets, acting out scenarios with masks, working with psychodrama and sociodrama, and exploring different levels of consciousness through artistic expression. This active involvement in the many facets of the creative process will enable them to regain a sense of hope, joy, and community involvement.

The art therapist is not afraid to descend with the client into the lowest depths of despair or to ascend with him or her to the peaks of "manic" elation because he or she is convinced that any genuinely effective type of therapy requires the sharing of the most intimate fantasies and "images." One of the reasons why traditional analytic techniques have frequently failed to reach the client consists in the rejection of certain fantasies as detrimental, "unhealthy," and "opposed to reality." As I (14) have pointed out, it is the subjective experience of inner and outer "space" or reality by the individual that determines his or her concept of "external reality." The images created by fantasies, dreams, daydreams, bodily sensations, memories, and archetypes are the true reflections of our life space. The art therapist is in tune with their symbolic meanings and reaches the client's unconscious and preconscious directly through this empathy. This deep level of communication opens up channels toward the re-evaluation of lifestyles, goals, and meaningful activities. It leads to the removal of anxieties and the eventual acceptance of risks permitting basic changes.

Otto Rank (38) has pointed out that art is the true method of education or the "drawing out" of inner experience. It is the task of every individuated person to become his or her own "artist-in-life" by integrating experiences into a particular lifestyle. Art therapy is not a means to "adjust" the individual to society. It is rather a way of living fully and creatively for the purpose of forging one's own peculiar existence. The goal of therapy is not to transform individuals into cogs in a smoothly functioning machine. It consists in the achievement of genuine individuation and self-transcendence.

Creative work is self-transcending and task-oriented. Art expression involves a confrontation with the psychic images of the realm of inner perception. It is an experience leading to symbol-making, symbol-digesting, and symbol-integrating processes. It is mediated by the *self* which is the *creator* within. Art products, like symbols, are derived from the unconscious, the preconscious, and the conscious components of creative expression. They are therefore understandable and compatible with the forms of logic and consciousness located in the left cerebral hemisphere. But they are also partly obscure, ghostly, mysterious, and ambiguous because they contain elements of unfathomable illumination from the realms of "inner space" located in the right cerebral hemisphere which can transform life-germinating chaos and turmoil into inchoate flows of energy into meaningful imagery.

Those art therapists who follow the humanistic approach I have outlined (13) are developing a specific philosophical orientation that perceives therapy as a continuous process leading to change and individuation through the harmonious integration of the basic faculties of sensing, thinking, feeling, and intuiting to achieve a rhythmically balanced personality. They encourage their clients to set out on the road toward a more compassionate and community-involved lifestyle based on the vision of the total person whose thinking is no longer imbued with cold logic and de-humanized "rationality." His or her thoughts and ideas become suffused with feelings of tenderness, compassion, and reliance on the faculties of empathetic sensitivity and imaginative intuition. The compassionate, integrated, individuated, and self-transcendent person is the genuine artist-in-life.

REFERENCES

1. *Art Psychotherapy: An International Journal.* New York: Pergamon Press.
2. Assagioli, R. *Psychosynthesis.* New York: Viking Esalen Books, 1971.
3. Betensky, M. *Self-discovery Through Self-expression.* Springfield, Ill.: Charles C Thomas, 1973.
4. Buck, J.N. *The House-Tree-Person Technique,* rev. ed. Beverly Hills, Calif.: Western Psychological Services, 1966.
5. Burns, R.C., and Kaufman, S.H. *Actions, Styles, and Symbols in Kinetic Family Drawings (K-F-D): An Interpretive Manual.* New York: Brunner/Mazel, 1972.
6. Campbell, J. *The Mythic Image.* Princeton, N.J.: Princeton University Press, 1974.
7. Frankl, V. *The Will to Meaning: Foundations and Applications of Logotherapy.* New York: New American Library, 1969.
8. Gantt, L., and Schmal, M.S. *Art Therapy: A Bibliography, January 1940-June 1973.* DHEW Publication No. (ADM) 74-51. Rockville, Md.: National Institute of Mental Health, 1974.
9. Garai, J.E. Applying the techniques of art therapy in student volunteer programs. *Synergist,* 3(3): 52-56, 1973.
10. Garai, J.E. Reflections of the struggle for identity in art therapy. *Art Psychother.,* 3-4: 261-275, 1973.
11. Garai, J.E. The use of art therapy in educational and vocational guidance. *Proceedings of the Fifth World Congress of the International Association for Educational and Vocational Guidance.* Quebec, Canada: Lavel University, 1973.
12. Garai, J.E. The use of painting to resolve an artist's identity conflicts. *Amer. J. Art Ther.,* 13(2): 151-164, 1974.
13. Garai, J.E. The humanistic approach to art therapy and creativity development. *New-ways,* 1(2): 2, 8, 19, 1975.
14. Garai, J.E. New vistas in the exploration of inner and outer space through art therapy. *Art Psychotherapy,* 3(3): 157-167, 1976.
15. Garai, S.H., and Garai, J.E. Techniques of family art therapy. *Group,* Nov.: 1, 5, 1974.
16. Hammer, E.F. *The Clinical Application of Projective Drawings.* Springfield, Ill.: Charles C Thomas, 1958.
17. Harris, J., and Joseph, C. *Murals of the Mind: Image of a Psychiatric Community.* New York: International Universities Press, 1973.
18. Jacobi, J. *Vom Bilderreich der Seele: Wege und Umwege zu sich selbst* [The Inner Kingdom of Images: Ways and Detours toward the Self]. Olten & Freiburg im Breisgau, Germany, 1969.
19. Jacobi, J. *The Inner Kingdom of Images.* Princeton, N.J.: Princeton University Press, in press.
20. Jung, C.G. Wandlungen und symbole der libido [Changes and symbolism of the libido]. *Jahrbuch für psychoanalytische und psychopathologische Forschungen,* 3 & 4, 1912.
21. Jung, C.G. *Collected Works,* ed. H. Read, M. Fordham, and G. Adler. New York: Pantheon Books, 1953-1974.
22. Jung, C.G. *Memories, Dreams, Reflections,* ed. and trans. A. Jaffe. New York: Pantheon

Books, 1963.

23. Keyes, M.F. *The Inward Journey: Art as Psychotherapy for You.* Millbrae, Calif.: Celestial Arts Press, 1974.

24. Kirsch, J. Remembering C.G. Jung. *Psychol. Perspectives,* 6(1): 54-63, 1975.

25. Kramer, E. *Art Therapy in a Children's Community.* Springfield, Ill.: Charles C Thomas, 1958.

26. Kwiatkowska, H.Y. Family art therapy and family art evaluation. *Psychiat. Art,* 3: 138-151, 1971.

27. Lystad, M. *A Child's World as Seen in His Stories and Drawings.* DHEW Publication No. (ADM) 74-118. Rockville, Md.: National Institute of Mental Health, 1974.

28. Machover, K. *Personality Projection in the Drawing of the Human Figure: A Method of Personality Investigation.* Springfield, Ill.: Charles C Thomas, 1949.

29. Morgenthaler, W. Ein Geisteskranker als Künstler [A mentally ill person as an artist]. *Arbeiten zur Angewandten Psychiatrie,* 1: 126, 1921.

30. Naumburg, M. *Schizophrenic Art: Its Meaning in Psychotherapy.* London: Heinemann, 1950.

31. Naumburg, M. *Psychoneurotic Art: Its Function in Psychotherapy.* New York: Grune & Stratton, 1953.

32. Naumburg, M. Art therapy: Its scope and function. In: *The Clinical Application of Projective Drawings,* ed. E.F. Hammer. Springfield, Ill.: Charles C Thomas, 1958.

33. Naumburg, M. *Dynamically Oriented Art Therapy: Its Principles and Practice.* New York: Grune & Stratton, 1966.

34. Perls, F. *Gestalt Therapy Verbatim.* Lafayette, Cal.: Real People Press, 1969.

35. Pfeifer, R.A. *Der Gesteskranke und sein Werk: Eine Studie uber schizophrene Kunst* [The Mentally Ill Person and His Work: A Study of Schizophrenic Art]. Leipzig, Germany: Kroner, 1925.

36. Prinzhorn, H. *Bildnerei der Geisteskranken* [Artistry of the Mentally Ill]. Berlin & Heidelberg, Germany, 1922.

37. Prinzhorn, H. *Artistry of the Mentally Ill.* ed. and trans. E. von Brockdorff. New York: Springer, 1972.

38. Rank, O. *Art and Artist: Creative Urge and Personality Development.* New York: Knopf, 1932.

39. Rhyne, J. *The Gestalt Art Experience.* Monterey, Cal.: Brook/Cole, 1973.

40. Shostrom, E.L. From abnormality to actualization. *Psychother.: Theory, Res. Prac.,* 10 (1): 36-40, 1973.

41. Ulman, E., and Art Therapy Association. Art in education, rehabilitation, and psychotherapy. *Amer. J. Art Ther.*

42. Ulman, E., and Dachinger, P. *Art Therapy in Theory and Practice.* New York: Schocken Books, 1975.

43. Winnicott, D.W. *Playing and Reality.* New York: Basic Books, 1971.

44. Winnicott, D.W. *Therapeutic Consultations in Child Psychiatry.* New York: Basic Books, 1971.

45. Zimmer, H. *Kunstform und Yoga im indischen Kunstbild* [Artform and Yoga in Indian Art Depictions]. Berlin: Springer, 1926.

The Role of the Group Therapist in an Evolving General-Systems Model for Group Psychotherapy

HELEN E. DURKIN

THE NEED FOR CHANGE

The rapid social, economic, and scientific changes of the mid-twentieth century, and the consequent worldwide turmoil, have had their repercussions in every field of human endeavor. In group therapy they led simultaneously to its vast expansion and its conceptual fragmentation. The Federal Law of 1963 extended mental health services to big hospitals and to the community at large. These new populations were not readily accessible to the traditional analytic group-therapy approach, which had dominated the field since its inception but was being challenged even in private practice. New techniques proliferated in an attempt to meet the needs. A period of theoretical confusion and sharp dissension followed which interfered with giving optimal service to patients and tested the credulity of the scientific community. It is only as we approach the mid-seventies that a growing core of group therapists is seeking to restore conceptual order and clarity. They are asking the question: Can we formulate an integrative theory of group therapy?

Today, then, there is urgent need for change. Unless we alter our models in accordance with twentieth-century changes in scientific principles and socioeconomic conditions, we wll gradually diminish our capacity to meet the conse-

117

quent needs of the group patients. As Levinson (21) has said, "Paradigms are time and space bound." Yet those who promote such basic changes must be ready to face resistance to their efforts; it will not be easy for group therapists to change models they have used successfully and in which they have a personal and professional investment.

WHY GENERAL SYSTEMS THEORY?

General systems theory, itself a product of the twentieth century, seems to have the ingredients for constructing a more timely paradigm for the group therapies. It is primarily a scientific metatheory which has already served to bridge the gap between the physical and the natural sciences. It can be expected to bring similar unifying trends into the present conceptual chaos in which we find ourselves.

What accounts for its capacity to serve the theoretical needs of group therapy? An appreciable number of scientists in a variety of fields have investigated the structural dynamics or the entire range of organized complex phenomena. As they focused on the organization rather than the content of these phenomena, they discovered that they consisted of entities whose parts and processes are in continous multiplicative interaction. They came to call them "systems," in contrast to sums or aggregates that interact additively (4). This radical change in viewpoint generated a whole new field of knowledge. A whole new set of relations among systems, their sub- and suprasystems, was brought to light and considerable new information was uncovered. Scientists were able to establish the laws of operation of systems in general. Even more significantly, they were able to make a conceptual leap forward to the recognition that all these systems are in constant flux and mutual interaction; that their structure is dynamic and determines their mode of operation. They had hit upon a new and unifying approach to the investigation of the phenomena of existence. Much in the manner of the person who solves a hidden picture puzzle, their changed viewpoint revealed not only new relations among the data, but brought into a focus a number of important phenomena, the meaning of which had been missed or vaguely grasped. Finally, they discovered some new phenomena. It is the intention of the author to establish the relevence of all these findings to work of the group therapist.

THE RELATION OF GENERAL SYSTEMS THEORY TO
PSYCHOANALYTIC THEORY

But first we must trace the historical development of this relation. During roughly the same period that group therapy was struggling with problems of expansion and specialization, general systems theory came into being.

Contrary to the opinion of some systems theorists, among them Watzlawick (33) and von Bertalanffy himself (4), general systems theory is harmonious in principle with psychoanalytic theory. Moreover, its new findings are complementary rather than contradictory.[1] For general systems theory has deep roots in the nine-teenth-century protest—in which Freud actively participated—against the restrictions of Cartesian science. Freud broke the taboo against investigating teleological phenomena and radically changed the psychiatric paradigm of his day. Out of this "Second Scientific Revolution" emerged a strong new emphasis on the principle of holism, on circular, reflexive cause-and-effect theory, and on the principle of function and relation.[2]

Freud and his followers subscribed to the new principles, but unfortunately the psychoanalytic literature continued to reveal traces of Cartesian modes of thought. Moreover, their new awareness of unconscious motivation influenced them to make preponderantly linear interpretations in terms of unconscious motivation and to lose sight somewhat of environmental factors and of the circularity of cause and effect in human relations. More important, they seemed, until recently, to remain relatively indifferent to the fact that systems scientists adhered more strictly than they did to the new principles and were, as a consequence, able to generate new concepts of energy and organization that account more adequately for the phenomena of human growth, creativity, and its complexity.[3] The gulf between them widened because psychoanalysts remained interested only in the organization of personality. The fact that both had started out with the same principles became obscured. It was not until the work of Ruesch and Bateson inspired the application of cybernetics to family therapy in Palo Alto,[4] that group therapists were forced to meet the impact of systems theory on their own work.

At present there are, in my opinion, two ways in which general systems theory may be employed to facilitate the evolution of a modern group therapy paradigm. It is my proposal that, for the present at least, it be employed as a comprehensive theoretical framework under which the major current approaches may be subsumed as conceptual subsystems. The latter, based primarily on the therapists' assumptions about the nature of personality, the causes of its pathology, and how it can be changed, would be expected to maintain their valid differences. For the sake of precision, internal consistency, and good communication, however, their present concepts would have to be reformulated in systems terms. I shall restrict myself to showing how the psychoanalytic group-therapy model can be modified and expanded within a general-systems-theory framework. But I believe that the same can be done with some of the other methods, such as humanistic experientalism, transactional analysis, Gestalt and communication theory, and that it may also provide a theoretical structure for the free-floating "innovative" techniques.

There is of course an alternative way of utilizing general systems theory in building a new model. The broad outlines of a more strictly systems model may be based primarily on the isomorphic structural characteristics of systems in general. But general systems theory alone cannot provide an adequate model for group therapy. It is, simply, too general. To make such a model practicable, we must avail ourselves of all existing information about the special systems of personality and small groups. Fortunately, psychoanalysis, human experimentialism, Gestalt psychlogy, and, more recently, communication theory have provided much information about personality systems, while group dynamics and systems family therapy fill us in on the unique characteristics of small group systems. Actually, both von Bertalanffy (4) and Miller (24) have themselves pointed out that no system can be fully understood without taking into account those unique characteristics that emerged at its particular level of complexity.

There are several such systems models under construction. Durkin (12) and Gray (17) are working on an emotional-cognitive systems model. Swogger is working on one that is based on information and feedback theory. The Vassilious (32) have developed one that is organized around group pictures produced by the members. Gruen (18) is attempting to construct one aroung the negentropic role of the therapist.

It seems to me that as sufficient information is accumulated and such systems models are tested out by clinical experience and experimental research the old terms of the traditional model with their imprecise and sometimes ambiguous conceptualizations may eventually disappear, but the relevant *empirical phenomena* behind concepts like unconscious motivation, transference, and the phases of personality development *must* continue to be taken into account.

BASIC GENERAL-SYSTEMS CONCEPTS

The Definition of a System

As mentioned earlier, von Bertalanffy defined a system as "a dynamic order of parts and processes standing in mutual interaction" (4). Frank Baker elaborated (1) on the concept in a way that helps us to understand personality and small groups which represent two levels of complexity in the continuum of living systems from "cell to society." He describes a system as "a *bounded* entity composed of units in continuous dynamic interaction" and he maintains that "each unit puts *constraints* upon the others" and that the product of their interaction is a distinct new entity with unique features of its own. It is a system at the next higher level of complexity. It is in this way that a group of individual members interact to form a new and distinct group system.

Miller (24) has pointed out that anyone who works in the systems field may choose his locus in the hierarchy of systems for study, but he must indicate the particular level of complexity at which he is working. In such a context, I treat the individual members as the "target" systems, because it is they who have come for help. The subdivisions of the personality constitute the "critical subsystems." The group is employed as an ad hoc therapeutic suprasystem. Other suprasystems in the environment, such as the family, social and work groups, and education or religious organization (suprasuprasystems) must be kept in mind as indirect sources on input.

The Structure and Operation of Living Systems

The most vital influence of general systems theory on the working group thera-pist is the discovery that living systems are always open, and that their structure is dynamic rather than static, for open systems are, in contrast to closed systems, cap-able and indeed dependent upon, continuously exchanging *matter, energy, and information* with other systems in their environment. (This includes the *"milieu interieur,"* i.e., their internal subsystem.) Structurally, they have been phyloge-netically programmed with more permeable and more flexible boundaries than are nonliving systems. Ontogenetic experience programs their individual patterns of transaction. A series of subsystems differentiate in the course of their historical development. The most important of these is the "decider" or organizing sub-system which serves the vital function of regulating input by controlling the boun-dary permeability. It operates through neurophysiological connections with the receptor and effector organs (kinesthetic and proprioceptive organs play a very im-portant role). Because of this dynamic structure and its functional aspects, living systems can respond selectively to a wide range of stimulation from the environ-ment (input). They are active systems, able to influence the environment as well as being influenced by it. By reducing their boundary permeability, they can reduce input and give the system time to reorder its internal interaction (throughput) in order to regain stability and maintain identity. When stability is satisfactory and the systems identity is assured, they can increase permeability. This is a *negentropic* process because the additional *input* may then be used for change and reorganiza-tion by the process of self-transformation. It counteracts *entropy,* the tendency to lose organization. More recently, the new cybernetics calls the former process morpho-stasis; the latter, morphogenesis (23). Normal systems keep these two forces in an optimal and flexible dynamic equilibrium or a "steady state." Human personality systems and social systems possess a high degree of capacity for morphogenesis, which has not yet been sufficiently exploited for therapeutic purposes.

SOME EARLY IMPRESSIONS AND CONCLUSIONS

I wish I could convey some of the excitement I experienced as I realized that the horizons of psychoanalytic theory could be expanded in this way. The uncomfort-able distance I had experienced between psychotherapy and the wider world of science seemed suddenly reduced and the hitherto blurred relation between my clinical data and the phenomena of science in general became clearer. But there was more. I found that I could use general systems theory to correct the ambiguity and imprecision of some of the analytic concepts that had bothered me for some time. And I learned to expand some analytic notions that were inadequate, such as adding the idea of dynamic equilibrium *(Fliessgleichgewicht)* to that of homeostasis in order to account more adequately for the creativity and complexity of the empirical data.

I also felt that many analytic group therapists still relied too much on substantive terms and content interpretations. A general-systems-theory framework would help to change that. Furthermore, although traditional group therapists had broadened their scope to include small group systems, they continued to regard these as obeying quite different operational principles from those followed by individual personality systems. General systems theory could serve to counter these tendencies, too.

Some Mutual Influences of General Systems Theory and the Analytic Model

While systems concepts are not entirely new, they are now more precisely articulated. For example, the analytic concept of the ego and its function of mediating between the intrapsychic needs and the demands of reality through its management of interpersonal relationships was an attempt to conceptualize the same structural phenomenon as that of the organizing subsystem with its function of boundary control. By virtue of its increased information, general systems theory has been able to spell out in more specific detail exactly how systems influence one another by transporting energy and information across permeable boundaries. Unlike "the ego," the terms are self-explanatory, more closely approximate the empirical facts, and are less open to anthropomorphic or vitalistic interpretations.[5]

General systems theory, with its telescopic view, was able to show that these organizational phenomena occur in systems in general. They thus provide the connecting link between clinical data and the empirical phenomena of other sciences. Psychoanalysis, with it's microscopic view, has been able to detect and conceptualize some of the less easily observable unconscious dynamisms of the human personality system, such as transference, the id, and the superego. Techniques to change these processes play an important role in bringing about transformations and reorganizations of the personality system and cannot, therefore, be omitted from our evolving model. It remains for group therapists to reconceptualize these phenomena. This can be done in systems terms.

Although general systems theory as such ignores unconscious phenomena, its view of open systems may be used to revise the concept of Transference and that of neurotic character defences (giving a more scientific account of it, and one which will make it more meaningful to other scientists). For example, my own first attempt, on the basis of clinical experience, makes the assumption that the exchange of matter/energy and information among personality systems takes the form of emotional and cognitive processes. The work of Durkin (12) and Gray (17) bears out this hypothesis, as does my own recent clinical testing of it.

To continue. From the time the infant system begins to separate psychologically from the parental suprasystem, it also begins to form internal images of "self" and "other" on which are based its patterns of transacting, which are later carried over into adult relationships with others. The internal images may be distorted because they have been influenced by the still global emotions generated by the earliest exchanges. Moreover, the transaction patterns are influenced by the fact that its perceptions, ability to discriminate, to generalize, and to comprehend (ego functions) are as yet relatively undifferentiated, and its decider or organizing subsystems (i.e., the synthetic ego function) are still immature. Consequently, the transaction patterns may have managed to serve chiefly the infant system's need for maintaining its identity. If such tightly boundaried morphostatic patterns become disproportionate in number to morphogenetic patterns, the child's capacity for growth may be diminished. Fortunately, most of these "transferential transactions" are reformulated in the course of later transactions, as the organizing subsystem matures and is better able to regulate them. But others may have become mechanized early by constant repetition, if the parental input is insistent, and especially if it reflects a large proportion of the parents neurotic needs, so that it is at variance with the growing system's inner state and must be excluded or distorted (mismatched). Growth continues to be sacrificed to stability, the essential dynamic equilibrium or steady state becomes precarious and the system dysfunctional. The person needs help and is likely to present himself at the door of the group therapist.

General systems theory puts a firm scientific foundation under the analytic concept of resistance and reinforces the technique of resistance analysis. As early as 1926, Trigant Burrow (7) protested that the analytic concept of resistance had no scientific foundation. General systems theory provides that foundation by its finding that systems of all kinds and levels of complexity need to maintain their identity in the face of change. Living systems do this by decreasing their boundary permeability. They thus offer a certain resistance to change. That constitutes *normal* resistance and must be respected. However, group-therapy experience shows that the members of therapeutic groups may have attached their sense or identity to their neurotic transaction so that they resist even therapeutic input essential to their growth. They avoid transformations and experience basic reorganization as a gigantic threat. In groups they "collaborate" to avoid change. We thus learn that the analytic concept constitutes a *special instance of dysfunctional boundaries.* The therapist, in exercising the control function, aims resolutely at thinning out such "sticky" boundaries and/or giving "active transport" of the therapeutic input across them. Nor can he afford to be dismayed by the anxiety, disorientation, and defensive hostility that precede radical reorganization. He must know how to distinguish them from true psychotic episodes and not retreat from carrying out his therapeutic contract.

In my experience in supervising analytic group-therapy trainees, I find that they tend to be very slow to recognize the more subtle forms of resistance and are often reluctant to deal with it firmly because of their uncertainty about how permissive to be. General systems theory counters this tendency by clarifying the active-passive dimension of the therapist's role. It insists on increasing boundary permeability and reinforces the technique of analyzing resistance. Within a general-systems-theory framework, however, the analytic group therapist has the option of selecting the techniques to facilitate "active transport" across thick boundaries. Gestalt and encounter techniques are at his disposal. Or he may decide to break through a rigid defense system by using the typical systems technique of deliberately creating disequilibrium (32). If so, he must be prepared for the emergence of strong anxiety and hostile defenses, but if he "contains" them, the systems boundaries will be likely to remain open to new input and their capacity for self-transformation will be stimulated.

The concept of equifinality. It is my conviction that the effectiveness of tracing transferential patterns of transaction to their familial origin has been established. When the connecting link with the past is restored to the patient's memory, his global infantile emotions tend to break through the temporal boundaries and the resistance is modulated. But it is true that too many practitioners have *overemphasized* the past. When the goal of understanding outweighs that of correcting the distortions, the effectiveness of Freud's brilliant technique is undermined. Looking back too much has been highly productive for research, but it can be disastrous for the goal of change. Worse, it leads to an error which has been called "the genetic fallacy of psychoanalysis."

In his attempt to account for the difference between closed and open systems, von Bertalanffy (4) formulated the principle of *equifinality*. In closed systems, he points out, conditions at the beginning determine the end state of the system. In open living systems, the development is not predictable. The state of the system may change at any point as a result of its regular exchanges with the environment. It becomes time-independent. That is, it is equifinal. Many of the present-day approaches, including family systems therapy, limit their interventions to the here and now. I have no quarrel with this in relation to normal systems, but I am convinced that in order to change personality systems that have become dysfunctional, the exploration of the historical origins of the transaction patterns is essential. Without it and the consequent uncovering of infantile fantasies, *durable* structure change is much less likely to take place. Moreover, it is in the patients' explorations into the past that their most poignant experiences occur. Many patients seem to regain some of their spontaneity at that point, and begin to develop a more genuine sense of identity. Nevertheless, history must not be allowed to become an end in itself.

Fortunately, Miller (24, 25) has reconciled von Bertalanffy's concept of equifinality with psychoanalytic theory. He recognizes the importance of early familial transactions in forming personality, as well as the later influences of the environment. Thus modified, the concept is harmonious with the analytic model and adds to its effectiveness.

The analytic therapist who accepts this concept will be deterred from allowing his interest in the past to interfere with his goal of effecting transformations. He will explore history only for the purpose of closing the patient's temporal boundaries because such transactions do not allow for change. They merely tend to reinforce each other's mechanized patterns.

Nor will he take for granted the group members' rationalizations that they cannot change because of the way their parents treated them. In other words, he will not be trapped by the "genetic fallacy." Instead he will make a point of demonstrating that in the group process, as in life, there are an indefinite number of choice points, and hold the members responsible for their behavior.

Flux equilibrium. Von Bertalanffy (4, 5) was critical of the psychoanalytic assumption that man's major motivation consists of need gratification for the purpose of tension reduction, and of psychoanalysis' reliance on the concept of homeostasis. He considered these sufficient to explain only the operation of closed systems. In an attempt to account for the fact that living systems are not merely reactive but have the capacity for change, growth, and creativity, he formulated his brilliant concept of *Fliessgleichgewicht.* (This construct has generally been called steady state, but in my opinion it is more accurately translated as flux or dynamic equilibrium.) In normal systems, as the control function regulates the exchange of emotion and cognition over time, it achieves a steady state which allows for both constancy *and* change; for the stability of the system *and* for its growth; for morphostasis *and* morphogenesis.

SOME BASIC ADVANTAGES OF A GENERAL-SYSTEMS FRAMEWORK FOR THE FIELD AS A WHOLE

General systems theory has made it possible to transcend certain artificial dichotomies that have created dissension among therapists. It recognizes their distinction but not their mutual exclusivity. (1) It brings into harmony the biological and cultural aspects of human behavior. (2) It brings out the natural connection between what has too often been thought of as the "intrapsychic" versus the "interpersonal" aspects of behavior. (3) but especially significant for group therapists is the fact that general systems theory transcends the fictitious dichotomy between those group and individual factors that influence change in groups and individuals. They may be seen as one set of phenomena, viewed from a different focus of interest or occurring at different levels of complexity. (4) Equally significant for group therapists is its demonstration of the essential interrelatedness of emotional and cognitive processes[6] in personality and social systems and in psychotherapy (19, 20).

SUMMARY AND CONCLUSIONS

In the face of the theoretical confusion in the field, there is need for an integrative framework. I assess the value of general systems theory for group psychotherapy and investigate the hypothesis that an effective overall theoretical framework can be constructed from general systems theory under which the major valid approaches may be subsumed as conceptual subsystems. The present study is limited to the relations between general systems theory and the traditional approach, but I believe it may serve as a model for determining which other methods can be included.

In order to reach a conclusion, the historical development of general systems theory and the psychoanalytic basis of traditional group psychotherapy is reviewed. There is then an assessment of their commonalities and their differences, and an attempt to evaluate some specifics of the mutual influences of their concepts upon each other.

Because of their common roots, their basic harmony *in principle,* and the complementarity of their differences, general systems theory can indeed be integrated with psychoanalytic theory. I believe that with due research the other valid major approaches may be included in this new, more comprehensive theoretical framework, and that it can then be expected to bring some needed unifying trends to the field without destroying the valid differences among the current approaches. A new paradigm is judged to be in the making, which may take the form of expanding the present methods or replacing them with a strictly systems model.

NOTES

[1] In my opinion, the same holds true for the other current methods.

[2] These principles are accepted by all modern approaches. It is to be noted that they shifted away from but did not replace analytic reduction, substantive thinking, or linear causation. They may both be used in accordance with the requirements of the situation.

[3] A case in point is the second law of thermodynamics, which is discussed below.

[4] I prefer to base the new model on von Bertalanffy's organismic theory, a living structure, because it is not a machine model.

[5] As Lewin (22) pointed out new concepts are at first approximate till tested experimentally and only later refined. Freud deliberately used Latin terms because they are more open-ended. Now we have enough information to refine them.

[6] Psychoanalytic theory originally emphasized the importance of continuous reciprocity between emotion and reason (15), but many practitioners became so eager to make accurate interpretations that they began to neglect the essential emotional context of "insight." The experiential modern approaches, sensitive to this error, blamed the method instead of the human error. They proceeded to make the opposite error. They usually intensified the emotional experience of group therapy but *eschewed* the *equally* important role of cognition.

REFERENCES

1. Baker, F. Review of general systems concepts. *Systematics,* 7 (3): 209-229, 1969.
2. Bateson, G., Jackson, D., Haley, J., and Weakland, J. Toward a theory of schizophrenia behavior. *Behav. Sci.,* 1: 251-264, 1956.
3. Bennis, W., and Shephard, H. The theory of group development. *Human Rel.,* 9: 415-437, 1956.
4. Bertalanffy, L. von. *General Systems Theory.* New York: Braziller, 1968.
5. Bertalanffy, L. von. General systems theory and psychiatry: An overview. In: *General systems Theory and Psychiatry,* ed. W. Gray. et al. Boston: Little, Brown, 1969.
6. Bion, W. Group dynamic - A re-view. In: *New Directions in Psychoanalysis,* ed. M. Klein et al. New York: Basic Books, 1955.
7. Burrow, T. Address Presented to American Psychoanalytic Society, 1926.
8. Durkin, H. Toward a common basic group dynamics. *Internat. J. Group Psychother.,* 7: 115-130, 1957.
9. Durkin, H. *The Group in Depth.* New York: International Universities Press, 1964.
10. Durkin, H. Transference in group therapy revisited. *Internat. J. Group Psychother.,* 21: 11-21, 1971.
11. Durkin, H. Group therapy and general systems theory. In: *Process in Group and Family Therapy,* ed. C. Safer and H. Singer. New York: Brunner/Mazel, 1972.
12. Durking, J. The Systems Structure of Group Psychotherapy. Unpublished Paper for Aspen Think Session Task Force, 1974.
13. Ezriel, H. A psychoanalytic approach to group treatment. *Brit. J. Med. Psychol.,* 23: 59-74, 1950.
14. Fenichel, O. *Problems of Psychoanalytic Technique.* New York: Psychoanalytic Quarterly, 1941.
15. Foulkes, S.H. *Group Analysis.* New York: International Universities Press, 1964.
16. Gray, W. Emotional cognitive structures. *Gen. Systems,* 18: 167, 1973.
17. Gruen, W. Group therapy as a system of energy transformaton: (unpublished paper).
18. Hartmann, H. *Essays on Ego Psychology.* New York: International Universities Press, 1964.
19. Kernberg, O. *A Systems Approach for Priority Setting of Interpretations in Groups.* article in *Int. J. Group Psychiatry 1974,* New York: International Universities Press, 1973.
20. Levinson, E. *The Fallacy of Understanding.* New York: Basic Books, 1972.
21. Lewin, K. *Field Theory and Social Science.* New York: Harper & Row, 1951.
22. Marayuma, M. The second cybernetics. *Amer. Scientist,* 5: 164-179, 1963.
23. Miller, J.G. *Living Systems: Basic Concepts,* ed. W. Gray et al. in General Systems Theory and Psychiatry. Boston: Little, Brown, 1969.
24. Ruesch, J. *Therapeutic Communication.* New York: Norton, 1964.
25. Ruesch, J., and Bateson, G. *Communication: The Common Matrix of Psychiatry.* New York: Norton, 1951.
26. Scheidlinger, S. Therapeutic approach. *Commun. Ment. Health Soc. Work,* 8: 3, 1953.
27. Schwartz, E., and Wolf, A. The mystique of group dynamics in topical problems. In: *Psychotherapy,* II. New York: Karger, 1960.
28. Slavson, S.R. Common sources of error and confusion. *Internat. J. Group Psychother.,* 3: 3-28, 1953.
29. Vassiliou, G. *A New Approach to the Use of Free Artistic Creation.* Ill.: Illinois Psychiatric Society, 1960.

30. Watzlawick, P., Beavin, J., and Jackson, D. *Pragmatics of Human Communication.* New York: Norton, 1967.
31. Weakland, J. Family therapy as a research area. *Family Proc.,* 1 (1): 63-68, 1962.
32. Weiner, N. *Cybernetics.* New York: John Wiley, 1948.

An Integrative Approach to
Family Therapy

NINA D. FIELDSTEEL

Therapy is concerned with change. Family therapy is a treatment modality that focuses on the family as a whole as an effective way to produce change. The family is here understood to represent a psychobiological complex of interacting systems. The family exists within the broader framework of social, economic, cultural, and historical systems. Though it is important for the therapist to be cognizant of this context, it is not germane to our current discussion. Our focus is on the family as the nexus of a complex of interacting systems, the individuals who make up the family. Each individual is a unique organization of biological and intrapsychic dynamics which have developed within a particular shared historical context. In broadest terms, family therapy is a treatment modality focusing on the family as a system, on the communications and interactions within the system that serve to maintain symptomatic behavior.

An integrative approach to family therapy works with the operations of the family system, but also considers it important to deal with the intrapsychic determinants of the behavior of the individuals within the system. Interactions between family members are not only expressions of the family system, they are also expressions of intrapsychic conflicts. The observable transactions of the family and the particular organization of the family as a system are related to and determined by both the conscious and the unconscious dynamics of the individuals within the family.

Techniques of family therapy based on systems and communications theory have focused primarily on the conscious behavior, observable interactions, and current events in the family. There has been less interest in relating pathological interactions to intrapsychic conflicts. Structural approaches to family therapy are based on the assumption that behavioral change occurs when there are changes in the system so that "it will not support the symptom" (1). Though Haley sees family therapy as representing "a discontinuous change in basic premises" (4), one cannot disregard all that has been learned about personality organization, individual dynamics, and particularly about the nature of the unconscious.

Psychoanalytic developmental theory is rooted in the family context. It is impossible to think of basic psychoanalytic constructs such as the Oedipus complex without thinking in terms of family organization. It is in the very structure and dynamics of family operations that the concept acquires meaning. It is equally impossible to think of ego development outside the context of the family. This phase of development implies the response and relation to others and external realities. All behavior is motivated by both conscious and unconscious forces, thus it is important to deal with both in any effort focusing on change. An integrative approach to family therapy is concerned with observable conscious behaviors and interactions and also with the meaning of these behaviors in terms of intrapsychic conflict.

This approach presents the family therapist with problems of choice. Not only must one decide where to focus with this complex of interactive systems, but one also needs to develop new techniques and a new language to effectively utilize these complex interrelationships. This problem is stated by Boszomenyi-Nagy (2):

> The family therapist needs further extension of conceptual frameworks. He needs a language that can express the private experience of relational transactions. There is also a need for genetic or developmental view of the long-range dynamics of family relationships. In summary, certain unconscious long-range determinants in family relationships cannot be understood without the construction of a comprehensive transactional, and at the same time, experiential language.

In support of an integrative approach, I have stated elsewhere that there are no easy ways to deal with these complexities (3). As psychoanalysts, we value individual history and individual intrapsychic dynamics, and as family therapists, we are committed to the consideration of the complex interrelationships within the family as a system. Though this presents us with an overabundance of clinical data, we can order it in a variety of ways and must be able to move from one conceptual framework to another.

The integrative approach to family therapy moves freely from the observable transactions to the intrapsychic dynamics and unconscious meaning of the transaction. The hallmarks of psychoanalytic therapy are to make conscious the unconscious, to analyze transferences, and to strengthen and develop ego functioning. These are also an important part of family therapy that integrates the systems and the psychoanalytic models.

I shall briefly discuss some techniques that may be used to explore and analyze both the individual unconscious and the shared unconscious family dynamics. The variety of transferences will also be discussed. An example of the way in which the analysis of transferences can serve to modify the family system is offered. The strengthening of ego functioning and its relation to the development of cognitive control will also be considered.

The task of making the unconscious conscious can be approached in a variety of ways. Slips of the tongue and humor are useful ways of making unconscious material conscious. Confusions of pronouns and gender and "errors" in proper names are common slips that can be analyzed. Family jokes are another fruitful area of exploration.

The analysis of dreams is particularly valuable in family therapy. Dreams can be worked with in a family in much the same way one works with them in groups. The dreamer reports his or her dream, associates to the dream, other family members are invited to share their associations, and the family then works out the meaning of the dream. This is a particularly useful tool in family therapy for several reasons. In the context of the dream, family members are able to communicate to each other previously unexpressed, unshared wishes, fears, and needs. It helps family members to listen to one another in new ways. It also increases their sensitivity to the voice of the unconscious and the multiple levels of meaning of behavior, so that they become much more aware of latent meaning in other exchanges. The dream can also become a metaphor for the complexity of individual functioning and leads to a mutual respect for what one does not know. The therapist's interest in working with dreams serves to reinforce their frequency. Family members become prolific dreamers and an important part of the family session is the work on dreams.

The analysis of transferences in family therapy requires working with a multiplicity of transferences, which operate on various levels. There are the transferences to the therapist, the transferences within the family, which are the very strong bonds that perpetuate and structure the family system, and the transference to the family as an abstract external entity.

We are particularly interested in analyzing and making available to the family members an understanding of the nature of cross-generational transferences. Parents often see their children as transference figures of their own parents, as well as of their siblings. Children too see parents not only as who they are in actuality, but also as transferential objects, for example, splitting the good and bad mother. Often the split may occur between parents, between parent and sibling, or between one parent and the therapist.

Transferences within the family are often revealed in slips of the tongue, confusion of proper names, or confusion of pronouns. For example, in a family session the mother may begin to talk about the father. As she talks about her husband, she may refer to her own father and the son in the family; suddenly pronouns become confused, and the listener is unable to sort out who is being referred to in any one instance. When this is examined, it becomes clear that the various male figures are merged; the husband is seen as the wife's own father. As this is explored in the family session, the expectations, disappointments, and distortions engendered can be examined and avenues for change developed.

In working with transferences, it is very useful for the family to see and to share the different ways in which they perceive the therapist. One family member may see the therapist as the good parent, another may see the therapist as a bad, depriving, punishing parent, and a third may see the therapist as a sibling from their own primary family. The power of the transferential feelings becomes very evident as they are shared. The fact that all the differing transferential responses are focused on one individual (in this case the therapist) illuminates the meaning of the projection. The ways in which the individual distorts reality become very clear in such an experience, and the family often moves then from the transferential distortions centered on the therapist to those existing within the family.

Another level of transferences operating in the family are transferences to the family as an external entity. These are often embodiments of maternal transferences. This is comparable to the phenomena occurring in group therapy. The family is seen as a source of nurturance, as a good and sustaining mother; or the family as an entity may be perceived of transferentially as a punishing or depriving maternal object. These transference distortions are often easily explored as differences in the ways individual family members experience the family constellation are shared. The sharing of the history of these transference distortions is an important experience leading to changes in the family system, shifting previously rigidly held positions and perceptions.

The use of history in family therapy is important for an understanding of both the unconscious meaning of behaviors in the family and of the transferences. One starts with the present observable behavior. To understand its meaning, it is often important to go back to not only the shared family history, but to the unique individual history of the family members. There are family therapists who feel that family therapy, to be most effective, must deal only with the "here and now." It seems apparent that what is often discordant or incongruous in family functioning is very much related to the inappropriate repetition of history and the force of history in the functioning of the present family.

In integrative family therapy, we work to make conscious not only the individual's unconscious dynamics, but also the ways they are shared within the family and the ways in which they operate to support the unconscious dynamics of the marital partners and the children within the family. The exploration of transferences within the family, the distortions of perception they foster, and the limitations that result from them become, in this instance, the avenue for doing both tasks.

An example of the use of the analysis of transferences in family therapy may be seen in the following, necessarily condensed summary of a family session. The R's were a family of three children and two parents. The designated patient was the youngest child. On initial interview, it was apparent that the entire family was having serious difficulty in their relations with one another and the outside world. The father was very unhappy at his job, which was a very prestigious one. He also expressed a great deal of unhappiness with his wife and particularly with their sexual relationship. The wife suffered from depressions and would very often shut herself away from the family, taking several novels with her to her room and not emerging for hours or days. Her way of communicating to her family was in terms of a sarcastic wit. She was extremely clever and could be very amusing, but often her humor was biting and harsh. The three children showed a variety of problems. The oldest, a daughter in her early teens, was doing very poorly in school, was very troubled by her mother's attitude to her, and had very low self-esteem. The middle child, who was just entering adolescence, was a very impulsive boy who seemed to be moving in the direction of socially unacceptable, acting-out behavior. He was also beginning to experiment with drugs. He was involved in truancy, in minor shoplifting incidents, and was defiant and hostile with both of his parents. The youngest child was referred initially to therapy because of learning problems. He was a hyperactive boy diagnosed as having minimal brain damage. He was extremely infantile in his social relationships and very clinging with both parents. The roles the parents assumed were that father was the "good guy" and mother, the bad one. The father allied himself with the children against the mother, pointing to her irrational behavior, her unreasonableness, and in subtle and yet consistent ways, encouraging the antisocial behavior of the older son.

When, after several meetings, the mother's hostility to her daughter was being discussed, her fear of her daughter and her readiness to see her as critical and rejecting was revealed. The mother then talked about her own childhood. She had never shared this directly with her children. She described her life with her mother, who suffered from very serious depressions, and her feelings when her mother was hospitalized frequently during the latter part of her adolescent years. Her fear of becoming like her mother emerged, as well as her perception of her daughter as her own rejecting mother. She feared punishment from her daughter for the guilt she had carried of being responsible for her mother's psychotic breaks. It was an extremely moving session because the children had not known what their mother had suffered. Her behaviors became more comprehensible to them. As the children in this family came to understand some of the mother's pain and fears, the structure that had been set up with father as the "good guy" began to shift. His role in separating the mother was questioned by the middle son who had formed his strongest conscious alliance with the father against the mother and her rules and limitations of his behavior.

In this session, powerful emotional information was shared, which on the deepest level had not been known to the children. As it was made explicit, it made behaviors more understandable, interactions more comprehensible. It provided for the possibility of cognitive control and change for all family members. For example, as the mother became conscious of her unconscious transference responses to her daughter as her own bad mother, their relationship shifted dramatically. At first, the daughter was moved to offer her mother comfort, acceptance, and mothering. The changes in affective climate then allowed for another shift. The daughter began to be able to elicit from her mother the nurturing and support she needed. The relationship finally shifted to the more appropriate one of mother and daughter, preparing the way for the separation and individuation that were part of the daughter's adolescent developmental tasks.

Along with working with transferences in family therapy, another crucial task for the family therapist is to be aware of and analyze countertransference responses. The family has a unique power to pull countertransferences from the therapist. We all grew up in families. We all have our own unfinished "family business." Almost all therapists who work with families are able to relate to the extreme power of a family to pull you into the system, in systems terms, or to arouse and evoke strong countertransference responses in psychoanalytic terms. Such responses are extremely useful to the therapist, making more explicit the dynamics within the family, and they can be shared with the family as a way of helping them understand what transpires in the session and the ways in which they elicit or evoke behavior, not only from the therapist, but from other family members.

Integrative family therapy is concerned with intrapsychic change and strengthening of ego development. Object relations, cognitive development, and reality testing must be part of the therapist's conceptual framework. As individuals change, there are changes in the total system, and the development of any one individual affects the total family functioning. In the family context, it is possible to make explicit the ways in which, as an individual moves to make changes based on insight and understanding, the unconscious motivations and the transferences that operated within the family change.

Systems can change when the unconscious motivations that have been responsible for the origins of the behaviors become conscious, and thus modifiable. This is not to say that changes in behavior do not also lead to insight, but it still becomes the task of therapy to develop that insight so that the individuals can develop cognitive understanding of their own behavior and of its origins. This enables them to become responsible and to control the direction and nature of the changes made.

The question has often been raised as to whether one can deal with unconscious wishes and fantasies in a family session. It has been my experience that, unless one or the other of the parents is psychotic, this is not a problem. More often, in my experience, there is timidity and a kind of often inappropriate secretiveness, rather than uncontrolled sharing of what might be destructive wishes or fantasies with young children. There are appropriate family secrets which should be kept. However, I do not believe this is usually the problem. More often than not, the "family secrets" parents feel they have to preserve are secrets that indeed are not secrets. Children in the family know or half-know the supposed secret, and the clarifications of distortions are more helpful than preserving the originally established "secrecy." There are appropriate family secrets or material that should not be shared with all family members. In our work, there is a great need to respect individual integrity, boundaries, and privacy. An important part of family learning is the understanding of individual boundaries and the respect for them.

Much of the material translated from the unconscious in family sessions is material that really has been known and shared by family members. Therefore, as one makes it explicit, conscious, and available, the possibilities for change become greater.

One of the reasons for discussing family therapy in terms of a psychoanalytic conceptual framework is to suggest that it is not necessary to develop an either-or approach. The concepts of psychoanalysis and systems theory are not necessarily mutually exclusive. The concepts are best understood as focusing on different aspects of observable phenomena. To enhance our understanding of families and to enable us to function more effectively as therapists, it becomes necessary to develop an overall integrative conceptual framework that allows the therapist to focus on different aspects of the behaviors observed, on different aspects of the symptoms causing distress, and on different styles of change which are not necessarily mutually exclusive. The goal is not to do individual psychoanalysis in the family group setting, but to accept that certain analytic principles are applicable to family therapy, much in the way that they have been made applicable to group therapy. We know that change comes about in a variety of ways. We are concerned with bringing about changes in behavior that allow individuals to live more fully and effectively. Our goal is to work toward change in such a way that the change once gained can be maintained and that further changes occur as they are needed in the life of the individual.

Integrative family therapy uses psychoanalytic concepts, but it differs significantly from psychoanalysis in many ways. For one, the role of the therapist is quite different. The family therapist is visible and of necessity more active than is the therapist in individual psychoanalytic treatment. We talked about the importance of the therapist working with his or her own countertransference responses. The therapist must be careful about which transference responses are shared and which are not. In a family where the pattern of communication is one of confusion and where there is particular emphasis on mixed and mutually conflicting messages, it becomes useful for the therapist to share with the family his or her experience of the confusion and what that confusion evokes in the therapist's feeling about family members and him or herself. This is sometimes a way of helping other family members who are suffering under the impact of induced confusion to be free to express what they feel. It also helps family members to reinforce their own reality testing. For example, if the child is confused by mother's statement, it may be helpful for him to know the statement is confusing not only to him but to others, and that he is not deficient because he cannot understand exactly what it is that mother wants. Again, this kind of response on the part of the therapist is very useful to the family and helps make certain explicit present behaviors understandable.

In training family therapists, we emphasize that it is important for therapists to "listen with a third ear" not only to the family, but also to themselves. It is helpful for the therapist to review the family session and understand the feelings evoked. The decisions about what to share have to be based on what would be good for the family and not on what is therapeutic for the therapist. Spontaneity, intuition, and immediate responsiveness are an important part of the family therapist's work. But therapy is essentially an intellectual discipline, requiring thoughtful and planful interventions that serve to move the therapy forward. The therapist must be free to use her or himself in all therapeutic situations, but it must be with an awareness of what is being used and why. The criterion for the value of an intervention must be in terms of the family's growth and development.

Implicit in this approach to family therapy are some assumptions of what is necessary for training in family therapy. Since we do not feel that family therapy is unrelated to the other forms of therapy, it is important to have a sound understanding of psychoanalytic concepts and the principles of analytic therapy. The therapist must also have had a personal analysis. An unfortunate result of the simplified language of systems theory or communication theory is that family therapy is often thought of as easier to learn or teach than individual analytic treatment. If one considers the multiplicity of stimuli, impressions, associations, and experiences the therapist must receive, sort out, and use, one sees that even if one is dealing with the conscious, here-and-now, observable phenomena, the therapist can experience being flooded with material. If one adds to that the expectation that the therapist will not only be attending the observable present, but also the latent meanings of the behavior and communications, verbal and nonverbal, then one sees that there is an even greater complexity. Our own experience has been that family therapy is much the most difficult treatment modality and that, therefore, more rather than less preparation and training are required.

An integrative approach to family therapy requires that the therapist have a broad range of understanding of theoretical concepts, a depth of understanding of self, and willingness to take the responsibility for making choices rather than following a rigid treatment format. Making choices represents accepting risk and responsibility. This is one of the things we try to teach our patients as part of the experience of individuation and increasing mastery of their own lives. As therapists, we also struggle with this task.

SUMMARY

Individual history, intrapsychic dynamics, the nature of the unconscious, and the structure of personality are all expressed in an interpersonal transaction. Observable transactions have their impact as causative factors, but to fully understand what is observed one must be willing to consider what is implicit. The analysis of dreams, of transferences and countertransferences, and the exploration of individual history do not lessen our ability to appreciate the unique character of the family as a system. An integrative approach to family therapy assumes that the family therapist will have available both the conceptual framework of systems theory and that of psychoanalytic theory, so that the therapist can choose which phenomena will be focused on at a particular time. It is the therapist's job to make a conscious choice as to where to focus, but also to maintain a conscious awareness that that particular focus is only that, a part of the picture and not the totality. This approach to family therapy allows for the most effective way to work for therapeutic change in the family as a whole and in the individuals who are part of the family system.

REFERENCES

1. Aponte, H., and Hoffman, L. The open door: A structural approach to a family with an anorectic child. *Family Proc.,* 12(3): 1-44, 1973.
2. Boszormenyi-Nagy, I. A theory of relationships: Experience and transaction. In: *Intensive Family Therapy,* ed. I. Boszormenyi-Nagy and J.L. Framo. New York: Harper & Row, 1965.
3. Fieldsteel, N. D. A new language for family therapy? The problems of an integrative approach. *Group,* January, 1976.
4. Haley, J. A review of the family therapy field. In: *Changing Families,* ed. J. Haley. New York: Grune & Stratton, 1971.

Saying Goodbye to Parents

RICHARD G. ABELL

Infants are born dependent. If their parents or parental surrogates do not take care of them, they will die. However, there comes a time in the life of everyone when, in order to gain one's own autonomy, one must say goodbye to one's parents. By saying goodbye, I do not mean the simple act of saying goodbye in the conventional sense. This kind of goodbye may be said over and over again to the same persons. In the transactional-analysis sense, saying goodbye to parents is a once and for all transaction. It is forever. It is the final step in the surrender of dependency on parents and the acceptance of self-support. It involves embracing the concept that "I am no longer dependent upon you, father and mother, for my self-evaluation." It includes giving up the existential position "I am not OK," and changing it to "I am OK." Unless this is achieved, it is impossible to give up dependency, since if I have not achieved this "I am OK" position I will be dependent upon others for my feelings of OKness.

Saying goodbye to parents, when done successfully, produces a state of mind in which I do not surrender the dependency I once had toward parents to someone else.

Essentially, saying goodbye to parents is a decision. It is what Robert Goulding[1] called a redecision. It replaces the earlier decision, "I have to depend upon you, father and mother, to take care of me in order to survive," with the decision, "I will now take care of myself."

To the young child, parents seem all powerful. Therefore, when they give him such counterscript drivers[2] as "Be perfect," "Try hard," "Hurry up," "Please me," and "Be strong," and such injunctions[3] as "Don't exist," "Don't be you," "Don't be a child," "Don't grow up," "Don't trust," "Don't make it," "Don't think," "Don't be important," "Don't show your feelings," "Don't have your feelings," "Don't belong," "Don't be sane," "Don't enjoy," or "Just plain don't," he usually feels that he must follow them in order to receive strokes and to survive.

This decision is made by the child, usually before the age of six, at a time when he is entirely or almost entirely dependent upon his parents for survival. He *must* take these parental messages into account and in most respects follow them or else he will be in serious trouble. A patient of mine, Jim, received from his father the counterscript driver "Please me" and the injunction "Don't show your feelings." His early decision was to try to please his father and to repress his feelings. By doing this, he adapted himself to the position he occupied in his family at that time.

A real difficulty in interpersonal relationship arose when Jim grew up to be an adult who earns his own living and who is no longer dependent upon his parents to fulfill his basic need for strokes, and who, in spite of this, behaves as if he is. Not only did Jim continue to try to follow his parents' directives by repressing his feelings (and in other ways), but this way of behaving generalized to include others in his environment, such as his employer, his colleagues, and the members of his family. It makes no difference that his parents are dead. He is now reacting basically to the aspect of his parents incorporated by his own Parent ego state. It will be impossible for Jim to "say goodbye" to his parents in the fundamental sense that I have previously described until he has nullified and reversed the effects of the counterscript drivers and injuctions he received from them.

How can this be done? I have found that a certain series of therapeutic steps is effective in producing this change. These are: (1) The identification of the problem, which in Jim's case is an exaggerated need to please others and the inability to express feelings appropriately. (2) The formulation of a contract to work on the resolution of this problem, with my help. (3) The exploration of the effect of the problem upon his behavior in his current environment. Such effects are frequently inappropriate anxiety toward authority figures and adapted reactions toward family members and friends. (4) Exploring earlier experiences and finding out how the patient's present reaction has developed from these earlier ones. This includes the isolation and uncovering of the counterscript drivers and injunctions that he received from his parents. It will then be necessary to abreact to the original family scene in such a way that the client expresses fully and completely his feelings and emotions toward his parents for the damaging messages they put upon him. (5) This is best accomplished in a Gestalt, double-chair fantasied confrontation with each of his parents. (6) During this confrontation, the patient regresses to the period of childhood in which the injunctions and counterscript drivers were given, and usually experiences such organismic disgust with the effect of them upon himself that he decides to break away from his parents, to get them off his back, to declare his independence from them. This redecision which is made in the Child ego state must be acceptable to both the Adult and Parent ego states if it is to be effective. A part of this step is feeding new information to the Little Professor (the Adult ego state of the Child of the child) of importance to him in making the redecision.

Until the steps outlined above or some other comparable ones have been taken, the patient is not in a position to "say goodbye" to his parents, since he will still be attached to them by unresolved problems. Premature encouragement of the client to "say goodbye" to his parents while he is still dependent upon them may lead to serious consequences, even hospitalization. There is thus a need for the therapist to be closely in touch with his patient in reference to the position he is in concerning the resolution of his problems before undertaking such a maneuver.

Experience shows that unless the client has vented his feelings of grief and anger toward his parents for the things they said and did to him as a child that caused him frustration and pain, and has gotten rid of these feelings to the point where he has uncovered and expressed his feeling of love toward them, "saying goodbye" will not be effective, and will not accomplish its purpose. As long as the client is angry at his parents, or as long as he is grieving intensely about the way they treated him, he cannot let them go. Such unresolved emotions produce what is termed in Gestalt the "hanging-on bite." The hanging-on bite is a state of immobilization or impasse. The person who is in this position cannot chew what he has taken in, he cannot swallow and digest it, and he cannot let it go. He can only hold on to it.

The way to break this impasse is to express these emotions freely and fully in "double-chair fantasied confrontations with parents." Such confrontations usually elicit deep feelings of grief and anger, expressed with tears, sobbing, and rage.

For example, Jim, who received from his father the injunction, "Don't show your feelings," was largely immobilized socially in adolescence. Under his picture in his high school yearbook was the caption, "A closed mouth catches no flies," which was certainly true of him at that time. This blocked him from having a girl friend, or, in fact, any close friend at all, and caused intense feelings of isolation, accompanied by repressed feelings of anger. What Jim was angry about he didn't know for sure. It turned out that he was angry at his father for giving him the injunction, "Don't show your feelings," and in addition "Don't be close" and "Don't exist."

This became clear when I did double-chair work with him. Part of the fantasied encounter is reproduced below:

> *Therapist:* Put your father on this chair in front of you and say to him in the present tense in fantasy whatever you would like to say to him. Be any age you want to be.
>
> *Jim:* I'll be my present age. [He looks at the chair as if his father were sitting on

it. His head is lowered and his eyes are looking up. It is obvious from this position that he is in his Adapted Child ego state.] I want you to listen to me, Dad. [Although he said that he will be his present age (30), it is clear that he is behaving like a child.]

Therapist: Say that ten times.

Jim: I want you to listen to me, Dad. I want you to listen to me. I want you to listen to me. [His voice is low, and there are tears in it.] I want you to listen to me. You are so cut off from me. You never say anything personal to me. You only talk about the weather or the stock market. I want you to ask me how I am, but I don't know how to get you to do that. My throat is dry.

Therapist: Be with your dry throat and give it a voice.

Jim: I don't feel as if Dad will listen, so what's the use of talking.

Therapist: Tell Dad what his not listening to you and talking has done to you.

Jim: When you don't listen to me I can.t talk to you, and when you don't talk to me I feel as if it's wrong to try to express my feelings, because you don't. So I don't. That hurts. I'm sick and tired of not talking. I'm fed up with it. Fed up. Do you hear me? [Jim's voice is much louder.] Do you hear me? Do you hear me? [Jim is now yelling, and his voice sounds angry.] I don't care what you do. I know people who will listen to me and talk to me. And be personal, too. [Yelling] I'm going to talk to them.

Therapist: Sit in your father's chair and play your father's role. [Therapist speaks to father's chair.] Dad, Jim says he suffered because you didn't listen to him and talk to him about personal things. Answer him with whatever comes to your mind."

Jim: [Playing Dad's role] I hear you and I understand. I suffer from that, too. I do care about you and love you, but I get anxious when I try to tell you. I learned not to talk when I was a little boy, too. My father never talked to me.

Therapist: Sit in this other chair, and be Jim and respond.

Jim: [Playing his own role. Looks surprised.] I didn't know that's the way it was, Dad. I didn't know. Now I understand.

It is clear that Jim recognizes at this point that no matter how much his father wanted to be different than he was, he could not, lacking therapeutic intervention, change, owing to his earlier conditioning. And since his father had died 12 years ago, there was no possible way of bringing such change about. Consequently, unless Jim himself changed and gave up his dependence upon his unfulfilled need for his father to talk in a personal way to him, there was no way out of his impasse. It is evident that he *did* give up the need for his father to change when he said, in his Gestalt work, "I don't care whatyou do. I know people who will listen to me and talk to me. And be personal, too. I'm going to talk to them."

A few months later I felt that Jim had worked through most of his problems with his father. When the group met and Jim brought up the subject of his father, I asked him if he was willing to say a final goodbye to him—to say goodbye once and for all. He said he was.

Therapist: Bring your father into this room in fantasy and say anything that you would like to say to him before you say goodbye. Then say goodbye.

Jim: I'm going to say goodbye to my father while we are standing on the bank of a creek. [Jim was talking quietly and evenly.] You taught me to swim when I was only about five years old. You loved to swim. You loved sailing, too. I remember how you took me sailing. I remember I was so small then that I could lie stretched out on the end of an oar. I remember everything just as if it happened today. We were in a small boat about 12 feet long. It seemed like magic to me, the way the small boat went through the water without our having to row it. I remember we sailed up a creek once and got hungry and didn't have any food. We saw a house and you said you would go up and ask if you could buy a sandwich or a loaf of bread. You came back with two sandwiches and we each had one and they tasted so good.

Jim was now recalling pleasant experiences that he had had with his father when he was a child. He continues:

Jim: I remember how we played catch once when I was a kid. You threw me the ball, and I felt proud when I caught it. I remember when we used to go camping, you and Mama and Ed [Jim's brother]. You and Mama would sleep in a hotel in the mountains, and Ed and I would sleep in a pup tent in the yard of the hotel. You would come out and look in the tent to be sure everything was all right after dark. You didn't say much, but I knew you were there. and now I know you cared.

As Jim was talking, his voice began to catch. He sat down on the floor and began to sob, first softly and then louder and louder, until he was in fact convulsed with sobs. After about five minutes he stopped and said softly, "I love you, Dad." Getting in touch with positive feelings toward a parent is an important thing to do before saying goodbye. Jim had achieved it.

Therapist: Are you ready to say goodbye to Dad?

Jim: [Jim was quiet for about half a minute. Then he spoke softly] Goodbye, Dad. Wherever you are, and whatever you are doing, take care of yourself. [Jim then began to sob again, long convulsive sobs. Eventually he stopped.]

Therapist: How are you feeling now, Jim?

Jim: Sad. I feel as if something important has just happened to me.

Therapist: It has. Will you look around the room at each person and see what you see?

Jim: [Looking at each group member.] I see concern. I see caring.

Therapist: Will you go to each person in the group and ask for what you want?

Jim goes to a man in the group. "How did you feel when I was working on saying goodbye to my father?" "I felt very close to you." Jim goes to a woman. "How did you feel?" He asks. "I cried when you cried. I was very deeply touched."

Jim goes to another man and asks, "Will you give me a hug?" The man hugs him.

Jim has just said goodbye to his father, and he is now able to say "Hello" to others, and to feel closer to them than ever before. Having rid himself of his feelings of anger at his father, he is now better able to experience feelings of intimacy to others, including his wife, who reports a dramatic change in his capacity to be intimate with her.

Jim said goodbye to his father four years ago. He is no longer in therapy but on occasion he calls me up and tells me how he is. He says that he no longer has feelings of anger toward his father. The thought of him occurs often, sometimes several times a day. Whenever he thinks of his father, it is with feelings of warmth.

Jim is now relating comfortably to other people. He has friends and an active social life. He is happy in it. People who knew him before he changed remark upon how different he is, and how much they like the difference. He accepts these strokes and is pleased with them. This in itself is a significant difference from the way he was before therapy, since Jim's capacity to receive strokes depends on the degree of his feelings of OKness about himself.

His feeling now is "I am OK." He has given up his dependency upon his parents for his self-evaluation. He has not surrendered his dependency to anyone else.

His earlier decision to depend on his parents in order to survive, and to please them in whatever way he must, has been replaced with the redecision, "I will now take care of myself." He is in the position of self-support. He is, in short, autonomous.

REFERENCES

1. Goulding, R. New directions in transactional analysis: Creating an environment for redecision and change. In: *Progress in Group and Family Therapy,* ed. J.S. Sager and H.S. Kaplan. New York: Brunner/Mazel, Chap. 9, 1972.
2. Kahler, T., and Hedges, C. The miniscript. *Transact. Anal. J.,* 4(1): p. 26, 1974.

Affective and Existential Application

Changes can be effected when patients are directly engaged by and involved with the therapist. Powerful emotions and experiences are encountered mutually by patient and therapist. The following chapters deal with a variety of active techniques that require the therapist's personal involvement.

Play Attention: The How Experience of Gestalt Psychotherapy

MICHAEL KRIEGSFELD

This paper was presented in a slightly different form at the First International Symposium on Non-Verbal Aspects and Techniques of Psychotherapy, July 29-31, 1974, Vancouver, B.C. Co-sponsored by: The World Psychiatric Association, Section of Psychotherapy; Canadian Psychiatric Association, Psychotherapeutic Section; Department of Psychiatry, University of British Columbia.

The late Dr. E. Schwartz, Dean of the Postgraduate Center for Psychotherapy, used to tell the story of his encounter with a hippy beggar who approached him with a plate full of coins. Preoccupied, Dr. Schwartz quickly brushed past, but the beggar chased him down the street and stopped him. "Listen man! You don't give! You don't take! The least you can do is relate!"

Relating, in a Gestalt psychotherapy encounter, implies the involvement of two people in a kind of performance. The psychotherapist, as an artist, draws into this creative experience many aspects of organismic response, including three basic processes I would like to bring into focus: (1) Attending, (2) Playing, and (3) Oscillating.

ATTENDING

A question I am often asked in demonstration of Gestalt is: "How do you attend to what is going on?" The verb may strike us as somewhat archaic; it means to heed, to listen to, as "to attend my words." The emphasis is clearly similar to the common parental instruction *pay attention,* meaning: my words are to be your guide. In school, the same message often leads to do-as-I-say-not-as-I-do conflicts of learning and teaching. In the army, of course, to be at attention means to be ready to receive the next order or command. And in the supervision of psycho-therapy, to pay attention to the patient sometimes means to stop what you are doing in order to follow the next verbal formula from the psychotherapy text.

To attend may also mean: to care for; to stay with; to be present with; to accompany actions or deeds with the capacity for special consideration, regard, courtesy, and awareness. The ability to attend is essential to a relationship between two people, and in fact to all human communication.

How does this process enter into the creative experience of the psychotherapist and patient, from the perspective of Gestalt psychotherapy?

I believe it is appropriate to introduce, at this point, an analogy which I will de-velop in the other two sections of this paper—the mystery of how two jazz musi-cians jam with each other. Improvising on the spot, each blows, first one taking the lead and then the other accompanies or follows. Sometimes they blow together simultaneously—speeding up, slowing down, modulating, getting louder or softer, more vigorous or calm, and finally agreeing to rest. The leader takes off with consideration for where the follower wants to go, concentrating on staying close to the follower without losing the lead. The follower goes along, but only in the style and direction in which he wants to go and where and how he is interested in follow-ing. The paradox and complexity becomes apparent.

The leader leads the follower by following the follower's lead. The follower fol-lows the leader by leading the leader in the way he will follow. They *attend* to each other and to themselves simultaneously, without thought, without judgmental in-junctions, without obligations, without stops, and without plans. They certainly don't talk to each other to discuss the issues pro and con, or to explain, or to jus-tify. When we listen to a jam session, we witness pure nonverbal communication and relatedness rooted in a style of attending involving consideration, regard, staying with, being present with, and simultaneously retaining an awareness of self and other. In this process, each is attending to what is at the moment, letting go of what has gone before, without inhibiting what is yet to come in new directions and new forms. They make contact and experiment by giving up the old and starting anew at each moment, fresh with the capacity to recognize and appreciate new beauty. Although clearly defining their separateness and their own parts, they fuse, integrate—harmonize—new creation into a whole that is meaningful and unique. Atonal dissonance, syncopation, silent rests, crashing, shrieking intrusions, jerkiness are all parts blended into a new whole that is pure improvisation, expression, and free flow.

Of course the jazz musician involved in improvisation represents only one of many different kinds of musicians. Some musicians need to read the music written for them by others, playing the notes according to the scripture of Gershwin or Beethoven, in prescribed structure and forms. Some can do both. I am thinking of Benny Goodman, a well-schooled musician who teaches at Julliard, and who has recorded a Mozart piece for clarinet and orchestra, using the classical approach. At other times, this gifted musician jams in the jazz improvisational approach. But in music, even the most classical of forms allows for some free flow. The composer may leave room for the musician to improvise in a small allotted section of the cadenza, though traditionally this has been a flourish or ornament not to be construed as significantly important to the major work.

The degree of improvisation in psychotherapy is also variable. The process of attending can be played in the style of the classical musician who first examines the musical notation or score, and then studies the history of the composer. In classical psychotherapy, the psychotherapist begins by looking at the patient's chart, record, intake material—a written history that serves as a guide to the next procedural steps. Or the psychotherapist may first make intense, careful attempts to make a diagnostic study of the patient. This approach may be characterized by alertness, as the psychotherapist makes an orderly progression from collecting data to interpreting, to exact fitting of label, to planning future treatment. Mozart is played one way, Beethoven another. The classical psychotherapist examines the score and identifies its source in order to determine the program and correct interpretation. The classical psychotherapist must guard against the danger of deviating from that which is written down. The key, the tempo, the shadings of interpretation are printed and to be followed exactly.

In *Psychology Today,* Manfred Clynes (1) writes:

> Let me give an example of the incredible precision and stability a good musician can achieve. The conductor, Arturo Toscanini, became a legend for his precise recordings of the Brahms-Hayden Variations with the NBC Symphony Orchestra. I had read that durations of his performances 1935, 1938 and 1948 were remarkably similar—so much so that they aroused my curiosity and doubt . . .

> I discovered after careful timekeeping that the total length of two performances differed by less than half a second in 16 minutes and 50 seconds, or about one part in 2,000. These two performances were recorded 10 years apart. The timing data also illustrates where Toscanini's conception of how the music should be conducted remained the same, there was great stability; but where the conductor changed his conception of one of the Variations, the difference in timing was obvious . . .

> Between the performance in 1935 and the one in 1948, both of which took place in the same hall, there was a world upheaval, Toscanini aged 13 years; there were

innumerable sources of instability—anxiety, fatigue, humidity, to name a few. One would expect, considering all these changes, that no two performances would ever have the same duration. But such changes meant little compared with the extraordinary precision and stability of the conductor's idiologs, actions and essentic forms. There can be no question, moreover, about Toscanini trying to remember how he had conducted the work 10 or 12 years before. A good artist feels his work anew; and besides, remembering would hardly allow accuracy. It was the precision of feelings that led to Toscanini's precision of execution.

In sharp contrast, improvisational jazz musicians like Fats Waller, even when playing their own compositions, have difficulty recording two similar takes in the recording studio, even on the same day. As much as he might admire the precision and craft of the classical artist, the Gestalt psychotherapist finds the jazz musician's approach more suitable and effective in his/her work. Using this approach, he/she is left free to attend to the patient; the patient, struggling to discover and define for himself/herself, his/her special, unique essence, is left free to play.

PLAYING

In our society, full freedom for play is often considered the prerogative of young children or of the idle rich. Those who make this judgment are involved with the concept of work as an ethical and moral precept.

Many theorists, including Erikson and Piaget, stress the value of play by pointing to some of its basic goals: physiological growth, expenditure of excess energy, practice, self-expression, restoration of energy, recreation, imagination, catharsis, and gratification of social needs. Unfortunately, play has not been generally acknowledged as a valid adult activity, and the term has been used in the pejorative sense to connote meaningless childlike activity. In fact, play can be the medium for the creative adult experience of striving to understand oneself and one's world. Erikson and Piaget give special recognition to play as the most significant process for self-instruction and self-cure. As a Gestalt psychotherapist, I consider the creative play experience a crucial ingredient for growth. In Gestalt terms, play takes the shape of contact experiments designed to facilitate new exploration and to allow awareness of impediments to exploration. These experiments involve not only content or verbalization, but also emotional absorption. The extent and quality of absorption is an indication of the vitality of the experience. In the creative play experience, the adult expresses both his/her understanding of and feeling about his/her original roles in life as he/she actually is; he/she expresses his/her willingness to actuate new performances with room and freedom for free motion and functioning. He/she can do this briskly, friskily, in jest, and with a variety of meaningful and sustained behavior.

We may now return to the image of the jazz musicians who play together. Improvising with each other is their most concentrated and exquisitely creative experience. They tune up together, adjusting to each other in relative pitch, or to a mutually agreed-upon outside standard. They take off without judgment to explore every facet of their own individual moods and joint harmony. The unthinking creative process within themselves as they attend to each other is so quick that action precedes thinking or planning. They play together without yielding their own uniqueness. Learning without teaching is taking place through the discovery and acceptance of what is. I would like to call attention to the fact that most psychological writings view the artistic experience as a solo or individual rite. Only in dance or in music is the creative experience the result of a joint or social encounter. Like these arts, psychotherapy—the distillation of communication and relatedness—follows the human love experience and I-Thou dialogue of living between two people.

The Gestalt psychotherapist and the patient, like two jazz musicians, look forward to new forms and new experiences rooted in the immediacy and improvisation of the moment. Instead of dwelling on predetermined judgments, habit patterns, or weaknesses, they concentrate on their abilities and skills to start anew, to risk a different configuration.

OSCILLATING

In my freely flowing capacity for imaginative play, I am fluctuating between passivity and activity. I thus oscillate back and forth between consciousness of how I am feeling, what is impinging on me, what is waiting in me to be expressed or fulfilled, and consciousness of what is going on in the other person, what he/she is like, with what qualities he/she touches me. This oscillating leads to contrapuntal harmony. As in jazz improvisation, psychotherapist and patient balance individual life melodies, accompanying each other. In the exchange, we both grow and become more in tune with ourselves, and with each other. I am attending and playing with all my skill, awareness, and interest in myself as well as in the other person. The patient in turn is attending, playing with his/her skill, awareness, and interest in himself/herself as well as me. What we interrupt, how we interrupt, how we create dissonance, how we create harmony, what we leave over for another session, bubble up in ever-changing flow from our individual figures and grounds as we discover infinite Gestalts in ourselves and in the other. This is not a premanufactured process in which we look for something to use or make in planned, contrived fashion. Implicit is the assumption that we are capable of nonjudgmental exploration of ourselves and each other in concert. This implies also interest, receptivity, openness to sharing, and daring to risk new polyphonic encounters. Since this is improvisational artistic creation between the two of us, I oscillate back and forth from my own production of pitch, tone coloration, intensity, duration, silence, rhythm, harmony to openness to his/her equally improvisational artistic creations. In Gestalt terms, I am experiencing myself as well as the other person *as we are.*

I am not an archeologist searching for ancient hidden causes, nor a super-spy catching glimpses of pathological distortion. The richness and vitality of the here and now leads to infinite contact, experimentation, and choice.

The kinesthetic sense for me is the chief medium for empathetic involvement. Traditionally this sense has been left undescribed, because culturally and professionally emphasis is placed on rational, verbal, intellectual issues. St. Vincent de Paul, the first social worker, instructed a novitiate: "It is not the loaf of bread that we give, but the love with which we give it that makes the other person able to accept it." In the here and now, I, as the psychotherapist, do not remain a detached outside observver seeking to match a fixed premise and diagnostic formulation with the programmed treatment plan. Rather I experience myself in relation to the actual sensations, organismic tensions, attitudes, kinetic energy, and psychomotor changes taking place. Like the jazz musician, I am ready to trust myself to play the next note, and to respond from my inner conviction of being alive, animated, and congruent with the other's responsive creation.

Another image may illustrate how Gestalt is played. At a jam session we watch with increasing excitement as the performance begins. The piano player is twisting his head and tapping his foot. The saxaphone player is beginning to weave and dodge. The bass player is slapping his bass. We see the drummer raising his arms ever so slowly. Perched precariously on the stool, the drummer is windmilling his arms in huge circles. Now the singer and one of the guitar players have begun a little dance step. Sliding, shuffling, hopping, bouncing, jiggling forward and backward, spinning and turning, they skillfully sway, with the momentum taking them almost horizontally. We, seemingly the nonparticipating spectators, are caught up in following the swinging and swaying. We shift in our seats, we snap our fingers, we clap our hands, we sing out or cheer, we stamp our feet, and the dancers in appreciation increase the frenzy and tempo. When we are almost certain the wild gyrations will lead them to crash into each other or fall off the stage, they suddenly exert some new energy, grab each other, and exchange places. Our own movements and facial expressions, as well as our vocal reactions, reveal our own projections into the scene. Expectant, with new energy, we are stretching, bending, reaching out to make contact again as we await the recapitulation of the exchange. We notice our own strain, tension, draining of energy and relief in the act of completion as we place ourselves in the place of the performers. We wonder how they keep their balance, how they time their exchange, and note the confidence and grace in their own self-support. Depending on our own sense of ourselves, we identify or avoid participation, but we are actively engaged with them.

Like the performance of the musicians, the encounter in Gestalt psychotherapy implies the recognition of a two-person performance involving attending, playing, and oscillating. The performance demands on the part of both performers skill and readiness to act together, risking open exploration and exchange, making contact through awareness and experimentation. Through self-discovery, self-acceptance, and self-affirmation, we are able to discover the infinite wisdom of the other person, and to discover, accept, and affirm his/her integrity, as well as our own.

EPILOGUE

I would like to close an unfinished Gestalt with a personal anecdote. Not too many years ago, as I was struggling to free myself from embeddedness in classical psychotherapy recitals, I had the privilege of working with a group at a rather prominent mental health rehearsal hall. Having worked at this mental Carnegie Hall from its inception, I was familiar with the many staff players and their traditional classical forms. After many years of playing various roles—individual psychotherapist, group psychotherapist, intake worker, researcher, supervisor—I became increasingly involved in avant-garde active psychotherapy. Encounter groups, sensitivity training, marathons, art therapy, Tavistock groups, and other modalities began to appeal to me from new horizons. Exploration, experimentation, improvisation—growth and change tore at me as I underwent the painful process of rebirth. I was making new music, and despite my own pleasure and satisfaction with the results, I began receiving bad reviews from my co-workers. This culminated late one night after a group session, when a therapist came out from the neighboring office where he conducted his own psychoanalytically oriented psychotherapy. "I have this woman inside on the couch trying to free associate and all we can hear is this terrible voice yelling 'I hate my fucking mother' and those horrible noises— what is going on? You simply have to stop!" Needless to say, I resigned soon after to continue my own artistic development. The group members chose to go with me. The house orchestral staff gave their relieved blessing.

After further experiences together, the original group members, with their own newfound autonomy, went their own ways. In following up with them, I hear about their good feelings and achievements. We stay in touch and laugh about the "good old days" when they threatened to picket.

One of the members of that group, who has gone on to complete academic training and undertake original research in this field, *attended* my reading of this paper at the First International Symposium on Non-Verbal Aspects and Techniques of Psychotherapy. I shared our mutual experience with the other participants in the symposium, speaking directly to that group member, but also expressing my own feelings about nonverbal aspects of psychotherapy:

> Meek, apathetic, apologetic, mousey, underachiever (that was your own melody line), you carried the image of St. Sebastian, inviting more and more flaming arrows shot into you. Will you forget the nonverbal techniques of psychotherapy which enabled you to release the locked-up fury and anger you never talked about till you punched and, in a frenzy that frightened us all, beat the stuffing out of the couch in the conference room? Will you recall the experiments in going around to others in the group unable to stand erect on your own two feet, body swaying without balance, trying to unfurl your assertiveness? Do you remember the gush of love and acceptance as members of the group hugged and embraced you as you sobbed spasmodically in pain and anguish? The balm and self-annointments you mixed to heal your own seared wounds, as you finally extinguished the flaming arrows, were a miracle of rebirth also. Talking never put out a fire such as

yours, nor stilled the terror and despair in hushed monotones. Thank you for allowing us both to play this gig. You are you and I am me and we have met and touched. Later we can hug, or laugh, or dance, or maybe beat the stuffing out of a couch together.

REFERENCES

1, Clynes, M. The pane pure of musical genius. *Psychol. Today,* July, 1974.

9

Primal-Oriented Psychotherapy

MAURY NEWHAUSE and MARY ANN H. FURDA

Primal therapy gained prominence in the early 1970's with the publication of Janov's *The Primal Scream* (2). He stated that after eight months of primal therapy, the patient is completely cured and never needs any therapy again. Cure includes the end of psychosomatic symptoms; the elimination of all defenses and tension; the cessation of all smoking, overeating, and drinking; the end of all symbolic behavior, including homosexuality; and the promise of a more meaningful life. Although some of Janov's earlier expectations have failed to materialize, results thus far do indicate that primal therapy is making a valuable contribution to the field of psychotherapy.

Interest in primal therapy, however, has waned since its auspicious debut. The major reason for this seems to be that Janov has refused to acknowledge the contributions of any therapies that preceded his discovery, and of any therapists not trained by his institutes. Since Janov has chosen to alienate himself from his colleagues, the result has been relatively poor communication among professionals, thus retarding the development of primal therapy. Instead of being accepted as an important new therapeutic process, isolated primal methods and techniques are being incorporated by therapists into existing therapeutic practices, often without a complete understanding of the process.

The Center for Feeling Therapy seems to be the major exception. The Center was started by a group of psychotherapists, some of whom had trained with Janov. Feeling therapy, like primal, relies heavily on affective abreaction. The differences in theory, method, and technique are discussed in detail throughout this chapter.

Perhaps a brief case study best illustrates some of the differences between primal-oriented therapy and primal therapy and what occurs in the therapy sessions. Karen's chief complaints when she came for therapy, at age 23, were being 100 pounds overweight, depressions with suicidal thoughts, and having to take care of many people in her life. Since, at that time, we were not practicing primal-oriented therapy, Karen did not come to us for that specific therapeutic orientation, nor had she read *The Primal Scream,* so that subsequently, when she experienced intense abreactions, she was not imitating what she had read about, nor doing what she thought would be expected of her. The sessions for the first few months were Gestalt-oriented, with Karen encouraged to lie on a mat whenever she appeared to be close to intense feelings. At other times, we both sat in chairs and talked.

Little seemed to be changing for Karen, either in therapy or in her life. Influenced by *The Primal Scream,* we decided to change the format of the session to help her to become more aware of and to express her feelings. She was asked to start a session lying on her back, which was her most vulnerable position, to breathe deeply, and to call for one of her parents. She began to quietly call "Daddy" and was urged to call his name louder and louder. (The client is always asked to use the name she called her parent as a child.) Whenever Karen wanted to stop she was encouraged to continue. Phrases like "keep going," "that's it," and "don't stop" helped her to express her feelings more intensely. After a few minutes, she was screaming with anger and rage at her father. Initially, her throat was closed and her screams choked. As her hate and anger poured out, her throat gradually opened and her voice deepened. This experience, building in intensity, lasted for about 35 minutes. At the end of this time, Karen felt exhilarated and temporarily free from anxiety. In each succeeding individual and group session for the next few months, Karen experienced similar intense abreactions.

Her first four abreactions consisted mainly of expressing hate and rage toward her father, without connecting to specific events of her past. In her fifth, she reexperienced two painful events. One was having to take care of her younger brother and being terrified when her father returned and screamed at her for letting her brother get hurt. The other dealt with having her mother die in her arms at age five and a half. Her mother's dying wish was for Karen to promise to take care of her father, so that both memories were related to taking care of others. In addition to re-experiencing the painful scene of her mother's death many times, Karen needed to scream with the full intensity of the repressed feeling, "Mommy, I can't take care of Daddy."

These abreactions were followed by insights about what had happened to her in her childhood, which up to this time had been almost totally repressed. Karen experienced the pain of the realization that her father did not love her in the way she needed to be loved, and had used her to take care of him and her younger brother. She had been able, however, to get his approval by becoming a very responsible child. Since as a child she could not face the pain that many of her needs were not being fulfilled, she made herself more unreal by becoming more responsible and taking care of more people. Her method of keeping this pain repressed was to stuff food in her mouth until she became obese.

In the 26 weeks following her first intense abreaction, Karen lost 96 pounds and went from three packs of cigarettes a day to none; her obsessions and compulsions completely disappeared, even though they were never discussed in therapy; a life-long sinus condition, which was serious enough to hospitalize her as a child, completely cleared up; on her job, she tripled her sales of the previous year; and her eyesight improved from 20/250 to 20/200.

We have learned in the years following Karen's treatment that her rapid gains were the exception. Most clients need much longer therapy and growth is usually more gradual and less spectacular.

Although most primal therapists would not work in the manner we have described—doing primal-oriented therapy in the 45-minute or hour-and-a-half session, we believe it to be a worthwhile experience. We have had to develop methods and techniques to assist clients in getting into intense feelings quickly. We have also found that most clients can be helped to experience intense abreactions without undergoing the costly three-week intensive program described by Janov (2).

In primal therapy, the primary aim of the three-week intensive program is to teach clients how to move into intense abreactive experiences. After this has been accomplished, the clients are expected to work on themselves in primal groups, with very little assistance from the therapist. It is our belief that many clients are not ready for this type of experience after only three weeks; they need to be seen for a more extended period of time individually. Primal-oriented therapy utilizes the 45-minute individual session once or twice weekly initially, rather than the three-week intensive program, for several reasons; our theoretical divergence from Janov concerning the handling of defenses, the time factor involved for both the therapist and the client, and the initial expense for the client. The purpose of the individual session in primal-oriented therapy is to assist clients in tracking their feelings, so that they gradually need less constant help from the therapist. When clients can utilize most of the 45-minute session by experiencing their present fully, feeling the source of their defenses, and expressing past feelings that were blocked, they no longer need individual sessions and enter primal groups.

These groups are an extension of the individual session; group members work primarily independently, with a minimum of interaction. The advantages of the group format at this juncture are: group sessions are longer than individual, clients in groups often trigger off feelings in one another thus facilitating abreactions, and group sessions are less expensive for the client.

We have incorporated several changes into our theoretical framework that make primal-oriented therapy quite different from primal therapy. Hart, Corriere, and Binder (1), much of whose contributions are also adaptable to the 45-minute session, describe a theoretical framework they call the feeling cycle. The first phase of this cycle is especially helpful with clients who abreact easily but who appear to be making few changes in their lives. Defenses should not be broken through, as in primal therapy, but must be felt and expressed as fully as possible. The function of the defense is to mask and reduce feelings that could not be expressed in childhood. The therapist helps the client initially to feel what it is like *not* to express his feelings and thoughts in the present, so that defenses are experienced fully. Once the client is able to be fully in the present, it is more possible to feel what the past was like. It is usually difficult to experience the disorder of one's past unless the present is relatively ordered. (Ordering is defined as the matching of feeling and expression.) Once the client has learned to differentiate between expressing a defense and expressing the feeling behind that defense, the choice between expressing a feeling or holding back becomes a more conscious one. This is counteraction; the first phase of the feeling cycle.

Providing an atmosphere of support, safety, and acceptance, the therapist assists the client in moving through the next phase of the feeling cycle, the abreactive phase. We do not share Janov's belief that abreaction is in itself curative. The release of tension and an understanding of how childhood experiences have disordered feelings, which is accomplished through intense abreactions, must be integrated not only with a conscious effort to distinguish between past sensations and meanings and present ones, but also with the choice to live fully in the present. Openness to one's feelings can only be maintained if present feelings with present meanings are expressed. The principle of balanced therapeutic movement assures that every expression of feeling from the past is matched by an equal expression of feeling in the present.

The next phase of the feeling cycle is the proaction, which is the first movement back toward feeling in the present. If the client remains in the regressed state of the child, it is difficult for him to function in the world. After the client has abreacted past repressed feelings, he must give adult expression to feelings that were blocked off in the past.

The final phase of the feeling cycle is the integration. Integration is living from the new level of feeling awareness and expressiveness that becomes available after completing a feeling. If the client does not live and respond from the new openness, he will not transform his life.

A client does not go through a feeling cycle in each session; many therapy sessions can involve a single phase. Sessions with experienced clients can be devoted to dealing with present feelings and on the difficulties a client has living from the feeling awareness already available to him. To transform his level of feeling, however, a client must experience all the phases of the cycle. By helping clients learn to move through the four phases of the feeling cycle independently, the therapist guides his clients toward the goal of becoming their own therapists.

The early stages of primal-oriented therapy are similar to conventional therapy. The client is usually lying on his back on a large cushion in a semi-darkened, sound-proof room. Each client begins the session in his own manner, sometimes relating his past, sometimes discussing present life difficulties. The therapist observes how the client defends himself against feelings and encourages the client to feel his defenses and subsequently express the feelings behind the defenses. As the client moves closer to his feelings, two kinds of resistances are likely to occur. One is that the client begins to try to talk about his feelings in an effort to push the feelings down. It is sometimes effective, at these times, if the client is encouraged to express himself in sounds rather than words. If, for example, a client wants to talk about how angry he is with his employer, he might be asked to express his anger with sounds and body movements. As the client experiences his present anger fully, often past connections to this angry feeling occur spontaneously. Using sounds instead of words sometimes permits connections to preverbal and nonverbal experiences.

The second resistance that often arises is physical. Most clients have learned to suppress and repress feelings by shallow breathing. Whenever the therapist observes that the client's breathing is shallow, he encourages deeper breathing. It is important that when exhaling, the client's abdominal muscles be relaxed. Often, as feelings emerge, the client tries to suppress them by gagging or choking. At these times, the client becomes frightened and needs support, usually through verbal encouragement and physical contact. Phrases like "push out a sound" or "stay with it" help the client overcome the fear of choking, and once a sound is expressed, the choking invariably subsides. The therapist should watch carefully for indications that the client is attempting to suppress feelings. Some signs are: restlessness, wanting to keep the mouth closed, putting hands to face, shallow breathing, excessive swallowing, gagging or choking, and headaches or other sudden pains in the body. When the therapist senses that the client is suppressing a feeling, it is sometimes helpful to reverse what the client is doing. For example, if the client wants to lie still, he is instructed to move around; if he wants to talk, he is encouraged to make sounds; if he wants to whisper, he is asked to shout, and so forth.

For some clients who have difficulty in connecting emotionally with their past, the early stages of treatment involve discussion of the theoretical framework so that they begin to understand how much their present difficulties have roots in their past. This intellectual preparation is sometimes augmented by the following techniques which further help clients to see how their relationships with their parents have influenced their present functioning. If a client is feeling hopeless, he is encouraged to hold the parent responsible who made the child of his past feel hopeless; if a client is close to tears but cannot cry, he is instructed to say this, in therapy, to the parent who discouraged him from crying; if a client is discussing how poorly he relates to others in his present life, he is told to tell that to the parent responsible for making it difficult to relate to himself, and therefore to others.

These techniques are not easily accepted by many clients who display great resistance to holding their parents responsible for their present-day emotional conflicts. They would rather blame themselves. Therapeutic progress is impeded as long as clients continue to blame themselves; they must connect to their three-, four-, or five-year-old child of the past who had no choice but to blame himself for difficulties in the parent-child relationship.

The purpose is not simply to blame one's parents; it is essential for the client to tell his parents, in the therapeutic session, *how* they made him feel hopeless, anxious, or inadequate. It must be pointed out to the client that helpful parents do not blame their children for their own shortcomings, but freely admit them. If, for example, parents have overindulged their child by giving him too much attention when he was young, he will have difficulty as he grows older in tolerating frustration, resulting in his making intolerable and unnecessary demands upon his parents. If, on these occasions, his parents blame him by saying, "What's wrong with you?" he will gradually internalize their words. Later, as an adult in therapy, it is likely that when he encounters difficulty, he will whine, "What's wrong with me?" It should be explained to the client that helpful parents would have admitted to the child that they made a mistake in overindulging him in his younger years. They would elaborate further that it was not his fault that he had become demanding or impatient in certain situations, but theirs, and they would now try to help him with these feelings. Just as in therapy, where the client must ultimately assume responsibility for changing self-defeating patterns and behavior, the child must also accept the responsibility for modifying his behavior. The child then does not blame himself for his difficulties, nor does he blame his parents. This nonjudgmental attitude permits the child to accept himself as he is, which then permits change to take place.

Many clients maintain that they have forgiven their parents because they did the best they could. It should be explained to these clients that perhaps the adult part of themselves has forgiven their parents, but the child within themselves still has varied unexpressed feelings about what occurred in childhood. They now, in therapy, have the right and the need to express these feelings.

From the foregoing statements, it can be seen that primal-oriented therapy is a gradual process that involves much more than just screaming by the clients. One misconception concerning abreactive therapies is that cure follows the scream. With most clients, the initial stages of therapy involve assisting them to experience themselves fully in the present, to become nonjudgmental about themselves and others, and to accept all their feelings. During the early stages of therapy, a wide variety of methods and techniques from Gestalt, psychoanalytic, hypnoanalytic, transactional, behavior, and client-centered therapies are used to help clients move toward more complete levels of feeling. This period may last from weeks to months, depending on the strength and nature of the client's defenses. Many clients believe that having only "big" feelings will cure them and try to have intense abreactions immediately. They need to learn that only complete feelings are therapeutic, because a person who lives from his complete feelings is being everything he is at every moment.

Most clients come into therapy with a belief system which must be continuously challenged by the therapist. They may believe, for example, that their lives would be better and their problems solved if only they had more money or were prettier or more handsome or had bigger and better orgasms or a different lover or spouse. The something to be changed or acquired is usually external. It may take months or perhaps years for some clients to take responsibility for how they live their lives and understand that they must live from complete feelings in order to transform their lives. Without transformation, clients replace solved problems with new problems. When a person limits, disguises, and pushes away feelings, he creates and lives out problems.

Another part of the belief system concerns living from images. An image is both a belief and a role, and conveys the social and personal expressions of insanity. For a person to become sane, he must give up the reasonableness and safety of images and live from complete feelings, not from images of who he should be or what he should do. Young children do not initially use images, but quickly learn to hold in feelings so that what is expressed is not what was originally felt. This process of checking natural expressions creates what Hart et al. (1) label the nonsense layer. In many ways this layer protects the child because there is no one in his life to help him with how he feels. What is deleterious about the nonsense layer is that the child can no longer give direct expression to what he experiences on the inside, nor can he receive anything directly from the outside. The child begins to replace his true feeling reality with his own reasonable insanity; he makes up reasons to explain what is happening to him. He begins to designate substitute meanings to sensations as he learns that in his family certain meanings, sensations, and expressions are not acceptable. The rules of reasonable insanity are: do not say what you feel; do not say what you mean; and do not follow your body sensations and impulses. Only when the nonsense is recognized and felt can a person begin to know himself and the world directly. The images translate the nonsense into functional and reasonable insanity. Unless a client is willing to enter this nonsense layer and give up his images and roles, no real change will take place in therapy or in his life.

One client's role in life was being a "nice guy." He would always try to do and say the right thing to avoid offending anyone. When he was a child, his mother discouraged any assertive or aggressive behavior. Since he needed her approval, he began to suppress and deny any feelings associated with assertiveness and aggressiveness and replace them with words that helped him to cope with his mother's neurotic behavior. He was not interested in playing football because he "could get hurt," he would not argue or fight with anyone because "the issue was not that important" to him, and he rarely asked for what he wanted because "if people care about you they would give you what you want without your having to ask." In therapy, his belief system had to be challenged, and he was encouraged to be assertive and aggressive in his everyday life. Only after he felt the disordering of his adult life did abreacting about his childhood have any meaning for him. He needed to give up his images so that he could begin to feel completely again and live from these feelings.

In primal-oriented therapy, clients are helped to feel and live from their feelings. They are not given anything new, but are helped to get back what they once had—complete feeling. Throughout the therapy, in fact within each session, clients choose either to move toward more openness or to close off and return to the safety of their defenses and belief systems. Some clients find transforming their lives too threatening and painful, and choose to accept the limitations of the way in which they are living. The clients who stay face the arduous but exciting task of living a life that is constantly changing and growing, and one in which they can participate more fully.

REFERENCES

1. Hart, J., Corriere, R., and Binder, J. *Going Sane.* New York: Jason Aronson, 1975.
2. Janov, A. *The Primal Scream.* New York: G.P. Putnam's Sons, 1970.

Encounter Therapy as an Existential Saga

CARL GOLDBERG

Group psychotherapy has reached maturity. Treatment in groups has come to be accepted in its own right as a decisive contribution to the study of and the relief from emotional disorders. Several decades of clinical work with patients in groups has convincingly demonstrated that experience in well-designed therapeutic groups may make contributions to the patient's therapeutic progress that are unattainable in individual sessions alone. Indeed, for an ever-increasing number of practitioners, group therapy is a more viable and powerful tool for a large portion of the patients they treat than are dyadic (individual) sessions (8).

Treatment in groups has become such a powerful treatment vehicle that the major challenges to group therapy have not come from other modalities of treatment—dyadic, milieu, chemotherapy, or any other—but from departures in treatment ideology and methodology among the wide array of group practices. Unlike dyadic psychotherapy, historically shackled by dedication to the theory and methodology of a few influential thinkers (26), the possibility for innovation in group treatment seems relatively unlimited. By means of innovative group techniques, it seems possible to successfully treat persons with a diversity of emotional disorders who have been resistive to the strategies of conventional psychotherapy (10).

THE INDIVIDUAL'S QUEST FOR MEANING

The magnitude and comprehensiveness of modern technology is such that only a relatively few scientists and technicians are actually required to serve the physical needs of the multitude. A century ago over 50 percent of the American population lived in rural areas and were engaged in agrarian endeavors. Today perhaps less than ten percent of the population reside on farms, although our food production is many times in excess of that of a century ago. A partial but salient reason for our large unemployment rate is the obvious fact that we do not require the large labor force of the less technological yesteryear. Moreover, as the crises in our large cities demonstrate, a minority of the denizen support the needs and economic well-being of the majority. An individual's existence today may be freely egocentric and asocial to a degree not tolerated a short while ago. Each individual today is not actually required, except perhaps in a moral sense, to maintain a trade and a life style forged on supporting the immediate and extended family. In the past, a man's destiny was always his family. They were the root and essence of his existence. He could no more evade this commitment than obviate the realization that he had produced offspring who required his care and protection. Today, with the high rate of changing families—through divorce and remarriage—a man may not be required by law to support the woman he took in matrimony and the children he produced from their union. If other persons do not take up his financial and social responsibilities, public agencies are designed to do precisely that (8).

These considerations suggest that the individual in American society today has been set emotionally adrift by the traditional anchoring institutions of his social system. In the past, these venerable ethical, social, and occupational concepts and beliefs of religious, family, and work-guild membership served to define the role and function of each societal member. The individual who was able to internalize these societal concepts derived a sense of identity and value as a member of society. Today our anchoring societal institutions are no longer able to absorb the intellectual and emotional energies of the denizen. The individual today must define for himself his place in an ever-changing world. Morality is now regarded as situational, tentative, and open to revision. Public and private commitments are no longer absolutely binding as they were within the more ordered and less questioned societal guidelines. The individual today is forced to question for himself the meaning of life: "Who am I?" "How did I get this way?" "Where shall I go?" The more the individual must rely on his own resources for solving personal difficulties, the more he is in touch with feelings of denigration, frustration, and anguish. The individual today feels that he is ailing, possessed by a sickness which is neither physical nor psychiatric, but rather a malaise of spirit, a sickness of alienation no less epidemic and socially contagious despite the absence of an organic etiology. The existential practitioner views this maliase of spirit as an ontological condition underlying all emotional and social disturbances—be they characterological or due to brief and situational crisis. Individuals possessed by ontological malaise have attempted conventional forms of treatment and remediation. They frequently languish in these situations, more frustrated and disillusioned than when they entered. The individual today seeks more than the perpetuation of his existence—he yearns for personal and transcendental meaning for his existence. Conventional psychotherapy, many patients feel, takes too long and is uninvolving. These patients feel that there is not enough give-and-take vis-à-vis patient and therapist to encourage them out of their alienation and characterological disillusionment (8).

Similarly, therapists have a difficult time reaching patients who appear to function adequately in their daily activities, but who at the same time are detached from their surroundings, having minimal involvement with any other person and no firm commitment to any endeavor (27). Insofar as these practitioners develop aversive reactions in their ephemeral struggles with these patients, conventional psychotherapy proves to be counterproductive for persons afflicted with ontological malaise.

The encounter movement, seen from this context, poses a powerful catalytic challenge to the mental health field. Encounter therapy is both a complex and elusive interpersonal endeavor which has stirred the excitement and anger, no less than the appreciation and compassion of its critics, defenders, and participants. In the last few years, the American scene has witnessed a profusion of innovative varities of group experience which until now have been too recent, too complex, and too controversial to be carefully studied. As a result, it has been unusually difficult to evaluate encounter therapy with any degree of objectivity, let alone with the empirical evidence the movement requires (3). Recently Morton Lieberman and his associates (21) have conducted an extensive investigation of encounter groups in which they studied 206 participants as they functioned in 18 groups with encounter leaders evincing a diverse range of encounter styles. Findings from this study are reported in this chapter.

If looked at with a healthy curiosity, the encounter movement challenges the conventional group practitioner to reconsider and seriously question his cherished beliefs about human conduct and amelioration of emotional suffering (16). In this endeavor, we must recognize the encounter movement as more than a passing social fad and a dissident social movement (3). The encounter movement is essentially, and most importantly for our purposes, a system of psychotherapy.

ENCOUNTER THERAPY AS A PSYCHOTHERAPY SYSTEM

Systems of psychotherapy are designed to come to terms with the distress afflicted by the dilemmas of contemporary society on our patients. Accordingly, systems of psychotherapy, if they are to be effective, are heavily shaped by the prevailing conceptions of the nature of man. The Freudian *Weltanschauung* held that man, as an object in the universe, is subject to unalterable natural and psychological laws. In sharp contrast, the world-view of the encounter movement places man at the center of the universe: Man is as much the lawmaker in the universe as he is subject of natural and psychological laws. As lawmaker, each individual is recognized as being capable of exercising choice over his own behavior (5). Need for societally recognized experts to decipher the strictures governing behavior, to enable the individual to deal with his personal distress, is less central in this worldview than in one in which man is perceived as subservient to a mysterious universal order. Consistent with this perspective, emotional distress is no longer regarded as an inscrutable condition rooted *within* the disturbed person, as exemplified in the demonological and constitutional notions of mental illness in the past and represented in the psychoanalytic concept of repressed libidinal urges. Encounter practices have focused increasingly on interpersonal relations and the influence of contemporary interactive patterns, rather than on the patient's developmental history accessible only by analysis of dreams, language slips, and other symbolic indications. Correspondingly, encounter therapeutic techniques emphasize working out conflicts by relying considerably on the resources of peers. Many encounter practitioners acknowledge that it is the group members themselves, rather than the therapist, who more frequently are the most salient therapeutic forces in the group (8).

In studying psychotherapeutic systems, it must also be recognized that therapeutic systems consist of essentially two interlocking dimensions. At the center of a therapeutic system, there is an ontological view of the nature of man and what he can become when self-actualized, as well as notions about the interplay of intrapsychic and societal forces on the actualizing process. Secondly, psychotherapeutic systems consist of techniques and methodology, based on the psychotherapeutic system's ontological notions, which are believed to be effective in helping the individual actualize his human potentialities. In terms of psychodynamic therapeutic practice, the ontological notions in Freud's writings stressed that removal of societally imbued neurosis would reveal an instinctually egocentric personality. This suggests that addressing the patient's conflictual nature may be necessary, but not sufficient, for his self-actualization. In practice, however, psychodynamic psychotherapy appears to assume a Rousseauian type of ontology. This position conveys the belief that if a patient were unfettered of his intrapsychic conflicts and distortions, he would spontaneously and naturally find a satisfying and harmonious existence. In recent years this contention has been seriously questioned from both within and outside the ranks of psychodynamic practitioners. These practitioners contend that psychodynamic practitioners are frequently not quite certain of what they wish their patients to accomplish, insofar as analytic treatment is based on a medical model, specified in terms of aberrance and pathology, rather than rooted within a constructive and definitive model of human growth and development (10).

The conventional practitioner, according to encounter practitioners, has been primarily concerned with the discovery and diagnosis of pathology. He operates from a genetic and constitutional bias which holds that most emotional disabilities are incurable. The best that can be done to improve the patient's condition is to transform severe pathology into less debilitating symptomatology. Diagnosis and in-depth exploration of the patient's life history is required to assess the life-space parameters within which the patient can successfully function. The encounter movement has risen in protest against conventional psychotherapy which has been content to imitate the principles and practices of general medicine. Encounter practitioners regard society as essentially unhealthy and a more legitimate "patient" than the solitary individual in psychological distress. Consequently, an increasing array of practitioners have asserted that in large measure the manner in which a person is regarded and treated by society's therapeutic agents determines his present behavior, more so than does his developmental history. If he is forced into a docile and dependent patient role, that is, if he is treated as a victim of social and psychological forces, he can not effectively deal with his situation (6, 7).

It is the thesis of this chapter that group psychotherapy currently requires a treatment system whose rationale and methodology are based on a realistic assessment of the ontological condition of contemporary man. The methodology of this system must teach patients and other concerned persons definitive skills which will enable them to administer to their own and their neighbors' loneliness and despair, to address the problems of alienation and existential exhaustion that characterize twentieth-century man (18).

Existential and humanistic psychology arose as a series of revolts against the image of contemporary man and his human condition embodied in the world-view of conventional psychotherapy. Existential psychology has been concerned with the *nature of inquiry* into the human condition. In this venture, existential psychologists have sought to understand the individual's behavior and experience in terms of the existential presuppositions about the human condition which they claim conventional psychotherapists tend to abuse or ignore in their treatment of ontological malaise (23). Unfortunately, existential psychologists have voiced their concerns in what seem to be rather poetic but unnecessarily vague terms. The quality of their terminology has resulted in considerable misunderstanding of existential concepts and intentions. This has exacerbated the usual difficulties of converting any philosophical or theoretical concept into viable psychotherapeutic practice. To my knowledge, existential psychologists have not been particularly fecund in developing a viable methodology from which to articulate their concerns. On the other hand, the encounter movement arose, as I see it, as an impatient attempt to spell out and implement the concerns of existential and humanistic psychology, by focusing on how patients and practitioners may best utilize each other as therapeutic agents. In this endeavor, encounter practitioners have developed a myriad of provocative social technologies to accentuate the therapeutic encounter. In short, the encounter movement has been an attempt to construct a model for generating positive growth and proactive development unfulfilled by conventional psychotherapeutic practice.

Unfortunately, a serious consideration of these encounter models is unpalatable to many conventionally trained practitiners. These practitioners simply reject the encounter movement as a fad, soon to be depleted and destined to disappear. In so doing, they maintain that encounter practitioners have failed to deal responsibly with fundamental issues of treatment and personal conduct. These practitioners see encounter experience as callously exploiting the ravenous need for human contact in America today. They view with pungent skepticism any social movement that claims unabashedly it has discovered the antidote to such resistive societal maladies as boredom, alienation, and the mendacity of our chosen leaders (16).

I, myself, do not believe that encounter therapy can be so easily dismissed, or that the ideas and practices of its more creative and responsible practitioners can be so unflinchingly ignored. Awareness of the limitations and abuses of these highly touted groups must not prevent us from critically examining and comparing their innovative and our own more conventional practices. To avoid operating in a social vacuum, insulated from the realities of our present culture, each system of psychotherapy needs to be challenged and openly curious in comparing its rationale, methodology, and results with those of innovative approaches. To view any therapy as a fad may be a denial of our patients' needs. The psychotherapist's craft is not intended to be eternal, to stand the test of time. The individuals we work with are finite, cast in a particular temporality, and forced to struggle with the conditions and realities of that particular period in time. The new group therapies have germinated and evolved in the present temporality. Encounter group practices may thus be in contact with current issues of human existence in ways that therapies formulated, conceptualized, and conducted by practitioners trained in yesteryear often obliquely fail to address. We may eventually reject the solutions the encounter movement offers us for dealing with human misery and the paths it suggests for personal and societal fulfillment. Nonetheless, the issues with which many of the encounter practitioners are struggling may be issues with which conventional practitioners have lost touch (10).

CONDUCTING AN ENCOUNTER GROUP

In converting philosophical and theoretical concepts to a treatment methodology, theoretical limitations and treatment problems soon become apparent. It is because of my concern that encounter therapy may be lost as a viable and legitimate, existentially oriented treatment modality that I have undertaken writing this chapter. In this chapter I will present my work with encounter groups as a rapprochement between the principles of existential psychology and what I regard as responsible therapeutic practice. I will begin my presentation by assuming that I have been requested to conduct an encounter weekend. I will share with the reader the issues and concerns that agreeing to conduct an encounter group evoke for me and how I attempt to deal with these concerns.

The phone rings and the voice on the other end of the line asks:

Dr. Goldberg? This is Dr. Daniels. We met at a professional meeting several months ago. I have been thinking about the discussion we had about encounter groups. I was intrigued by some of your ideas about encounter therapy. But, as you know, I have some reservations about these groups. I regard myself as a conservative psychiatrist. Nonetheless, a number of patients I have been seeing for some time are presently in some sort of impasse. I have been wondering whether it would be worth a try to have them experience a more intensive group experience than the 90-minute weekly therapeutic groups I have available. I have also received phone calls from people who don't want conventional therapy and are, instead, interested in experiencing an encounter group. You told me, I believe, that you conduct time-limited encounter groups from time to time. Would you be interested in . . .

Group functioning may be seen as operating along three salient dimensions: the intentional, the ephemeral, and the subtle. The *intentional* aspect of an encounter group refers to the planned goals of the group experience and the methodology the group practitioner employs to achieve these goals (2). As I put down the phone receiver, I realize that from my discussion with Dr. Daniels I am unaware of who the people are who will be participating in the weekend encounter. I also realize to plan a group efficaciously I must know what expectations the particpants have for the weekend. Moreover, I need to know what each participant will bring to the encounter weekend in terms of experiences, perspectives, strengths, and limitations. At the present time, I am certain only that the encounter is limited to a weekend—Friday evening to mid-day on Sunday. Will this time period be an opportunity for each participant to deal differently with his personal concerns than he has in the past or will the time constraints be a built-in limitation? This concern raises the issue of meaning of time in a therapeutic experience.

Denial of "Immediacy" in Human Experience: The Existential Dilemma

Despite its critical nature, time is a relatively unexplored dimension in the practice of psychotherapy. Only quite recently have such topics as suicide and thanatos, inseparably adjoined to the meaning of time and purpose in human experience, been forced upon the attention of the mental health practitioner. Concerns about suicide, death, and nonbeing reveal quite baldly the irreducible condition of human existence which therapist and patient share in common. Our time is limited—the past cannot be held onto without cost to our present and our future. Nonetheless, each of us quite habitually tends to deny the reality of time in his own existence. The crux of our existential dilemma is that whereas the use and structuring of time is essential in seeking meaning in human existence, the fear of contaminating and dissipating our precious time by probing the dimensions of temporality has led to our pervasive disuse and denial of time. We tell ourselves that the present is neither ripe nor opportune—we are not presently ready to live fully or openly; tomorrow will be more expedient. Some of us may even say that our opportunities for happiness and fulfillment are already exhausted. In more critical moments, we are faced with the realization that only the present is immediate and real. If we question our right to utilize and live fully in the present, for even an instant, that moment—its potentialities and opportunities—is lost forever. Without appreciating the meaning of time in human existence, our attempts at a meaningful definition of ourselves as finite, purpose-seeking beings are doomed to futility. To ignore the individual's phenomenological experience of time, that is, how he uses and structures his existence, is to deal with artifacts of human existence, oblique to the mercurial uncertainty of "lived" existence. These notions should enable us to recognize that guilt, integrally related to the failure to find meaning for persons afflicted with ontological malaise, involves the individual's sense of failure in living up to his own human potential. Conventional practitioners frequently are unconcerned with the existential source of guilt, treating guilt instead as the patient's experienced residue of forbidden thoughts and urges. The pangs of existential guilt cannot be ignored in a viable therapeutic endeavor for they hold fast to the individual's intentionality. An individual's purpose and meaning are predicated upon his use and structuring of time. The question of human purpose is only meaningful to an existent—someone who is finite and will someday cease to be. Consequently, an individual gains purpose by seriously grappling with his finiteness and his mortality (11).

Role-Modeling

To enable the participants to become personally involved in an encounter experience, it is necessary that I, too, become ego-involved and model the processes I am seeking to evoke during the encounter experience. During the encounter, I will try to get in touch with and articulate the personal meaning of time within my own life and in my therapeutic practice. I have come to recognize that however I behave in an encounter, my behavior is intended to deal with my own anxiety. Such behavior is not necessarily counterindicated. All of us act in ways intended to avert our anxiety and maximize our comfort. It is not that I am trying to avert my own anxiety that is important, but that I realize that it is I who am uneasy and that it is I who strives to become more comfortable (8).

Early in the encounter I plan to discuss my own involvement in time-binding collusion with the participants in order to alert them to my possible collusion with their own resistive patterns. I have come to realize that unless I avoid colluding with a patient in guaranteeing him a future as a patient, therapy will never begin—for both of us will fuse in the magical notion of acting as if that which is not born cannot die. This consideration has serious implications for the encounter group. I realize that my levels of comfort and anxiety as a facilitator shape in large part whether or not a meaningful encounter ever begins and how long it will be tolerated by me. I must not overlook or deny my own needs in how I conduct the group, but rather employ them purposively as hallmarks of my own intentionality, that which is uniquely me (8).

That which I enact in my encounter with another in an encounter group is not simply a professional role—which I can conveniently turn on and off. That aspect of my being enacted in my encounter with another in distress and struggle is an integral part of my personality. But at the same time it is an aspect of my personality that is *time-limited*. I have come to realize that I cannot maintain the requirements of the role of facilitator for long and highly concentrated periods of time. Time has meaning for me in a group because time brings into startling immediacy my own finiteness. Time forces me to maintain an aspect of my personality that causes me tension and strain. The encounter group, more than the conventional 45- and 90-minute therapy sessions, forces me to extend the boundaries of my ego-often beyond a point at which I remain comfortable. Time therefore vexes my narcissistic and irrational conceptions of myself, forcing me to feel my finitude (13).

Personal Preparation of the Encounter Practitioner

Not knowing who the participants are who will attend the encounter, I cannot at this juncture of my encounter preparation develop a working plan directed at the particular needs of each participant. Indeed, the only person attending the encounter for whom I have access to personal data is myself. In my preparation for the weekend, I experience a need to concentrate on my own being-in-the-world. I consider the concerns and issues I am currently working on in my own life. I explore how well I am doing with these issues, to assess what my pressing needs are and the impediments in my making progress with these concerns. These subjective data inform me of what may interfere with my effectiveness as a facilitator for others during the encounter weekend. Following this reflection, I interpolate my personal concerns with what I am struggling with as a practitioner. To avoid being overly didactic and detached in the encounter, I must cast aside for the time being that which I have already figured out about neurosis and human nature. I realize that my preconceived formulations and firm convictions about my work will issue forth more quickly than is necessary when I become uncomfortable during an encounter. To be most in touch with the struggle of the people with whom I will be working, I am aware that I must stay as persistently as I can with my own dissatisfactions and unfinished work.

This brings me to the issue of the *disclosed presence* of the encounter practitioner. As a psychotherapy supervisor and educator, I find that most of the practitioners I know are caring and socially concerned people. In contrast, I find that many of these practitioners lack a clear idea of their own values and have a perfunctory awareness of the effect their conduct has on the people with whom they work. These practitioners are best able to deal with specific issues and concerns as they are brought up in sessions by their patients, but they demonstrate a befuddling myopia as to what working on these issues will bring them and their patients.

In my view, it is not enough for a therapist to be there for a participant in an encounter without some accentuated awareness of how he wants and is prepared to be there for the participant. *The practitioner must stand for something.* He must represent and embody some values. His presence must offer meaning to their encounter together or else the participant will be left alone to find meaning in the presence of another who is denying his own values and struggles for meaning (15). My values need to be enacted in my being-in-the-world with a participant. To make informed choices, the person with whom I am working requires honest and relevant information about how I am experiencing him. It is not enough for me to "understand" and "care" for another in an encounter. I must express my concerns in a manner in which they can be perceived and deeply felt. A therapist who knows what is wrong with a patient, psychodynamically, but is unable to foster a relationship with him, cannot meaningfully influence the patient.

"Since existence is a process, man cannot really understand himself once and for all time, only from moment to moment" (20). When "experiencing freely," I tend to experience the encounter situation more emotionally than when feeling comfortable. I experience choking up, giddiness, irritation, anxiety, sensuality, and other emotional reactions which my more clinical and "professional" formulations and notions of certainty of what I should be attending to in a therapeutic encounter apperceptively filter out. It is only from an immediate and continuing commitment to the real possibility of a relationship with the person with whom I am involved in an encounter, which is not bracketed off by oaths of conduct and statements of clinical interest and responsibility for the other (rather than responsibility for my own intentionality), that I am aware of a deep sadness and personal loss from our separation in the world. The closer we come together, the more we are aware of our separation. The more we get in touch with that ultimate estrangement, the more we can appreciate what we are currently sharing together and the preciousness of the present moment. In the enduring of a risky ordeal experienced together, people come to truly know one another and develop, as a result, a genuine liking and respect for one another. At the moment at which we lose the sense of certainty and security of theoretical and clinical procedure, so that we can no longer predict the outcome of our being together, the possibility of a meaningful encounter lies before us. It is the degree to which the participant senses that the practitioner, as enacted in his relationship with him, is willing and able to negotiate how the participant is to be regarded and treated that both agents within an encounter can cast aside reactive fears and the need for safety and each can accommodate himself to the other; in so doing, each explores their interpersonal situation, coming to experience himself and the other with increased meaningfulness.

The journey into self requires the presence of another. We come to know ourselves through the other. The journey in quest of meaning is, in my view, most productive in a setting in which each agent seeks an increased awareness of his own identity (14). For many practitioners, unfortunately, the exploration of the practitioner's being-in-the-world within the encounter is an unconscionable endeavor, as if the practitioner were without existential anxiety and concern that might be decisively shaping the encounter. Denying one's own identity becomes entrenched in many practitioners. We have been led to believe that a practitioner should not want anything for himself other than to be fairly remunerated. He should only be there to deal with the patient's concern. Issues of existential concern are denied in a setting in which the therapist suppresses his own intentionality.

Location: The Scenic Respite

The encounter weekend will be held at Dr. Daniels' scenic and isolated country lodge on a mountain top in rural Virginia. I muse about the serenity and beauty of these environs which I have once visited. I feel warmed by the prospect of sharing the personal, intimate concerns of a presumably very bright and creative group of people. I contrast this setting with the now monotonous decor of my psychotherapy office, where I have experienced the same patients almost daily—some for a number of years. I contrast the encounter weekend to the daily struggles for gains in my therapeutic practice. I fantasize that the weekend group will unfold smoothly, almost poetically. I know from experience, however, that my musing is more wish than reality.

The struggle to find out where I am, prior to convening a group, is an endeavor I attempt in planning my therapeutic groups as well. There is a subtle but important difference, however. In planning a therapeutic group I don't have the psychological luxury of staying just where I am. I am too aware from the onset of who the patients in the group will be and their pressing concerns.

Encounter: An Ongoing Existential Saga

I do not conceive of the encounter group as an isolated moment in time, divorced from the ongoing existence of each of the participants, as many encounter practitioners appear to view the experience. Or why else would these practitioners be unconcerned about historical information about the participants with whom they work? I view each participant's behavior at any moment in the group as part of a process. Each behavioral event needs to be understood within the context of what has gone on before and what direction present behavioral patterns portend for the next moment. Behavioral events within the encounter cannot meaningfully be explained as discrete and independent events. For each participant in an encounter group there is a plot, as in a theatrical drama (1). Working out this plot requires the cooperation of the other group members, who serve as co-actors with each participant, who represents himself as a protagonist. In developing his plot, each participant, as protagonist, reveals character attributes. The manner in which protagonist, group leader, and the other participants blend the unique strengths and limitations of the protagonist's character to his human condition determines the therapeutic success of the encounter experience for each participant (10).

Contemporary group therapists did not, of course, invent the drama theme as a modality for working out the human condition of the individual in quest of meaning for his existence. Playwrights and novelists throughout the ages have been concerned with drama as an arena for the struggle of reshaping the human condition (3). In Sophocles' plays the protagonist is asked to come to terms with his character flaws in interface with the chorus, which represents the attitudes and sentiments of the community. Sophocles, perhaps more successfully than Shakespeare, realized that the protagonist's tragic dilemma could not be fruitfully borne through solitary struggle with his own intrapsychic processes, or even in dialogue with his deity. Parenthetically, this may be one reason why Shakespeare's tragic heroes—Hamlet, Macbeth, Othello, and Lear—are forced to collude with external forces in their own self-destruction. Sophocles' protagonists, on the other hand, appear to find meaning in their fate (10).

Sophocles' existential arena is an encounter modality. He realized that the protagonist must come to terms with the values and sentiments of the *modus vivendi* in which his human condition is situated to make his struggle meaningful. In this respect, a person may be regarded as acting irresponsibly—that is, disregarding his ontological responsibility—to the extent that he fails to question his socially induced roles and the sanctions that reinforce adherence to role demands and expectations. No individual can develop a durable value system and philosophy of life without coming to terms with the values and norms of the groups in which he holds membership and to which he has reference, as well as appreciating the effects these incentives have upon others with whom he is involved. The agendaless, simple structure of the encounter group, in contrast to the well-ordered structure of everyday life, enables participants in an encounter group to come to grips with their deep-seated reasons for coming together with other people (3, 8).

Existential Concerns in an Encounter

During an encounter experience, I focus on the existential concerns being revealed or denied by the participants. *Existential concerns* are attempts by those involved in an encounter, by means of dialogue, inquiry, and interaction, to explore whether the behavior and sentiments being enacted in the encounter are in keeping with the understanding and agreement of the agents involved as to why they have come together and what they seek to derive from being together. If these dialogues and interactions fail to elicit the goals and ways of being together each of the agents seek, such conduct begs the question of a *therapeutic encounter*. According to my view, a therapeutic encounter is an endeavor that seeks to broaden the participants' willingness and ability to make informed choices in the conduct of their existence (15).

The collaborative interface of protagonist and chorus in a therapeutic encounter requires an understanding of the history of the protagonist in such a way that the other members of the encounter group are enabled to participate meaningfully in the protagonist's ongoing and proactive saga. To know a person, I must know from whence he came. I am concerned with where each of the participants is in his own psychological development at that moment in which we will encounter each other in the group. I am interested in the previous therapeutic experience he may have had, as well as the educational endeavors in which he has been involved. This information forms the basis for appreciating the kinds of psychosocial interventions and learning endeavors that have succeeded and those that have failed in each participant's saga. Concomitantly, this information provides data on the skills each participant will bring to the encounter. Whereas I am concerned with each participant's history, I am even more interested in his proactive saga. I believe, as do many encounter practitioners, that an individual's hopes for the future—his future projection—shapes his present view of himself as much or more than does what has gone on in the past. I am therefore concerned with how the participant has prepared himself to achieve his specific long-range and immediate goals in terms of present and future object relations. Without these data, I cannot responsibily decide whether I and the encounter weekend can be helpful for any individual who may wish to participate in an encounter group. I would not want to have a person convene with the group and sometime during the encounter weekend have him painfully discover that this group is not the place he needs or where he wants to be.

The conditions surrounding many encounter groups make it difficult to envision the goals for the participants in accordance with the needs of each. Nonetheless, I will not take this easy repudiation of clinical procedure. My therapeutic responsibility requires that prior to convening a group I be aware of the participants' goals and formulate a methodology to address these goals. Having some definitive ideas about the participants' goals, I will be able to explore the kinds of group experience necessary to implement these goals and the risks and probabilities for success—based on my resources and limitations, as well as those of the participants. It is therefore necessary to meet with Dr. Daniels prior to convening the encounter weekend and discuss with him each of the participants.

The information I obtain prior to a face-to-face interchange I regard as preliminary data. This consists of the implicit contract the participant will be bringing to the encounter (as I understand his contract at this time). Consequently, I cannot be a responsive facilitator until a participant is enabled to make *explicit* his contract with me and the other participants. I need to know what the participant is seeking, rather than what I believe he should be seeking. Articulation of the participant's covert agenda—his assumptions, expectations, and demands about what is going to take place during the weekend—permits his hopes and fears to become public and accessible to open negotiation among the participants and myself to establish a productive modality in which to work (9).

As in Greek drama, it is the presence of other group members as community representatives that renders an encounter-group member an inherently real and meaningful opportunity to come to terms with the values and norms of the groups in which he holds membership. The representation of society in an encounter, however, is not alone a reflection of the meaningfulness of the situation. This requires an intimate understanding of the protagonist as a unique individual. The tacit assumption that all men require the same qualities of living, in the same quantity and in the same fashion, which is underscored in many encounter groups is antithetical to this understanding (10). It is my understanding that the considerations and concerns I have expressed about acquiring prior knowledge of the participants' existential saga would be regarded as unnecessarily conservative by many encounter practitioners. As I gather from the presentations of other encounter practitioners, they require no prior information about the people with whom they work in conducting an encounter group. Practitioners like Schutz (29) and Shepard (30), who have undaunted confidence in themselves, seem to believe that they can work successfully with anyone who has the "smarts" to find his way into an encounter group. These practitioners would appear to have little or no concern for the specificity of the participant's psychological needs (35). They begin their "treatment" of the participants without initially educing what brought them to the encounter, and what the participants want and expect for themselves during the weekend (2).

Those Who Come to be "Encountered"

It should be apparent that the motivation of persons joining encounter groups may vary considerably. Some participants may be making a sincere effort to find out what they are "all about," others seek an intimate but, nonetheless, time-limited emotional adventure. Many participants regard an encounter group as an inexpensive substitute for psychotherapy, or a vehicle for getting attention for their disabilities, while at the same time denying the seriousness of their difficulties; still other participants recognize the encounter group as an opportunity to get intimately acquainted rather quickly with persons of the opposite or same sex (depending on how they "swing"). Also in attendance (of the greatest concern to me) are a considerable number of participants who feel compelled to attend because of subtle or clear directives from their employer or sometimes from their spouse (4).

Operating from a blithe ignorance of the participants' motives, many encounter practitioners inform the participants, who are strangers to them, that whereas the participants have the opportunity to try out new kinds of behaviors in the encounter, they are on their own in dealing with these new experiences.

> If you want to resist instructions or group pressure, that is up to you. If you want to bow to pressure, it's your decision. If you want to be physically injured or go crazy, that, too, is up to you. You are responsible for yourself [29, (p. 131].

It would appear that encounter practitioners, like Schutz and Shepard, who use the encounter group as a platform for espousing abstract social and political ideologies, have neither the time nor the inclination to come to grips with the real concerns of the people with whom they are working. Lieberman and his associates (21) report that encounter practitioners whose style is characterized by high aggressiveness and high charisma are particularly insensitive in identifying casualties in their own encounter groups. Indeed, they frequently indicated that the participants the investigators reported as casualties have profited considerably from the encounter experience (p. 176). The important question for me is whether the encounter practitioner is the participant's agent (which a participant might assume in paying a fee) or the agent of his own social and political philosophy.

The concerns raised here require some consideration of the composition of participants that I find most productive for an encounter experience.

The Size and Composition of an Encounter Group

I generally prefer to work with eight to 12 participants in a weekend encounter group. I want a group that is large enough so that no one feels compelled to interact or speak, and small enough so that no one needs to have to wait their turn to be heard. The group, in short, should be of such size and composition that interactions can freely and spontaneously ensue. An encounter group works best for me when the membership is heterogeneous. Variance in the background of the participants insures that the participants will attend to the exploration of current group tensions and concerns. A group composed of participants with similar vocational and personal interests frequently spends considerable time and energy in banal chatter about what they have in common outside the group. This serves to reinforce existing behavioral patterns. Under these conditions, the participants avoid exploring concerns influencing their present group behavior. In heterogeneous groupings, on the other hand, participants rarely tolerate participants who pursue issues that fall beyond the pale of the present group situation, for these are issues of concern to only a few participants. In this configuration, the participants are more amenable to exploration of the present group situation because it, not extragroup situations, is what the participants have in common. An encounter group begins to seriously work together as an ensemble the moment participants become aware of common feelings rather than common experiences (8).

Variance in psychological maturity is also salient in the unfolding of viable encounter experience. But, more than in a therapeutic group, a fair degree of psychological maturity is required for a participant to profit from an encounter weekend. I have found that to benefit from a therapeutic group experience a person requires a fair degree of insight and analytic reasoning skill and a willingness to be accountable for his own behavior. An additional factor must be taken into consideration. The majority of participants who dropped out of the encounter groups investigated by Lieberman and his associates (21) were found to be persons "who are highly conflictual about aggression, who are fearful of the expression of anger, who do not feel that it is important to express anger or to confront others directly" (p. 209). Participants must therefore have sufficient ego strength to form a relationship with several other persons in which the participant can tolerate critical scrutiny of himself and be willing to disclose his painful, threatening, as were as tender and compassionate concerns to others.

Once having discussed with Dr. Daniels the participants who we have mutually agreed may profit from an encounter experience, I enter into the ephemeral dimension of encounter-group planning. The *ephemeral* aspect of a group relates to issues groups raise about the participant's and group leader's relationship. In planning an encounter weekend, I am concerned with issues encounter groups raise about the participants' ("inalienable") right to know what kinds of treatment they are being subjected to, the risks involved, and the roles and responsibilities I, as an encounter practitioner, am willing to assume in the encounter experience. The terms under which the participants and I enter into a relationship to achieve some specifiable goals must be open to rational and mutual negotiation (2).

Encounter as an Influence Process

It is the nature of human interaction that people try to influence one another. Many of these endeavors are conducted in such a way that people can choose whether or not they will be influenced. In many other instances, however, people have little or no choice about the nature and the impact of how others will try to influence them. All forms of psychotherapy, group training, and education are special cases of the more general category of influence. How people are influenced by one another is determined by the implicit and explicit agreement in their relationship. It does not matter, therefore, whether an encounter-group experience is referred to as "treatment," "group training, " or "education" *as long as* the persons involved are cognizant that it is their explicit and implicit agreement as to what roles and responsibilities the group leader and the participants are willing to assume that determines what will take place in an encounter group.

For the participants to understand what kinds of treatment they may be subjected to, what risks are involved, and the probabilities for success, the participants need some appreciation of the conditions in a group that produce psychological risk and how these risks may be reduced.[1]

This raises the very important issue of *contract negotiation.*   The encounter practitioner, in addition to group-dynamic and psychotherapeutic skills, must have the ability to effectively negotiate a *working contract* with the participants. Working parameters must be made explicit for utilizing the encounter experience as a *designed, experiential learning situation* in which roles, responsibilities, skills, and procedures for working together as a group are specified (16, 17). Without a clear set of objectives as to what constitutes appropriate task behavior and what constitutes resistance, statements about "irresponsible" behavior in the group are merely subjective value judgments on the part of the encounter leader and the other group members. Critical evaluation and attempts to deal with dissatisfactions are difficult to render effectively without clarity about what each of the participants seeks and how he conceptualizes the means of achieving these ends during the weekend. Consequently, in reaction to what I regard as an attitude of irresponsibility among encounter practitioners in whose workshops and groups I myself have participated, the group leader and the participants in a viable encounter experience need to concern themselves with a realistic assessment of the nature of a relationship in a time-limited experience (2). They need to consider what can be realistically accomplished in a two-day group: the nature of disclosure and the extent of intimacy that is reasonable or desirable to permit oneself with people with whom a relationship may not extend beyond the bounds of the weekend, or, indeed, may extend to situations in which knowledge of one another's intrapsychic struggles is experienced by one or the other as highly threatening (16).

In my view, for an encounter experience to be a viable therapeutic endeavor (call it "growth," "influence," or "education," if you prefer), the encounter practitioner needs to respect his contract with the participants in terms of what they have agreed to do and not to do. He needs to suppress his own urges to use the group as a "political" arena. Too frequently encounter leaders operate from abstract theories of social order. By procrustean manipulation, they shape the participants to match the group leader's requirements. Along these lines, it has been suggested that the encounter culture has launched a campaign to exorcise the superego of modern man (31). Sometimes skillfully, often unwittingly, core values and attitudes society has deemed essential to a regulated society are being reshaped, cavalierly disregarded, or brutally removed by means of group pressure and identification with the "guilt-liberated" group leader. This subtle form of societal change doesn't appear to work. Ignorant of the literature, these group practitioners are unaware that public compliance does not in and of itself lead to internalized behavioral change. I suspect that many of the practitioners associated with the encounter movement are unaware of what others in the encounter field and those in the more established group practices have tried to do with groups and the results of these endeavors (2).

Instead of operating from a sound conceptual base, many encounter practitioners rely entirely on "gut" feelings. "I know I am a good leader," said one, "because I have a 'gut' feeling for people" (4). Such encounter leaders believe that their most significant contribution to ameliorative endeavors is their intuitive sense of knowing *when* a technique or structured exercise is required, *which* technique is best indicated, and *how* to effectively engineer the technique. In an encounter experience I anticipate that the participants expect I will bring to the group a wide assortment of structured exercises and techniques to bear upon difficult moments in the encounter-to break through impasse and resistance. This brings into consideration the issue of social technology. According to Leiberman and his associates, "incorrect technology" was the fundamental problem in the encounter groups investigated (p. 451).

The Social Technology of Encounter Therapy

It seems to me that despite the lip service both psychotherapists and encounter practitioners give to the notion of behavioral change, people come to a therapeutic situation not to be made different, not to be compelled or taught how to act differently, but to become more accepting of what they already are. My clinical and encounter experience suggests that an individual does not "change" dysfunctional aspects of himself until he comes to *accept and understand himself as he is*. To do otherwise he would unpropitiously expend his energy in denying and defending against what he is. I have become skeptical about pervasive personality changes as the result of a single experience—no matter how intensive the encounter might be! I have come to realize that people "change" when they are ready to change. This, of course, does not imply that behavioral change is an endeavor inimical to conscious effort or external facilitation. It does suggest, however, that efforts at behavioral change evoked (or compelled) during an encounter experience may be premature and lack durability. This contention seems strongly confirmed by Lieberman and his associates' study.

There appears to be a definite developmental progression to psychological growth (Freud's libido theory and Erikson's identity crises are but two theoretical delineations of this idea). Each developmental step requires a well-timed and relevant response from significant others in the interpersonal field of the individual in the throes of change. An effective encounter practitioner takes into account the participant's pattern of growth, as well as his style of resistance. He respects both the participant's right to proceed at his own pace, or to remain as he is, if that is his professed wish (2).

In obviating these ethical and therapeutic considerations, encounter practitioners frequently circumvent problems of resistance by simply ignoring them or getting the participant involved in a nonverbal exercise. They seem to feel that if they can get the participants to put their feelings into action, then there is no need to explore these feelings cognitively. Frequently, in these groups, once emotion is expressed, it is dropped. There is no endeavor to explain the meaning of these feelings. These group leaders' objective is apparently to induce the participants to express emotion but not to learn what the emotion is all about, or to attain a sense of mastery over these feelings (2). What these practitioners fail to realize is that experience remains largely unconscious and inaccessible to rational action unless the opportunity for cognitive processing is available. It is understandable then that the assumptions made by the encounter practitioners investigated by Lieberman et al. concerning the importance of structured exercises and other action-oriented interventions in influencing desired behavioral change in participants were not substantiated. The "high learners" in Lieberman's study reported significantly more incidents involving the presence of insight and the reception of cognitive information than other types of group events.

I am not overly concerned with exercises and techniques. Techniques, as I have tried to indicate, are meaningless without some understanding of what is going on in the encounter. The utilization of a technique presumes the knowledge of a goal. Before suggesting exercises in a group, I need the opportunity to observe and interact with participants. I am concerned with such considerations as where each of the participants is at any point in time: What are their unexpressed needs? Where are the participants as a group? What are the normative conditions and the collusive hopes and fears of the participants at this moment in time and how are these factors shaping behavioral events in the group? And, most importantly, where am I, as facilitator, in the group? How am I involved? How am I colluding with the participants in avoiding some of the meaningfulness of the encounter for each of the protagonists? To know this I must ascertain what I am anxious about and have been avoiding (10).

Only at the moment in which I get in touch with these dynamic and therapeutic concerns can I judiciously decide where to go in the group. By knowing what my contract is with each of the participants as protagonists—derived from an awareness and an agreement of how we will collaborate as authors of specific plots in their personal saga—and from an awareness of what is impeding progress at that particular moment in the encounter, I sense what needs to be done to redirect our efforts. By utilizing myself as a trained, sensitive, and responsive conductor, I sense at what moment to: (a) help induce a climate in the group in which trust and sincerity are experienced by the participants as both possible and desired; (b) not intervene in the process, for example, let the group stay with a difficult silence; (c) encourage fantasy material and associations to release repressed data; (d) induce rational discussion to cognitively process material; (e) use statements and interpretative interventions to describe the dynamics of the situation, permitting the participants to process the material as they will; (f) encourage interactions among the participants and/or participate myself in interactions with others in the group, to provide relational possibilities in the group; or (g) take an active and directive role in the group and suggest behavioral actions and involve participants in nonverbal and other structured exercises to facilitate awareness of material being avoided.

Encounter practitioners have been particularly fecund in developing group exercises to provide participants with the opportunity to experience salient interpersonal processes which may require a long development in conventional psychotherapy. In my view, however, the ethos of these techniques emphasizes individual assertion, regarding inclination toward social responsibility as a neurotic manifestation. Lieberman and his colleagues (21) found that the potency of structured exercises as a form of leader intervention was not particularly impressive. They believe that the effects of structured exercises are transitory because the participants do not experience what happens in the encounter group as a product of their own endeavors (p. 419). Consequently, the most important structured exercises or "simulated situations" (as I prefer to call them) would appear to me to be those that enable each of the participants to master skills enabling each to come to terms with their human condition by means of an interpersonally cooperative endeavor. The simulated situations I will be discussing are designed to get the participants in touch with their own and their fellow participants' loneliness and despair, to address the conditions that present themselves in an encounter group in which the participants take each other seriously, rather than regarding their concerns about one another as neurotic manifestations (12).

Simulated Existential Situations

All systems of psychotherapy and psychosocial education seem to share the aim of increasing the client's choice in the conduct of his life. Each person has a choice of how much of himself he is willing to experience deeply. Experiencing the deeper recess of oneself is frequently painful, as it reveals unbuttressed the loneliness and dread our ontological responsibility evokes in a world of uncertainty. The defenses we erect provide a respite from ontological pain inasmuch as the probe of our deeper existential concerns is averted. *Man's basic choice is one of choosing how he wishes to experience his life* (8).

I have developed several simulated situations which I have utilized in groups to explore the choices described above. The first of these is called the *Lifeboat Situation.* In this exercise I am interested in enabling the participant to become more aware of how he uses or avoids himself and others in facing the immediacy of his situation in the world. The second simulated situation is referred to as the *Epitaph Exercise.* This exercise gives the participant an opportunity to review his values and intentions and the extent to which these sentiments have been actualized. The *Except For! Exercise* is integrally linked to this review. In this exercise the participant has the opportunity to explicitly spell out those situational demands he has tacitly responded to over such a long period of time that they have become an entrenched attitudinal stance. The final simulation situation I will discuss is called the *Potlatch Exercise.* This exercise seeks to uncover those character traits and personality attributes the participant employs to avert probing his existential concerns. As there is not sufficient space to describe these exercises in detail, only the Lifeboat Situation will be discussed. For a detailed description of all the exercises mentioned above, the reader is referred to my other writings (11, 12, 15).

In the Lifeboat Situation the participants are told:

> In keeping with the notion that only the present is immediate and real, I would like each of you as best you can to consider as immediate and real the following situation: You and the people in your group are in a lifeboat in the middle of the Atlantic Ocean, far off from the shore and without any real hope for immediate rescue. You find that the boat is springing water. There is too much weight in the boat. Someone has to be dropped overboard. There is no way to avoid this problem, so please don't spend your time planning ways to avert this dilemma! You have 30 minutes to handle this immediate situation.

I try to discourage any "solutions" to avoid or deny the "reality" of the Lifeboat Situation. Nonetheless, the participants invariably first view the Lifeboat Situation with amusement and intellectual excitement. Participants inevitably spend the first moments in the situation planning ways to avoid having to consciously struggle with what their life means to them and whether or not they wish to fight for or justify their existence in the presence of other persons also struggling with the meaning of their existence. Each of us, in our own way, tries to escape the awesome responsibility of our creative and destructive powers (8). Intellectual solutions having failed or been discouraged, the feelings elicited in the Lifeboat Situation become emotionally heavy, similar in some respects to a long-term psychotherapy group at work.

Near the end of the 30 minutes the participants were given for their task, I tell them:

> Apparently a serious error has been made! The boat is taking in water at a rapid rate. It appears that only *one* person in the lifeboat can be saved. You have 15 minutes to handle this situation.

At the end of the 15 minutes, I move the participants out of the lifeboat and encourage a discussion in terms of the following questions:

1. Were any of you actually able to get yourself into the situation and experience the situation as immediate and real?
2. What was the situation like for you?
3. How did you experience yourself?
4. What did you learn about yourself?
5. What values and meanings did you get in touch with in this experience?

The Lifeboat Situation reveals that human meaning and purpose cannot be separated from interpersonal encounter. As Haigh (19) notes, "The search for interpersonal encounter is a central human quest. Perhaps the most pressing existential crisis of our age is the pervasive sense of aloneness which so many of us feel so much of the time."

Although man is born in aloneness, his ontological responsibility does not require separation from others. Indeed, separation from human company makes man's ontological responsibility more difficult as a process, unrewarding as an experience, and a meaningless exercise as an ethical concern. A man's separation from his fellows makes the ethical concerns of his life unknowable to others. Man may best choose what he intends to be by making himself known to others. G.H. Meade, several decades ago, brilliantly described man's need for the mediation of another's perspective in order to participate consciously in his own choice. Disclosing is vital because in the act of disclosing himself to another man makes his intentions known to himself as well. Correspondingly, man permits himself to become that which he does not intend to be through passive collusion with others. When man withholds himself from others, others, in experiencing him and trying to make meaning of their experience, define him as they will rather than as he who is being defined seeks to be known. Man is defined by his own actions. He is defined by others to the extent that he remains passive and undisclosed (8).

The simulated situations described above are designed to enable the encounter participant to get in touch with the "immediacy" of his "lived" existence by helping him pursue the following concerns: (1) What am I actually experiencing?

(2) What does the experience mean in terms of the person I intend to become—that is, what is the relation of my experience to my own core values? (3) What fears and conditions are interfering with my experiencing my existence directly? (4) How can I re-experience my experience, bringing my experiences into fuller awareness—that is, what experiments, exercises, and ways of being will help me complete my experiences? (5) Having re-experienced and completed my experiences I should have a more lucid conception of who I am—how do I put these values into action?

Simulated situations are, of course, no more the most propitious modality for addressing existential concerns in an encounter experience than are any other of the various possible interventions at the purveyance of a well-trained encounter practitioner. Each type of intervention has its judicious time and place. An encounter practitioner becomes skilled when he has learned to temper his knowledge of technique and theory with intuition and interpersonal sensitivity. In my encounter practice, exercises involving some psychological risk for participants are generally confined to the involvement of no more than two or three participants at a time. This gives me the opportunity to evaluate whether each of the participants is willing to be involved, how he needs to be involved, how he is prepared to be involved, and finally, how he experiences the exercise. When I suggest exercises that involve several participants, if not the entire group, these techniques are generally psychologically supportive, rather than involving risk for the participants.

Encounter as Psychosocial Education

Discussion of technology to deal with resistive behavioral patterns in an encounter group raises for me the issue of psychosocial education.

Analysis of resistance and transference is not sufficient to inform participants in an encounter group of their task responsibility. The same holds true for psychotherapy. My experience in both psychotherapy and encounter groups has led me to believe that participants work more profitably when they are educated about therapeutic work. They require clear orientation about productive therapeutic roles and behaviors, as studies of preparing patients for psychotherapy have indicated (32, 33). I find it fatuous to relegate all rational concerns about the treatment process as intellectualization and requests from patients for expected psychotherapeutic behavior as passive-dependent resistance. I have been increasingly impressed that much of what practitioners frequently regard as resistance is simply the patient's ignorance of therapeutic behavior, as well as a legitimate reaction to inconsistent and nondirective approaches. We are clearly aware that therapists cannot avoid imposing their values in their work. Nondirective approaches are therefore contradictory. Rather than trying to remain neutral, we need to reinforce the therapeutic and facilitative responses patients elicit in order to help shape therapeutically productive postures (10).

Encounter-group experiences are time-limited. The concern for efficacious technology is perhaps more accentuated in an enounter group than it is in long-term therapeutic groups. In my experience, behavioral patterns and improved psychosocial functioning may be profitably taught in an encounter experience, provided that the social technology is predicated on conversance with the needs and goals of each participant involved in the endeavor.

The encounter movement, despite a wide variation in origins,[2] is based upon two rather divergent ontological notions. Indeed, one of the most impressive things about practitioners of encounter therapy is their willingness to borrow theory, method, and techniques freely. In so doing, they have not been as conscientious as we might like in specifying the ontological concepts and rationale behind the techniques they employ. Neither of the two ontological notions upon which encounter technology is based, while having serious consequences for encounter practice, has been sufficiently differentiated from the other.

The first ontological approach is primarily concerned with teaching *social technology* that will effect lasting changes in the participant's interpersonal skill and functioning after he leaves the encounter experience. The second ontological approach is an appeal to *deep emotional needs* that have been unsatisfied during the participant's tender years. Conventional psychotherapies have, in my view, failed to adequately address these two significant areas of psychological concern.

The techniques I categorize as falling within the social-technology approach focus upon such skills as learning to read metacommunications; being aware of one's own body language and that of others; fighting fairly by setting up rational rules; ceasing to impose unrealistic demands on oneself and others by checking one's irrational attitudes against psychological lists constructed, for example, by rational-emotive practitioners; and learning to interpret one's own life script and those of others by being aware of the games described by transactional-analysis practitioners. Each of these techniques is based on the assumption that there is an available model for improved interpersonal functioning. Interactive-skill training and learning how to learn in an interpersonal setting teach the participant the required steps in assuming leadership functions in the family and other natural groupings. This is an example of what Miller (24) has referred to as "giving away psychology": changing people through education rather than therapeutic practice. Consequently, a salient characteristic of this approach is the assumption that understanding and skill in human relations can be taught. The emphasis is not on changing the psychodynamics of the participants, but on *teaching* participants to use therapeutic, psychological, and educational concepts and principles in order to have greater influence in affecting situations outside of the group.

The second approach appears to be an answer to what the transactional-analysis practitioners have referred to as the "Child ego state." The emphasis is on deeply felt emotional experience generated within the group situation. In psychodynamic therapy, the emphasis appears to be on diluting and more manageably reintroducing the psychological states originally experienced as traumatic by the patient. In the new group approaches, the attempt appears to be to induce sudden and complete diminution of defenses against instinctual urges formulated at the patient's preverbal level of functioning. The result is that the originally traumatic events are experienced again, directly and undiluted. But they are experienced, concomitantly, in the present, with the warmth and caring of the other group members rather than with the rejection or indifference of the original objects of the past. The primal scream, yelling, guided fantasies through childhood, and other such techniques attempt to create intensive emotional experience, as well as to circumvent impasse with resistive participants, with little or no cognitive processing of the experience.

Practitioners of both approaches must concern themselves with the style they wish to employ in having the participant experience new learning opportunities. These styles vary, of course, from "letting it happen" to "making it happen" (22). The practitioner in the second approach, although he may be rather active in the session, unlike the group leader in the first approach, tends to avoid taking responsibility for the learning experience. Group leaders in this position insist that they are not there to cure or to take care of participants. Instead, they are together with the participants in order to share a growth experience with them (8). Group leadership, as a result of the therapist's sharing responsibility with group members, tends to be egalitarian, rather than based on authority and expertise as in the psychodynamic or the first approach. Where the egalitarian notion is practiced, every group member, be he patient or therapist, is seen as one who heals and who is healed by others in the group. In these groups, there is stress on the group leader's openness, disclosure, and congruence of feeling rather than his withholding of strong affect. The group leader's role-modeling of self-disclosure is designed to encourage open communication among the group members. Feedback is accentuated in contrast to interpretation. Emphasis is on how a person is perceived by his peers and what he chooses to do about how others see him, rather than "what he is" and "why he became that way."

The emphasis on feedback transforms the issue of countertransference to a new level. How a patient fares in a group cannot be explained simply by a consideration of the pathology and psychodynamics of the participants in attendance. Examination must be directed to the role, style, and personality of the group leader (2). In the mental health field today there is increased awareness and attention to how group leaders subtly influence what happens in their groups (2). Taking this into account, many encounter group leaders regard the group members as powerful counteractors to countertransferential tendencies by the group leader (8). Those psychodynamic psychotherapists who emphasize the contamination of patient perceptions due to transference, projective identification, and other distortions are less apt to utilize this monitoring capacity by group members. Generally, encounter group leaders underscore the group members' capacity for offering a different, but no less valuable, perspective of process in the group from that of the group leader. '

In contrasting the two encounter-group approaches, it should be noted that the leadership and fellowship roles are more clearly defined in the social-technology approach than in the deep-emotional-needs approach. In the former, the group leader takes considerable responsibility for the learning experience. Modalities for peer interaction must be taught in this approach since knowledge of how to effectively function interpersonally is not assumed to be an instinctual or natural tendency. In the latter approach, the group leader presents himself as being responsible for himself and insists that group members are responsible for themselves. He encourages group members to act spontaneously and on "gut" feelings. This would suggest that the role model for assuming harmonious and satisfying functioning is obtained by experiencing oneself in different ways— by participating in awareness exercises, processing feedback from other group members, and trying to emulate behaviors the group leader models. Reliance upon verbal and nonactive interaction is viewed as ineffective or too slow (10).

Most encounter practitioners (most psychotherapists, for that matter) appear to emphasize one or the other of the two ontological approaches I have described. In maximizing available time in an encounter experience, I attend an even balance to each of these positions.

Having explored the technology of the encounter group, we need to consider those dynamics and processes in a group that the encounter practitioner focuses his interventions on in order to bring into the participants' awareness their own involvement in what is occurring in the group. There are in all groups a host of preconceived assumptions and expectations made by the participants about what should happen in an encounter group. The *subtle* aspects of an encounter group relate to how these predominantly unconscious notions become pooled and shared by the entire group membership, often in very subtle and obscure ways. It is on the basis of these unconscious notions that group members operate in rewarding and rejecting one another's behavior (2). To the extent that these unconscious notions about group behavior are shared by participants—either because of similar personal orientations or through social contagion—they are referred to as "common group tensions." These tensions are the shared, covert aspects of group process in which the needs and defenses of the group members are at odds with one another. The manifest content of group activity may embrace any conceivable issue, but regardless of the manifest content, there always rapidly develops an underlying group tension or emotion that the participants are unaware of, but which significantly influences their behavior. Common group tensions, if not brought to awareness, block participants from working effectively on the goals for which they have convened. In this endeavor, knowledge of the principles of body language are crucial to the practitioner's work with groups. Nonverbal signals often transmit powerful and urgent emotions from participant to participant, from group member to the group as a whole. One of the encounter practitioner's major tasks is to reveal these group tensions and delineate their meaning to the work of the participants. His task, then, is not to make the participants comfortable, to enable the participants as a group to make a decision, to minimize or to maximize conflict and tension. Participants in an encounter group require some appreciation of the uncertainty, frustration, anger, alienation, anxiety, and other intrapsychic discomfort they experience in the group and the roles, attitudes and defenses they evince in relation to these feelings (5).

In poorly conducted encounter groups, group tensions remain hidden agendas. This aversive condition leads to group regression and depersonalization of group members. If the goals the participants are seeking are impeded because of primitive emotions evoked in pursuing these goals, and the participants are unable to communicate these feelings to one another in an open manner, then frustration, anger, and social contagion break through with full fury.

Levels of Analysis in an Encounter Group

An in-depth investigation of a group may be seen as falling within three general approaches. The group leader may focus on the entire group as an entity. He may instead concentrate on a subgroup within the larger composite of the group. Or he may simply disregard the group as a configural reality and instead concern himself with each member of the group as an individual entity in a situation where other social objects are present (8). In conducting encounter groups, I do not maintain any of these three perspectives exclusively. My focus periodically shifts during the course of a group. It is incumbent upon the encounter practitioner to know when to appropriately work with one level of group analysis rather than another. During an encounter experience, I select exercises and techniques to elucidate dynamics and processes at each of these levels of group functioning.

I will illustrate this rationale in terms of an encounter-group workshop I conducted at the Fifth International Congress of Group Psychotherapy in Zurich a few years ago (16). I first sought to delineate how a togetherness situation, comprised of strangers, is transformed into a group situation in which participants are decisively interrelating. This was accomplished by asking for volunteers early in the workshop to move chairs and tables in order to create more space in which the participants could work. Delineation of nonverbal and symbolic expression of the participants' changing mood was utilized to contrast the climate of the group before and after this deceptively innocuous "warm-up" exercise. Following this warm-up, *milling* (8, pp. 194-196) was employed to demonstrate early group sociometric configuration, a reflection of the level of relatedness and the cohesion of the group as a whole. The *Magic Shop* (17) was employed later in the session to illustrate interpersonal contract negotiation among several members (a subgroup) of the group. Still later in the group the *Reflected-Image Technique*[3] was selected to elucidate repressed material and ego defenses of a participant who asked the group to help her make some behavioral changes. I suggested that before she tried to make psychodynamic changes she might wish to simply experience herself differently. This intervention reflects the intrapersonal level of group analysis.

The Problem of Re-entry

Intensive group experiences are short-lasting unless the issue of re-entry is built into the methodology. Encounter practitioners, even those with psychoanalytic backgrounds, seem to believe that the "working through" so integrally a part of psychodynamic therapy can be accomplished by the participant on his own in the period following the encounter experience. These optimistic practitioners seem to believe that if behavioral change is to occur, it will occur "now"—in the immediacy of the encounter session (28). This fundamental principle of encounter therapy is a marked departure from conventional psychotherapy. The circumvention of the problem of participant re-entry is, I believe, a major theoretical limitation and treatment problem of encounter therapy. The problem stems from several self-defeating, if not dubious, philosophical notions:

1. The world outside of the encounter movement is not a nice place. The encounter group is a nice, growful environment.
2. Psychotherapy is a microcosm of the world outside. Therefore, avoid psychotherapy and its conservative tenets.
3. Individual assertion is synonymous with personal responsibility. If an individual isn't getting what he wants, it is because he isn't assertive enough. If the other person becomes threatened by one's assertiveness, it is the other's problem because he needs encountering and isn't doing anything about it.

I , on the other hand, feel that in working in an encounter group with a participant's deep concerns about himself, rather than primarily focusing on group process and group training. I am involved in a psychotherapeutic endeavor. As an encounter practitioner, I am still a psychotherapist. I do not wish to help participants insulate themselves from the world outside of the encounter group, but to enable them to develop social and personal skills for coming cooperatively to terms with other people. To foster a social modality in which each participant may effectively review, experiment, or, if he chooses, modify and revise his personal strategies and core attitudes about himself and his existential condition, the climate and composition of the group must represent the realities of the society in which he is seeking to come to terms. A confrontation group in a Synanon program may, with some justification, "brutally" strip away the last remnants of defenses and reshape the participants' character to fulfill Synanon's ideal ethos. The goal of Synanon is to build a better self-contained subculture and not to return residents to the "addictive" society at large. On the other hand, for an Esalen-type group to do such reshaping for a weekend marathon is both unrealistic and dangerous (10). Encounter experience is a therapeutic experience, not a substitute for it. Paradoxically, overly "successful" encounter experience—where the group leader and fellow participants are too reasonable, too accepting, and too caring—creates an insulation of treatment, separating it from life. Why should a participant have to risk hurt again from objects in his daily existence who lack the caring, reasonable understanding of his group leader and fellow participants? Whereas severe anxiety and depression blot out time and annihilate the future in his everyday world, the proliferation of encounter experience (or psychotherapy, for that matter) guarantees the participant the security of a future as long as he continues to identify himself as in need of "encountering." Group-encounter leaders and participants alike slip too easily into role relationships in which the group leader and the other group members take on the functions and responsibilities the participant and his significant others in his daily world have been assuming or should be assuming (14).

This brings up the issue of an *application period* in concluding an encounter experience. I believe that it is neither responsible nor useful to leave pendulous serious concerns issuing from an encounter experience.

Encounter Application Period

I conclude the weekend with some exploration of how the processes that evolved during the encounter weekend can be applied to the participant's daily roles and functions. I view one of the major values of the encounter experience to be the inculcation of interpersonal knowledge, both on an affective and a cognitive level, with which the participants can effect mature working conditions in the daily membership groups they attend. Unless the encounter practitioner attempts to bridge the encounter experience with the participant's daily life, the value of an experiential group as a generalizable learning experience is lost. There are also concerns raised by the participants during the weekend that require continuing psychological attention. I make recommendations to these participants as to how they may follow up these concerns in working with Dr. Daniels.

CONCLUSIONS

In my view, when appropriately involved at its task, the encounter group, like the Greek chorus, enables each of its participants to understand his personal saga— his personal and interpersonal strategies, assumptions, expectations, wishes, hopes and fears—by which, as protagonist, he has attempted to live and, frequently, for which he has been ready to die. Once this preliminary work has begun, the chorus and the protagonist begin to revise the saga, to express it and act it out with greater authenticity, openness, and congruent awareness of the information and sentiment protagonist and chorus have shared together. The encounter practitioner may suggest techniques or provide behavioral models to facilitate resolution of areas of conflict or to develop skills that the protagonist and chorus have recognized as essential for becoming the person the protagonist seeks to become. The warmth and intimacy found in the best of encounter groups serve to reinforce the integration of the protagonist's new learning into his ongoing saga. The encouragement for developing intimate and satisfying relationships among the participants effectively serves this endeavor, provided that practitioner and participant keep clearly in mind that lasting satisfaction is derived from relationships in the community, not from exclusive encounter-group relationships that require hopping from one encounter group to the next. Within the presence of community representation in an encounter group, each protagonist's revised saga can be socially validated. The other encounter participants, as representatives of present and future relationships, provide the opportunity for each participant to struggle with, contract, and negotiate for the conditions he seeks. But only within the community, where the "patient" role cannot be evoked to provide false safety, can his saga be actualized (10).

NOTES

[1] Lieberman and his associates (21) found that of the 206 participants who started in the encounter groups studied, 7.8 percent of the total number of participants and 9.1 percent of those who attended one half or more of the group sessions suffered "significant psychological injury."

[2] The historical roots of the encounter movement should be well known by practitioners and need not be reviewed here. For the reader interested in this history, see Yalom (34) and Goldberg (3, 8).

[3] This is a technique in which a participant selects another person in the group with whom he or she identifies conflict areas similar to his or her own. The two participants sit facing each other. The first participant is asked to look intently at the second participant as if looking into a mirror and relate what is seen in this reflected image.

REFERENCES

1. Anthony, E.J. The history of group psychotherapy. In: *Sensitivity Through Encounter and Marathon,* ed. H.I. Kaplan and B.J. Saddock. New York: E.P. Dutton, 1972.
2. Goldberg, C. Encounter group leadership. *Psychiat. Soc. Sci. Rev.,* 4(11): 2-8, 1970.
3. Goldberg, C. *Encounter: Group Sensitivity Training Experience.* New York: Science House, 1970.
4. Goldberg, C. An encounter with the sensitivity training movement. *Can. Ment. Health,* 19(5): 10-17, 1971.
5. Goldberg, C. Group counselor or group therapist: Be prepared. *Psychother. Soc. Sci. Rev.,* 26(8): 24-27, 1972.
6. Goldberg, C. A community is more than a psyche. *Can. Ment. Health,* 20(3, 4): 15-21, 1972.
7. Goldberg, C. Reply to Dr. Hoffer. *Can. Ment. Health,* 20(5): 36-37, 1972.
8. Goldberg, C. *The Human Circle—An Existential Approach to the New Group Therapies.* Chicago: Nelson-Hall, 1973.
9. Goldberg, C. Courtship contract in marital psychotherapy. *J. Family Counsel.* 3: 40-45, 1975.
10. Goldberg, C. Peer influence in contemporary group psychotherapy. In: *Group Therapy 1975,* ed. L.R. Wolberg and M.L. Aronson. New York: Stratton Intercontinental Medical Books, 1975.

11. Goldberg, C. Existentially oriented training for mental health practitioners. *J. Contemp. Psychother.*, 8(1), 1976.
12. Goldberg, C. Existential training for group therapy practitioners. In: *Group Therapy 1976*, ed. L.R. Wolberg, M.L. Aronson. New York: Stratton Intercontinental Medical Books, 1976.
13. Goldberg, C. Termination—A meaningful pseudodilemma in psychotherapy. *Psychother.: Theory, Res. Prac.*, 12(4): 341-343, 1975.
14. Goldberg, C. *Patient-Therapist Partnership in Co-therapy—A Systems Perspective,* In: *Systems Science and the Future of Health,* ed. J. Bradt. Washington, D.C., Groome Center, 1976, 153-155.
15. Goldberg, C. *Therapeutic Partnership*—Ethical concerns and responsibilities of the psychotherapeutic relationship. New York: Springer, 1977.
16. Goldberg, C., and Goldberg, M. Encounter group experience workshop. *Proceedings of the International Congress of Group Psychotherapy,* Zurich, August, 1973.
17. Goldberg, C., and Goldberg, M. The psychodramatic magic shop as a technique in contract negotiation. Presented at the meeting of International Congress of Social Psychiatry, Athens, September, 1974.
18. Goldberg, C., and Kane, J.D. A missing component in mental health services to the urban poor: Services-in-kind to others. In: *Mental Health Issues and The Urban Poor,* ed. D.A. Evans and W.L. Claiborn. New York: Pergamon Press, 1974.
19. Haigh, G.V. Psychotherapy as interpersonal encounter. In: *Challenges of Humanistic Psychology,* ed. J.F. Bugental. New York: McGraw-Hill, 1967.
20. Hora, T. Existential psychiatry and group psychotherapy. In: *Psychoanalysis and Existential Philosophy,* ed. H.M. Ruitenbeek. New York: E.P. Dutton, 1962.
21. Lieberman, M.A., Yalom, I.B., and Miles, M.B. *Encounter Groups: Firsts.* New York: Basic Books, 1973.
22. Lennung, S.A. Implicit theories in experiential group practices—A pedogological approach. *Interpers. Develop.*, 5(1): 37-49, 1974-1975.
23. May, R., Angel, E., and Ellenberger, H.F. *Existence.* New York: Simon & Schuster, 1958.
24. Miller, G.A. On turning psychology over to the unwashed. *Psychol. Today,* 3(7): 53-54; 66-74, 1969.
25. Ruesch, J. Communication and mental illness. In: *Communication: The Social Matrix of Psychiatry,* ed. J. Ruesch and G. Bateson. New York: W.W. Norton, 1951.
26. Ruitenbeek, H.M. *Group Therapy Today: Styles, Methods and Techniques.* New York: Atherton Press, 1969.
27. Ruitenbeek, H.M. *The New Group Therapies,* New York: Discus Books, 1970.
28. Schaffer, J.B., ˚and Galinsky, M.B. *Models of Group Therapy and Sensitivity Training.* Englewood Cliffs, N.J.: Prentice-Hall, 1974.
29. Schutz, W.C. *Here Comes Everybody.* New York: Harper & Row, 1971.
30. Shepard, M., and Lee, M. *Marathon 16.* New York: Pocket Books, 1971.
31. Stone, A.A. The quest of the encounter culture. *Internat. J. Psychiat.* 9: 219-226, 1970.
32. Truax, C.B., Shapiro, J.G. and Wargo, D.G. Effects of alternate sessions and vicarious therapy pretraining on group psychotherapy. *Internat. J. Group Psychother.*, 18: 186-198, 1968.
33. Yalom, I.D. Preparation of patients for group therapy. *Arch. Gen. Psychiat.*, 17: 416-427, 1967.
34. Yalom, I.D. *The Theory and Practice of Group Psychotherapy.* New York: Basic Books, 1970.
35. Yalom, I.D., et al. *Encounter Groups and Psychiatry.* Task force report. Presented at the meeting of the American Psychiatric Association, Washington, D.C., 1970.

Thinking and Feeling in Transactional Analysis: Three Impasses

ROBERT L. GOULDING

All impasses seen by the therapist and the client seem to relate to archaic impasses, and these seem to be specifically of three kinds, when viewed with a transactional-analysis framework.

The first which I call a first-degree impasse, originally relates to the message from the Parent ego state of the parent, called by T.A. theorists the counter-injunction, and is usually what the parent asks the child to do so that the parent can be proud of her/him, as "Work hard so that you can get into medical school (so that I won't be totally sorry that you were born)." This is illustrated in Figure 1. We see this in many of the therapists we train, who are still working hard, not enjoying, at 30-40-50 years of age. This is one of the impasses that many encounter leaders work with when they do all the general "experiments" they do. Working with this impasse is fairly simple, and is seen as being between the Parent ego state and the Child ego state, solved by a simple dialogue between Child and Parent,

Reprinted from *Voices: The Art and Science of Psychotherapy*, Vol. 10(1), Spring 1974, pp. 11-13.

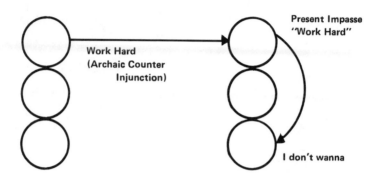

Figure 1.

Reprinted from *Voices: The Art and Science of Psychotherapy,* Vol. 1, Spring 1974, pp. 11-13.

and with the Adult making the decision to knock off working so hard. The client then allows himself to work only 50 hours instead of 70 or 80, and starts playing golf or tennis or going fishing more often. However, what may happen is that he then finds himself working very hard at golf, or trying to catch all the fish in Yellowstone Park.

We then run into the second-degree impasse, which is originally between the Child ego state of the parent and the Child ego state of the client, and is introjected into the Child ego state by the client as illustrated in Figure 2. This is usually a far earlier message than the first illustration and may well be, in this case, "Don't exist," experienced as being given in such statements as, "If you hadn't come along I wouldn't have had to marry your no good father," or "I could have been an opera singer," or "My troubles are all your fault." As long as the client is working hard, listening to the counter-injunctions, he can avoid listening to the injunction not to exist; when he stops working hard, a little voice in his head may say, "If you're not working hard, you might as well not be here," and he begins to get depressed. (This is the danger of working through the first-degree impasse in an encounter session, where the leader doesn't know enough to recognize the danger of letting the client go home without at least some awarenesses—the encounter devotee depresses himself when he is not getting strokes for working so hard and may end up driving off a cliff on the way home from the encounter.) In a dialogue between his introjected Child of his parent and his own little Adult (called the Little Professor, that part of us that makes a decision around the injunction in order to survive in a hostile environment as a child), he may then be able to say, in an affective manner, "I am not listening to you, I am not going to die, or kill myself, to please you." Usually the

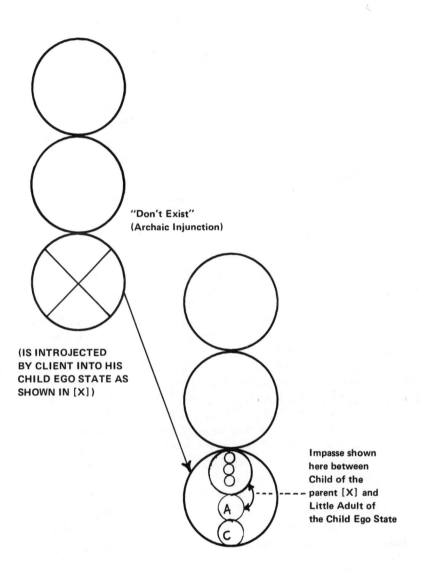

"Don't Exist"
(Archaic Injunction)

(IS INTROJECTED
BY CLIENT INTO HIS
CHILD EGO STATE AS
SHOWN IN [X])

Impasse shown
here between
Child of the
parent [X] and
Little Adult of
the Child Ego State

Figure 2.

I'm no good   I'm Great

Figure 3.

therapist in this impasse encourages some regression, asking the client to remember earlier and earlier scenes, until he fantasizes a real scene of childhood when he first decided it might be easier to die than to tolerate his environment (which is what will please mother anyhow). In this real scene, he experiences all the feelings he did in the original scene, so that his new decision to exist comes from his Child ego state, with tremendous affective relief.

The third-degree impasse is between the Adapted Child and the Free or Natural Child, as in Figure 3. I don't know how to draw a structural diagram to illustrate this impasse, and have changed the diagram of the child into the functional one seen here. (The Adapted Child may be further divided by showing positive adaptation and rebellious adaptation.) Here the injunction not to exist is so early, perhaps even prenatal, that he feels himself as not worthwhile, as valueless, as deserving death. A recent example of this kind of work was done in a dream in which the client dreams he has a cancer which is killing him. As he takes the part of the cancer, he feels himself being the killing agent, and as the dialogue develops he claims both parts, then overcomes that killing part of himself—saying as his *Free Child*, "I am not going to let me kill me," and as his adapted self, "I am feeling weaker and weaker," first with rage at himself, and finally with laughter, as he breaks through the impasse.

A knowledge of these three degrees of impasses will help the therapist in creating his environment with the client, and will help the client to cognitively understand his work after the Gestalt work is done. We have found, and Yalom and Lieberman found in their recent work with "encounter" groups, that the therapist who gives maximum cognitive feedback, who stimulates affective experience moderately, who cares, and who is moderately executive in his work, gets the highest gain. Such cognitive feedback as the script matrix, the drawing of the level of the impasse, is important for the patient after he works through his affective experience, in consolidating his gains.

Body Related Approaches

While Freud, the father of psychoanalysis, spoke of the body ego, many psychoanalysts and psychotherapists have not given attention to the body in their work with patients. In the last decade a new attention to the body has emerged. The body is no longer viewed as separate from the mind, and is seen as an important dimension not to be ignored in psychotherapy. Some of the papers presented here relate the body directly to psychotherapeutic work, while others work with the body more as an adjunct to other forms of therapy.

The Alexander Technique and Gestalt Therapy (Gestalt Synergy)

ILANA RUBENFELD

The sea has waves ... waves are the sea. Sea and waves are one. To speak of the waves apart from the sea or the sea apart from the waves is an illusion ... mind and body are one.

In the last decade, there has been an important shift in focus in the field of psychotherapy. The focus, once only on the verbal aspects of a person, has come to encompass the nonverbal. Because we have no word that recognizes the integral nature of a human being, this split view still exists. In the last four or five years, however, the evidence that this is changing is slowly and steadily mounting.

For many years, my colleagues and I have been working with people in the areas of posture, nonverbal communication, body work, and grounding. At first, response to this work was less than enthusiastic. "Well, that's very interesting ... " became a stock answer. Then, authentic interest began to emerge with a more than occasional "What is this work that you do?" Now it's just the reverse: "What do you do? Where can I get it? How can I train others to do it?" What once was the era of the "baby" boom is rapidly becoming the era of the "body" boom.

This chapter deals, first, with an early psychophysical explorer named F. M. Alexander whose work and theories have provided some of the conceptual seeds that comprise my present work. Secondly, the reader is invited to participate in some experiments to enhance an understanding of this work. Lastly, I have included some studies of individuals whose work in a group setting illustrates the relation of body-mind awareness to psychotherapy and psychotherapy to body-mind awareness.

IN THE BEGINNING

Frederick Matthias Alexander was very much a child of the Victorian era. Born in Tasmania, Australia in 1869, he had been interested in theater and recitation from the age of six. At 19 he traveled to Melbourne where he had hopes of becoming a professional actor. In pursuing his work, he would often give Shakespearean recitations; during this time his voice recurrently failed him.

His problematic voice prompted him to seek medical advice to correct his malady, but all of the doctors he consulted gave his the same advice: "Stop talking and your voice will come back." Alexander tried this several times, but each time, after regaining his voice, he would soon lose it again.

Determined to solve his problem, he began to observe *how* he was speaking. He hoped that through understanding his own process of talking, he might find a clue that would lead to the restoration of his voice. Sitting in front of a set of mirrors, he painstakingly observed himself in the act of speaking—taking in the subtleties of his every movement. As he watched, he noticed that the minute he began to "think" about a movement, the muscles in his body were already preparing for that movement. Also, he realized that certain movements were not reflexes, as he had erroneously thought, but learned habits. He concluded that if these movements had been learned, they could also be unlearned.

Alexander discovered, through his patient self-observations, that there was a complex set of actions that always preceded the beginning of his speech process. For example, when he went to make a sound, he would throw his head back and down and gasp. The gasp limited him to a very shallow intake of air and made him aware that he was cutting himself off by depressing his larynx even before he uttered a sound. This activity seemed far more obvious to him when he was performing than when he was speaking normally. Regardless of whether he was talking or performing, this pattern of pulling his head back, depressing his larynx, and sucking in breath was present.

When Alexander realized that these three activities were causally related to his loss of voice, he set about to change himself. At first, this led to confusion and newly discovered questions: Was the sucking of breath responsible for the depression of his larynx and the pulling back of his head? Or was one of the other two factors the culprit?

Unable to solve his problem, he went on with his self-observation. After several months, he came to the realization that while he could not directly control the sucking of breath or the depressing of his larynx, he could consciously control pulling his head back and down, thus shortening his neck and depressing his chest. He wrote: "The importance of this discovery cannot be overestimated, for through it I was led on to the further discovery of the primary control of the working of all the mechanisms of the human organism, and this marked the first important state of my investigation" (1, p. 143).

Alexander began to understand that his throat problem was not a local problem, but one that concerned his entire body. The movement of his head and torso were integrally connected. After dealing with the dynamic relationship between head, neck, and torso, he observed how they were holistically interconnected with how he used his limbs, the position of his pelvis, and the relation of his feet to the ground.

This discovery led him to examine his total posture. Now that he was aware of the misuse of his body, the next task was to find a way to alter his old habit patterns and consciously choose a more economical way of using himself.

For more than ten years, Alexander's experimentation and development continued. During this period, he returned to the stage, where he received enthusiastic responses about the extraordinary control he exhibited over his breathing. Soon he had earned a reputation as the "breathing man."

Some 16 years after beginning his process of self-observation, Alexander left Australia and traveled to London. Here he taught his technique and published a book entitled *Man's Supreme Inheritance*. In 1914 he began to divide his teaching time between England and America. In America he met, taught, and befriended John Dewey, who vigorously promoted his work.

In the years that he taught, he gathered some of his most famous pupils: George Bernard Shaw, George Coghill, and Aldous Huxley, Huxley (2) was so impressed with his method or re-education that he wrote:

> Mind and body are organically one; and it is therefore inherently likely that, if we can learn the art of conscious inhibition on the physical level, it will help us to acquire and practice the same art on the emotional and intellectual levels. What is needed is a practical morality working at every level from the bodily to the intellectual. A good physical education will be one which supplies the body with just such a practical morality. It will be a curative morality, a morality of inhibitions and conscious control, and at the same time, by promoting health and proper physical integration it will be a system of what I have called preventive ethics, forestalling many kinds of trouble by never giving them the opportunity to arise ... So far as I am aware, the only system of physical education which fulfills all these conditions is the system developed by F. M. Alexander.

THE TECHNIQUE

Alexander continued with his work until the age of 86, when he died. He developed a method encompassing body-mind awareness, conscious control, and organismic thinking by re-educating himself to speak and through diligent self-observation.

I have summarized some of Alexander's principles that continue to have enduring effects on the future of psychophysical therapies:

1. Without awareness, we cannot change.

2. In performing an action, the minute you "think," the muscles receive the message to move.

3. The posture you're habitually used to-the one that "seems" right—may not be. Thus, you could be unknowingly hurting yourself.

4. Habit patterns, in general, are not reflexes; they are learned.

5. The use of one part of your body can affect your whole body. In Alexander's case, the use of his whole body affect his voice—particularly the relationship between his head, neck, and torso, which he called "primary control."

6. "Conscious control" can be exerted over habit patterns.

7. You have the ability to "inhibit" habit patterns and choose an alternate route. Paying attention to *how* you get to your goal means being with your process rather than being with the goal itself. Alexander used the term "means whereby" for "process" and "end-gaining" for "goal."

The intellectual knowing of these principles is not enough for structural change. In order to change, we need a kinesthetic experience accompanying the intellectual knowing. The following ideas used in the teaching of the Alexander technique are guides in the process or re-education and are some of the more important tools for change:

1. Become *aware* of what you do, how you think, and how you habitually act.

2. *Do nothing.* Suspend judgment and be willing to leave yourself alone. (I sometimes call this the "neutral" space.)

3. Imagine other actions, other alternatives.

4. Give yourself the "directions." (These are very specific sets of word symbols through which guided physical experiences come to have kinesthetic meaning. They reflect a dynamic and postural balance of movements.)

Emotions and memories are often stored in our bodies, resulting in tension and imbalance. These tensions, and the habits they foster, interfere with flexible functioning of the whole organism. Release of these tensions establishes new structural patterns which change alignment and posture.

The teacher's tools are skillfully trained hands in concert with specific Alexandrian "directions" tailored to the individual needs of each student. In conjunction with the use of specific words, the teacher touches, guides, and provides the student with a kinesthetic experience that demonstrates the meaning of the words in physical language.

In order to use the "directions," the student needs to be kinesthetically educated. Many people think they are moving their neck when, in fact, if they looked in a mirror, they would discover that they are moving their head. Also, many people *think* they are in a relaxed state and are surprised to find that they are not when touched by a skilled hand.

Some basic Alexandrian directions are:

1. *Let the neck be free and move back.* First think about the neck moving back in space . . . and then allow it to move back.

2. *Let the head go forward and up.* First think of nodding "yes" . . . this motion gives you an idea of the word "forward" . . . then think of moving up from the top of your head like a helium balloon. These two directions are interdependent. When the neck is free, it moves back in space and the head goes forward and up, the spine then has room to lengthen.

3. *Let the torso lengthen.* This is the opposite of spine shortening and arching at the lower back.

Misunderstanding these words can lead to further misuse of yourself. The teacher thus guides you on a journey toward discovering the relationship of each part of your body-mind, separately and together, so that finally you experience yourself as an integrated total person.

In body-mind awareness, we discover that nothing is local. What is necessary is the practice of physical ecology—the full awareness of the synergistic means your body uses in daily functioning and their consequences. We are never still. We are always moving and adjusting to gravity. The following story illustrates what I mean. While in a boat, I noticed several gulls in the distance on the land. The closer I came, the more at peace they appeared. Finally, as I rowed very near them, I noted that they were not still at all, but constantly shifting from leg to leg, always poised and ready to move in any direction. Perhaps we can all be like these gulls—never finishing an act—constantly integrating the dynamic processes of head, neck, torso, pelvis, limbs, feet, and emotions.

AN OPPORTUNITY TO EXPERIMENT

Since skilled hands are probably not available to you at this moment, I will attempt to guide you toward a better understanding of Alexandrian directions. Since this work has been traditionally taught on a one-to-one basis, it was necessary to create an experiential method for presenting this work to groups, workshops, and very large audiences. The work can be classically presented by a lecture-demonstration. However, it is also possible to add experiments designed for an entire group, so that individuals may have a better understanding during the demonstration. Moshe Feldenkrais has been a great inspiration to me in creating many of these experiments.

Right Thumb/Third Toe

There are parts of our bodies that seem vague or unknown to us. The first experiment I want to do with you addresses itself to this fact and gives us an opportunity to experience a body-mind concept.

Right now, I would like you to close your eyes. With your eyes closed, I would like you to focus and think your right thumb. Now, very gently go down to your left foot, focusing and thinking your third toe in your left foot. I invite you to do whatever you need to do to sense and feel the third toe in your left foot. Now, open your eyes gently.

How did you experience your right thumb? Did it become more vivid by just thinking about it? How did you experience the third toe in the left foot? Did you wiggle the toe or touch it to make it more vivid?

This illustrates an important concept: we all have the ability to know parts of our bodies by thinking and consciously using them. We often use our right thumb, but we don't usually think of the third toe in the right foot.

Through touch and movement, you acquire kinesthetic awareness, which imprints a new path in your brain. Eventually you can just think about a part of your body without moving it. There are yogis who have been practicing this approach for many years and are able to connect with and control various organs in their bodies. Through touch and movement, each part of your body becomes more kinesthetically aware.

Grounding and Balance

Take a few moments to stand. While standing, notice how your weight is distributed throughout your body and your feet. Lean forward, shifting your weight onto the front part of your feet. Notice which parts of your body stop you from falling over . . . which parts of your body compensate to keep you upright. Now, begin to lean backward, shifting your weight onto your heels. Notice which parts of your body stop you from falling backward . . . which parts of your body compensate to keep you upright. Repeat this sequence several times and then return to your original stance. Notice if you experience any changes now. How do your feet feel? How is your contact with the floor now?

This experiment exaggerates what subtly occurs in your body and in your grounding constantly. By experimenting with these extremes, you develop an awareness about your everyday posture and words like "head," and "neck," gain meaning.

A Neckwalk

Take the tips of your fingers and touch the back of your neck, starting at the lowest point you can reach, and, slowly, contact each vertebra up your neck . . . keep going up higher and higher.

Your neck is probably longer than you realize. You may discover this by the differences in texture between the base of the head and neck. People are frequently surprised to discover just how long their necks are and how high the head is balanced on the neck. If you ask a large group of people where their heads begin, they will usually touch the middle of their necks. When we refer to "head directions," we mean the back, the sides, and the top of the head.

Where is Your Head?

The relationship of the head, neck, and torso is critically important to the rest of the body. If your head is "off," you are left unaligned, ungrounded, and disconnected from the use of gravity.

The following experiment will help you experience extreme head-and-neck positions. You may find that one or a combination resemble your own habit pattern. The Alexandrian directions will have more meaning after these experiments.

1. Stick your neck forward while pushing your chin out. In our culture, the verbal counterpart for this position is "sticking your neck out." Take your fingertips and just trace them up and down the back of your neck and head. Let your fingertips give you information about how this position affects your body. Become aware of what happens to your breathing . . . eyesight . . . voice . . . balance . . . in this position. Now slowly allow your neck and head to move back onto your body and notice what happens to your breathing . . . voice . . . eyesight . . . and balance now.

Have you noticed the tension and strain of your head and neck after a day of work with clients? this could be due to the head-neck-and-torso position just described.

2. The next position is the one in which the back of the head is *down* and the chin is slightly up. Again, use your fingertips to trace the back of the neck and head. Become aware of how this position affects your breathing . . . eyesight . . . voice . . . and balance. Walk around the room and notice how this position affects your coordination and posture.

Shorter people and children find themselves in this stance when they have to "look up" in order to communicate. In both these positions, the head is cut off from the rest of the body.

3. In the third position, bring your chin down upon your chest. Notice how difficult it is to move from right to left and look around when your head is facing the floor. See what this position does to your eyes when you want to make contact with others. once more, notice how this head-and-neck position affects your breathing . . . voice . . . eyesight . . . movement . . . and balance.

Spinewalk with Partner

This experiment requires two people. Standing up, you face your partner's back. Find the lowest point of the spine and gently touch each vertebra moving up slowly. While you are touching your partner, both of you simultaneously think the word "spine." When you get to about the shoulders, think the word "neck." (Note: "neck" is still part of spine.)

If you get tense or tight, remove your hands slowly and let them hang loosely at your sides while you rest. This is *extremely* important because your tension could be transmitted to your partner.

Your touching gives your partner a kinesthetic experience as you allow yourself to sense the structure of the spine. Gently tap the entire back, sides, and top of the head. Both partners think "head." Be aware of how you are breathing while you are doing this task.

A CHAIR LESSON

A way to demonstrate many of the Alexandrian principles is during a "chair lesson." A chair is used here as a Western symbol of how one gets from here to there. All of us get in and out of chairs many times during each day. If, through conscious control, we can change our patterns, release our tensions, and integrate some of the Alexandrian directions, we can move in and out of a chair in a flowing and balanced way.

Observing and touching a student in the activity of getting in and out of a chair provides the teacher with valuable information about a student's process. Before introducing the directions, I ask students to sit down and to get up in their own habitual pattern, making sure that they notice "how" they use themselves. I may ask them to exaggerate these movements to acquire an even greater awareness. Once a student is able to "inhibit" the usual way of getting in and out of the chair, a different experience becomes possible. In this way, I introduce the idea that the *process* of getting into the chair is as important as the *goal* of sitting. As the use of the entire body becomes foreground, the act of sitting becomes background.

I begin to guide the student in and out of the chair with words and touch. These instructions help integrate the complex relative movement of the head, neck, and torso as well as all the other parts of the body involved in this activity. The word "inhibit" is used here to mean the ability to stop using the old habit patterns, a willingness to leave yourself alone, and to subsequently experience a different total pattern.

A TABLE LESSON

In this part of the lesson, the student is lying down on a low table. This position allows the person to experience a maximum degree of release from tension in relation to gravity. During this part of the lesson, a particular sense of trust is developed.

During a lesson, I will concern myself not only with the head and neck relationship, but also with each part of the body—shoulders, arms, pelvis, legs, back, ankles, feet, hands, etc. There is a whole new adjustment made by the torso, head, and neck when the relation of legs to pelvis changes.

TOUCHING

Touching, in this work, is a very special skill which may take up to three years to learn. It is a unique kind of touching, waiting to see where the person is.

I do not push through resistances. I wait until the person gives me permission to enter and consents to change. The responsibility for change rests within the person. The will to change is communicated from the inside. It moves outward toward me, while my touch from the outside moves inward to meet the person.

This is a cooperative effort and is as necessary for change in body alignment as the therapeutic alliance is in psychotherapy. To the observer, it might appear I am doing something "to" the person, I am moving limbs and muscles around. It is, in fact, the person, himself, who releases and allows me to move them.

I call this type of touching "open hands" since the teacher can sense nonverbally what is happening to the musculature and the skeletal system. The "open hand" is not tense and pushy, but rather a hand that leaves and allows enough space between teacher and student for movement and change.

GESTALT SYNERGY

The seeds of integrating Gestalt with the Alexander technique began in the 1960's when I first met Fritz and Laura Perls. They encouraged me to combine the "body-mind" work with Gestalt therapy. Using Gestalt seemed to be a natural progression in integrating stored emotional material that had been released through the body work.

The client will be able to process emotional situations and experience new ways of being. The position that a client assumes on the table may bring about the spontaneous release of emotional material. The following are examples of such a spontaneous release.

When a client was on the table, I asked her to lie on her back and bring both knees up. The woman began crying. When I asked her what she was experiencing, she reported that she was reliving an abortion that had happened many years before. This painful position had brought back the memory.

In another instance, I was working on a client's shoulders in order to broaden her chest and free her breathing. As I guided her shoulders, this young woman's arms became longer. she became frightened and began to cry. I asked her what she was afraid of and she reported that she was scared of her arms becoming longer. She reported that she might then be able to touch herself. When I asked her where she would touch herself, she indicated her genitals. During this work, this client looked and sounded much younger. Her voice had become quite high-pitched. I asked her how old she was and she responded that she was about two or three. When I asked her where she was, she answered that she was in her crib. "I'm frightened that my hands will touch my vagina and I'll masturbate." At this point, the client was crying and screaming. She later reported having contacted for the first time in her adult life the memory of her mother tying her hands to her crib with colored ribbons to prevent her from masturbating.

Integrating body-mind awareness with psychotherapy is fundamental to our holistic nature. This synthesis does not treat the individual in terms of a series of structural and postural changes. Rather, it includes the realms of emotions, thinking, body structure, spatial concepts, and movement.

Some key sentences that have emerged from my integrative work have been- "I have a right to my own space!" "I have a right to my own head and I don't have to give it away!" "I can stand on my own two feet!" "I can look at you and still be me!" "I own my own body. It's mine and you can't have me!" "I can be big and wide!" "I can take up more space!" Once, a client with asthma released his chest— his key sentence emerged as: "I have a right to breathe and be alive!"

At the end of some workshops, clients described some aspects of my integrative process with the following themes:

1. Body architecture—exploring inner and outer space.
2. Centering—balancing mind, body and emotions.
3. Achieving awareness in the "here and now."
4. Seeing life attitudes reflected through body patterns.
5. Risking changes in body and emotions.
6. Working with gravity—dynamic balance.
7. Redistribution of energy flow—achieving natural body equilibrium.
8. Conscious control—learning means for dealing with habit and change.
9. The language of the body—how thoughts interfere or coincide with body functions.

The Alexander technique essentially deals with the body-mind mode. It is one of the oldest Western systems of body-mind integration. My blending of the Alexander technique, Gestalt therapy, and Feldenkrais exercises creates additional gateways for contacting, expressing, and working through deep feelings, adding the emotional counterpart to this integration shifts the work into a psychophysical synthesis that is a holistic view of our total organism.

SELECTED BIBLIOGRAPHY

Alexander, F.M. *The Resurrection of the Body* Selected and Introduced by Edward Maisel. New York, Delta-Dell, 1969.

Carrington, W.H.M. *Balance as a function of Intelligence* Systematics. 1970, pp. 7, 295-306.

Dart, Raymond, A. *An Anatomist's Tribute* to F. Matthias Alexander London: The Sheildrake Press, 1970.

Feldenkrais, M. *Awareness Through Movement* New York: Harper & Row, 1972.

Feldenkrais, M. *Body and Mature Behavior: A Study of Anxiety, Sex, Gravitation and Learning.* London: Routledge & Kegan Paul, 1949. (Also, New York: International Universities Press, 1969.)

Jones, Frank Pierce, *Body Awareness in Action* New York: Schocken Books, 1976.

Barlow, Dr. Wilfred. *The Alexander Technique* New York: Knopf, 1973.

Fagen, J. Anne and I. Shepard. *Gestalt therapy now.* Palo Alto: Science and Behavior Books, Inc. 1970.

Latner, Joel. *The Gestalt therapy book.* New York: The Julian Press, Inc. 1972.

Lederman, J. *Anger and the rocking chair: Gestalt awareness with children.* New York, Random House, 1969.

Perls, F.S., *Gestalt Therapy Verbatim,* Lafayette, Calif.: Real People Press, 1969.

Perls, F.S., Hefferline, R.F. & Goodman, P., *Gestalt Therapy,* New York: Julian Press, 1951. (Republished: New York Dell, 1965.)

Polster, Miriam & Erving, *Gestalt Therapy, Integrated, Contours of Theory and Practice,* Brunner/Mazel, N.Y. Publishers, 64 University Place, New York, 1973.

Fagen, Joan; Sheperd, Irma Lee., *Gestalt Therapy Now,* Harper, Row, Collophon, 1971.

Stevens, John., *Gestalt Is,* Real People Press, 1975.

The New Sex Therapy: An Interim Report on a Changing Discipline

BARBARA K. HOGAN

The treatment of sexual dysfunctions may well have begun when a human male first found himself ejaculating earlier than he wished and tried to do something about it, or when a human female was first troubled by the snapping shut of her vagina at an inappropriate time. Certainly the use of aphrodisiacs to cure impotence goes back almost to the start of recorded history. The actual treatment of sexual dysfunctions by trained therapists using rational procedures, however, had to await the 1960's.

Psychoanalysts and similar professionals had of course been treating patients with sexual disorders much earlier, starting with Freud and continuing to the present. The results, for most of the specific sexual dysfunctions, were disappointing enough to leave many therapists and patients unsatisfied. The behavioral and interpersonal approaches that followed and differed from the intrapsychic methods pioneered by Freud appeared to be somewhat more successful, but only in relative terms.

So matters stood until 1970. In that year, Masters and Johnson (9) published the results obtained in their sex-therapy program, and two things happened. The actual treatment of sexual dysfunctions was revolutionized, and the discrete, specific discipline of sex therapy was born.

It has grown vigorously. In 1964 Dr. Helen Singer Kaplan began treating the sexual (and other) problems of ghetto patients at the New York Medical College-Metropolitan Hospital Center, of which she was Chief of the Psychosomatic and Liaison Services and which serves one of the poorest sections of New York City. Utilizing many of the techniques of Masters and Johnson but adapting their format to accommodate outpatient treatment, she was able to achieve remarkable rates of success. Her findings were amplified and expanded, and the results sharpened and refined, in the Sexual Treatment and Education Program of the Payne Whitney Psychiatric Clinic, Cornell University-New York Hospital Center. This approach to treatment, which combines all the previous approaches—self-treatment, intrapsychic, interpersonal, and behavioral—has become known as the "new sex therapy," after the title of a book by Kaplan (3). The description of the new sex therapy in this chapter is based on my continuing participation in the Sexual Treatment and Education Program, starting in 1971. The lengthy case history that makes up the core of this chapter illustrates the procedures pioneered in that program.

SEXUAL FUNCTIONING AND DYSFUNCTIONS

Before discussing treatment, it is necessary to know what is disordered and what normal functioning is like. Masters and Johnson (9) have described normal sexual functioning, for both men and women, as occurring in four stages: excitement, plateau, orgasm, and resolution. The excitement phase is characterized subjectively by erotic feelings and physiologically most spectacularly by erection in the male and lubrication of the vagina in the female. Other physiological manifestations are vasocongestion and myotonia, and increase in rate of breathing, blood pressure, and pulse rate. In the male, erection is accompanied by thickening of the scrotum, flattening and thickening of the scrotal sac, and elevation of the testes. In the female, the breasts begin to swell, the nipples become erect, and mottling may occur.

The plateau is, in effect, the excitement stage carried further. The physiological effects are caused primarily by vasocongestion reaching a peak. In the male, penis and testicles are fully engorged, and a few drops of mucoid fluid may appear; in the female, the labia minora swell and change color, and the entrance to the vagina thickens to form the "orgasmic platform" (9). Finally, just before orgasm the clitoris rotates 180 degrees and retracts behind the symphisis pubis.

The major difference in the physiological response of the two sexes appears in orgasm. The male orgasm consists of two phases, emission and ejaculation. Emission is primarily a function of the vascular system, and entails the collection of the ejaculate in the urethral bulb; ejaculation is essentially a muscular reflex, the contraction of the perineal and bulbocavernosus muscles at a frequency of 0.8 second to expel the ejaculate. Subjectively, the emission phase is experienced as the sensation of "ejaculatory inevitability."

The female does not have an emission phase; orgasm consists of contractions of the circumvaginal and perineal muscles—also at a frequency of 0.8 second. As is well known, following orgasm the male experiences a refractory period during which further orgasm is impossible; the woman has the capacity to have orgasms indefinitely, the number being limited only by her physical endurance.

Resolution encompasses the return of the body to its resting—i.e., pre-excitement—phase. Full return of all bodily functions to the unaroused condition varies with age, but is about 30 minutes for younger individuals of both sexes.

The Masters and Johnson presentation, while very descriptive and physiologically much more detailed and accurate than any that preceded it, shares with earlier presentations the assumption that "the sexual response consists of an orderly sequence of a unitary and inseparable event" (8). This concept corresponds well with the subjective experience of sex, and is certainly useful in aligning the subjective and the physiological. On the other hand, "clinical and physiologic evidence suggests an alternative formulation—that the sexual response of both genders is actually biphasic" (3). The two phases are the vascular and the muscular; that is, a "genital vasocongestive reaction which produces penile erection in the male and vaginal lubrication and swelling in the female; and the reflex clonic muscular contractions which constitute orgasm in both genders" (3). The biphasic formulation does not replace the Masters and Johnson description but rather represents a further synthesis of the elements involved in sexual functioning.

This is not only of theoretical importance, but also has clinical significance. "The two components involve different parts of the nervous systerm. ... Furthermore, vasocongestion and orgasm differ with respect to their vulnerability to the effects of physical trauma, drugs, and age. Finally, the impairment of erection and ejaculation in the male and of lubrication and orgasm in the female results in distinctly different clinical syndromes .... which respond to different treatment procedures" (3). Thus, for a long time premature ejaculation was considered a type of impotence, and was supposed to be amenable to the same kind of treatment. But in fact, premature ejaculation represents a muscular dysfunction and impotence (erectile problems) a vascular dysfunction, and the treatment modalities are entirely different for each.

What, then, are the sexual dysfunctions? The new sex therapy considers that there are six, divided equally between the male and the female. Sexual dysfunctions of the male are impotence (erectile dysfunctions), whether primary or secondary; premature ejaculation; and retarded ejaculation. Sexual dysfunctions of the female are general sexual dysfunction (lack of arousal); vaginismus; and orgastic dysfunctions. It is to be noted that most sex therapists in the past lumped lack of arousal and orgastic dysfunctions together, as manifestations of a general sexual dysfunction. But they are clearly distinct conditions: distinct in their physiological origins and distinct in their treatment.

Male impotence and female general sexual dysfunctions are vasocongestive dysfunctions, and are comparable in that both involve a lack of arousal. Retarded ejaculation and orgastic dysfunctions are muscular dysfunctions, both involving overcontrol, an inability to "let go." Premature ejaculation and vaginismus are also muscular dysfunctions. Until very recently no correspondence between these two conditions was assumed; but it appears that both involve involuntary, reflex muscular action occurring prematurely; and other, intrapsychic correspondences may be found. In this respect, it may be of interest to note that premature ejaculation and vaginismus are the easiest of the dysfunctions to treat.

APPROACHES TO THE TREATMENT OF SEXUAL DYSFUNCTIONS

Almost every therapist is eclectic to *some* degree, borrowing concepts and techniques that appear to be both useful to his patients and compatible with his own approach. Just as the new sex therapy is a "therapeutic amalgam" (10), so the behavioral, intrapsychic, and interpersonal therapies have altered to accommodate promising outside material. Indeed, as Sollud points out (11), "In the last decade, a beginning rapprochement between behavioral and psychoanalytic approaches has developed. ... One development has been the appreciation by some of the significance of psychoanalytic concepts to behavior therapy. ... There is a realization among some analysts that factors relating to learning theory could play a role in analytic therapy."

Nevertheless, with this rapprochement, the interpersonal, behavioral, and intrapsychic schools are still quite distinct and likely to remain so, since each addresses most efficiently a different class of problems. All, however, have been and are being used to treat patients whose primary (presenting) problem is sexual. Intrapsychic therapy—psychoanalysis, Gestalt therapy, any therapy that aims at a global psychodynamic reorganization of the patient—by its very nature does not directly address the sexual dysfunctions. As a result of the changed psychodynamics, the patient may be cured of his sexual problems; however, this is by no means certain, and in some cases—notably, premature ejaculation—is not very likely. Where comparative data exist, the success rate of intrapsychic therapy is usually lower than that of other therapies, and the treatment time is almost invariably longer. It appears, however, that patients who have experienced otherwise successful intrapsychic therapy make excellent candidates for sex therapy.

Nor is this to be wondered at. Behavioral dysfunctions, including the sexual dysfunctions, have remote, immediate, and physiological causes, and the efficacy of treatment depends on the proper choice of the target. For example, in premature ejaculation the remote cause may lie in unconscious, oedipal-derived, sadistic feelings toward women and a desire to rob them of pleasure; the immediate cause may lie in the nature of the dyadic transaction; but the (very successful) treatment in sex therapy lies in identification of the premonitory sensation—which is a learned response. Psychoanalysis can proceed for years with the psychiatrist never mentioning—or thinking of—the premonitory sensation and its recognition. On the other hand, when the remote causes of premature ejaculation or any other dysfunction are still potent in the patient's unconscious, previous psychiatric treatment can have helped to resolve these conflicts and pave the way for sex therapy. Further, intrapsychic problems can often impede the course of sex therapy; and when this happens the insights and techniques of psychoanalysis can be very useful. Similar considerations apply to interpersonal (or dyadic or marital) therapy. Marital therapists tend to locate the causes of sexual dysfunctions in the marital transactions, and to treat such dysfunctions by treating the interpersonal problems. Again, intervention into the dyadic transactions may yield some positive results with sexual functioning; the sexual problems of many couples have indeed been traced specifically to dyadic conflicts, and case histories have been presented in which premature ejaculation has been cured by marital therapy and nothing else (6). Thus, while it is possible that interpersonal therapy may achieve some success where intrapsychic does not, it is not as consistently successful as sex therapy. Clearly, however, where destructive dyadic transactions interfere with sex therapy, insights and approaches from interpersonal therpay can often make a crucial difference.

Traditional behavior therapy is characterized by three factors. First, the therapist identifies the specific behavioral pattern he wishes to modify; then he interprets that behavior in terms of extinction or reinforcement characteristics; and then he prescribes appropriate reinforcing or extinguishing exercises or procedures to bring about the modification in behavior. The therapist thus intervenes directly and actively into the therapeutic situation; furthermore, positive reinforcement for approved behavior very often comes from the therapist's approval as well as from the patient's own satisfaction. On the other hand, like the interpersonal and intrapsychic therapist, the traditional behavioral therapist concentrates his treatment on the events that occur in his office. The success rate of behavior therapy in treating sexual dysfunctions appears to be as inconsistent as that of interpersonal and intrapsychic therapies. The reason may be that behavior therapy requires a clear field in order to be effective. But all experience indicates that resistance to the therapy often arises, sometimes with great force. The behavior therapist deals with such resistance through behavioral strategies, as the psychoanalyst and marital therapist deal with resistances using their own appropriate strategies. But behavioral strategies may be ineffective in countering interpersonal or intrapsychic resistances, and the therapy is hampered. "Often this approach is effective in modifying specific (sexual) symptoms; often it is not" (3).

Masters and Johnson elaborated and applied behavioral principles in specific ways to create the new field of sex therapy. In terms of what has been called the new sex therapy, the Masters and Johnson approach represents traditional sex therapy. Masters and Johnson combine a fixed and a flexible format. Patients are treated as couples by male and female co-therapists. The couple is expected to devote two full weeks to therapy, away from home and living in a hotel or motel near the treatment center. The couple is seen every day. Treatment begins with a round-table discussion between all four parties, proceeds with individual discussions between patient and therapist of the same sex, and then consists of the exercises and feedback sessions with the therapist.

Regardless of the presenting symptom, the first exercises are always "sensate focus," nondemand. This takes two forms. In sensate focus I, both partners are nude and one caresses the other's body nongenitally, with the caressed partner indicating the pleasurable and nonpleasurable sensations. Then the partners reverse roles. The partners are specifically instructed not to proceed to intercourse. Sensate focus II includes the genitals; again, however, intercourse is prohibited. Following sensate focus, exercises are prescribed directed to the specific sexual complaints.

Although the treatment is quite successful (Masters and Johnson report an over-all success rate of 80 percent), on a practical level it poses some difficulties. First is the requirement that the couple reserve two weeks exclusively for treatment. This is not easy for many couples, and represents a substantial expense. Next is the use of co-therapists as a matter of course.

In terms of use of exercises, type of exercises, and the focusing on the target symptom—the direct treatment of specific sexual dysfunctions—the new sex therapy is based on Masters and Johnson. It differs, however, in several respects, of which three are considered significant. First, patients are treated on an outpatient basis, and are not required to devote two weeks exclusively to therapy. Next the treatment is tailored specifically to the needs and symptoms of each couple. And finally, the nature of the therapeutic intervention is different. (In addition, treatment is almost always by a single therapist; co-therapists are brought in only under unusual circumstances.)

In the new sex therapy, patients visit the therapist's office and are given exercises to do at home. The sessions are continued (and new exercises are usually prescribed) until the treatment is terminated. The number of office visits ranges from 5 to 15 sessions; the patients can continue their private lives without interruption. The treatment format varies: a specific treatment format is designed for each individual and each couple.

The difference in therapeutic intervention has to do with the handling of resistances. Resistances always arise during the course of treatment, and can be quite severe. The Masters and Johnson therapists tend to deal with resistance by behavioral means: bypass, repetition, positive reinforcement, concentration of insight on the behavior exhibited in the exercise. In contrast, the new sex therapy deals with patients' resistances in whatever mode seems most suitable: intrapsychically, interpersonally, or behaviorally. The new sex therapist is trained in the application of these techniques, and will not hesitate to use the most appropriate. It should be emphasized, however, that these interventions may or may not be intended to resolve intrapsychic or interpersonal problems (although sometimes they must); they are specifically in the service of sex therapy, and they are utilized only insofar as they are necessary to clear the way for sex therapy.

THE NEW SEX THERAPY

The new sex therapy aims at the rapid treatment of sexual dysfunctions through exercises targeted at specific sexual problems, prescribed by a single therapist and performed by the patients at home. Fundamentally behavioral in method, it gains effectiveness by its ability to dispel patient resistances that frequently disrupt standard behavioral therapy, utilizing an extensive armamentarium of techniques and methods. While entailing less therapist time and less interruption to the normal life of the patients, results to date indicate a success pattern roughly the same as that of Masters and Johnson (3).

The behavioral orientation of the new sex therapy is evident. "It focuses on attaining certain specified goals through the application of specific behavioral techniques, which differ according to the nature of the presenting problem. The often contractual nature of the new sex therapy as well as the specified operational nature of the procedures used place the new sex therapy within the tradition of the behavior therapies. . . . . Behavioral principles are incorporated in the prescribed sexual exercises and can account, to a large extent, for their effectiveness" (10). These behavioral principles include desensitization, shaping, extinction, and reinforcement. The treatment for vaginismus, for example, consists of inserting objects of increasing diameter into the vagina until it can tolerate the male phallus—clearly a desensitization procedure. With its proscription of intercourse, sensate focus removes the demand-for-coitus element from the couple's interactions, and is thus a form of desensitization; it also helps shape the couple's response to stimulation, and provides positive reinforcement in terms of the (usually) pleasurable sensations it results in.

But note that almost every behavioral exercise can be evaluated in terms of other approaches. Sensate focus is clearly a way of modifying the dyadic interaction to foster better communication; in intrapsychic terms, prolonged gentle contact and being "taken care of" hold great significance in light of infantile needs and expectations. Even the treatment for vaginismus, which appears almost entirely behavioral in effect, assumes the ultimate presence of a partner and thus a dyadic relationship, and has obvious references to early sexual explorations.

When the exercises are performed with little resistance, or when the resistance is of a situational, anticipatory, or performance variety (Will it work? Will he/she cooperate?), progress is often very rapid. Many cases fit into this category: the couple arrives with good intrapsychic and marital functioning and achieves good sexual functioning with gratifying ease. For other patients, the resistances can take several forms, but appear to arise in two contexts: resistance to the process of the therapy and resistance to the outcome.

In the treatment of couples where one partner is considered dysfunctional, resistance to the outcome of the treatment can arise in both partners and is most commonly expressed in interpersonal modes. The typical fear of the "healthy" wife, for example, is that once the husband becomes sexually adequate he will no longer need her to tolerate his inadequacies and will leave. Males, of course, have the same fear with respect to their wives. The typical fear of the treated spouse is that the process of change will be irreversible and accelerating: change in sexual functioning somehow means that he or she will "have to" change his or her whole life style. One anorgastic woman feared that if she ever achieved sexual success she would be in a constant state of sexual excitement, and would want to have sex "with every man and woman I see."

Resistance to the process can have intrapsychic origins, in which case the manifestations are almost endless, or interpersonal origins. Many of the latter resolve into a giving up of power in the relationship: for men, often the power to dominate, for women, often the power to resist. Thus, many men do not like the idea of their wife (or a female therapist) "ordering them around"; many women feel that their only defense against their husband's assertiveness is their abillity to remain aloof. One woman resisted the sensate-focus exercises because she didn't want to become sensitive to her partner's needs; she would become too involved and that would be bad for her. (When she began to progress, the husband began to wonder whether he was "man enough" to satisfy her.) For either sex, where closeness is threatening, the process of sex therapy will almost inevitably arouse resistances.

In dealing with resistances, as stated, the new sex therapist uses whatever technique seems most appropriate. The simplest and most rapid are preferred, and so the therapist will consider first the behavioral techniques. Resistances may be bypassed or the exercise repeated—or both. With one couple starting out with sensate focus I, the man found it difficult to assume the "passive" role, but the woman had a very positive experience. The next assignment was sensate focus II, bypassing the man's resistance. This time both partners resisted, the woman interpreting all of the man's comments with complete literality, the man being short-tempered and touchy, and both feeling unaccountably sleepy at crucial times. During the therapy session, the couple was confronted with the implications of their behavior and the third assignment was a repeat of the second: sensate focus II. The result was vastly improved communication, and the specific "dysfunction" exercises were then begun.

Where behavioral techniques do not work because the resistance is too intense, then the intervention is interpersonal or intrapsychic. If the former, the focus may very well be on the couple's patterns of communication (more usually, lack of communication), on the possibilities and rewards of negotiation, and in general on such destructive interaction patterns as emerge. In these cases, the therapist's contribution lies chiefly in providing insight, in establishing the office as a safe ground for communication, and in tailoring the exercises to aid in the dyadic interaction. The therapist can thus emphasize the importance of notifying one's partner of one's responses to either of the sensate-focus, or any other, exercises.

For interventions on the intrapsychic level, the therapist uses the appropriate therapeutic mode: if a dream seems relevant, then it is interpreted or discussed; if

Gestalt role-play is indicated, it is done. For this reason, the new sex therapy is beginning to be called "psychosexual therapy."

Probably the most important factors in overcoming the patient's resistances, however, are the attitude and support of the therapist. It bears repeating that in psychosexual therapy, transference—especially the kind of positive transference feelings that result in trust (as between surgeon and patient)—is exploited in the service of the treatment. Often all that is required is the reassurance that feelings, behaviors, desires, fantasies, fears, etc., can be tolerated and the patient is ready to proceed.

A striking example was the husband of a woman with vaginismus, whose marriage had remained unconsummated for five years. Both husband and wife were virgins when they married; the treatment was successful, the vaginismus was cured—but when the husband finally entered and began to thrust, he became terrified. He suddenly felt that his penis was a piston in the cylinder of his wife's vagina, that his thrusting was forcing air into her organs, and that she should explode if he continued. This was surely a fertile field for a display of the therapist's knowledge of symbolism, psychodynamics, and automobile manufacture; but the patient was instead provided with the relevant information on anatomy and physiology and assured that there was nothing to worry about, and the problem was solved. An exploration of the possibly sadistic feelings of the patient toward his wife (and toward women in general) was totally bypassed—as was his resistance. Thus, the new psychosexual therapy, with its emphasis on rapid treatment and limited therapy hours, demands thorough grounding of the therapist if it is to succeed. It also demands a highly organized effort on the part of the therapist; the therapist must know not only what to prescribe but what to look for. Sex therapists differ in their procedures as much as any other therapists; as a way of focusing the therapist's attention and awareness, however, the procedure followed in the Payne Whitney Sex Education and Therapy Program has proven very valuable.

This procedure begins with an intake and evaluation interview, in which certain information is always gathered for each partner of the couple: target symptoms, presenting problems, family history and attitudes, childhood development, adolescent development, premarital development, marital history, and medical and psychiatric history. Specific sexual questions, always included, involve masturbation, premarital experiences, sexual problems, etc. If the couple is accepted for treatment, the therapist describes the ground rules for the therapy and the general approach, provides any education information that seems called for, and arrives at a therapeutic "contract" with the couple. This is simply an agreement by the couple to take responsibility for their sexual development, do the exercises, and attend the office sessions; in effect, to give the therapy a chance to work. If both patients have sexual problems, the therapist explains that they will work on the more tractable problem first and the more recalcitrant one next. The session concludes with a "sig" (short for "signa," the directions provided on pharmacist's prescriptions for the patient to follow). The sig is a description of the first set of exercises the couple is to perform. Any other appropriate information is given, and an appointment is made for the next visit, usually a week away.

At this next session, and at every subsequent session, the therapist directly or indirectly evaluates three factors: the sexual, interpersonal, and intrapsychic functioning of the couple. Based on an appraisal of these factors, the therapist offers any interpretations, insights, interventions, clarifications, reassurances, permission, etc., that appear warranted, and gives another sig.

Succeeding sessions follow this same general form, and continue until the condition is alleviated or the prognosis is negative. A termination interview is then held, and an appointment is made for a follow-up interview, usually six months away. During the treatment period, many patients continue in individual or conjoint therapy concurrently with the psychosexual therapy.

The patients usually return to their previous therapy, or to their private lives, not only with improved sexual functioning but also with a greater degree of closeness and intimacy. The emphasis throughout the therapy is not on performance but on pleasure, and this comes as the lifting of a great burden for many couples. Relieved of the need to prove oneself or satisfy the other, they are further relieved by being held responsible for their own pleasure—which means, of course, that the partner is held *not* responsible.

The emphasis on pleasure, and the removal of responsibility and the need to perform, have the effect of placing the dysfunction "outside" the relationship. Whereas premature ejaculation, for example, was previously a problem for the man to try to control and the wife to try to put up with, it now becomes something for them both to work on, while still asking for and giving the great pleasures and tenderness that remain available. The problem is no longer between the couple, an obstacle to their relationship; it is external, the object of their mutual efforts. The feelings of warmth and love that bring couples together and persist sometimes in the face of great adversity now often come to the surface. The couple is happier and more secure as a couple, more intimate, more sharing. The improvement in sexual functioning that usually results from the therapy intensifies the warmth and closeness. The sex therapist—certainly the psychosexual therapist-treats the dysfunction, but sometimes the greatest satisfaction comes in seeing not only the relief of symptoms but also the strengthening and pleasuring of a relationship.

The best way of elucidating a treatment technique is through case histories. A single case history follows, selected to illustrate the number and variety of resistances that may be encountered, and the range of therapeutic responses sometimes called for. Because of its complexity, it is presented in greater than usual detail.

CASE HISTORY: EILEEN AND CHARLES WALTERS

Eileen and Charles Walters have been married for four years. He is 33 years old, a former architect now studying patent law; she is 29 years old, a history major in the graduate school of an Eastern university. Both have part-time jobs. The nominal patient is Eileen; her problems are low libido and secondary orgastic dysfunction. Charles has no sexual problems. Both are Irish Catholics.

Intake and Evaluation

Eileen was brought up very strictly by a quiet, aloof, and difficult mother and a warm and affectionate father. She has two brothers, one older (a priest) and one younger. Sex was never discussed in the house. She attended parochial schools until she was 18 years old, dating a little in high school and engaging in petting. At those times, she lubricated and felt aroused, but never went on to intercourse or orgasm. She masturbated only once, when she could hear her father and brothers talking in the next room, and had the first of the two orgasms she has so far experienced. She suffered guilt feelings for a long time. Her mother died when Eileen was 15 years old and beginning puberty. When she was 18, Eileen entered a convent, but left when she was 24 because she realized it was an unsatisfactory life. That year she started in graduate school, and is close to fulfilling her Ph.D requirements. A year later she married Charles. She was a virgin at the time.

Charles Walters was also a virgin when he married. The middle of three male children, he was raised very strictly by an "efficient" mother and a shy, quiet father who died quite suddenly a few months after the marriage of Charles and Eileen. Charles received a degree in architecture, worked several years in a large engineering company, and then began the study of law. He is finding it arduous and often dull, but is close to receiving his degree.

Charles began to masturbate at the age of 19 after his older brother had warned him against it. This spurred him to try. He masturbated intermittently after that, usually with guilt feelings. He started dating at the age of 26.

The marriage of Charles and Eileen was not consummated until a few weeks after the wedding, because Eileen was vaginismic. On the advice of a gynecologist and after sequential dilation, penetration was finally achieved. Although she had no orgasm, Eileen was excited by the foreplay and felt that, as a whole, it was a very lovely experience. She feared, however, that it might take a long time for her to achieve full satisfaction. Charles's reaction to his first intercourse was apprehension: he knew that there were problems, but had no idea what the solutions might be.

Once they started, intercourse proceeded at a satisfactory frequency, two or three times a week. At first, Eileen felt that she too would soon learn to relax and enjoy the experience. But after a time she became jealous of Charles's orgasms and disappointed at not having orgasms of her own; and when he ejaculated she would cry. She began to ask for more sexually—more time, more attention, more stimulation. Charles then felt pressured to "perform" and was angry at being ordered around by his wife. He expressed his anger indirectly, however, and so they began to fight.

On a vacation two years after their marriage, they attempted oral stimulation of Eileen. Eileen had the second of her two orgasms, but Charles objected vehemently:

she was "very foul" down there. This was the start of many violent arguments. The arguments are continuing. They now have intercourse about once a month, with Charles usually (but not lately) taking the initiative. Foreplay is inadequate for Eileen. Eileen is aroused with difficulty and easily distracted, especially when Charles changes course—which he is very abrupt about. Charles is aroused by genital stimulation, but is depressed when Eileen isn't aroused. During foreplay, Eileen's lubrication is erratic; but she never masturbates herself and has never had an orgasm. When they do have intercourse, they try various positions. Eileen's favorites are the side-to-side and the female superior, where she feels more in control; Charles prefers the male superior.

Two years ago, after their summer vacation, Eileen entered individual psychotherapy with a female psychiatrist; Charles occasionally participated in conjoint therapy. Therapy continued for Eileen for two years, with no improvement in either the marital condition of the couple or in Eileen's sexual functioning. Because of Charles's rigidity toward change and resistance to anything he considered a demand, Eileen's therapist suggested that he enter individual psychotherapy also, but he refused, saying: "I'm not ready." Finally, Eileen's therapist recommended sex therapy. Their explicit goals for sex therapy are not incompatible. Charles wants Eileen to be aroused more easily and more reliably, and not be subject to so many whims; he thinks the sex problems will work themselves out. Eileen wants to achieve orgasms in any way during sex, and she wants sex more frequently.

The treatment will be for orgastic dysfunction and low libido in the woman, and what is therefore relevant *at this point* are the indications with respect to Eileen. The immediate causes of her problems are severe parental and religious prohibitions, which she has not overcome; fear of loss of contol, which she masks by allowing herself to become distracted; and marital discord. The remote cause is likely due to the unresolved trauma of her mother's death, which occurred at an unfortunate time for a young girl—the onset of puberty. Considering this fact, and the fact that she has previously taken steps to help herself, her resistance will most likely be to the outcome of the therapy. Enjoyable sex for Eileen will be an act of rebellion against her mother. She will be accepted as a patient because she seems highly motivated and because her intrapsychic difficulties seem neither insumountable nor used as a defense against sexual functioning. Charles has exhibited pathological rigidity and defensiveness, and this might interfere with treatment. On the other hand, he has previously undertaken conjoint therapy with Eileen, and this indicates some degree of flexibility. Also, having an orgasm in coitus ultimately demands the cooperation of the male. On balance, then, treatment will begin conjointly.

Finally, what should the pattern of treatment be? Considering the marital pathology, the first exercises will be nondemand sensate focus, primarily as a probe to determine the suitability of continuing conjoint treatment. This will be followed by specific exercises for Eileen for orgastic dysfunctions. To some extent, the exact format of the exercises will be determined by the results of the probes.

The sig, then, is sensate focus I. Eileen and Charles are to perform the exercises at least twice, once with Eileen initiating and once with Charles. They are to return for their next office meeting in one week.

Conjoint Session 1—One Week Later

The first series of exercises had promising results. The exercises were actually performed, and both Eileen and Charles appreciated the experience of contact and sharing. Eileen was aware of some sexual feelings, and in general enjoyed the exercises, especially the relief from the pressure of having to achieve an orgasm. She was able to assuage a beginning sense of guilt by reminding herself that she was simply following professional advice. Charles was aroused to the point of erection while touching and being touched, and during both series urged Eileen to have intercourse. At those times Eileen began to feel pressured.

It is to be expected that Charles will resist changes over which he has no control, and it is clear that his urging of intercourse with Eileen is a manifestation of this resistance, an attempt to sabotage the process. On the other hand, he has reported positive feelings of sharing and contact. The decision is to bypass the resistance and proceed to the next step. The sig is sensate focus II, performed at least twice (each initiating once); the second time they are to talk about what they are seeing and feeling.

Conjoint Session 2—One Week Later

Resistance and sabotage. The first series of exercises saw a fight over the instructions: Eileen initiated, Charles began to talk, Eileen took exception to this, and they quarreled. Finally they agreed on a procedure (talk).

During the exercises, when Eileen touched Charles's genitals, he pulled away (he was "ticklish"). Eileen was much more receptive to Charles's caresses than the first time, but now she had two complaints. First, Charles spent too much time on the rest of her body and not enough on her genitals; and next, when he did approach her genitals, he kept trying to put his fingers in her vagina against her wishes.

So Charles has flouted both the letter of the sig (to talk) and the spirit of the exercises, their nondemand, "pleasuring" aspect. I ask each of them to have a fantasy about the meaning of success in the therapy: the best outcome, and the worst. For the best, each says that they will become closer as a couple. For the worst, Eileen fears that she will become more vulnerable: Charles will attack her (in her genitals), reject her, or leave her; even if she retaliates, she will be abandoned. For Charles, the bad outcome is that he will be dictated to, controlled by his wife.

The sig is to repeat sensate focus II, with some ground rules added. First, if either one wants to stop an exercise, it stops; and next, if they have any questions about the sig, they are to telephone me for clarification.

But the session does not end with the sig. Charles has been very inattentive and distracted in the past 15 minutes, and when confronted he admits (1) that he doesn't like being told by a female therapist what the rules are; and (2) that he doesn't like being told by Eileen when to do the exercises. So a complicated procedure is arranged wherein each can initiate on certain specified days. The issue of control is noted and bypassed.

Conjoint Session 3—One Week Later

The first series of exercises went well: Eileen was more relaxed and slightly more aroused; Charles was less ticklish and also experienced greater pleasure. The second series, to be initiated by Charles, never happened. On one of the appointed days, when Eileen came home from work, Charles was in bed. On another day, Eileen was depressed at some events on her job. On the third day, Charles was depressed and angry with Eileen, but wouldn't tell her why. He thought, however, that the therapy was a waste of time. Eileen was angry with Charles for not initiating the exercises; she walked around nude for a time, but Charles did not respond.

Charles's resistance must be dealt with directly, otherwise he will sabotage the entire procedure. I confront him with the facts that he is setting up a self-fulfilling prophecy, denying that the therapy will work and making sure that it won't. The sig is again sensate focus II, and again a complicated initiating procedure is arranged.

Conjoint Session 4—One Week Later

Mildly promising. Charles did initiate the first series of exercises, although Eileen was anxious and jittery, closing off her genital areas, pushing his hands away. The second time she was less anxious. For both times as toucher, Charles was disappointed in her reactions. As the touchee, however, Charles was very aroused both times, exclaiming with pleasure. This surprised and dismayed Eileen at first, but later she was pleased that she could have such an effect on him. There was also a third time: they both got drunk, started petting, became aroused very quickly, and were about to have intercourse when the telephone rang. They ended with no orgasm for either, but "great sex."

Eileen and Charles are colluding in sabotage, but it may be helping their sex lives. The best course seems to be to take over the resistance in the service of therapy. The sig (to be repeated twice) is to begin with sensate focus II concentrating on the genitals, and to achieve penetration with the penis using vaseline if they both agree and want it. Eileen is to be aware of unpleasant sensations should they occur, and to verbalize her reactions. The strategy is to help Eileen focus on her vaginal sensations while allowing Charles to break the "rules" (and have his own orgasm) in a way that may be constructive.

Conjoint Session 5–Five days Later

All resistance remobilized, in full virulence. Charles had problems in school, drinking and cutting classes. Eileen was anxious about therapy: she felt vulnerable, something has been missing in her past, she is closed off, despairing–it was easier not to face these feelings. With regard to the first exercise, Eileen asked, "Are we going to do the exercise?" Charles replied, "I'm very tired. What are we supposed to do?" The exercise was discussed; Charles started, stopped, and fell asleep.

That was the extent of their homework. Both were angry; Eileen was disappointed; neither talked about it or took responsibility for his or her actions. Charles was doing the exercises for the therapist's sake; Eileen was doing the exercises because she was paying for them.

It is time to evaluate the probes. It is clear that minor progress one week evokes tremendous resistance the next week, and that most of the resistance, and the sabotage, comes from Charles. Troubled and anxious though Eileen is, she has persisted in at least trying to do the exercises, while Charles has persisted in trying to avoid them.

If this were marital therapy, I would continue to see Charles and Eileen conjointly. But this is sex therapy. Eileen wants to learn to have orgasms, and the conjoint sessions are not helping her, but rather are used in the service of resistance. I therefore suggest, and they agree, that I see Eileen for a number of sessions alone. I give Eileen her first individual sig: self-exploration (alone) of her genitals using a mirror; and masturbation using vaseline and concentrating on her sensations. These are standard beginning exercises for orgastic dysfunction.

Individual Session 1–One Week Later

The exploration of her genitals seemed to Eileen like a clinical examination. But she felt no anxiety, which had not been the case when she had used the dilator for vaginismus.

She had masturbated twice. The first time, in bed and under a blanket; she felt awkward, worried, ignorant, and self-conscious, the spectator of her own activities. The entire experience was unpleasant and boring, there was no arousal, and she wanted to stop almost as soon as she started. The next time she masturbated in front of a mirror, and this was an improvement. She could at least do something (distracting herself from her anxiety)–and she was able to see the physiological signs of arousal: puffiness of the vagina, color changes, and the like. She didn't feel aroused, however. In fact, this entire sig left her feeling like a victim: trapped into doing something she didn't want to do and had never wanted to do; it had not been pleasant; and if she never had another orgasm she would never miss it.

Eileen's vaginal anaesthesia is a sign of great anxiety, of which the immediate cause is probably the religious proscriptions against masturbation. I confront her on this level, reassuring her that it is all right to have pleasure and to give herself pleasure, not to depend on somebody else. Eileen's response is encouraging: she becomes very upset and starts to cry, but it is clear that this has reached her. I then suggest that she try replacing her negative fantasies of abandonment with positive fantasies of success and fulfillment. The sig is to masturbate at least twice using vaseline, at least once in front of a mirror.

Individual Session 2—One Week Later

This has been a very hard week for Eileen in all areas except sex therapy. Her younger brother has been seriously injured in an automobile accident; Charles has been cutting classes and skipping assignments in school and acting very strangely. The only person he has spoken to all week has been Eileen—who suggested he see a therapist. But Charles refused.

The exercises, however, yielded moderately positive results. The first time was neither pleasant nor unpleasant, because her mind seemed to be wandering. The second time, however, she masturbated as an escape from her problems, and she found it peaceful, soothing, and pleasant.

With her initial anxiety abated, Eileen may benefit from fantasy. Fantasies "are very useful . . . . They serve concomitantly to stimulate and to distract from anxiety . . . . Digital stimulation of the clitoris plus distraction by fantasy often produce orgasm with a few weeks" (4). The sig is to purchase an erotic book and to use fantasy while masturbating; that is, read and masturbate, read and masturbate, etc.

Individual Session 3—One Week Later

Eileen couldn't find an erotic book and had trouble producing her own fantasies, but the masturbation itself was pleasant enough until the last (third) time. Then she began with more vigorous stimultion, and suddenly: "I felt I had to stop. I felt I had to curl up and grab my knees and hold them tight together." She stopped and felt a tingling sensation in her genitals, started again . . . and then came the feeling that if she continued she would achieve orgasm—and an overwhelming guilt. She mentally spoke the words, "I will never do this again," and some relief came, and with it the thought that if only someone would forgive her, all her problems with sex would vanish.

I congratulate Eileen for persisting in the exercise, and move to tackle the resistance head-on. For it turns out on questioning that the people who could forgive Eileen are her priest, her mother or her father. Working in the Gestalt mode, I ask Eileen to take the role of the priest. "Don't do it again," says the priest; "It'll be all right if you never do it again." No forgiveness there. Eileen starts to cry: the priest will not forgive her, and neither will her mother or father. Now she is very upset. She feels very angry with her mother, but sees this as an act of defiance, an acknowledgment that her mother has left her without *ever* giving Eileen the right to experience pleasurable sexual feelings. I indicate the conclusion: to "own" her own sexuality, Eileen will have to separate from her mother.

Eileen has much to think about. The sig for the next week is the same as for the previous week: buy an erotic book, read, masturbate.

Individual session 4—One Week Later

A week of working through the resistances. Eileen masturbated once without a book, but was distracted thinking about the last session. Then she bought an erotic book (a compendium of fantasies), read it, thought it distasteful, finally found an appealing fantasy, started to masturbate, and then stopped—she had to do some reading in history!

No masturbatioan for the rest of the week, and her erotic book again seemed too "coarse." So Eileen began to make up her own fantasies: of watching a man's body while he is playing tennis; of masturbating while talking to someone on the telephone; of sitting at a restaurant table with one man while another is under the table performing cunnilingus on her—and just as she climaxes all the lights go out. The fantasies have two elements in common, secrecy (nobody is supposed to know what's going on) and passivity—the passivity of the passive-aggressive. The secrecy is equated with "getting away" with something, and this feels to Eileen like assertion. Now the therapist provides the meaning: Eileen is acting not for her own sake but against someone else, and therefore she is not free to choose what is best for her. She can have an orgasm only when rebelling, not for herself; but this also evokes strong guilt feelings. The passive fantasies tie in with her passive behavior, and with the suppression of anger at her mother. The way out is to take an active role: first, to become angry with her mother, facing and sharing the pain and loss; and next, to be good to herself, to be a good mother to Eileen, to be grown up.

The sig is more reading and masturbation.

Individual Session 5—One Week Later

Eileen has had orgasm. It was a complicated week, fighting with Charles and her friends, problems at her job and in school. All alone finally, Eileen began reading her erotic book, masturbated, felt the urge to stop and curl up her legs, continued the stimulation, felt the orgasm coming, continued, climaxed—and cried and covered her face. What were her feelings at the time? Terror, guilt, fear of the pleasant sensations she was experiencing, and pride that she had experienced orgasm, that she had fought her way through. Why had she covered her face? "Because I thought I was going blind."

Insights begin to flood Eileen. What will happen if she goes blind? "I won't see how ugly I am." She also feels ugly when she is angry, she doesn't know what she will say, and it feels as though a lot of garbage is coming out. For Eileen, then letting go is to be ugly. Why has she been arguing with her friends? Because she has become less accommodating. She has always been known as a "very giving" person, who let herself be imposed upon because that was the only hope she had of being taken care of. But she sees now that she must give to herself, that she is a big girl and can take care of herself.

A sharing of good feeling between patient and therapist. The sig is more of the same, perhaps using a vibrator.

Individual Session 6—One Week Later

Another orgasm (reading in addition to manual stimulation), no crying, some tightness in her chest, some stiffening but persistence through this . . . very exciting, somewhat unnerving.

A new development occurred. Charles, who had never questioned Eileen on her individual sessions, began to pressure her for intercourse and she has been refusing, not wanting to handle more than one thing at a time. They quarreled, and Eileen developed another worry: Can she experience orgasm again?

Conjoint sessions will soon be necessary, but Eileen needs more practice having orgasms. The sig is to continue masturbating, and to try using a vibrator.

Individual Session 7—One Week Later

Manual masturbation to orgasm—Eileen doesn't care for the vibrator.

On her own, Eileen began to include Charles in the exercises. They talked together for a time; then Charles masturbated Eileen manually, and she found it pleasant but too distracting; then each masturbated to orgasm. Eileen externalizes. She cannot understand why Charles wants to stimulate her: "It takes such a long time." He may say that he wants to, but Charles does many things he would rather not do. She doesn't deserve this attention.

These are problems, but this has been a very positive development. If the previous pattern holds, Charles will exhibit some resistance this next week, but perhaps this is evoked by being confronted with his behavior and feelings in a treatment context. I will continue seeing only Eileen, but I will suggest exercises for both of them.

The sig is for Eileen to read and masturbate, and then for Charles to enter and finish off by thrusting.

Individual Session 8—Two Weeks Later

They had trouble finding a position; also, Eileen had vaginal itching and burning when Charles entered; she may have an infection. They attempted intercourse three times. Once they each reached orgasm through masturbation; once Eileen stimulated her clitoris while Charles was inserted and they both had an orgasm; and once

Charles had an orgasm by himself—Eileen was in too much pain.

Eileen is essentially orgastic. During sex itself, Charles appears to be a good partner. But Eileen is troubled about their relationship now: apart from intercourse Charles is withdrawing from her—he goes to sleep, he doesn't talk, he doesn't share his feelings, and he avoids closeness. I decide to bypass Charles' resistance, to help Eileen continue to have orgasm in coitus. The next step in this direction is the bridge maneuver. "Most coitally inorgastic women who are orgastic on clitoral stimulation can climax if they are stimulated (to orgasm) at the same time the penis is contained in the vagina . . . . The bridge maneuver is different in that the basic idea is to provide the woman with clitoral stimulation *up* to the point of, but not actually to, orgasm, and then let coital thrusting trigger off the orgastic reflex. Thus the 'bridge' between clitoral stimulation and coitus" (4).

The sig is the bridge maneuver (which is usually performed in the side-to-side position). Since Charles appears fairly cooperative in strictly sexual matters, there are hopes for a good result. Conjoint therapy will be resumed starting with the next session.

Conjoint Session 6—Ten Days Later

Encouraging. Various outside problems kept Eileen and Charles separated during most of this time, and they attempted intercourse only once. Eileen was very tight and at first Charles couldn't enter; when he did, however, there were not many problems. Eileen did not have an orgasm, but came close; Charles did have an orgasm, but with difficulty. Neither one felt as much stress as in the past. Eileen feels now that she is less demanding that every time be successful; she can wait and work for a good outcome. They feel closer, more intimate.

The sig is the same, with the suggestion that Eileen guide Charles's penis into her vagina when she is ready.

Conjoint Session 7—Two Weeks Later

Negotiating problems. Eileen and Charles had trouble deciding on positions, times, and procedures, and no satisfactory sex of any kind took place. At the same time, she began having violent quarrels with her older brother: he wants to be an uncle right away, and never mind any of her thoughts about a career!

Eileen is aware of a fear of being cheated. At best, her life with Charles can be close and cooperative; at worst, it is a power struggle. At best, sex can be warm and close; but at some level she is afraid to have Charles inside her. It seems to be tied in with her sense of powerlessness: the superior power of Charles's penis; the superior power of her brother's age and status in the family.

For his part, Charles is withdrawing, behaving erratically and unpredictably, finding ways of sabotaging and spoiling every move toward togetherness she initiates.

The sig is a repeat of the bridge maneuver.

Conjoint Session 8—Two Weeks Later

Power struggle. According to Charles, Eileen raped him: masturbated to orgasm when he was sleeping, woke him, and insisted on sex—twice. He obliged, full of fury, had an orgasm, and turned away. He has not initiated sex for some time now; this is always left to Eileen, who is growing angrier and angrier.

Charles is afraid of his anger, will not express it directly, saves it up—and days or so after the event he acts it out in some way to punish Eileen. Eileen is furious: she does not believe that Charles will ever change and is not sure how much she herself can change into a totally independent person. What she can see is that sex is not the cause of her problems but the focus, the place where her (and Charles's) other problems are brought.

It is apparent to them both that this is no longer a problem for sex therapy. Eileen has become orgastic and her libido appears to have increased: the sex therapy has been successful. The relationship may or may not improve; but Eileen is in treatment with a therapist whom she trusts. A termination session is scheduled for two weeks later.

Termination

Charles and Eileen arrive half an hour late; their car has broken down. Charles is charming, but nervous and tense. He has been doing some thinking, confronting the results of his withdrawing behavior. He has also been thinking about Eileen, the improvement she has realized, the fact that she wants still more satisfaction out of life. He wants that same satisfaction, and is ready to take responsibility for getting it. Charles has decided to enter individual psychotherapy.

Evaluation

Eileen's therapy has been a success; she is consistently orgastic, and is taking responsibility for herself in new areas. For Charles, the therapy has been successful also, especially considering the context. He is moving to take care of himself—in the circumstances, a triumphant conclusion.

And the therapeutic program? It was a difficult case with many decision points. Perhaps Charles should have been confronted earlier, rather than allow so much time to go by before really addressing the problem of his sabotage. Perhaps the therapist was not confronting the clear evidence of his resistances, but was hoping unrealistically that they could be helped directly as a couple with a relationship rather than as two people living together with a sexual problem. But these are too many perhapses, and the outcome of the program, at least, was satisfying.

NEW DIRECTIONS IN THE NEW SEX THERAPY

The future of sex therapy has two aspects: developments within the field of sex therapy and the impact of the new sex therapy on related disciplines. What is newest about the new sex therapy is its amalgam of psychotherapeutic approaches in the behavioral sciences into one specific therapy that is highly effective. It seems very likely that similar amalgams, combining behavioral goals with interpersonal or intrapsychic procedures, will have application in many areas apart from sex therapy. As Sollud has stated (11), "As these goals are achieved, an initial therapeutic momentum is created. The patient comes to believe in his ability to change aspects of his life, and the neurotic cycle of powerlessness and suffering is interrupted."

Success in achieving a goal can of itself have beneficial ramifications far beyond those originally sought; and it is common, after successful sex therapy, for couples to report improved interpersonal and intrapsychic functioning. In a follow-up session four months after sex therapy had been successfully terminated, one couple reported the feeling that now they could "lick anything." They indicated some disagreement between themselves as to when to start having children, but they were quite confident that they could work this out.

No claim is made that the new sex therapy initiated the movement toward the integration of separate therapeutic techniques into flexible treatment procedures; Marks and Gelder (7) were pointing in this direction at least ten years ago. The new sex therapy does, however, provide a large significant body of consistent data that leave no doubt as to its success. It is known informally that some psychiatrists and family therapists, exposed to the new sex therapy, have begun incorporating the experiential, behavioral-task approach into their own treatment procedures. It can only be expected that this movement will continue.

Within the new sex therapy, advances are sure to be made. This chapter has been written as though treatment is afforded only to couples, not to individuals. The reason is that statistically significant data have been collected only for couples. Work has been done, however, and is continuing, on the treatment of individuals in individual sessions, the treatment of individuals in group sessions, and on the treatment of couples in group sessions.

One dysfunction, orgastic difficulties, does not always need a partner to be treated (although treatment to result in coital orgasm does). Treatment of women patients with orgastic problems has, based on initial results, been as successful as treatment in couples. The group treatment of single males for premature ejaculation has been attempted; it has not achieved the spectacular success of treatment in couples because the exercises do require a partner. Some males, however, were able to find partners and effect their cures, while others, reinforced by the emotional support of the group, were able to comtemplate the thought of finding partners with reduced fear. It is also worth pointing out that the success rate for such groups—about 50 percent—is still higher than that achieved by any other treatment. The group treatment of couples with premature ejaculating males has been attempted, with apparent success (5).

Treatment of all-male or all-female groups for other dysfunctions is being explored, as well as treatment of mixed groups of single females and males. Treatment of homosexuals with sexual dysfunctions is almost inevitable. Treatment of persons with physiological sexual handicaps, such as paraplegics, has begun in some places; I myself have with Raul Schiavi, M.D. just undertaken a program at Mount Sinai Medical Center, funded by a grant from the National Institute of Mental Health to investigate and evaluate sex-therapy techniques for men with organic and psychogenic impotence caused by diabetes.

Treatment of patients for whom sex therapy has hitherto been contraindicated will most likely be attempted. "Although these are relative criteria, we do rule out patients and partners with serious medical illness which precludes sexual functioning; drug addicts; severe active alcoholics; active schizophrenic, paranoid or acutely depressed patients; couples engaged in highly destructive or imminently dissolving marriages. . . . We also try to rule out those patients who may not be too seriously or acutely ill to prevent their cooperation in therapy, but show sexual symptoms which clearly constitute defenses against the eruption of major pathology" (3). It will be noted that in the two years since this statement was published (1974), sexual therapy for the physiologically handicappped has begun. It is likely that treatment for other "denied" patients will also be attempted, as results of existing procedures accumulate. Well-compensated schizophrenic males (with cooperating wives) have already been cured of a variety of dysfunctions, as long as treatment was undertaken during periods of remisssion of the pathology and was carried out with extreme attention to the psychodynamic factors.

Finally, as more is learned of the actual sexual responses (important details of the sexual functioning of women are still to be elucidated), and as clinical experience with the dysfunctions and their treatment accumulates, it appears likely that the therapist will be able to more confidently select the optimum combination of approaches. Thus, retarded ejaculation appears to have a 50 percent success rate when treated using intrapsychic methods, and a 60 percent success rate when treated by Masters and Johnson. On the basis of these data, the sex therapist treating retarded ejaculation may very well emphasize psychodynamic insights and techniques more than normally, in the expectation that this would prove more than normally helpful.

One more point should be made. Sex therapy as an independent field is quite recent, the new sex therapy is very new, the need for sex therapy is very great, and effective means for satisfying that need now exist. What this implies is that, at present, there are many competent sex therapists whose approaches will differ to some extent from the one described here. it also means that the future of sex therapy is far from predictable. Just as the descriptions I have provided apply to only a part of the sex-therapy field at present, so my outline of the directions in which sex therapy is proceeding can illuminate only a small portion of its future.

REFERENCES

1. Fensterheim, H. Assertive methods and marital problems. In: *Advances in Behavior Therapy.* New York: Academic Press, 1972.
2. Hogan, P., and Hogan, B. Family treatment of depression. In: *The Nature and Treatment of Depression,* ed. F.F. Flach. New York: John Wiley, 1975.
3. Kaplan, H.S. *The New Sex Therapy: Active Treatment of Sexual Dysfunctions.* New York: Brunner/Mazel, 1974.
4. Kaplan, H.S. *The Illustrated Manual of Sex Therapy.* 1975.
5. Kaplan, H.S., et al. Group treatment of premature ejaculation. *Arch. Sex. Behav.,* 3: 443-452, 1974.
6. Levine, S.B. Premature ejaculation: Some thoughts about its pathogenesis. *J. Sex Marital Ther.,* 4:326-334, 1975.
7. Marks, I.M., and Gelder, M.G. Common ground between behavior therapy and psychodynamic methods. *Brit. J. Med. Psychol.,* 39:11-24, 1966.
8. Masters, W., and Johnson, V. *Human Sexual Response.* Boston: Little, Brown, 1966.
9. Masters, W., and Johnson, V. *Human Sexual Inadequacy.* Boston: Little, Brown, 1970.
10. Sollud, R.N. Behavioral and psychodynamic dimensions of the new sex therapy. *J. Sex Marital Ther.,* 4:335-340, 1975.
11. Sollud, R.N. The new sex therapy: An integration of behavioral, interpersonal, and psychodynamic approaches. Unpublished manuscript, 1975.

Biofeedback Applications in Psychotherapy

IVAN WENTWORTH ROHR

Recent changes in the practice of psychotherapy have included the application of a variety of new techniques (17, 29, 47, 52). The new techniques have come from modifications of traditional personality theories and methods, from laboratory research with animals and humans, and from outside the fields of psychiatry and psychology. Among the sources are Gestalt therapy by Perls (33), hypnotherapy (20), the biofeedback of Kamiya (26), and varieties of relaxation methods (4, 5, 23). Applications of these methods as a part of psychotherapy often accelerate and enrich the process through symptom reduction and increased affectual experience.

An essential ingredient in these new methods is also basic to verbal therapy: *feedback* to the patient by the therapist, or by the patient himself, of the patient's experience in the form of new and useful information. In verbal therapy, information from the patient is processed and returned by the therapist as he questions and interprets the patient's presentations. This kind of feedback is limited by the therapist's theoretical commitment, his perceptiveness, and his goals; and the patient's endeavors are restricted by his anxiety, confusion, transference, and defenses. These limitations and occupational hazards of traditional psychotherapy, for both therapist and patient, handicap its effectiveness. An additional restriction is imposed by the fact that many symptoms that develop out of unconscious conflicts remain autonomous after the growing and changing person, in or out of therapy, has resolved the conflicts. There is also abundant evidence that for some people symptoms can be "learned" without any direct origin in unconscious conflicts, and can be "unlearned" through re-education (3).

The limitations and hazards of traditional psychotherapy have sharpened the need for therapy methods that give patient and therapist more reliable and clinically useful data. Biofeedback training (BFT) of psychophysiological functions meets some of the needs and is becoming a significant clinical procedure in the treatment of a variety of disorders (6, 15, 22, 28, 38, 49). Where some of the techniques of traditional psychotherapy (18) and of the recently devised, active therapies (16, 32, 34, 36) are incorporated during particular biofeedback applications, each of the general procedures is enhanced by the others.

The differences between BFT and the use of BFT in the context of psychotherapy is of major importance. Various procedures have their own clinical uses and returns; when combined, their returns are increased. Their differences and combined uses will be discussed in detail, essentially in reference to clinical issues. The theoretical problems of psychodynamics, behavior theory, etc., are beyond the scope of this chapter.

BIOFEEDBACK

Biofeedback originates in Cannon's conceptualization of homeostasis in *The Wisdom of the Body* (14):

> Repeatedly I have called attention to the fact that insofar as our internal environment is kept constant [homeostasis] we are freed from the limitations imposed by both internal and external agencies that could be disturbing. The pertinent question ... is freedom for what? It is chiefly freedom for the activity of the higher levels of the nervous system and the muscles they govern. By means of the cerebral cortex we have all our intelligent relations to the world about us.
>
> They are made possible by such automatic regulation of the routine necessities that the functions of the brain which subserve intelligence and imagination, insight and manual skill, are set free for the use of these higher services [pp. 302-303].

Biofeedback techniques attempt to return homeostatic processes to normal balances, thereby freeing the mind of burdensome malfunctions of physiology.

The basic concept of biofeedback application is that of a closed-loop method of controlling a dynamic system by reinserting into the system the result of its past performance (45). In biological feedback systems, the growing organism uses psychophysiological feedback as a normal and necessary process of establishing patterns of competent relationships with the environment. The growing child learns through physiological feedback, *in vivo,* to stand, walk, speak, and to regulate social, emotional, and mental functioning (21). The use of sensitive electronic instruments in electronically enhanced biofeedback is merely the refinement of providing the subjects with appropriate information about the functioning of the physiological systems they wish to modify. The instruments provide an easily recognizable signal, or information, that is otherwise out of the subject's awareness.

The biofeedback machines pick up such signals, usually bioelectrical, amplify, rectify, and convert them into visual and auditory forms. These are then fed back to the subject, thereby giving him immediate and useful information about his physiological functioning (Fig. 1).

The subject attempts to modify volitionally the ongoing activity of his physiology in terms of one or more of its attributes. For example, *rate* (of heart beat or muscle contractions), *intensity* (of body surface temperature, autonomic arousal level, muscle tone), *direction* (of flow of blood throughout the circulatory system, blood pressure), *percentage increase* (of given brain waves, such as alpha, theta, or other frequencies in specified cortical areas), and *shift in the predominance of one subsystem over another* (from sympathetic-nervous-system predominance in reactivity to increased predominance of the parasympathetic nervous system) are among the attributes of various physiological systems that are responsive to BFT.

THE LEARNING PARADIGM

When a signal is made available to the subject, his first task is to comprehend that the signal is a reflection of the ongoing activity of the system being monitored by the feedback machine. This is remarkably easy to accomplish, even by children. Routinely, during the first session, the subject has learned through self-demonstration that the signal does change in the relevant attribute by means of his internal desire for a change to take place in the physiological process. The clearest example is the EMG signal, say rate of clicks or deflection of a needle, that the subject can voluntarily control by tightening or relaxing muscles being monitored: the higher the tension level of the muscles by tightening them, the faster the rate of clicks, or the wider the deflection of the needle being observed. When the subject has learned that simple concept, the initial demand characteristic of BFT has been completed: returning continuously to the subject a discernible signal concerning moment-to-moment changes in a physiological activity. The second demand is the immediate feedback of the signal in analog form (the signal covaries with the physiological activity), or in binary form (the signal indicates a right or wrong response) of the moment-to-moment changes. As the physiology changes, the signal changes virtually immediately. The subject is then able to reinsert into the feedback loop changes based on his immediate past performance. As the signal varies, he knows whether

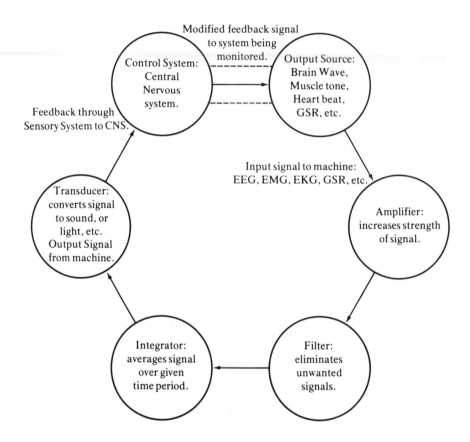

FIGURE 1: Schematic of the electronic biofeedback system.

his physiology is changing in the desired fashion; and he begins to identify and to emphasize the internal operation he uses to bring about such change. Incidentally, most subjects can barely articulate the nature (imagery? sensation? emotion?) of the internal operation, even though they can become highly skilled in the biofeedback procedure.

The last requirement in BFT is the subject's motivation. Most adults are motivated by the need to relieve distress or by the intrinsic rewards of curiosity or achievement. Others are motivated by extrinsic rewards of approval or money. Subjects of the higher education-intellectual levels tend to use intrinsic rewards;

subjects of lower levels are peculiarly lacking in the motivation necessary for prolonged periods of training, even if their complaints are serious and dangerous and they are being paid to participate.

BFT thus appears to fit the operant-conditioning paradigm (39): immediate knowledge of the results of one's performance through feedback, shaping of the desired response through successive approximations, and reward as the reinforcer of correct responses. In this paradigm, the subject continues to engage increasingly difficult levels of physiological activity, throughout each session, and session-by-session, as the sensitivity (gain) of the instruments is increased and, simultaneously, as he gradually masters his ability to regulate his physiology.

INSTRUMENTATION AND PHYSIOLOGY

Electronic BFT in itself, or when strengthened with even minimal techniques from the realm of psychotherapy, has demonstrated its value in revising malfunctions in various physiological systems. Brudny et al. (9) reduced spasmodic torticollis through electromyographic (EMG) biofeedback. Jacobs and Fenton (22) relaxed spasms in injured upper trapezious muscles; other applications of EMG-BFT in rehabilitative medicine have been conducted (1, 25, 31). Budzynski, Stoyva, and Adler (12) also used the EMG in frontalis muscle placement to train tension-headache patients to lower the muscle tension in the head area, thereby reducing the headaches. Other spasms secondary to the pain of cluster headaches, and to tension throughout the head, neck, and shoulders, respond to EMG-feedback relaxation (48). The electroencephalogram (EEG) has been used in the treatment of epilepsy (40), and in achieving states of relaxation through increasing the percentage of alpha-theta waves. The thermister, measuring surface body temperature, has been applied in training migraine and Reynaud's disease patients to increase blood flow to the periphery from the head for symptomatic relief (51). The electrocardiogram (EKG) in BFT assists heart patients in changing the rate or rhythm of some cardiac disorders (46). The dermagram—or the galvanic-skin-response (GSR) machine—has specific applications in monitoring stress levels mediated by the autonomic nervous system (43) in order to diminish anxiety, achieve hypoarousal, and reduce resistances and release affect to consciousness.

Many other applications of each feedback instrument have been reported in the literature; the foregoing examples merely relate each machine to a given physiological system. The issue of the relative independence of each physiological system, or the independence of attributes within a system, is an open question in BFT and psychophysiological research. That is, does a change in one system cross over to produce a change in another system? The answer is mixed. For example, reducing the density of beta rhythm (which is sometimes a reflection of worry, fear, tension, anxiety) through EEG feedback concurrent with increase in density of alpha-theta rhythms (which are often associated with "feelings" of relaxation) does not invariably reduce smooth- or skeletal-muscle tone to significant levels of relaxation, let alone reduce a localized spasticity. Nor does achieving autonomic hypoarousal through GSR feedback invariably cross-over to cause vasoconstriction of arterioles in the head and vasodilation in the periphery to relieve migraine. This issue is of considerable importance in both research design (13) and clinical applications (7). Currently, clinicians appear to be pragmatic in developing treatment plans for any complaint, adding instrumentation and psychotherapy techniques as they assess clinical progress. Generally, though, system specificity holds true in biofeedback applications. If the complaint is a reflections of malfunctioning in the musculature, the EMG is applied; in autonomic malfunctioning, the GSR; in circulatory disorders, the EKG or the thermister; in brain-wave activity, the EEG.

Cross-over or generalized beneficial changes in another system can occur as the targeted physiological system returns to within normal parameters of homeostatic functioning. Needless to say, the clinical rule of thumb regarding prognosis holds in BFT: the healthier the patient, the more efficacious the treatment technique being used, for the target symptom and for co-existing symptoms as well.

Expectations of cross-over are included in some treatment plans for some patients. A common inclusion, for example, is the expectation of improvement in sleep for sleep-onset insomniacs through EMG-induced muscular relaxation of frontalis. This application usually includes reduction of autonomic hyperarousal and increase in alpha-theta density. In the event hyperarousal and muscular spasms in the head region are closely causative in the insomnia, and the EMG application accompanied by relaxation also results in the reduction of autonomic hyperarousal, the insomnia is likely to remit. However, so many individual differences appear in symptom formation and the kinds of responses patients have to BFT, that economical routine applications and reliable treatment plans remain to be clearly established.

EFFECTIVE AGENTS

The identification of the effective agents in BFT is confounded by the numerous variables influential in human functioning. Blanchard and Young's (7) review of both research studies and clinical case studies of BFT concluded that the "soundest" evidence for the efficacy of BFT was confined to EMG applications in areas of muscle rehabilitation, the reduction of subvocalization and tension headaches, especially when the latter is continued with home practice of relaxation exercises. EEG feedback from the sensorimotor cortex is also helpful in epilepsy. The reviewers appear to assess the research and clinical applications from the viewpoint of BFT as they attempt to sort out the effective agents in biofeedback as a clinical treatment procedure in psychosomatic and other disorders of physiology.

Their finding of limited experimental support for establishing BFT, in itself, as a clinical procedure is on firm ground. In fact, BFT in and of itself has limited, but useful, value in the treatment of physiopathologies. In psychopathologies, reducing a psychophysiological malfunction, such as tension headache, hyperarousal, muscle spasticity, or changing cerebral rhythms, may alleviate some of the presenting symptoms. The application in neurotic and psychotic persons may also leave behind the psychic distress, the defective ego or self-image, the guilt, anger, fears, the anatomic change, or whatever, that may have caused or contributed to some of the symptom formations in the first place. Notably, most, if not all, successful BFT applications in psychosomatic disorders are multimodality procedures, drawing on relaxation techniques and behavior therapies. These latter techniques obviously utilize the psyche as a major agent in the treatment of psychopathologies and physiopathologies (8, 30).

Whatmore and Kohli's (49) work in EMG-BFT appears to come closest to being an exception in regard to the extent of their recognition and inclusion of cognitive and emotional variables in their applications. They use multichannel EMG as the primary agent in retraining physiology. Even here, where there is some use of "verbally reassuring and quieting a patient in a phobic situation" (p. 150), the emphasis is still on BFT. The marked de-emphasis of psychotherapeutic techniques may account for the extraordinary number of sessions their procedure runs. For 50 patients presented, the range was 116-517, the median was 204; each session was 90 minutes, twice a week. Daily practice at home was also used. Many of their patients suffered from severe and long-lasting disorders, which may have extended the duration of the treatment procedures. Also, the criterion for remittance or cure may be of a higher level of demand, such as total change in all complaints, than other clinicians maintain—hence the excessive time involved. However, what may well have taken place over the extended periods of their treatment procedures is a gradual and vital, concurrent change in affect, cognition, and attitudes as the "mind" is gradually freeing the body from the restrictions and debilitations of severe physiological disorders. Obviously, an interactive process of change in the mind-body relationship is set in motion during the conscious use of BFT. Attempting to determine which is cause and which is effect is akin to the chicken-egg puzzle and will not be attempted here.

The Whatmore-Kohli approach in clinical practice serves as a model of one end of the continuum of BFT applications in "physiopathologies," as Whatmore prefers. That is, revising the altered functions of physiology due to errors in signaling of the nervous-endocrine systems, as opposed to structural, anatomical alterations. The following model may serve as an example of the other end, but it includes applications to symptoms of primary and secondary relationship to altered structures as well as altered functions in various physiological systems.

APPLICATIONS IN PSYCHOTHERAPY

Applying BFT in psychotherapy involves existential issues of importance to the patient, in addition to symptom reduction. Usually patients have decided on referral as to what they wish to deal with—symptom or self. Some will revise goals in midstream, in either direction, when more complex, intrapersonal material emerges during BFT. They must then decide on the kind and extent of their participation in the clinical procedures. Those who are engaged in psychotherapy will have already made a commitment to the introspective model and proceed to use biofeedback applications to enhance an internal search to the end of intrapersonal change.

When the patient is viewed as a totality of thinking, feeling, and behavioral processes that interact, biofeedback applications are used in attempts to release him from the handicaps of crippling symptoms and limited self-knowledge. In this model, the instruments have two clinical functions: direct applications in BFT to revise psychophysiological functioning, including symptom reduction, and to create more efficient, intrapersonal communications and personality integration. These communications include all parameters of thinking, feeling, and conduct; the last in the sense of both physiology (muscle tone, body sensations and awareness, homeostasis, etc.) and psychic interaction with one's environment (relationships, activities, attitudes, affects, etc.). The instruments of biofeedback are used to create psychophysiological conditions under which psychological processes can be explored, conceptualized, and revised through self-experience and self-knowledge.

A basic condition that accelerates personality integration as well as symptom reduction is a state of relaxation. Research and clinical findings in varieties of relaxation states confirm the healthy consequences of muscular and autonomic states of calm (4, 11, 35, 42, 44). Emotional and mental calm, or the absence of anxiety and poorly integrated affects, are often achieved in relaxed states and can bring additional rewards of lowered blood pressure, improvement in disturbances of sleep, appetite, and sexual functioning, among other changes in both primary and secondary symptoms.

Relaxation Through Focal Attention

Experience with a variety of diagnoses, complaints, and biofeedback applications has led to establishing a verbal relaxation technique that is routinely suitable in most clinical situations. The method consists of teaching the patient to concentrate his attention passively on various regions of his body, the regulation of his breathing and mental contents, and the relaxation of muscular and autonomic levels of functioning. The relaxed state, accompanied by an increase in the self-control of one's own mind and bodily processes, intensifies intrapersonal communication and potentiates biofeedback techniques in themselves, as well as in their applications in psychotherapy.

The patient is informed that the relaxation method can be learned quickly and easily, in about 20-30 minutes, that he can use it to reduce daily stress, and that it will be applied as one of the procedures in treating his complaints. While sitting erect, legs uncrossed, hands in lap, or supine, the patient is instructed to allow his eyes to close and to bring to mind a real life scene that includes feelings of adequacy, calm, well-being, and self-acceptance. The patient is encouraged to recall any details of the scene, the time, place, people, and emotions. He is requested to allow the memories to return, without forcing his thoughts, but to relive the scene as effortlessly as possible; and to allow the feelings that return to grow stronger and stronger, to let the sense of well-being and adequacy permeate his mind and body. After several minutes of reinforcing the recollection, the instructions continue:

> Now tuck that experience in the corner of your mind and bring your attention to your forehead; just be aware of your forehead, of what it feels like. This method is one of passive concentration; of allowing your attention to focus where you want it focused. Allow your forehead to relax; let the tension drain out of your forehead without forcing anything. Let your attention focus easily and passively, and allow yourself to let go. If other thoughts or images come to mind, just let them drift through, don't try to remember them, or to understand anything that comes along.

The therapist continues to guide the patient's attention slowly to major bodily areas: cheeks, jaw, front and back of neck, right shoulder, upper arm, forearm, hand, fingers; and down the front and back of the torso, and then down the other side of the body, including the lower limbs. The procedure is applied slowly, quietly. The patient is occasionally reminded to *allow* his attention to focus quietly on the body area being targeted, and to let his attention return to his body if other thoughts enter his mind. Self-attention to breathing is introduced when respiration rate and depth have obviously lowered, commonly after the head area has been attended to. The patient is instructed: "Be aware of your breathing. On the fringe of your attention, you can recite to yourself various words in rhythm with your breathing: calm, quiet, relaxed, peaceful; or you can count, one—two, one—two."

A goal of the procedure is to train the patient to regulate his thoughts and to direct his attention, while his ego observes its own functioning. Moreover, removing unwanted thoughts from the mind can't occur by direct attempts to push them out. They are best removed by being replaced by other mental contents and the reduction, eventually, of disturbing affects and attached anxiety.

Each patient responds individually to the procedure, in terms of motivation, level of anxiety, the intactness and strength of the ego, the nature of the defenses, and the kind and severity of the psychopathology. Neurotics are rarely disturbed by the release of suppressed or repressed material. The response of psychotics, or other patients with ego defects, is only slightly more variable and unpredictable, but still not disruptive.

The purpose of the recall and enhancement of an experience of personal adequacy is to be able to reintroduce the recollection of such a state into the patient's consciousness in moments of anxiety or distress that may disrupt the relaxation procedure, and during internal searches. Occasional patients cannot utilize this relaxation technique and Jacobson's (23, 24) procedure in a highly abbreviated form is then applied. Home practice in relaxing is encouraged in order to develop skill in self-relaxation. An audiotape of the office session can be useful to many patients in their practice sessions. After the procedure has been applied, the patient should continue the self-involvement for several minutes. Finally, the therapist instructs him to "return your attention, slowly, gradually, to the present. Let your eyes open slowly."

Most patients achieve quite deep states of mental and physical relaxation. Those who appear to achieve minimal progress in the first application are usually rather rigid and not given to introspection. They fear a loss of control and are likely to be externalizers rather than internalizers. Jacobson's progressive relaxation method is then usually effective since it uses active, controlling efforts, alternating with letting go of tensed muscles.

Patients should be asked after the procedure as to what they experienced mentally, emotionally, and physically. What images came to mind? Did any region of the body seem particularly tense? These data are incorporated in further clinical procedures. The therapist can monitor, or use as feedback, the relaxation procedure through GSR or EMG instruments.

Clinical Use of Biofeedback

Once the patient has achieved a significant level of relaxation, various psychotherapeutic techniques can be applied. The techniques are selected in terms of the complaints, ego strength, etc. Systematic desensitization while muscularly relaxed (53) is a commonly applied behavior technique in cases of phobias, with best results in animal and object phobias (27, 50). Severe social anxieties and agoraphobias, which are suggestive of chronic, diffuse anxiety and poor egos, are more difficult to remit. These patients appear to require more time, interspersed with an analysis of historical events and relationships that prevented the development of normally differentiated egos and defenses. GSR feedback for relaxation in treating phobias and diffuse anxiety, and for monitoring by the therapist of autonomic responses to anxiety-provoking stimuli, provides the therapist with a signal that is below the patient's awareness, and tracks the fight-flight character of sympathetic activity. Frontalis muscle tension is questionable as an index for measuring anxiety level (2). Probably an increase in frontalis tension level from above 2 to 3 microvolts (μV) once any spasm in frontalis has been reduced (through BFT) is a measure of normal response to any stimuli. Three to 4 μV, usually considered a moderate level of muscular tension, may be a function of the increase in facial muscle tension as inhibitory of internal emotionality that the patient does not want to reveal through facial expressions, rather than a sign of anxiety alone. One simply masks one's feelings by tightening muscles—the "poker face." Consequently, tracking changes in anxiety level in patients may require monitoring to be conducted through other physiological systems; through EMG electrode placement elsewhere (e.g., sternocleidomastoid, occipital muscles); or in the symptom-specificity response model-response stereotypy of Sternback (41). That is, most patients manifest one or more stereotypic symptom formations (tension in neck, butterflies in the stomach, hyper-arousal, obsessive ruminations, etc.), and a patient's particular symptom recurs under stress. Using the patient's stereotypic response as the target for BFT *and* as the "thermostat" for anxiety manifestation, during the application of other thera-peutic interventions, provides an idiosyncratic and reliable output signal for track-ing anxiety responses during treatment.

The Toomims' (43) use of the GSR is an outstanding example of the clinical use of a biofeedback instrument in uncovering anxiety-laden fantasies and repressed emotions, the indications of which are difficult to identify through free association, or through the traditional observations of the patient by the therapist. Changes in the GSR's output signal, as the sympathetic nervous system reacts to internal and external stimuli, can be modified in complicated ways by anxiety and other affects. Apparently inexplicable deviations in the GSR signals are clues to sympathetic re-activity that are out of the patient's awareness. Consequently, in this procedure, the patient and therapist are able to identify hidden emotional reactivity as it occurs and to then enhance self-awareness and search out the mental contents.

Some Case Examples

An example of a GSR signal of profound and severely repressed anxiety is re-flected in the case of a 36-year-old, single woman whose seven years of psycho-analysis removed many difficulties in living but left her still feeling empty, often depressed, and with mild, recurrent episodes of derealization. She was referred for hypnosis and biofeedback after the analysis had run its course. While relaxed, through GSR feedback, she was guided in imagery toward a beach to desensitize her to her fear of water. The GSR signal suddenly increased in amplitude and the pa-tient began to undergo an acute anxiety episode. She explained later that she had visualized an enormous wave suddenly advancing over the ocean toward her. She associated the wave with her mother's psychotic episodes of rage and violence during her childhood. The patient had discussed those terrifying experiences with her analyst many times, but she had not been able to re-experience physiologically and emotionally the traumatic events which, when repressed, also repressed emo-tionality, leaving her in a chronic state of depression. Probably the deep, relaxed state achieved through GSR feedback lowered repression sufficiently to release the primitive terror. Repeated applications of the procedure released increasing amounts of anxiety and emotionality, with concurrent reduction in the derealization, empti-ness, and depression, and with improvement in living.

One example of the use of GSR and relaxation techniques, in an attempt to per-mit the use of psychotherapy, involves a case of alcoholsim and self-isolation. Mrs. T. had suffered a right-side cardiovascular accident 11 years previously. Five years later she fainted on the street with no recollection of any cause. She returned home and stayed in for six years, drinking heavily to relieve anxiety. She was finally hospitalized and referred for adjunctive treatment of diffuse anxiety and agoraphobia. In the initial interview, she complained of sleep-onset insomnia, recurrent palpitations with restlessness and nausea, headaches related to premenstrual depression, and muscle tension across her shoulders and scalp. Mrs. T. was taught the relaxation method in the first session, with good response, and was treated with a combination of GSR and EMG training and verbal therapy. At the beginning of treatment, the focus was on lowering her general level of tension through use of relaxation techniques. She responded very well, often going into a near-trancelike state. An attempt was made to set up a hierarchy to reduce the agoraphobia, but no circumscribed fears seemed to be involved and any hierarchy was not useful. As she became more relaxed, however, she was able to go out, first accompanied and then occasionally alone. She often had her husband walk her part way to the hospital, and then she went the rest of the way—perhaps 6 blocks—by herself. After a dozen sessions, she was discharged to outpatient status for further BFT and psychotherapy.

Mrs. T.'s hyperaroused state appeared to be a crucial basis for some of her current disabilities in living, but not the sole cause. The therapist's termination note reported:

> It became apparent in talking with Mrs. T. that her husband had a stake in keeping her helpless, as he frequently accompanied her when it was not necessary, and that she herself was reluctant to become more independent. While much of the agoraphobia had disappeared, Mrs. T. still seized on any excuse to avoid going out by herself. She felt trapped, tied down, and impotent to control her life, but when she had begun to improve she began to cancel therapy sessions and retreated more and more to her house. She was very depressed about her living situation and felt that only when she and her husband moved would she be able to be really well; however, she also used the move as a way of escaping therapy and became unreachable. It was thus impossible to work with her on reasons for her retreat.
>
> Although general relaxation aided by the GSR was the main technique used in therapy with Mrs. T., the EMG, placed on the neck, was also tried to help reduce neck tension. Mrs. T. never achieved good control over the EMG output, but seemed to become less bothered by neck pains, although her basal level remained at around 9 μV.
>
> Mrs. T. improved considerably during the course of treatment. She was able to use relaxation techniques at home and became able to go outside alone for the first time in 6 years. However, there was also a dynamic resistance to improvement which ultimately led to termination before the considerable gains Mrs. T. had made were really consolidated. It has been impossible to reach her since termination to determine how she is doing at present.

Using the feedback machines and relaxation to decondition autonomic hyperarousal appeared to diminish the diffuse anxiety and agoraphobia, thereby improving her competence in interacting with the environment and permitting an attempt at self-understanding.

The second illustration of biofeedback applications, relaxation, and an internal

search is that of a professional woman who was clearly more accessible to psychotherapy. She was referred for treatment procedures adjunctive to her psychoanalysis. The analytic procedure had encountered a plateau in that, when she would
"search into her fantasies and regress" in analytic sessions, she would begin to
"drift off" saying she felt "nebulous." Experiences of "drifting off" in classes as a
young child had been recalled as early examples of these episodes. Evidently, a
significant degree of anxiety erupted and interfered with emotional recall during
the analytic sessions. The process and its consequences were tentatively viewed as a
lack of intergration of somatic and affective experiences with consciousness, due to
the onset of the anxiety. Techniques considered were hypnosis and biofeedback
(EMG and GSR).

In the initial interview, M. presented herself as a coherent, intelligent, highly
motivated woman, who had enjoyed good success in most areas of living. Maturation was uneventful. There were no other outstanding complaints except for
periods of feeling that she was "rushing through the day, gritting my teeth." She
sometimes awakened with her teeth clenched, and she had undergone a marked,
prolonged depression a few years before, without known cause.

Biofeedback monitoring was utilized with EMG surface electrode placement on
the frontalis and GSR monitoring of autonomic arousal level, without feedback
signals. EMG baseline fluctuated 3.0-7.5 μV, with a rapid (20") decrease to 1.5 μV:
GSR baseline was average with equally rapid decrease. Both changes indicated a
deep and quick response to muscular and autonomic relaxation. EMG-feedback
signal was nulled toward the end of the session, and she was able to maintain the
relaxed state without feedback reinforcement. At the end of the session, she reported feeling at ease, though she had felt a need "to perform" in lowering the
feedback signal. She used mantras to offset the inappropriate mental effort.

In the next session, EMG application was repeated, frontalis baseline was 3.0 μV,
indicating a moderate tension level. Hypnotic induction was utilized to recall and
reinforce an event of adequacy and well-being. She was then asked to revisit her
home at age five to six, to visualize herself standing as a young child of 5 in some
important spot in that house, and that various important people would come by
and interact with her briefly. She reported: "First, Daddy. Joy; reassurance;
loving . . . Second, big brother. Protected." (Anyone else?) "Couldn't find Mom.
She was giving a lesson . . . Third, another brother, Mad. Then I found Mom and
she was annoyed. She was giving a lesson . . . Fourth, the cook. Friendly, warm;
place of refuge."

She was instructed to dream and to remember everything upon awakening. After
terminating the trance, M. reported feeling deeply relaxed and "that this is my
body," as she touched her arms and legs. "I feel connected together, this is all me."
She had not dreamed, but had recalled a recurrent childhood nightmare of being
attacked by a dog. She had also experienced the "important spot" as "being stuck
in the hall." Her mother's studio opened off the hallway.

During the third session, machine monitoring was not used; the session focused on her recall of the "hallway" scene and its ramifications. Under a moderate trance, she was asked to go back in time, stopping when and where she chose to. Within a few minutes she reacted with a smile of pleasure and said she was back in "1967; peace, love, by everyone; undemanding love; didn't have to perform; just be self."

The feeling was enhanced through suggestion and "stored," and she was then instructed to return to the hallway, to stand facing the door of her mother's studio, and to see her mother standing in the doorway, looking at her. "She just looks at me. Not angry. Just looking, 'You know better.' So why do I make noise and disturb her?" [What do you feel now?] "I don't know what's really expected of me, and why she's not mine and why can't I go in there. Her students do. I'm feeling scared—and angry—at the same time. How can I know, if no one tells me? Mother went back in the room. It happened again, and I still don't know why. And why does she belong to those people and not me? I don't see what's so sacred about that room."

She was asked to focus on the two feelings and to let the stronger one intensify. After several minutes, her associations were elicited: "She doesn't like me! I never thought of that. I'm mad." The trance was removed and M. continued to reiterate her surprise at her anger and her thought that her mother didn't like her.

The following session was confined to further recall of the hallway scene and use of guided fantasy under hypnosis. She could visualize her parents' interacting in the hallway: "Can see them; she's beautiful. I can't discern her mood. He's jealous of the men [mother worked with]. He's mad. They're going to have a fight. I always felt they would fight about something other than what they talk about." (Such as?) "What she does all day, whom she sees. He's getting affectionate, but she doesn't want it—not in front of the kids. She pushes him away. He looks puzzled. He's one of those cuddly people." (What else takes place?) "They have arguments about money. I'm on Daddy's side. He always looks so hurt; as though he can't understand why she pushes him away."

The trance had lightened and signs of affect had diminished. M. was returned to the present; the trance was deepened, and she was instructed to visualize herself sitting in an empty theatre and to write and conduct a short scene. She saw her mother on the stage giving a concert, and she felt proud of her mother. M. then began to compare herself to her mother. "You never measured up. You can always do better [according to her mother]. I was fat. I wanted to lose weight but she wouldn't let me diet. She didn't want me to be pretty."

M.'s associations continued freely: her mother thought girls are trouble, boys are bad; her father liked her, no matter what; her mother didn't like her; and that made a difference to M., although she didn't know how. M. wanted to be like her grandmother as a person, but beautiful and smart like her mother. "I am smart; that's the only thing I could be sure of." (After a long silence she was encouraged to speak.) "I'm thinking of wanting to be loved for myself and not what I can do." (What feeling now?) "I feel lost, like in the hallway. Mother never saw me, only my performance. I feel alone; nothing under my feet." M. was weeping and after a few minutes the trance was reduced. Her first thought was of being angry with her father and her analyst, accusing them both of being ineffectual.

The next two sessions were devoted to reinstituting the experiences of isolation and helplessness and attempting to induce through recall and intensification of attached affects a sense of well-being. Under hypnosis, she was instructed to recall another real event during which she felt a sense of competence and well-being; then she was told to visualize herself in a thick fog and as the fog thinned she would find herself alone on a vast, empty plain. She reported feeling "empty, rootless." The image of the plain was removed and, upon being asked to recall her house, she reported, "I have a doll—hanging on to it. Feeling hopeless. Three, four years old. In my crib, rocking. No use crying; no one is going to hear it. I want anybody to hear it. Feel alone, hopeless; like you're going to die, or be lost forever." (Have you felt this way recently?) "Yes, on and on." (What do you do to change it?) "I don't do anything. I've thought of going out windows." (What does your body feel like now?) "In my chest and stomach I feel hollow."

M. then had an image of a rosebush growing "flowers and thorns. Beauty and self-protection."

She was then instructed to recall the event of well-being and to intensify the affect. After trance reduction, M. expressed her fear of losing control and wanting to cry—meanwhile wiping her eyes. She said she now felt "more solid; usually I feel vague." Her emotional involvement in her recollections had obviously been profound, as judged by her body movements and tone of voice.

EMG monitoring was used in the next session, without feedback, to assess somatic response. Frontalis was low at onset (3.5 μV) and lowered to less than 1.0 within 10 minutes. Trance induction proceeded quickly. She was taken back to the hallway, her attention cleared of associations to anyone but her mother. (You're looking at the studio door; your mother comes out and walks toward you, smiling, and picks you up.) "I can't imagine that scene." (Can you feel anything?) "I can't feel her. I feel cold inside." (Anything else?) "It's like I'm holding her around her knees and she won't pick me up. I feel angry, frightened, bad. I don't understand." (Call your mother.) M. whispered, "Mommy." (When encouraged to call louder) "I'm scared. I don't know. She won't hear me. She's stiff; doesn't want me to touch her. She's mad. I don't know why. She's still not mad about pushing my brother down the stairs. She thinks I don't need her."

The frontalis level rose sharply during this session. Time was allowed for M. to integrate the recollections. She was then relaxed to a deep level and the trance was removed. M. reported that she couldn't remember what her mother's body felt like; only her knees. Nor could she remember being picked up or held by her; as she could by her father, on whose lap she would sit as late as age 12.

The next session was confined to analysis of her current, spontaneous reactions of anger toward members of her family, especially one brother who had caused her father to slap her, and toward her contemporaries. M.'s childhood desire to be like her mother, to dress like her, and her ambivalent feelings toward her mother were also re-explored.

The central problem of her self-image was reassessed under hypnosis in the following session. While in a moderate trance, M. was asked to recall the three women in a dream she had had in analysis, to approach each in turn and inquire, "Who are you? What do you feel about who you are? Which of the three does each one like the best?" Frontalis tension level increased moderately during the ten-minute period. She was asked to recall any sensation that went with each dialogue and then to focus her full attention on the "thing" one of the three women had kicked into the quarry. GSR level increased sharply. When asked to report, she said, "I couldn't figure out what I kicked, but kept remembering Bob—the first guy I went out with. He was the first one to make me pay attention to what I feel, and that I feel something. The kitchen scene comes back—when we split. I didn't want to feel because I couldn't imagine life without him, so I didn't feel anything. It's the same with Leo when I got his postcard and got angry. I will not have him in the future and so don't want to feel anything regarding him." (At this point M. was crying and overtly distressed.) "The reason I kicked that thing in the dream—I kick things away before they become important."

Several minutes of silence elapsed before M. was asked about the dialogues with the three women: "One I liked, and she liked herself. The second one liked what people think of her. The third one—a bitch—one who kicked the thing. The bitch hiding behind the child. The two sitting down said, 'Whatever you kicked over the edge was important and you don't have the right to kick it over so thoughtlessly, without thinking of it.' The third one is the woman who is threatened by the thing."

After trance reduction, M. said, "The thing is men; I kicked them away. Bob first, because our backgrounds were so different. Fred called off the engagement because he was going to be drafted."

The last session was opened by M. reporting "separation anxiety. My stomach is in a knot. I've been sighing; I feel like crying, I'm going away on vacation and don't know where." Relaxation was applied with rapid reduction of the stomach spasm. She reported, "feeling safe, protected, feel sure of myself now; both my feet are on the ground."

The general impression was that M. had not established her self-identity as a female, as an intellectual, or as a professional in any firm fashion. She appeared to have rejected her mother as an object of identification and to have substituted a brother, who she soon realized was not as loving as she had believed him to be; and to have identified with personal traits of her father (passivity and gentleness). She pictured herself growing up as "ugly, smart, unappealing as a girl." The rejection of her excellent intellectual capacities may be related to the rejection of her mother, who was considered bright.

The EMG-GSR monitoring indicated that emotionality directly experienced produced anxiety and led to an acute experience of "loss." She would emote and not be conscious of internal affect. As the sessions progressed, she became more rapidly aware of emotionality and the accompanying body sensations, and more consciously able to identify the particular feelings, their contexts, and some of their antecedents. She continued her analysis with increased emotional responsiveness.

The adjunctive procedures appeared to have diminished the isolation of affect from thought and conduct as the patient became increasingly in touch with somatic, physiological processes.

Reintegrating autonomic arousal and cognitive functioning, as in these three cases, can also be useful in treating psychotic patients for whom autonomic instability is a common finding.

Mrs. S. was a 28-year-old, married woman, mother of two, who presented lifelong complaints of pervasive anxiety, many phobias, fainting spells, low self-esteem, impaired social judgment, depressive episodes, and "feelings of coming apart at the seams." She was twice hospitalized for depression and agitation, diagnosed as schizophrenic, and treated with medication and ECT during the first hospitalization. Her private psychiatric care had not changed the crippling symptoms and she had become increasingly withdrawn and fearful. During the second hospitalization she was referred for adjunctive treatment of the chronic anxiety and the agoraphobia. She reported feeling despairing of any change, having suicidal thoughts, dizziness, sleep disturbances, and loss of appetite and interests.

Mrs. S. was treated in the hospital and followed privately in collaboration with her psychiatrist. Procedures included relaxation techniques induced and monitored through GSR and desensitization for specific phobias and imagery of anxiety-provoking situations (streets, stores, crowds, buses) by visualizing herself in such situations while deeply relaxed. When anxiety levels increased, she was re-relaxed until she could imagine herself applying simple coping devices to deal with the situations and people she found threatening in those contexts. Many ordinary scenes were recalled while deeply relaxed, and the identification of her emotions and thoughts was searched out in order to help her identify what she felt and thought, and how she could regulate and express these reactions with reasonable success. She managed in varying degrees to generalize, *in vivo,* many of the changes gained in the office procedures. Within a few weeks she could abort severe anxiety attacks through self-relaxation by "telling myself to relax." There was a lessening of the agoraphobia, although she was still restricted in the distance she could travel from her house by herself. Some feared situations were experienced with a significant change in anxiety (school conferences, taking her son to a clinic for medical care, moving into her own apartment away from her parents, staying alone in her apartment, some social relationships) over the 22 treatment sessions.

On termination, Mrs. S. still suffered periods (minutes to a few hours) of varying levels of anxiety, recurrent episodes of feelings of isolation and purposelessness, reactions of frenzy when planning social events with parents or in-laws, claustrophobic episodes, states of emptiness, and preoccupations with her future. Except for occasional episodes of acute, severe anxiety reactions, and the limitations in distance from home, the patient reported that most of the remaining complaints were manageable. She continued in psychotherapy with her psychiatrist who had confirmed the reported changes.

A 35-year-old, male, homosexual schizophrenic presented problems on referral of pervasive and crippling anxiety attacks, low self-esteem, obsessive ruminations including fantasies of pederasty, disruptions in work, and marijuana abuse of 10 cigarettes per day. The therapist's treatment plan was relaxation training, GSR and EMG feedback, desensitization of anxiety reactions, reduction of ruminations through thought stoppage, and elimination of the drug abuse through daily record-keeping, and developing a recognition of the connection between drug use and anxiety episodes. In 12 sessions, once a week, the patient had reduced smoking to one to two times a day; he could prevent or abort most anxiety attacks and ruminations; and he was reported as being more realistically related in his concurrent group-therapy sessions.

In the treatment of a former chronic alcoholic, who was manic-depressive, several methods were also used concurrently or in sequence. She was a 45-year-old woman who had a 20-year history of alcoholism and psychiatric complaints, including hypertension, migraine, multiple phobias, chronic insomnia, and severe morning nausea. There had been two hospitalizations for acute, agitated depressions with three courses of electroshock therapy and a sympathectomy for the migraine. She was referred privately for biofeedback application for her tension headaches, migraine, and multiple phobias.

The alcoholism and agitated depressions had been brought under control, but she still suffered from such severe muscle tension throughout her head and shoulders that she could barely sleep and arose each morning feeling nauseated. Her phobias interfered with traveling, remaining alone, and her social activities. The tension in her forehead was so intense that she could not use hairspray. If the spray dried on her forehead, the constriction of her skin would cause excruciating pain. Her blood pressure was abnormally high, and the dosage of some of the medications she was taking was close to dangerous levels.

She was taught the relaxation procedure and placed under a light hypnotic trance. EMG feedback was used to reduce the severe muscle spasms in the upper and middle trapezious, and GSR feedback was used to reduce autonomic hyper-arousal and to monitor her ongoing response to various behavior and autogenic techniques, and hypnotic suggestion, The headaches and phobias diminished, the morning nausea abated, she reduced the dosage level of several medications, and her blood pressure returned to near-normal limits. She accomplished these gains within a dozen sessions.

Treatment Considerations

EMG frontalis placement was less useful in these cases of psychosis for achieving relaxation than GSR feedback. Evidently the patients were autonomic responders when made anxious, as opposed to those whose anxiety resides predominately in the skeletal musculature.

Goldstein (19) studied psychotics, neurotics, character disorders, and normals in various physiological systems, and nonpsychotic depressives, nondepressives, and normals, and hysterics, nonhysterics, and normals as second and third groups for similar inter- and intragroup comparisons. Physiological systems studied included motor-action potentials of seven muscle groups (EMG), palmar resistance (GSR), respiration, heart rate, and blood pressure. The EMG and GSR findings are specifically relevant to the present clinical method. Goldstein found the psychotics (most of them schizophrenics) and depressives to be most highly responsive in both skeletal muscle and autonomic systems to stressors (inescapable white noise). Moreover, "there was no evidence of hypo-reactivity among the patients. For the autonomic nervous system, there was an indication that depression was actually characterized by hyper-responsiveness at rest. Group differences were less apparent with the resting motor action potentials. Presumably, emotionally disturbed individuals are able to relax their skeletal muscles as well as normals. On the other hand, relaxation of the autonomic nervous system is more difficult" (p. 48). Notably, anxiety level was controlled across groups, which further establishes autonomic hyperarousal as being related to psychosis and depression, as such, as well as being related to anxiety, as such.

The multimodality, symptom-oriented treatment of choice for anxiety-ridden patients, depressives, and psychotics in the present model consists of: (a) general relaxation augmented by appropriate biofeedback instruments, (b) EMG reduction of specific muscle spasms, (c) GSR-induced hypoarousal, (d) desensitization of specific or diffuse anxiety reactions, and (e) cognitive search and change in affects and attitudes through developing coping methods during states of relaxation. This model is also applicable to the nonpsychotic patients, as previously illustrated, In some instances, where intensive psychotherapy is the primary treatment procedure, this multimodality model serves as an adjunctive procedure to reduce resistances, to enhance intrapersonal communication, or merely for symptom reduction.

Follow-up of a sample of cases characterized by mild to severe degrees of psychopathology revealed acceptable stability in desired changes, provided the anxiety supporting the symptoms, whether bound or free-floating, was significantly reduced, and that cognitive understanding and coping mechanisms had been acquired to deal with real or imagined situations that had been previously disorganizing, especially in schizophrenia.

Symptom reduction is necessary but not sufficient to maintain a desired change in ego functioning. An example of failure in symptom relief is the case of a 65-year-old woman inpatient who was unable to walk because of a 7-year spasm in both legs, diagnosed as conversion symptoms. She was also liable to severe, generalized body spasms. She was referred for EMG applications and hypnotherapy. The patient was treated with Jacobson's relaxation technique in order to develop conscious control over muscle groups, and with EMG placement on the frontalis to enhance relaxation, and on various muscle groups of both legs, to reduce the chronic muscle spasms. The left leg, more severely and chronically tense, began to relax and straighten out within a few sessions, and the large knot at the left ankle diminished and her foot returned to a normal angle. She soon began standing and walking with some direct assistance. The psychopathology became more accessible to consciousness, although she was incapable of insight. A psychic trauma then occurred causing a body spasm, resulting in a fall and an injury, and the treatment procedures became less effective. There was also a recurrence of asthma. Her planned discharge to her family and to private care was carried out in hope of avoiding increased dependence on the hospital. A follow-up found her to have regressed in all areas, and she was again bound to her wheelchair. Evidently, the inability to bring about a change below the symptom level accounted for her regression.

Many other clinical applications have been attempted with lack of success or limited returns. Determining the precise causes of failures is as difficult as determining the precise reasons for successes. Some of both have been suggested throughout this report; they all need careful investigation, variable by variable. Clinical experience strongly indicates that the relatively healthy, monosymptomatic patient responds satisfactorily to noncomplex procedures. Conversely, the more seriously disturbed patients, particularly the psychotics, require a multiplicity of methods in combination or sequence, each of which presumes to influence thinking, feeling, or conduct, in varying degrees and interactions.

SUMMARY

Biofeedback applications in psychotherapy have a wide range of efficacious applications for both primary and secondary symptom relief in a wide variety of complaints. The question of "cure" of neuroses or psychoses is not at issue as a clinical or theoretical problem at the present time in these applications. Clinically speaking, theoretical issues are moot questions when a clinical procedure is found to be helpful, especially in cases where standard procedures have failed or have run their course. If the clinician concentrates on the applications appropriate to the presenting problems and complaints and adds useful techniques as he progresses through the course of treatment, the issue of etiology, diagnosis, and cure are of immediate concern only in terms of the clinician's recognition of the limitations of biofeedback applications in psychotherapy and in the rehabilitation of anatomically injured patients. The clinician will focus his applications on the primary or secondary symptoms arising from the basic problem, or from the behavioral reactions to the problem, thereby permitting a realistic selection of treatment procedures. Experimental studies will eventually resolve many of the questions now confronting clinicians in this area. Meanwhile, creative applications that are harmless to the patient will probably continue to be reported in the literature and will add more answers and more questions in the fields of biofeedback and related treatment techniques.

REFERENCES

1. Andrews, J.M. Neuro-muscular re-education of the hemiplegic with the aid of the electromyograph. *Arch. Phys. Med. Rehab.,* 45: 530-532, 1964.
2. Basmajian, J.V. *Muscles Alive,* 3rd ed. Baltimore: Williams & Wilkins, 1974.
3. Beech, H.R. *Changing Man's behavior.* Baltimore: Penguin Books, 1969.
4. Benson, H. *The Relaxation Response.* New York: William Morrow, 1975.
5. Bernstein, D.C., and Borkovec, T.D. *Progressive Relaxation Training: A Manual for the Helping Professions.* Champaign, Ill.: Research Press, 1973.
6. Birk, L. *Biofeedback: Behavioral Medicine.* New York: Grune & Stratton, 1973.
7. Blanchard, E.B., and Young, L.D. Clinical applications of biofeedback training: A review of the evidence. In: *Biofeedback and Self-Control,* ed. L.V. DiCara. Chicago: Aldine, 1975.
8. Brown, B.B. *New Mind, New Body.* New York: Harper & Row, 1974.
9. Brudny, J., Grynbaum, B.B., and Korein, J. Spasmodic torticollis: Treatment by feedback display of EMG—a report of nine cases. *Arch. Physiol. Med. Rehab.,* 55: 403-408, 1974.
10. Budzynski, T.H., and Stoyva, J.M. An instrument for producing deep muscle relaxation by means of analog information feedback. *J. Appl. Behav. Anal.,* 2: 231-237, 1969.
11. Budzynski, T.H., and Stoyva, J.M. Cultivated low arousal—an antistress response? In: *Limbic and Autonomic Nervous System Research,* ed. L.V. DiCara. New York: Plenum, 1974.
12. Budzynski, T.H., Stoyva, J.M., and Adler, C. Feedback induced muscle relaxation: Application to tension headaches. *J. Behav. Ther. Experiment. Psychiat.* 1: 205-211, 1970.
13. Campbell, D.T., and Stanley, J.C. *Experimental and Quasi-experimental Designs for Research.* Chicago: Rand McNally, 1963.
14. Cannon, W.B. *The Wisdom of the Body.* New York: W.W. Norton, 1939.
15. DiCara, L.V., Barber, T., Kamiya, J., Miller, N.L., Shapiro, D., and Stoyva, J. (eds.). *Biofeedback and Self-control: An Aldine Reader on the Regulation of Bodily Processes and Consciousness.* Chicago: Aldine-Atherton, 1974.
16. Fagan, J., and Shepard, I.L. *Gestalt Therapy Now.* Palo Alto, Cal.: Science and Behavior, 1970.
17. Glick, B.S. Conditioning therapy by an analytic therapist. *Arch. Gen. Psychiat.,* 17: 577-583, 1964.
18. Glover, E. *The Technique of Psychoanalysis.* New York: International Universities Press, 1955.
19. Goldstein, I.B. The relationship of muscle tension and autonomic activity to psychiatric disorders. *Psychosom. Med.* 27: 39-52, 1965.
20. Gordon, J.E. (ed.) *Handbook of Clinical and Experimental Hypnosis.* New York: Macmillan, 1967.
21. Harlow, H.F. *Learning to Love.* San Francisco: Albion, 1971.
22. Jacobs, A., and Fenton, G.S. Visual feedback of myoelectric output to facilitate muscle relaxation in normal persons and patients with neck injuries. *Arch. Phys. Med. Rehab.,* 50: 34-39, 1969.
23. Jacobson, E. *Progressive Relaxation.* Chicago: University of Chicago Press, 1938.
24. Jacobson, E. *Self-operations Control.* New York: J.P. Lippincott, 1964.
25. Johnson, H.E., and Garton, W.H. Muscle re-education in hemiplegia by use of an electromyographic device. *Arch. Phys. Med. Rehab.,* 43: 320-322, 1973.
26. Kamiya, J. Operant control of the EEG alpha rhythm and some of its reported effects on consciousness. In: *Altered States of Consciousness,* ed. C.T. Tart. New York: John Wiley, 1969.

27. Lader, M.H., and Mathews, A.M. A physiological model of phobic anxiety and desensitization. *J. Behav. Res. Ther.,* 6(4): 411-421, 1968.
28. Lang, P. The application of psychophysiological methods to the study of psychotherapy and behavior modification. In: *Handbook of Psychotherapy and Behavior Change,* ed. A.E. Bergin and S.L. Garfield. New York: John Wiley, 1971.
29. Lazarus, A.A. *Behavior Therapy and Beyond.* New York: McGraw-Hill, 1971.
30. Lazarus, R.S. A cognitively oriented psychologist looks at biofeedback. *Amer. Psychol.,* 553-561, 1975.
31. Marinacci, A.A., and Horande, M. Electromyogram in neuromuscular re-education. *Bull. Los Angeles Neurol. Soc.,* 25: 57-71, 1960.
32. Masters, R., and Houston, J. *Mind Games.* New York: Viking, 1972.
33. Perls, F.S. *Gestalt Therapy Verbatim.* Lafayette, Cal.: Real People Press, 1969.
34. Perls, F., Hefferline, R.F., and Goodman, P. *Gestalt Therapy.* New York: Dell, 1951.
35. Reinking, R., and Kohli, M.L. Effects of various forms of relaxation training on physiological and self-report measures of relaxation. *J. Consult. Clin. Pyschol.,* 43: 595-600, 1975.
36. Schutz, W. C. *Joy: Expanding Human Awareness.* New York: Grove Press, 1967.
37. Schwartz, G.E. Biofeedback as therapy: Some theoretical and practical issues. *Amer. Psychol.,* 666-673, 1973.
38. Shapiro, D., and Schwartz, G.E. Biofeedback and visceral learning: Clinical applications. *Serv. Psychiat.,* 4(2): 171-184, 1972.
39. Skinner, B.F. *Behavior of Organisms.* New York: Appleton, 1938.
40. Sterman, M.B., and Friar, L. Supression of seizures in an epileptic following sensorimotor EEG feedback training. *Electro-encephal. Clin. Neurophysiol.,* 33:89-95, 1972.
41. Sternbach, R.A. *Principles of Psychophysiology: An Introductory Text and Readings.* New York: Academic Press, 1966.
42. Stone, R. and DeLeo, J. Psychotherapeutic control of hypertension. *New Eng. J. Med.,* 294(2): 80-84, 1976.
43. Toomin, M., and Toomin, H. *GSR Biofeedback Response Patterns in Psychotherapy.* Los Angeles: Bio-feedback Research Institute, 1975.
44. Wallace, R.K. Physiological effects of Transcendental Meditation. *Science,* 167: 1751-1754, 1970.
45. Weiner, N. *Cybernetics.* Cambridge, Mass.: M.I.T. Press, 1961.
46. Weiss, T., and Engel, B.T. Operant conditioning of heart rate in patients with premature ventricular contractions. *Psychophysiol.,* 8: 263-264, 1971.
47. Wentworth-Rohr, I. Symptoms, insight and behavior techniques in psychoanalytic psychotherapy. *Psychoanal. Rev.,* 57(1): 48-59, 1970.
48. Wentworth-Rohr, I. Clinical Case studies in biofeedback and psychotherapy. Unpublished manuscript, 1973.
49. Whatmore, G.B., and Kohli, D.R. *The Physiopathology and Treatment of Functional Disorders.* New York: Grune & Stratton, 1974.
50. Wickramasekera, I. Instructions and EMG feedback in systematic desensitization: A case report. *Behav. Ther.,* 3: 460-465, 1972.
51. Wickramasekera, I. Temperature feedback for the control of migraine. *J. Behav. Ther. Experiment. Psychiat.,* 4: 343-345, 1973.
52. Wolpe, J. *The Practice of Behavior Therapy.* New York: Pergamon, 1969.
53. Wolpe, J., and Lazarus, A.A. *Behavior Therapy Techniques.* New York: Pergamon, 1966.

Integrative Therapeutic Approaches

Often proponents of different systems of psychotherapy have been at war with one another, each asserting that one system is better than another. There has been a need for a bridge of this schism and for unbiased assessment of what therapy is most effective for which patient. This section on integrative approaches to psychotherapy serves as an illustration of how different therapies can be combined to enhance the therapeutic outcome.

Remarks on Integrating Psychotherapeutic Techniques*

CLEMENS A. LOEW**

I would like to share with you some of my experiences in using a number of therapeutic approaches. Some of the complicated issues to be faced are what technique is best for what kind of problem, how the patient is affected by multiple techniques, and what, if any, internal conflict the therapist experiences in the use of different approaches.

Let me present a fictitious case which will illustrate some of these complexities in practice and training.

A woman comes for therapy to a clinic with the complaint of blushing. Her face becomes deep red when she meets new people. This is upsetting socially and at work where she is required to mingle with people. She feels very embarrassed and self-conscious, as you can imagine. She is eager and highly anxious to get rid of that symptom.

---

*Reprinted from *Psychotherapy: Theory, Research and Practice,* 12(3): 241-242, Fall, 1975.
**Based on presentation at the New York Society for Clinical Psychologists' (NYSCP) 26th Annual Conference: Integrating Psychotherapeutic Techniques.

The therapist assigned to her is open to various modalities, but is analytically oriented. The case is presented for discussion at the weekly case conference attended by therapists from diverse treatment modalities. The therapist suggests that the patient see a behaviorist in conjunction with her analytic therapy to help with alleviation of the symptom. Here is where things become interesting.

The supervisor, who is an analyst, vehemently disagrees. He says blushing is of course not the patient's real problem, but only a symptom of underlying dynamics—perhaps oedipal conflict and sexual anxiety. He argues against sending her to a behaviorist on the following grounds: (1) it would interfere with transference, (2) encourage resistance, (3) dilute the therapeutic relationship, and (4) encourage the patient to see the therapist as an authority in that the behaviorist will act as a teacher and direct the patient.

Here the behaviorist takes issue angrily and says:

> But that is exactly how I want to be seen: as an expert, a teacher or authority from whom the patient will take guidance and instruction. I want to help her get rid of the symptoms of blushing—that's what she came for, isn't it? I would use such techniques as desensitization, relaxation, and fantasy production. Besides, who cares about the unconscious. And of what relevance is transference?

The Gestalt therapist, watching all this, gets very indignant. He says:

> First of all, she is not a patient—but a person. It is really very important for a Gestalt therapist not to use the medical model—as you do. Secondly, what is important is simply what she experiences and where *she* wants to go with it. *She* has to take responsibility for whether she wants to focus on blushing or masturbation, or religion or her father.

The bioenergetic therapist is standing with his feet planted firmly on the ground. He is watching all this with a smirk, and says, "I don't care about her blushing. What I care about is her posture, the way she stands—whether she can be pushed over easily, etc."

I suppose you are wondering what happened to the patient. She was turning purple in the corner. Actually, she went to a psychic healer who said that he could not work with her because she did not believe in him, and did not want to get cured anyway.

This example is, of course, part fantasy and part reality of what might happen at a conference of therapists from diverse treatment modalities.

From my point of view a therapist can incorporate a variety of techniques. It is difficult, but possible. What is not feasible is for a therapist with a particular training and orientation to switch horses in midstream. Thus, if a psychoanalyst were suddenly to suggest a Gestalt technique, the patient would see it as artificial and phony. The patient would react with suspicion—"Why are you doing this suddenly? Have you been to a workshop over the weekend?" By the way, the few analytically trained therapists who are successful in integrating have been doing so from the beginning of their work; they have a reputation for using a variety of therapies so that the patient who comes to them already expects this kind of treatment. This is in contrast to the expectations a patient has coming to an analyst, or any other therapist with a single orientation.

Unfortunately, the "active" therapies lend themselves more to mechanical and incompetent use. The reason is that workshops are always available in transactional analysis, Gestalt, hypnotherapy, etc. People take one weekend in one of these and call themselves experts. Responsible therapists from these orientations object to such misuse, of course. Brief psychoanalytic "workshops" are relatively rare—training usually lasts four years in a typical program.

I have been trained as an analyst. That means that I work with making the unconscious conscious, analyzing transferences, encouraging cathartic experience and working through. What is often diluted and underplayed is that all the therapies have their own specific philosophies and models from which the therapist operates. These models may not be explicit, but they do exist. Thus, for one therapist to utilize a different approach requires also different kinds of thinking related to that approach. The therapist may then feel splintered between the various systems.

An analogy will clarify this point: It is difficult to be a Catholic and an orthodox Jew at the same time. It may be more useful for the therapist to become a Unitarian.

Perhaps a new theoretical framework is needed to integrate the relevant techniques. This new system would extrapolate valid principles and theories from various schools into a universal framework. Adequate training of therapists would take many years and would need to be rigorous and selective. This is because it is at least as difficult to become expert in an integrated approach as in a single theoretical orientation.

Beginning students tend to misuse the theory and technique of a particular school. Language and jargon, such as analytic or T.A., is used as a way of keeping distance between therapist and patient and to avoid relating to the patient and his needs. Perhaps it would be wise in teaching the beginner, to take a more humanistic, nonjargon, nonformal approach. To use the analytic system as an example, focus should be on developing communication vs. interpretation, relating vs. analysis. After the abilities of listening and sensitivity are developed, training could focus on providing the theoretical framework with its necessary language.

If we are going to consider various techniques as valid and useful, then we must start training students with this integrated approach from the beginnning. That is, to enable the therapist to view a person from different perspectives. A clinician should be trained to become not an analyst, not Gestaltist, not a behavior therapist, but someone who combines some of these—according to his ability and personality.

A Total Approach to Psychotherapy and Medications: Sensory Awareness and Physical Exercise

RICHARD M. CARLTON

THE NEED TO WAKE UP THE ORGANISM

Early in my training as a psychiatrist I became aware of profound limitations in the classical techniques of analysis, and in fact with all verbal techniques. While I saw their value in helping a patient uncover facts, ideas, and theories about his behavior, I noted that the patient was then left high and dry at the threshold of actual *experience*. While the translation of those ideas into "gut-level" insight was known to be essential for the process of psychotherapy, there were no specific skills or techniques for working directly in that realm of experience itself. It was as if everybody were talking about the sun, but no one knew for sure how to get out into it. The patient was told he would have to "find that out for himself," since no help was available.

I noticed that when the *discussions* of verbal psychotherapy failed to result in these experiences, this was ascribed to "resistance" on the part of the patient, or to his "not being ready." But on the other side of the question, it seemed to me that the verbal approach was like the Beatle's Day Tripper: "She's a big teaser, she took me half the way there." While "half the way" was infinitely superior to no progress at all, there was still that other part of the journey, both for me personally and for the patients I was treating.

I noticed also that psychiatric medications, for those who needed them, were just not enough. The medications did do a magnificent job in alleviating excessive anxiety and depression. But obviously medications should be used only to buy time during which something else can happen in the patient's life to help him develop autonomy, and that "something else" often failed to materialize. Those patients who required medications often had the greatest difficulty in utilizing interpretation, so that the verbal techniques were just not helping enough. Clearly, some additional approach was needed.

So early on I was looking for ways to directly explore the nonverbal levels. I felt that if more work were done on those deep levels, we would not produce those millions of people who can expound on their family dynamics like the analysis of some play, and yet have not experienced the flesh-and-blood person who holds his breath and flinches in pain at those same dynamics.

Through my exploring, I have found an approach that fits my needs and the needs of most of my patients extremely well. It is a new and an excellent approach for people in psychotherapy, whether on medications or not. It is a total and safe way of coming into contact, through combining sensory awareness and physical exercise with the verbal techniques of psychotherapy.

Sensory awareness is a process that helps one actively explore these nonverbal levels of feelings, emotions, and sensations. It works down on the level of the ground, where the breathing, the real world, and the "self" really are. I came to understand that in our society we often think of the "self" as some abstract concept, and very few of us experience it down on the level of the weight and movement of our muscles and bones. And that *is* the problem. We look for it in the realm of ideas, where it isn't to be found, and don't look for it in the organism, where it patiently awaits us. Down in the totality of the organism is the only place where the self *can* be. Yet until one experiences it there, "it" might as well have been on some distant planet.

For the past five years now (the time that I have been studying sensory awareness), I have had that feeling of "of course—it was so simple. Why didn't I ever see it before?" The answer to that question is that the conditioning of our culture and of our families makes it (1) easy for us to career around our minds and manipulate ourselves, and (2) frightening for us to sit still for even a moment and really trust, really *feel* what's going on inside.

Sensory awareness is a study I *gave* myself to. While most of us, patients and therapists alike, have an immediate response to it and are greatly impressed by the relaxation and joy it can bring, we soon discover that there are deeper levels that can be explored. That is where the real work begins, although the work is to do no work. Therefore we must not work hard at doing no work. What is involved is essentially this: to allow the ever-present sensations from the organism to each in their turn enter consciousness, and if we get stuck on any of these sensations, to find out what it is that is interfering. In thus allowing *consciousness to flow* (e.g., from contact with the ground, to a thought, to the sensation of movement, and so on), the organism is allowed to open and to take care of itself in a totality that few of us had even dreamed possible. Breathing takes care of itself, posture takes care of itself, and anxiety and pain dissolve as we become absorbed in full contact with the inner life *and* the outer world.

There is no "tuning out" here. There is certainly no asceticism in this work, no enforced suffering, no costumes to wear, no teachers to revere. There are no "stress positions" to make your body tremble and shake, no manipulations intended to make you experience your repressed sense of horror, as there are in bioenergetics. No one tears apart the connective tissues of your muscles and attempts to "restore" you to functioning, as happens in rolfing. The opposite happens here: you learn to *restore yourself,* by attending fully to what's going on in the moment.

I came to perceive that this level of total functioning, which we reach through sensory awareness, is something *natural* to all animals, including of course human beings. When we study the behavior of dogs and cats, and little children, we see from the way they sit and the way they move around that they are in solid contact with the ground and the moment. It is only through years of conditioning that young children are induced to give up their rich contact with the self and accept (with suppressed heartbreak and rage) the idea that "others know best." But through the sensing work, we can regain the ability we had as children to be present in the moment, and from that we can rely on ourselves and not on others for views as to how to live our lives.

My teacher of sensory awareness for these past five years is a wonderful woman named Betty Keane. Betty studied sensory awareness for 15 years with Charlotte Selver (who brought the work to this country from Germany), and has been teaching it privately and at institutions such as the New School For Social Research for many years. She has mastered the art of *inviting* you to experience, rather than pushing you to it or demanding it of you; and that, along with her joyousness and vitality make her a very special person to me.

I will concentrate on how a psychotherapist can experience this field for himself and how he can apply it to clinical situations with his patients. I want to emphasize that if the therapist has not himself had a direct experience of this level of being, then he will not be able to help his patients reach it. For this reason, when we resume the discussion of sensory awareness after the section on medications, I will include some sensory explorations for you to try *while* you're reading.

After these explorations and additional thoughts on sensory awareness, we will then turn to some physical exercises and see how they combine with the sensory work to further awaken the organism and promote total health. The exercises are relatively easy to do, and have tremendous leverage—that is, they produce (or liberate) far more energy than is put into them.

We will then examine some clinical applications of this combined approach, ranging from the treatment of obsessive-compulsive disorders to a unique approach to overeating and smoking problems. This will be follwed by case histories and a concluding section.

AN APPROACH TO PSYCHIATRIC MEDICATIONS

This section deals with a philosophy of dispensing psychiatric medications, and a discussion of such issues as the modes of actions and side effects. I have found in my consulting work for several clinics that nonmedical personnel have many questions as to when medications are indicated, what can be expected, and how to keep the patients motivated to stay on the medications. I hope that this section will fill the need not only of these therapists, but also of persons who are on medication and would like to know not only how the medication can help or hurt them, but also how they can help *or hurt* their own course on the medication.

A Philosophy of Medicating

There are many people who are unreal and out of touch, to the extent that their lives are stifled and miserable. I am not referring to those people who are overtly psychotic and who are obiously in need of hospitalization, but rather to a fairly large group who will probably never need hospitalization, but yet whose lives are filled with quiet desperation. Many of these need psychiatric medication very badly and respond well to it, but would have "survived" without it.

In my own practice, I would estimate that about one fourth of my patients are in need of medication. In addition, I see each week an average of two to three new consultations sent by several referring psychologists, who will continue with psychotherapy but have detected that medication may be needed. In about nine out of ten cases, they are right about the need for medication.

I have found, over and over again, in treating this large group of people, that the smallest possible dosage range is usually quite effective. By raising dosages slowly, and by using the smallest possible doses (e.g., 10-20 mgm Mellaril per day, 1-3 mgm Haldol per day), sedation and other side effects are kept to a minimum. Further, by taking just a little bit of time during the first evaluation and the first follow-up session to teach the basic six suppling exercises of Dr. Kraus (see below), tension is reduced even further and this helps enormously in keeping the dosage level down.

What the medications do essentially is to *lower the noise level* of the distress. They bring the level of tension down from something grossly unmanageable to something that is more life-size and workable. They help us buy time, during which the patient can learn new methods of coping. I advise patients who are going on medication that they are likely to be on it for six to nine months, and that during this time, they will discover new ways of experiencing and coping with their anxieties and problems. I stress that they should really get to *feel* what this new way of being is like, so that they can try to keep it going once they get off the medication.

This approach to medication is quite different from the one we sometimes see, where the patient is given the medication in order to "be still" and to stop "bothering people." There are physicians who prescribe copiously but do very little to help the patient gain insight. This unfortunate approach may help with the anxiety of the acute crisis, but it adds a new long-term problem, that of becoming dependent on medication for many years.

Clearly, the desirable approach is to give medications during an interim period, buying time so that the patient can grow on all levels through the psychological insights that will be learned, and through the focusing that physical exercise and later on sensory awareness will help him to achieve.

Categories of Medications and Their Indications

1. *Major tranquilizers.* This group is also known as the antipsychotic tranquilizers. Some commonly used examples are Thorazine, Mellaril, Stelazine, and Haldol. The first three are phenothiazine compounds; the last one is a butyrophenone, with a slightly different chemical make-up but with similar effects; it has proved very effective. These drugs revolutionized and humanized the management of the severely disturbed patient. Since their introduction, their use has extended to include less severe disorders, such as certain borderline situations, neuroses, and even depressions. One drug from this group, Mellaril, is said to have the best antidepressant effects of this group, and so it is used in certain types of depression; Mellaril is also successfully used in very small doses to control the agitation of presenile dementia. Because this group is used on such a large range of problems, from mild to severe, a patient who finds that he is using one of these medications should not assume that he has been labeled "psychotic." There is much less of a tendency for people to abuse these major tranquilizers, as compared to the minor tranquilizers, which are massively abused.

2. *Antidepressants of the Tricyclic Group.* Examples of this group are Elavil and Tofranil. These are used very effectively in the treatment of moderate and severe depressions. Within two weeks, there is a marked improvement of the common symptoms of depression, such as feelings of sadness and hopelessness, apathy, and the vegetative disturbances, such as loss of appetite, weight loss, constipation, and insomnia. Also relieved by these medications is the agitation present in some types of depression.

3. *Lithium.* This salt is very helpful in cyclical mood disturbances, meaning the elations and/or depressions of manic-depressive illness. Lithium will abort and prevent recurrences of manic episodes. While it will not abort a current episode of depression, there is strong evidence that it will prevent future episodes from emerging. (Therefore, a tricyclic antidepressant will usually be combined with lithium in the treatment of a current episode of cyclic depression.) Lithium has also been used in the treatment of certain alcoholic conditions. However, lithium is a very difficult

drug to use because it becomes readily toxic to the kidneys (causing frequent urination), the stomach (causing nausea and vomiting), and other organs. It must therefore be closely monitored through blood tests to detect high serum levels before the patient becomes toxic. When it can be well-regulated in this manner, it is the treatment of choice for the manic-depressive illness.

4. *Antidepressants of the MAO Inhibitor Type.* One example of this group is Parnate. These drugs are very dangerous. On the one hand, they often cause a severe drop in blood pressure when the person stands up. On the other hand, they can cause a severe and sometimes fatal elevation in blood pressure, when combined with a variety of other medications, or when certain fermented foods are eaten, such as aged cheese and certain wines. Because of these dangers, these drugs should not be taken unless other drugs have failed to work after extensive trials at sufficiently high dosage levels.

5. *Minor Tranquilizers.* Some members of this group, such as Valium, Librium, and Miltown, are among the most widely abused drugs in the world. I seldom prescribe these, because I feel that if the problem is of such a mild degree as to require only a minor tranquilizer, then probably the patient can achieve a significant reduction in levels of tension through the program of exercises. This avoids the risk of habituation and also of side effects such as bone-marrow depression, which can sometimes occur. I cannot justify taking even the small risk that may be involved, when exercise will provide relief. If the person won't exercise, in other words if he wants a "miracle cure" and won't work to take care of himself, then that is grist for the therapeutic mill. Meanwhile, firm limits should be set and the patient's childlike attitude should not be given in to. The exceptions to this are those situations where major tranquilizers or antidepressants were indicated and were tried, but where side effects of these could not be adequately controlled. It does happen that some patients are highly reactive and develop pronounced side effects, and under these conditions, minor tranquilizers can be given as an alternative. They can also be given to mildly psychotic persons who need such a small dose of major tranquilizer that a minor tranquilizer would suffice and would have fewer side effects.

Clinical Effects

For reasons of space, we will confine this discussion to the major tranquilizers and the tricyclic antidepressants.

1. *The Major Tranquilizers.* In the more severe cases, where there are delusions or hallucinations, within a few days to a week these manifestations fall off rapidly. In some of these cases, the manifestations seem to persist on a very low level, like a "radio turned down," and no longer bother the patient or his family. For example, in one classical case, a woman still had the delusion that she was Jesus Christ, but now that she was on the medication she was able to care for herself and her family, rather than walking around the streets of Brooklyn all day heatedly trying to convince people that she was Christ. In other cases, the psychotic manifestations disappear completely. In both types of cases, the patients often make statements

within the first week to the effect of "I was really crazy back then, and I'm glad it's over." In other words, the psychotic material has rapidly become ego-dystonic (meaning that the patient now sees this material as abnormal and undesirable).

In the less severe cases, where for example scattering and moderate disorganization are the underlying difficulties, the tranquilizers bring about a rapid improvement in the ability to concentrate, to work, and to relate to others.

2.*Tricyclic Antidepressants.* In the case of moderate to severe depression, the tricyclic antidepressants are used and have two phases of effects. In the first few days there are antianxiety effects, which fact is very much appreciated by the patients because a great deal of anxiety or agitation usually accompanies depression. Then, in seven to ten days, the antidepressant effect kicks in; this is how long it takes to modify the balance of chemicals in those nerve cells where the action takes place. Therefore, it may be one to two weeks before the patient's mood brightens, appetite returns, and sleeping patterns improve. The patient starting on an antidepressant must be told that it may take two weeks before he feels significantly better. Telling him this increases his cooperation and his chances of following up on the medication. It should be noted that once these medications are discontinued, it takes seven to ten days for the effects to wear off.

Side Effects

The referring therapist and the psychiatrist should both actively encourage the patient to tolerate the side effects, especially since many of them will disappear within one to two weeks, and the few that persist can usually be controlled with other medications. I have noticed in giving lectures to professional groups that people in the audience look aghast when they hear about these side effects. I therefore want to emphasize that the incidence and scope of these side effects is not that great, but they must be mentioned because the therapist and the patient must be informed of what can happen. Further, in my approach of using the lowest possible doses and in promoting exercise, the more severe side effects are unlikely to occur. And in any case, the benefits of these medications are so spectacular as to make the side effects worth tolerating. If the referring therapist should detect too many side effects, he should report this immediately to the prescribing psychiatrist, so that a change in medication can be considered. If he feels that he cannot discuss these problems of management freely with a particular psychiatrist because of the latter's attitudes, he should consider referring elsewhere.

Here is a list of the side effects in common to the major tranquilizers and the tricyclic antidepressants: Drowsiness, sedation, dizziness, and headaches are fairly common, but usually disappear in a few days or a few weeks. Nasal congestion can occur. Occasionally seen, but significant when it occurs, is "paradoxical worsening," where after starting the medication the patient becomes confused or suffers a worsening of the presenting symptoms; this condition must be thought of, so that rather than raising the medication under the assumption that the illness is worsening, the medication can be lowered or discontinued. With very large doses of either group, confusion and staggering of gait can occur. Allergic manifestations can occur, such as skin rash, bone-marrow depression, and liver damage; these are unlikely to occur at the lower dosages, and they can be tested for through periodic blood tests; of course if frequent sore throats develop or the patient becomes jaundiced, blood tests must be done immediately and the medication re-evaluated. Medications from both of these groups can lower the seizure threshold, and thereby induce seizures. If there is a family history of seizures, dosages should be raised very slowly. If the patient himself has had a history of seizures, in most cases anticonvulsants should be given prophylactically; these anticonvulsants will control this, and again, the results are most often worth it. Other side effects include orthostatic hypotension, wherein the blood pressure drops when the patient stands up too rapidly. Both groups of medication can produce weight gain, and therefore the patient should be encouraged to watch his diet and to exercise regularly. EKG changes can occur in older patients. Narrow-angle glaucoma will worsen with these medications (wide-angle glaucoma will not), and therefore the major tranquilizers and the tricyclic antidepressants are contraindicated in this condition.

There are side effects particular to the major tranquilizers: muscle reactions of the Parkinsonian type can occur, wherein we see one or several of the following symptoms: tremor of the hands, rigidity or stiffness in movement, grimacing around the mouth, or restlessness and pacing which resemble nervousness but are the expression of a muscle hypertonicity. In the vast majority of these muscle reactions, the patients respond instantly to anticholinergic medication such as Artane or Cogentin. Once needed, these should be taken on an ongoing basis along with the tranquilizer.

In severe crises, which seldom occur on the usual outpatient dosages and are extremely rare under the very low dosages, the patient may have severe twitching and may not be able to make voluntary movements at all; of course this is frightening to all concerned, and if it develops, the patient should be taken to an emergency room where intramuscular or even intravenous Benadryl will immediately control these side effects. If such a severe reaction should occur, then of course the tranquilizer must be reduced drastically or discontinued, with another type of medication substituted. These severe muscle reactions are extremely rare, but you must be informed of what can occur. The milder muscle reactions described above are seen more often—in my experience in about one third of those treated—but Artane or Cogentin will control this and they are very much worth taking!

Photosensitivity is another side effect that is particular to the major tranquilizers of the phenothiazine type: patients on these medications are more likely to develop sunburn, and this can be quite intense. Therefore, in the warmer seasons, the referring therapist and the psychiatrist should each remind the patient to avoid heavy exposure to the sun, especially the first few times that he goes out into it. In addition, large amounts of suntan lotion should be used, particularly sun blockers with PABA. People who are on Thorazine should be the most concerned with this problem; those on the other major tranquilizers will not have to worry as much about it.

Length of Time Medication is Needed

We said above that the course of medication is usually six to nine months. The main reason for this is that the natural course of many of the major psychiatric disturbances runs about that long and then subsides. To discontinue prematurely is to invite a resurgence of the distressing symptoms with consequent demoralization and disorganization. Even if medications are promptly resumed, there is no guarantee that the patient will recover fast enough to avoid hospitalization. Why take the risk?

A classic study demonstrated that for patients who had already been hospitalized, those who stayed on the medication for a minimum of nine months had a relatively low return rate, whereas those who discontinued the medication before the first nine months had a massively higher rate of rehospitalization. The message is clear, and applies whether or not hospitalization has been indicated: the patient should stay on the medication until the danger period is over.

Some patients may need to stay on for longer periods of time, even years. This would apply for example where the patient has a process thought disorder. In contrast, other individuals may have had only an acute crisis, with very little in the way of underlying pathology, and for these persons one or two months on the medication may suffice. The important consideration for the psychiatrist is that he be willing to go along with a trial discontinuation if the patient feels strongly that he is ready and is being realistic about it. And the important consideration for the patient is that he be willing to recognize that if symptoms recur a few months after discontinuation, it was no harm in trying but it is now time to get back on the medication.

Why Some Patients Stop Taking Medication

Some patients discontinue the medication out of ignorance, in that they "feel better" (thanks to the medication!) and think they no longer need it. Others discontinue out of self-destructive reasons, usually unconscious in nature. Often it is that they literally cannot tolerate the health and good feelings that the medication has made possible. They are afraid of the contact they feel with themselves and with others. Some of those in this group wish unconsciously to return to a period of disorganization in which they did not have to take responsibility for themselves. If the therapist can repeatedly interpret this tendency to the patient, and if the patient is open enough to hear what the therapist is saying, the discontinuation may be prevented.

Other patients want to go off the medication because they "want to do it by themselves." Here again, the therapist should explain to the patient that he needs additional help *for now,* and he should help the patient find out *what is interfering* with the patient's perception of this reality. The interference often has to do with confusing the therapist with parents (transference): the mistaken assumption is made that to "comply" with the therapist is equivalent to "giving in" to the parents and losing the fight to maintain individuality. The patient does not see that this endless fighting with his parents (real or introjected) is actually destroying his chances of autonomy. Of course, another source of interference with accepting the need for medication is the feeling instilled by the parents (and later often reinforced by the spouse) that to "get better" is to betray the relative by leaving him behind in his pathology. In other words, if the patient gets better, the relative may get worse. Such abandonment has been strictly policed against by a strong system of taboo, which the patient is terrified of violating. If the therapist can help the patient to understand that he is being "ripped off" by the bind, the patient may be better able to stand his ground and stay on the medication.

Pharmacologic Modes of Action

Due to considerations of space, this discussion is confined to the modes of action of the major tranquilizers. Some simplifications will be made for the purpose of clarity. Those interested in greater detail can consult *Biologic Psychiatry* by J. Mendels (6).

We said earlier that patients experience the effect of the tranquilizers as a turning down of the noise level of a radio. This is very interesting, because in terms of the actual pharmacologic mechanism, this is also what seems to take place: the excess activity of a particular area of the brain is inhibited. The particular area involved is thought to be the nigro-striatal tract in the limbic system. This tract is involved in the regulation of tension and aggression. The limbic system it is a part of is a spherical area located near the bottom of the hemispheres; it and the hypothalamus together comprise what is called the vegetative center. This center is the seat of the emotions and drives, and if there is a physical counterpart to the Freudian concepts of id and libido, this is it. This vegetative center has millions of connections not only within itself but also to all important areas of the brain, including the cerebral cortex (where thinking and associating take place), and the nerves that control the voluntary muscles. (It is this latter fact that explains why the major tranquilizers can have a side effect on muscle tone.) When electrical stimulation is given to laboratory animals in these areas of the vegetative center, marked changes in behavior will occur, such as increased aggression and rage, increased sexual activity, and increases or decreases in the intake of food and water.

One of the current theories about the types of emotional illness that respond to major tranquilizers is the following: The nerve cells in the nigro-striatal tract are hyperactive, which means that they are firing too rapidly and too readily. This could be because they are hypersensitive to dopamine, or because excess amounts of this transmitter substance are present. This excess firing in turn throws off the regulation of aggression and tension, which this nucleus is responsible for. The major tranquilizers work by plugging up the receptor sites, which blocks the action of dopamine and thereby restores the organism to a more stable level of functioning.

It is as if a defective key were used to plug up the ignition lock in a car, thereby making the car unable to start. Through this quieting down of an entire system of regulation, stresses that would previously have staggered a patient are now taken in stride.

I urge any person on medication reading this section to understand that the fact of a biochemical imbalance does not mean that the imbalance has *caused* the illness. The illness may in fact have caused the imbalance. Therefore, you should not draw foolish conclusions such as: "Since I have an imbalance, I might as well just take the medications and skip psychotherapy." There is every reason to believe that coping better with stress and reducing tension will help the imbalance to be corrected. The purpose of the medications is to make this even easier for you, and thus to hasten the day that you will have found your own way to becoming self-reliant and will no longer need the medication.

GENERAL GUIDELINES TO COMBINING MEDICATIONS WITH PHYSICAL EXERCISE AND SENSORY AWARENESS

What you as a mental health professional should especially retain from the previous section on medications is that at certain times in the lives of some of your patients, they will be *unable* to effectively utilize the insights and limits you are trying to establish. This failure is not to be blamed on the patient or on yourself. Neither of you is "doing anything wrong."

It is that the patient's mind (actually his entire organism) is too bombarded by stimuli from within and without for him to be able to hear and make use of what goes on in the therapy sessions. Thus, when you find yourself with a person who does not appear overtly psychotic (no hallucinations or delusions), but who is nevertheless flooded with anxiety, scattered in his thinking and functioning, and consistently unable over a period of months to utilize the therapeutic interventions, then it is time to do proverb testing, get projective drawings, get an MMPI, and consider psychiatric consultation. With medications, if indicated, the "wall" you seem to be talking to may come down in a matter of weeks, sparing the patient months or years of crippling disorganization, and sparing yourself the frustration of trying to "get through." Remember, there has to be *somebody there* in order for you to make contact.

If, in addition to his taking the medication, you can motivate him to get started on the suppling and vigorous exercises (which will be detailed in later sections), and after that if you can help him work with sensory awareness, you will witness an even greater improvement in his ability to cope. And you will have favored an earlier and more successful withdrawal from the medication. If medication was not indicated, or if it was tried but could not be tolerated because of side effects, then this same combined approach will help the patient to reduce tension and cope better, without the aid of medication.

One of my major findings in the use of exercise and sensory awareness to supplement psychotherapy is that through these the patient discovers that there is something he can do for himself and that *he is not helpless.* There is a magnificent uplifting of mood, outlook, and self-reliance. This improvement in the experience of the self and the simultaneous decrease in the overall level of tension combine to lower the need for medication and of course to enrich the growth that is the goal of psychotherapy.

I strongly recommend that for severely disturbed persons the sensory work be held off until the patient is stabilized by the medication and the physical exercises. This may mean a wait of several weeks or months before introducing sensory awareness. The reason is that for some very disorganized patients the mere fact of closing the eyes may increase the already high level of terror. Furthermore, the increased sense of contact with the self may prove to be too frightening if the patient is not ready for it. Naturally, I am talking here about the very disturbed patient.

I find the best approach is to allow the medication to quiet the person's fears, and to allow the physical exercises to begin the work of returning the patient to the ground. Every time he walks or jogs, or lies down on the mat for the suppling exercises, he is increasing his contact with the ground (i.e., with reality). Without his even knowing it, he is beginning to shift his attention away from the cartoons of his mind and back to his movement in the real world.

Then, as he trusts himself and you more, you can begin slowly introducing sensory explorations as *part of* the physical exercises. For example, you can ask him to spend a little more time letting his weight down on the mat in between sit-ups. Or you can ask him to close his eyes while he is bending forward to touch his toes, and to feel how his weight is shifting. In this way, you can test his responses and see how ready he is to work on this level of deeper contact.

Naturally, with another patient who is not so fragile, you can begin the sensory work much sooner. As with any therapeutic technique, you must feel your way as to each individual's readiness. The psychotherapist should remember that his role is different from that of a full-time teacher of sensory awareness. The patients who have come to him have not come for sensory work or for physical exercises, and many of the patients the psychotherapist sees are lightyears away from a real experience of the organism. If these people had a stronger experience of the organism, they would not be where they are at the time.

So even though the therapist may know that this work will help the patient in the long run, he must respect the patient's limitations, which include fear of letting go, fear of deep contact, and prejudices about anything "different." Remember that the verbal-analytic work, which was radical 50 years ago, is widely accepted today; and patients come in expecting to talk and think and think and talk. *The therapist must know that it may take some patients six months, one year, or even longer before they can begin work on a deeper level.* As the patients become ready, for sure they will let the therapist know. In the meantime, great patience is needed.

Naturally, the patients who come to your practice with good ego strength, and for whom medication is not even a question, can begin the sensory work immediately. I am trying here to sensitize the therapist to recognize a continuum of readiness for this sensory work, from "stay the hell away" to "let's get to it." In contrast, the work with the suppling and vigorous exercises can be begun immediately, no matter what the patient's level of functioning.

SENSORY AWARENESS AS A MEANS TO TOTAL FUNCTIONING

I came to sensory awareness at a time in my life when pressures were mounting and I was having difficulty handling them. I found that I was dwelling on my problems and that pains were developing in my neck and back. The combination of both of these was distracting me and making me irritable. Within one to two months of starting the sensory work with Betty Keane, I had begun to clearly experience the ways in which I was literally holding on to these problems, throughout all levels of the organism. In addition to sensing the thought patterns of worry and doubt (the basic thing I had noticed at first), I was now able to sense the tightening in the abdomen, the holding of the breath, and the further pulling away from the sense of the ground, which were all taking place. I learned how to return to the sense of the ground and how to strengthen it. I discovered how to stay in contact with the distressing sensations and to just let them be, without judging them or trying to change them. This acceptance led *without effort* to the letting go that was so needed. I could not *make* it go away! But if I remained open, staying with the sensation, then the distress went away by itself. In other words, I had learned *to get out of the way* and let the organism take over and do what it knows how to do.

I hope that this conveys to you a sense of what goes on in this work, and how important it is for all of us to be able to reach this level of acceptance of ourselves. How often we find ourselves and our patients struggling to "make the problem go away." We seldom see that the struggle itself perpetuates the problem.

Sensory awareness addresses the widespread problem of living without a sense of being. What's happened is that many people have lost touch with their inner nature, in other words, with this sense of being. The fundamental way in which this comes about is by inducing people, while they are young, to greatly exaggerate the importance of *doing things*. The child that has been treated this way will soon pay little attention to his own feelings, and a great deal of attention to his worries about doing things "right" for others. Soon his sense of worth is based on how well he is doing things, and is no longer grounded in his inner being and presence. How do *you* feel about your own self-worth? Do you have a strong sense that if you didn't do this for your parents, that for your self, and such and such for society, that you wouldn't really be *worthy?* Think about that for a moment. Do you see what I mean?

We can describe briefly three sources in our culture for the unhealthy emphasis on doing and the subsequent split of the self:

1. Society's goals: In every culture there is enormous pressure placed on each individual to conform and to contribute to the "common good." The "good" being sought by most people in our society is productivity, expansion, wealth, and power. This places a stigma on just *being,* and produces a lifestyle akin to walking into a cold, hard wind: we have the feeling that we can never get enough to breathe.

2. Parents' attitudes: The more insecure the parent, the more he will reinforce in the child his society's emphasis on doing as opposed to being. Take as one common example the need of many mothers to see the child "finish the plate," in total disregard of the child's feelings and of the fact that there is no impending famine. When this sort of interfering goes on for many years, the child can no longer find his own way in relation to eating, smoking, drinking, and all other areas of his life where he needs to know what his own limits are. Many of my patients have expressed this confusion by saying "Not only don't I know what I want, I don't even know how to *find out* what I want." The rage that the child experiences about this interference is enormous, but of course in most cases is repressed and finds expression only in attacks on the self-through self-hatred, psychosomatic disease, and various addictions.

Another burden of "doing" commonly placed on children by parents is the message that the "happiness" of the child is supposed to come from giving "meaning" to the parents' lives and from "saving" the marriage. Since no amount of the child's servicing could ever get the parents in touch with themselves, the parents will never be able to give the real approval that the child needs. The tables are fixed. Later on, he will try to get approval from his own self by endless doing, such as the pursuit of money, or the trying out of every therapeutic fad, and so on.

3. The underlying Western view: this is a third source of the splitting of the self, for it pretends to divide man into separate parts, such as mind ("good") and body ("bad"). Once we are raised with that split, it takes enormous trust and patience to experience the wholeness once again. We must remember that the men who formulated the split—such as Plato and Aquinas—were just frightened people like you and me, trying to make sense out of a bewildering universe. Their notions are a major source of our confusion.

One of the important ways out of this confusion is found by turning our attention to the ground that we are in contact with, and following the flow of breathing. In allowing the consciousness to flow and sensing anything that tends to restrict the flow, we return to a simple place inside where what we need can be made very clear to us, and where self-approval comes naturally because it is related to the mere fact of our existence and not to anything that we are doing.

Sensory Explorations

Here are some suggestions for trying out these explorations. Find a place where you can have quiet and privacy. Have someone you're comfortable with read the guidelines to you very slowly, or you yourself can read them slowly into a tape recorder. If neither of these is possible, then simply try to remember the basic activity and do not push to recall everything. Put aside the book before you start the exploration, so that you are not tempted to come back to it and read about what you "should" be feeling.

For reasons of space, I will present two explorations here. For further explorations, see the book *Sensory Awareness* by Charles Brooks and Charlotte Selver (1). The movements and the sequence of movements in these explorations are not that important in and of themselves, and only serve as a means of getting in touch with the self.

Exploration: Getting quiet, experiencing arms and shoulders: Come close to the edge of the chair, the harder the chair the better. Close your eyes and find out what you are experiencing at this moment of time. Do not try to modify anything you may notice; it is essential that you first experience what is going on. When you have sensed what your sitting is like, slowly raise one arm out to your side to the horizontal. Notice the sense of weight, and feel the activity in your shoulder that has to do with holding up this weight. As you let the arm come back down after a few moments, allow the weight of the arm to settle where it wants to, and try to stay open in the shoulder. You might try this two or three times, each time allowing the arm to come to rest where it wants to, even though this sensation may be awkward for you. Open up to the sensations that are coming in from the side you have just moved. Do not struggle to find words for these sensations, for that may interfere with the perception. After a while, compare the sensations from the side you moved with the sensations coming from the other side. Notice if one arm feels more present (more "there"), find out which shoulder, if either, feels higher; when ready, repeat this exploration on the other side, raising that arm and letting it down a few times. Be sure to allow the sensations on this side to be different from those on the first side, so that you don't make demands on the organism for sameness. All along the way, find out what happens to your breathing and find out if you can let your weight rest on the chair (ground).

Discussion: Don't read this until you finish the exploration. But if you can't participate now, then go ahead with the reading. Quite commonly, during this first exploration, people experience a strong sense of awareness, presence, and "being more there" on the side that was just moved. This simple process of paying attention to the organism, and of allowing subtle movements, opens up the area. It can bring increased blood flow, relax previously tense muscles, and most important of all, it can enhance the sense of presence. While *relaxation* is a wonderful byproduct of this work, it cannot always occur, and *should not be considered the goal of the work*. We must not make demands on the organism to feel "relaxed," for that repeats the demands our parents placed on us, for example to suppress our anger and to "sit still" when we were frustrated with them. The purpose of this work is to become deeply present in ourselves, to stay present even though we may be bothered by certain sensations, and through this to allow whatever is needed to take place.

Exploration: Opening to breathing and weight: In sitting, let the head have weight and come slowly over the knees, as far as is comfortable. Feel if the weight has shifted forward from the sitting bones to the feet. Sense what the breathing is like, and let the breathing help you up to sitting once again. As you come up, feel how the weight shifts back and how the spine unfolds. Allow the head and neck to go through a range of motion, that is to be in balance, rather that to fix on any one "correct" position.

This is an excellent exploration to do when you are confused or tired, because it allows the mind to clear and become settled. It also helps introduce you to what your breathing is like. One of the truly unique features of sensory awareness is that it teaches you to stop interfering with your breathing. All other modalities, such as the various types of yoga, teach one form or another of continued *manipulation* of the breathing. For example they tell you to assign fixed periods of time to breathing out, to holding the breath, and to breathing in again. But here at last is a method that allows the organism to do exactly what it needs. No one has to tell dogs and cats, or young infants, how often and how deeply to breathe in and out. And no one has to tell you, either. In situations as diverse as jogging a mile, making love, taking an exam, or responding to a dangerous situation, your breathing will change all by itself. Our goal then, is to get out of the way and allow it to happen. What a waste it would be to distract ourselves at those times by "thinking" if we should be breathing in for the count of six or out for the count of eight. Let's stop interfering!

Some Basic Principles of Sensory Awareness

To come to a statement of the basic principles of sensory awareness, let's begin by examining what's happened in those persons who experienced *nothing* during the sensory exploration we just presented. This may have been the case for some of you, and it is not uncommon. If you experience "nothing," the idea is to stay with the organism and that experience of "nothing happening." If you remain alert and open, rest assured some perception will enter your consciousness. For example, as you are waiting, you may experience a tightening someplace, which may represent the demand to "make something happen." Well, if you look at this from a different viewpoint, it is *wonderful* that you detected this tightening, because now you have caught on to what it is that actually happens in you when you push yourself: you stiffen up! Stay with the stiffening now, and allow something else to happen— perhaps it suddenly "lets go."

This leads us to the statement of three of the most important principles of this sensory work:

1. *The organism's response to the* demand *to experience is to turn off. But the organism's response to the* invitation *to experience can be to become alive and present.*

2. *Openness is reached by staying present for what is.* Those of you who have read Eastern thinkers such as Krishnamurti will now understand on a deeper level why they emphasize staying with "what is."

3. *The organism will take care of itself if you get out of the way.* In my experiences as a physican, I have seen many illustrations of this principle, but one of them in particular stays in my mind. When I was a medical intern, I was covering the emergency room one very busy Sunday. A young German woman walked in and asked for treatment of an infected toenail. When I asked her how it had become infected, she told me that eight days before she had been bitten by a shark. I told her not to put me on. She explained that she had been scuba diving, and had stayed on in the water after her buddy had gotten out and had urged her to come out. She was completely engrossed with a reef and was not paying attention, when suddenly she felt a sharp pain in her right foot. *Without knowing what was behind her,* she pulled out the knife that was strapped to her calf, and swung it around behind her. The knife plunged into the eye of a shark that was coming back for its second try! On the first try all it had gotten was her entire fin and a tiny little chunk from her toenail! As the shark thrashed around, you guessed it, she swam rapidly back to the boat. And here she was, eight days later, standing alive in front of me with both legs in place, and only an infected toenail with a piece missing to show for it. This girl *never saw* the shark, so she must have been guided by some incredibly strong force or presence to have even hit it, let alone to have hit it in the eye! This force is available to each of us, in the organism. Most of us only experience the tip of the iceberg, because the conditioning has gotten us in the way of this force. This conditioning can be reversed by waking up the organism.

We will turn now to a discussion of the importance of physical exercise and the role exercise can play in facilitating the goal of psychotherapy.

PHYSICAL EXERCISE

The Need for the Suppling and Vigorous Exercises

Exercise is essential for total health. To think that you can achieve "mental" health without having "physical" health is to be fooled by a trick of the mind, because the separation of the two is merely a concept of the mind.

Much of our excessive tension is related to lack of exercise. Without exercise, the body stores up tensions like a wound-up spring. Various hobbies and forms of meditation may give us some relief, but they can't discharge the tension and stimulate the body systems (cardiopulmonary, digestive, and endocrine) to the degree that exercise can.

Let's be clear about one thing: there is no such thing as a life without any tension at all. It is natural that some things will pull you one way and other things will pull you the other way. You experience that pull as a tension within the organism, such as tightness in the chest, squeezing in the abdomen, and so on. Since you can do nothing about the *existence* of tension in your life, then your energies should go to keeping it to a minimum and to coping well with it as it arises. That is, you should develop your best way of relating to it.

With proper exercise, you will be better able to meet the demands that life makes on you. When you tense a muscle, the fibers of that muscle slide over one another so that the muscle can shorten and do its work. But if you remain tense, the muscle stays shortened, and after long periods of this *the muscle becomes chronically shortened.* This is scientifically demonstrated. The muscle you habitually tense at the back of your neck, when you want to tell off your boss but can't do it, has become shorter. After a few years of this, your head is being pulled back and down, and if you think about it, your head needs to be able to move freely to the midline (and lower) in order for you to look someone right in the eye and convince him that you mean business. Any drag on this free forward movement (due to shortened muscles at the back of the neck) makes you feel that there is something "holding you back." So you see that what is going on at the "psychological" level corresponds to something at the "physical" level of the organism. There is no way it can be otherwise.

It is not just assertiveness that is interfered with by these restrictions of the muscles. All emotions are affected, including love, joy, and the sense of wonder. If we understand that emotion is a sensation that flows within the organism (e=*motion*), and that muscular holding will literally choke off that flow, then we see that the freezing of the "body" is the same thing as the freezing of the "mind."

That is why psychotherapy—of the "mind" alone—is not enough. Even sensory awareness, strong as it is in itself, is not enough. Transcendental meditation is not enough, yoga is not enough, and all these things put together are not enough.

There is just no substitute for the suppling and the vigorous exercises, which are integral activities of the species. We are primates, whose remote ancestors swung in the trees. Until this century, all of mankind had to walk and run thousands of miles every year, had to chop wood, carry heavy loads, stoop down, and so on. These activities kept the organism vigorous, supple, and well-balanced. We are so under-exercised and so tense that the population as a whole is ravaged by a disease—"hypokinetic disease." The lead article of the *New York Times* of January 12, 1976 carried the headline "U.S. Study . . . sees peril in lack of exercise." There is general consensus in the health field that for those who don't exercise regularly, there is an earlier incidence of degenerative diseases (such as diabetes and arthritis), and a shorter life span due to premature heart attacks and strokes.

Description of the Suppling Exercises

Dr. Hans Kraus describes this "hypokinetic disease" in his enlightening book *Backache, Stress, and Tension* (4). Kraus is one of the great experts in the field of exercise, and headed the first President's Commission on Physical Fitness. He is a vigorous and joyful man who, even with a lot of grey hair, still climbs the Swiss Alps, and I admire him tremendously.

You should read his book, with special attention to the sections on Fight or Flight and on the Six Basic Warmup Exercises (pp. 87-92). This book is not just for people with backaches. It's an excellent guide to getting back on the road to physical fitness. One of the most important points he makes in the book is that in doing the suppling exercises, you must *let go* of a muscle after you have contracted it. This means waiting between movements, hanging out, staying loose—letting go. Here is an example: shrug your shoulders up, without straining; now let the shoulders down slowly, and let go for several moments; then shrug up again, and down again. That's the correct way. Now try the incorrect way, which is to shrug and then let the shoulders a little of the way down but then immediately shrug them up again, without ever coming to rest. Try the correct way again, and feel the difference. We have gotten our muscles (and ourselves) into the habit of tensing and staying tense whenever there is an irritation, and in our modern urban life, there are plenty of irritations. So we must learn to let go.

As Kraus points out, the physiologic tendency of the organism is to release its tension through fight or flight: fighting discharges tension, and so does running until one is out of danger. But in our overly civilized society we do not use "fight or flight," we "sit and stew," as Kraus says. Doesn't this pattern sound familiar? You hold on to problems, you brood over them, you swallow your anger, you take it out on the wrong person (your spouse, yourself), and every little irritation becomes magnified. In order to break that habit of holding on, we must teach the muscles to let go. This is the key to the exercises.

I want to point out that suppling exercises alone are not enough. Vigorous exercises are necessary too, in order to fully restore the muscles to their proper length and tone. However, those of you who are very out of shape should spend several months just building yourselves up with the suppling exercises, taking up walking as the only type of aerobic (vigorous) exercise at this stage.

I also want to point out that the goal here is definitely not to become a musclebound jock, but rather to come from way under par back up to the barest minimum standards of physical fitness. Most of the population is far below minimum standards, and this fact is clearly reflected in the high levels of obesity, addiction to drugs and alcohol, and mental illness in our society. So, with these ideas in mind, let's get to the basic six suppling exercises. All you will need is a firm chair or stool, and a mat or towel to lie down on. Beginners are advised to place the mat on a rug, not on the bare floor.

Warning: If you suffer significantly from pains in the back, neck, or shoulder areas, or if you have a history of slipped disc or other medical problem, *do not start yet.* You can hurt yourself. See your physician first, and ask him to perform the Kraus-Weber test (4). This is a widely accepted measure of the limitations imposed on you by the degree of tightness and weakness you may have in your muscles—for example, not being able to touch your toes, or not being able to do a sit-up.

If you don't have significant pains, you can proceed for now with the simple exercises listed below, and take the Kraus—Weber test as soon as you get the book. You will find here some slight modifications from the exercises as listed in Kraus's book. Here are some of the ground rules:

1. In the first few weeks especially, make all these movements as small as possible. Most people (especially men) try too hard and some go into spasm. Try to make it pleasurable.

2. Hold each of these movements for a count of three, and do each movement a series of three times. Always let go after each movement.

Exercise 1. Sit toward the edge of a hard chair. Try to feel your sitting bones making contact with the chair. Slowly shrug your shoulders up, hold for the count of three, then slowly let them down and come to rest, letting go completely (3X). Now shrug your shoulders up and forward (3X). Then up and back (3X). Make the motions smooth and continuous, not jerky. Now turn your head slowly to the left without straining, then back to the middle and let go. After pausing for a moment, turn your head to the right, then back to the middle again and let go (3X). Then let the weight of your head come forward and down toward the chest, without straining; then back to the middle and rest; then futher back just one or two inches, and back again to the middle and let go (3X). Finally, let your head come slowly over the left shoulder, making especially sure not to strain in this motion; come slowly back to the middle and let go; and then let the weight of your head go over the right shoulder, then back to the middle again and let go (3X). Try to make these movements small, remembering that less is more. If any of the movements in this series of exercises causes pain or spasm, skip that particular movement for several weeks.

Exercise 2. Lie on your back on a mat or towel. A bed is too soft. Feel the floor underneath you. As you take a deep breath in, shrug your shoulders up toward your head, and when you reach the maximum inspiration, let go of the breath and the shoulders at the same time (3X).

Exercise 3. Stay on your back, but bring your knees up with your feet on the floor a foot or so from the buttocks. Bring the left knee toward the chest, then extend that leg out with the heel almost touching the ground, and when you reach full extension let your leg rest on the ground for the count of three. Then bring the leg back to the starting position and let go again. Repeat this with the right leg. In this way, alternate for a period of three times on each side. Try to feel the letting go that takes place in the hips whenever the leg comes to rest, and also feel where the stretch is (in your legs, lower back, or elsewhere) when you bring the knee up toward the chest. Avoid strain.

Exercise 4. Come over on your left side, in fetal position, your right hand along your right side. Bring your right knee toward the chest, then extend the right leg down to full length then back to start and let go. After doing this three times, turn over on your right side and bring the left knee toward the chest, extend it out, and then bring it back to start and let go. Again, feel the degree of stretch and don't overdo, and feel the letting go in your hips.

Exercise 5. Over on your stomach, face on one side resting on the floor, let your shoulders and the rest of you come to as much contact with the floor as possible. Now squeeze your buttocks and your thighs together, hold for the count of three, and let go (3X).

Exercise 6. On your back, knees again in the air with your feet on the floor. This time bring both knees toward the chest at the same time, and then bring both together right back to the starting position and let go. There is no extension of the legs in this exercise. Again feel the stretch and the letting go.

Now go backward doing six again, and then five, four, three, two, and one.

You must make time for these exercises in your daily life. To make it easier to get started, only a basic program is presented. Later on, as happens with so many people, you will begin to crave the exercises and then you will turn to the section in Kraus's book where you can find an additional series of four to eight exercises to add to your basic six. Follw Kraus's guidelines as to how to add on these additional exercises.[2]

These exercises make so much sense to me now that it's hard to understand that others can't see the value of it. But then, I went for many years without exercising, using the same excuses that you do. When I went to see Dr. Kraus for the pains in my upper back, I discovered that these had developed because I had gone for years without regular exercise, while meanwhile the hours I spent in a chair were steadily increasing, first because of studying and later because of my professional duties. Naturally, the tensions in my life played a role in the development of these pains, but the pains might not have started if I had been exercising regularly. When I first began the exercises, I could not come closer than six inches to touching my toes. Within a few months, I was able to reach the toes and now I can almost touch my palms to the floor. This means that I have added more than eight inches of stretch to my legs, back and shoulders. There is no question in my mind that the tremendous increase in emotional freedom that I have noted in the past few years has come along with this increase in physical freedom. I hope that this will inspire you to try it out. Remember that the first two months are usually the period of greatest resistance, so stick it out.

Vigorous Exercises (Aerobics)

I teach all of my own patients how to exercise, and I do the same for the patients referred for medication, providing the referring therapist is in agreement. This method has proven extremely successful.

But I want to report to you an astonishing phenomenon that I have observed again and again: even though it is true that most patients are from the beginning delighted with the way exercise makes them feel, and most others warm up to it in a month or two, there is an almost universal tendency to slack off when the next wave of worry or pressure hits them. *Just when they need it the most, they exercise less!* Usually all it takes is a pep talk to get them moving again, and after resuming they realize they could have handled the situation more easily if they hadn't stopped. But what is going on here? Why this denial of the self just when it needs to be affirmed?

For now, I don't want to deal with the psychological reasons for this—such as a strong need to suffer in order to maintain contact with negative parental introjects. Rather, given the space limitations, I'd like to consider the societal contributions to this problem, which must be explained to the patient.

In a nutshell, the sports field in general and the physical education system in particular are so off-the-wall that they turn off hundreds of millions of sensitive people. When I tell my patients that they can find *their own way* of engaging in sports, this is truly a revelation and an inspiration to them. They had never considered the option. Consider what happened to them in high school: when they couldn't do chin-ups they were mocked and got a "zero" from the coach instead of a concrete plan to develop strength, coordination, and pride. And even the kids who did well in sports were burned by the system. They were trained in sports like football, which made them muscular but rigid (inviting back problems later on), and further, these sports were not the kind of activity that would teach them *daily habits of exercise!* So this weekend one person throws his back out in a touch football game, and next weekend another rips the knee cartilages playing tennis.

On top of all that, the spirit of "winning is everything" kills off most of the benefit people (other than promoters) can get from sports. After the Philadelphia Flyers had attacked the Russian hockey team like wild boars, their captain said, "That's the only way we know how to win." Really, it's no wonder people don't exercise!

I encourage you to read George Leonard's book *The Ultimate Athlete* (5) for a picture of the new movements under way in the field of physical education, and also for encouragement:

> Lifelong physical activities can be provided for every body type . . . the short-term excitement and intensity created by the overblown desire to win at all costs can be replaced by a more durable excitement and intensity springing from the heart of the athletic experience itself . . . this may provide us the best possible path to personal enlightenment and social transformation in this age [pp. 19-20].

One of the major points I would like to bring out in this chapter is: *deep sensory experiences of the self along with vitalizing movements will awaken the organism. When we are fully participating in the organism, we can go beyond relaxation, physical fitness, and better adjustment, and enter a new realm of consciousness.*

By all means, get started on the ground floor of fitness, which in and of itself is essential for you. But also be open, as you are ready, for these new dimensions of experiencing your self.

For guidance in the vigorous activities that will contribute to your fitness, the best book I know of is *Aerobics* by Kenneth Cooper, M.D. (2). Cooper wanted to find a way to standardize exercise, so that each individual would know how far to run or swim, for how many minutes, and at what speed. His research results took all the guesswork out of it. It's all there, in tables that will tell you—after you take a simple jogging test—what category of fitness you're in, and how to proceed from that level.

Cooper assigns point values to each exercise, and tells you how many points to go for each week. On pages 51 and 52 of *Aerobics,* he shows you several combinations of exercises that will give you the points needed and in a manner that suits your disposition and your time schedule. The maintenance level that you should reach within a few months is 30 points per week. You should get these points in not less than four days of exercise per week, and not more than six days per week. *You must give yourself a minimum of one day off a week, to allow the body to rest.*

For those of you who are just starting out, even ten points a week will be a lot. For example if you play handball twice a week for 35 minutes, or if three days a week you walk one and a half miles in 29 minutes twice daily, either of these would give you about ten points a week. That's a lot of activity for many of us. So, before you go out and hurt yourself by pushing too hard, take the test in the book, and follow your category of fitness scrupulously.

You can see from the above discussion that this is another one of those areas in which developing your sensory awareness is valuable, because it will help you avoid injuries. As you're getting back into shape, it's better to go a little easy on yourself than to push too hard. Remember that you're not trying out for the Olympic races.

Whereas with the suppling exercises we can offer a standardized basic six, with the vigorous exercises that is not possible. So use Cooper's book as a guide, and most important, use your own inner sense as your best guide. Conduct yourself *feelingly,* so that you listen, on the one hand, to the organism's need for exercise, and, on the other hand, for its need to slow down, lay off for a while, or try something different. Find your own rhythm and balance.

SOME APPLICATIONS OF THE COMBINED APPROACH

In each of the applications, sensory awareness and physical exercises will be used to systematically enhance the individual's strength, flexibility, and sense of presence and of continuity.

1. *Overeating.* After getting quiet, the person places a small amount of food (such as a small piece of cracker) in the mouth, and with patience he or she soon notices that by itself the jaws begin to chew the food and the swallowing motion takes place, without the person having to "do" anything. People are astonished by this, and by the sense of taste that they had previously ignored, and also by the pleasant sense of fullness that can be achieved with eating a ridiculously small amount of food. With a combined approach of sensory awareness and exercises

(such as calisthenics and swimming), several patients have lost 30 to 40 pounds within four months. Feelings of deprivation did not become severe for these people, and the weight loss has been maintained. I have never seen any other approach to diet that helps the individual experience what eating actually is, or that helps to increase the pleasure and satisfaction from the food.

2. *Schizoid Detachment.* This work sensitizes the patient so that he can detect subtle sensations, including the emotions that he has been out of touch with. It helps him to trust the ground, his sense of self, and the process of letting go, all of which are prerequisites for the integration of the schizoid personality.

3. *Scattering, Hysterical Traits, and Hyperventilation.* When people with these problems discover that contact with the ground slows them down and soothes them, and is alway available to them, tremendous relief is provided.

4. *Smoking.* After getting quiet, the person is encouraged to gradually breathe out more and more deeply, each time allowing the next breath to come in as it wants to. Most often, the next breath in is considerably deeper, but it is deeper without requiring any extra exertion. At times, gentle pressure from the hand is applied to the breastbone, or a light stone is used for pressure. If the hand is used, it is removed when the person is about to breathe in again. People smoke when they become tense and need a release. The tension is associated with air hunger, which comes from the constriction of the chest. In order to get more air, the smoker sucks in a great deal of smoke (and air) and then lets out an even greater exhalation. Whereas the usual exhalation is quite small, when the person smokes, he breathes out such a large volume that the entire room gets clouded up with smoke. It is very similar to the long breath out of a meditator when he says Ooommm. The organism knows that this long breath is needed; the smoker just needs a different way of allowing it to take place, so that the holding up of the chest can be released.

5. *Obsessive-compulsive and Phobic Behavior.* A person with these problems confronts a fear and a void when he tries to stand up to the problem, and is plagued with a sense that there will be nothing left of him to survive that confrontation. But when he engages in the sensory work, even as he experiences these feelings of doom and void, he reminds himself to pay attention *also* to the contact that is coming in from the ground. He comes back to the sense of breathing, he feels his own movement, and he senses his own presence. He experiences the unpleasant feelings of doom as mere *sensations* taking place somewhere within the organism. He learns to trust himself and to doubt the validity of the superego's threat that he will not survive. Through all this, the power and strength of the entire organism are harnessed and are allowed to work *for* him rather than against him.

6. *Failure to Reach Orgasm.* Betty Keane reports that the experience of letting go and of trusting the continuity of sensations has enabled several women she has treated to achieve orgasm, often for the first time in their lives; for some this occurred after just a few sessions.

7. *Back Pain, Sinus Headaches, and Psychosomatic Disorders.* I believe that the single most damaging force to the total health of the individual is that he allows tension to interfere with his breathing, and this completely throws off the move-

ment, balance, and natural flow of energy in the organism. By exercising and by staying open to the breathing and other sensations, the health is mobilized and emotions such as anger will be sensed and dealt with before they can be turned inward. It should be especially noted that the freeing of the breathing breaks the vicious cycle of pain-clutching-more pain.

8. *Sensory Break Instead of Coffee Break.* In between patients or phone calls you can arrange for periodic breaks of three to five minutes in which you can close your eyes and raise your arms out to the side or lean forward in the manner described in the sensory exploration. If there are people near your desk, small movements of the shoulder can be made instead. This activity will recharge your batteries. Other days you may want to do a brief version of the basic six suppling exercises.

9. *Countertransference Problems.* It is of the utmost importance to you as a psychotherapist that you be aware of the feelings that arise in you while you are working with a patient. This will help you not only to be in better contact with the patient, but also to prevent your being drained by hours on end of needy people. You must become aware of your own tendencies to hold your breath and freeze your motion in the presence of someone who is making demands on you. You should remember also that the task of just sitting in a chair all day long is in and of itself exhausting, and is without any of the physical activity that would replenish your energy. It is therefore vital that you tend to yourself so that you can keep breathing and moving, and keep alive. Dr. Hans Kraus, the back specialist, has told me that whereas the average person may come in with three to five painful trigger points, the average psychiatrist doesn't come in until he is riddled from head to foot with seven to ten or even more of these trigger points! We do tend to get "out of it," and sensory awareness is the best means I know of for getting back in.

10. *Space Travel.* In any situation where there is weightlessness or sensory deprivation, if the individual can find a continuous reference point within himself, he is much more likely to maintain his sanity. The one reference point that is always with us, throughout our lifetime, is the sensation of the movements of breathing. Even when there is no sense of contact with the ground, no smell, no sound, there is still that sense of gentle pulling, pushing, flowing, and ebbing that is the breath. Like a fix on the North Star, I believe this attending to the breathing will help men navigate their own precarious existence in the disorienting new reality of space.

CASE HISTORIES[3]

Neal

Neal is a 23-year-old, single graduate student who started therapy one year ago with a chief complaint of "feeling numb." He was in a state of confusion and apprehension so intense that at just the ring of a telephone his skinny body would jump and cringe. He was utterly preoccupied with the question: Should he or should he not go to Israel for a "vacation"? I pointed out that he was not *supposed* to make a decision, in that he had a need to perpetuate this state of confusion. He posed endless questions, which further perpetuated this confusion. He had never kissed or embraced a girl and was afraid to do so.

Figure drawings had no shoulders, so that the arms more or less came off of the neck. The female figure had a breast coming out of the arm, in the manner of a large biceps. The haste with which he drew the figures corresponded to and resulted from his parents' teaching: happiness is *not* possible during this lifetime; so just "buckle under" and try to become rich and famous even though *you* will never make it.

Because of a wall of panic that was for all intents and purposes impenetrable, he was started during the second month on small doses of a major tranquilizer. The response to Mellaril was immediate, and the doses never had to exceed 30 mgm per day. He felt calmer, and was increasingly able to set aside that decision-making preoccupation about going to Israel. He reported that even though the thoughts "*could* come flooding down on him," nevertheless they were being held at bay. He caught on quickly to the physical exercises and to the sensory work. He responded especially well to a sensory exploration of lying on the floor and letting the weight settle and the breathing open. He jogged regularly, and delighted at his sense of increasing strength.

Within half a year, he began to look like a man, as he became more comfortable and visibly more present in the chair. His voice lowered and he no longer mumbled. A spark came into his eyes. At nine months, his projective drawings had improved considerably, with shoulders now being present. He reported an inner sense, while drawing the figure, that "this person is three-dimensional."

At ten months, a trial discontinuation of the Mellaril was attempted, but a steady increase in confusion indicated that he wasn't ready. Mellaril was resumed, but at even smaller doses of 10 to 20 mgm per day, and within one week he was back on the track.

In the twelfth month, he began to get interested in dating girls, and then he made a truly liberating decision: he accepted an invitation from good, positive friends to spend a few months at their farm in New Hampshire. He went, fully in contact with his fears of separation and individuation, and anticipating a very good time. That's where he is now, and I hope he is gaving a great time.

I asked him to write down a few things about his experiences in therapy, and here are excerpts (emphasis mine):

> The sensory work gives me a sense of myself—before I never knew when I was tense . . . I'm able to exert more force and *presence* in my relations with other people . . . *I've begun to see that I am more than my thoughts and that the world exists on deeper levels* . . . with the physical exercises my body feels better—less tense—after I've done them, even though I still resist and put them off . . . I'm developing a sense of wanting to do them because it feels good rather than because they're good for me.

Greg

A 30-year-old single male with great bushy beard, Greg held his eyes wide open and his head back, in frustration and rage. Prior to coming to me, he had had a total of *ten years of analysis,* but he had never had an experience of the reality of his organism. He spoke often of feeling himself an abyss, an emptiness, a vast hole, and a "brick" in his brain. He was exceptionally resistant to physical exercise. His days were spent recoiling from loss of ego boundaries, in that as he passed people on the street he felt he was becoming merged with them. In response, he would fantasize knives. This reflected his desperate attempts to stave off an overwhelming mother. Perfectionism and rigidity were severe, but he was an excellent accountant!

He was hypersensitive to a wide variety of major tranquilizers, suffering intolerably spacey and remote feelings on each of them. So even though he needed this avenue of help, it couldn't be used.

One day, in frustration, I let him have it about his resistance to exercising outside of these sessions. He was stunned but went home and started doing them. At the next session three days later, he was a new person. One month later, during a sensory exploration in the office, he reported that he had just felt for the *first time in his life* his own "boundaries" and had experienced that he was "a separate person from everybody else." A few months later he had the first positive relationship he had ever known with a woman. Later on he fulfilled a dream of many years: he left New York City—which he hated but had been unable to leave—and moved to a quiet place in California. Here is an excerpt from a letter he sent me from there:

> I keep on experiencing more and more of the moment. Except for moments when I feel depressed (I still don't know why), I feel serene and peaceful most of the time . . . I wonder if I could ever tell you how much you enabled me to feel and experience. It's almost hard to believe I ever felt different. I've become more aware of experiencing the moment. It's great!

Mary

Mary is a 25-year-old single woman with pretty red hair, constant sadness just under her face and ulcerative colitis. Her father committed suicide two years ago, but her colitis had started prior to that. She had had two hospitalizations for the colitis, and strong medications were needed to stop the bleeding. Her alcoholic mother has a voice that "goes right through me"—she points to her abdomen to show where it is that it goes through her.

Right around the time that she started therapy, Mary had to discontinue her colitis medication because of severe side effects. It was therefore imperative that she begin a program of exercises to reduce tension, but with the warning that overdoing it and fatiguing herself could cause the colitis to flare up. She went at the exercises with great gusto, starting with the suppling exercises and a few weeks later getting to easy jogging. To her relief and mine, this regimen alone controlled the bleeding. This was accomplished without recourse to any psychiatric medications (although of course these would have been given if the bleeding had not been controlled).

Mary has made steady progress on all levels. The tearfulness is now gone from her face, and the clutching of the abdomen has lessened greatly. Only six months into therapy now, she is ready and able to move out of her mother's very close-knit home. In the fourth month, I asked her to write down some of her experiences, and here in its entirety is her fascinating letter (emphasis mine):

When Dr. Carlton asked me if I did any exercises, I just shrugged my shoulders and replied no. I thought to myself—here comes another easy pat solution that one hears on the T.V. or can read every month in a magazine. It's not that I've never tried exercise—it's that I've never succeeded. I've gone on diets and tried the 20 sit-up routine. It usually lasted a grand total of two days.

When the first six exercises were introduced to me, all I could say is that I would try. I had the feeling that I would do my old routine—exercise two days and stop. Perhaps the fact that I was told that the exercises would make my body relax made me a little more anxious to test them. My job as a junior high school teacher often makes me very tense. So I started trying the exercises in the morning. These are exercises you can do in a semi-sleep state. Sometimes, I listen to some soft, slow music and exercise to the rhythm. After two months a strange thing has occurred. I no longer have to force my body to do the exercise. My body wants to do them because I don't feel good if I skip them. Often during the lunch hour, I do some of the exercises in my classroom, lying on a beach towel. *It helps me feel more alive.*

About a month ago, I tried running in the park after work. At first, I'd run about the equivalent of a long block. I was huffing and puffing but I had to walk the mile track to get home. Over the last month, I have improved to running between one-quarter to one-half miles. *It's not particularly far, but I always feel good when I pass the park house where I stopped the first day.*

Before I started exercising I had a routine—come home from work, turn on the T.V., drink a cup of tea, and sleep two hours. I don't always find it easy to run. Last week I arrived home really beat. I was having company and the house still needed to be cleaned. I was tempted to take a quick snooze. I had not done any of the exercises so I decided to do the easy exercises and skip the running. Yet, once I finished the easy exercises, I was ready to run. After running, I came home and cleaned. I stayed up until about 1:30 without feeling tired.

The running instead of making me feel tired, makes me wake up. I feel I can run off and forget the students who drove me crazy all day. The cold December breeze makes me feel like a kid who goes out to play and comes home only because it's time to eat.

These statements from my patients—and that last sentence in particular—have deepened my conviction that the addition of these experiential approaches gets through to the individual's health sooner, more deeply, and in more dimensions than is possible through the verbal approaches alone. This is an application of that old adage: "Give me a fish and I eat for a day. Teach me to fish and I eat for a lifetime."

I make a present of three paperbacks to all my patients: *Backache, Stress and Tension* by Hans Kraus (4); *Aerobics* by Kenneth Cooper (2); and *Bodymind* by Don Ethan Miller (7). These books celebrate the vitality and self-reliance that come in restoring the organism to a state of suppleness and conditioning.

In addition, I teach elements of sensory awareness to my patients. The depth that we go to is determined by the patient's readiness, which is clearly visible in his responses along the way. The therapist must know that what the patient is actually experiencing is goldmine enough to explore, and that he must resist temptation to push beyond that.

Through this combined approach of exercises and sensory awareness, within a matter of weeks there is a massive reduction in anxiety and tension. I have seen this occur in patient after patient, and I have shared with them their joy in this sense of well-being. This approach has been very successful in reducing the dosages of tranquilizers and antidepressants, when these were indicated. In addition, for a number of patients who needed medications but could not take them because of excessive side effects, this approach served as a very reasonable substitute for the medications.

It is necessary, though, to get beyond relaxation, and into another dimension of experience. If relaxation alone were sufficient, then the very effective relaxation techniques of biofeedback, behavior therapy, or T.M. would be enough. The basic objection to focusing on alpha waves, or on a pleasant scene, or on a mantra (as in T.M.), is that in the long run precisely the *opposite* is needed. We need to stop focusing on isolated thoughts or functions; we need to stop manipulating. We can derive far more benefit from freeing the consciousness than from fixing it on something. For instance, at this moment, I might sense my contact with the ground; the next moment I might discover a holding in the shoulder; and by staying present there, I allow it to let go without my "doing" anything to it. In contrast, if I merely concentrate on alpha or on a mantra, I might become relaxed but I will block out these all-important sensations from the organism. *What we are trying to reach here is total, moment-to-moment functioning, and not just "relaxation."* After all, we can't stay in alpha or recite a mantra all day long. But, we can stay quietly in touch with letting the weight down and with keeping open around the breathing. We owe it to ourselves to stay in touch, because the price of getting "out of it" is too great!

We must be aware of our cultural tendency to rush to "make the problem go away" (relax), and recognize that there is a childlike indulgence behind that attitude. A far more useful lifetime strategy is to learn how to remain fully present, even in the face of unpleasant feelings of tension. And we must learn to get out of the organism's way so that it can handle this tension without making itself sick—it knows how to do this! We interfere with the organism's work when we permit ourselves to lose contact with the ground and the breathing, and focus instead on "what's wrong" or "what has to be changed."

The reasons the physical exercises are so important for enabling the organism to do its work are that:

1. The physical (outer) level of the organism needs strength and endurance in order to stay healthy.

2. Exercise prevents excessive build-up of tension and thus the dwelling-in-the-mind that is our habitual reaction to that tension.

3. Exercise lengthens the muscles that tension has chronically shortened. An example of the latter is the pulling back of the head and slumping of the shoulders we see all around us. Conditions like these drain energy and *cause* tension, even when there's "nothing wrong," and can be corrected through exercise.

4. The exercises work hand-in-hand with the sensory work to make the organism come alive. Everyone who works out regularly knows this feeling of aliveness.

While the physical exercises are strengthening the outer, the sensory explorations are strengthening the inner. It is particularly the inner strength of breathing that we need to develop. Years of holding have weakened the breathing, which is why hardly any of us can sit up straight unless we hold ourselves up (try it). In contrast, animals and small children sit up beautifully without holding. It is this holding of the breathing that produces most of the *intensity* of the distress and panic we feel. Hours on end of constricted breathing will produce feelings similar to that of holding the breath underwater for several minutes: We begin to scream inside for air! In other words, if we can "come up for air" as often as we need to, we may still feel the tensions but we will lose 90 percent of the *distress* about them. Wouldn't that be enough for you? It is the *strengthening of the inner* that allows us to stay open in the breathing, no matter what's happening.

Finally, a clear distinction must be made between the approach to the physical exercises and to the sensory explorations. In the exercises, the movements and letting go of movements are all-important. Doing these in a feeling manner helps, of course, but sensation is not what the work is about. Whereas in sensory awareness, sensation *is* what we're after. Movements are only a means to wake up sensation. When we become absorbed in the process of the sensations, the strength and presence of the organism emerge. This presence is 99 percent of what we need in life. It is nice to have comfort and to have loved ones, for sure. But without this tangible sense of presence, comfort and love are not *felt*. Without presence, people become unreal: They are endlessly driven to "achieve," to "prove their worth," and to justify an existence that they do not experience from the inside.

With this sense of presence restored, we can rest in a quiet place and take whatever comes our way, because we have the full *experience* of that which is solid and enduring in us—the organism in its totality.

NUTRITION

The subject of nutrition is so vast that writing about it risked making this chapter far too lengthy, and yet it is so important that I felt this discussion of a total approach could not be complete without at least a few major points being made. For further details, check the reference section for several of the fine books on the subject (8, 9, 10, 11). You should read these books "with a grain of salt," because the pioneers in this as in any field tend to get carried away at times. Take their ideas as guidelines, and follow only those that seem sensible and comfortable to you.

Here then are some of the major points:

1. Total health will be immensely improved by limiting the intake of sugar. The average American consumes a third of a pound of sugar per day, and because the organism was not designed to process these staggering amounts, many people become toxic. This toxicity can be physical (arthritis and other degenerative changes) and/or emotional (hypoglycemic mood changes). The more needy and "oral" types would naturally tend to consume more sugar than average, and become more vulnerable.

2. Health will also be improved by eliminating as much as possible the food additives such as artificial colors and artificial flavors, MSG, calcium propionate, and so on. There are conservatively ten million American school children afflicted with hyperactive disease, and Dr. Ben Feingold of Kaiser-Permanente has demonstrated (11) that more than 50% of them will clear up when additives are removed. In my experience, these additives cause unusual physical and mental symptoms in adults as well as children. Parents should as much as possible prevent their children from eating these foods, and should be wary themselves. Most important of all, pregnant women should totally abstain from foods with these additives, because the nervous system is at its most sensitive to toxins during embryonic development. Feingold has also found that salicylates in drugs (aspirin) and in nature (e.g. apples, oranges), and certain compounds acting chemically like salicylates (e.g. Indocin ® and Yellow Dye #5) can induce symptoms similar to those of the food additives, and should have trial eliminations. Ritalin ®, used for hyperactives, contains color additives to which they are sensitive.

3. Many persons who have depression, anxiety or fatigue in a chronic form, and who have not responded adequately to psychotherapy and medications, might consider supplementing those modalities with moderate or large dosages of vitamins and minerals. They may need far more of these than normal because their

chronic stress tends to deplete vitamins, and in addition they may have higher biologic requirements (9, 10); and in any case, even a good diet cannot provide enough vitamins and minerals, because our foods are not *adequately* enriched after all the processing that is done.

Three case histories will help demonstrate the importance of nutritional awareness for people generally and for health professionals in particular:

1. Margaret: A 58 year-old married nurse had a twelve year history of severe right upper quadrant abdominal pain, associated with frequent syncope (fainting) which would be followed by debilitating diarrhea and nausea. Extensive workups for porphyria and other organic illnesses, carried out by fine physicians at excellent hospitals, were negative. Forty-two electro-convulsive treatments had failed to help her in any way. When referred to me in suicidal despair, she began keeping a diary and discovered that the fainting and subsequent diarrhea and nausea followed within four hours any meal or snack containing additives, which were eliminated. She has been free of pain for an entire year, at the time of this writing. On the average of once per month she will have episodes of syncope and diarrhea/nausea, but these occur one-to-one with careless lapses in eating offending foods, such as certain breakfast bars, chicken fried in packaged batters, hams wrapped in plastic, and so on. She is also made ill by Indocin ®, given by another doctor as a pain reliever for her arthritis, which confirms Dr. Feingold's observations (see above). It is interesting that her syncopal attacks are followed by several minutes of what appears to be post-ictal (seizure) behavior, during which she cannot move voluntarily, makes groaining noises, breathes heavily, and is unresponsive when her husband passes his hand in front of her eyes. Thus it seems these additives are capable of inducing seizures.

2. Allan: An 8½ year-old boy with a two year history of encopresis (defecating in his pants), and learning disabilities. Treatment by a psychiatrist and later a psychologist was ineffective. He was overweight, and helped himself frequently to the kitchen full of "junk food" that his parents stocked. The soiling, which used to occur two to three times every day, has at this writing occurred only three times in the month since additives have been eliminated: the first in the first two days while offending foods were being weeded out; the second and third followed two separate occasions where the parents gave him hot dogs despite warnings that these are major offenders. These two cases have led me to formulate that the additives can cause a profound discharge of the autonomic nervous system, which in the nurse resulted in a syncope or seizure and diarrhea, and in the boy resulted in sudden evacuation of the rectum.

3. John: A 49 year-old writer was chronically depressed and unable to function, and drank fairly steadily. Moderately large doses of vitamins (e.g. 50 mgm B_1) and minerals brought some improvement in mood but drinking continued. One day he reported a chronic pattern wherein his rectum would fill up with only partially digested material which was hard to evacuate, and this would be accompanied by stuffiness of the sinuses. On the assumption that there wasn't sufficient stomach acid to properly digest and assimilate food and vitamins, a hydrochloric acid supplement was given. Within a week, digestion was more complete, sinus problems had stopped, and he reported the following: "The craving for alcohol

is gone. My hand reached for the bottle, but I realized that I didn't want any." The vitamins could not be fully effective until properly absorbed; and the psychotherapy could not be fully effective until the nutritional and metabolic status was brought under control.

CONCLUSION

It is important to be open to new approaches. Each therapist must decide if he is going to stay in the "traditional" modes because that is the way he's been trained to help, or whether we will explore new modalities because that is what his *patients* may need. I think the flight from the traditional therapies into all the new (and sometimes freaky) modalities results largely from dissatisfaction with the slow pace and over-intellectualized tendencies of the traditional. Some leave under poor motivation, such as wanting "instant cure;" but larger numbers of people these days are well-motivated to seek total well-being, and so look elsewhere.

My primary concern has been to find a system in which to use psychotherapy as a solid base, but where the insights gained could be made real through the direct experience of the organism; and, at the same time, a system that would fully respect the patient's defenses, and be free from the desparate manipulations of so many of the "hands on" approaches. I find that the combination of sensory awareness and physical exercise fulfills these needs. It accelerates and enriches the process of psychotherapy in ways that are very gratifying for the patients: they *love* the work. It leads them naturally to heed their needs in areas of nutrition and elsewhere. This combined approach is very satisfying to me as a therapist, because the sessions are varied in content; because the patients become self-sufficient as they come to sit in and occupy their own space and therefore do less "leaning" on me, which is great for both of us; and because they develop a balance, endurance, and well-being which are beautiful to behold.

REFERENCES

1. Brooks, C., and Selver, C. *Sensory Awareness.* New York: Viking, 1974.
2. Cooper, K.H. *Aerobics.* New York: Bantam Books, 1976.
3. Kraus, H. *Clinical Treatment of Back and Neck Pain.* New York: McGraw-Hill, 1970.
4. Kraus, H. *Backache, Stress and Tension.* New York: Pocket Books, 1974.
5. Leonard, G. *The Ultimate Athlete.* New York: Viking, 1975.
6. Mendels, J. *Biologic Psychiatry.* New York: John Wiley, 1973.
7. Miller, D.E. *Bodymind.* New York: Pinnacle Books, 1974.
8. Airola, Paavo, Ph.D., N.D. *How To Get Well,* Phoenix:Health Plus Publishers, 1974.
9. Pfeiffer, Carl, Ph.D., M.D. *Mental and Elemental Nutrients,* New Canaan, Conn:Keats, 1975.
10. Hawkins and Pauling *Orthomolecular Psychiatry,* San Francisco:W.H. Freeman, 1973.
11. Feingold, Ben M.D. *Why Your Child is Hyperactive,* New York:Random House, 1975.

Regression as an Agent of Change:
An Integrative Perspective

HENRY GRAYSON

Regression is a natural, spontaneous means by which the organism attempts to protect, and then heal or restore its equilibrium.

Many people do not share this point of view. Through numerous clinical discussions with colleagues over the years and in classes of students I have taught, I have found many view regression as usually a negative or pathological phenomenon. They seem to think of it as a sign that a person's condition has worsened, and do not seem to realize that the organism has gone into that state as a purposeful, though perhaps unconscious act.

Common restorative forms of regression in human beings include the need for sleep and dreaming, and the desire for rest and care when sick. On a larger scale, we know that besieged armies have generally tended to retreat in order to recoup their forces. Whether an individual or an army, to persist foolishly in the face of grave danger would lead to inevitable annihilation.

It is my thesis that the organism is innately self-enhancing unless there is a physiological or learned interference. For example, when children have been allowed to eat whatever they wished, they have not confirmed many adults' fears that the children's cravings would remain largely with candy and other carbohydrates and fats. Instead, the child's desires for foods change according to the nutritional needs of the child. This is valid, of course, only if the child has direct access to various foods from which he can choose readily, and if the child is not strongly influenced by previous ideas about food.

When there is fear, the organism may learn blocks to inhibit the natural movement toward self-enhancement, including blocks to the use of regression as a restorative function. Even so, the regression is purposeful in that it serves to protect the organism from what it perceives to be inevitable destruction.

Developmentally, regression indicates, according to Eidelberg (5), that under certain conditions, the repressed wish or its energy may 'regress,' to be discharged on an earlier stage of development . . . . It seems that regression, by interfering with the normal development and disposition of instinctual energy, makes it more difficult to become aware of an infantile wish, and mobilizes other defense mechanisms" (p. 108).

Take the case of Nathan, for example, As a child, he viewed his father as a powerful, cruel giant who could castrate him or even destroy him. At the time when he would have moved into the oedipal conflict, his father was beating him and threatening to send him away to a children's home when he did something his father disliked. Nathan, in order to protect himself, repressed any oedipal wishes and retreated to earlier levels of adaptation—a manic state of working as hard as he could all the time to earn love and avoid rejection. Hence the infantile sexual wish was lost to awareness.

Regression, itself, is not to be seen categorically as either healthy or pathological. On the pathological side, it can be generally said that less neutralized energy is available for the functions of the ego and superego when regression occurs. In extreme forms, the observable result is what we commonly call schizophrenia. As Arieti (1) put it, "The specific reaction consists of the adoption of archaic mental mechanisms, which belong to lower levels of integration. Inasmuch as the result is a regression to, but not an integration at lower levels, a disequilibrium is engendered which causes further regression, at times to levels even lower than the one in which certain perceptions are possible."

On the other hand, as noted above, regression may be considered a normal and even creative process. It is a regular nightly experience in the form of sleep, without which we cannot expect to function in a normal way. Dream research has revealed that a certain amount of REM time is necessary for the person, or he will begin to evidence signs of psychoticlike behavior (3, 4, 20).

As early as 1938, Freud wrote, "A dream is a psychosis, with all the absurdities, delusions, and illusions of a psychosis" (9). This temporary psychosis seems to give us the chance to re-experience pleasures and fears of childhood and infancy, which are forbidden to conscious awareness during our waking state. It is as if we have to indulge in a temporary psychotic experience in our sleep in order to be normal the next day.

Regression, therefore, as Kris (15) has noted, may be either in the service of the id, as in psychosis, or in the service of the ego. In the latter sense, regression may actually aid ego functioning, because this form of regression is controlled. Ego function is not submerged or lost, and the id derivitives remain under ego control. Regressions of this type are the hallmark of creativity, including imagination, creative thinking, and intuition. It is not unlike George Kelly's (14) concept of "loosening" or the Gestalt notion of inverse perception of the figure and ground (18). Greater integration of the personality is possible with this kind of regression, since the ego is not fighting with the id derivitives, but rather the mobile catheses of the primary process become available for secondary-process utilization (15).

One further way of distinguishing between healthy and pathological regression is by the length and breadth of the regression. In psychosis, there is sweeping regression involving many aspects of the person's personality, which may last from a few minutes to many years. Even here, we cannot classify all such regressions as pathological. If the person is able to use the psychotic regression to integrate more adequately at earlier levels, then the ego is strengthened, rather than further weakened. Very often ego support may be needed during or after such regression. Healthy or ego-controlled regression is usually of short duration, and may be stopped with minimal effort by the ego at any time. It might be called, more aptly, a temporary regressive experience.

Since regression has been considered not only as a normal experience in many forms, but also as one which is potentially creative or integrative, it has been considered central in more than one form of psychotherapy. Let us now turn our attention to some of these.

The use of regression has always been at the heart of psychoanalytic technique. In the beginning, Freud used hypnosis, catharsis, and abreaction. Later he moved to the use of the regression in the transference neurosis in the analytic situation. He put it thus: "The analysis of the transference neurosis is the keystone of psychoanalysis" (8). In addition, Freud (10) and his followers have given considerable merit to the use of dreams in psychoanalysis. Both, in essence, are the therapeutic utilization of regression—the affect and symbolization of the primitive instincts, wishes, and defenses experienced in dreams and in the transference.

Slavson (21), the pioneer in group psychotherapy, was even more adamant concerning the place of regression in psychotherapy: "... there is no psychotherapy possible without regressive movement which can be achieved only in a therapeutic setting of a regressive type."

Reich (19), recognizing that some defenses did not seem penetrable by verbal analytic means, went on to propose that the physical body itself may house various defenses—hence his movement into physical activity as a means of breaking through the body armour to facilitate a regressive experience. Based on Reich's ideas, Alexander Lowen (17) further developed physical and verbal techniques, called bioenergetic analysis, in the attempt to facilitate breaking through the body armor and therapeutic regression.

Perhaps the most extreme proponent of regression as being not only therapeutic, but necessary for real change is R.D. Laing (16). In the early 1960's, he shared his ideas with a professional audience at Columbia University during the American Psychological Association meeting in New York. He spoke of the possibility of therapists actually helping their patients to go mad and come back again. Anything else, he contended, was aborting the process and was not done with the patient's best interests in mind. Needless to say, at that time his talk was received with a stony, hostile silence.

In my own clinical practice, I have several times observed verifications of Laing's hypothesis—not that I helped my patients to become mad, but rather that their psychoses were useful to them in reintegrating at earlier levels. For example, two different patients were treated analytically with minimal progress for over a year. Both terminated prematurely and abruptly after not being able to get past certain resistances. Within three months of their termination, each became psychotic with full-blown delusional systems. One returned to therapy during the episode; the other after the symptoms had remitted. In each case, the patient entered therapy with a deeper degree of involvement and made significant progress in personality reorganization in the years that followed. It seemed that the sweeping regression of their psychoses not only broke through old defenses and brought about disintegration, but also the possibility of a healthier reintegration. Their "forbidden" impulses and primary-process thinking were less frightening to them and did not need to be repressed. Hence they were more readily able to use this awareness for further integration and stronger ego functioning.

A viewpoint similar to Laing's has been advanced by Arthur Janov (13). A number of years ago, Janov was in a group session with a patient who was talking about an act on the London stage where a man, dressed up in diapers, drinking milk from bottles, went around yelling, "Mommy! Daddy! Mommy! Daddy!" as loudly as he could. Janov asked his patient to do the same, because he seemed so fascinated by it. He began, with Janov's insistence, to cry out, "Mommy! Daddy!" As he did he became quite upset. He began writhing in agony on the floor; his breathing became rapid, spasmodic, and his words came out of his mouth almost involuntarily. It was as if he were in a hypnotic state or trance. Janov (13) describes what follows:

> The writhing gave way to small convulsions, and finally, he released a piercing, deathlike scream that rattled the walls of my office. The entire episode lasted only a few minutes, and neither Danny nor I had any idea what had happened. All he could say afterward was, "I made it! I don't know what, but I can feel!" [p. 10].

Janov said that this man was neither a hysteric nor a psychotic, but rather a poor 22-year-old college student who was withdrawn, sensitive, and quiet.

This episode aroused Janov's interest considerably. In search of an explanation, he tried it with other patients, and invariably "it" happened—what he came to refer to as the "primal scream." Janov, rather arrogantly, proclaims that his method, called primal therapy, is *the cure* for neurosis, which he defines as: ". . . the dynamic and continuous struggle to mask a potentially catastrophic reality that could not be safely integrated in childhood without shattering the psychophysical integrity of the organism" (p. 16). He feels that his approach is revolutionary because it "involves overthrowing the neurotic system by forceful upheaval. Nothing short of that will eliminate neurosis" (p. 11).

In some ways, primal therapy seems to smack of early Freud, i.e., catharsis and abreaction bring about the cure. Janov, in a telephone conversation in October, 1971, told me that he has research evidence that primal screams excite certain brain centers far more than a general catharsis does. He also claims the screams are directly attached insightfully to the early childhood traumas that resulted in the neurotic adaptational style in the personality, and are not merely an experience of emoting.

In two previous papers, I discussed the place of regression, or rather regressive experiences, as central elements in strengthening the ego. In the first (11), it was noted that the process of decathecting infantile wishes "involves essentially the same mourning process as that necessary for separating one's self from a tangible lost object." Mourning is always a regressive experience. In the other paper (12), it was noted that:

> Encounter techniques combined with psychoanalytic work may aid those with character disorders to have an experience comparable to the transference neurosis of the neurotic—though not of the same time duration. Through temporary regressive experiences facilitated by various well-timed encounter techniques the person is able to break through his denial and repression and to gain more awareness of his infantile wishes and introjects and to bring them under ego control. It is in the fully experiencing the defensive patterns, the archaic wishes, and the introjects in the present with affect and insight that the patient becomes more free to see other options open to him as an adult.

In addition, I have found such techniques, which are as well-chosen and well-timed as a good analytic interpretation, to be helpful for other types of patients than those with character disorders. Let us turn to some clinical examples.

CLINICAL EXAMPLES

Ambulatory Paranoid Schizophrenia

Jean B., with paranoid delusional symptoms, had been my patient for one year in psychoanalytic psychotherapy three times a week when she terminated abruptly and prematurely, unable to gain insight into the nature of her transference resistance. She returned to treatment, however, after two months, reporting that she had heard a lecture in graduate school on anaclitic depression. She realized by her emotional reaction to the lecture that she had repressed her strong dependency needs and that this had been a part of her premature termination. Her treatment this time consisted of one individual and one group session each week. Most of her delusions subsided within the next year.

In one of her analytic group sessions about one year after resuming treatment she was *gvetching* about her work and living crises, but fending off any kind of help as rapidly as the group members tried to give it to her. I pointed this out to her—that she seemed to be pleading with one hand and pushing away with the other. She then spoke of how she was afraid to be given to—afraid of becoming completely helpless and remaining that way. At that point, I wondered if she might like to try something that might be helpful to her, but before I could say what it was, she quickly said, "No!" With this, she suddenly saw the way in which she may often masochistically deprive herself. After some discussion of this, she asked what my suggestion was, at which point I told her: lifting and rocking. I explained that in this exercise, the person lies on the floor, eyes closed, and the group slowly lifts the person and then gently rocks her for a period of time. Again, she said, "No." What she feared most was that she would "put the group members out" and that she would "want it to go on forever." In essence, her fear was that uncontrolled regression would take over. Finally she said, "OK, I'll take the risk and see what happens." She was able to tolerate the experience for only three or four minutes and asked to be put down. Later she said she had really wanted more, but feared that she was getting too much from the group. This led to more associations of feelings of low self-worth—not being worthy of love.

This seemed to be a major turning point in her therapy, for in the remainder of that session and the months that followed, she became much more assertive with both her negative and positive feelings in the group. She became able to ask for help in ways that were clear and to which people could respond appropriately. She sought out and obtained a new job with a $2,000 increase in salary. In addition, she reported that she had been touched by a woman in a subway station to ask directions. She suddenly became aware that she had not felt her customary rage inside her over being touched, for any touching previously had been anathema to her.

It seems, for her, that the learning had become generalized—which often seems to occur from some experiences with well-timed action techniques. However, the most important insight and learning from the experience was a fuller acceptance of her dependency needs and a testing out of her mistrust by letting herself experience both more directly—a major benefit of a carefully chosen action technique in lieu of an interpretation. By the regressive experience, her dependency became less frightening to her. This in turn led her from her characteristic masochistic passivity to more productive activity, both in the group and in numerous practical ways in her outside life. Correspondingly, in her individual sessions, she became more open than ever before to begin looking at many of her previous delusions and projections in her life.

Psychoneurosis

George, a psychiatrist in his forties, was in a series of training groups for professionals I led on the use of nonverbal methods in group psychotherapy. In the third session, he stated that he still didn't feel like he was really a part of the group—that even though he had been participating, he felt like an outsider. He stated that he had had a very stiff neck for a couple of days and that it seemed to be getting worse. His facial muscles were extremely tense and his entire posture revealed extreme somatotized tension. He talked flatly about several conflicts, but apparently without real insight—and certainly not combined with any affect.

I decided then to try working with him physically. He lay on the floor on his back with his eyes closed while I gave him relaxation instructions for several minutes. Then I gently lifted his head and let it turn as slowly as it would go in the other direction, then gradually back to the straight position, and then slowly lifted it and lowered it to the floor. this was repeated two times following relaxation intervals, after which the group lifted and rocked him. A considerable amount of the muscular tension had been reduced, but much was still apparent. Following these exercises, however, he said he was not able to relate a problem about which he said he had wanted to talk, but had been unable to do so. He told the story of having a fight with his wife two weeks before in which he had given her a black eye. It was the only time he had ever hit her, and he had felt extreme guilt over it. But more than that, he feared his rage breaking through again—feared he might harm her more seriously.

An "encounter drama" was set up after he picked a woman to play the role of his wife. The encouter drama differs from traditional psychodrama in that it is more structured and takes place in one position. Sitting closely, but opposite each other on the floor, the working patient takes the clasped hands of his partner and presses them as hard as he can continuously. The working patient's eyes are closed and he and his partner call each other by name, back and forth, with various spontaneous feeling intonations until the working patient feels he can say to the other ("mother," "wife," "father," "husband," etc.) what he has always wanted to say, but has not been able to say. A pillow or cushion is kept handy for the working patient to beat or choke if rage begins to emerge.

Some anger came through in the encounter drama, but much more apparent was the hurt over his wife's being distant, unresponsive and uninvolved with him. This was accompanied with intermittent sobs as he talked, while being held in his "wife's" arms. When they finished, the group observed that he sounded much more like he was talking to his mother than to his wife. This led to more regression and opened the way for numerous associations to his childhood relations with his mother—which in turn led to associations to his older brother, whom he esteemed, but also sorely resented because he felt his parents preferred him. Another encounter drama was set up and he chose a man who reminded him of his brother to play the role. This drama led from tremendous infantile rage, wanting to kill his brother, recalling memories of wanting to, and one experience when he felt he would have killed him if a friend had not stopped him by taking his gun away from him. This in turn was followed by his feelings of hurt and the desire to obtain love from his brother. At this point, he clutched his "brother" and sobbed bitterly. This led him to recall memories of homosexual dreams he used to have about his brother—dreams that had been repressed for many years—and his wish to get affection from his brother.

Following the encounter drama, it was apparent to all the group members that his facial muscles were totally relaxed as well as the remainder of his body. This he confirmed by saying, "I don't think I have ever felt as relaxed in my whole body." He said that he felt he had gotten to more important insights combined with feeling than he had gotten in the three and a half years of his conventional training analysis—but that he was also going back into analysis to continue working through the insights and feelings opened up by this experience.

Discussion

With George, it seemed that his experience was threefold. The focus on the body symptom was necessary in breaking through the body armour and in facilitating regression. As Reich notes, " . . . it is striking to find how the dissolution of a muscular rigidity not only liberates . . . but, in addition, also brings back into memory the very infantile situation in which the repression had taken effect" (19). Secondly, the encounter game of lifting and rocking allowed George to develop more trust in the group to open the door to working on his problems; and last, the encounter drama led to further regression with catharsis, recall, and insight.

In both cases, regression was facilitated by direct work with the body ego defenses as well as the verbal confrontation of defenses. Without the regression, there could not have been the insight with affect and consequently the chance to do reintegrative work at earlier, developmental levels.

Innocuous experiences do not produce therapeutic change. Deep feelings must be experienced with insight in order for a reworking to be valuable. Regression can be an effective means of bringing about insight with affect.

Frankl (7) often quotes Nietzsche as saying, "that which does not kill you, makes you stronger." In regression, what keeps the person from being "killed" is an ego that is strong enough to tolerate or even allow it, or the assistance from another strong ego which can be "loaned" to the person temporarily. Perhaps as we develop more effective means of facilitating therapeutic regression, more change can take place in psychotherapy with less time and expense.

SUMMARY

Regression, in itself, is seen as neither healthy nor pathological. It may be in the service of the id or in the service of the ego. In the latter case, it has been a central element used for therapeutic change in numerous forms of psychotherapy, from psychoanalysis to primal therapy. Clinical examples were cited to show how temporary regressive experiences and even sometimes sweeping regressions in psychoses, are useful in helping the patient move toward further insight and reintegration of the personality at earlier levels.

REFERENCES

1. Arieti, S. *Interpretation of Schizophrenia.* New York: Robert Brunner, 1955.
2. Arlow, J.A., and Brenner, C. The concept of regression and the structural theory. *Psychoanal. Quart.,* 29:603-605, 1960.
3. Dement, W., and Kleitman, N. The relation of eye movements during sleep to dream activity: An objective method for the study of dreaming. *J. Experiment. Psychol.,* 53: 339-346., 1957.
4. Dement, W., and Wolfert, E.A. The relation of eye movements, body motility, and external stimuli to dream content. *J. Experiment. Psychol.,* 55:543-553, 1958.
5. Eidelberg, L. *An Outline of Comparative Pathology of the Neuroses.* New York: International Universities Press, 1954.
6. Eissler, K.R. The Chicago Institute of Psychoanalysis and the sixth period of the development of psychoanalytic technique. *J. Gen. Psychol.,* 42:103-107, 1950.
7. Frankl, V. *Man's Search for Meaning.* Boston: Beacon Press, 1959.
8. Freud, S. Analysis terminable and interminable. In: *Collected Papers.* London: Hogarth Press, 1950.
9. Freud, S. *An Outline of Psychoanalysis.* New York: Boston, 1949.
10. Freud, S. *The Interpretation of Dreams.* New York: Basic Books, 1953.
11. Grayson, H. Grief reactions to the relinquishing of unfulfilled wishes. *Amer. J. Psychother.,* 25:287-295, 1970.
12. Grayson, H. The psychoanalytic use of encounter techniques. *Psychiat. Annals,* in press.
13. Janov, A. *The Primal Scream.* New York: Dell, 1970.
14. Kelly, G. *The Psychology of Personal Constructs.* New York: W.W. Norton, 1955.
15. Kris, E. *Psychoanalytic Explorations in Art.* New York: International Universities Press, 1952.
16. Laing, R.D. *The Politics of Experience.* New York: Pantheon Books.
17. Lowen, A. *The Betrayal of the Body.* London: Collier Macmillan Ltd., 1967.
18. Perls, F., Hefferline, R., and Goodman, P. *Gestalt Therapy.* New York: Julian Press, 1951.
19. Reich, W. *Character Analysis.* New York: Noonday Press, 1967.
20. Schiff, S., Bunney, W., and Freedman, D. A study of ocular movements in hypnotically induced dreams. *J. Nerv. Ment. Dis.,* 133:59-68, 1961.
21. Slavson, S.R. Common sources of error and confusion in group psychotherapy. *Internat. J. Group Psychother.,* 4:3-30, 1953.

Some Similarities and Differences Between Transactional Analysis and Psychoanalysis

JOHN J. O'HEARNE

When I first discovered transactional analysis (T.A.), I did not like it. It was too mechanistic for me. I thought it silly to draw three small circles on a page, label them Parent, Adult, and Child, and think that the complexities of a human being could be reduced to such a simple diagram. However, when I first saw it in operation, I changed my mind and decided to learn more.

Many of my colleagues in the field of group psychotherapy have had experiences somewhat similar to mine. A great many of them felt that T.A. was simplistic and too mechanistic; many of them changed their minds when they saw it at work. Some of these colleagues have learned T.A. and integrated it with their more traditional methods of psychotherapy. Some have learned a little bit about it, but do not integrate it with their work. A few became so enthused that they left the traditional methods behind (I have never seen this condition last very long). A small number learned a little bit about T.A. and convinced themselves that it would not work. Some do this by saying it's not deep enough to effect lasting character change. Others are more like a medical student who heard one lecture on T.A. He then said he did not need to learn it because he would never use it. His teacher asked him why and he replied, "It won't work." The teacher asked him how he knew in the first year of medical school that it would not work. He answered, "It can't work; it's too simple!"

As I learned more about T.A. than the Parent-Adult-Child circles, I appreciated the many similarities between T.A. and psychoanalysis. I shall discuss these likenesses first and later discuss the dissimilarities in the two methods.

Both are analytic methods.

Both have specific terminology which can easily lead to jargon—for example, "He's really sick, what a sadist!" can be as much jargon as "You are playing games with me."

Some of the most important key concepts in each method are difficult to define in words that can be understood by an eight-year-old child. For instance, the philosophic construct called *ego* in traditional psychoanalysis is difficult to define. So is the term *ego state* which T.A. borrowed from psychoanalysis.

What seemed simple when first discovered rapidly became more complex. For example, Freud's libido theory evolved in interesting and sometimes complex fashion. In T.A. the three ego states, Parent, Adult, and Child, were at first simple to understand. Soon, however, they became differentiated on a functional basis into Nurturing Parent and Critical Parent, plus both Adapted Child and Natural Child.

The theories of formation of symptoms are similar in each of these methods. They both stress conflict within the individual in relation to the inside private world of the individual and/or between that private inside world and the outside world of reality. If we take depression as an example, we can see that both methods talk about a loss, plus anger directed back against the individual himself. Psychoanalysis does this in terms of object loss and introjected hostility. T.A. would diagram a Parent, Adult, and Child showing that the Child has sustained a loss and that the Parent of that individual is figuratively beating upon the Child.

Both methods of treatment *may* emphasize the metacommunication that tells us how to interpret the verbal message the person transmits. T.A. pays a great deal of attention to these nonword aspects of communication. Psychoanalysis may or may not, depending upon the school. Psychoanalysts may focus more attention on the words than on the rest of the communication. Some people in T.A., however, may pay at least that much attention to the words. They disregard Berne's warnings, which included such statements as "Think sphincter." Perhaps the methods of supervision involved have something to do with psychoanalysts' paying a great deal of attention to words. Analytic seminars may focus a great deal on "process recording," using as good a verbatim account as the candidate can make after the interview is over. Analytic group therapists usually are as alert to nonverbal communications as any clinicians I have ever seen work. Since a competence examination in T.A. involves actual tape-recorded segments of the candidate's work, T.A. therapists must pay attention to voice tones and sentence structure, not just the words themselves.

Both the psychoanalytic organizations and the T.A. Association certify certain candidates as to their competence at the end of their training. I believe that a good clinician can acquire a great deal of competence in T.A. in a two-or three-year period of instruction and supervised experience. I believe most psychoanalysts will agree with me that even if the individual is already a good clinician it will take that person more than three years of study and supervised experience to become a certified psychoanalyst.

One of the great virtues of T.A. is that it is understandable by children as well as the Child ego state in our patients. One need not be a transactional analyst to ask a patient to speak in words that an eight-year-old child can understand. Everyone has known a parent, an adult, and a child. Nobody has ever seen an id or a superego walking around. They are philosophic constructs. I believe they are more difficult to comprehend than the simple phenomenologic realities described as Parent, Adult, and Child. In treating families, I have often been told that one of the children said to a parent something like, "You are really in your angry Parent tonight, aren't you?" I have known many an older child in a family warn a younger one by saying, "Mom's really saving up some anger stamps for you. You better play it cool."

These few, simple, technical words I have used here will be seen by many as part of the jargon some associate with T.A. I do not believe that T.A. sponsors any more jargon than any other method of therapy. People who are new to T.A. may use the terms Parent, Adult, and Child; Stamps and Racket; Game and Script, in an almost magical way. They remind me of the way I used to see dermatology at the time I graduated in medicine. My view of dermatology at that time was that if you knew enough Latin to hang a fancy Latin name on the condition, some miracle was supposed to happen and seldom did. In the same fashion, naming an ego state or a game does very little good. I am entirely convinced that naming a game does virtually no good. As a matter of fact, I instruct my patients and my trainees not to accuse anyone of playing a game unless they can specify the first three moves. I use this warning with them because the concept is "catchy." However, I believe that the Adult ego state of the individual is not aware when a game is started. Therefore, to say to a person, "You are playing a game" is no more effective than calling the individual a dirty name or telling him he has lacunae in his superego.

Because of the simplicity of the concepts involved and of the language used to describe them, the rudiments of T.A. can be quickly taught to businessmen, teachers, and others who deal with many people who might never be inside a therapist's office. For a businessman to clearly predict what will happen if he tries to help a help-rejecting complainer, and to be able to teach this to his subordinates, is something I find a great deal more difficult to do using traditional psychoanalytic theory. Likewise, to teach the concepts of the unconscious is more difficult for me than teaching that the Child will remember but may not trust us enough to tell us a "secret."

As I began to use T.A. a great deal in my practice, I saw in consultation a young man who had held up a store. The gun he used only fired blank cartridges for starting swim meets. After the robbery the young man fled the store. When he encountered a red traffic light, he stopped and waited for the light to change. By that time the police arrested him. From the psychoanalytic frame of reference, I thought that certainly this intelligent-enough young man must have had an enormous unconscious need to be caught. I asked him, in fact, if he wanted to be caught, and he thought the question was silly and laughed, saying, "Of course not." I thought about the significance of his using a pistol that would only shoot blanks, and predicted that he would have a rivalry with his father, from which he had retreated. From this frame of reference, I thought that he would certainly remain unconscious of his reluctance to compete in a world of men, beginning with his father, and also that he would remain unconscious of his motivations, both to rob the store and to be caught.

From the T.A. viewpoint, I could get another perspective. I quickly taught the young man that none of us are one individual, but we are each three people—specifically a Parent, Adult, and Child. Having taught him this, I asked him how he felt as he stood outside the store. He replied, "I don't know." I said, "That's the Adult part of you, the one who deals only in facts. I agree, he does not know. I would not be surprised if the little eight-year-old boy in you knew how he felt. Will you ask him?" He thought a moment, said, "I don't know." I repeated, "From watching your face, I believe you are still in your Adult ego state, dealing only with facts. Will you remember how you were when you were about eight years of age and held a toy gun in your hand?" He smiled. I said, "I believe that's the Child ego state you are in now." He nodded and said, "You're right. I felt excited outside the store." I then asked, "When you went inside and pointed the gun at the man behind the cash register, how did you feel?" He said, "I still felt excited." I said, "How did you feel when he handed you the money?" He looked puzzled and said, "I felt let down." I replied, "Yes, you would have had lots more excitement if there had been a shoot-out." He agreed.

To show him that we feel, think, and behave differently in each ego state did not require but 20 minutes. Teaching him how to use his Adult ego state to regulate expression of Child feelings began right away. Helping him see that the Child in his father didn't want him to surpass him—and that Mother supported this family system—took longer. I believe I was a better therapist for him because I also know some psychoanalytic theory.

After experiences similar to mine with this young man, many people being introduced to T.A. begin to question whether there actually is an unconscious or whether the Child is simply not willing to tell us his secrets yet.

DIFFERENCES BETWEEN PSYCHOANALYSIS AND TRANSACTIONAL ANALYSIS

The contract betwen the patient and therapist is quickly made explicit in transactional analysis. In psychoanalysis, the therapeutic contract is regarded by some as nonexistent and by many others as an implicit contract.

Since this is one of the major departures T.A. makes from traditional psychoanalysis, let's examine it in some more detail. Consider the case of a 21-year-old student who dropped out of college before finishing the first semester of his senior year. His grades were everything from failures to excellent, both in high school and college. His summer work history was spotty. His love relationships were characterized by "falling in love," spending a great deal of time with the young woman involved, beginning early discussion of marriage, and then losing interest in her. If this young man came for treatment, I would think along psychoanalytic lines that we could have an *implicit* contract in which I would agree to help him study his emotional reactions so that he could choose better responses to them. I would predict to myself that at first he would find his treatment enjoyable and stimulating; that after a while he would begin to feel hostile feelings to me and at first that he would not tell them to me, unless we were following the rule of free association. Whether using this rule or not, I would be listening for his voice tones and the interruptions in his speech as he talked with me. I would not be surprised if he began, fairly early in the treatment, to have dreams in which he focused on damage to some objects in the dream, including perhaps his own body. I would not be surprised if he would fall in love several more times and make great new beginnings at some job. I would not expect him to follow through on either of these, and would look closely for his acting on his impulses, rather than bringing them for the treatment sessions. I would expect that as he gained insight into his fear and resentment of me and his father that he would despair of ever feeling adequate. I would anticipate that we could work this through so that his sense of adequacy increased. I would expect him to start making friends with women near his age instead of regarding them primarily as sex objects or miraculous gratifiers of his dreams. I would expect him gradually to begin feeling friendly to other men, then to say something friendly to or about his father and me. About this time I would expect him to get a job that he liked, hold it, and begin to enjoy working. As we decreased the frequency of his visits, concomitant with his increasing success, I expect that he would feel grateful to me, angry that I hadn't cured him sooner, and sad at leaving.

If I saw the same young man and was treating him from the T.A. viewpoint, I would ask him how he wanted his life to be different, both in the near and intermediate term, as well as the long term.[1] I might ask him how he wanted to be living differently in six months, a year, two years, and ten years. I might write these goals so that he could see them. Then I would ask what behavior *he* would have to change in order to reach these goals. I would list the behaviors he named. Then I would say, "As you make these changes in your own behavior, how will you be seen differently by those who know you best?" I would ask this about both work and love situations. As he talked about his planned successes, I would ask what his parents might say about them. He would probably answer, "They would like it." I might then ask him to close his eyes, picture his parents as he knew them when he was a young boy; then to fantasy telling them of his success, while watching carefully for a change on their faces in his fantasy. I would ask him if both parents are smiling or only one. Not infrequently, in the first session, the patient is surprised at discovering (which he has known for years) that one parent would not be smiling in approval. If he recovers such awareness, I tell him we'll come back to that, and ask another question: "How will you tend to stop yourself from reaching this goal?" Some patients answer quickly and directly; others are mystified. If mystified. I can ask such questions as "Will you procrastinate? Will you say that you'll change and not do it? Will you get discouraged and give up?" I then probe as to whether he is waiting for some Santa Claus to make him well, strong, and happy, or whether he is waiting for rigor mortis to deliver him from his earthly troubles. If he is waiting for death to deliver him, he will have considered suicide. He will almost always tell me this in the first several sessions, even in the absence of clinical depression. At that point it is extemely important to make a no-suicide contract with him (1). Since I have used this type contract, none of my patients have committed suicide.

I then ask the patient, "When are you going to make the changes you described above?" The patient usually answers, "Now." I review the difficulties that the patient predicts in his growth, and I ask him how he will tend to defeat me in my efforts to help him. I say something like this: "You have a very bright Child ego state. If you did not, you would not have survived this well, this long. You've almost certainly spotted ways in which I will probably be of assistance to you. You have probably also spotted some ways that I won't quite do the job as you might like. How will you tend to defeat me in my efforts to help you?" "What check-points can you set up for yourself for three months, six months, and 12 months in the future?" It is at this point that the patient begins to be most evasive. The patient will use "soft" concepts, such as, "I'll be feeling happier." At this point I will press for objective behavioral checkpoints, such as, "I will have lost ten pounds and kept it off for two months without feeling depressed," or "I will make two A's and three B's in school this semester." The treatment contract is now becoming explicit.

In discussing this contract, please note the emphasis on time in the T.A. version. Here we give checkpoints, both in time and behaviorally, for the patient to observe his own behavior within a certain time frame. Contrast this with the apparent time-lessness and the implicit nature of the contract in some psychoanalytic methods. Likewise, because of the objectiveness of the checkpoints and the plan in the T.A. contract, as well as other features in this mode of working, we will expect very little regression in the T.A. model of treatment, in contrast to a greater amount of re-gression in the psychoanalytic model. I personally feel freer using T.A. than I do a psychoanalytic model of treatment. One reason in addition to those above is that T.A. mixes well with other methods of treatment. It mixes particularly well with the Gestalt approach popularized by Frederick Perls. If our young man, described above, complained of feeling "walled-in" in a therapy group, I can try a traditional T.A. approach. I might have him tell me which ego state he is in, how he is dis-counting the solvability of his problem. I might get him to go into his Adult ego state by asking him to cross the room and draw on the board the transaction be-tween him and me or the rest of the group in which he is presenting himself as a helpless Child and trying to get us, as parents, to rescue him. I have many other options such as asking him to describe the wall, to speak about it in a metaphor. I might use an action method, such as asking him if he will consent to have a wall placed around him in the group and let us know what he feels like being inside. If he agrees, I ask other group members to make a circle around him, linking their arms at the elbow. Their faces are directed inward. I ask him if this is what his wall is like. Then I ask him to use his eyes as eyes, and tell what he sees as he looks at the people in the group. If he feels his wall is less personal, I may ask the people in the group to turn their backs to him, again linking arms at the elbow, and ask him if that's what he feels like. People who feel very isolated will say that the latter model represents their wall.

This is a tiny sample of the complementary relationship between T.A., which can be done as a left-lobe therapy, and the Gestalt approach, which can be done as largely a right-lobe therapy (2, 3). I believe that psychoanalysis is largely a left-lobe therapy. By left lobe, I am referring to a monitoring and analysis of sequential bits of behavior as contrasted with right lobe, which is more holistic. I believe that there is some integration of these modes in all good practices of psychotherapy. I further believe that such integration is most apparent when the patient reaches the moment of "aha!" as he suddenly puts feelings, thoughts, memories, attitudes, etc., into a shift in perception, perspective, and behavior.

In both T.A. and the psychoanalytic models, I do expect that the patient will seem to go backward at times in his treatment. I expect working through to be necessary in both forms of treatment, most particularly with the regression in psychoanalysis. Some of the working through might be extremely important to do in T.A. Working through is commonly neglected in T.A. therapy and training. It is seldom mentioned by Gestalt therapists.

If I thought a period of extended treatment time were necessary for the patient's resuming his growth, I would not hesitate to invite him to join a marathon therapy group. Here I would expect some regression to occur (limited), perhaps some group contagion, an enormous amount of group sharing, a large amount of "deep" material, by which I mean oedipal and preoedipal material. In the marthon as well as in both individual and group therapy sessions, the patient will see me using all three of my ego states as I use T.A. plus Gestalt or occasional encounter or psychodrama techniques. If I were using a psychoanalytic approach, the patient would not be so aware that I have a Child ego state. He would encounter primarily my Adult ego state with some Nurturing Parent. Only rarely would he meet my Critical Parent.

I believe that a well-trained, powerful, creative therapist depends more on the person than on the theory espoused. However, I also believe that some theories are easier to learn and to use than others. I believe that T.A. is easier to learn than is psychoanalytic treatment. I'd like to illustrate some of these principles by way of a case example.

A urologist referred a man in his late twenties for psychiatric consultation before considering further the young man's request for sex-reversal surgery. After making a diagnosis, I invited him to attend a weekend marathon and set up a follow-up visit two weeks later.

At first, he was quiet in the marathon. One of his first interventions was made from a Nurturing Parent as he sought to help someone else. When he heard someone talking about how her parents were disappointed at her birth because they had wanted a son, he began to cry softly and then to talk. He was the fourth son and last child born into his family. Father taught the other three sons how to help him run the farm. Mother had wanted a daughter. The parents made an implicit agreement that this child was "hers." She clothed him in dresses at times; his long curly blond hair was not cut until he went to the first grade. Mother taught him how to run a home. He cried as he realized that his father probably had not wanted another child at all while his mother had wanted a daughter. He had pleased her in many ways but always felt something was missing because he was not a girl. He said, "I've always felt like a girl in a boy's body."

By this time in the marathon, he knew about ego states and script analysis. A summary of the work follows:

Therapist: Is it true that your mother wanted a girl?

He: Yes. She brought me up as a girl and was happiest when I was with her and she treated me like a girl.

Therapist: What ego state in your mother wanted you to be a girl?

He: I see now it was her Child.

Therapist: Did her Adult teach you how to do girl-like things?

He: Yes. Dad didn't teach me how to do boy things. I felt he didn't want me around. He didn't play with me either. At times, I felt like I didn't exist for him, even when I got real good grades at school.

Therapist: When you were a boy and realized Mom had wanted you to be a girl, did you decide to do anything about it?

He: No, only to please her when I could. And when I read now about sex-reversal surgery, I think she'd like for me to be her little daughter and I'd feel better too.

Therapist: Would Mother's Adult believe you were really a girl if you had this surgery? Or, would you only look like a girl?

He: [Crying] I really wouldn't be a real girl.

Therapist: No, you wouldn't. Mother's Adult would know the difference and so would yours. Does Mother's Adult like you now?

He: Yes. I am her favorite still.

Therapist: Does Mother's Parent approve of you now?

He: Yes. She thinks I'm great like I am.

Therapist: So the little boy in you always wanted to please a part of your mother— her little girl state that always wanted a daughter.

He: That's right. And I can't turn the clock back. That's what the little girl part of her wanted, like there was a part of me that felt I could really make her happy by becoming a girl.

Therapist: And now you face the fact that there is no way you can become a real girl, even though you might look like one. [He cried softly as he nodded, yes.]

Therapist: You have every right to be sad. You've cherished this dream since you were a little boy and even decided to give up your maleness to please your mother. [After a long, respectful silence] What do you think of surgery now?

He: It's no use. It wouldn't work. I wouldn't be the real thing. And she loves me like I am.

Therapist: Right. You will grieve at the death of this wish. A little later on, we'll teach you what we mean when we say that you can't *make* anyone happy.

The therapist then drew a script matrix to simplify his working through, showing how the Child ego state in his mother had given the message, "Don't be the sex you are. Don't be you." She followed this with, "I'll show you how to be a girl." His father's Child ego state did very little with him. The Parent ego state in both parents had taught him how to work and study hard. He could then see that the Child in him had truly wanted to please his mother at all costs. The other two ego states in him knew that she felt he was great just as he was.

The therapist believed he would need a long working through which would be painful. When the patient returned for a follow-up visit, he felt great. He had remembered his discoveries at the marathon. He had already finished much of the grieving needed to relinquish his cherished childhood wish. He further confided that he had been on such large doses of female hormones that his breasts had been enlarging and becoming painful several weeks before the marathon. Since the marathon, he had cancelled future treatments with the urologist and his family doctor. Amazed at this, the therapist scheduled several more visits and was surprised at the rapidity of the reversal in his attitudes. Within six months, he was regularly dating a young woman. He asked if she could come to a marathon with him. In accord with our policy that therapy is too good to save just for sick people, we consulted with her and agreed that she could be in a marathon. Her "breakthrough" was not nearly so impressive as his. Two children have resulted from their marriage. In chance encounters with him at his work since that time, he seems to be a good loving parent to his children.

A chart is included to summarize some similarities and differences between transactional analysis and psychoanalysis (Table 1).

TRAINING

I believe that there is no substitute for extensive, well-supervised training in psychotherapy. I believe that therapists should be trained in depth as well as in variety. This depth is always present in good psychoanalytic training. I cannot always say the same about T.A. training. Here, more depends upon the trainer since I have never seen anyone who did "pure" T.A. therapy.

I pity the therapist who knows a little about many different therapeutic modalities but is not solidly grounded in any.

I also pity the therapist who knows how to use only one therapeutic modality. Such therapists have the attitude, "There's only one road to Rome." By contrast,

TABLE 1

Comparison of Psychoanalysis and Transactional Analysis

Features	Psychoanalysis	T.A.
Analytic	Yes	Yes
Jargon potential	High	High
Key concepts difficult to define	Yes	Yes
Simple ideas rapidly became complex	Yes	Yes
Importance of childhood	Yes	Yes
Importance of meta-communication	Variable	Great
Working through	High	Variable
Competence certification	Yes	Yes
Time required for training	Beyond 3 years	2-3 years if already good clinician
Treatment contract	Implicit or none	Explicit
Emphasis on time	Low	High
Regression	High	Low
Transference neurosis	Encouraged	Discouraged (the child usually remembers)
View of ego/ego states	Philosophic constructs	Phenomenologic realities
Understandable by children	Low	High
Easily comprehensible in nontherapeutic setting	Low	High
Mixes well with other treatment methods	No	Yes
Emphasis on unconscious	High	Low
Therapist as role model	Rare	Common

I believe that all roads lead to Rome. Or, in the language that we North Americans learned as children, "There is more than one way to skin a cat."

Therapists with prior psychoanalytic training find that their prior training combines well and quickly with T.A. For those therapists whose personality and training suit them for it, I believe that T.A. offers a simpler and less regressive mode of treatment than does either psychoanalysis or psychoanalytically oriented therapy.

REFERENCES

1. Drye, R., Goulding, R., and Goulding, M. No suicide decisions: Patient monitoring of suicidal risk. *Amer. J. Psychiat.,* 130:171-174, 1973.
2. Fagan, J. The gestalt approach as right lobe therapy. In: *The Growing Edge of Gestalt Therapy,* ed. E.W.L. Smith, New York: Brunner/Mazel, 1976.
3. Galen, D. Implications for psychiatry of left and right cerebral specialization. *Arch. Gen. Psychiat.,* 31:572-583, 1974.

Psychoanalytic or Experiential Group Psychotherapy: A False Dichotomy

RUTH C. COHN*

Often a young group therapist will speak to me of a personal dilemma engendered by having more than one supervisor. For example, one supervisor may say to him: "If you hide, how do you expect your patients to dare to become and be themselves? You have a right to your feelings as a human being; and these feelings will help your patients learn to be authentic individuals, unashamed of their thoughts and emotions." The second supervisor might say the opposite: "You can't expect to help your patients with their problems while you are burdening them with your own; they have a right to your full attention. Check your own feelings silently and discover whether they are induced by the patient's pathology or by your own unresolved problems, and speak only when reasonably certain this is purely in the patient's interest."

*333 Central Park West, Apt. 32, New York, N.Y. 10025.

"Reprinted from THE PSYCHOANALYTIC REVIEW, Vol. 56, No. 3, Fall 1969, through the courtesy of the Editors and the Publisher, National Psychological Association for Psychoanalysis, New York, N.Y."

I would like to share with you my own viewpoint with regard to this controversy within our profession. This is my hypothesis: All correct therapeutic interventions initiate curative processes which affect the patient's total personality. This occurs when the intervening stimulus facilitates the patient's recognition of any significant part of important personal reality that he was previously unaware of or detached from. Such curative processes occur when the patient receives messages that help him to: 1) repair distortions in his perceptual and cognitive world, 2) add emotional content to previously deprived or depleted personality areas, 3) free physical mobility from prior rigidity.

While therapists offer differing stimuli with greater or lesser emphasis on each of these three levels according to their various orientations and personalities, the patient's innate tendency toward health will expand the curative process so as to affect his total organism. Such processes may be likened to giving injections to a physically ill patient; almost regardless of where the drugs enter the body, the total organism will be affected through the therapeutic intervention.

I believe that the psychotherapeutic process can be initiated by a variety of interventions, such as the use of interpretation to promote insight or a realistic encounter geared toward a curative experience. It may, for instance, be promoted by a therapeutically oriented total here-and-now experience, by an analytic weaving of threads between the past and present, or by emphasis on values, future goals, or working directly with body defenses.

Individual preferences do not relieve us from searching for and refining optimally effective methods and professional skills. We have to investigate, explore and increase our knowledge as to what techniques may be most helpful to a given patient at a specific time. Consideration must be given to the patient, the therapist, and to the methods in all their intricate specificities and variant conditions. Each patient has permanent as well as temporary *patterns of receptivity to therapeutic interventions,* which are determined by his constitution, by his character, his immediate energy level, acute motivations, tensions, etc. Correspondingly, each therapist has typical patterns of activity and response, specific trained skills and variant convictions in different periods of his life, as well as moods of the hour. Analysts may conceptualize patterns within the framework of libidinal cathexis, transference matrix and resistance, while experientialists may define the same phenomena as relating to growth potential, inauthenticity of encounter, and avoidance patterns. *The therapist's task is to strive towards establishing procedures which aim at meeting up with the patient's optimal receptivity and to recognize how he can best function in the patient's interest.*

My hypothesis is that the patient's innate growth potential responds positively to the recognition of any important factor of his personal reality. Therefore the therapist's acceptance of the patient's reality initiates a fluid curative process. If the therapist misconceives an important facet of the patient's reality, an obstacle to the curative process occurs. Even such error, however, is not fatal to the therapeutic process if the patient has achieved an autonomy level which allows him to react positively to a negative stimulus.

"Match or Miss" interventions connote the therapist's skill at recognizing the patient's receptivity and reality. The matching intervention presupposes the therapists' ability to recognize health as well as pathology, and to accurately gauge the patient's optimal receptivity and energy level at any given moment. The point in time when such recognition occurs may be accompanied by an "aha" experience, a glow of heightened awareness, or just a fleeting surprise that a disagreeable head or neck tension has disappeared. The "miss" intervention is generally (although not always) countertherapeutic. It may occur through faulty communication processes, which miss the patient's reality on any one level or through failure to recognize the patient's limitations on psychological or somatic levels.

I then perceive the curative process in therapy as a fluid intrapsychosomatic event which is derived from an interactional here-and-now experience and involves the totality of the there-and-then of past and future. It proceeds towards a new here-and-now which has integrated the therapeutic stimulus and process of the recent therapeutic event. Such stimulus is derived from an interactional process between the patient, therapist(s) and/or a group.

CASE EXAMPLE: THE SAME CASE IN TWO GROUP THERAPY SETTINGS

I would like you to follow me on an imaginary trip with a patient, Dina, into the group therapy sessions of Dr. Allen Ashley (analytically-oriented group therapy) and Dr. Eric Emory (experiential group therapy). Let us follow Dina (a real person) as she interacts with these two therapists and their groups (who are also real). However, for the sake of essential rather than factual truth, let us take poetic license and create two episodes which occur simultaneously.

Dina is the patient on whom I would like you to focus your attention. She is 35 years old, married and has one two-year-old child. She speaks in a barely audible voice without intonation whenever she talks about herself at any length. But she is capable of sounding vigorous and vivacious when speaking about others. Her facial expression, accordingly, is either masklike and dead or quite animated.

(In this episode, all italicized material relates to the *thoughts* of therapist and patient.)

Psychoanalytic Group Therapy

Dina: (I must force myself to talk . . . I feel so terrible . . . it's difficult . . . but I have to push myself . . .) Bob . . . my husband . . . last night again he came home late . . . I was up . . . the baby had just gotten up for a glass of water and when the door opened I tried to smile and act casual . . . not as if I was hurt. *(They also know why he was out . . . he must have another woman . . .)* He was furious with me and walked out of the kitchen *(Maybe he's jealous of the baby . . . but I can't help that—I won't neglect him.)* Afterwards, in bed . . . he turned to the wall . . . and I cried all night. *(I need his body next to mine ... I need to cuddle up ... I don't want to tell this to the group.)* I just can't help being so depressed when he comes home late.

Sharon: Oh, why don't you break it off ... get rid of him. You have no idea how much better off I am since I separated from my husband. He used to run around with women like that ...

Dina: (Sharon doesn't understand ... I can't be without Bob ... I love him ... being next to him ... and I need him for Freddy ... maybe I'm not bright enough for him, or sexy enough and he found someone better.)

Craig: You know, I don't blame him a bit. If I had to put up with Dina's whining and nagging, I wouldn't bother to come home either. Blah blah blah ... all the time ... nothing the poor guy ever does is right ... and that crying voice ... just like my mother ... she just keeps going on and on ...

Dina: (I feel tight ... my stomach ... throat ... choking ... don't move, it hurts too much ... Craig hurts ... what did he say? I don't know what he said.)

Jane: Craig, how can you be so cruel? Don't you hear how upset Dina is ... she can hardly talk.

Craig: Ah! You're another one to talk ... another ball breaker ... you, Dina, Sharon ... you're all experts in the art.

Dina: (Why doesn't Dr. Ashley say something ... help ... he is silent ... he must feel the same way as Craig about me ... what did Craig say?)

Morty: I can't see this at all, Craig ... I'd be upset too if my wife came home late every night ... but ... there's something about Dina's voice ... that low voice ... you have to strain. I want to listen and I can't.

Dina: (Morty is nice ... Now I remember what Craig said ... he accused me of nagging Bob.)

Jane: Whenever Dina speaks, I feel like I shouldn't take up time with my stupid problems ... her's are so much worse ...

Dina: (Oh, Jane ... I'm sorry ... she needs Dr. Ashley more than I do and I take up all the time ... Damn, I need him so—right now and he just sits there.)

Dr. Ashley: (Dina's crying. She looks confused ... bewildered ... it's better than that whining ... I can't stand that voice ... it gets on my nerves ... sickening masochism ... guilt as a defense. If only she fought people openly ... I'll be cautious.) You seem to be close to tears. Dina, I wonder what is going through your mind.

Dina: I feel awful ... just awful ... I think Bob feels ... you know ... like Craig said. And it's my fault. If I were more cheerful ... if I could smile like Jane ... my little sister is that way, always smiling even when it hurts ... and I can't and I know Bob hates it.

Dr. Ashley: (Her conscious guilt acts as a defense against showing any aggression.) You think it's all your fault?

Dina: I know it is and I don't really feel like talking here because *(because they'll jump on me)* .. because I get on everyone's nerves.

Dr. Ashley: (Maybe she does . . . she often gets on mine.) Craig was the only one who said you get on his nerves. You seem to have a radar system for negative judgments . . . you always hear only the negative.

Dina: (What is he saying? . . . can't think . . . speak somebody! . . . please . . . I can't talk.)

Dr. Ashley: (I guess she went blank . . . heard me negatively, too . . . maybe I can help her see where this defense comes from . . .) I wonder why you go blank now . . . what of your childhood comes to your mind with regard to "negative judgments"?

Dina: (Nothing . . . nothing . . . they're going to bed next door . . . Mummy, Daddy . . . radar station for the negative . . .) No . . . nothing . . . They . . . my parents . . . they just didn't pay any attention to me . . . I had to be quiet when Daddy came home . . . except for when I had good report cards. I had to be quiet . . . always . . . when my parents went to sleep I had to whisper to my dolls so they wouldn't hear me . . . and I couldn't wake Sis up . . .

Dr. Ashley: Perhaps if your dolls could speak, they would tell us how angry you were at your parents for having to be quiet, for having to give so much to your sister and to them. And how you lost your voice.

Jane: Dina, your voice was loud just before . . . I wonder why.

Dina; (Damn it . . . why does she interrupt? . . . blank . . .) I didn't notice my voice.

Sharon: Dina is being a good girl . . . answering all of Dr. Ashley's questions.

Craig: I'm glad he's giving it to her . . . she needs to be told plenty . . .

Dr. Ashley: (I gave her an important interpretation . . . a connection from the hostility she knew about and told to her dolls to her withholding aggression now . . . to Craig, Jane, Bob . . . I guess me, too . . . her choked voice . . . I let it rest at that and go to Craig; he's so blind to his hatred and is setting me up as his male ideal, not mine . . .) Craig, you really have it in for Dina . . . for Sharon and Jane, too . . . they must do something to your system . . .

Craig: You bet they do!

(Later that evening at home)

Dina: (Dr. Ashley doesn't like me as much as Jane or Craig . . . he only gave me such a short time and he stayed with Craig all evening. I know he doesn't really like me but he never says so. He must really, really hate me . . . and Bob, he can't stand me either . . . I don't care. No, I do care. Why doesn't Dr. Ashley stay with me? I hate him . . . I hate him . . . I feel like smashing my fist on his bald head . . . How can that be? I'm not that way . . . Freddy loves me . . . my dolls come to my head . . . they used to love me, too . . . that's funny . . . now I talk to myself as I did to Irmie and Edith, my dolls . . . and they liked me . . . even when I thought of letting the faucet run over and drown everybody, the whole house except me and Irmie and Edith . . . I'm really funny . . . if I listened to myself like my dolls did . . . I'd like me. Funny . . . I like that thought: "I'd like me. I'd like myself." Go ahead, Dr. Ashley . . . just ignore me . . . hate me . . . see how much I care! I hate you all

... that's a good one ... "my dolls like me and I like me and I hate you" My head feels good now.) Bob, did I ever tell you that I used to sing? That was before I got these lousy headaches ... when I was still in school ... I was the best singer ...

Bob: No, I didn't know that ... but I know you've got a great voice ... I like your voice when you sing.

In this brief episode, Dr. Ashley intended to lead Dina toward the recognition of her repressed hostility which manifested itself in her masochistic way of torturing Bob by her as-if-crying reproaches, and torturing the group and analyst by her manner of speech. The method used here is: 1) professional attitude—the therapist speaks to and about the patient without revealing his own experiences; 2) leading questions which go along with Dina's resistance of guilt feelings defending against hostility ("You think it is all your fault?"); 3) leading questions oriented toward important memories; 4) interpretation of Dina's repressed anger.

Although the analyst had promoted a process of insight into the dynamics of repressed hostility, Dina was emotionally preoccupied with the feeling of transference illusion and a perception of Dr. Ashley's unexpressed annoyance which she interpreted into the transference connection of his disliking her. This kept her awake and worried. Her awareness of her own hatred for Dr. Ashley's "disliking" her and preferring "other children" fused with the memory of her revealing her rage about her parents to her dolls and their successor, the husband, and the baby, Freddy. This heightened awareness deepened into the experience of a recognition, here manifested with an awakening sense of humor and an ability to communicate with Bob on a nonmasochistic level.

Experiential Group Therapy

Dina: (I must force myself to talk ... I feel so terrible ... it's difficult but I have to push myself.) Bob ... my husband ... last night again he came home late ... I was up ... the baby had just gotten up for a glass of water and when the door opened I tried to smile and act casual ...

Dr. Eric Emory: Please speak louder! Do you smile when you are angry?

Dina: (Push ... voice choked ... I can't ... I can't talk louder.) I don't want to upset Freddy with our problems.

Morty: You know that can't be done ... not upset our children ...

Dina: (I'm not going to let Freddy suffer like I did, Morty doesn't understand ... he hasn't got any children.)

Craig: What a phony! She is the phoniest.

Dina: (What did he say? I can't understand ... he's angry ...)

Sharon: Craig's at it again ... ignore him, Dina. So what happened between you and Bob?

Dina: He was ... just furious ... when he got into bed, he turned to the wall ... *(I can't tell them this. I can't stand sleeping alone.)*

Eric: (I feel irritated, annoyed.) Dina, I really can't hear you without straining a lot . . . I feel irritated now.

Jane: It's difficult to hear her . . . but I understand . . .she's choked up . . . it's painful to talk about it.

Sharon: So maybe it wouldn't kill you to strain a little, Eric . . . After all, you're not having her troubles.

Eric: I don't want to strain. Dina can talk louder.

Dina: (I want Eric to listen . . . to help . . . and Eric looks so pleased with himself . . . he doesn't care about me . . why should he?)

Jane: You should stay with Dina, Eric . . . really you should.

Eric: (Jane plays Dina's voice.) What troubles you, Jane?

Jane: I think Dina needs you now and you should stay with her.

Eric: I don't want your "shoulds." I don't need them. I want to stay with you now. Speak for yourself, Jane!

Jane: My problems are not big like Dina's. They don't involve a husband and child.

Sharon: Right! My problems were cut in half the day I left Mike. I keep telling Dina she should get rid of Bob . . .

Dina: (Eric doesn't care about me, he doesn't like me. What's wrong with me? He's so nice to everyone else.) Sharon, I can't leave Bob. Everything that's happened is my fault. If I were cheerful and agreeable like Jane, Bob might come home on time.

Morty: You don't know what you really feel, Dina. You whisper when you talk, and you want to smile when you're hurt or angry.

Dina: (Morty confuses me . . . I feel like crying . . . I don't want them to know.)

Eric: What is it, Dina?

Dina: Nothing . . . go on to someone else.

Eric: You look as if you're crying.

Dina: (I won't.) No.

Jane: The group isn't Freddy. He is little. But we can take it.

Dina: I don't want to cry here . . .I cry all the time when I'm alone . . . last night . . . all night.

Eric: An image flashed through my mind just now . . . the huge ocean . . . with just one little boat . . . way out . . .

Dina: (crying) (I'm in that boat . . . all alone.) Nobody listens . . . they never listen . . . when you need someone . . . nobody is ever there . . . you, Eric, you don't care either, with your pleased self-adoring smile on your face . . . you never, never care . . . all you care about is the money you take home to your wife.

Eric: Yes, Dina, I do care about my wife and my money. But I care about you too. And your rage hit me right now. It hurts. But now you speak for real and I can hear you.

Dina: No, you don't. you never do.

Eric: You can say this now. I feel relieved.

Craig: She thinks you are as phony as she is.

Eric: For heaven's sake, Craig, can't you see when someone is real?

Craig: You must know that she is phony.

Eric: I wonder if there isn't more to you, Craig, than this one-way track.

Dina: (There he is again . . . he takes on Craig . . . I shouldn't feel so jealous . . . but he always does it . . . he always drops me . . .)

(Later that evening at home)

Dina: (I just.don't get Eric . . . I got so furious . . . he always listens to everyone but me. I guess I do talk in a low voice . . . but Jane always manages to hear me. He did look sad though . . . and he helped me cry . . . the boat . . . I am in a boat . . . far way, Mummy and Daddy in their bedroom, that's when I used to talk to my dolls. I was so lonesome I told them how I felt about Sis getting everything . . . she was just like Jane, so concerned and cheerful and sweet . . . no, but maybe they didn't really care about her either, she says so, they were too egotistical, money, money, money, that's all they ever talked about and screamed at each other for. Mummy complained she couldn't buy clothes for us . . . I didn't want any clothes . . . All I wanted was for them to stop screaming . . . Egoistic? I never thought of that . . . like Eric, money, money . . . .he doesn't want to "strain" himself for me, just wants money, who cares . . . I don't want to talk to him. No, that's not true. I say he doesn't want to listen but I really don't want him to know how I feel. When I screamed at him, I felt better though . . . and he said he did . . . Maybe I should have told my parents, they might have listened and understood, about my not wanting them to scream, not wanting clothes . . .) Bob, I wonder . . . no . . . I'd like to know how you felt when you came home last night.

Bob: Fine, until I got a look at that expression on your face. I was really sorry to be late again, but you looked as if you didn't give a damn about the reason . . . so I just didn't feel like explaining.

Dina: I feel so unsure . . . about your loving me.

Bob: This is the one thing I can't stand about you—it hurts me when you don't trust me.

Eric (therapist) openly stated his needs. He stressed what was comfortable for him together with his thoughts, imagery and feelings directed toward Dina (and the other group members). This openness was used by Eric as a major tool for stimulating the curative process. He offered Dina, by his frank expressions, the opportunity to give vent to her own impotent rage. Dina, whose life history indicated that she was most creative in solitude, reconstructed the group process later on in her mind and made meaningful connections from the therapeutic session to her childhood. She pondered about Eric's seeming callousness, which appeared inconsistent with his relatedness to her and him empathic imagery. From there, Dina was able to consider her parents' "egocentricity" in the light of their marital problems and relatedness to their children. She was now on the way toward the recognition of her own "egoistic" magic formula: "Parents and therapists must live for their children and patients, and must understand them without spoken words." Having dimly recognized this feeling, she spontaneously communicated in a direct verbal way with Bob.

In both therapy sessions, Dina experiences a process of recognition, which was initiated by the therapist's interactions. Dr. Allen Ashley maintained a primarily objective attitude and led Dina directly toward insight of dynamic connections between the repression of hostility in the past and her present defensively masochistic behavior. Dr. Eric Emory presented himself as a man with personal feelings and subjective needs and he facilitated Dina's awareness of her own feelings by this authentic encounter.

In both instances, the fluid curative process involved the patient's total personality. Dr. Ashley's patient worked from induced insight towards emotional and physical release; Eric's patient used her encounter for gaining insight.

People are psychobiological entities whose past experiences and future anticipations meet at the pinpoint of the here-and-now. This little space-place, however limited, is the only moment of freedom and action which is ours in living. This crosspoint of past and future is therefore also the only meeting ground in which therapist and patient can interact. All psychotherapy therefore occurs in the here-and-now of intervention and receptivity—a two-way road with a one-way emphasis. However, since the here-and-now, as defined by the fluid process of the there-and-then, is past and future, the therapeutic process involves all previous experiences and the anticipated future of both the therapist and the patient.

Although I hypothesize the therapeutic effectiveness of all therapy as based upon the fluidity of curative processes, I do not wish to understate differences and effectiveness of the two methods. I would like to propose that experientialism, if based upon psychodynamic concepts, is not a departure from, but a continuation of, Freud's search.

Freud, in his practice and theoretical framework, came steadily closer to the application of the here-and-now principle of modern experientialism. His discovery of the phenomenon and concept of transference established the present as the forum of therapeutic intervention. His concept of resistance served to pinpoint, within the here-and-now of psychoanalysis, the power of defenses as operant in the analytic process. Correspondingly, the emphasis in the doctor—patient relationship, which had initially been seen as representative of the medical model, also underwent changes. The analyst's personality was seen as contributing, for better or for worse, to the therapeutic process. Concepts of "the therapeutic personality" and the "educational experience of psychoanalysis" rely heavily on the "corrective experience" of an interpersonal event. However, the psychoanalyst's tools are still primarily seen as his using questions, comments, dynamic interpretations and a professional accepting attitude.

The experiential viewpoint has taken the personal involvement of the therapist in the corrective experience one step further. Intensification of personal communication and exploration of the immediate encounter are continuations of Freud's conceptualization of transference and resistance as active agents of the past in the present. The experiential psychotherapist's primary tools are his perceptivity of the patient's feelings, his acuity in understanding verbal and nonverbal statements and his revealing his personal experience of the patient to him. Such revelation fuses subjective and objective perspectives of the patient's personality and behavior. *The effect of authentic, open communication replaces one-sided patient-related interpretations. The therapeutic means is seen as interpersonal rather than intrapsychic truthfulness. If, however, experientialists neglect the meaning of the past as operant in therapeutic processes, unrealistic denial takes place which is countertherapeutic.* (This holds equally true for today's frequent denial of the significance of intellectual insight in the therapeutic process. As Freud states: the voice of the intellect is low, but penetrating.)

While, in psychoanalysis, interpretations foreshadow future insight and integration, experientialism uses interpretations as cementing forces for the just-experienced therapeutic intervention. This is a natural outgrowth of Freud's maxim of "staying with the surface" (the immediacy of the here-and-now) and interpreting "just a step ahead" of the patient (but not more).

Both analytic and experiential schools use participant group members as assistant therapists. Analysts speak of multiple transference; experientialists of group encounter. While patients are inclined to gear their behavior toward therapists' theoretical and practical expectations, the history of group therapies parallels the general historical trend toward experiential emphasis within the psychoanalytic process. Group therapy as a method has been highly instrumental in helping the classical psychoanalyst to accept the efficacy of greater experiential openness. The powerful force of transference distortions becomes most obvious in groups when patients continue to see their peers with their subjective-colored glasses, regardless of the fact that they know each person's history and characteristics. This is equally true for the continuation of transference projections onto group analysts, whose behavior is more exposed to their groups than to individual patients.*

SUMMARY

The seeming juxtaposition of psychoanalytic versus experiential group psychotherapy is seen as a false dichotomy. The author hypothesizes that all curative processes are fluid. All therapeutic interventions are effective if they lead to the

---

*In a group analytic cotherapist setting with my colleague, Dr. Max Markowitz, we discovered that our patients, for long periods of time, continued to see us as dominant or submissive according to their transferential matrix; some patients assigned the role of the domineering partner to my male colleague, some to myself.

integration of personally significant aspects of reality previously unavailable to the patient. The intrapsychosomatic curative process guides constructive processes from one personality level to all others. Thus, psychoanalytic insight leads to release of emotional and physical tension, and experiential encounter promotes psychoanalytic insight. Differences—but not a dichotomy—exist and relate to the role of the therapist and the emphasis on the here-and-now versus the there-and-then within the therapy session. The author sees a historical trend beginning with Freud's conceptualization of transference and resistance and evolving toward more experiential attitudes in psychodynamically oriented individual and group psychotherapy.

Index

"I represent the Republic's Department of Alien Affairs, which is based far from here on Deluros VIII." Gruening paused and wiped the sweat from his forehead. "I have been instructed to remind you of certain promises that were made in your name, and to urge you to reconsider your decision to allow our mutual enemies from the Canphor system access to your world."

"I made no such promises," said Jalanopi.

"I happen to know that you did," said Andrew McFarley.

"Just translate what I have said, Man Andrew," said Jalanopi coldly. "Great things are at stake here, and I will not have you jeopardize them."

McFarley shrugged and translated Jalanopi's statement.

"Mike Resnick makes no secret of the fact that he draws heavily on African history, tradition, and culture to help create some of his alien cultures, which not only provide an authentic exotic setting for his readers but also provide a unique opportunity for us to examine the foibles of humanity through a kind of artificial distancing. . . . You can read PURGATORY as a straightforward novel, or you can read it as a commentary on the self-destructive impulse of human expansiveness, but whatever your viewpoint, you should certainly read it."

—*Science Fiction Chronicle*

PURGATORY

MIKE RESNICK

A TOM DOHERTY ASSOCIATES BOOK
NEW YORK

This is a work of fiction. All the characters and events portrayed in this book are fictitious, and any resemblance to real people or events is purely coincidental.

PURGATORY: A CHRONICLE OF A DISTANT WORLD

Cover art by Martin Andrews

A Tor Book
Published by Tom Doherty Associates, Inc.
175 Fifth Avenue
New York, N.Y. 10010

Tor® is a registered trademark of Tom Doherty Associates, Inc.

ISBN: 0-812-53535-9
Library of Congress Catalog Card Number: 92-43881

First edition: March 1993
First mass market edition: February 1994

Printed in the United States of America

0 9 8 7 6 5 4 3 2 1

To Carol, as always,

And to Barbara Delaplace,
fine friend, fine writer

Contents

Foreword

There is a parable that Zimbabweans, white and black alike, sometimes tell when they sit around a campfire at the end of the day:

It seems that there was a scorpion who wished to cross a river. He saw a crocodile floating a few feet away and asked to be carried across the river on its back.

"Oh, no," said the crocodile firmly. "I know what you are. As soon as we're halfway across the river you'll sting me and I'll die."

"Why would I do that?" scoffed the scorpion. "If I sting you and you die, I'll drown."

The crocodile considered the scorpion's answer for a moment and then agreed to ferry him across the river. When they were halfway across, the scorpion stung the crocodile.

Fatally poisoned, barely able to breathe, the crocodile croaked, "Why did you do that?"

The scorpion thought for a moment, and then, just before he drowned, he answered, "Because it's Africa."

I have exercised my author's prerogative and related this anecdote to you only because it is an amusing story. It obviously has nothing at all to do with this novel, which is about the mythical world of Karimon rather than the very real nation of Zimbabwe.

M.R.

I

JALANOPI'S
TREE

One

Jalanopi's tree was almost five hundred years old.

It reached to a height of nearly half a mile and was a full one hundred feet in circumference at its base. Once it had been surrounded by many trees like itself, tall and stately, but now it was the last, and it could be seen for more than five miles in every direction. Its trunk and limbs were a deep purple, smooth and glistening in the sunlight. Its circular leaves had been falling for almost a month, and its silver flowers were a distant memory.

The tree had been there for three centuries before the coming of Jalanopi's people. Huge animals had rubbed against it and eaten of its bark; small animals had burrowed into it and lived in its base. Later, prisoners had been tied to its bole and hanged from its branches. Dwellings had been made of its bark, medicines from its leaves, and poisons from its blossems. Its twigs and branches had supplied the firewood that lit the village Mastaboni at nights, its fruit had been eaten by untold generations of villagers and animals, and its sweet sap was prized by the local children.

Over the years all of its branches, to a height of more than seventy-five feet, had been removed for various pur-

poses, but it was home to more than one hundred avians,
nesting far above the ground. Untold generations of
Tailswingers had been born, lived, and died in its branches
without ever descending to the ground. Dozens of green-
and-gold lizards sunned themselves on the branches. A
huge serpent had made its home in the tree when
Jalanopi's people first arrived; no one had seen it for almost half a century, but since no Tailswinger or lizard
corpse was ever found on the ground, the villagers were
convinced that it was still up there, a thousand feet or more
above their heads.

Every section of Jalanopi's tree was a page in the living
history of his people. The first human explorer, Robert
Elroy, had carved three long notches on its bole to mark his
path almost two centuries ago, only to fall prey to a pack
of Devildogs two miles farther on. The first human mission-
ary, Father Patrick Dugan, had made his first convert beside the tree, then died of fever a month later. Jalanopi's
grandfather had been killed beneath this tree, chopped to
pieces by his enemies. Years later Jalanopi's father had
retaken the area, pinning his rival chief to the trunk of the
tree with a spear and leaving the body there until the
raptors and insects had picked the bones clean.

Jalanopi himself had been born less than a quarter mile
from the tree. As a child he had broken a leg trying to scale
it, which left him with a slight but permanent limp. He had
used the tree for target practice when he first learned to
hurl a spear, and had happily lost his virginity one spring
evening in the shadows cast by the tree's enormous purple
branches. It was beneath this tree that he himself had been
proclaimed king when his father died, and beside this tree
his father had been buried. As king, Jalanopi had held
court and passed sentences, made treaties and declared
wars beneath his tree.

And so it remained a very special tree, viewed with an
almost religious awe by the members of the Tulabete, who

were Jalanopi's people. It was said that as long as the tree lived they would survive and prosper, and that if the tree should ever die, then so too would the Tulabete.

Jalanopi himself was an imposing sight, and commanded even more awe than his tree. He stood fully seven feet tall, and wore a tunic of spun spider-silk and a cloak made from the skin of a Wildfang that he had taken while armed with only his spear—an act that had cost him one of the long pliable fingers from his three-digited hand. He had just completed the annual shedding of his old skin, and the tiny new scales on his green-tinted body glistened in the sunlight, emphasizing the rippling of his enormous muscles. Atop his bullet-shaped head sat the copper crown that signified he was the rightful king of the Tulabete, a crown he had defended twice in war and three times in personal combat, and for which he had not been challenged in more than a decade now.

He viewed his world through striking orange cat's-eyes, and all that he could see, to the horizon and beyond, was his domain. It stretched from the ocean in the east all the way to the broad river hundreds of miles out to the west, from the northern desert to the southern mountains. Jalanopi was certain that there was more to his world, but he had sent out scouts and none had ever found any land worth conquering. There were deserts out there, and mountains, and salt water, and jungles where the rain never ceased and the sun never shone, but he had no interest in them. There was no tillable land that he did not rule, no game animals that did not graze on the Tulabete's vast savannahs, no fresh water that did not flow through his domain.

There were rivals for his land, of course—once-powerful clans that now scratched out a living on its outskirts, and, it was rumored, a huge, powerful tribe beyond the mountains to the south—but he had beaten back challenges

before, and he knew that as long as his tree stood the Tulabete were invulnerable in battle.

He leaned back against his tree now, lazily surveying his domain, as a flock of avians took off from the upper terraces. It was a warm day, dry and clear, as almost all the days were. In a few minutes he would have to sit on his wooden throne and hold court, but for the moment he was content just to stare out across the lush green fields, dotted here and there with the domiciles of his people, each dwelling constructed in the mystic shape of a coiled serpent.

Finally a man clad totally in black approached him.

"Good morning, Jalanopi," he said in the language of the Tulabete.

Jalanopi stared at him but said nothing.

"I trust you slept well," continued the man.

"I always sleep well," said Jalanopi, his long, lean tongue flicking out to capture an insect that flew too near his face. He reeled in his tongue and brought his teeth down on the insect's carapace with a loud crunching noise.

The man looked away, trying to hide his distaste for the Tulabete's dietary habits. "I would not sleep well if I were you," he said. "Not with that party of Canphorites camped just a couple of miles away."

Jalanopi continued staring at the man. "You are a very unusual servant of your god," he said, dwelling sibilantly on the *s* sound in each word. "He preaches love, and you preach suspicion."

"My god did not create the Canphorites," replied Reverend Andrew McFarley. "They are a vicious and duplicitous race."

"They came from the stars," answered Jalanopi. "*You* came from the stars."

"And there all similarity ends."

"Do not fear for us, Man Andrew," said Jalanopi easily. "The Canphorites are in Jalanopi's kingdom; they will obey Jalanopi's laws."

"I doubt it."

Jalanopi flicked away an insect that had landed on his face, leading McFarley to wonder once more why certain insects were considered delicacies by the Tulabete while others were viewed merely as pests.

"Then they will suffer the consequences."

McFarley's expression reflected his doubts on the matter.

"But in the meantime, they have brought me many gifts," continued Jalanopi.

"They seek to buy your friendship with trinkets," said McFarley.

"As you yourself gave me a hat?" suggested Jalanopi.

"I wish only to live among your people and educate them in the ways of Jesus Christ."

Jalanopi stared at him with expressionless cat's-eyes, his features more alien and inscrutable than usual.

"You are wasting your time, Man Andrew," he said at last.

"It is mine to waste."

"How long have you been here?"

"On Karimon? About four months."

"And have any of my people accepted this Christ of yours?"

"Not yet," said McFarley. "But they will."

"You seem both friendly and harmless, Man Andrew, and you are welcome to remain—but they will not accept your Christ," said Jalanopi. "Why should a race of warriors worship a being of a different race who was unable to defend himself and let himself be killed by his enemies?"

"It is not that simple," said McFarley.

"It is that simple," said Jalanopi with a cold reptilian smile. He pointed to the cross that hung around McFarley's neck. "You even wear the instrument of his destruction. How can a man who worships death preach to beings who worship life?"

"I do not worship death," answered McFarley, "but rather what he died for."

"You have learned our language, and you have brought us medicines, and you have helped us care for our old and our infirm, and for that we are grateful," said Jalanopi. "But you had best keep those books you brought with you; there is no wisdom in them for the Tulabete."

"There is wisdom in the bible for *all* sentient beings," said McFarley, stepping aside as a pair of Tallgrazers, the local meat animals, wandered by, almost brushing against him. He noticed recently healed scars at their joints and wondered how they survived when the Tulabete inserted narrow tubes and drained them of their marrow—a substance that, along with the insects, formed the Tulabete's staple diet—on a monthly basis.

Jalanopi looked at him, his face still an unreadable green mask. "Do you truly believe that?"

"Absolutely."

"In a few minutes I must hold court and sit in judgment," said Jalanopi. "One of the cases that will be brought will be from an outlying area. Two females both claim to be the mother of the same infant. His father has been away fighting a tribe called the Rakko and cannot say which of them is the true mother. The father is very wealthy, and the day will come that all he possesses is passed on to his progeny. It can reasonably be expected that the son will favor his mother more than the other woman, which is doubtless why they both claim to have given birth to him." He paused. "What is there in your book to deal with *that*?"

McFarley smiled. "As I said, there is wisdom enough in the bible for *all* races." He wiped some sweat from his forehead, flicked away a flying insect and barely got his hand out of the way of Jalanopi's amazingly swift tongue, then continued. "Once, a very long time ago, there was a king named Solomon, who was praised far and wide for his

wisdom. And into his court came two women, each of whom claimed to be the mother of the same baby."

"Truly?" asked Jalanopi, his eyes narrowing, his earholes pulsating, both signs of sudden interest.

"Truly. He questioned both of the women, but they each kept to their story."

"As these will do today."

"Finally, he announced that he could not tell which of them was the true mother, and that the only fair decision was to cut the baby in half and give one half to each woman."

Jalanopi exhaled a long, high-pitched hiss, which McFarley had come to recognize as a display of contempt.

"This king was *not* wise," said Jalanopi at last.

"Hear me out," said McFarley. "When he announced his decision, one of the women came forward and said that she could not allow him to kill an innocent child, and that she would forsake her claim to motherhood. And Solomon immediately knew that she was the mother, for no mother would allow her baby to be slaughtered."

"Your Solomon was a fool, Man Andrew."

"Why?"

"Do you know what would happen if *I* made that same judgment?"

"Suppose you tell me," said McFarley.

"Neither female would say a word, and then, because a king does not retract a threat made before his tribe, the infant would have to be cut in half."

"Surely the real mother would protest."

"The penalty for disputing my judgment is death," said Jalanopi. "Do you really think they will protest?"

"Try it," urged McFarley. "You'll see that you're wrong."

"And if I am *not* wrong?" said Jalanopi. "Will *you* kill the infant?"

"No."

Jalanopi hissed again. "You see, Man Andrew? You wish

to offer your god's advice, but if it proves wrong you do not wish to bear the consequences."

"How will *you* solve the problem?" asked McFarley.

"It would be foolish to reach a decision before hearing both females, would it not?"

"Yes," said McFarley. "Yes, it would."

"You are both fair and honest, Man Andrew. Very few beings of any race are willing to admit when they are wrong."

"*I* may be wrong," said McFarley. "I have never claimed to be infallible. But my religion is *not* wrong."

"It is well that you should feel that way," continued Jalanopi. "It is a matter of belief. I should no more be able to talk you out of worshiping your gods than you can talk me out of worshiping mine."

"God," McFarley corrected him. "One god."

"He must feel very overburdened at times."

"But He persists."

"An admirable trait. And now it is time for me to put on my ceremonial headdress and hold court."

"Do you mind if I watch?" asked McFarley.

"You wish to compare my judgment to that of King Solomon?"

"I'm just curious to see how you handle the problem."

"Then come," said Jalanopi, walking off across the short brown grass to his intricately winding dwelling, which seemed to curve back on itself time and again. Twice he sidestepped small rodents that were in his path; a third time, for no reason McFarley could fathom, he went out of his way to step on and mortally wound an identical rodent, which he ignored as it lay there writhing in its death throes.

Upon reaching his dwelling, Jalanopi crawled into it with a slithering motion, retrieved a huge feathered headdress, wrapped a cloak made from the skin of a Nightkiller around his shoulders, and returned to his tree. The members of the village followed him to the carved wooden

throne, also in the shape of a coiled reptile, where he sat down and waited for them to fall silent. Finally he nodded to one of his counselors, who stepped forward.

"What have we today?" asked Jalanopi.

"First, there is a petition from the human, Fuentes, to continue hunting on your land for three more months." The counselor nodded to an assistant, who placed three bags at Jalanopi's feet. "He offers this salt as a gift."

"He may hunt for ten days," said Jalanopi. "No longer."

"It is a large amount of salt, my king," noted the counselor.

"True," agreed Jalanopi. "And it is very valuable to us." He paused and allowed himself the luxury of a cold, totally reptilian smile. "But it is obviously not very valuable to *him*, for he has given us salt the last three times, and he has not left our world for almost a year, which means he came with a great supply of it in his ship. Salt must be very easy for him to obtain on his homeworld, and we must take that into account when bargaining with him."

"What if he says no?"

Jalanopi scooped up a handful of dirt. "If I offer you this in exchange for something I want, and you tell me you must have two handfuls, am I likely to walk away simply because I know dirt is valuable to you?" He smiled and let the dirt fall to the ground. "Fuentes will be back with more salt in ten days' time."

"Yes, my king."

"Next?"

"Three members of the Fani tribe claim that a party of Tulabete warriors attacked one of their merchant caravans."

"Good. Our warriors are to be commended," said Jalanopi. "Where did this take place?"

"Along the Karimona River, just south of the Pundi Pools."

"Offer the Fani my apology, and tell them such incidents

will continue if they persist in penetrating so deeply into my territory."

"They want compensation, my king."

Jalanopi shook his head. "They had no business being where they were," he said in his sibilant manner. "There will be no compensation."

"They claim that to avoid the river would force them to traverse the Tenya Mountains, which would double the length of their trip and seriously cut into their profit."

"They should have considered that before they went to war with me seven years ago."

"May I make a suggestion?" asked McFarley.

Jalanopi turned to him. "Would your Solomon have paid them recompense?" he asked caustically.

"No."

"Well then?"

"Your land is sparsely populated, and the Fani don't seem to be in a position to do you any harm. If it is really in their best interests to use this route, why not charge them a tribute for each crossing?"

"No," said Jalanopi. "Give them no thought, Man Andrew," he continued, hissing his contempt. "The Fani are burrow-dwellers who lack the courage to stay above the ground at night. They are not worth your consideration." His long tongue suddenly shot out, though no insects were near him. "Further, the day would come when they choose not to pay the tribute, and then I will have to go to war again to punish them. It is far better not to let them cross my land in the first place." He stared at McFarley. "You disapprove, Man Andrew?"

"It seems a bit harsh."

A frown crossed Jalanopi's lean reptilian face, and the constriction of its muscles forced beads of thick, glistening oil to the surface of his forehead and cheekbones. "It was harsh when they tortured my grandfather, or when they mutilated our livestock, or when they poisoned our wells.

This is not harsh." He turned back to his counselor. "Next?"

"We have two females, Tagoma and Sagara, who each claim to be the mother of the same infant. They are both wives of Kabulaki, who owns much land and many animals, all of which the infant will inherit when Kabulaki dies. You must decide which is the true mother."

McFarley watched and listened as each female, amidst much wailing and cursing, adamantly held that the infant was her own. One of them, Tagoma, was in the process of shedding her skin, and looked as if she had been brutally mauled by predators; the other, Sagara, had just acquired a new skin, and looked as sleek and shining as Jalanopi.

There had been no witnesses to the birth, and Kabulaki was still patrolling one of the frontiers. Jalanopi questioned each female perfunctorily, grunted at their answers, and finally reached out for the infant, which one of his minor counselors was holding.

"He is a good, strong, healthy child," said Jalanopi, staring at the infant. "See how he refuses to lower his gaze before my own?" He turned to McFarley. "And your King Solomon would have cut him in half?"

"He would have *threatened* to," answered McFarley. "There's a difference."

"What is your judgment, my king?" asked the senior counselor, who sensed that Jalanopi had no further questions to ask.

"A strong grip, too," said Jalanopi, holding out a finger for the infant to grab. "Someday this child shall become a mighty warrior, whose fame will terrorize his enemies and whose word will bear great weight with his king. See the fearlessness in his eyes!"

"Your judgment, my king?" persisted the senior counselor, who seemed to feel a need to keep Jalanopi's schedule moving.

Jalanopi stared at the two females.

"One of you is lying," he said. "And you are lying because you know that this child will someday be a wealthy and powerful warrior, and that as his mother some of his wealth and power will accrue to you. This cannot be permitted."

"Then which is the rightful mother, my king?"

"I cannot say," answered Jalanopi. "Therefore, from this day forward, the child will become *my* son. He will live in my house and be cared for by my wives, and since I am the wealthiest member of the Tulabete, the infant will inherit more land and more cattle than he would inherit from Kabulaki." He paused. "His true mother will realize that her child will fare better in my house than in her own, and her mother's heart will be content. His false mother will have gained nothing by her lies. That is my judgment."

Both females backed away, neither displaying any emotion, and Jalanopi proceeded to the next case, which had to do with the joint ownership of some domestic animals. When that was done, he waved his hand imperiously, indicating that he was through making judgments for the day and, as the villagers dispersed, he walked over to McFarley.

"What would King Solomon say to *that?*" he asked.

"He would say that you have robbed the true parents of their child," answered McFarley without hesitation.

Jalanopi's lips parted in what passed for a smile among his race. "The child will be back with his true parents before the long rains."

"How can you say that? You've already admitted that you don't know which one is the mother."

"We cherish children in our society, Man Andrew," answered Jalanopi. "When Kabulaki returns home and realizes that one of the females cost him his son, he will determine which is the true mother, and when he does, the child will be returned."

"You mean he will beat the truth out of her?" said McFarley distastefully.

"Does not such a lie deserve a beating?"

"Then why didn't you save him the trouble and do it yourself?"

"A king does not soil his hands thus," answered Jalanopi. "Besides," he added, "I am not the aggrieved party."

Jalanopi was about to remove his headdress when, from across the short brown grass, his senior counselor approached him.

"Yes?"

"The Canphorites wish an audience, my king."

"Again?"

"Yes, my king."

"I am hungry now. Tell them I will meet with them after I have eaten."

"Yes, my king."

Jalanopi turned to McFarley. "Will you join me, Man Andrew?"

"I'd be honored."

They walked over to Jalanopi's dwelling, where one of his wives had prepared a meal of still-moving little *things* covered with a sauce made from the pulp of some of the local fruits and flowers. McFarley took one look as Jalanopi inserted his tongue into the mixture and allowed some of the insectlike creatures to slither onto it, then averted his eyes just before Jalanopi drew his tongue back into his mouth.

"Perhaps you are not hungry," suggested Jalanopi.

McFarley listened for the hiss of contempt and watched for the quivering nostril that signified amusement; he thought he heard and saw both signs, but he wasn't quite sure.

"Perhaps later," he said.

Jalanopi nodded his head. "Or perhaps not," he said, and now McFarley was certain that he was an object of distaste and ridicule to the king.

"Tell me," he said, hoping to change the subject, "what do the Canphorites want?"

"The same as usual."

"And that is?"

"They will offer me many gifts in exchange for permission to dig in my hills."

"What's *in* your hills?" asked McFarley.

"Various metals that we use for decoration," answered Jalanopi; he secreted a clear liquid that caused more of his lunch to climb eagerly onto his tongue, then brought them back into his mouth. "They must have many people to decorate, because they have offered much more than the metals are worth."

"How much have they offered you?"

Jalanopi pointed to a pair of his domestic meat animals. "They have offered two thousand Tallgrazers, plus fifty bags of salt." He shook his head in disbelief, as if only a race of madmen would make such a munificent offer for the stuff of armbands and necklaces.

"Have they told you how much metal they plan to remove from your hills?" asked McFarley.

Jalanopi shrugged. "What difference does it make? They are fools."

"Then why have you not reached an agreement with them?"

"Because every day I wait, they increase their offer." He looked expressionlessly at McFarley. "They have also warned me not to treat with members of your race."

"I can believe *that*," said McFarley.

"They say that you eat infants of your own race, and conquer innocent races, and torture your enemies."

"Do you believe them?"

"I do not believe that you eat infants, for if you did, where would all your people come from?" said Jalanopi thoughtfully. "As for their other statements, it is only fitting that you should conquer races that are weaker than

your own, and if your enemies try to kill you, why should you not torture some of them as an example to the others?"

"We torture no one," said McFarley. "And we do not conquer races that are weaker than ourselves. We protect them from races like the Canphorites, races that *do* believe in conquest."

"And Men never conquer or exploit other races?"

"If anyone—Canphorites or Men or anyone else—should try to exploit your people, I will do everything in my power to prevent it."

"You have been here only a short time, Man Andrew," noted Jalanopi. "What have we done to bring forth such love of our people and our planet?"

McFarley considered his reply for a moment. "Meaning no offense, it is not that I love you but that I hate the exploitation of innocent races—by Canphorites *or* Men."

"Do you truly believe that the Canphorites wish to conquer the Tulabete?"

"At the very least they wish to rob you."

"In what way?" asked Jalanopi.

"You remember the example you used earlier today, in which you picked up a handful of dirt?"

"Yes."

"Well, the metals in your hills may be worth very little more than dirt to you, but on other worlds—both mine and the Canphorites'—those metals are among the most valuable things one can own. And on their world, like mine, salt is almost as easy to obtain as dirt."

"But you have no Tallgrazers on your world," said Jalanopi, "and they have offered a number equal to that which I already possess."

"They have weapons that would seem like magic to you," said McFarley. "It would take almost no effort for them to go to a distant village, kill everyone in it, and return with all the Tallgrazers that village possessed."

"Truly?" Again Jalanopi's eyes narrowed and his ear-holes began pulsating.

"Truly."

"Tell me more about these weapons."

"They are terrible weapons of destruction, each of them superior to a hundred warriors with spears."

"If such weapons exist, why have not the Canphorites simply taken what they want from the Tulabete?"

"If there were no humans on your world, or in this sector of the galaxy, they would do just that, for they have done so on many other worlds," answered McFarley. "But they know that if they did, we humans would tell our government, and they would have a war on their hands—a war they could not possibly win."

"And your race also possesses these magical weapons?" asked Jalanopi.

"We do. But we use them only when there is no alternative."

"I can conceive of many situations in which no alternative presents itself," said Jalanopi with a dismissive wave of his three-digited hand. "Now explain, Man Andrew: why do Fuentes and the other human hunters not use such weapons? It would seem that with them they could slay thousands of animals in a single day."

"They hunt for sport, and it is not sporting to employ these weapons."

"But Fuentes sells the skins of the animals he kills, and the horns of the Horndevils, does he not? So it is not entirely sporting."

"These weapons would obliterate horns and skins."

Jalanopi was silent for a moment, lost in thought. "They are *that* powerful?" he said at last.

"They are."

"Then I now know what price to extract from the Canphorites," said Jalanopi.

"They will not give you such weapons," said McFarley.

"Then they will not be permitted to take metal from our hills."

"Or if they *do* give them to you, they will give you defective weapons, or weapons that work only for a brief period of time and will be useless once they have taken what they want and left your world."

"Perhaps," said Jalanopi. "But if I am to possess such weaponry, I have no alternative but to deal with the Canphorites." He stared, almost mockingly, into McFarley's eyes. "*Have* I, Man Andrew?"

Two

"This is a dangerous path you are treading," said Paratoka, Jalanopi's chief advisor.

The king was sitting beneath his tree, in conference with his closest associates.

"The humans seek to exploit us, do they not?" answered Jalanopi, his long tongue darting out to capture a small flying insect that got too near his face.

"Yes."

"And the Canphorites would do the same?" continued Jalanopi, his strong jaws crushing the insect.

"Yes, my king, but—"

"They think of us as their inferiors, as being but a step above the beasts of the forests and savannahs," said Jalanopi. "This will be our advantage, for they will not believe that we have the foresight to realize what they are attempting to accomplish, and they will never credit us with the wisdom to capitalize on our mutual animosity."

A hot breeze swept through the village, carrying a cloud of dust past Jalanopi's tree. None of the Tulabete moved or attempted to speak until it had swirled past, and then Paratoka leaned forward and spoke again.

"I have studied the situation, my king. It is the Men we must be wary of, not the Canphorites."

"They both wish to exploit us," said another advisor.

"True," answered Paratoka. "But the Canphorites control only their home planets, Canphor VI and VII, and a handful of worlds—no more than twenty—that oppose Man's Republic. The Republic itself has conquered or otherwise assimilated some *forty thousand* worlds. They are much the stronger race, and they have had far more practice at conquering worlds than we have at withstanding such empires."

"They have made no attempt to subdue or subjugate us," said a third advisor.

"*Yet*," said Paratoka.

"But if they are as strong as you say, then it would be better for us to be associated with them than with the Canphorites."

"We will not be the satellite of *any* race," said Jalanopi firmly. "I do not intend to sit idly by while Men *or* Canphorites plunder my world."

"You have heard of their weapons," said Paratoka. "And surely what they have told us must be true, or else how could they have conquered so many worlds? How can we oppose them?"

Jalanopi looked coldly at his circle of advisors.

"Since we cannot be stronger than they are, we must be wiser." His tongue darted out again, capturing a crawling insect from the bole of his tree, and he carefully plucked it off his tongue and held it up. "I have already told you: our advantage is that they view *us* the way we view *this*—as mindless insects to be plundered and used."

"Man Andrew seems a friendly and respectful being," said yet another advisor. "I see no signs of aggression in him. Possibly we are being hasty."

"If I were to send one member of the Tulabete to a world I eventually wished to dominate, I would not send Kabulaki

or one of our other great warriors, for their first instinct would be to fight." He paused. "No, I would send our gentlest member, a friendly and respectful being, as you say, to ease their fears. I would have him befriend their king, and offer help in their hour of need, and I would never allow him to suggest that we might someday wish to extract payment for that help." His lips parted in his version of a smile. "They have sent us just such a man, and never once has he suggested that payment might someday fall due for Man's help."

"Even knowing all this, how are we to protect ourselves against it?" asked the advisor.

"We must create a situation whereby it is in Man's best interest to help us," answered Jalanopi. "We will make them literally beg to arm our people with their weapons, and we will make a treaty that explicitly states that they do this of their own free will, and that no payment will be demanded, now or forever."

"*Can* this be done?"

Jalanopi nodded an affirmative. "I shall take the first steps this afternoon."

"Even if we obtain their weapons, will they not retain even more powerful ones—weapons that can destroy our entire world?" persisted the advisor.

"Almost certainly," said Jalanopi. "*I* would."

"Then I repeat: how are we to protect ourselves?"

"By being wiser than they are," answered Jalanopi. "We know that they have an empire of forty thousand worlds. We know they wish to add to it. From this, we can conclude that they do not want a dead, lifeless rock, but a living, breathing world that can be exploited." He paused. "So let them *have* their weapons that can kill the planet. We know that they will not use them."

"We *hope* that they will not use them," amended the advisor.

"We *know* it," repeated Jalanopi firmly. "For if they be-

lieved in the destruction of their enemies, why are the Canphorites, who have lost three wars with them, still alive?"

Paratoka got to his feet and emitted a low whistling cry of triumph.

"We shall triumph, for we have the greatest and wisest king of all!" he hissed. "Long live Jalanopi, warrior king of the Tulabete!"

The other advisors took up the chant, and after a moment Jalanopi stilled them by raising his hand.

"Now we must prepare," he said. "Pass the word to Kabulaki and my other generals that I wish to see them tonight. Send runners to those who are patrolling the borders that I want them to be on the alert, and that they will soon receive new orders."

"What do you plan to tell our people, my king?" asked Paratoka.

"That we are going to war."

"Against whom?"

Jalanopi leaned back against his tree, his face an expressionless mask even to his closest advisors. "I will know by nightfall."

"But—"

"I have issued an order," said Jalanopi. "See that it is carried out. And have Man Andrew brought to me."

Paratoka bowed. "Yes, my king."

"The meeting is over," announced Jalanopi. "Go about your business, tend to your land and your animals, and speak of this to no one."

One by one his advisors left, and a few moments later Andrew McFarley approached him.

"You wished to see me?" asked the man.

"Indeed, it is time that we had a serious discussion," said Jalanopi, getting to his feet. "Come, walk with me as we talk, Man Andrew."

"Is something wrong?" asked McFarley, as Jalanopi led

him through the nearby pastures, passing within a few yards of the huge brown, placid Tallgrazers.

"I am afraid that I must ask you to leave Karimon, Man Andrew."

"*Leave?*" repeated McFarley, startled. "Have I done something to offend you, Jalanopi?"

"No," replied Jalanopi. "You have been an exemplary guest."

"Then why . . . ?"

"Tonight I shall issue a declaration of war against both the Fani and the Rakko, our two most formidable enemies. Against either one, I know we would emerge victorious . . . but we will be fighting a war on two fronts and we will be severely outnumbered, and I cannot guarantee your safety."

"Why don't you let *me* worry about that?" said McFarley, brushing some flying insects away from his face and trying to ignore the odor of the Tallgrazers' pungent droppings.

"I do not want any incident to destroy the friendship between our races," said Jalanopi. "Especially the death of an honored friend. You will have to leave."

"What of Fuentes and the other hunters?"

"If we can find them, we will send them home. Their whereabouts are currently unknown."

"And the Canphorites?"

"The Canphorites have offered us weaponry with which to defend ourselves."

"*We* could give you far better weapons."

"But they have already agreed to do so, and for no cost: the weapons are a gift to cement the friendship between us."

"I told you not to trust them, Jalanopi," said McFarley. "They will want something in return. Mark my words."

"So would your Republic," replied Jalanopi, carefully watching McFarley out of the corner of his eye.

"How many weapons have the Canphorites offered you?"

Jalanopi paused, trying to think of a plausible number. "Three thousand now, five thousand later if we still need them. And experts to show us how to use them and keep them functioning."

"You are letting them buy your world for three thousand weapons," said McFarley. "And I can assure you that after the battle, the weapons will cease to function and the parts needed to repair them will not arrive."

"You have always been honest with me, Man Andrew," said Jalanopi. "But they *are* the enemy of your blood, as the Fani and Rakko are the enemies of *mine*. On this one matter I am not certain that you are to be trusted."

"Will you at least let me contact my people and see if they can match the Canphorites' offer?"

"So that *your* weapons will fail to function after the war, and *your* race can purchase Karimon for a trifling price?" replied Jalanopi with an expression that McFarley assumed was sardonic among the Tulabete.

"If *we* support you in this war," said McFarley, "we will give you not only weapons and advisors, but written guarantees, backed by the full power and prestige of the Republic."

"The *Republic* is just a word," said Jalanopi. "If it exists at all, it exists many trillions of miles from here. What recourse have we if you do not keep your pledges?"

"What recourse have you if the Canphorites break *their* word?" shot back McFarley. "*We* have not asked for mineral rights. We have not asked you to join our Republic. If you let us help you, there will be no strings attached."

"I do not understand."

"It's a human expression," said McFarley. "It does not translate very well. What I mean to say is that we will help you for only two reasons: first, because we wish to be friends to *all* races, and second, because we do not wish to see any

world subjugated by the Canphorites. We will ask for no recompense of any kind."

They reached the end of a pasture. Jalanopi made a strange trilling sound, and a small avian that had been perched atop the broad back of a Tallgrazer, picking insects from its hide, flew over and landed on the broad palm of the Tulabete's outstretched hand.

"Do you see this avian, Man Andrew?" said Jalanopi.

"Yes."

"He came to me because he trusts me, just as your Republic wishes us to come to you because we trust *you*. Is this not so?"

"Yes," said McFarley, wondering what point the Tulabete was making.

"Five hundred times this avian has come to me, and never have I betrayed its trust. We have a special bond between us, this avian and I. It knows I am far bigger and stronger, and that it has no defense against me, but it willingly places itself in my hand." Suddenly Jalanopi closed his hand; the startled avian let out a single, panicked shriek and died, and Jalanopi carelessly tossed its corpse onto the ground before the eyes of the shocked human. "The 501st time was not so lucky for it, was it, Man Andrew?"

"What was the point of that little demonstration?" demanded McFarley.

"How many times must we put ourselves in your hand before you decide to squeeze?" asked Jalanopi. "What recourse have we if you break your pledge to us? We are as helpless before you as the avian was before me. . . . But we are wiser than the avian: we know better than to willingly perch upon the Republic's hand."

"All I can do is repeat what I said."

"But what are your assurances worth?" continued Jalanopi. "If a million Men should land here tomorrow to enslave my people, to whom can I go to say: 'This is not part

of our agreement. Talk to Man Andrew, and he will tell you what he promised on your behalf'? Who will believe me?"

"Doesn't the same situation exist with the Canphorites?" asked McFarley, stalling for time while he tried to think of an acceptable answer.

"Canphor controls how many worlds, Man Andrew?"

"Twenty-seven."

"And how many worlds are in your Republic?"

"The worlds in the Republic are willing partners in a great galactic enterprise," said McFarley firmly.

"I am sure they must be," said Jalanopi. "How many willing partners do you have?"

"Forty thousand."

"There you have it."

"In numbers there is strength, and in strength there is security," said McFarley.

"I do not need strength to fight against the Republic's enemies, for they are not *my* enemies," said Jalanopi. "I need only the strength to fight against the Fani and the Rakko."

"You are making a serious mistake, Jalanopi," said McFarley.

"Then I shall have to live with it. I want you off the planet before sunrise, for beyond that I cannot promise to protect you."

"Will you at least let me contact the Republic?" persisted McFarley. "We may be able to make an offer that meets with your approval."

"It seems a waste of time," said Jalanopi. "I have already reached an agreement with the Canphorites."

"Let me *try*," said McFarley. "What harm can it do?"

Jalanopi pretended to weigh the offer in his mind for a long moment, then shrugged his entire body expressively.

"You may try," he said at last. "But I warn you that it is a waste of time. We are satisfied with the Canphorites' proposition."

They turned and began walking back to Mastaboni, where McFarley left Jalanopi and went over to the small church that housed not only his bibles and his religious artifacts, but also his subspace radio. Jalanopi stopped at Paratoka's dwelling long enough to tell his advisor to keep the Canphorites out of the village until otherwise instructed, for he didn't want an angry McFarley accusing them of making offers of which they were ignorant; then he wandered over to a nearby stream, where he waded into the water, sat down, and amused himself by catching the darting red-and-gold fish with his hands.

He did not throw them ashore, for the Tulabete did not eat fish, but it was an exercise that kept his mind alert and his reflexes sharpened, and none among his people could catch as many fish as he. They carried sharp teeth, these fish; one had cost him the middle digit of his hand before the last monsoon, and it was just now growing back, a phenomenon that the Tulabete took for granted but which seemed to astound both McFarley and the Canphorites, neither of which could regenerate any portion of their anatomy.

McFarley came by almost an hour later and squatted at the edge of the stream.

"I've been looking all over for you," he said.

"I have been here all along," answered Jalanopi. "Do you eat fish, Man Andrew?"

"From time to time."

Jalanopi's hands shot out beneath the rippling surface of the water, and an instant later he pulled a large red-and-gold fish out of the water and flipped it onto the bank near the human, where it flopped four or five times and then lay still, gasping in the bright sunlight.

"It is my farewell present to you," said Jalanopi. "Beware its teeth until you are certain it is dead."

"I've spoken to my people," said McFarley.

"And how many regiments of so-called advisors do they wish us to accept?"

"None."

"Very wise, Man Andrew," said Jalanopi. "That way we will never learn to use your weapons."

"Hear me out, please," continued McFarley. "We will give you eight thousand hand-weapons; we will ship as many or as few advisors as you request; and we will present you with a document, signed by the naval commander of this sector and witnessed by members of six other races, that at no time, now or in the future, will we attempt to extract payment in any form for the weapons or for our services. We want only to be your allies, and to prevent you, in your innocence, from falling under the influence of the Canphorites."

"That *is* a handsome offer, Man Andrew," said Jalanopi. "And you require absolutely nothing in return?"

"One thing."

"Oh? And what is that?" asked Jalanopi, repressing the urge to part his lips in his equivalent of a grin.

"The Canphorites must be told to leave."

"To be replaced by you?"

McFarley shook his head. "We will not come until we are invited."

"And if we should never invite you?"

"Then, except for the Men who unload your weapons and those you request to act as advisors, myself and the few hunters and explorers already on your planet are the only Men you will ever see."

"And I assume you have no objection to remaining hostage to our agreement, Man Andrew?" said Jalanopi.

"I don't believe I understand," replied McFarley.

"You will remain with the Tulabete until long after the war is over. If the agreement is broken, your life shall be forfeit."

McFarley swallowed hard, then nodded his head. "My people do not lie, Jalanopi. I will consent to remain hostage to your agreement."

"Then tell them I accept their offer," said Jalanopi. "How soon can the weapons be here?"

"By noon tomorrow."

"Have the ship land near my village."

"What about advisors?"

"We will accept five hundred advisors," said Jalanopi. "They will be under my direct command, and they must leave the moment the war is over. Does your Republic agree to that?"

"I am certain they will," replied McFarley.

"It would appear, Man Andrew, that you and I are to become allies against the Fani and the Rakko." His hands darted beneath the water once more, then emerged and tossed their squirming prey onto the bank. "Have another fish."

Three

The war—*slaughter* would be a better word—took exactly nine days, after which the decimated Fani and Rakko sued for peace.

Jalanopi brought their leaders to his tree one by one. Each was given the opportunity to swear fealty to him and to pay tribute to the Tulabete. Those who did were allowed to leave in peace; those few who refused were chopped to bits where they stood. None of the enemy's warriors were killed or incarcerated; each was given free passage back to his homeland.

On the tenth day, Jalanopi informed McFarley, who had come to act as a liaison between the king and the human advisors, that it was time for the advisors to leave. McFarley suggested that the Tulabete, though they had wrought enormous havoc among their enemies with the weapons, hadn't properly learned to maintain them, and that the advisors would be delighted to remain for as much as a year until such time as Jalanopi's army had mastered the art of weapon maintenance.

"That would not be a good idea," replied Jalanopi. "I do not wish alien wars to be fought on my soil."

"I do not understand," said McFarley.

"I have told the Canphorites that they may return in three days' time," explained Jalanopi. "It would be best if your soldiers were gone before the Canphorites arrive."

"I thought you signed an agreement—" began McFarley.

"I agreed to deport the Canphorites before accepting your gifts, and I kept my word," said Jalanopi. "There is nothing in the agreement that said they must be barred from Karimon for all eternity."

"Thirteen days is *not* comparable to all eternity."

"Your race has been a good friend to the Tulabete, as you have been a good friend to me, Man Andrew," said Jalanopi. "I have no quarrel with them. This is a simple disagreement between myself and your king, and you need not concern yourself about it." He paused. "I will send Paratoka, my chief advisor, away with your advisors. He will represent me and speak to your king and the matter will be resolved." He parted his lips. "Who knows? Perhaps he will come back and advise me to join your Republic."

"I will convey your message to my people immediately," said McFarley, walking off to his church and his subspace radio.

Jalanopi next sent for Paratoka.

"How may I serve you, my king?" asked the chief advisor upon arriving at Jalanopi's tree.

"I want you to accompany the Men back to see their king."

"What shall I say to him?" asked Paratoka.

"He will do most of the talking," answered Jalanopi. "I have informed him that I intend to allow the Canphorites to return immediately; he will surely find this unacceptable. You will argue that he has no right to tell us whom we can befriend, and gradually you will allow him to make his points and win the argument."

"Is that all, my king?"

"Of course not," said Jalanopi. "We have not seen the last of Men yet. While you are there, you will find out what the metals in our hills are worth to them."

"They have said they will not return until you invite them," noted Paratoka.

"They will return," said Jalanopi with certainty. "What I must know is how much to charge them for the privilege."

Four

Seven weeks passed before Paratoka returned with the information Jalanopi required. The hills, he explained, were filled with many kinds of metals, some highly prized by Men, some virtually worthless to them. There was no way they could know how much of each existed until they allowed some Men to land on Karimon and run a thorough survey.

"Go back," said Jalanopi, "and tell them that we will allow them to come and make their tests—but that they are not allowed to bring any weapons with them."

"I think they will insist, my king," answered Paratoka. "The Men who conduct the tests are in a branch of the military."

"It is *they* who want the metal, not *I*," said Jalanopi confidently. "We shall see who possesses more patience, their king or yours."

"They have no king," noted Paratoka.

"His name is Solomon," replied Jalanopi. "How could they function without a king? Probably he does not consider the Tulabete important enough to be granted an audience; he will soon realize that he is in error."

Paratoka went back to the Republic with Jalanopi's answer, and nothing more was heard from Men for five months. A few more hunters applied for permission to go after trophy animals, and a handful of missionaries were allowed to set up shop, but every day Jalanopi waited for the Republic to give in to his conditions, and each new day brought forth nothing but silence.

"They need encouragement," he announced to his advisors one night. "Invite the Canphorites back."

"We agreed not to," noted Paratoka.

"When the Men return, we will deport the Canphorites again," said Jalanopi.

"That is not fair to them," offered another advisor.

"What are they to us?" asked Jalanopi. "Since Man is the strongest race we have encountered, and since Man covets our metals, then we must use everything at our disposal to bend the race of Man to our will."

"Surely others have tried," said the advisor. "And yet they have forty thousand worlds in their empire."

"*I* am not others," said Jalanopi. "We will invite the Canphorites back again."

Five

The reappearance of the Canphorites had the desired effect upon the Republic. No sooner had the news reached them than a party of human diplomats and ranking military officers requested permission to land on Karimon and meet with Jalanopi.

Jalanopi set the time for the audience, which, of course, was held beneath his tree. As the moment approached, he donned his ceremonial headdress, sat upon his serpentine throne, and assembled his warriors—all armed with the Republic's weapons—in such a way that they appeared to be even more numerous than they were. Finally, satisfied, he allowed his guests to be brought before him.

A party of seven men and women, five in military uniforms, walked across the dry, grassy plains toward Jalanopi's village of Mastaboni. A member of Jalanopi's own race led them, beating the tall grass with his spear to frighten away any poisonous snakes. By the time they were within sight of Jalanopi the entire party was covered with sweat and dust. They stopped some twenty feet from Jalanopi's tree as the Tulabete formed a ring around them, and finally one of the two men who wore civilian clothing stepped forward.

"Greetings, King Jalanopi," he said. "My name is Arthur Gruening, and—"

Jalanopi held up a hand, and the man immediately fell silent.

"These fools have not even bothered to learn our language," he said to Paratoka. "You will translate."

"My Terran is not very good, my king," replied his chief advisor. "I suggest we summon Man Andrew."

Jalanopi nodded his acquiescence. "But you will remain and listen, for when all is said and done, he is one of them."

"Yes, my king."

McFarley arrived a few minutes later, was apprised of the situation, and began translating for both sides.

"My name is Arthur Gruening," recommenced the man in civilian clothing, "and I represent the Republic's Department of Alien Affairs, which is based far from here on Deluros VIII." He paused and wiped the sweat from his forehead with a handkerchief, and silently wished that he had brought a hat. "I have been instructed by my government to remind you of certain promises that were made in your name, and to urge you to reconsider your decision to allow our mutual enemies from the Canphor system access to your world."

"I made no such promises," said Jalanopi.

"I happen to know that you did," said McFarley.

"Just translate what I have said, Man Andrew," said Jalanopi coldly. "Great things are at stake here, and I will not have you jeopardize them."

McFarley shrugged and translated Jalanopi's statement.

"Your own representative gave us your assurances that the Canphorites would be permanently barred from Karimon," said Gruening.

"He had no authority to do so," said Jalanopi.

"Nevertheless, he spoke on your behalf."

Jalanopi held up his hand once more.

"Bring Paratoka before me."

Three of his warriors immediately walked over to a serpent-shaped dwelling.

"But he is sitting right before you!" said McFarley.

"Man Andrew, if you wish for these seven members of your race to survive the day, you will limit yourself to translating," said Jalanopi. "And do not forget that the real Paratoka will tell me if you have properly translated what I say."

A blindfolded Fani warrior, his hands bound behind him, was dragged out of the dwelling and over to Jalanopi's tree.

"Here is Paratoka," announced Jalanopi.

He waited for McFarley to translate, then withdrew a long sharp blade and, before anyone could react, lopped the Fani's head off.

"As you can see," continued Jalanopi calmly, as he sheathed his blade, "Paratoka is incapable of speaking for himself, let alone for me." He stared at McFarley, his orange cat's-eyes wide and unblinking. "Thus do I treat *anyone* who misrepresents me."

Gruening and the diplomats averted their eyes, while the military men watched with no show of emotion.

"Have we anything further to discuss?" asked Jalanopi after a momentary silence.

"Yes," said Gruening, forcing himself to look away from the corpse. "We have given you our weapons and our friendship. We have kept our promises to you. We have proven ourselves to be your friends. Why are you once again opening your planet to the Canphorites, whom you know to be our enemies?"

"I offered your race the chance to survey our hills and make your various tests for our metals," answered Jalanopi. "When you failed to reply, I naturally assumed that these things held no interest for you. We are a poor people, and if we cannot sell our metals to you, then we must sell them where we can."

"The Canphorites are surveying your hills right now?" asked Gruening, startled.

"The Canphorites are in our hills," said Jalanopi. "I have no idea what they are doing there."

"We would like to survey them also."

"Then why did you not reply to me when the offer was made?"

"Because of the conditions you imposed," answered Gruening. "You have many wild animals on your world, and you have not yet conquered all of your enemies. It would be foolhardy to send a party of Men out, totally unarmed, to survey your hills."

"All problems are capable of solution when peace-loving beings meet together and talk," said Jalanopi, and only McFarley recognized the open lips and the tightness around his eyes as a contemptuous smile. "Had you simply voiced your concerns, we could have solved this particular problem months ago. I will send an armed party of my warriors into the hills with you to act as your guards."

"We would prefer that our men carry their own weaponry," answered Gruening.

"You sound distrustful," said Jalanopi. "This is not the statement of a friend."

"One moment, please, King Jalanopi," said Gruening. He turned and conversed with his companions in low tones for a minute, then faced Jalanopi again. "We accede to your conditions, King Jalanopi. A team of forty surveyors will land here the day after tomorrow, and we will place their security in your hands."

"I accept this burden," said Jalanopi formally.

"And the Canphorites?"

"Soon they will leave."

"How soon?" asked Gruening.

"When it pleases me to send them away."

"They are a duplicitous race, King Jalanopi. If I were you, I would keep them under constant surveillance."

"I thank you for your advice."

There was a brief silence.

"Perhaps," continued Jalanopi, "your surveyors had better bring another thousand weapons with them, that we may better protect them from the Canphorites."

"We have total faith in your ability to protect us with the weapons you have," said Gruening.

"But *I* do not," answered Jalanopi. "I will require one thousand more weapons to guarantee your team's safety."

"McFarley!" snapped Gruening, turning to the translator. "This is blackmail! You tell him so!"

"That might not be wise, sir," responded McFarley.

"We won't be held up by this savage!" continued Gruening. "We've played by the rules, we've fulfilled our end of the bargain, and now he's trying to hold us up again! If we go home empty-handed, I guarantee we'll be back in force!"

"You won't go home empty-handed," said McFarley.

"What are you talking about?"

"You're facing more than a thousand of his warriors, armed with Republic weapons. If you don't agree to his demands, you'll never make it to the ship."

Gruening suddenly became aware of his surroundings. A single avian screeched in the upper terraces of Jalanopi's tree as the diplomat looked from one savage reptilian face to another.

"Surely he doesn't think he can get away with killing us!" he said at last.

"I've come to know him very well during the year I've been here," answered McFarley. "I think he is convinced he *can* kill you. He'll kill me as well, and blame the whole thing on the Canphorites. All that will happen is that the Republic will give him more weapons to protect himself against the Canphorites who are on the planet, and perhaps go to war with Canphor itself."

"By God, they'd *do* it, too!" muttered Gruening slowly.

"He's a clever bastard for an animated snake that walks around half-naked."

"Do not make the mistake of underestimating him, sir," said McFarley.

"That wasn't Paratoka he killed, either, was it?"

"I am not at liberty to say, sir," replied McFarley.

"So he speaks Terran?"

"No, sir, but *somebody* does."

Gruening looked around at the assembled Tulabete, trying fruitlessly to spot the Terran-speaker.

"Just whose side are you on, McFarley?"

"I'm on the side of peace," answered McFarley. "But if I have to tilt to one side or the other, I usually favor the underdog."

"All right," said Gruening. "The old bastard's got us over a barrel. Tell him we agree to all his conditions."

McFarley did as he was instructed.

"You had quite a conversation with him, Man Andrew," said Jalanopi, his lips slightly parted. "I assume you were explaining his options to him."

"His lack of options," McFarley corrected him.

"What more shall I demand of him, I wonder?" mused Jalanopi.

"If you push him hard enough, he'll leave."

"That would not be wise."

"Oh, he'll promise to give you everything you ask for, but he'll send in the Navy instead. If I were you, I'd quit while I was ahead."

"But you are not me," answered Jalanopi. His tongue flicked out and captured an insect. He chewed it thoughtfully for a moment, then looked up. "Ask him how he intends to pay us if we allow him to take our metal from our hills."

"We can pay in the Republic credit, or any of the 1,279 currencies currently accepted by the worlds of the Republic," answered Gruening promptly.

"What is a credit?" asked Jalanopi.

"A unit of barter," answered Gruening.

"Like our Tallgrazers?" asked Jalanopi, indicating a herd of the animals in a nearby pasture.

Gruening smiled. "The credit comes in paper form, like this." He pulled some bills out of his wallet and held them up for Jalanopi to see.

"That is not acceptable," answered Jalanopi. "It would take millions of them to make one Tallgrazer."

"Actually, you could buy a Tallgrazer for about two hundred of them, I should think," said Gruening.

Jalanopi shook his head. "Not from the Tulabete. And once you have obtained these credits, what do you do with them? Can you extract the marrow from their bones?"

Gruening tried to give Jalanopi a rudimentary education in economics, but the king would have none of it.

"It will not work, Man Gruening," he announced at last. "If I were to go among the Rakko and the Fani, or even my own people, and offer them your pieces of paper in exchange for their Tallgrazers, they would think me crazy."

"Then what *do* you want in payment?" asked Gruening.

"I will decide when the time comes," answered Jalanopi. He got to his feet, towering over them. "Now you will join me for the midday meal, and then you will return to your Republic and send me both your surveyors and your arms."

The meal was a disaster, as both McFarley and Jalanopi had known it would be, but the Tulabete king was enjoying his visitors' discomfort too much to cut it short. When they had finally reboarded their ship and were racing out of orbit, McFarley again approached Jalanopi.

"I would have thought Paratoka would have learned *something* about a cash economy during his time in the Republic," he said.

"He did."

"Perhaps he and I can clarify it for you now."

"Why bother?" replied Jalanopi. "I already understand it."

"Then—"

"If they give me credits, Man Andrew," said Jalanopi, as if speaking to a schoolchild, "they will never allow me to spend those credits on weapons; they will remain here until the paper rots. Therefore, I will play the fool until they decide that the only fee I will accept for our metal is more weaponry."

"Just who do you intend to use all this firepower against?" asked McFarley.

"Initially, the Rakko and the Fani. Then the other tribes. And eventually, if they prove to be too bothersome, I will use them against the Men who come to my world."

"That would be a mistake."

"I have no quarrel with your race, Man Andrew," said Jalanopi. "In fact, we are very much alike. I know how their minds work, I know what motivates them. But between us, there is a difference."

"And what is that?" asked McFarley.

"They crave money and power. I, who have no use for money, crave only power. If I can use them to secure my power on Karimon, they may use me to secure their money."

"And what of *their* craving for power?"

Jalanopi's lips parted with a slight hissing sound. "Let them exercise it over worlds that do not understand them as well as I do. We will be partners, Men and my people . . . but *I* will be the senior partner."

McFarley smiled grimly. "I wish you luck, Jalanopi."

"You think they will take advantage of me, do you not?"

"Yes, I do."

"It is good of you to warn me."

"I have not warned you, Jalanopi," said McFarley, "for I have no idea how they will do so. I have merely answered your question."

"Is this not disloyal to your own race?" asked Jalanopi, always trying to learn more about his enemy.

"To my race, perhaps. To my God, no. He teaches us to love our neighbors."

"At the cost of betraying your own people?"

"I have betrayed no one, Jalanopi," answered McFarley. "Nothing I can say to either side will make any difference in the long run. This scene has been played out many thousands of times on many thousands of worlds. Many of them had monarchs who thought they knew how to manipulate the race of Man, but almost all of them are now members of the Republic."

"*Almost* all," said Jalanopi. "Some were different. So shall I be."

"I wouldn't count on it, my friend," said McFarley. "Today you won. If I were you, I would savor it, for your victories over Man will be few and far between."

Jalanopi paused thoughtfully. "What will they do next?" he asked.

"Next? They'll bring in their surveyors and make sure your world is worth their effort."

"And if it is?" said Jalanopi. "Then what?"

"I don't know," answered McFarley. "Men are very creative."

Six

I t took four months for Man's creativity to manifest itself; once they found out that the Tulabete's hills were
rich in gold, platinum, silver, copper, and fissionable materials, they pulled all their surveyors out.

Then disquieting news began to arrive. A village of Tulabete had been massacred by the Rakko on the southern
frontier of their territory. A party of warriors sent out to
examine the carnage had never reported back. The males
from a trio of large northeastern villages were killed by the
Fani, and more than three hundred females were stolen.
Tiny tribes that had never caused any trouble were suddenly attacking the Tulabete, and successfully.

Finally the word reached Jalanopi, as he sat brooding
beneath his tree: the Fani and the Rakko and the others
were all in possession of Republic weapons, in far greater
quantity than the Tulabete possessed.

Jalanopi accepted the challenge, marched his men out
to war, and engaged the enemy. It was only due to his
superior generalship that he came away with a draw—a
very expensive draw, both in terms of warriors and weapons
lost. Two weeks later he committed to another battle, only

to discover that his enemy had been resupplied. He re-treated back to the heart of his kingdom, there to consider his options.

For two days and two nights he sat alone beneath his tree, lost in thought. Finally he summoned McFarley.

"You were right, Man Andrew," he said bitterly. "Men are more creative than I had anticipated."

"I am sorry, Jalanopi," said McFarley sincerely.

"It is both too late and too early for regrets," replied Jalanopi. "I must contact your Republic and make the best deal I can."

"My radio is at your disposal."

"Tell them I must have more weapons, and that I am willing to cede them the rights to take the metal from my hills if they will agree to stop arming my enemies."

"I will do so immediately," replied McFarley, hurrying off to his church.

He returned some twenty minutes later.

"Well?" asked Jalanopi.

"Let us say that your request was not unanticipated," said McFarley wryly.

"What was their response?"

"They have leased all mineral rights on Karimon to the Spiral Arm Development Company, which is run by Violet Gardener. Have you ever heard of her?"

"No. She is a *female*?" The tone of his voice was clearly contemptuous.

"So I gather."

"What use is a female to me?"

"Money knows no gender," answered McFarley. "I gather she is prepared to sign a treaty with you, by which you will give her the mineral rights she craves and she will assure your primacy over the tribes of Karimon."

"What good is the promise of a female?" said Jalanopi. "Females are little better than Tallgrazers. If a warrior

wants one, he buys one. They have no brains. They are good only for preparing meals and producing babies."

"They have no *rights*," said McFarley, "which is quite a different thing than having no brains. You waste half of your race's potential by keeping them in such servitude." He paused. "Among my own race, females are treated as equals, and frequently prove themselves to be superior to males."

"This may be true of Men, Man Andrew," said Jalanopi firmly, "but not of the Tulabete. Our females are capable of nothing more complicated than cooking and weaving cloth."

"That is because the males rarely speak to them, and there is none among them capable of teaching them more. I assure you, Jalanopi, that there is no difference in ability between a newborn Tulabete male and a newborn Tulabete female, only in opportunity."

"With my own spear I have killed many Wildfangs and Nightkillers," said Jalanopi. "What Tulabete female could do that?"

"I do not know," answered McFarley. "Nor will *you* ever know what they are capable of doing, as long as you treat them no better than you treat your Tallgrazers." He paused for a moment. "Besides . . ."

"I know . . . I have no choice," said Jalanopi. His facial muscles contracted spasmodically, forcing a greasy fluid to the surface.

Long after McFarley had left, Jalanopi remained motionless, wondering if he would be the last king of the Tulabete to sit beneath his tree. Eventually his natural confidence reasserted itself, and he began thinking of ways to manipulate this female that the Republic had seen fit to reward with *his* hills.

II

GARDENER'S DREAM

Seven

Her name was Violet Gardener, and though she was hardly the seventh son of a seventh son, she was something quite special the day she was born: the only child of a father who'd made half a dozen fortunes mining the Frontier Worlds before he'd settled down in the heart of the Republic, and a mother who had tried her hand at acting, playwriting, and poetry, and been successful at all three. Great things were expected of the child of Lawrence Gardener and Belore Ivor, and she did her best not to disappoint.

She grew up on Lundquist IV, a gentle green world that was almost a bedroom suburb of Deluros VIII, the huge planet which was already on the brink of becoming the capital world of the race of Man. Her grades were such that not even her exceptional parents could object, and she excelled in most sports, though none truly interested her. She possessed bright red hair and a temper to match, and spent a goodly portion of her time trying to keep it under control or coping with the consequences of it.

When she was seventeen, she went to the university planet of Aristotle, from which she emerged seven years

later armed with degrees in literature, metallurgy (her father had insisted), and political science, but still with no serious notion of what to *do* with her life.

She made the social scene on Deluros VIII and Earth and the other fashionable worlds of the race of Man for the next two years. It was said that she had taken a string of lovers, but if so, she was discreet enough that none of them were ever identified. It was also said that she twice enlisted herself in detoxification programs, but there no records to prove *that*, either. It is known that she briefly underwent analysis to learn to control her emotional outbursts; it is assumed the sessions were successful, because she never returned.

Then, as she drifted through the worlds of the Republic, trying her hand at this and that, never quite satisfied with her life, something happened. Her many biographers still disagree about the event, but something convinced her to return to Aristotle for another two years, after which she emerged with one more degree—cartography—and a driving sense of purpose.

Man's expansion through the galaxy had always been inward, toward the Core. Born on the Spiral Arm, where the stars are not closely clustered, he had moved farther and farther from his home planet, finally choosing Deluros VIII as his new headquarters world. He had meticulously assembled his empire in a number of lines of political, economic, and military conquest, each stretching out from the Deluros system. He had pushed toward the Core of the galaxy, the worlds of the so-called Inner Frontier, and toward the galactic Rim—the worlds of the Outer Frontier— but for some reason, probably simply the unthinkably vast scope of his operation, he had never made much headway in the Spiral Arm from which he had come.

At age twenty-nine, Violet Gardener set out to change that.

She had a vision—a dream, if you will—of expanding

Man's empire throughout the Spiral Arm. Her knowledge of cartography had shown her the most practical way of achieving her goal, for cartography had become an almost political science, dealing not only with maps but with alien races and lines of transport and power. Her studies of politics, especially interstellar and alien politics, imbued her with the requisite knowledge for dealing with human and alien governments alike. Her knowledge of mining, plus the occasional advice she sought from her aging, planetbound, but still mentally alert father, showed her a way to make her dream pay its own way. And her own intelligence and all-consuming drive—some biographers have implied that it was merely her wild temper, properly directed and channeled—made her initial successes almost inevitable.

While most of Man's expansion up to this point in his galactic history had been undertaken by and for the military, it was Violet Gardener who convinced the Republic to lease her the economic rights to seventeen star systems in the Spiral Arm, and she acted as almost a private arm of Mankind's empire-building machine. She was not concerned with lines of military force, but rather with lines of economic dependence and communication. By the age of thirty-two, her dream was no longer an ephemeral vision, but a logical, rational, well-reasoned 672-page tract that was almost a bible to her subordinates, explaining as it did precisely why seventeen specific star systems would spread Man's influence throughout the Arm, how and in what order each of the systems must be approached, the cost of each conquest, and the profit potential therein.

Violet began with Pirelli and Doxus II, a pair of seemingly insignificant, totally uninhabited oxygen planets whose sole function was to serve as fuel and munitions suppliers. Then she moved on to Castlestone, a planet rich in gemstones and fissionable materials. It took her three years to introduce a monied economy among the intelligent marsupials she found there, and though the exports

from her mines on Castlestone were more than enough to capitalize her next few ventures, she had contracted both cancer (which was curable) and a very rare blood disease (which probably wasn't) in the interim. Always a realist, she decided that Time was her one irreplaceable commodity, and that she couldn't afford to spend as much as three years on any one world.

She refined and brutalized her approach on Narabella and again on Sugarmoon—an oxygen satellite of the huge, gaseous Borgo XI—and by the time she set her sights on Goldstone, the true cornerstone upon which she meant to build her little trading empire, she was prepared for any eventuality.

What she found when she landed was a primitive humanoid race, its various nations constantly at war, totally devoid of a monied economy. After two meetings with leaders of the most powerful nations had proven fruitless, she began working in concert with the Navy, bringing about various improvements in the inhabitants' lifestyles. They built bridges and roads, imported fertilizer and hybrid crops, even brought in a team of exobiologists to provide the inhabitants with sophisticated medical care.

It didn't take long for the natives of Goldstone to adapt to the innovations that had made their harsh lives more bearable, and during the interim she opened up two more worlds. Then one day, without any warning, all humans left Goldstone, all aid stopped, and most of the improvements upon which the inhabitants now depended began to crumble.

The leaders of the various nations sought her out—she had always made herself available to them—and begged her to restore what had been taken away from them. She explained that such benefits cost money, and that the Republic had cut off all funds to the Spiral Arm. Since they did not possess a monied economy, they obviously could not give her the money required to buy their way out of

their current predicament. She sympathized with them, of course, but what could she do?

There followed a month of negotiations. Goldstone was willing to move to a currency-based economy, but the governments had no tax base since the civilian population had no way of earning money. Violet listened thoughtfully to their problem, then announced that she might have a solution: if they would cede to her all mining rights to Goldstone's mineral wealth, she would pay them a stipend of ten million credits per year or ten percent of her profits, whichever was greater. Furthermore, if they would guarantee her a work force of two million native miners to begin with, gradually increasing to an eventual five million, she would pay their salaries, in the amount of thirty credits per worker a week, with more for supervisors, thus creating a tax base for the government. With these two sources of revenue, the government could, in one enormous leap, move to a monied economy and would be able to afford to bring back the conveniences and necessities that had heretofore been supplied gratis by the Republic.

Within a year, Goldstone's mines were operating around the clock, more were being opened up daily, and Violet Gardener was wealthy beyond her wildest dreams. But her dreams were not of wealth, but of a human empire stretching from one end of the Spiral Arm to the other, and she realized that she still had work to do.

And so, standing on the roof of her recently erected office building, she turned her eyes skyward and saw, flickering faintly in the distance, two yellow stars around which circled two planets that she planned to assimilate into her financial empire. Though she had never set foot on either of them, she knew them as well as she knew the reflection of her own face, grown tanned from the sun and lean from disease, in the mirror.

Before long, *they* would know *her* even better.

Eight

"Throw Jalanopi's image up on the holoscreen," ordered Violet Gardener, sitting at the head of the table in her spaceship's conference room.

"Working . . . done," announced the computer.

As the image appeared, the overhead lights automatically dimmed and the portholes that looked out at the galaxy became opaque. Violet sat at one end of a long chrome table that was magnetically linked to the metallic floor of the conference room; six men and three women were clustered at the other end. "He looks like a snake with limbs," she remarked.

"Well, he *thinks* a lot like a Man," said Arthur Gruening bitterly. "He's a cagey old bastard."

"Yes," said Violet dryly, making no attempt to hide her contempt for Gruening; he was not in her employ but the Republic's and was therefore instantly classified as both an incompetent and a spy. "I understand he more than held his own with you."

Although barely five feet tall, her bright red hair turned an unstylish gray, and a sallow tint to her skin that reflected the early stages of her blood disease, her displeasure still inspired a sense of terror in her subordinates.

"What could I do?" said Gruening defensively. "The Republic had tied my hands. I wasn't authorized to act until the Spiral Arm Development Company signed its lease with the Republic and took control of Karimon." He smiled. "The poor devil doesn't know what he's in for."

"Linus?" said Violet, turning to Linus Rawls, a tall, lean mustached man who sat slumped in a chair, his formal outfit already wrinkled, a smokeless cigarette dangling from his lips. He'd been with her for almost ten years, and was the only one in the room who was unafraid of her, or at least able to keep his fears to himself.

"Yes?"

"Tell me about the inhabitants."

"*I* can do that, Madam Gardener," said Gruening.

"I'd rather hear about them from someone who has lived with them for a few months than from a man who was outmaneuvered in his only meeting with them."

"I've already explained that to you—" began Gruening petulantly.

"Yes, you have," said Violet. "Therefore, you've no need to do it again. Linus?"

"Well," said Rawls, "I spent three months hunting the northern part of Jalanopi's kingdom with Fuentes, as per your instructions. The game is phenomenal: they've something called a Redmountain that—"

"I'm not interested in the animals, Linus," she interrupted.

"Sorry," said Rawls. He swallowed and began again. "We used a batch of snakes as gun bearers, cooks, skinners, trackers, camp boys, everything, so I got to know some of 'em pretty well. By and large, they're a pretty malleable lot."

"You call them snakes?"

"Fuentes does, so I picked it up. They don't live in huts or houses, you know; they slither into these twisted, serpentine mounds when they go to sleep, and they've got tongues

you wouldn't believe. They can pick an insect out of the air at twenty inches. Strange voices, too: they hiss a lot."

"They look humanoid," noted Violet.

"Well, *I* wouldn't call them human. They spend a lot of time in the water, and in those crazy mounds, and no human ever ate what the Tulabete eat."

"Minor differences," she said with a shrug. "How strong are they?"

"Well, Jalanopi can probably mount an army of twenty thousand on a week's notice. As for the others . . ."

Violet shook her head. "No, I meant how strong is an *individual* snake?"

"They can lift a pretty heavy load."

"Their shoulders seem very narrow and somewhat sloped."

Rawls nodded his head. "Yeah, I guess they are."

"Good. We'll give them .975-caliber projectile rifles."

"Madam Gardener, they can't shoot straight with the hand weapons we *gave* them," said Rawls. "They'll never learn to shoot those. For one thing, even Fuentes' bearers haven't figured out, after all the years they've been with him, that jerking the trigger as hard as they can doesn't make the bullet go any faster." He paused. "All that's going to happen is that they're going to take one shot, blow a huge hole in something they weren't aiming at, and have the recoil break a shoulder."

Violet stared at him expressionlessly. "What is your point, Linus?"

He stared back at her, and suddenly he grinned. "No point, Madam Gardener. Just an observation."

"Jalanopi will doubtless want weapons from us," she said. "I see no reason why we shouldn't give him the most powerful rifles available." She turned to another assistant. "Mr. Lohmeyer, I believe you have the surveyor's reports?"

A gray-haired, nattily dressed man got to his feet. "Yes, Madam Gardener. Gold in profusion, some platinum,

huge copper deposits, some rare stones; we haven't come across any diamonds yet, but we know they're there."

"Fissionable materials?"

"There may be some uranium beyond the mountain range on the Tulabetes' southern border. We didn't get a chance to thoroughly explore it, but the geologic conditions seem right for it."

"How long before we can make the planet start paying for itself?"

Lohmeyer furrowed his brow as he considered the various factors. "I can't see it showing a profit for at least five years, Madam Gardener. We're starting from scratch here: no industry, no commerce, no spaceport, no dwellings or conveniences for the human supervisors. Everything will have to be built or imported. There's not much water in those mountains, either; we're going to have to find a source and divert it. And all that is assuming we don't have problems organizing a local work force." He shook his head. "No, I can't see us showing a serious profit any sooner, and my estimate may well be optimistic."

"That's not soon enough, Mr. Lohmeyer," replied Violet.

"Actually, I don't know how we can do it any faster, given the conditions we are presented with," answered Lohmeyer.

"You have your timetable, and I have mine," answered Violet, who had not shared the information that her blood disease, while not an immediate threat to her life, was incurable, and would leave her weaker and less able to stand the frenetic pace of her life with each passing year. "I have made it my business and my destiny to bring the Spiral Arm under Man's control, and I cannot allow each world to take five years to pay for itself."

"I would be happy to entertain any suggestions concerning how you think we might put Karimon on a paying basis in less time," said Lohmeyer.

"Simple," said Violet. "We open it for colonization—not only to farmers, but to miners. We will bring in our equipment and put our own people to work, but we will also allow any Man to put in a claim in exchange for a certain percentage of his profits."

"*What* percentage?" asked Rawls curiously.

"A fifty-fifty split, I think."

"Fifty-fifty?"

"That's right."

"How many miners will buy *that*, I wonder?" said Rawls with a chuckle.

"Anyone who wants to mine the world will," answered Violet. "Otherwise we will mine the entire planet ourselves; it will take longer, but we'll be richer for the waiting." She paused. "I think you can count on any number of miners signing up. Doubtless some farmers, too, since the miners will need food."

"We thought we'd open up Belamaine for farming," put in Gruening. "It *looks* like a sister planet to Karimon, but the only mineral deposits it has in any quantity are copper and iron. There's enough of a galactic market for copper that we can turn the concession over to the planetary government in exchange for farming rights on their northern continent. It's all but uninhabited, and the climate and soil samples indicate an excellent farming world."

Violet shook her head. "You don't understand these native races, Mr. Gruening. They have no monied economies, and precious little use for metals . . . but they understand the value of *land*. We will begin mining the copper on Belamaine, and we will open shops for our miners. As always, with planets controlled by the Spiral Arm Development Company, barter will not be acceptable in any of our stores. Once the natives understand that there is money to be made in mining, and things to spend it on, they will demand their mines back. We will give them some, in exchange for agricultural concessions, and we will create jobs

for them in the mines that we still control." She grimaced contemptuously. "No wonder the Republic has had to go to war so often. You must understand the people you plan to subjugate, Mr. Gruening."

"You've had your share of little battles, too, Madam Gardener," he replied defensively.

"True," she replied. "But never at the outset. Never before we were ready for them, or before a substantial number of the native populace was enlightened enough to fight on *our* side. You don't waste Men in a war with aliens if you can enlist other aliens to fight on your side." She stared coldly at him. "And you don't decimate entire worlds to the point where they are of no economic value to the Republic. Otherwise they become just so many meaningless numbers added to your total, rather than functioning, economically integrated cogs of a vast human machine."

Gruening shifted uneasily in his chair. "This is not the best time for a political debate," he suggested.

Rawls chuckled aloud. "On Madam Gardener's ship, it's time for anything she wants it to be time for."

Violet turned to Rawls. "Thank you, Linus, but Mr. Gruening is quite right. Our purpose is to determine what actions we will take in regard to Belamaine and especially to Karimon."

They discussed the matter for another hour, at which time her pilot announced that they had entered orbit around Karimon and would be landing momentarily.

"Do you want to meet Jalanopi in his village, or would you rather he came to you?" asked Rawls.

"We're dealing from strength," answered Violet, studying Jalanopi's holograph once more. "Let's leave him a little dignity among his people and go to him."

Rawls nodded, and set about organizing a landing party.

The ship touched down about three miles from Jalanopi's village, and a few moments later a trio of sleek

groundcars carrying Violet Gardener and her party emerged from the hold and began driving toward Jalanopi's tree.

"Very pretty planet," commented Violet.

"To tell the truth, I'd have been happy to stay out in the bush another three or four months with Fuentes," replied Rawls with a smile. "It's a lovely world. Exquisite scenery, and some truly fabulous big game."

"I believe I saw an enormous waterfall as we were coming down from orbit," remarked Violet. "It seemed almost four miles wide, though I could be mistaken about the size."

"Yes, I know the place. It's along the Karimona River, an awesome sight. They say you can hear it from as far as twenty miles away."

"Has it got a name?" she asked.

"The natives call it Doratule."

"An evocative name. What does it mean?"

"Thundermist."

She wrinkled her nose. "This is going to be a human world. It ought to have a human name."

"Have you one in mind?"

She was silent for a moment. "Did Johnny Ramsey ever hunt on Karimon after he resigned as Secretary of the Republic?"

"No," answered Rawls. "I believe he confined his hunting to Peponi and one or two other worlds, all closer to the Core."

"All right," said Violet. "Let's call it Ramsey Falls. It's a nice way to honor a good politician—and who knows? If he hears about it, he might take a hunting trip here and write it up in his memoirs. A little publicity never hurts."

"I've been meaning to speak to you about that," said Rawls.

"About Johnny Ramsey?"

He shook his head. "About hunting."

She smiled. "It sounds like Mr. Fuentes has a convert."

"You've never seen game like this, Madam Gardener," he said, trying to control his enthusiasm. "Redmountains twenty feet tall, carnivores like Wildfangs and Nightkillers, behemoths like Horndevils—it's a hunter's paradise." He paused uneasily. "So I was thinking . . . well, you don't really need me to manage the mining concession, and . . ."

"And?"

"I'd like to take a couple of years to set up a hunting industry on the planet. I found that I really enjoyed the time I spent with Fuentes. I think a string of lodges and camps, properly advertised back in the Republic, would quickly return your investment."

She considered the notion for a long moment. "That might not be a bad idea, Linus. It would get us written up in some of the popular journals, it would create a need for hotels and all the other businesses connected with the safari industry; it would probably even make a second spaceport cost-efficient." She paused. "How long will the game hold out?"

"I beg your pardon?"

"How long before you kill it all, or leave so little alive that we have to create parks and start selling the climate and the view?"

"No problem, Madam Gardener," said Rawls confidently. "The game will last forever." He pointed to a trio of gazelle-like creatures grazing a quarter mile away, oblivious to the groundcars. "See those Fleetjumpers there? When I was with Fuentes, I saw a herd of them that was so large it took a full day to pass by."

"Nothing lasts forever, Linus," she replied. "I've been to many worlds like this one. In less than half a century they change from planets with islands of natives in a sea of animals to isolated islands of protected animals in a sea of natives."

"That can't happen here," he assured her. "You can't

imagine the sheer *quantity* of game out there on the plains."

"It happens everywhere," she replied. "Just make sure that we're prepared for it."

"I'll make sure," he said earnestly. "I'd like to run it myself, once we get the mining operation set up."

"I assume you'll want a percentage?"

"I'll earn it," he assured her.

She nodded. "All right. Are you happy now, Linus?"

"Yes, Madam Gardener."

"Then perhaps you'll start concentrating on our upcoming meeting with Jalanopi. I think we're almost there."

The three groundcars came to a stop about one hundred yards from Jalanopi's tree, which had been visible for the past five miles. The king, clad in his headdress, was sitting on his serpentine throne, surrounded by Paratoka and his other advisors. Andrew McFarley stood off to his left, some ten feet away.

Violet waited while the door was opened for her. Then, striding between two of her bodyguards, and followed by the rest of her party, she approached Jalanopi, stopping fifteen feet from him.

McFarley stepped forward.

"Good morning, Madam Gardener," he said. "I am the Reverend Andrew McFarley. Jalanopi has asked me to serve as his translator."

"I'm pleased to meet you, Reverend," said Violet, extending her hand. "How long have you been on Karimon?"

"A little less than two years," he replied.

"And how do you find the climate and the natives?"

"I find both to be admirable."

She smiled. "Do I detect a note of partisanship, Reverend McFarley?"

"I know what you plan to do to this world," he said. "I've seen it before, and I don't like it."

"Reverend McFarley, outside of saving your friend

Jalanopi from his foolishness and implementing a mining concession, even *I* don't know what I plan to do with this world."

"Why don't you just leave them alone?" he demanded.

She arched an eyebrow. "Why don't you?"

"I bring them the word of the Lord," he said. "I don't rape and plunder their planet."

"Just their minds," suggested Violet. "You will bring them guilt and shame. I propose to bring them the more positive benefits of human civilization. We shall see who does the most harm in the long run."

McFarley seemed about to say something else, then evidently thought better of it, and Violet turned to Jalanopi.

"King Jalanopi," she said, shielding her eyes against a sudden gust of wind that brought a cloud of fine reddish dust with it. "I am Violet Gardener, representing the Spiral Arm Development Company. I am delighted to make your acquaintance."

"I am pleased to meet you, Man Violet," said Jalanopi, once her message had been translated. "Welcome to Mastaboni."

Violet turned to McFarley. "Mastaboni?"

"The name of his village," answered McFarley.

"What does it mean?"

" 'The Killing Place'," said McFarley. "It is where his grandfather's people were slaughtered."

She made no comment, and turned back to Jalanopi. "You know why we are here, of course?"

"Yes, Man Violet," he replied. "I know why you are here. You have brought weapons?"

"I have brought weapons," she replied. "And more."

"More?" replied Jalanopi. "I did not ask for anything more than weapons."

"It is a gift of friendship," said Violet.

"And what is this gift?" he asked suspiciously, flicking out his tongue to capture an errant flying insect.

"We wish to be your friends," answered Violet. "Friends do not let other friends suffer needlessly. So along with bringing you five hundred weapons for your own warriors, I have instructed the Spiral Arm Development Company to transfer five thousand members of our private security force to Karimon. Your enemies are our enemies, and we will fight beside you until they have been subdued."

"I requested no help, only weapons," protested Jalanopi.

Violet smiled at him. "What are friends for?"

"How long will your security forces remain on Karimon?" asked Jalanopi.

"For as long as it takes to establish you as the most powerful king of the most powerful nation on the planet."

Jalanopi listened to the translation, then turned to McFarley.

"Does she speak the truth, Man Andrew?" he asked as one hundred feet above his head a Tailswinger family suddenly began screeching at a golden lizard that was scurrying up the huge trunk of the tree.

"Yes, she does," answered McFarley. "But she does not speak the *whole* truth."

"And what is that?"

"You will be the most powerful king of the most powerful tribe on Karimon," said McFarley. "But you must remember that she is not a king, and the Spiral Arm Development Company is not a tribe or a nation."

Jalanopi considered the human's remark for a moment.

"She expects me to be her puppet, then?"

"In essence."

"And I must agree, must I not?" continued Jalanopi, closing his eyes as the warm wind brought another cloud of dust. "For if I refuse, she will then make the same offer to the king of the Fani." He stared at McFarley, who did not answer, and finally he spoke again. "I could kill them all right now."

"Then you will lose the war against the Fani and the

Rakko, a war you are in the process of losing right now. And there will be severe retribution for killing Violet Gardener."

"*How* severe?" asked Jalanopi, still considering his options.

"More severe than I hope you can imagine," answered McFarley. "You have no choice, Jalanopi."

"For the moment," answered Jalanopi. "I will make this treaty because I must, but I will study my enemy and search for weakness, just as the Nightkiller studies the herds of Twisthorns and seeks out the weakest. There must be weakness here as well, and I shall find it."

"You are defeated, my friend," said McFarley sadly. "You have never undergone anything like this before, but for Man—and especially for Violet Gardener—it is an almost daily occurrence. She has seen it all, and has devised ways to combat whatever you may do."

"She has not experienced Jalanopi before," said Jalanopi firmly. "The day will come when she will wish she never had. This I promise you, Man Andrew." He turned back to Violet. "Tell her that I am happy to accept her warriors, and that they will, of course, be under my command."

"She will never accept that, Jalanopi," said McFarley.

"Tell her anyway."

McFarley translated Jalanopi's statement.

"My forces have weapons and procedures that are unfamiliar to you, Jalanopi," replied Violet. "It would be far better for them to be placed under their own command."

"I insist that they obey *my* orders, since they fight for my tribe," said Jalanopi.

Violet stared down at two warring insects next to her foot and considered his demand for a long moment, then looked back at him and nodded her agreement. "If it is that important to you, they will be under your command."

"Are you sure that's a good idea, Madam Gardener?" whispered Gruening.

"Not now, Mr. Gruening!" she said abstractly, without taking her eyes from Jalanopi.

Gruening instantly fell silent.

"Now," continued Violet, "in exchange for our help, and as an act of friendship, you will cede sole mining rights on Karimon to the Spiral Arm Development Company."

"I appreciate your coming to my aid in this minor skirmish with my enemies," answered Jalanopi. "It is truly an act of friendship—" he paused, "—but hardly one that is deserving of my entire mineral wealth."

"We are prepared to pay for what we get."

"I am listening," said Jalanopi.

"First, for the sole right to mine your world, we will give you two thousand more weapons, the highest-powered projectile rifles yet invented by the race of Man," said Violet.

"What of your *other* weapons?" asked Jalanopi.

"Other weapons?"

"The ones Man Andrew has told me about, and that my advisor Paratoka saw when he visited your Republic: laser rifles, sonic pistols, molecular imploders."

"We are forbidden by law to give such weapons to members of any race that has not officially joined the Republic," she answered. "But I think you will find our help and our weapons quite sufficient to your needs." She paused. "In addition, we will give you five thousand credits on the first day of every month, for as long as we remain here."

"They do not yet possess a calendar, Madam Gardener," interjected McFarley.

"How do they determine the seasons?" she asked.

"The long rains and the short rains."

"Tell him that I will give him twenty-five thousand credits on the first day of the long rains and on the first day of

the short rains, for as long as Men continue to take minerals out of his hills."

McFarley did some quick mental computing and stared at her. "That's a very small drop in a very large bucket," he said.

"Are you the translator or the negotiator?" asked Violet irritably. "Tell him what I said."

McFarley translated her offer.

"What is your opinion, Man Andrew?" asked Jalanopi.

"It is a drop in the bucket."

"I do not understand."

"It is not enough."

"How much should I demand."

"A million credits before each rain," said McFarley. "The problem is, you've nothing to spend it on."

"I will find something," said Jalanopi, his lips parting.

"Oh?"

"Do not the Canphorites manufacture weapons also?" he asked.

McFarley turned back to Violet and relayed Jalanopi's counter-offer.

"*You* had something to do with this," said Violet disapprovingly.

McFarley stared at her without answering, and she continued: "For one thing, they only have three fingers on each hand. I find it highly unlikely they would have developed a decimal system, and without it, how would Jalanopi come up with such a nice, round number?"

"You're a very quick study, Madam Violet," acknowledged McFarley with a wry smile. "It took me almost a month before I realized how they counted things." Suddenly the smile vanished. "You haven't responded to his counter-offer yet."

"Believe it or not, Reverend McFarley, I have no wish to be your enemy or Jalanopi's," said Violet. "Tell him I agree

to his terms and will pay him one million credits or its
equivalent on the first day of each rain."

"Its equivalent?" said McFarley quickly. "In what—horse
manure, chlorine tablets, granite?"

"You are a very distrustful person," said Violet. "This is
a bad trait in a Man, and an especially bad trait in a man
of the cloth. I will pay the agreed-upon sum in Republic
credits or its equivalent currency."

"What's the catch?" asked McFarley.

"There's no catch. I am willing to write all this down in
our treaty with Jalanopi. In fact, my investors will insist
upon it. All agreements must be documented; I am sure
you will be happy to represent Jalanopi if he does not read
Terran."

"I will."

"I further assume that the Tulabete have no written
language?"

"That is correct."

"Then you will tell him I agree to his terms, and that we
will create a document and both sign our names to it.
There will be four copies of this treaty. He will keep one
copy, I will keep one copy, one copy will remain with the
Spiral Arm Development Company, and one copy be filed
with the Bureau of Alien Affairs on Deluros VIII."

McFarley presented the proposition to Jalanopi.

"It is the best deal you're going to get," he added on his
own. "I think you had better accept it."

"Where are these documents?" asked Jalanopi, looking
around, not quite sure what a "document" was.

"They will be created in Madam Gardener's ship once
you have agreed. Then she will return, we will go over the
treaty line by line and word by word so that there can be no
misunderstanding, and then, if both sides are in agreement, you will each put your mark upon each copy."

"And she is bound by the laws of Men to obey the
treaty?" asked Jalanopi.

"That is correct," said McFarley.

Jalanopi parted his lips again and emitted a high, hissing sound that McFarley couldn't interpret.

"I am bound by my laws, too," he said at last. "But between us there is a difference: I *make* my laws, and I can change them at my will," he said at last. "This female has much to learn, Man Andrew."

"I get the distinct impression that this female has almost nothing left to learn," said McFarley grimly.

He conveyed Jalanopi's agreement, the human party returned to the ship for an hour, and when they returned they had with them the documents that would legally empower the race of Man to begin mining the mineral wealth of Karimon.

Jalanopi made his mark on the treaties, Violet signed them, and then Paratoka and various humans, including McFarley, signed as witnesses. Before sunset Violet Gardener and her party were on their way to the nearby world of Belamaine and a call had been sent out for five thousand members of her security forces to be transferred from Goldstone to Karimon.

And nothing would ever be the same again.

Nine

I t was officially the Spiral Arm Development Company Security Force, but it quickly became known as The Column—and an impressive column it was, stretching for almost three miles.

Jalanopi had gone out to survey the situation on his northern frontier for himself and had brought McFarley along to translate. He did not like what he saw and immediately sent for Linus Rawls.

"Man Linus," he said harshly, "I demand an explanation. We agreed to the presence of five thousand Men. There are at least thirty thousand here, and my advisors tell me that there is an equal number marching to the south against the Rakko."

"If you'll read the treaty carefully, as we did," answered Rawls easily, "you'll see that we promised to provide a security force of five thousand men, and so we did. There are three thousand here, prepared to do battle with the Fani as soon as their orders come through, and two thousand more to the south of us, ready to secure Jalanopi's kingdom against the Rakko."

"I tell you there is a minimum of thirty thousand soldiers

here!" insisted McFarley, without waiting for Jalanopi to reply.

Rawls looked out across the broad savannah, where his men were encamped for the midday meal.

"You are mistaken, Reverend McFarley," said Rawls. "There are only three thousand members of the security force here. All the rest are functioning as support, not soldiers."

"What's the difference?"

"Only the soldiers will do the actual fighting," replied Rawls. "That was our agreement, and we intend to keep it to the letter. The rest of these men are drivers, cooks, doctors, supply clerks, and the like. Many of them aren't even armed."

"And two or three days from now, when you've defeated the Fani and the Rakko, they all become miners, is that it?"

"Oh, I would think some of them will become farmers," drawled Rawls. "If I were you, I'd be more worried about the battle lasting more than two days."

"With *your* armaments?" said McFarley with a contemptuous laugh.

"We haven't made contact with the Fani yet," noted Rawls. "Our best information is that they're almost two hundred miles north and west of here, and that they're beating up Jalanopi's forces pretty badly."

"When will you meet them in battle?"

"As soon as we're ordered to," answered Rawls. "Read your treaty."

He went off to the mess tent to order lunch.

"You foresaw this, Man Andrew?" asked Jalanopi, when McFarley had explained the gist of the conversation to him.

"Not quite," answered McFarley. "I knew they were duplicitous. I just didn't know what form it would take."

"*I* foresaw it, when they allowed Men to come under my command," said Jalanopi.

"I'm afraid there's not much you can do."

"I can order them to attack."

"I don't know their codes," replied McFarley. "And you may be sure everything will be scrambled."

"What does that mean?"

"It means I can't radio orders to them."

"They are right here," said Jalanopi. "I will give them orders, and you will translate."

"I do not think they will obey you," said McFarley.

"They *must.* It is in their precious treaty. Summon Man Linus; he will support me."

"I doubt it."

"Are you my friend or my enemy?" demanded Jalanopi.

"I am your friend. You know that."

"Then summon Man Linus."

McFarley went off to the mess tent and returned with Rawls.

"What can I do for you, Jalanopi?" asked Rawls pleasantly.

"Bring me the highest-ranking officer among all those present," ordered Jalanopi.

"This is a security force, not an army," answered Rawls. "We don't have officers."

"You are playing with words," said Jalanopi. "Bring me the soldier who commands all the others."

"Certainly," said Rawls. He summoned a stocky, bearded, gray-haired man, who walked over and snapped to attention. "Jalanopi, this is Chester Michaels, the man you wished to speak to."

"Man Chester," said Jalanopi, "you are aware of the treaty I signed with Man Violet?"

"I haven't read it, but I know the gist of it, sir," replied Michaels.

"You know that your army is under my control?"

"I don't have an army, sir," answered Michaels. "I have a security force."

"It is the same thing. You are under my command."

"That is my understanding of the situation, sir," said Michaels.

"Then I order you to attack the Fani."

"Certainly, sir." Michaels looked around the barren savannah. "Where are they, sir?"

"They are to the north and west!"

Michaels shaded his eyes and looked northwest. "I don't see anything, sir."

"They are two hundred miles away," said Jalanopi.

"I'm afraid I'll need a more exact location then that, sir," replied Michaels. "Two hundred miles to the north and west is too vague. It encompasses literally hundreds of square miles, sir."

"Are you refusing my order, Man Chester?"

"Absolutely not, sir," said Michaels. "If you'll pinpoint the enemy's location, I will be happy to lead an attack against them."

"You have machines that can locate them."

"That is true, sir," said Michaels. "They are currently under your command. If you would like to examine them, sir, and thereby locate the enemy, the attack can proceed immediately."

"I cannot read the machines, and while Man Andrew can operate a radio, he tells me that he does not possess the necessary codes."

"Well, that does present a bit of a problem, sir."

"I order you to give him the codes."

"That would be a breach of security, sir. Reverend McFarley is neither a Tulabete nor a member of our force. I would be happy to give the codes to *you*, sir. They are quite complex, but once you have written them down—I assume you know how to read and write, sir?—I cannot legally stop you from turning them over to anyone you choose, including Reverend McFarley."

Jalanopi waited for McFarley's translation, glared at

Rawls and Michaels through his orange cat's-eyes, worked the muscles in his face until it was covered by a clear secretion, and stalked off, followed by McFarley.

"What would you have done if he could read and write?" asked Rawls curiously.

Michaels grinned. "Even if he *did* read and write, he only speaks snake, not Terran."

"Well, enjoy your lunch and get your men ready to move," said Rawls, returning his smile. "I have a feeling that our green-skinned friend is undergoing what we in the trade call 'an agonizing reappraisal'."

"Yes, sir," said Michaels, saluting smartly and returning to the mess tent.

Twenty minutes later Jalanopi ceded control of the column to Linus Rawls, who immediately turned over all operations to Chester Michaels and his aides.

Rawls returned to Mastaboni with Jalanopi and McFarley, where he kept in constant communication with both the northern and southern segments of the column. It took exactly four days for the security forces to subdue the Rakko, and two days after that the Fani surrendered. Eleven thousand inhabitants of the planet had died, with about twice that many wounded; only four Men were killed, three of them by errant bullets from the high-velocity rifles which had been delivered to the Tulabete.

The column regrouped about fifty miles outside of Mastaboni and remained there for a month until Rawls was sure there would be no further uprisings among Jalanopi's enemies. Then the security forces returned to Goldstone, and some of their "support troops" dispersed to other worlds. The bulk of them, over twenty thousand in number, opted to remain on Karimon, filing mining claims, establishing huge farms on the vast plains to the east and west of Mastaboni, starting small businesses, or simply occupy-

ing themselves by hunting the vast array of animals that stalked the plains and hills of Karimon.

Violet Gardener returned six weeks after the war, with a treaty from neighboring Belamaine securely tucked away in her safe on Goldstone.

"How are things proceeding?" she asked as Rawls came out to greet her as she emerged from her ship.

"About on schedule," he answered. "The bad snakes have been pacified, and the good snakes are starting to get an inkling of what a credit will buy them. I think within two years' time we won't have to import any food, either; there were more would-be farmers in the column than I had anticipated. We may even be able to start exporting grain in four or five years."

"Good," she replied. "Pirelli, Doxus II, and Castlestone can always use more grain. Nothing grows there except rocks." She paused. "How is our friend Jalanopi taking all this?"

"I think he's adjusting. He is, after all, the king of all he surveys—as long as he doesn't look in any Man's direction," said Rawls with a smile. "How did things go on Belamaine?"

"A bit of a slaughter, I regret to say," answered Violet. "Still, it's in the fold, and that's the main thing. It's not much of a world, really—just endless fields filled with animals and savages, waiting for Men to come and farm it. It has none of the beauty of Karimon."

"You've only been here for a few hours," replied Rawls.

"That's not so, Linus," she said. "In fact, I was here last month. I spent a week touring the Tulabetes' kingdom with your friend Mr. Fuentes as my guide."

"I didn't know that," said Rawls, surprised.

"There's no reason why you should," she answered. "I frequently make unscheduled trips to my worlds." She

paused. "Between paying for the security forces and leasing
the mining equipment and purchasing the exploitation
rights from the Republic, Karimon has already cost me
more than two billion credits. I thought I'd like to see what
I'd purchased for my money."

"And?"

"As I said, it's a beautiful world. Temperate climate,
gravity just a little lighter than Galactic Standard, lovely
mountains and rivers, an unlimited source of cheap labor.
A Man could live like a king on Karimon, Linus." She
paused. "Also, it's perfectly located—halfway between
Goldstone and Earth. We can do a lot more than pillage its
mineral wealth; I can see us settling and populating the
entire planet."

"You *were* impressed, weren't you?" said Rawls, amused.

"Others will be just as impressed," she said confidently.

"First you've got to convince them to come here and see
it for themselves," said Rawls. "Just how do you propose to
do that?"

"You know that river—the one that eventually goes over
Ramsey Falls?"

"The Karimona, yes," said Rawls.

"Fuentes and I followed it from the falls for almost six
hundred miles," she said. "Finally we came to a lovely
valley, perhaps fifteen miles in diameter, surrounded by
hills on three sides, warm by day and cool by night, with the
river flowing right through it."

"And?"

She smiled. "That's where I'm going to build my city."

"Your city?" he asked, surprised.

Violet nodded. "I've already designed it. There will be
every attraction to appeal to the right kind of colonist: a
modern hospital, theater, opera, eventually even a sporting
stadium. It's in Fani country, and they're not about to
protest, as long as we give them jobs and pay their leaders
off with a few weapons that don't function very well."

"You're *really* going to build a city?"

"I plan to break ground next week on the very first structure."

"And what will that be?" asked Rawls.

"I've been living in offices and spaceships for a long time, Linus," she replied. "I'm getting older, slowing down. It's time I had a permanent residence. After I've built it and made it perfect, I'll build the city around it— and when I'm through with that, I'll build the whole planet around the city."

"I'll believe it when I see it," commented Rawls with an amused smile. "Me, I could spend the rest of my life here once we get the hunting concession established. But you—I just can't see you settling down in one spot after all these years."

"I'm *dying*, Linus," she said. "Oh, not very rapidly and not yet very painfully . . . but the day is not that far off when I won't have the energy to keep flitting from one world to the next looking after my interests. I'll need one world to be my headquarters."

"Why not Goldstone?" asked Rawls. "That's where all the action is these days. And from what I saw of the surveys, this world will never be able to produce metals and precious stones to equal what Goldstone is turning out."

"I've already tamed Goldstone," she replied. "And I learned a lot from it."

"And now you want to tame another world?"

She nodded. "Only this time I'm going to make it perfect."

Ten

Athens didn't look like a typical colonial town. Violet Gardener had chosen the name well, and had hired architects to match. It sprouted up from the long grasses in the valley and rapidly spread outward from a central core, white and elegant and pristine.

The animals had been the first problem. Huge Redmountains, fifteen to twenty feet high, some weighing as much as twelve tons, used the valley as a migration route. She offered Fuentes a bounty for each of them, but he was a sportsman, not a killer, and eventually she imported a twelve-man team to eradicate them from the valley.

The Redmountains, for all their size, were no serious threat to Man. They were herbivores and herd animals, gentle and trusting even as they were being decimated, and within a month some seven hundred of them were dead and the rest had deserted the valley forever.

The predators proved more bothersome. There was the Wildfang, a huge catlike creature that weighed some six hundred pounds, could sprint up to half a mile with unbelievable speed, and feared absolutely nothing. And in the evenings there were the Nightkillers, those semi-arboreal

creatures that were equally at home on land or in trees. They had huge, many-faceted eyes that could see as well in the dark as in daylight, and they rarely gave any indication that they were in the vicinity before pouncing on their hapless victims. Violet lost her entire team to Wildfangs and Nightkillers during the first three months of the city's construction. The Wildfangs, especially, made a habit of lurking around construction sites and waiting for their breakfast—Men—to come to them. She was about to send for another team when Fuentes, who could not resist the challenge, came and spent another month wiping out the last Wildfangs and Nightkillers in the vicinity, adding considerably to his status as the greatest hunter of his era.

The Rivertooth and the Water Horse still posed serious problems to the Fani females, who insisted on standing waist-deep in the river while indulging in their ritual bathing or fetching water for their families. Not a week went by that a lurking reptilian Rivertooth didn't make off with some female or child, and rarely were there more than forty-eight hours between attacks on native canoes by the huge, ill-tempered Water Horses. But since Men knew enough to stay away from the river and only the Fani were lost, Violet decreed that there had been enough killing of animals and allowed the amphibians to live. She never realized that placing her city in the path of the annual Brownbuck migration would reduce the size of that particular herd from well over a million to just under five thousand in something less than a decade, but even if she *had* known, it wouldn't have made much difference to her. Athens had become her passion, and while it was being constructed all other considerations were secondary to it.

· At the foot of the hills, perhaps two miles from Athens, she simultaneously constructed Talami, the natives' quarters named for the village that had existed on the same spot. She had bulldozed the old Talami to erect a new city for the Fani, a city composed of row upon row of small

rectangular dwellings, neatly laid out in orderly lines, each equipped with a water source and a power source.

She tore them down a month later when none of the Fani would live in them, preferring their serpentine-shaped dwellings and burrows. Her architects studied them, tried to construct them, but never managed to produce one in which a Fani would consent to live. Eventually she simply gave up, at which time a new Talami, identical to the original Talami in almost every way, grew apace with Athens.

Three days before the four-block central city of Athens was completed, Violet received word of the first mining disaster. Seventeen Tulabete had been buried alive some two hundred feet beneath the surface when a mine wall collapsed; by the time they could be reached, those who hadn't died of other injuries had suffocated.

She flew to Mastaboni in her private aircraft and landed at the newly built airstrip, where Linus Rawls was waiting for her.

"What went wrong?" she demanded as he escorted her to a nearby groundcar. The control tower, which was surrounded by a herd of Fleetjumpers and a crowd of scruffy-looking Tulabete children, glistened new and white in the late morning sun.

"Mine collapsed," answered Rawls. "Had to happen sooner or later. Just bad luck that it happened sooner."

"Are the snakes giving you much trouble over it?"

He shook his head. "We gave five thousand credits compensation to each family."

"They accepted it?" she asked as they began passing the Tulabete's serpentine huts and burrows near the broad new road.

"A year ago they wouldn't have known what a credit was;

today you can see most of the grieving families blowing their money at the company store."

"The benefits of a monied economy," she said wryly. "How much damage was done to the mine?"

Rawls shrugged. "We won't know for a couple of weeks. There's a lot of stuff to clear out."

"Hire more snakes and work them around the clock," said Violet. "I want that mine producing on schedule."

"I don't know that we're going to get *any* snakes back to work until we can show them that the mines are safe."

She stared at him coldly. "I don't recall wording that as a request, Linus. Do whatever must be done, but get that mine operating again."

"Jalanopi may object."

"Pay him off."

Rawls sighed heavily. "We might have a little problem there. He's already figured out that the guns we gave him are virtually useless, and he knows that there's also a limited supply of ammunition. I think it's safe to say that he's not our most rabid supporter."

"He doesn't have to support us. He just has to keep from hindering us."

"I can give him more money," said Rawls tentatively, "but . . ."

"But?" demanded Violet.

"He doesn't have anything to spend it on. Most of the snakes are making next to nothing, but Jalanopi already has enough money to buy everything that's for sale on the whole damned planet." He paused uncomfortably. "We could appropriate some Tallgrazers from the Fani, I suppose."

"Do whatever you have to do," she said, closing the subject. "But get that mine up and running."

"I rather thought I'd leave it to Klein and Schindler," said Rawls. "I've got enough work of my own."

She shook her head. "*This* is your work; the hunting

concession is your reward. You are the most senior member of my staff on this world, Linus; *you* will make sure the mine is operational."

"But—"

"No arguments, Linus. I'm delighted that you found something you want to do, and I'm sure it will turn a profit—but it will have to wait its turn. The mines come first."

"If you say so."

"I do."

The next morning McFarley stalked over to her temporary office and demanded an audience with her. She made him wait until she had finished her breakfast and taken her various medications, then flooded the room with soothing music, ordered the walls to become translucent to usher in the muted rays of the sun, and finally allowed him to be brought into her presence.

"What can I do you for, Reverend McFarley?" she asked, looking up from her computer.

"You can shut down your mining operation until it's safe," he replied, brushing the dust from his outfit.

"It's safe enough now," said Violet, staring idly at the holographs of her parents that seemed to float just above the surface of her desk. On the wall behind her was a framed copy of the treaty she had signed with Jalanopi, one of the hundreds that were posted in every Spiral Arm Development Company office across the planet.

"You mean it's safe enough for the Tulabete," he shot back caustically. "I don't see any *Men* working it."

"You didn't see any Men working before the accident, either. The Men are there to supervise."

"The Men are here to exploit," said McFarley.

"To exploit the mineral wealth of the planet," she agreed.

"You know exactly what I mean!" snapped McFarley. "You hire these poor souls for a pittance, provide them

with no protection, pay off their families with another pittance when there's a disaster, bribe Jalanopi to look the other way, and continue working under the same unsafe conditions as if nothing had ever happened."

"Sit down, Reverend McFarley."

He looked around, found the only other chair in the room, and seated himself.

She stared at him for a long minute, studying his face in the muted light, and finally spoke: "You *look* like a Man, Reverend McFarley," she said. "Why is it that you continually take the snakes' side against your own people?"

"Men are not supposed to do what you're doing to these poor, primitive beings!"

"You are wrong," said Violet. "Men do precisely what I am doing. It is our destiny to achieve primacy in the galaxy, Reverend McFarley. Already we have gathered some forty thousand worlds into the fold, and more are joining us every day. Not one of them was better off before it joined the Republic."

"That's a matter of opinion."

"History will prove you wrong, Reverend," she replied, fighting back a wave of the dizziness and nausea that always followed her morning medication. "We will bring these poor unfortunates the gifts of literacy, and technology, and medicine, and eventually even self-government—but Man has spread himself too far and too thin to do it gratis. Each world must pay for itself, and Karimon will pay by providing us with its ores and precious metals."

"If your motives are so pure, why can't you wait until the mines have been made safe?"

"Because I'm not in the philanthropy business," answered Violet. "Karimon has already drained billions of credits from the Spiral Arm Development Company; it has to start showing a return on our investment."

"Rubbish! You have tens of billions of credits in your various banks. How much could waiting an extra month or

two cost you? What harm is there in seeing that no Tulabete will ever again die in an avoidable disaster?"

"I'm operating on a much tighter schedule than the Republic," she said. "This planet could be an oasis of human civilization in the vast emptiness of the Spiral Arm. Its mineral wealth and farmland could make it the premier world of this sector. I can foresee the day when Athens becomes the financial and cultural center of the entire Arm. That is my vision, Reverend McFarley, and I will bring it into being during my lifetime."

"And a month or two makes that much difference?" demanded McFarley.

"It might," she said bluntly. "I have a lot to accomplish in the Spiral Arm, and Time is always the one irreplaceable commodity."

"And what about the thousands of Tulabete who might die for this vision of yours?"

"I am not a monster, Reverend McFarley," she replied. "Of course I hope that no one dies, and I will do my best to protect them—but if a handful *should* die to achieve Karimon's destiny, then their heirs will reap the benefits that much sooner."

"How much comfort do you think they will derive from that?" he asked sardonically.

"Precious little," she admitted.

"Well, then?"

"These are not Men you are talking about," said Violet. "They are aliens who eat insects, wantonly brutalize small animals, have yet to discover the wheel or the lever, and live in burrows. Would you have them remain at this stage of social evolution forever?"

"Certainly not—but I would not *force* change upon them."

"Oh?" she said sardonically. "Then may I presume that you have not attempted to spread the word of Our Lord Jesus Christ among them?"

"That is not the same thing."

"Of course not. *You* are doing it, not I." She smiled. "I believe the word for that is 'hypocrite'."

"I resent that!" he snapped. "I am attempting to bring comfort and solace to them, not to exploit them!"

"Nonsense," she said, suddenly weary. "I have had this argument and fought this battle many times before." She waited until another wave of dizziness had passed. "Let me suggest, Reverend, that in all the time you have been here, you have not made a single convert."

"No, I have not," he admitted defensively.

"Has it occurred to you that this is because they do not share human values?"

"They share a desire to live," said McFarley. "That is enough."

"To live, and to eat, and to procreate," said Violet. "So do the beasts in the field and the insects that the Tulabete feed upon."

"There is a difference," said McFarley. "The Tulabete are intelligent beings."

"No, Reverend McFarley," said Violet firmly. "They are *sentient* beings. As we bring them the benefits of human civilization, we will turn them into intelligent beings. We will teach them to *use* their minds, to read and write, to work with sophisticated machines, to run an economy that is acceptable to other societies, and to farm their land rather than ignore it."

"You are trying to turn them into something they are not," said McFarley.

"I am turning them into something they would have eventually become without our interference," said Violet. "And I will save them untold generations of ignorance and suffering and disease." She paused again. "I will turn them into a race that will live its potential lifespan. Before we arrived, there was not a wheel on the entire planet; I will turn them into users of tools, so that eventually they need

never perform the kind of labor to which you object so strongly. They are totally without power: electric, solar, fusion, or any other kind; I will create dams and power sources so that the most remote village will have light at night." She looked across her desk at him. "And once I have done these things, maybe *then* you might have more success convincing them that our God is worth worshiping."

"I'm not sure that you and I worship the same God," said McFarley.

"I can live with that if you can," replied Violet.

"I don't know if *they* can," he said.

"I know a little something about them," said Violet. "Karimon was *not* Eden when you arrived, and you did not find a bunch of innocents living in a state of grace. They go to war, they kill and torture their enemies, they worship half a hundred gods. They are not a batch of Adams and Eves waiting for us to leave so that they can return to lives of peace and innocence." She paused and stared at him. "Their society has been evolving slowly, but it has been coming closer and closer to what we would term civilization each day. All I am doing is speeding up the process."

"By swindling them out of their natural resources and appropriating their land?" demanded McFarley.

"No one is swindling anyone, Reverend McFarley," she replied calmly. "We have paid their government for the right to establish our mines, and we have appropriated no land that was under cultivation."

"It was *their* land nevertheless—and as for paying their government, you have taken a completely unsophisticated leader and paid him a pittance to let you pull billions of credits out of his land."

"We have a treaty, Reverend McFarley," responded Violet. "If you feel it was unfair, why didn't you inform Jalanopi of your objections?"

"He had no choice, and you know it," McFarley shot

back. "If he hadn't signed, he'd have been overrun by the Fani and the Rakko, and you'd have dealt with them."

"Then you agree that he's better off for having signed the treaty."

"He'd be better off if you had never landed on Karimon."

"I doubt it," said Violet. "He'd probably have been killed by an enemy or a subordinate in the next year or two, and even if he survived, he'd spend the rest of his life sitting beneath that ridiculous tree wrapped in a blanket and making pronouncements that had no effect five miles away. I have made him the richest and most powerful snake on the planet, and as long as he continues to abide by the treaty, he will remain so."

McFarley struggled to keep his temper in check. "You've got all the answers, haven't you?"

"No, Reverend McFarley," she replied. "Only God has all the answers. All I have is a dream that I plan to realize."

"No matter what the cost."

"I expect it to show a profit."

"You don't know what I'm talking about, do you?"

"I know precisely what you are talking about," she said. "Do you think you're the first Man who has turned his back on his own race and tried to thwart me? Eventually most of them have come to the realization that what I am doing is for the good of both Men and aliens."

"Well, this is one man who will never agree with what you're doing," he said firmly.

"Doubtless you would have preferred to see Karimon become a satellite of the Canphorite empire."

"I would have preferred that neither Men nor Canphorites exploit Karimon."

"One or the other was bound to."

"I don't know why," he said stubbornly.

"Then you are a fool." Violet got to her feet. "And I have

already spent enough time listening to your foolishness. This interview is over."

"You won't reconsider your decision?"

"If a member of your congregation—assuming you ever *have* a congregation—were to collapse and die in the heat of religious fervor, you wouldn't stop doing God's work, would you? Well, I won't stop doing Man's work."

"You haven't heard the last of this," promised McFarley.

"I'm sure I haven't," replied Violet. "But perhaps, before we speak again, you will take a long look in a mirror. You are a Man, Reverend McFarley, as much as you may wish you weren't. You may be tolerated by the snakes, but you will never be one of them. You do not look like them, you do not think like them, you do not share their values or even their gods. What possible good can come of denying your own humanity? Whether you approve of them or not, changes are coming to Karimon. It will become a modern world, a working member of the Republic. You can make the transition from savagery to civilization easier, or you can make it more difficult, but you cannot stop it." She paused and stared at him once more. "I'd like you to think about that before we have our next conversation."

She dismissed him with a wave of her hand and went back to conversing with her computer. After lunch, she received assurances from her engineers that the collapsed mine could be reopened the next morning and she took her private plane back to Athens, where she checked into the one room of the hospital that was already operational for her monthly blood transfusion.

She floated above the floor on her airbed, one tube carrying her own blood to an atomizer while another delivered a fresh supply of the life-extending fluid into her veins. She marveled, as she always did, that medical science had kept her alive and functioning this long, at the same time wondering what demons within her could so pollute this fresh blood that within four weeks it would be as use-

less and diseased as that which was now being drained from her. McFarley, she decided, would call it the curse of ambition. She preferred to think of it as the price of greatness. From time to time she wondered whether time would prove her or McFarley correct, or whether her condition was simply the result of an indifferent God in an indifferent universe.

She was always surprised when she emerged from the transfusion feeling weak rather than vigorous with her renewed blood supply, and she elected to recuperate in solitude at the small cottage she had built for herself, overlooking the Ramsey Falls.

She arrived in late afternoon, spent the few remaining hours of sunlight strolling through the countryside accompanied by a trio of bodyguards, then returned to the cottage, where her personal chef had prepared her dinner. Later, under the light of Karimon's two moons, she sat on the raised porch outside her front door and watched as huge Redmountains and majestic Twisthorns and light-footed Fleetjumpers came down to the Karimona River to drink. The air was cool and crisp and clear, and she felt, for a pleasant few moments, as if she were the only person on the planet.

She spent two days and two nights at the Falls, renewing her depleted energies, and was fully prepared to spend another week there before returning to Athens.

Then she received a message from Rawls that jolted her back to reality.

Eleven

"Strike?" she repeated. "They don't even know what a strike *is!*"

Rawls' holographic image hovered above her computer, looking more annoyed than worried.

"They do now," he replied wryly. "I have a feeling that a certain gentleman of the cloth has been giving them a crash course in labor relations."

"That man is getting to be more trouble than he's worth," she said grimly. "Place him under house arrest and restrict him to his quarters while we get this situation sorted out."

"On what charges?" asked Rawls.

"Find one and make it stick."

"He hasn't broken any Karimon laws, and human laws don't apply here."

She was silent for a moment as she considered the situation. Finally she made her decision.

"Put the whole place under martial law," she said. "Send for the security force from Athens to back you up. I'll let them know the request is coming through; they can be there in three hours." She paused. "Arrest McFarley for

breaking some violation. Treat him with courtesy, and make sure he's comfortable, but keep him isolated. I don't want him talking to any of the Tulabete."

"I'll need some legal basis for declaring martial law," noted Rawls.

"The basis is planetary security. We have received word that the Canphorites may attack at any moment. And of course, we can't have them disrupting our production of vital material for the war effort, so you have the authority to conscript all able-bodied snakes and put them to work in the mines."

"I'd hate to defend this in a Republic court," remarked Rawls.

"The Republic has nothing to do with this," answered Violet. "Karimon isn't a Republic world. It is an independent planet that has signed a treaty with a private company."

"What if there's resistance?"

"There won't be."

"But if there is . . . ?"

"Then take Jalanopi into protective custody, and do the same with any other snake that has the authority to call a strike. Treat them with every courtesy, but don't let them near any of their people." She paused again. "I'll be there sometime tomorrow to take charge."

"Maybe you'd better stay where you are," said Rawls, "or go back to Athens. Things could get ugly here."

She shook her head. "They haven't had time to organize," she replied. "Remove Jalanopi and McFarley and you'll find that there won't be any trouble." She grimaced and added, "*This* time."

Twelve

The strike lasted for three days.

The Tulabete, who didn't quite know why they had to work in the mines in the first place, seemed equally unaware of why they suddenly had to stop. Rawls jailed the five who seemed to be the ringleaders, though he was sure they were taking their orders from Jalanopi, then shut down all the services that the Tulabete had grown used to. When this didn't have the desired effect, he had his security forces take one hundred Tulabete males to the mines, and released them only when they had produced their day's quota. The next day he took two hundred, the day after that three hundred, and since there were less than six hundred able-bodied males in the area, the strike was virtually over.

He waited another week to make sure there were no further problems, then released Jalanopi and the ringleaders with a stern warning that further agitation would result in further confinement.

Two days later he paid a visit to McFarley's church, where the Reverend had been held incommunicado since the strike began. A guard let him in, and he found McFarley sitting on the steps leading up to the pulpit, reading a bible

in the dim light that filtered in through the high windows.

"Good morning, Reverend McFarley," said Rawls.

"What are you doing here?" said McFarley suspiciously.

"I bear glad tidings," said Rawls with a smile. "The state of emergency is over, and Mastaboni is no longer under martial law. You're free to go."

"You broke the strike," said McFarley. It was not a question.

"Strike?" repeated Rawls. "What strike?"

"Don't play games with me," said McFarley. "I was confined to my church because of the strike in the mines."

Rawls frowned. "I don't know what you're talking about, Reverend. You were confined for your own safety because of a very real threat of invasion by the 5th Canphorite Fleet. Fortunately, the Republic's Navy was able to frighten them off."

"How long did it last?"

"They just turned away this morning, so I would estimate that we were in a state of emergency for twelve days."

"You know what I mean," said McFarley irritably. "How long did the strike last?"

"You keep mentioning a strike," said Rawls. "There was a mild disturbance when the mine collapsed, but everyone was back to work just as soon as the mine could be reentered. I have nothing but admiration for the grit and determination of your parishioners."

"What about Jalanopi?"

"I give up," said Rawls. "What *about* Jalanopi?"

"Is he alive?"

Rawls chuckled. "Of course he's alive. He's probably eating bugs beneath that stupid tree of his. You're welcome to visit him."

"This isn't the end of it, you know," said McFarley, getting to his feet and brushing some dust from his clothing.

"I tend to agree with you, Reverend," said Rawls. "You

never can tell when the Canphorites will threaten us again. We'll simply have to remain in a state of preparedness."

"Where's Violet Gardener? I want to speak to her."

"She's in the hospital at Athens," answered Rawls. "I'm told it's nothing serious. I'm sure she'd be happy to speak to you once she's released. That will be sometime tomorrow morning, I believe."

McFarley looked around the church. "You say I'm free to go now?"

"We'd never keep you against your will," Rawls assured him.

"You just did, for the better part of two weeks."

"That was for your own safety, Reverend," said Rawls. "*You* may think you're a snake, but we know better, and Men always protect their own."

"How comforting," said McFarley caustically.

"I'm glad you appreciate it, sir," said Rawls.

"Are my movements to be restricted in any way?" asked McFarley.

"Absolutely not, sir. You are free to go wherever you please."

"Including off the planet?"

"Certainly. We have no desire to keep you on Karimon." Rawls paused. "In fact, it might be better all the way around if you were to leave. You were doing noble work here, sir, but it's time to turn it over to the experts."

"Thank you, Mr. Rawls," said McFarley, making no attempt to mask his dislike of the man. "Then if you will step aside, I'd like to go outside."

"I can drive you to your ship if you like, sir."

"I think I'd like to visit my friend Jalanopi first," answered McFarley. "If I find you've harmed him in any way, I have every intention of reporting it to the Bureau of Alien Affairs on Deluros VIII."

"That's certainly your privilege, sir," said Rawls. "If

Jalanopi tells you he was physically mistreated, I will personally seek out and punish the man responsible for it."

McFarley seemed about to say something else, thought better of it, and walked down the aisle and out of the church. Rawls nodded to the guard at the door, who stepped aside to allow the Reverend to pass by.

"Follow him," said Rawls. "I want to know every place he goes and every snake he sees."

The guard saluted and left, and Rawls, wondering if he would *ever* get a chance to sit beside a fire and plan the next day's hunting, put through a call to Violet Gardener.

"How are you feeling?" he asked as her image, surrounded by a sterile hospital environment, appeared over his computer.

"I'll be all right," she replied, displaying an arm that was attached by tubes and wires to half a dozen sleek new machines. "We've got a new medic here from Earth who specializes in exotic blood diseases, so he's doing some tests."

"Can he cure you?"

She shook her head. "Nothing can cure me, Linus. But possibly he can see to it that I don't tire so easily. There's a lot of work still to be done, and I can't live on amphetamines forever." She shrugged. "That's neither here nor there. Why have you contacted me?"

"I released McFarley twenty minutes ago."

"And?"

"He's talking about leaving the planet. I don't like it. Men like him don't give up that easily."

Violet frowned. "I agree."

"What do you think he's up to?"

"I don't know."

"Do you want me to keep him here?"

"No," she said with a sigh. "He'll just foment more trouble, and eventually we would have to do something very unpleasant to him."

"He's meeting with Jalanopi right now. I can't imagine he's going to talk the snakes into another strike, not after we broke the first one so easily."

"No, he's brighter than that," agreed Violet. "He's got something else in mind."

"The Bureau of Alien Affairs?" suggested Rawls.

"I doubt it. We're developing a primitive planet and we haven't harmed anyone. The mining accident was just that—an accident. They'd back us to the hilt."

"But does *he* know that?"

"If he doesn't, he should."

"Maybe this is his first alien planet."

"I'm sure it is," said Violet. "Men like McFarley, they decide they're all that stands between alien Edens and human corruption, and they become more alien than the aliens they're misguidedly trying to help. Once they land on a planet, they stay there."

"Well, then, what do you want to do?" asked Rawls.

"I suppose we'll just have to wait. The next move is up to him." She frowned. "Time is so precious. If there's one thing I hate, it's *waiting.*"

"Perhaps it won't be too long," he reassured her.

And it wasn't.

Thirteen

Seven uneventful weeks and two blood transfusions later, Violet Gardener was summoned from her house in Athens to Mastaboni.

"What's up?" she asked Rawls, when she was finally able to raise him from aboard her private plane.

"The other shoe just dropped."

"Explain yourself, Linus."

"McFarley's back, and he's got a couple of high-level officials from Deluros VIII with him. They've been speaking to Jalanopi all morning."

"Who are they?"

"No one that we've dealt with before. A man named Willis Gaunt, from the Bureau of Alien Affairs, and a woman named Katherine Njobe from the Department of Cartography." He paused. "I ran a check on them, and they're legitimate."

"Have you any idea what they've got in mind?"

"None . . . except that we're probably not going to like it much."

"I *already* don't like it," she said. "If the Republic is willing to accept all these worlds we've brought into the

fold, you would think they'd finally be willing to let us simply do our job, instead of constantly throwing obstacles in our path." She sighed wearily. "All right. I'm due to land in less than an hour. Have someone there to meet me."

"I'll meet you myself."

"No," she said. "I want you to stay at your computer. Find out everything you can about Gaunt and Njobe. Where they've lived, where they were employed before they got their current jobs, if any complaints have been filed against them. See if you can run a financial check, too."

"You're not giving me a lot of time," he said.

"Do what you can," she replied, ending the connection and silently cursing her one true enemy, Time. Jalanopi, McFarley, these bureaucrats, the entire Spiral Arm, all were nothing but irritants. But just as Rawls had a limited amount of time to probe for weaknesses with his computer, so, too, did she have a limited amount of time to pursue her vision. The blood tests had shown some promise, but it would take more time—her nemesis again—to study the results, to create a formula, to effect a change in her condition.

And the Republic which she was trying to serve was the greatest waster of time. If it didn't assimilate Karimon today, it would do so tomorrow, or next year, or next century. She felt like the ephemeral servant of an eternal master, which, if it blinked its eyes, would miss the entirety of her lifetime. The only way to prove she had existed at all was to make a mark, leave something behind so people would know that Violet Gardener had been here, had lived and breathed and *accomplished* something with her brief span of years.

She was still dwelling on such thoughts as her plane glided in for a gentle landing, then accelerated and shot skyward at the last moment.

"What's the matter?" she demanded.

The pilot looked back at her and grinned. "Horndevils

on the runway. This isn't exactly Earth or Sirius V. The sound of the engine scattered them; we won't have any problems on our next approach."

She looked out the window as a dozen of the huge, two-ton beasts lumbered off in fright. *Before I die, I will look out at this same spot and see nothing but cultivated farmland, land that will feed the millions of Men who will emigrate here to make their lives and their fortunes.*

The plane touched down, one of Rawls' assistants escorted her to a groundcar, and a few moments later they reached Mastaboni, which had changed considerably in the two months since she had last seen it. The human community, formerly a row of assay and claims offices and a pair of hastily erected rooming houses, now comprised three long blocks, with stores and restaurants and a pair of small hotels lining the main street, and perhaps three hundred quickly erected geodesic domes forming an adjacent residential area. There was even a small office building, and some entrepreneur had set up a groundcar dealership next door. Eight or nine large, substantial homes were being constructed half a mile away, overlooking the river. The embryonic human city was still surrounded by miles and miles of empty, uncultivated scrubland, an occasional Fleetjumper or Twisthorn still wandered through the streets, and it hardly compared to her spotless, shining Athens, but the sight of it comforted her nonetheless. Change was movement from one point in Time to the next, and when you stopped moving, so did Time.

"I've lost my bearings," she said. "Where is Jalanopi's tree?"

"About three miles downriver," said her driver. "They're not going to leave that damned tree, and nobody wanted to live next door to them, so the town kind of developed right here. We don't go among the snakes unless we're invited, and they don't come here. Works out just fine all the way around."

"Well, I've been invited. Let's pick up Linus and pay Jalanopi and his guests a visit."

They walked to a small shop, not yet opened to the public, that displayed a vast array of hunting gear and weaponry in its windows. The door scanned them, identified them, and slid back to allow them inside, where Rawls sat behind a small desk.

"How are you feeling?" he asked.

"Annoyed as hell," she answered.

He grinned. "Okay, you're fit for duty. Let's go." He got up from his desk and led her out to a groundcar, leaving his assistant behind.

"What did you manage to find?" asked Violet as they left the new city behind them and headed south.

"So far, not much," answered Rawls. "They seem to be exemplary civil servants. If there's any hint of impropriety, I haven't been able to find it yet. Of the two, I'd watch out for Gaunt."

"The Alien Affairs representative?"

Rawls nodded. "He seems to be a passionate advocate of alien causes, and he's got a hell of a legal staff behind him."

"What about Njobe?"

"She's been in Cartography for sixteen years. I still don't know what the hell she's doing here."

"Well, we'll find out soon enough," said Violet.

Halfway there Rawls had to stop to allow a small herd of Redmountains to finish crossing the road.

"They're awesome, aren't they?" remarked Violet, staring at the huge beasts. "I can't imagine why you and Fuentes take such pleasure in killing them."

Rawls made no answer, and after another moment they were once again speeding along the road. A few Tulabete children waved at them as they went past, and soon they came to a halt some fifty yards from Jalanopi's tree.

Jalanopi himself, wearing his ceremonial headdress, sat

upon his wooden throne, flanked on one side by Andrew McFarley and Paratoka, and on the other by Willis Gaunt, a slender man dressed in a dust-covered white outfit, and Katherine Njobe, a smallish woman with short black hair and a much more sensible khaki garment.

Rawls helped Violet out of the groundcar and accompanied her to the little group, then stood aside as she came to a halt directly in front of Jalanopi.

"Good morning, King Jalanopi," she said. "I understand that you wish to speak with me."

"I will let others speak for me, Man Violet," answered Jalanopi in broken Terran. He gestured toward the two emissaries of the Republic. "These are Man Gaunt and Man Njobe."

Violet turned to face them. "Welcome to Karimon," she said. "I trust you will enjoy your stay."

"We do not plan to remain here very long, Madam Gardener," said Gaunt, his diction precise and clipped. "We are here for business, not pleasure."

"There is no reason why you can't combine both," replied Violet. "Karimon has many scenic wonders, and if you are a sportsman, I'm sure Mr. Rawls can arrange a hunting or fishing vacation for you."

"I am afraid not."

"Then perhaps we can at least entice Miss Njobe to sample the beauties of our world," said Violet pleasantly.

"May we get down to business, Madam Gardener?" said Gaunt. "It is precisely to determine whose world this is that I have come all the way from Deluros VIII."

"I could have sent you a copy of our treaty and saved you the voyage," said Violet. She turned to Katherine Njobe. "Might I ask what a representative from Cartography is doing here?"

"All in good time," said Gaunt. "Miss Njobe and I have agreed that I should speak first."

"As you wish," said Violet with a shrug.

"Some weeks ago, Reverend Andrew McFarley visited the Department of Alien Affairs with some disquieting information," said Gaunt.

"That's not surprising," replied Violet. "Reverend McFarley finds most things disquieting. I suspect it goes with his profession."

"Please let me continue," said Gaunt severely. "Reverend McFarley brought to our attention the fact that you had conscripted native labor to work in your mines, and—"

"They are not *my* mines," Violet interrupted him. "They are the property of the Spiral Arm Development Company."

"Of which you are the majority stockholder," he replied.

"Nor were any Tulabete conscripted," she continued. "Everyone who works in the mines has been paid, and the Spiral Arm Development Company can produce records to prove it."

"Let us cut straight to the heart of the matter," said Gaunt. "A mine collapsed, the laborers refused to work until their safety could be guaranteed, and you incarcerated Jalanopi, Reverend McFarley, and five members of the Tulabete community. Do you deny that?"

"Certainly I deny it," answered Violet. "Karimon was under threat by a Canphorite fleet, and Jalanopi was placed in protective custody for his own safety, as was Reverend McFarley."

"And the other five?"

"Suspected Canphorite sympathizers. They were released as soon as the threat was over."

"On what authority did you declare martial law?" continued Gaunt.

"The treaty that Jalanopi signed with the Spiral Arm Development Company gives us the authority, in fact the duty, to protect his people and assure his continued sovereignty."

"Reverend McFarley says that Jalanopi was manipulated

into signing this treaty because you interfered with the internal politics of Karimon, and that had he not signed it, his nation would have been defeated by other nations that you yourself had armed. Jalanopi supports Reverend McFarley's explanation."

"Jalanopi had no objection to that treaty when it was all that stood between him and military defeat," answered Violet. "I don't see any reason why it is invalid now."

"Madam Gardener, it is invalid because my department has ruled it to be invalid," said Gaunt. "I only wish I had held my current position when you bludgeoned Goldstone into accepting your terms. I have reviewed that treaty, and unfortunately it is too late for me to disallow it, but I promise you that I cannot and will not allow you to subjugate or exploit either the Tulabete or any other alien races. Do I make myself perfectly clear?"

"You make yourself perfectly clear, but I do not think you established a legal basis for your actions," replied Violet. "I have a legal treaty that was signed by both myself and Jalanopi, and the fact that he no longer wishes to abide by it does not make it any less legal."

"That is a matter for the Department of Alien Affairs to decide."

"No, Mr. Gaunt. If anything, it is a matter for the courts to decide. I have been this route before, on both Doxus II and Sugarmoon, and I assure you that the courts will support our right to be here."

"I have reviewed your entire career, Madam Gardener," said Gaunt. "In the cases of Doxus II and Sugarmoon, you had the support of the Bureau of Alien Affairs. I assure you that this is no longer the case."

"Your support has always been welcome, but it is hardly necessary," said Violet. "I repeat: I have a valid, legal treaty with Jalanopi."

"Not as of this moment," said Gaunt sternly. "If you wish to go to court to reverse my ruling, you are certainly free

to. The Bureau will fight you every step of the way. I should imagine it will take the better part of thirty years to get a reversal, perhaps longer—*if* you get one at all. If I were you, I would channel my efforts into helping aliens rather than exploiting them."

"Mr. Gaunt," said Violet, "pardon my bluntness, but you are a desk-bound bureaucratic fool. I *am* helping to elevate the natives of those worlds controlled by the Spiral Arm Development Company—and I am doing it without bombing them into submission, as the Republic has done on so many other worlds. I have not installed a puppet government—another favorite Republic ploy—and I have not found it necessary to appeal to the Navy to support the handful of Men who have emigrated here. I am doing what your cherished department *ought* to be doing, and I resent your blind, hostile ignorance as much as your illegal interference. Have I made *my* position perfectly clear?"

"Your position was clear to me the first time you exploited the innocent natives of the first world you set foot on," said Gaunt with open hostility. "It is the conclusion of the Department of Alien Affairs that you manufactured the conditions that led Jalanopi to sign the treaty with your company, that you willfully misled him about the extent of the powers the treaty allowed you, that you broke a legal strike of native workers, and that you illegally incarcerated one Man and six Tulabete, including King Jalanopi, to further your company's financial gain." He stopped for breath and stared directly into her eyes. "The treaty is invalid. You have legal recourse if you wish to pursue it, but until such time as my decision is reversed in a court of law, you will be criminally libel for any action you take on Karimon based on rights granted to you by the treaty." He paused. "I will allow all Men one month to make their personal accommodations with King Jalanopi or leave the planet." He turned to Jalanopi. "Is that acceptable to you, King Jalanopi?"

"Yes, Man Gaunt," said Jalanopi, who had been listening to McFarley's translation of the conversation, his own comprehension of Terran not being up to the task.

"I ask you, Madam Gardener, not whether you agree with my ruling, but whether you understand it?"

"I understand it," said Violet.

"And will you abide by it?"

She stared at him without saying anything.

"I repeat," said Gaunt. "Will you abide by my ruling?"

"I don't answer insulting questions," said Violet. She turned to Katherine Njobe. "What has the Department of Cartography to do with all this?"

"We have been speaking as if Jalanopi is the ruler of the entire planet," said Njobe. "But this is not the case. He is the king of the Tulabete, but there are other nations here as well. When Cartography was informed of the Bureau of Alien Affairs' ruling, we were instructed to create a map delineating the various nations on Karimon." She paused, and smiled uncomfortably. "The Republic realizes that you have a considerable investment on Karimon and suggests that you might wish to make an accommodation with one of the other nations rather than abandon the world entirely." She shifted her weight uneasily. "Such an accommodation would of course require the approval of the Bureau of Alien Affairs."

Violet smiled in amusement. "That's the Republic for you," she said. "While they're letting Mr. Gaunt and his department slap my right hand, they're telling me to dig in with my left and save them the trouble of conquering Karimon fifty or seventy years from now."

"In essence," agreed Njobe.

"It's a moot point," interjected Gaunt. "Given your prior record, I think I can guarantee that my department will look with disfavor upon any treaty you may sign with any alien race. There has been no complaint from the neighboring world of Belamaine, and so we are not free to inter-

vene there, but before I leave here this afternoon you will
be given an official edict requiring the Spiral Arm Development Company to submit all future treaties to the Department of Alien Affairs before they can be enacted." A smug
smile crossed his face. "I hope you are satisfied with the
empire you have built upon the shoulders of oppressed
alien races, because it will extend no farther."

"We shall see," said Violet. She turned once again to
Katherine Njobe. "How long will your work require you to
remain here, Miss Njobe?"

"Perhaps three days, possibly four," she replied. "My
understanding of the political structure of Karimon is that
the actual borders are in a state of constant flux. I will
create a broad generalized map to which the the various
nations agree and then station two members of the Department of Cartography on Karimon to refine it. Hopefully,
with the aid of the various local governments, they can
create a definitive map within half a year."

Fat chance, thought Violet. *Not a one of these snake rulers
has ever even seen his boundaries.*

Aloud, she said, "I have an apartment in Mastaboni and
a house in Athens. They are at your disposal for the duration of your stay here."

"Thank you," she said.

"I will provide you with a guide for the Tulabete's country, and will supply you with a security team for those
borders that are not considered secure."

"That is most generous of you, Madam Gardener."

"We have no disagreement with the Department of Cartography," replied Violet. "In fact, I hope you will join me
for dinner in Athens prior to your departure."

"If I have the time."

"Mr. Gaunt, have we any further business to discuss?"

"We have not," said Gaunt.

"Then, if you don't mind, I'll take my leave of you." She

turned to McFarley. "Are you satisfied, Reverend McFarley?"

"Totally," replied McFarley with a triumphant smile.

"Good," she said.

"What are you staring at?" he asked.

"I just want to make sure I remember that smile," she replied pleasantly.

Then she turned and walked back to her groundcar.

Fourteen

Violet flew back to Athens as soon as the meeting was over and summoned Rawls there the next morning. He arrived at her newly completed mansion just before noon and was ushered into her private office. It was decorated with certificates and citations from the Republic, holographs of herself in the company of both human and alien leaders, and various awards she had won for her accomplishments over the years. The holographs of her parents sat on her desk, and floating some four feet above the floor was a three-dimensional display of the Spiral Arm. Those planets she had opened and brought into the fold glowed a brilliant green, those she still needed to assimilate to bring her dream to fruition blinked a bright blue at regular intervals.

She sat behind an imported desk made of shining alloys, her various computers and vidphones hidden from sight.

"Much nicer than your office at Mastaboni," said Rawls, surveying his surroundings. "I don't see the treaty, though."

"It's invalid, in case you've forgotten already," she said wryly.

"I haven't," he replied. "Do you mind if I sit down?"

"Please do," she said, as he commanded a chair to float over to him. "I trust that Mr. Gaunt has taken his leave of us?"

"Yesterday."

"Good. I have developed a serious dislike for him."

"I have a feeling that it's mutual."

"Doubtless," she agreed.

"Well," said Rawls after a brief silence, "what's our next step?"

"We're certainly not going to go to court," she replied. "I couldn't afford the time even if I were in perfect health and assured of twice my normal lifespan."

"I suppose we could just ignore the ruling," suggested Rawls. "I can't imagine that the Navy would actually be ordered to attack Men who are developing an alien world."

Violet shook her head. "That's stupid, Linus," she said. "We're dealing with a fanatic who has the support of one of the most powerful departments in the government. He'd make it a point of honor for the Navy to do just that." She snorted contemptuously. "Hell, it might even catapult him to elective office. I'd hate to have *that* on my conscience."

Rawls chuckled. "You just might have a point there." Suddenly he leaned forward, serious again. "So what *do* we plan to do?"

"We plan to obey Mr. Gaunt's edict to the letter."

"You're not seriously considering leaving the planet," said Rawls firmly. "I know you better than that. You've never backed away from a fight in your life."

"Who said anything about leaving?" replied Violet. "Karimon is my home now. I plan to live out my life here, hopefully in peace and tranquillity."

Rawls leaned back comfortably. "You've got it all figured out. I knew it wouldn't take you a whole day to come up with a solution." He paused. "What's our plan of attack?"

"What would *you* do, Linus?" she asked.

"Me?"

She nodded. "One of these days there's going to be a crisis while I'm in the hospital or visiting some other world. You've been with me longer than any of the others. I'd like to think you can get your mind off killing helpless animals long enough to take charge if you have to."

Rawls shifted in his chair and considered his options. "Well, you can't appeal to Gaunt," he said. "That's obvious. And McFarley would sooner dance on your grave than help you across the room. That leaves Jalanopi." He paused, frowning. "But you've got to cut him loose from McFarley, and you've only got a month to do it."

"That's right."

"Wait a minute," he said. "There's Katherine Njobe, too. She's still on Karimon." He frowned again. "But what the hell can *she* have to do with anything? She's just a mapmaker."

She turned to stare at her display of the Spiral Arm. "Linus, Linus," she said wearily. "It's as plain as the nose on your face, or the horns on one of your trophy animals. *Think!*"

He lowered his head in thought for a moment, then looked up. "I'm sorry. I was a little slow today, wasn't I?" He smiled. "It doesn't have a damned thing to do with mapmaking. It was her offer, right?"

"Certainly."

"That's what stumped me for a minute. There isn't a damned thing worth pulling out of the ground up in Fani country."

"You know it, and I know it . . ." said Violet, returning his smile.

"But Jalanopi doesn't know it, and neither does McFarley!" concluded Rawls triumphantly. "So we sign another treaty, this time with the Fani, and we make a lot of noise and fuss about moving our whole operation up there. We close down the company stores and the native infirmary, we

shut off the power, we do everything we can to make Jalanopi think that he's lost our money, our weapons, everything, to the Fani."

"I think it should work," said Violet. "The Republic practically begged us to stay."

"There are a couple of problems," said Rawls. "Even if Jalanopi wants us back, there's no way the Department of Alien Affairs will okay any new agreement you sign with him." He paused. "And after what Gaunt said, I don't see how you're going to slip a treaty with the Fani past him."

Violet smiled. "There's a big difference between signing a treaty with the Fani and letting the Tulabete know we are *willing* to sign it." She paused. "As for Jalanopi, why would we want to sign a treaty with him?" she continued with false innocence. "We'll be hellbent on moving our base of operations to Fani, remember? Jalanopi's caused us a lot of trouble with our own government; we're not going to give him so much as a credit."

Rawls looked puzzled. "Then I don't quite see . . ."

"Put yourself in Jalanopi's place, Linus," she said. "He'd like us off the planet, but we're not leaving. Furthermore, we're about to spend all our money with the Fani. Not only don't his people know how to locate or work a mine without instruction—and McFarley isn't the one to tell them how—but even if they managed to pull some ores out of the mines we've already started, they have no market for them. We own the only spaceships on Karimon, and McFarley wouldn't begin to know where to go to get a price for anything they wanted to sell." She paused. "All right. You're Jalanopi, and you know all this. You see the Fani becoming rich and powerful, and your own mines deserted by the one race that could reestablish your primacy on the planet. What would you do?"

"I'd look for an investor," said Rawls. "A human investor."

"Right."

"But there aren't any. McFarley doesn't have any money, and everyone else on the planet works for us, or spent everything they had to emigrate here."

"Wrong," she said.

He stared at her curiously. "Who am I missing?" Then, suddenly, he grinned. "Will she do it?"

"*You* ran the financial check on her," said Violet. "What do you think?"

"Katherine Njobe: thirty-seven years old, unmarried, spent her whole career in Cartography," recited Rawls. "Net worth: seventy-two thousand credits."

"Not much to show for fifteen years, is it?" suggested Violet. "Especially if I can show her a way to make a million credits in one month."

"Sounds good to me," said Linus. "How do we work it? Set up a dummy corporation in her name, filter a few million credits into it, have her pay it to Jalanopi as a show of good faith for signing a new treaty . . ."

"And then have her sell us the rights she's purchased," concluded Violet. "She'll have a legally binding treaty with the Tulabete, and we will deal directly with her corporation and not with Jalanopi at all, thereby obeying Mr. Gaunt's dictum to the letter."

"What if she says no?"

"Then I will gently explain to her that I will fly to Goldstone and return with the first Man who *doesn't* say no, and the only difference is that someone else will make a million credits that could have been hers."

Rawls lit a smokeless cigarette and shook his head sadly. "That poor snake," he said at last. "He'll never figure out what's happened."

"He'd be a poor snake if we let the Republic run us off the planet," Violet corrected him. "I'm going to make him the king of the most powerful country on a major planet. If he'd thought things through and stopped listening to

fools like McFarley and Gaunt, he'd realize that he's much better off with us than without."

"I wonder . . ." said Rawls.

"What do you wonder?"

"If he wasn't happier before we arrived. Maybe his kingdom was just a tree and a patch of barren ground, but his word was law and he took orders from no one."

"Of course he was happier before we arrived," she said irritably. "Just as Men were happier when all they had to do was fill their bellies and keep warm and dry. They didn't have neuroses, they didn't fight wars, they didn't worry about nonessentials." She paused. "But on the other hand, they lost more than half their children in infancy, they succumbed to every disease that came around, they had no language, no history, no art—and they were hunted by everything that was bigger and stronger. They may have been happier, but they weren't better off. You learn to take the bad with the good, Linus."

"I suppose so," he agreed. "But it does lead to another question."

"Oh?"

"Which are we—the bad or the good?"

"That all depends," said Violet.

"On what?"

"On who writes the history books."

Fifteen

Two weeks had passed when Linus Rawls drove up to
Jalanopi's tree, got out of his car, and walked over to
where the Tulabete king and the human minister were
awaiting him.

"Good morning, Jalanopi," said Rawls, bowing his head
slightly. "Morning, Reverend."

"I had rather hoped we had seen the last of you, Mr.
Rawls," said McFarley distastefully.

"Well, that's what I'm here to speak to you about," said
Rawls easily. He turned to Jalanopi. "I know you've been
learning Terran. Are you comfortable enough with it for
me to speak directly to you, or would you rather have
Reverend McFarley translate?"

"You may speak to me, Man Rawls," said Jalanopi. "If I
do not understand, I will ask Man Andrew."

"Fine," said Rawls. "Let me know if I'm going too fast for
you."

"I will do so." Jalanopi stared at Rawls out of his orange
cat's-eyes. "Why are you here, Man Rawls?"

"I'm here to talk a little business with you," replied
Rawls, pulling a large Antarrean cigar out of his tunic and
lighting it.

"We are not required to do business with Violet Gardener or her Spiral Arm Development Company anymore," interjected McFarley heatedly. "I thought that Mr. Gaunt of the Department of Alien Affairs made that quite clear."

"I'm no longer working for her," said Rawls. "I'm here on my own behalf."

"A falling out among thieves?" suggested McFarley.

"Let's say a reassessment of goals," answered Rawls. "She has hers, I have mine."

"I do not wish to deal with *any* Men," said Jalanopi.

"Oh, I think you do," said Rawls, unperturbed. "I very much think you do." He shrugged. "But if you don't want to listen to me, well, that's your problem. Thank you for your time, and I'm sorry to have bothered you."

He had started to leave when Jalanopi said, "Wait."

McFarley turned to Jalanopi. "Why have you stopped him?" he asked in the Tulabete dialect.

"Let us hear what he has to say," answered Jalanopi. "I do not like his attitude. He seems very sure of himself."

"You do not have to listen to him," warned McFarley. "Remember: we have the Department of Alien Affairs on our side."

"True," said Jalanopi. "But it cannot hurt to listen. I want to know why he speaks with such confidence." He turned to Rawls. "I will hear your proposal, Man Rawls," he said in Terran.

"Thank you," said Rawls. "I don't suppose it's any great secret that I want to set up a safari company on Karimon. I had taken some tentative steps in that direction before our little contretemps two weeks ago." He paused. "I'd still like to start my company, and I'd like to lease the area that you call the Baski Plains."

Jalanopi understood the gist of it, but turned to McFarley for a precise translation.

"What is that to me?" he answered at last. "I am not required to enter into any transactions with you."

"Hear me out," said Rawls. "I am prepared to pay you a fee of one hundred thousand credits, renewable annually, as well as ten percent of my gross profits. This is not a treaty, as Reverend McFarley will tell you. It's a straight business deal. The land will remain yours; all I want is the exclusive right to hunt on it."

"I am not interested in what you want, Man Rawls," said Jalanopi, "nor do I trust you."

"Look," said Rawls, "if it's Violet Gardener you're worried about, I'll agree to a stipulation that none of her people will be allowed to cross the Baski Plains."

"They are leaving in twelve more days," interjected McFarley. "Why would they want to cross the Baski Plains?"

"Hadn't you heard?" asked Rawls. "She's moving her operations to Fani."

McFarley and Jalanopi exchanged surprised glances.

"No," said Jalanopi. "We had not heard."

Rawls nodded. "Yeah, she's pulling everything she's got out of Mastaboni—every Man, every machine, every generator. I guess she's got to leave you the roads, even if there won't be any vehicles here to use 'em."

"She cannot treat with the Fani," said McFarley. "Mr. Gaunt assured us of that."

"Mr. Gaunt is cooling his heels back on Deluros VIII," Rawls pointed out. "Besides, I think she took his warning to heart. She's offering the Fani a much more favorable treaty. Something like fifty million credits a year, free hospitals and schooling, more weapons than you can shake a stick at—weapons that *work*, not the kind she foisted off on the Tulabete—and she's agreed to pay the miners a hell of a lot more than she was paying them here." He paused. "She's had a couple of weeks to cash in a batch of political favors she's owed back on Deluros. My understanding is that she went over Gaunt's head and has gotten the Bureau

of Alien Affairs' approval." He stared at McFarley and Jalanopi in open surprise. "You really didn't know?"

"This is the first I've heard of it," said McFarley, frowning.

"How many weapons?" asked Jalanopi.

Rawls shrugged again. "I don't know. Twenty, thirty thousand. Maybe more."

"Why have you left her service?" demanded McFarley suspiciously.

"Despite what you may think, we parted on friendly terms," answered Rawls. "She's a driven woman; she won't stop until she's put together her string of worlds in the Spiral Arm, and she'll die before she's finished. I took a long hard look at the situation one day and realized that I'm *not* a driven man. I have enough money to live comfortably for the rest of my life, and it suddenly occurred to me that I'm nearer the end than the beginning. It's time to start enjoying the fruits of my labor, and during the time I spent hunting with Fuentes, I discovered what I enjoy the most."

"Then why start a safari business? Why not just go out and hunt for the rest of your life?"

Rawls smiled. "I may not be a driven man, but I'm not a *stupid* man, either. I haven't the skill or the reputation to get contracts from the huge Republic museums like Fuentes can, but I see no reason why I shouldn't make a profit on my hobby if I can."

There was a momentary silence, which was broken by Jalanopi.

"What of Athens?" he asked. "She cannot move an entire city to Fani country."

"You're not dealing with some amateur," said Rawls. "This is Violet Gardener we're talking about."

"What's your point?" asked McFarley.

Rawls grinned. "Since she couldn't move Athens to Fani country, she moved Fani country to Athens."

"I do not understand," said Jalanopi.

"The Fani border was officially moved two hundred miles south last week, and somewhere out there is a Republic mapmaker who's about five million credits richer than she was the last time you saw her."

"I don't believe you," said McFarley.

"I have copies of the map in my office back in Athens, with the Department of Cartography's seal on them," said Rawls. "I'll have one sent to you."

"That's illegal!" shouted McFarley.

"Since it falls within the domain of the Department of Cartography, it's perfectly legal," replied Rawls. "Oh, you could challenge it in court, or get Mr. Gaunt to do it for you, but Katherine Njobe can tie it up for as long as Gaunt can tie up the treaty. We'll all be dead and buried before any of it gets resolved."

"Then I will go to war and reclaim my land," said Jalanopi.

Rawls looked amused. "With what? The weapons you've got will kill more Tulabete than Fani."

McFarley stared at him for a long minute. "Why have you told us all this, Mr. Rawls?" he asked at last.

"Because you asked, and because it's in my best interest that you realize I'm the only source of Republic credits you've got. If Jalanopi wants to buy weapons, or bring back any of the conveniences his people have grown used to before they get annoyed with him for sending Violet Gardener away, you might as well deal with me."

"We have much information to evaluate," said Jalanopi. "I will give you my answer in ten days."

"I'm afraid I'll need it by tomorrow," said Rawls, deciding the time had come to bait the hook and dangle it before them. "I have a partner who's anxious to move quickly. If we can't get a hunting concession here, we'll have to deal with the Fani or the Rakko." He paused. "I'd

much prefer the Baski Plains. Fuentes says it's the best hunting area on the planet."

"Who is your partner?" demanded McFarley. "Violet Gardener?"

"I told you before," said Rawls. "I am no longer associated with Violet Gardener."

"Then who is it?"

"I don't suppose there's any harm in telling you," said Rawls, after pretending to weigh the question for a moment. "It's Katherine Njobe. She saw no reason to keep working on salary after her little windfall last week, and she wants to invest her money on Karimon. *I'm* perfectly willing to wait ten days, but she's never had this kind of money before, and as the old saying goes, it's burning a hole in her pocket. She wants everything to get started yesterday." He paused and smiled. "You know, the crazy thing is she doesn't even *like* hunting. Thinks it's immoral to go around shooting animals for anything but food. But she wants her money to start working for her, and she doesn't like the thought of being one of Madam Gardener's minority stockholders." She chuckled. "Probably afraid Violet will find some way to do to her what she did to the border."

"I see," said McFarley thoughtfully.

Rawls looked at both faces, human and alien, trying to hide their thought processes from him, and decided that his job was done.

"I've got to go back to Athens and close out some accounts—it's my last official act as a Spiral Arm Development Company employee—and I probably won't be able to get back until tomorrow evening," he said. "Katherine is due to land at Mastaboni later this afternoon. Since she's putting up the bulk of the money, and she's the one who knows the exact dimensions of the Baski Plains, she's empowered to finalize an agreement with you."

"We will consider meeting with her," said Jalanopi.

"Fair enough," said Rawls. "We've had our differences in

the past, but I'm sure you'll see that my business proposition can benefit both of us. I look forward to a long and prosperous relationship with you."

"We shall see," said Jalanopi.

"Just consider the alternatives," said Rawls. "That's all I ask."

As he drove back to the airport, he was certain they were doing just that: considering the alternatives. And long before Katherine Njobe arrived, they would realize that the only alternative to becoming an economic and military backwater while the Fani were prospering through their mythical treaty with the Spiral Arm Development Company was to make the best deal they could with the cartographer.

It was not the first time in his life that he felt a twinge of sympathy for anyone who was foolish enough to stand in the path of Violet Gardener's dream.

Sixteen

On the 183rd day of the year 1826 G.E., Jalanopi, king of the Tulabete, signed an agreement giving Katherine Njobe's newly formed Karimon Development Corporation limited farming and homesteading rights and unlimited mining rights to the kingdom of the Tulabete, as well as a hunting concession in the Baski Plains, in exchange for a fee of five million credits per annum to be paid in perpetuity to Jalanopi and his heirs.

On the 186th day of the year 1826 G.E., the Spiral Arm Development Company purchased one hundred percent of the stock of the Karimon Development Corporation, including all of its assets and liabilities, for the sum of one million credits, and Katherine Njobe was given a seat on the board of directors of the Spiral Arm Development Corporation.

On the 304th day of the year 1826 G.E., Katherine Njobe submitted her maps of Karimon and the neighboring world of Belamaine to the Department of Cartography.

On the 316th day of the year 1826 G.E., the Department of Cartography approved Katherine Njobe's recommendation that the names of Karimon and Belamaine, the sister

planets that specialized in mining and agriculture, be changed to Rockgarden and Flowergarden in honor of Violet Gardener, whose efforts on behalf of the Spiral Arm Development Company had brought so many new worlds into the Republic's eager embrace.

And Violet Gardener was two steps closer to the realization of the dream that burned so fiercely within her.

III

FUENTES' GLORY

Seventeen

Fuentes, his rifle cradled in his arms, crawled across the sunbaked ground, trying to ignore the sweat that rolled down his forehead and into his eyes. After he had progressed some five yards he stopped and peered ahead once more.

The small herd of Brownbucks was still grazing about forty yards ahead of him. Twelve—no, make that eleven females, nine of them with young, and one male. About three hundred yards to his left were another half dozen males, bachelors who were biding their time until one felt capable of challenging the herd bull.

He wished they would all go away.

Because one hundred yards past the herd was his prey, a huge Redmountain that had so far remained unaware of his presence. It was a magnificent beast, standing fully fifteen feet at the shoulder, covered with coarse reddish hair, its long narrow ears tight atop its head, twitching constantly, listening for danger. The eyes—small, blue, distrusting, peeking out from beneath the rudimentary horns on its forehead—weren't of much use to it, but it was said those ears could hear a bush rustle a mile away. And the

huge nostrils, set at the end of its enormous, oblong head, could smell water from fifty miles away.

The Redmountain had no natural enemies, not until the natives of Rockgarden had developed weapons, but it was almost as if Nature had anticipated this, for no animal on the planet was better equipped to pinpoint danger, and none was so quick to flee from it.

Which, concluded Fuentes, was what made them worth the effort in the first place. Merchants within the Republic paid good money for the horns, which were then transformed into jewelry . . . but Fuentes had more than enough money. It was the challenge he craved, and that was why he hunted Rockgarden, as he had hunted Peponi and Serengeti and a dozen other worlds before he had landed on this one.

He really should have been out dispatching a family of Blue-and-Golds, those oddly striped herbivores of the northern plains, to fill a commission for the Natural History Museum on Far London. In fact, he had a lot of commissions still to fulfill, but Bandakona, his tracker, had spotted this particular Redmountain late yesterday afternoon, and he had dropped everything else to go after it.

Slowly, carefully, he withdrew a small cloth bag filled with cigar ashes from one of his many pockets and tapped it gently, then watched the ash float gently past him, away from the Redmountain.

Fuentes sighed. The wind was right, the sun was so bright that the Redmountain couldn't tell him from a tree stump, not at this distance . . . but if he stood up, he would panic the Brownbucks, and the second they took off the Redmountain would flee into the nearby thornscrub. It wouldn't hide him, but it wouldn't have to: no Man could keep up with a Redmountain, and only a hunter with a death wish would walk alone into the shoulder-high bush, where he'd be at the mercy of any carnivore that chose to stalk him. There was no visibility, no room to maneuver,

too many chances of hanging himself up on the six-inch thorns.

He put the ash bag back into his pocket, then froze as the Brownbuck bull suddenly raised its head and stared in his direction. An insect crawled up his shirt, attracted by the scent of his perspiration, and bit him painfully on the side of his neck. He grimaced, but made no other movement, and after what seemed an eternity the bull went back to its grazing. Fuentes waited another ten seconds, then carefully moved his hand up to his neck, found the insect, and pulped it between a thumb and forefinger.

He looked ahead again and saw that the Redmountain's grazing was slowly taking him farther and farther away. Fuentes estimated the Redmountain's distance at two hundred fifty yards. For a moment he considered leaping to his feet, yelling to scatter the Brownbucks, and taking a quick quartering shot as the Redmountain raced off toward the thornscrub. It was possible, of course—he'd made more difficult shots in his career—but the likelihood of dropping the Redmountain with the first shot was minimal. Probably he'd have to go for a lung shot; with the Redmountain racing hell-for-leather in the opposite direction, there was too much chance of having the bullet deflected by a massive hip or leg bone . . . and even a lung shot would be unlikely to kill it before it reached the thornscrub, and then he'd have to follow it into the bush, where the advantage would be all with the Redmountain.

No, he'd just have to wait where he was, inch forward whenever he could, and hope that the Brownbucks would disperse or the Redmountain would move off in a new direction. Otherwise, it would simply be another unsuccessful hunt; he'd had hundreds before, he'd have hundreds in the future.

He looked behind him. There was Bandakona, his tracker, laying motionless some sixty yards away. The Tulabete saw Fuentes staring at him and looked at the hunter

questioningly. Fuentes shook his head and motioned the tracker to remain where he was.

Then his attention was taken by the Brownbucks. Suddenly they seemed nervous and uneasy. They would graze for a moment, then suddenly look around with wild, staring eyes. The herd bull snorted a few times and walked a few steps in Fuentes' direction, its ears tight on its head, flicking constantly.

Fuentes knew that he had done nothing to alert the Brownbucks to his presence, and a quick glance back showed him that Bandakona had remained absolutely motionless. No, something else was disturbing the herd. Possibly a Wildfang or a Nightkiller in the tall grass.

Even the Redmountain was getting uncomfortable now. It bellowed, that resonant, low-pitched bellow that, once heard, could never be forgotten, and began looking around restlessly.

Fuentes noticed some sweat on the stock of his rifle and slowly, gently wiped it off with his sleeve. If there *was* a carnivore out there, and the herd suddenly broke and ran, he might, just might, be able to get off two aimed shots before the Redmountain made it to the thornscrub.

Then the Redmountain looked straight in his direction, bellowed again, turned on its heel, and raced off. An instant later the Brownbuck raced off after it.

"Fuentes!" cried a voice, and he turned to see a Tulabete racing across the flat dry grass toward him.

"Damn it, Bandakona, what the hell got into—?"

Fuentes stopped, puzzled, as Bandakona stood up, looking every bit as disgusted as the hunter.

"Fuentes!" cried the running Tulabete again, and now Fuentes could see that it was Ramaloki, one of his camp attendants.

Fuentes stood, hands on hips, and waited for the Tulabete to reach him.

"You'd better have a damned good reason for frightening off that Redmountain," he said at last.

"Message you," panted Ramaloki, who had only recently mastered a very rudimentary Terran.

"It couldn't wait?"

"Big message. Very important."

"All right. What is it?"

"You come back to camp, you see and hear."

"Why don't you just tell me?"

"Can't. Violet Gardener not to confide."

"Violet Gardener?" repeated Fuentes. "Are you sure?"

"Yes. Very sure."

Fuentes sighed, slung his rifle over his shoulder, and began the two-mile walk to where he had parked his groundcar. Once there, he waited until Bandakona and Ramaloki climbed onto the roof—their favorite seating area—and followed the barely discernible track back to his camp, which had been pitched in a small clearing beside a stream. Three of his assistants were working on skins he had taken the day before, scraping the insides with knives to remove the last vestiges of flesh and fat, and his cook, a native with an unpronounceable name from a tiny tribe that was distantly related to the Fani, started making a pot of coffee the instant his groundcar arrived.

A small, slight woman was sitting on a chair in front of his bubble tent, and he had to stare at her for a moment before he realized that it was Violet Gardener. She had lost some thirty pounds from her stocky frame in the three years since he had last seen her, and she now supported herself with a cane. Her hair was almost totally white.

"Good morning," she said. "I'm sorry to disturb your hunt, but it's imperative that I speak to you."

"I'm always happy to speak to you, Madam Gardener," said Fuentes, handing his rifle to one of his bearers, who took it off to clean and oil it. "Shall we go into my bubble?"

She nodded, turned with some difficulty, and had barely

reached the entrance before he caught up with her and helped her through.

"Won't you sit down?" he asked, pulling up a chair for her.

"Thank you," she said, seating herself gently and breathing an exhausted sigh.

"I almost didn't recognize you," said Fuentes.

"Incurable blood diseases will do that to you," she replied wryly. Suddenly she smiled. "At least I don't have any trouble keeping my weight down these days."

"You don't look well, Madam Gardener," said Fuentes. "Whatever you have to say, you could have done it via our camp video receiver. You didn't have to come in person."

"I think I did," she replied. "I have a proposition to put to you, and I cannot take No for an answer."

He eyed her warily. She may have been old and weak and sickly, but she was still Violet Gardener.

"How long have you been out here in the wilderness?" she asked, returning his stare.

"Four or five months," he said. "Possibly six. Time doesn't have much meaning out here. I get into Athens during the rains, to ship out my trophies, deposit my commissions, and pick up new assignments."

"But for all practical purposes, you just stay for a few days and then come out to the bush again?"

He nodded, wondering what was coming. "That's right."

"So you're not aware of the political situation."

"*Is* there a political situation?" he asked. "I thought you secured the rights to exploit Rockgarden almost six years ago."

"I did."

"Well, then?"

"We have a problem on our hands," said Violet, shifting painfully on her chair, trying vainly to find a comfortable position.

"The Republic?" asked Fuentes. "Most of my contacts on Deluros VIII are dead or retired."

She shook her head. "The problem is right here on Rockgarden," she replied.

"Who's causing it?"

She sighed again. "Part of our agreement, the operative part that allows us to function here, is that we have been paying Jalanopi an obscene amount of tribute each year for the right to mine and homestead his land."

"He's demanding more?"

"No."

"Well, then?"

"He wants all Men to leave Rockgarden immediately."

"He did that once before, and it didn't work."

"Before, he hadn't spent twenty million credits on Canphorite weapons," noted Violet grimly. "He's got a fully equipped army. They've taken over some of our outposts on the Rakko border."

"How big an army?"

"Who knows? At least thirty thousand, possibly four times that many, not counting collaborators and fifth columnists in every native village."

"All right," said Fuentes. "You've got an armed native uprising on your hands. I'm sorry to hear about it. But why does this concern *me*? I live out here in the bush; I didn't even know what was going on until you informed me."

"Fair question," acknowledged Violet. "Straight and to the point." She paused. "I want you to take command of our armed forces."

Fuentes laughed. "Me? I've never spent a day in uniform in my life."

"That's not important."

"Then why are you joking about it?"

"I'm not joking. We need a hero to rally around, and you happen to be the only hero we've got."

"Why don't you just do the reasonable thing and ask the Republic to send the Navy?" said Fuentes.

"We could," admitted Violet. "But once you let the Republic in, it's damnably hard to make them go away again." She shook her head. "No, we have the manpower and the weaponry to put down this uprising. What we need is a bona fide hero that Men want to follow, a hero who will inspire them to do what they have to do."

"I'm no hero," protested Fuentes. "I'm just a hunter."

"You are a hunter with four best-selling books circulating through the Republic. They've written two biographies of you, and even made a syndicated holo show of your adventures. They've—"

"Those weren't *my* adventures," interrupted Fuentes. "Some scriptwriter dreamed them up."

"It makes no difference," said Violet firmly. "They're yours now." She paused. "You have been honored on Earth and Deluros VIII. One of your hunting companions was Johnny Ramsey, the most popular Secretary the Republic ever had. There's not a man on Rockgarden who doesn't know your face. You're T. J. Fuentes, the greatest hero on Rockgarden, maybe in the whole Spiral Arm, and you're the man I want for the job."

Fuentes spent a moment considering his reply. "I'm flattered, Madam Gardener," he said at last. "But I don't know the first thing about military strategy."

"You think Jalanopi does?" she shot back.

"At least he knows his territory."

"So do you," said Violet. "Better than any Man. Perhaps even better than Jalanopi himself."

"I'm not qualified to command men in battle."

"Then I will surround you with officers who are, and you can rely on their advice. But I need *you* to rally the people and lead our men into battle."

"And if I say no?" he asked.

"Then we'll lose an outpost a day, and our colonists will

be tortured and killed, until I can find someone else to lead us."

"How many colonists have we lost so far?"

"Thirty-seven."

"That's not very many."

"I know," said Violet. "But I want you to know *how* they died."

She handed him a trio of cubes, each with a holograph taken at the scene of the carnage. Fuentes, who had seen death every day of his adult life, winced as he stared at the first two and returned the third without looking at it.

"When and where do I report for duty?"

"Tomorrow morning, at Government House, in Athens."

"I'll be there," he promised.

Eighteen

Fuentes sat in his bubble, examining his weaponry: laser pistol, sonic pistol, plasma rifle, molecular imploder.

He shook his head sadly. If there were four less sporting weapons in existence, he didn't know of them. He missed his projectile rifle, just as he was sure he would miss the *thunk!* of a bullet striking home.

He sipped his coffee and studied the map once again. No one knew quite where Jalanopi was, but Paratoka, Jalanopi's most trusted advisor, had the main body of Tulabete forces encamped on the Karimona River, about eighty miles north of the Ramsey Falls. It was good terrain for them: heavily forested, too damned hilly for Violet's engineers to have gotten around to building roads yet, lots of meals on the hoof, plenty of water, a couple of hundred villages where any wounded snakes could find aid and succor.

The problem was, he didn't know *why* they were there. There were no human habitations within forty miles, and the snakes had no vehicles. They were hundreds of miles from Mastaboni, almost a thousand miles from Athens.

Whenever he hunted a new world, he always gave himself a few months to study his prey, to learn how it thought, before going out with rifle in hand to take his trophies. But now he had eight thousand Men under his command, almost a third of the human population of Rockgarden, and they—and Violet Gardener and the politicians—were itching for battle, hungering for a victory to brag about.

He looked out the open entrance of his bubble, at the hustle and bustle of the encampment. There were so many Men! It made him uneasy. He was used to being virtually alone, accompanied only by an alien camp staff, neither knowing nor caring what day of the week it was, or even where he was. For more years than he cared to think about, his life had been structured around two necessities: a source of water and a source of trophies. He begrudgingly carried a video transmitter, but he had never once sent a message on it; he used it only to receive the rare transmission from civilization.

And now he was surrounded by officers awaiting his orders, by farmers and miners turned soldier who had probably been handling these strange weapons all their lives, by radio and video operators who were in constant contact with Athens and Mastaboni, by a small army of chefs and orderlies who were required to tend to the larger army that looked to him for leadership.

How had it happened? One moment he was lying on his belly in the dry grass, waiting for a clear shot at a Redmountain, and then suddenly he was a commanding general, wondering not only why he and he alone was qualified to lead his Men against Jalanopi, but also what Jalanopi had gone to war for in the first place. Normally taciturn, he had become positively close-mouthed. Normally given to a drink before supper, he now consumed almost a pint of alcohol each evening. Normally given to walking twenty and thirty miles under the blistering sun of Rockgarden, he now rode in the back of his command vehicle, surrounded

by officers and communications equipment that were more alien to him than the Redmountains and Wildfangs that he hunted.

A uniformed man entered his bubble, stood before him, and saluted smartly.

"Yes?" he said.

"Colonel Marston requests permission to speak to Commander Fuentes, sir."

Fuentes sighed. "Then just say, 'I want to talk to you, Fuentes,' " he said. "And skip the salute. And the sir."

"But—"

"You know I'm the boss here, don't you?" asked Fuentes.

"Yes, sir."

"And I know you know it. And there's no one else around to impress. So forget the pomp and ceremony and just tell me what's on your mind, Mr. Marston."

"Yes, sir . . . ah, yes, Fuentes," said Marston with an expression of disapproval.

"That's better. Now let's have it."

"We caught a Tulabete spy about three miles from here, sir," said Marston. "We thought you might like to be present for questioning."

Fuentes nodded and got to his feet. "Where is he?"

"It's a she," said Marston, stepping aside as Fuentes walked past him and out into the open. "We've got her in the guardhouse." He paused. "We haven't been able to get a word out of her yet."

"Let's go," said Fuentes, turning to his left. He walked with the same easy, ground-eating stride he had developed over the years, and Marston had to trot to keep up with him.

When he reached the guardhouse, two soldiers saluted him, and one opened the door of the lightweight titanium structure for him. He stepped inside, waited until his eyes became accustomed to the poor light, then turned to Marston.

"Where is she?"

"Cell number three, sir."

"Open it."

Marston walked to the third cell and hit the combination that caused the door to slide into the wall. Seated on the chair was a female inhabitant of the planet, her jaw swollen, her left eye blackened and shut. Her hands were cuffed behind her, and she sat on a small, uncomfortable stool.

"Turn her loose," said Fuentes.

"You mean take off the cuffs, sir?" asked Marston.

"I meant what I said. Take her back to where you found her, set her free, and give her our apologies."

"But, sir—"

"Look at the tattoos on her legs, and at the totem on her necklace," snapped Fuentes. "Can't any of you fools tell a Fani from a Tulabete?"

"She's a Fani?" asked Marston, surprised.

"Of course she's a Fani. *That's* why she wouldn't talk to you. She doesn't understand the Tulabete dialect."

"But she looks just like a Tulabete!" said Marston defensively.

"And you and I probably look alike to her," said Fuentes.

"How will I convey our apologies to her, sir?" asked Marston.

"Take my personal chef along with you," said Fuentes. "He speaks some Fani."

"Yes, sir," said Marston, saluting.

"And Colonel Marston," said Fuentes.

"Sir?"

"Next time, *look* first. We're here to fight the Tulabete. We don't need a war with the Fani, too."

Marston took the Fani female by the arm and left without another word, and Fuentes, dreaming of empty places and silent nights, returned to his bubble, opened his bottle a few hours earlier than usual, and poured himself a tall drink.

Nineteen

I t was an hour before dawn when Fuentes gave the signal to halt.

The woods were silent, all the predators having fled before the approach of his army. He gave the signal to his chief lieutenants, who began dispersing in a huge semicircle. Suddenly a Tailswinger screeched, and one of the soldiers instantly silenced it with a sonic pistol.

Fuentes checked his timepiece. Marston's men should have positioned themselves about four miles to the south. He'd give his own men twenty minutes to circle the Tulabete encampment, and then he'd call for the predawn attack.

It had been worked out in minute detail by his advisors, a classic example of military encirclement. The Karimona River was running fast and deep at this time of year, and they would be attacking from three directions, with the river itself cutting off any possible retreat. Paratoka was supposed to have close to six thousand Tulabete here; a quick, decisive victory might convince Jalanopi to call off the war and sue for peace.

Nonetheless, Fuentes felt uneasy. Maybe this was the way

Men fought against each other, or against the Canphorites and Lodinites, but the Tulabete were creatures of the wilderness, even more at home in it than Fuentes himself. *He* couldn't be caught in a trap like this, and he had some difficulty believing that *they* could. Just the absence of predators' growls and coughs should have told them something was amiss, as should the fact that no avian or Tailswinger screeched a second time.

He'd left three thousand men back at his main encampment, going through drills for the benefit of any spies Paratoka might have sent up there—*real* spies, not poor Fani females who didn't even know there was a war going on—and had come down here with one hundred boats silently riding the swift river current. One boat had capsized, one had been attacked by an enraged Water Horse, but the other ninety-eight had made it intact, and he now had a force slightly larger than Paratoka's own, and far better armed, almost in position to strike.

His advisors were manning the communication devices, making sure each unit was properly placed, and still he felt uneasy. They may have been primitives, these Tulabete, but they weren't stupid, and only stupid soldiers allowed themselves to be completely surrounded in the bush.

Still, he wasn't able to put his doubts into the form of valid objections, objections that his lieutenants would understand, and so he stood, his back against a small tree, peering ahead into the darkness, trying futilely to spot a flickering light from a Tulabete campfire.

Finally the moment came for him to signal the attack, and still he waited. It *felt* wrong, and he hadn't lived this long in the wild by not paying attention to his instincts.

"Sir?" said an advisor, crawling over to him. "Is something wrong?"

"I don't know," said Fuentes.

"The men are all in position, and it will be light in

another eight or ten minutes, sir," said the advisor. "If we wait much longer, we lose our advantage."

Fuentes waited silently for another moment, and finally nodded.

"All right," he said. "Pass the word."

"Thank you, sir."

Timepieces were synchronized, communications were passed, and ninety seconds later thousands of Men stormed the Tulabete camp.

It was deserted.

Fuentes arrived with his advisors five minutes later.

"I was afraid of this," he muttered.

"How could they have known?" said one of his advisors bitterly.

"We must have a traitor in the ranks," said another.

"We don't have any traitors," said Fuentes.

"Then how could they have known, sir?"

"The same way I'd have known."

The man stared at him, but made no reply.

Fuentes saw two soldiers approaching a hut.

"Tell those men that no one enters any dwellings," he ordered.

"But sir," said an advisor, "they may have stockpiled some weaponry in—"

The explosion drowned out the rest of his sentence, and more than one hundred Men fell to the ground. Most lay still; a few writhed weakly.

"Medic!" screamed an officer.

As the sun came up, three more dwellings exploded, and Fuentes, leaving only his explosives experts behind, ordered a retreat to the boats.

"But shouldn't we try to pick up their trail, sir?" asked an advisor.

"They're long gone," said Fuentes. "They've got a ten- or twelve-hour head start on us, and they've had time to lay a booby trap every half mile. I've lost over three hundred

Men here without even sighting the enemy. I think that's enough for one disaster, don't you?"

"Then we're just going to turn tail and run?"

"That's right."

"I request permission to take a party out after them," insisted the advisor.

"Permission denied," said Fuentes. "You and your brethren are military men, and I'm sure you know what you're doing in a conventional military situation, but you're overmatched here. As long as I'm still in charge, I'm going to do what I should have done in the first place."

"And what is that, sir?" asked the advisor sullenly.

"I'm going to fight this war the way it *should* be fought," answered Fuentes.

Twenty

Fuentes leaned against the corral rail and looked at the herd of Blue-and-Golds.

"Well," asked Alex Hawkins, standing beside him.

"How many have you got?" asked Fuentes.

"Maybe a hundred here, probably four hundred more roaming the north pasture."

"And they've all been broken to bridle and saddle?"

"That's right."

"You showed remarkable foresight, Mr. Hawkins."

"Foresight, hell," chuckled Hawkins. "I took one look at your armored column when it moved through four months ago, and I knew you couldn't sneak up on a deaf man with it." He paused and lit a small, thin cigar. "So I asked myself, what are these guys gonna need if they really plan to fight the Tulabete? And I said, they're gonna need some way to approach 'em without alerting every living thing within ten miles. Well, I'd been raising Blue-and-Golds for meat—I've got a contract with a couple of restaurants, plus your pal Rawls' safari camps—and I figured, hell, they're half-domesticated anyway, so why not see if they can be broken for riding? Could be worth even more to me that way."

"It was a very smart move."

"I knew sooner or later you'd need something to ride, and I figured, well, they could import horses or some other riding animals, but they're not native to Rockgarden. Those that disease don't kill right off will alert every avian and Tailswinger around—whereas if you ride through the bush on Blue-and-Golds, animals that *belong* there, hell, none of the other animals figure to raise any kind of a ruckus at all, and you don't need to carry any special feed with you. They'll eat whatever the land's got to give 'em."

"How much are you asking for the batch?"

"Well, I've got to keep at least a half a dozen stallions and maybe sixty mares to form the nucleus of a new herd," said Hawkins. "And then I have to figure my expenses. I mean, hell, they put fifteen of my wranglers in the hospital at Athens." He lowered his head in thought for a moment, then looked up. "Twelve hundred credits apiece, in lots of fifty."

"I'll take all that you have."

"Just like that?" asked Hawkins, amused. "You don't want to argue price?"

"The government's paying for it," said Fuentes. He pulled out a pocket computer, dictated his agreement, sealed it with both thumbprint and voiceprint, and ordered it to supply a hard copy, which he handed to Hawkins. "Just transmit this to the Department of Defense at Athens. I'll need an accurate count of them before I leave, and they'll deposit the money in your account within ten days."

"When will you take them away?"

"I'll be back in an hour with my men."

"Hey, Fuentes!" called Hawkins as Fuentes walked to his armored groundcar.

"Yes?"

"I ain't got more than a dozen saddles and bridles."

"I ordered five hundred in Athens. They arrived at my camp this morning."

"Then you knew all along you were buying my Blue-and-Golds."

"That's right."

"Maybe I should have asked for more money."

"But you didn't."

Hawkins shrugged. "Well, what the hell, I sure as hell ain't gonna go broke on the deal."

Fuentes returned an hour later with a dozen Men and herded the Blue-and-Golds back to his camp. Four hundred thirty-six hand-picked men and women, each of whom had had some experience riding horses or other animals, were waiting for them. Within an hour all of the Blue-and-Golds had been saddled and mounted. A few were initially skittish, but Fuentes gave his team a full week to get used to working with their animals, and by the end of that time they were as well behaved as any cavalry mounts back on old Earth.

Each night he had one of his aides contact his base camp and find out where the enemy's warriors were located. Finally, on the eighth day, when he decided his team was ready for battle, he pinpointed the nearest of Jalanopi's armies, a force of about four thousand Tulabete that was encamped at the foot of the Tenya Mountains some forty miles to the east of him.

"Summon the troops," he ordered another aide, then went out to the center of the camp and waited for them to assemble.

"Your training period has ended," he announced when the last of them had arrived, and they were all lined up at attention. "Tomorrow morning we will ride to the Tenya Mountains, where we expect resistance from one of Jalanopi's armies. They have Canphorite weaponry, but I think we can anticipate that not one in ten of them will have mastered it, whereas you have all demonstrated proficiency with your own weapons."

He paused, and accepted a small box from one of his

aides. "Our Blue-and-Golds will allow us to traverse any type of terrain without calling undue attention to ourselves. They are of this world, and I think I can guarantee that this will not be a repeat of the fiasco that took place two months ago at the Karimona River.

"Some of you," he continued, "may question just how easy it will be to approach the enemy, even mounted on native animals. Each of you, upon returning to your bubbles, will find a box identical to this on your bunk." He held the box up, then opened it. "Each box contains an outfit identical to *this*"—he produced a form-fitting blue-and-gold–striped bodysuit—"and from this day forth, you will wear your camouflage suit at all times. I guarantee that at eight hundred yards, you will be indistinguishable from your mounts, especially since we will not be marching them in formation, and once you are closer to the enemy than eight hundred yards, I trust you will know what to do and there will be no further need for camouflage or secrecy."

There was a murmur of surprise at the sight of the outfit.

"Let me impress upon you once again that once I pass the word that we are nearing the enemy, only myself, Colonel Nichols, and Colonel Calthrop are empowered to lead the team. One of us will always be in the vanguard, and your animals will follow us at their own speed and in their own way. Should they appear in any recognizable formation, our advantage will be lost. Is that understood?"

There was a general nodding of heads.

"Are there any questions?"

"What are we to do with our prisoners, sir?" asked a young woman. "Since we've been living off the land, we don't have any provisions for them, or even any extra Blue-and-Golds for them to ride once they've been captured."

"The answer to that should be obvious," answered Fuentes. "We cannot afford to have any survivors escape and inform the rest of Jalanopi's armies that we have employed the strategy of approaching and attacking on Blue-

and-Golds." He paused and looked around at his troops. "If there are no survivors, there are no prisoners. Is there anyone who does not understand what I am saying?"

. Silence.

He dismissed them then and had them awaked about an hour before sunrise. The camp was bustling with chefs and aides-de-camp and grooms rushing all over, but Fuentes got them moving by daybreak.

"We might as well find out what kind of stamina these beasts have when they're carrying full loads," he announced about a mile out of camp. "Let's take them at a trot or a slow canter for the next few miles and see how they hold up."

Within two miles even the fittest of the Blue-and-Golds were covered with lather and panting heavily.

"Well, that's that," he remarked. "They've got a fine turn of speed for a little more than half a mile, enough to take them well clear of a Wildfang or a Nightkiller, but they can't remain in motion all day like the Fleetjumpers or the Brownbucks."

He had his team dismount and walk beside the Blue-and-Golds for the next mile. Then they were back in the saddle, making their slow, easy way to the foothills of the Tenya Mountains. They didn't seem to be making much progress, but nightfall found them only ten miles from their destination.

Fuentes made each member of the team responsible for his mount. They attracted a family of Wildfangs early in the evening, but the scent of Men drove them away. A Nightkiller made a run at one of the Blue-and-Golds just before dawn and fell to the laser pistol of one of the camp guards.

They were off again just before sunrise, and Fuentes cautioned them to let their mounts graze and proceed at their own pace.

"Do you think they can see us yet, sir?" asked a female

aide when the bulk of the Blue-and-Golds were within two miles of the enemy's camp.

Fuentes nodded. "They've got to have lookouts posted higher up the mountain. Yes, they can see us all right."

"Then shouldn't we pass the word to charge?"

"No. The animals would be exhausted long before we reached our destination. Let's just let them keep grazing and edging closer." He paused. "Our only problem will come if one of the Tulabete comes out to shoot some meat for his camp."

"What do we do then?"

"Kill him as quickly and silently as possible."

But no Tulabete came to meet them, and when they were finally able to see the camp, Fuentes pulled out his sonic pistol, the predetermined sign for a charge, and a moment later more than four hundred humans, wearing striped outfits that matched their steeds, were riding hell-for-leather into the middle of the Tulabete stronghold.

Laser weapons hummed, sonic pistols destroyed with silent sound, plasma rifles hissed, and the surprised Tulabete began dropping in huge numbers. Here and there members of Fuentes' team fell to the Canphorite weapons, but the boldness of the daylight attack had caught the Tulabete by surprise, and the scene passed from attack to carnage to a simple mopping-up operation in a matter of ten minutes.

Finally silence reigned, and one of Fuentes' lieutenants approached him with the news that all but two hundred of the enemy were dead. A pair had fled up the mountain, but posed no immediate threat.

"They pose a very definite threat," Fuentes contradicted her. "We can't have them coming down after we leave and alerting the remainder of Jalanopi's soldiers to the method of our attack."

"What of the two hundred prisoners, sir?" she asked.

"I told you when we began this enterprise that we could

not afford to take any prisoners," said Fuentes. "Execute them."

"Have you any preference?"

"Preference?" he repeated, confused.

"The form of execution, sir?"

He shook his head. "Just do it as quickly and painlessly as possible."

She saluted. "Yes, sir."

He gave orders to confiscate all the Canphorite weapons, then entered his opposite number's hut, hoping to find some hint as to what they were doing here in the mountains, what their next target might be. He found nothing, but remained for almost two hours, long enough for the executions to be completed.

When he emerged he found his team's leaders waiting for further orders.

"Even the dead can inform the living," he said. "I want you to turn your molecular imploders on the corpses until there's nothing left of them. Then do the same to the huts and all other signs that there was ever an army or a battle on this spot." He paused. "You," he said to one of his aides, "get me my rifle."

"You mean your plasma weapon, sir?"

"I mean my *rifle*," said Fuentes.

She returned with it a moment later and handed it to him. He took it from her, thrilling to the feel of it in his hands after all these months.

"I should be back within two days," he said. "Set up camp out on the savannah about ten miles west of here and wait for me."

"Where are you going, sir?"

"Up there," he said, jerking his head toward the mountain. "There are two Tulabete up there, remember?"

"It's a huge mountain, sir."

"I'll find them," he replied confidently.

"They may be armed."

"I hope so," he said, walking toward the mountain, rifle in hand.

"Shouldn't we send a party out with you, sir?"

He stopped in his tracks. "There's nobody on this team who can read a trail or shoot a weapon as well as I can. The bush turns to dense forest about a quarter mile up the mountain. I won't risk human lives unnecessarily."

"We just don't want you to risk your own, sir."

He smiled. "Risk it? Hell, I'm reclaiming it."

"I don't understand, sir."

"No, I suppose you don't."

And with that, he started off again toward the mountain, his stride a little springier, his eyes a little brighter.

After five months of engaging in the follies of Men and aliens, Fuentes was going hunting once again.

Twenty-one

Fuentes followed the trail, spotting a patch of crushed grass here, a piece of shed skin hanging from a thorn branch there. They were running aimlessly, panicked, using up too much energy. He knew from his long association with the Fani and the Tulabete how far they could run under normal circumstances . . . but the Tulabete were plains-dwellers, and the higher they climbed, the more difficulty they would have as the air became thinner. They'd drop, exhausted, in another mile and a half, possibly less.

He surveyed the landscape, the contours and ridges of the mountain; he'd hunted it a year ago, and he knew it fairly well. They'd never make it up past the treeline, nor would they want to. They'd feel safe in the forest and would wait for his team to depart. That meant they'd need a vantage point, a place from which they could observe his cavalry's departure. And water, of course; they couldn't know how long the Men would remain in the area, and they'd have to have water.

His keen eyes sought out and found the three likeliest spots from which the two Tulabete could watch their camp

without being spotted from below. One had the wrong kind of shrubbery, a dryland bush that required minimal water; it would never have grown up there if there had been an ample supply. That narrowed it down to the other two sights, one quite steep, one a much easier climb. They couldn't know they were being followed, and they'd be exhausted by now, so he opted for the latter.

When he was half a mile away from it, he left the more obvious route and began silently climbing up through the bushes and trees that clung to the mountain. After a few moments he hit a thick grove of thornscrub and stripped down to his shorts and shoes, leaving his outfit and his socks behind. He'd rather have his body take the scrapes and wounds from the thorn than give himself away by a sound of ripping fabric.

The site was empty when he arrived half an hour later, but that didn't surprise him. He had analyzed where they'd go, but they would arrive only after some trial and error. He felt he had at least an hour before they showed up, and he spent the time creating a blind behind the thick bushes and then waited patiently inside it.

And it was an hour later, almost to the minute, that two Tulabete cautiously approached the site, obviously exhausted from their exertion. He waited until they were almost on top of him, then fired his rifle once and instantly trained it on the second Tulabete as the first dropped to the ground. His finger was tightening on the trigger when he recognized the Tulabete's insignia, and instead of firing, he stood up.

"Don't move!" he said in Tulabete.

"Go ahead and kill me, as you killed all the others," answered the Tulabete in excellent Terran.

"I have no intention of killing you," said Fuentes, stepping out of the blind. "You are Paratoka, Jalanopi's most trusted general. You are worth more to me alive than dead."

"Jalanopi will not ransom me," answered Paratoka.

"Jalanopi will not be given the opportunity to ransom you," answered Fuentes. "You possess much valuable information. We want it."

"I will not speak under torture," said Paratoka.

"No, you probably won't," answered Fuentes. "But you will tell us what we want to know under the influence of certain drugs."

"I will tell you nothing."

"You're welcome to think so, if it brings you comfort," said Fuentes. "Now," he added, prodding the Tulabete with the tip of his rifle, "let's climb back down the mountain and find out which of us is right." Suddenly he stopped and fired a shot in the air.

"What was that for?" asked Paratoka.

"My men know I came up here after two of you. If they spotted you before they saw me, and they hadn't heard that second shot, they might think you had murdered me and be tempted to kill you themselves."

They began climbing down the mountain. After some forty minutes of silence, Paratoka turned to Fuentes.

"Do you really have drugs that will force me to tell what I know?" he asked.

Fuentes nodded. "Your central nervous system is different than ours, so they're not the same drugs, but every sentient being is susceptible to *some* truth serum. If the medics in Athens haven't isolated it yet, your presence will give them a reason to redouble their efforts."

"I cannot let you give such drugs to me."

"You should have thought of that before you went to war."

"You should not have come to our world, and we would not have *had* to go to war."

"I never caused you any trouble," replied Fuentes. "I've always dealt fairly with Jalanopi."

"If it was just *you*, we would have had no cause for war.

But your people have virtually enslaved the Tulabete, and as Athens expands you are doing the same to the Fani. You plunder our hills, you take away our land, you make us work for you so that we can pay the taxes that you impose, and each of you lives in more luxury than Jalanopi." He paused. "Is it any wonder that we have gone to war?"

"I'm no politician," answered Fuentes. "The reasons you took up arms are your business. Ending the war as quickly as possible is mine."

"You may win this battle, and the next one, and the one after that," said Paratoka. "But in the end we will win the war. It is our world, and you are the intruders."

"It's my observation that God usually favors the side with the best weapons."

"Then your god is a fool."

"We shall see," said Fuentes, as the trail narrowed and they found themselves walking at a steep angle down a precarious path.

"No, Fuentes," said Paratoka. "*You* shall see. I cannot go to Athens with you. I will not betray my people."

And with that, he calmly stepped out into space and fell some three hundred feet into a gully.

It was then that Fuentes began to wonder if the war would ever truly end as long as a single Tulabete or Fani remained alive.

Twenty-two

Fuentes spent the next day and night alone in his bubble, considering the implications of Paratoka's death, the fanaticism of a man—*snake,* he corrected himself—who would rather throw himself off a mountain than betray an army that was obviously doomed to defeat.

When he emerged after breakfast the next day, he was a changed man, a man who knew what had to be done. The snakes must be taught, now and for all time, that resistance was futile, because if that lesson wasn't driven home, promptly and unequivocally, they might have continual war until the last snake was killed. He didn't care what happened to the planet—it would never be an untouched wilderness again, and if he survived the war he knew that he'd be heading off in search of another paradise, hopefully a few years ahead of the colonists—but he was a Man, and he knew that it was his duty to do what he could to see that Men didn't get thrown off the planet, because if it could happen on Rockgarden, it could happen on Flowergarden and Goldstone and Peponi and Walpurgis III and all the thousands of other worlds on which the race had gained a toehold.

So Rockgarden wouldn't be Paradise anymore, which was simply evolution, to his way of thinking. As long as he could stop it from becoming Inferno, he'd have done his job, fulfilled his obligation to the race, and then he could move on. He was a realist, and in this case, outnumbered hundreds to one by the snakes, he'd settle for stopping the slide at Purgatory.

That afternoon he studied the map again. There were twenty-seven Tulabete villages between the Tenya Mountains and the Fani border. Twenty-seven lessons to be learned by the snakes, before they became so powerful that only their extinction could prevent the slaughter of every Man on the planet.

This time the Blue-and-Golds marched in formation. They came out of the savannah and burned the first three villages they came to. Those snakes who remained to fight were killed; those who fled were left alone, to spread the word of what happened to innocent snake bystanders when Jalanopi dared to take up arms against Man.

The fourth village he bypassed entirely. Let the snakes wonder about that, let them search for fifth columnists among their own, let them destroy every last member of the village simply because Fuentes had seen fit not to attack it.

He leveled the next nine, burning crops wherever he found them. He then bypassed two more, and followed that by destroying every Tulabete village all the way to the Fani border.

Then, because he didn't want a war with the Fani at some future date, he marched his squad through the heart of Fani country. They killed no one, destroyed no dwellings or farmfields, killed only those animals they needed to eat . . . but they represented an irresistible force, and when he returned to Tulabete land three weeks later, he did so with the confident knowledge that those Fani who harbored thoughts of revolution had seen the future and didn't like the shape of it.

Jalanopi was waiting for him, enraged at the slaughter and destruction of twenty-four Tulabete villages. His forward scouts brought word of Jalanopi's presence back to him, and drawing upon a lifetime's bushcraft, he and his squad melted into the night and reappeared thirty miles behind Jalanopi. He waited until he had been spotted again, then began a zigzag retreat across the western hill country, never getting more than forty miles ahead of Jalanopi's army, never allowing the Tulabete to get within ten miles of him.

This cat-and-mouse pursuit continued for almost a month, as he drew Jalanopi closer and closer to the main body of his own army. He knew that the humans' weapons of destruction would work to best effect on a broad, flat field, so he gradually led Jalanopi to the Baski Plains, a broad savannah some three hundred miles long and fifty miles wide. Jalanopi followed him up to the edge of the Plains, then halted, not willing to expose his army to the superior firepower of his enemy.

Fuentes tried feint after feint, but to no avail. Jalanopi was willing to fight a guerrilla war, but he was no fool, and he knew that the humans had had ample time to reinforce their army and add to their weaponry.

Fuentes even came up with the stratagem of driving a wild herd of Blue-and-Golds to within a quarter mile of Jalanopi's main encampment and laying a trap for the retreating Tulabete, but Jalanopi spotted the ruse and held his ground. Fuentes then considered sending his cavalry in an earnest charge in the hope that Jalanopi might consider it another trick, but as well-armed as his squad was, he couldn't ask them to face nine thousand entrenched Tulabete.

And so the standoff continued, until a single radio message from Athens changed everything.

Twenty-three

Fuentes approached the airbed that floated gently some three feet above the hospital floor and wondered what was keeping its occupant alive other than her indomitable will.

Violet Gardener lay on her back, attached to half a dozen monitoring devices. Tubes and pumps constantly recirculated fresh blood through her veins, machines performed the functions of her heart, her lungs, her pancreas, and her liver. There was so much medical paraphernalia crisscrossing the bed that the patient herself seemed almost an afterthought.

"I came as soon as I heard," said Fuentes softly.

"It had to happen sooner or later," replied Violet weakly. "Even the best machine can run only so long on rotten fuel, and my body was never the best of machines even on its good days."

"There's nothing they can do?"

"They've been doing it for thirty years," she said wryly. "The stockpile of miracles finally ran out."

"What if they shipped you to Deluros?" asked Fuentes.

"This is my world. I'd rather die here."

"Has anyone told you . . . that is . . . ?"

"Two days, maybe three," she answered. "If it's any longer than that, I won't know about it: I'll be too heavily drugged because of the pain."

"I'm sorry," said Fuentes. "I wish there was something I could do."

"There is," whispered Violet.

"What?" asked Fuentes, suddenly alert.

"If I have to die, and I do, then I want to die knowing that Rockgarden is once again safe for colonization. This world can be the center of human commerce and culture in the Spiral Arm. That has been my dream. Now you have to take the next step toward making it a reality."

"We're not going to lose the war, Madam Gardener," he assured her.

"That's not enough," she said with something like her old strength. "I want to die knowing that we've *won!*"

The effort left her weak and gasping for breath.

"Two days . . ." mused Fuentes.

"One more thing," she said in a barely audible whisper.

"What is it?"

"If Jalanopi surrenders, so much the better . . . but if he should die, I want him buried next to me."

"He's your enemy."

"We have to live with the snakes," she said. "We must triumph over them, but we must also be magnanimous in victory. Bury us side by side. It will be a gesture they understand—two leaders who respected each other."

"I'll see to it," said Fuentes, as a nurse entered the room, took some new readings, and changed some of the medications that were dripping slowly into Violet's body.

"Thank you," said Violet, just before fading into unconsciousness.

Fuentes remained with her for a few more minutes, then had a driver take him back to the airport, where he rode a small military plane back to his encampment, wrestling

with the problem of how to keep his promise to Violet Gardener. The two sides had been at a standoff for close to a month. Eventually the humans' superior firepower would win the war, but first it would become a battle of attrition. He had nothing against wiping out Jalanopi's entire army with saturation bombing, but they were dispersed in small groups, and the landscape precluded the possibility of a successful mission. He'd kill two hundred thousand trees and level forty hills and pollute the Karimona River before he killed half of Jalanopi's warriors, nor did he have the military capacity to deliver a tenth of the bombs required before Violet Gardener died.

When the plane landed, he went directly to his bubble and spent another fruitless hour trying to devise some strategy to defeat an army that had stood against him for half a year, in less than two days' time. Finally he called in his most trusted advisors, put the question to them, and rejected one half-baked suggestion after another.

The consensus, after three hours of brainstorming, was that it couldn't be done, even without allowing for a safety factor. Besides, Violet Gardener, if she hadn't expired already, was almost certainly in a coma by now; what difference could it make to her whether they won in two days or two weeks or two months?

"I gave her my word," said Fuentes at last, closing the matter.

His aides walked out, one by one, and then, on a hunch, he sent for Bandakona, his former tracker who now served as his personal aide. The Tulabete arrived a moment later, and Fuentes gestured for him to sit down.

Bandakona was even more apolitical that Fuentes. He had lived in the bush all his life and felt loyalty neither to his own race nor to the race that now employed and protected him. All he wanted was for the war to end, not out

of any humanitarian reasons, but so that he and Fuentes could go back to hunting once again.

"Bandakona," began Fuentes, pouring himself a drink but not offering any to the tracker, whose metabolism couldn't handle alcohol, "I need your advice."

"You want, I give."

"You know that Jalanopi's army is dug in forty miles to the north of us."

"Yes," said Bandakona, nodding his head and pointing to the north. "In forest."

"For almost a month I have been trying to lure him out onto the Baski Plains, but I have been unsuccessful. Now it is imperative that we meet in battle in the next two days. How can I get his army to meet mine?"

Bandakona, whose Terran was too limited to comprehend some of the terms used, merely stared at Fuentes, who then translated his question into Tulabete.

"You cannot entice his army out of the forest," answered Bandakona in his native tongue, "for he knows that you have more men and better weapons. You must go in after him."

"We couldn't *find* him in that forest, let alone fight him," said Fuentes, shaking his head. "My men would be just as likely to shoot each other by mistake."

"No," said Bandakona. "You do not understand."

"Then explain to me, please."

"What I said: *you* must go in after him."

"I just told you why we can't."

"Not *we*," said Bandakona. "*You*."

Fuentes frowned. "I don't understand."

"You must enter his camp alone, or at most accompanied by myself, a Tulabete."

"I'll be an easy target the second I enter the forest."

"He will not have you killed. You are too important. He will want to know your mind."

"All right," said Fuentes. "So I enter his camp. Then what? He takes me prisoner. What good does that do?"

Bandakona parted his lips in a reptilian smile. "No, Fuentes," he said. "Go back to 'Then what?' "

"All right," said Fuentes. "I walk into his camp. Then what?"

"Then you challenge him."

"I *challenge* him?"

"In front of his own army. He cannot say no, for this is how he became king, and how he retains his kingship."

"Are you saying that if I win, I become king of the Tulabete, and can order the armies to disperse?"

"No," answered Bandakona. "You are not a Tulabete, so you cannot become king. But you one make condition: if he wins, all Men will leave Rockgarden. If you win, the Tulabete surrender and return to their villages."

"You're sure he'll do it?"

"He has no choice. If he does not accept your challenge, he is no longer king."

"You mean I could have done this at any time, and he'd have accepted the challenge?"

"Yes."

"Why the hell didn't you tell me before?" demanded Fuentes.

Bandakona looked at him, puzzled. "You never asked," he replied.

Fuentes considered the proposition. "I'm fifty-four years old," he said at last. "I don't know how you measure age, but that's not young for a Man. Jalanopi's almost a foot taller than I am, and he must outweigh me by close to one hundred pounds."

"That is another reason he will fight you," agreed Bandakona.

Fuentes sighed. "What chance have I?"

"Depends."

"Depends on what?" asked Fuentes quickly.

"If he chooses weapons, you have a chance."

"If *he* chooses weapons?" repeated Fuentes. "Why can't *I* have the choice of weapons?"

"Because you are not the king."

"What if I bring a weapon anyway?"

"Then you will be killed before you have a chance to fight him."

"I see," said Fuentes. Suddenly he got to his feet. "Let's go," he said.

"Right now?"

"If I think about it, I'll find five hundred reasons not to go."

"Violet Gardener was right," said Bandakona as they walked to the corral.

"About what?"

"You are a great warrior."

"Only if I win," said Fuentes grimly.

After they saddled their Blue-and-Golds, Fuentes summoned six of his officers to the corral.

He briefly explained the situation to them, then concluded: "I'm telling *you* this precisely because you are not settlers or colonists. You came to Rockgarden to serve in the military, and you have no vested interest in this planet. If Jalanopi defeats me in fair combat, you *must* find a way to disperse the troops and keep my word to him. I'm acting with the full power and authority of Violet Gardener."

"We'll go with you, sir!" said the youngest of them.

He shook his head. "Bandakona says if anyone except himself accompanies me I'll never make it to Jalanopi alive."

"Can you trust him, sir?"

"Jalanopi?"

"Bandakona. After all, he's a Tulabete."

"I've trusted him with my life many times in the past. He has never given me cause to regret it."

"How do you know they won't slice you to ribbons once you get there?"

"If they do, Bandakona will tell you so."

"If they don't kill him, too."

"Sir," said another lieutenant. "You really must take some of us along as observers. With all due respect to your special relationship to Bandakona, I do not believe that the Men will disperse because a Tulabete says Jalanopi defeated you in fair combat."

Fuentes considered the statement, then nodded. "You have a point. All right. Colonel Montgomery and Major Williams, get your mounts and join me."

Bandakona walked over to Fuentes. "The Tulabete will not like it, these two coming with you."

"I'll instruct them to leave their weapons behind, but we have to have a pair of credible observers. That young man was right: none of my troops will believe you."

Bandakona shrugged, and made no reply.

A few moments later Colonel Montgomery and Major Williams, a young woman who had been promoted twice by Fuentes for bravery and initiative in the face of the enemy, rode up to him.

"Do I understand that we are to be observers at a personal combat between you and Jalanopi?" asked Montgomery incredulously.

"That's right."

"And that this fight will decide the outcome of the rebellion?"

"So I have been led to believe."

"Why in the world aren't you sending Carruthers, or one of our other martial-arts experts?" persisted Montgomery.

"According to Tulabete tradition, it can only be decided by personal combat between the two leaders."

"I take it Jalanopi's met you?"

"Many times," said Fuentes. "No doubles, no ringers."

"Pity."

"I agree," said Fuentes grimly. "On that happy note, let's go off and end this war one way or another."

He turned his Blue-and-Gold to the north and urged him to a ground-eating trot.

Twenty-four

Fuentes led his little party into the forest. He was aware that the Tulabete were watching his every move, though Montgomery and Williams couldn't spot the telltale signs. Bandakona brought up the rear. Fuentes waited until he was more than halfway to Jalanopi's camp, then slowly unbuckled his gunbelt, held the holster and weapon above his head for his unseen observers to see, and let it drop to the ground, ordering the two officers to do the same.

"Let me discharge it first," said Williams, referring to her laser pistol. "Then it won't be any use to them."

"Don't," said Fuentes sharply. "If they hear it start to hum, they'll turn you into a pincushion."

"But there aren't any Tulabete around," she protested.

"You'd be surprised."

"How many?"

"More than fifty."

"Well, I'll be damned!" she muttered, and followed Fuentes' example with her own weapon. Montgomery hesitated for a moment, and then dropped his sonic pistol to the forest floor.

"Good," said Fuentes. "You're not supposed to be ac-companying me at all, but that should convince them you've only come as observers."

Bandakona, who disdained human weapons, hurled his spear into a tree and dropped his knife to the ground.

They rode in total silence for two more hours, and finally reached a large clearing that had five Tulabete dwellings that seemed to have been hastily erected some time ago and were already falling into disrepair. Some sixty Tulabete were in the camp, and Fuentes dismounted and held one hand up in the air to show he was unarmed, while he held his Blue-and-Gold's bridle with the other.

"Dismount, please," he said to his officers.

Montgomery and Williams did as he said, and stood by their mounts.

A Tulabete, wearing the insignia of an officer, ap-proached them.

"I have come to speak to Jalanopi," said Fuentes in the Tulabete dialect.

"I speak for Jalanopi."

"Do you also fight for him?" asked Fuentes.

"I fight in his army," said the officer, not understanding the implication.

"I am tired of fighting his army," said Fuentes. He raised his voice so that everyone could hear it. "I have come here to challenge Jalanopi in personal combat. If he chooses not to meet me, he is a coward, and I will claim victory before all of his people."

"I will give him your message," said the officer.

"You do that," said Fuentes. He turned his Blue-and-Gold's reins over to Bandakona and waited, hands on hips, for Jalanopi to appear.

Finally a vast number of soldiers approached, with Jalanopi, wearing his ceremonial headdress and walking with his characteristic limp, at their head. He came to a halt some ten feet from Fuentes.

"We meet again," said the Tulabete.

"We meet again," said Fuentes.

"You were a hunter of animals, Man Fuentes," said Jalanopi. "How did you come to be a persecutor of my people?"

"It happened when you became a torturer and murderer of *my* people," replied Fuentes.

"Your people have no right to be on Karimon."

"That's what I have come here to decide," said Fuentes. "If you win, Men will leave your planet. If I win, we stay. Either way, the war ends."

"You are a fool, Man Fuentes," said Jalanopi. "With my own hands I have slain a Nightkiller and killed four Tulabete, all stronger than you, who aspired to my throne."

"I believe you."

"You slay animals from great distances. You do not pit your strength against them."

"That is true," acknowledged Fuentes.

"Why, then, have you challenged me?"

"I promised Violet Gardener the war would end before she died. She will die in the next few days."

"The war will end," agreed Jalanopi. "And your race will leave Karimon forever."

"The name of this world is Rockgarden," said Fuentes, removing his hat and tossing it to Bandakona, "and nobody's leaving it. Choose your weapons."

"You hope, perhaps, that I will choose rifles at four hundred yards?" asked Jalanopi, parting his lips and hissing.

"It makes no difference to me," said Fuentes with an air of indifference. "But before we begin, I want you to instruct your people that they are to disperse and return to their homes after I kill you. Their weapons will of course be confiscated, but they will not be punished for having followed you."

Jalanopi nodded curtly to his lieutenants. "It is done.

And these two, and the traitor who holds your hat, will tell your army to return to the stars from which they came when I place my foot on your neck and claim victory?"

"They will."

"Then it is agreed, and now I will kill you, as I have killed all the others who thought they could defeat Jalanopi." He paused and drew himself up to his full seven-foot height. "We will fight with no weapons at all."

Fuentes stared at the glistening scales on Jalanopi's massive, muscular body and wondered at his own audacity. Aloud he said, "That is acceptable."

Jalanopi spread his arms wide, and his soldiers backed away, forming a huge circle of perhaps seventy feet around the two combatants. Then the king of the Tulabete lowered his head and charged the slim, gray-haired man.

Fuentes sidestepped the charge and kicked Jalanopi's game leg as the huge Tulabete passed by him. Jalanopi stumbled, fell briefly to the ground, and was up on his feet instantly.

Twice more Jalanopi charged, and twice more Fuentes narrowly avoided him and went after his bad leg. But at the end of the three charges, Jalanopi showed no sign of pain or frustration, while Fuentes was panting heavily.

This time Jalanopi approached Fuentes slowly if not cautiously, his massive arms spread out to catch the human if he tried to sidestep or avoid him. Fuentes backed away slowly, then at the last moment reached down, grabbed a handful of powdery dirt, and hurled it into Jalanopi's eyes. The Tulabete brought his hands to his face, and Fuentes, mustering all his strength, hurled himself, head and shoulder first, at Jalanopi's game leg. The *crack!* was loud enough for every soldier gathered in the circle to hear.

He felt no pride in his accomplishment. He had merely done as the predators he had hunted all his life had done: find the weak link and attack it. Besides, his shoulder was throbbing so badly he could barely lift his arm, he was

having difficulty catching his breath, and the huge being on the ground wasn't dead yet.

"I have no wish to kill you," panted Fuentes. "If you will surrender, I will let you live."

Jalanopi's answer was to lunge forward and deliver a powerful blow that was aimed at Fuentes' head but landed on his shoulder as the Tulabete lost his balance at the last instant. Nonetheless, the force of it sent Fuentes rolling across the ground, and he scrambled to his feet just before Jalanopi, dragging his broken leg behind him, could catch him.

Fuentes felt the energy leaving his aging body and realized that he could take no more chances. Instinct and a bit of wrestling and kickfighting had gotten him this far, but now he had to finish the job, and he doubled up his fists and began circling Jalanopi, always keeping just out of the Tulabete's reach, feinting now and then, and stepping in to deliver his devastating punches only when the Tulabete's leg caused him to turn too slowly or to struggle to keep his balance. He saw a rock on the ground, a large enough rock to do some serious damage, but to use it he would have to get close enough so that Jalanopi might be able to take it away and use it against him, and he decided to wait until the Tulabete was further weakened.

It was a slaughter, but a slow slaughter. Within ten minutes Jalanopi's face was bleeding in half a dozen places, and one of his eyes was swollen shut. Five minutes later the other eye closed, and blind and crippled, the Tulabete still refused to yield, hurling himself blindly at where he thought Fuentes was standing.

Twice Fuentes pleaded with Jalanopi's lieutenants to surrender on behalf of their king, and twice they merely stared at him as if he were quite mad. Finally, nearing exhaustion himself, he picked up the large rock he had spotted earlier, cautiously circled around behind Jalanopi, and brought it down on the back of the Tulabete's head with all his re-

maining strength. Jalanopi grunted and plunged forward on his face. Fuentes dropped to his knees, brought the rock down twice more, and the Tulàbete Uprising was officially over.

Twenty-five

V iolet Gardener and Jalanopi, king of the Tulabete, were buried side by side beneath Jalanopi's tree two days later, and Fuentes, who would have preferred to be left alone, was forced to undergo a triumphal parade through the streets of Athens, the conquering hero of the Tulabete War.

"Thanks to you and you alone," said the mayor of Athens during the ceremony in which Fuentes received the medal which had been created expressly for him, "Rockgarden has truly become a planet for Men. Never again will the duplicitous, cowardly snakes take up arms against us. Never again will they have the courage to challenge our primacy. This is truly a glorious and historic day."

It took all of Fuentes' self-control not to laugh aloud at that statement.

Three weeks later he landed on the jungle world of Ascardi II and went hunting for Greendevils, the huge carnivorous amphibians that were coveted by so many museums within the Republic.

He never returned to Rockgarden.

IV

WILCOCK'S CASTLE

Twenty-six

I t was twenty-seven years after Violet Gardener's death that Richard Wilcock stumbled upon the castle.

Progress during the preceding quarter century had been steady, but not phenomenal. Six hundred thousand Men now lived on Rockgarden, all but a handful of them colonists who had made the commitment to live out their lives there. Fully a third of the planet was under cultivation, and far from importing food from the neighboring world of Flowergarden, Rockgarden exported almost half its produce to the other mining worlds in the vicinity.

Athens was the cultural center Violet Gardener had envisioned, populated by more than four hundred thousand Men, and the neighboring shantytown (shanty*city*, actually) of Talami had grown apace, housing more than two million snakes, most in the employ of the men who lived in Athens.

Fuentes had lived long enough to write two memoirs of Rockgarden, one of the war and one of his hunting experiences, and Linus Rawls' son and two daughters now managed an enormous safari operation, catering to the wealthiest sportsmen and tourists in the Republic.

Faniland and Tulabete Country were crisscrossed with networks of roads and powergrids, the desert continent on the other side of the world was finally being exploited, and Mastaboni and Athens both boasted large up-to-date spaceports.

There was still land to be had, too—millions of square miles of it, and there was no shortage of immigrants willing to spend their savings to purchase it. There were planets such as the university world of Aristotle, where people came to study; and planets such as Peponi, where the rich and the idle came to pursue their pleasures; and planets such as Buddha II and Luther and Inshallah IV, where people came to practice their religions; but the people who came to Rockgarden came to work, to plow the earth, to extract the metals from the hills, to form a merchant class that catered to the needs of those who farmed and mined.

Richard Wilcock was no different from most of them. He had come to Rockgarden with his parents at the age of fifteen, had spent four years on their farm outside of Mastaboni and another seven as a mining engineer until he had accumulated enough money to buy a homestead. It was his misfortune to be in the market for land during one of the periodic inflationary spirals that tended to hit the colony worlds, and rather than pay the exorbitant prices being asked for farmland near Mastaboni, he packed his few belongings in his groundcar and headed south to the still-undeveloped Rakko Country.

He drove more than two thousand miles, the last seven hundred without roads or even tracks, shot his own dinner each night, made rudimentary maps of the area through which he traveled, even learned the Rakko dialect well enough to make himself understood. The journey took him the better part of eight months, but finally he found the property he was looking for: it was a large plateau, perhaps six miles in diameter, buttressed up against huge rocky outcroppings which were not quite mountains but more

than hills, to the south and west. A river flowed across the eastern side of the land, and the climate seemed temperate.

He surveyed the property, staked his claim, discovered to his delight that he was able to afford such a remote piece of land, and spent the remainder of his money buying the farming machinery he needed. It was all secondhand, since the shipping costs exceeded the cost of the equipment itself, but it worked, and, filled with the pride of ownership, Richard Wilcock set about the business of establishing the farm he had always dreamed of owning.

He knew that his situation wasn't unique on the planet, that other young men and women who could not afford the more desirable land in nearby Faniland and Tulabete Country would be looking about for less expensive locations, and that within a handful of years there would be a hundred or more farms down in Rakko Country. The roads would follow, then the first small trading centers, then the huge granaries, and finally a city or two. He planned to be ready when they arrived.

The only problem was that, despite the land's flat surface, there were an awful lot of rocks in it, most of them just beneath the surface. They slowed down his equipment, broke his blades, pierced his tires. They were not big rocks—most of them could easily be lifted with one hand. But there were so *many* of them, the more he pulled out, the more there seemed to be.

Curious, he dug straight down some twenty feet, and still the profusion of rocks continued. Wilcock had no degrees in agriculture or geology, but he thought he knew good virgin farmland when he saw it, and he'd never come across anything like this.

Finally, in frustration, he contacted Mastaboni, gave them his coordinates, and chartered a plane to take some soil samples back for analysis to determine if he could expect to continue finding myriads of these rocks in what he had fondly hoped would be rich, fertile soil.

The plane returned three days later with his soil samples and Professor James Ellery.

Wilcock walked out to the grass landing strip, and was surprised to see the big, burly, bearded Ellery emerge from the plane, a huge pack on his back.

"Richard Wilcock?" said Ellery.

"Right."

Ellery extended his hand. "I'm James Ellery of Gardener University."

"But that's in Athens," said Wilcock, frowning. "I sent my samples to Mastaboni."

"And they consulted with experts in Athens," said Ellery.

"Well? What's the verdict?"

"This soil can't contain those rocks."

"They sent you all the way here to accuse me of faking a sample?" demanded Wilcock heatedly.

"Not at all," replied Ellery. "Since such stones don't occur naturally in such soil, they sent me here to find out who put them there." He smiled. "I'm from the Department of Archaeology."

"You think someone *put* them there?" repeated Wilcock.

"We're quite certain of it," answered Ellery. "The only questions are who and why."

"How long do you think it will take you to find out?"

Ellery shrugged. "I have no idea."

"I have to warn you: I'm not really equipped to handle a guest." He smiled apologetically. "In fact, I'm still living in a camping bubble."

"Oh, that's quite all right. I can camp out until my staff gets here."

"Your staff?"

"I'm just the advance guard, so to speak."

The pilot waved to Ellery, who waved back as the little plane sped by them on its takeoff.

"Well," said Ellery energetically, "suppose you show me where I can find these stones?"

"Just dig straight down," answered Wilcock.

"Right where I'm standing?"

Wilcock snorted disgustedly. "Anywhere within two miles of where you're standing."

"Excellent!" exclaimed Ellery.

"Have you eaten lunch yet?" asked Wilcock.

"I haven't even had breakfast," admitted Ellery. "I've been too excited."

"Well, come on back to my bubble and I'll fix something for us to eat."

"Lovely place here," said Ellery, looking around as they walked the mile to Wilcock's camp. "Well-protected from the elements, dependable source of water, altitude of forty-seven hundred feet so the summers don't get too hot. I can see why you chose it." He paused. "I wonder who chose it before you?"

"You're absolutely sure that somebody did?" said Wilcock dubiously.

"Those rocks don't belong here, and certainly not in that quantity," said Ellery.

"And you base your hopes or theories or whatever they are on that?"

"Not entirely," answered Ellery. "Though the rocks are certainly a strong indicator."

"But not the only one?"

Ellery shook his head. "No."

"What else is there?"

"There are also some things that *should* be here, but aren't," said Ellery.

"What?" asked Wilcock, surprised.

"Trees."

"Trees?"

Ellery nodded. "Given the conditions, there should be trees here, Mr. Wilcock. But look out across the valley; not a single one as far as the eye can see."

"That's one of the reasons I chose it," explained Wil-

cock. "I didn't want to waste the first few months deforesting the land."

"Someone did it for you."

"How can you be sure?" asked Wilcock as they arrived at his camp and Ellery gratefully took off his enormous backpack. Wilcock led his visitor past the sheds that housed his equipment and over to his bubble. He gave a brief order to his kitchen computer, then pulled up a pair of chairs for himself and Ellery.

"You drove here, Mr. Wilcock," said Ellery. "You went though hundreds of miles of Rakko Country and stopped when you found what seemed to be a flat empty field of tillable land. I *flew* here, and once we pinpointed your location I had my pilot fly in increasingly larger concentric circles, always using the river as a starting point. There are perhaps twenty other valleys just like this one within a radius of seventy miles, and each of them is covered with trees. Also, I studied the animals we saw: we passed over Redmountains, Horndevils, Twisthorns, Fleetjumpers, three species of Brownbucks—all browsers. We didn't see a single Blue-and-Gold or Brownbison, or any other grazer. The reason we didn't see them is they are not native to this area, and the reason they're not native to this area is that there is no savannah. There are forests, and scrubland, and some swamps, but *you* have the only grassland for a hundred miles." He paused. "Do you know how unusual that is, Mr. Wilcock?"

"Evidently not."

"Well, let us say that it would be enough to get me here, even without the rocks."

"What do you expect to find?" asked Wilcock, walking to the kitchen area for a moment and returning with a sandwich for Ellery and canisters of beer for each of them.

"Some evidence of a prior civilization."

"You mean a snake civilization?"

Ellery sat down on a folding chair. "Oh, I doubt it. The

snakes hardly strike me as a race of sentient beings that has reverted to barbarism."

"Then what?"

"There are more than ten thousand sentient races in the galaxy, Mr. Wilcock," said Ellery, "and more than eight hundred of them achieved space flight before we did. I suspect one of them posted a colony here sometime in the past."

"That's an awfully farfetched conclusion to draw based on a few rocks and a lack of trees," said Wilcock skeptically.

"Oh, there are other reasons too," said Ellery, sipping his beer.

"Such as?"

"The soil samples you sent."

"What about them?"

"Very poor in nutrients."

"I don't understand," said Wilcock.

"You may think you're the first young man who set out for Rakko Country to make his fortune, but in fact there have been about forty others. Many of them have sent soil samples to Mastaboni or Athens, so that experts could analyze them and suggest the best combinations of crops and fertilizers." He paused and took a bite of his sandwich. "In every case, their soil samples contained far more nutrients than yours did."

"So I picked a spot with poorer land."

"True—but there has to be a *reason* why it's poorer."

"And what do you think the reason is?"

"I should think that would be obvious from everything else we've discussed," answered Ellery. "This land was overused."

"I just run in luck, don't I?" said Wilcock disgustedly. "I spent every credit I've got buying what looks like the most idyllic farmland on the planet, and there are so many rocks I can't plant anything, and even if I could, the soil couldn't support it."

"Not to worry, Mr. Wilcock," answered Ellery. "If we find what I think we're going to find, the government will be more than happy to resettle you elsewhere."

"Why should the government give a damn whether someone lived here hundreds or thousands of years ago?"

"If my theory is correct, we are not the first race to colonize Rockgarden. Someone else was here first."

"So you said—but that doesn't tell me why the government should take an interest in it?"

"I should think that would be obvious to you, Mr. Wilcock," said Ellery with a smile. "They may come back." He paused. "They may even think that Rockgarden belongs to them."

Twenty-seven

E llery's crew arrived a week later, by which time the archaeologist had thoroughly examined the site and was able to tell them where to begin work.

At first the digging seemed haphazard, and Wilcock, an interested spectator now that he knew the government would recoup his losses, thought that Ellery had been wrong, that, all his arguments to the contrary, this was simply a patch of ground with a lot of rocks buried in it.

But after a month it became apparent that they were indeed unearthing an ancient structure that had been made entirely of stone. There was a main area, surrounded by walls some forty feet high, that Ellery called the Castle, filled with large courtyards, labyrinthian passageways, cisterns, and grain storehouses. But as the scope of the dig continued, they found stone fencing extending entirely across the valley floor. Whoever or whatever had built this forgotten structure hadn't done it overnight.

The bubbles that had temporarily housed Ellery's staff of thirty soon became more permanent structures, and doubled and redoubled within five months. The Rakko themselves began coming to the valley to watch the dig, and

many of them hired on as servants or laborers on the project, and a village of huts and burrows sprang up a mile away from the humans' houses.

Each night, after dinner, Ellery would preside at a meeting where his staff described what they had discovered that day and discussed its meaning, and Wilcock sat in rapt fascination, assimilating what he could.

After the initial work had disclosed that the structure was made entirely of millions of stones carried from the rocky outcroppings some fifty miles away from the valley, the brunt of each discussion concerned the builders of the Castle. About half of the crew felt that it had indeed been created, perhaps a millennium ago, by the Rakko or a related tribe, but Ellery and a number of others insisted that the structure was far too sophisticated, that the Rakko—and indeed every other tribe of snakes—gave no indication of being a once-powerful civilization that had fallen into barbarism, but rather appeared to be a primitive race that was just now, with an enormous boost from Man, emerging from it.

The problem facing those on Ellery's side of the question was quite simple: what had become of the builders? If they were Rakko, they were still in the area . . . but if they were Men or another starfaring race, why was there no sign of them? They had found the skeletons of a few snakes, but not enough to imply they had been the only inhabitants; more likely, concluded Ellery, they were laborers or servants, possibly even slaves. If some plague or war had wiped out the builders, where were *their* remains? And if they had migrated elsewhere, where had they gone to?

"Back home," suggested Ellery when Wilcock, who was still struggling to comprehend some of the terminology, asked the question again one day at breakfast on the veranda of the permanent structure Wilcock had built for himself while all the digging was going on.

"Then why didn't the Department of Cartography have

a map of the planet, or even a name for it, before Violet Gardener opened it up?" persisted Wilcock. "*We* haven't reverted to barbarism since reaching the stars. There should have been a record of it."

"*We* never colonized Rockgarden prior to Violet Gardener," answered Ellery. "I gave up on that hypothesis weeks ago. This is simply not the kind of structure Men would build, not even Men who had been stranded here without weapons and were desperate to protect themselves from hostile snakes." He shook his head. "No, it had to be some other race."

"Then where are they?"

"Either they're dead, in which case we will come across their remains someday, if not here, then wherever they migrated to; or they went back home, wherever *home* may be."

"I still don't know why the place couldn't have been built by the Rakko," said Wilcock. "It would answer the question of what happened to them."

"Not really," said Ellery. "If they built it, why did they desert it? It was virtually impregnable, it had a supply of water, it had cultivated land. Only something catastrophic could have made them leave." He paused. "Have you seen any signs of a catastrophe?"

"No," said Wilcock. "But perhaps a disease . . ."

"Would you leave a city and go back to subsistence farming and living in burrows if a disease struck?"

"I'd want to get away from it."

"You'd be carrying it with you."

"But if I was so primitive I didn't know that," said Wilcock, "if I had no notion of medicine or hygiene . . ."

"Then you'd also be too primitive to have built the castle," answered Ellery with an air of finality. He got to his feet. "No, it has to have been another race, a race about which we know nothing."

"Perhaps they were a native race—not snakes, but some other race—that became extinct," suggested Wilcock.

Ellery chuckled. "And didn't leave a trace of themselves anywhere on this entire planet except right here?"

"You won't know that until you dig up the whole planet," replied Wilcock stubbornly.

"I'm glad you're showing such an interest in our work, Richard," said Ellery. "But perhaps you should leave the hypothesizing to the experts."

"I didn't mean to annoy you," said Wilcock. "It's just very difficult to watch what's being dug up every day without becoming curious."

"I'm not annoyed," said Ellery. "But I really must get back to the site. We'll speak again later."

He walked off, leaving Wilcock to ponder the unanswered questions of the Castle while Tbona and Mbani, the two Rakkos he had hired as servants a few weeks earlier, cleaned up the breakfast table. He watched them idly for a few minutes as they carried plates and trays off to the kitchen, scrubbed the table, and swept and washed the veranda floor.

He was still daydreaming when Tbona approached him gently.

"Man Richard," he said in the Rakko dialect.

"What?" asked Wilcock, startled.

"Do you wish your tea now?"

"Oh, yes, thank you, Tbona."

Tbona disappeared into the kitchen and returned a moment later carrying a tray on which sat, in neat order, a cup and saucer, a tiny pitcher of cream, and a pot of steeping tea.

"You do not go to the dig today?" asked Tbona.

"Oh, I'll get by there a little later," answered Wilcock.

"My two brothers were hired yesterday," said Tbona.

"I'm glad to hear it," said Wilcock.

"Yes," said Tbona. "They will live with me at the far end

of the valley. I have not seen them in many days. It is good that we are all together again."

"I'm sure you will all be very happy," said Wilcock, pouring himself a cup of tea.

"I am happy, because I like to work in the house." He paused. "They are not very happy."

"Well, if I hear of anyone else needing houseboys, I'll recommend your brothers," said Wilcock, adding some cream and stirring his tea.

"Oh, no," said Tbona. "They do not like houseboy work."

"Why do they work here at all if they are not happy?"

"They are working over by the fences," answered Tbona, pointing toward a spot at the edge of the valley, "and they wanted to work at Castle Karimon."

"Is that what you're calling it—Castle Karimon?"

"That is what we have always called it," answered Tbona.

"You mean, since Professor Ellery discovered it," said Wilcock.

"No—always."

"Just a moment," said Wilcock, putting down his tea and staring at Tbona. "Are you trying to tell me that you knew about the castle before I arrived?"

"Yes, Man Richard," answered Tbona. "And always it has been called Castle Karimon, by my father and his father too."

"Have you told this to Professor Ellery?"

"No."

"Why not?"

"The Men who work at the dig, they do not talk to the Rakko, except to give orders." He paused and parted his lips. "That is why I like being your houseboy. You are nicer than the others."

Wilcock frowned. "Bring Mbani here for a moment, please. I'd like to speak to him."

"Have we done something wrong, Man Richard?"

"No."

Tbona went into the house and emerged a moment later, followed by Mbani.

"Mbani," said Wilcock, "what do you know about Castle Karimon?"

"Nothing, Man Richard," answered Mbani.

"You've never heard of it before?"

"Oh, everyone has heard of it," said Mbani. "But I know nothing about it."

"How long has it been here?"

They each shrugged.

"Forever," said Tbona at last.

"Who lived in it?"

"Great kings," said Mbani with complete assurance.

"Rakko kings?"

Again they shrugged.

"Snake kings?"

"Yes, great snake kings," said Mbani.

"What became of them?"

"I do not understand."

"The kings who lived in Castle Karimon," said Wilcock. "Where are they now?"

"They are dead, Man Richard."

"What about their descendants?"

"What is a descendant?"

"What happened to their sons and grandsons?" amended Wilcock.

"They have been dead for more rains than you can count, Man Richard," answered Tbona.

"What killed them?"

"Who can say?" replied Tbona. "Wildfangs, Nightkillers, sickness, hunger, war. What kills any of us?"

"Would you be willing to repeat to Professor Ellery what you have said to me?" asked Wilcock.

"He will not listen," said Tbona.

"Why do you think not?"

"I have learned a little of your language," said Tbona. "Not enough to speak, but enough to understand some things. And I know he thinks that the snakes are not smart enough to have built Castle Karimon."

"Will you tell him anyway?"

"Will he beat us?" asked Mbani.

"Of course not."

"Many of the Men on the dig beat snakes."

"You are *my* servants. I will not permit anyone to beat you for following my orders."

"Will he beat *you*, then?" persisted Mbani. "You have been good to us, Man Richard. If he kills you, we will have to work on the dig, or perhaps for another Man who will beat us."

"No one is going to beat anyone!" snapped Wilcock in frustration. "I just want you to tell him what you told me."

"If that is your order, Man Richard," said Mbani unhappily.

"It is my order," said Wilcock with a sigh.

"Then we shall do so," said Tbona. "But it will make no difference."

"It might."

Tbona shook his head. "For Man Ellery to believe us, he would have to admit that we could build such a castle, and he will not do that."

"Why should that bother him?" asked Wilcock. "He's a scientist. If he finds his theory is invalid, he will move on to the next theory."

"But he is also a Man."

"I don't understand."

"If he admits that Castle Karimon was built by my people," said Tbona, "then he must agree that it is ours and he must give it back to us." He stared at Wilcock, and suddenly Wilcock could see the bitterness in his servant's face and hear it in his voice. "Do you think he will do that?"

Twenty-eight

Within three years the entire area had been fully excavated, the crumbling walls of Castle Karimon had been reinforced, and the debate over the structure's origins continued unabated.

Wilcock was absolutely certain that the structure had been built by the snakes. Once, perhaps a millennium ago, they had migrated south—long before the tribes called Rakko, Tulabete, or Fani existed—and built this outpost in the wilderness. They had traded with snakes who lived even farther south, and they had prospered; at one point, some four thousand snakes had lived within the huge enclosure. It was a thriving city, perhaps the first ever on the face of the planet, and it had survived for centuries.

But the exhaustion of the soil, which had led Ellery to conclude it had been overfarmed, was to Wilcock the key to why the city had been abandoned. It was neither war nor pestilence nor a reversion to barbarism: it was the simple fact that after a couple of centuries the land could no longer feed the city's inhabitants, and it was this that eventually caused them to leave in search of more fertile land.

It seemed a simple and elegant conclusion, and Wilcock

found that a number of archaeologists had arrived at it independently. But Ellery and other senior members of the team insisted that snakes simply could not build a city of such complexity, that its design and construction were forever beyond their capabilities.

The argument wasn't confined to Wilcock's property. It extended to Athens and Mastaboni, where the daily newstapes presented arguments on both sides of the question. Wilcock himself "wrote" a book about his discovery of the city—which is to say, he sat down with a ghostwriter and poured out his thoughts, findings, and reminiscences into a recording device—and offered his conclusion, which was that what he had found was an ancient city built by the natives of Rockgarden. Even the name lent force to his argument, he said, for the Rakko had no word for the world they lived on, yet they called the place Castle Karimon— and since Karimon was the Tulabete and Fani name for the planet, he decided that the word had existed in some previous language that had split up into the three major dialects sometime after the desertion of the city.

Dozens of linguists then leapt into the fray, most of them claiming that Wilcock didn't know what he was talking about, and that he should leave the evolution of nonhuman languages to those who studied them for a living.

Early on, the government had expressed its willingness to reimburse Wilcock for his trouble and offered him a farm in Faniland, but he decided not to part with his valley. He had become fascinated with Castle Karimon, and to support himself—the land, after all, wasn't producing any income—he built a small hotel for tourists and visiting scholars who wished to explore the ruins. Then, because Violet Gardener had done her groundwork properly and forced the snakes to convert to a monied economy, he built a smaller, less elegant second hotel, about two miles away, for the occasional snake that wished to see the castle.

And then, seven years after first stumbling onto the val-

ley, Richard Wilcock contracted an exceptionally virulent tropical disease. He was shipped to Athens, and for three weeks it was touch and go, but eventually the doctors effected a cure. When he emerged from the hospital, he had lost almost half his body weight, all of his hair, and most of his health, and had been told that he was inviting certain death if he returned to the valley. His immune system had been seriously compromised, and he was informed that he would have to spend the rest of his life in the city as a semi-invalid.

His immediate response was to ignore the advice of his doctors and return to his home in Rakko Country. For three months he seemed fine, and then the disease struck again.

He died on the plane that was flying him to the hospital.

He left behind no wife or children, no relatives of any sort. His book had made enough money to pay for his funeral and satisfy his various debts. He was, in truth, a relatively unimportant man who had not made much of a mark on Rockgarden during his brief life. All he had really done was find a tract of land laden with rocks and call in the experts.

But if his life left no lasting marks on Rockgarden's history, his death was another matter altogether.

Twenty-nine

Richard Wilcock died intestate. He made sure there was enough money in his estate to pay his creditors, but having no heirs, he never saw any purpose in making a will.

The government waited the mandatory two rains for any claimants to Wilcock's estate, which for all practical purposes meant the valley that held Castle Karimon, and then set in motion the legal machinery to reclaim the land.

At the same time, one Milton Jnoma, one of the first members of the Rakko tribe to receive a higher education, and the very first to hold a law degree, petitioned the court to award the land to the members of the Rakko nation as a whole, with himself and a select committee of Rakko elders as executors.

The land, he claimed, housed a historical artifact of vast importance to the Rakko. Using Wilcock's book as evidence, he argued that the Rakko or their progenitors had built Castle Karimon, and since the land was worthless as farmland, the government could have no objection to turning it over to his people, who viewed themselves as the spiritual heirs to the ancient city.

James Ellery immediately stepped forward as a friend of the court, arguing that Wilcock had been mistaken and that the structure had been created not by snakes but by aliens. He brought in seventeen experts who agreed with his conclusion, which was simple and to the point: no snake society in the history of the planet, up to and including the current one, had the sophistication and expertise to create such a structure.

Jnoma suggested that it was even more difficult to obtain a law degree than build a stone castle, and pointed out that he had graduated fourth in a class of fifty, ahead of forty-six Men. Was Ellery saying that none of those forty-six Men had the sophistication to build a stone wall?

The trial went on for two weeks, with witnesses on both sides contradicting each other so thoroughly that at last the judge threw her hands in the air, ruled that insufficient information existed to determine who had built Castle Karimon, and put the land in a government-administered trust until such time as the original builders could be identified beyond any reasonable doubt.

That settled the matter . . . for six days.

Then Jnoma asked for another hearing, based on new evidence. He had located Wilcock's two houseboys, Tbona and Mbani, who were willing to testify that Wilcock, after returning from his hospitalization in Athens, had expressed the desire that the Rakko eventually take possession of Castle Karimon and indeed the entire valley.

The judge refused to allow their statements to be read into the record, as snakes did not have the same rights or status as Men under the constitution of Rockgarden, and hence their testimony could not be used to contradict any human testimony.

That night there were riots in Athens, Talami, Mastaboni, and even the small snake colony just beyond Ramsey Falls, and suddenly, by the next morning, Castle Karimon had become a planet-wide symbol of equality for

the snakes. Tulabete who had never been to Rakko Country, as well as Fani who had never even seen a Rakko, began picketing the government buildings, demanding that Castle Karimon be turned over to the Rakko. Richard Wilcock, whose name had been unknown to them a week earlier, was mourned as the one unprejudiced Man on the planet, and rumors were rife that the government had actually had him assassinated before he could legally turn the land over to his two Rakko servants—who had been elevated, in the snakes' minds, to his two staunch Rakko friends and co-workers, and who themselves had become legal martyrs to the cause when they were not permitted to speak in court.

Eventually one leader emerged, as one leader usually does in such cases. His name was Robert Gobe, he was a Fani who had spent some years off-planet, studying in the better schools of the Republic, and upon his return he inflamed his followers with a series of fire-breathing speeches demanding that the government turn Castle Karimon over to the snakes' keeping, that anything less was not only an insult and an injustice but was the equivalent to an official government position that the snakes were nothing but animals in the eyes of the ruling race.

Gobe's problem was that the snakes *were* nothing but animals in the eyes of the ruling race, and especially in the eyes of their legal system, and he was arrested after a week of less-than-gentle suggestions that he moderate his rhetoric.

Since he was a Fani, it was decided to incarcerate him in Tulabete Country, far from his followers, and so he was shipped off to jail in Mastaboni. When he arrived there, the government found, much to its surprise, that a crowd of almost ten thousand worshipful Tulabete had surrounded the jail.

Gobe stood at the door to the jail and raised his hand for silence.

"They can lock me away," he said, "they can starve and

beat and humiliate me, just as they can jail and beat and humiliate you, but they cannot make us less than we are. Castle Karimon is ours, and justice must eventually prevail." And then, as they dragged him off, he decided to say one last thing to solidify his bonds with this particular audience: "Jalanopi's tree still stands!"

Very few of the Men on the scene understood the reference, but the cheer from the Tulabete could be heard for miles in every direction.

Thirty

Robert Gobe was locked away without a trial and kept incarcerated for two years.

He put the time to good use, laboriously writing a book entitled *Karimon Will Be Ours,* which included not only the moral justification for returning Castle Karimon to the snakes, but a long and detailed section cataloguing the abuses his people received at the hands of their human rulers, and finally, a truly frightening account of the regular beatings he had received since his arrest.

Somehow he managed smuggle the book out, a few pages at a time. The government caught wind of it just before it went to press in Talami, arrested everyone involved in the project, and destroyed the plates.

What they did not know was that a second copy of the manuscript existed, and that it was being printed on Earth even as they were confiscating all the primitive printing presses in Talami. Copies soon spread throughout the Spiral Arm, the human press took up the snakes' cause, and within another year the Secretary of the Republic, half a galaxy away on Deluros VIII, wrote a strong letter of protest to Rockgarden concerning the treatment of the snakes in general and Gobe in particular.

The government of Rockgarden, with their race still outnumbered hundreds to one by the snakes, decided that since the problem wouldn't go away on its own, they would solve it in the most efficient way possible. Robert Gobe was finally charged with inciting to riot and insurrection, was found guilty, and was hanged from Jalanopi's tree the next morning.

Those protesting his treatment—and there were many—were arrested on the spot. Some were beaten, some were released unharmed, and some were never seen again. The protests became less frequent and less violent, Wilcock's castle was made off-limits to snakes, and within a month things were back to normal on Rockgarden.

Except that the name Karimon, which had virtually vanished from the language prior to Violet Gardener's death, was once again in fashion when Men were not around and the snakes spoke, with renewed purpose, among themselves.

V

PETERSON'S LAKE

Thirty-one

E mily Peterson stood atop a bluff, overlooking the Punda River as it flowed through a small valley in the northern sector of Faniland.

"Well?" asked her foreman.

She continued looking at the river for another moment, then turned her attention to the holographic map that her pocket computer projected in the air just in front of her.

"I think we'll do a series of five small dams, rather than the two larger ones," she said, instructing the computer to make notes on the map. "The river is too small for any commercial traffic, and it'll do less damage to the fish and wildlife this way. After all, we're doing it for *their* benefit in the first place." She shook her head in wonderment. "You'd think if they were going to gazette a new national park, they'd choose an area that isn't subject to annual droughts—or at least that they wouldn't import four hundred Redmountains that have to drink eighty gallons of water apiece every day."

"Well, that's the government for you."

"I think we'll also create a number of permanent lagoons," she added, displaying them on the map. "The

Punda is very narrow here, and it's the only water for fifty miles in the dry season. No sense making the predators' job *too* easy."

"Good idea," replied her foreman. "They can rename it the Punda Pools National Park. It's got a nice ring to it."

"All right, Alexander," she said, deactivating the computer. "Go on back to the hotel, tie in to our office computer in Athens, and start running a cost analysis."

"Aren't you coming back with me?"

She shook her head. "I want to look around a little more and pinpoint exactly where I want those dams."

"All right. I'll see you later, then."

He turned and walked toward his groundcar, and Emily spent the next two hours walking beside the Punda, her experienced eye examining the landscape, the flow and depth of the water, the routes the animals would have to take to reach the lagoons she planned to create.

Suddenly she heard something moving in the bush. For just a moment she realized that she was alone and unarmed in the midst of an untamed wilderness area, but even as she was looking for a convenient tree to climb she decided that no animal would approach that clumsily.

"Alexander, is that you?" she said. "I thought I told you to start running a cost analysis."

"No, it isn't Alexander," said a voice, and a moment later a middle-aged man, lean and wiry, with a deep scar on his chin, came into view. "They told me I'd find you here," he said, and then smiled. "But nobody told me how big 'here' was."

"Have you any idea how ridiculous you look?" asked Emily, chuckling at his elegant city outfit. "What in the world is John Blake doing out in the bush?"

"Looking for you," he said, brushing the dust from his clothing. "Isn't it against the law to be walking around on your own in a national park without a communicator?"

"Is that another of the many laws you've passed this

year?" she asked, as a small herd of Fleetjumpers peered at him and then leaped off in the opposite direction.

"Probably," he said. He shrugged. "What the hell. I was never very good with a compass anyway. Even if I had raised you, you couldn't have told me how to find you."

"How *did* you find me?"

"I pulled up next to your groundcar and started walking along the river." He paused. "Thank heaven you were going south rather than north, or I might have been walking forever."

She laughed. "All right, now that you've found me, what's so important that you had to fly all the way out from Athens? Has the Wildlife Department changed their mind about the dams, or did you simply cut their budget again?"

"Neither," he replied. "The dams will be built—but if I have my way, they won't be built by you."

She frowned. "Oh?"

"I've got a more important job for you," he continued. "Quite possibly the most important job on the planet."

"I've been listening to your speeches," answered Emily. "I thought the most important job on the planet was keeping the snakes in line."

"It is."

"I run a construction company, not a prison," she answered.

"Then hear me out," said Blake. "The snakes are Rockgarden's problem, and we'll solve it ourselves. The one thing we do not need is someone coming in and telling us what we must or must not do."

"So the Republic's finally gotten into the act," said Emily.

"The Republic has no business telling us what we have to do," insisted Blake. "We are not a member world."

"I may not agree with all your policies," replied Emily, "but I agree with *that*. Rockgarden's problems are Rockgarden's, not the Republic's." She looked out over the river,

where a trio of Twisthorns had just come down to drink.
"What have they demanded?" she asked.

"Equal rights for all sentient beings," answered Blake.
"One being, one vote."

"I assume the government has refused?"

"Give every snake the vote and they'd kick us off the
planet by sundown," he said. "Of course we refused."

"Well, that's very interesting, John, and more than a
little bit disturbing—but what has it got to do with me?"

"The Republic won't bring military force to bear," he
said. "They've overextended themselves throughout the
galaxy, and they're very sensitive to charges of militarism
these days." He paused. "But they have no compunction
about using economic force to make us comply with their
edicts."

"What have they threatened?"

"Nothing specific yet . . . but we are not without our
sources of information. When dealing with planets like
ours, their first step is always to cut off sources of energy."

"Planets like ours?"

"Rockgarden is very poor in fossil fuels, and those minimal amounts that we have are in environments that are very
difficult to work. We've been depending on shipments of
fissionable materials from the Republic for ninety percent
of our power."

"Then why don't we simply use our own fissionable materials?" asked Emily.

"It's never been cost-effective to mine and refine them."
He paused. "More to the point, given the current situation,
we can't afford to let any fissionable material fall into the
hands of the snakes."

"Then what *do* you want?"

"We want to convert to a safe power source that will last
as long as Rockgarden—and we want to do it fast."

She stared at him, puzzled, as he took out his own computer and had it create a map of the continent.

"Here is the Karimona River, all forty-six hundred miles of it," he said, tracing a winding strip of blue with his forefinger. "And *here*," he said, "is the Zantu Valley, three hundred miles long, eighty miles wide, with the Karimona passing right through the middle of it."

"So?"

"I want you to build a dam," said Blake. "I want that dam, plus the Ramsey Falls, to supply all the power that Rockgarden can use for the foreseeable future."

"I don't think you understand what you're asking," replied Emily. "To create that much power—"

"—you'd have to turn the Zantu Valley into a lake three hundred miles long, eighty miles wide and four thousand feet deep in the middle," he concluded for her.

"Precisely."

"The government has just voted to use the Zantu Valley for that purpose."

"What about all the snakes who live there?"

"We'll move them."

"And the animals?"

"We'll move them, too—as many as we can."

Emily stared at the map for a long moment. "What kind of timetable are we talking about here?"

"Our target date is five years from now."

"It could take me three months just to develop some feasibility studies and to cost it out."

"It is feasible, because it *must* be feasible," said Blake firmly. "As for money, that's no object. You will be given everything you need, and you yourself will emerge from the project an extremely wealthy woman."

"It's a hell of an undertaking," said Emily, still studying the map.

"That's why I came to *you*," said Blake. "But you must remember that this is a matter of paramount importance. This dam *will* be built and this lake *will* be created. You are my first choice, but your refusal will not halt the project."

"I quite understand," replied Emily. "Let me speak with my associates, and if we decide that your project is feasible, then I will accept your commission."

"That's all I ask."

"I don't think you realize half of what you are asking," said Emily.

"I beg your pardon?"

"At a time when relations between the races have never been more strained, you propose to move perhaps a million snakes from their tribal homeland and turn it into a lake. At a time when our hunting and tourist industries are in decline, you are proposing a project that will almost certainly kill off ten to twenty million game animals. In the middle of a drought, you are proposing a project that will lower the Karimona River, the lifeblood of the entire continent, by perhaps fifty percent. And while you're doing all this, you're also thumbing your nose at the Republic."

"Suppose you let *me* worry about all that," said Blake.

"I just hope *some*body in Athens is worrying about it," said Emily seriously.

Thirty-two

The surveys took five months. The cost analysis took another three. The creation of a work force, a million strong, mostly snakes supervised by Men, took another two. Every problem, and there were many, was pinpointed, analyzed, and solved.

Except one:

The seven hundred thousand Fani who lived in the Zantu Valley were relocated, or hired onto the work force.

The two hundred thousand Fallani, a Fani subgroup, who lived in the Zantu Valley, were relocated.

The seventy-eight thousand Golomba who lived in the Zantu Valley were relocated.

That left twenty-two thousand snakes of the Polombi tribe, impoverished even by snake standards, who made their meager living by fishing in the Karimona River. Their entire culture was based on the river; even their god, a huge four-armed fire-breathing deity, was a river god.

And they refused to leave.

"They are a royal pain in the ass," complained Blake at his weekly meeting with Emily Peterson in her Athens headquarters. "I've offered the entire tribe one thousand

credits apiece and the guarantee of a new homeland, and they simply won't budge."

"Obviously they prefer their old homeland," replied Emily.

"Their old homeland is going to be submerged under trillions of tons of water in another couple of years," answered Blake. "What they like isn't important."

"It is to them."

"If I have to move them forcibly, I will," said Blake. "I would just prefer to find a less controversial solution."

"I don't know why you've come to us with your problem," said Emily. "I was hired to create a lake and build a dam. *You* were supposed to take care of the political aspects of the situation."

"I thought the creator of the Peterson Dam might care to have some input," said Blake coldly.

"I didn't ask for this to be called the Peterson Dam," responded Emily. "In fact, I expressly asked you *not* to use my name. You insisted on it so that the snakes' anger would be directed at me rather than the government—but I'm telling you now that I will not be held responsible for whatever you finally do to or with the Polombi."

"You could help by hiring at least some of them to work on the project," said Blake.

"We catch fifteen or twenty of them every night, doing their damnedest to *sabotage* the project," answered Emily.

"I wasn't aware of that."

"Well, now you are."

"We'll have to put a stop to it."

"I wish you luck," said Emily. "They think they're doing the bidding of Gantamunu, and that he'll protect them."

"Who's Gantamunu? Their king?"

"Their god."

"Wonderful!" spat Blake. "Just what I need. A bunch of religious zealots trying to destroy the project."

"They're a bunch of innocent primitives who can't understand why you are destroying their river."

"I've had interpreters explain it to them again and again," complained Blake. "They'll be better off for it. Once we create Lake Zantu, we plan to stock it. In fifteen years, we'll be pulling a hundred tons of fish out of it every day."

"Well, that's one reason your arguments don't work," said Emily.

"I don't understand."

"Why don't you go look at the absolute poverty in which they live?" she suggested. "Not one in five of them will be alive in fifteen years."

"If they'll move, we, give them all the medical attention they need."

"Probably they'd prefer spiritual attention, which is what you're taking away from them."

"How? They can build churches or whatever they use for worship wherever we relocate them."

"Gantamunu is a river god," said Emily. "If you destroy the Karimona River, you destroy *him*."

Blake shook his head in disgust. "And the Republic wants *them* to run this planet!"

Thirty-three

M atunay, the king of the Polombi, walked along the moonlit bank of the Karimona River.

Here was the spot where he was born, over there the place where he underwent the Adulthood Ritual, half a mile back the spot where his father had died and he himself had become king. This mound of dirt was where he had taken his first wife in marriage, that tree over there where he had hidden as a youth when a Water Horse attacked him, three hundred yards upriver the spot where a River-tooth had killed his daughter.

This was more than land, it was a history book of his life and his people. What audacity the Men had to think that Gantamunu would sit idly by and let them destroy it, bury it under untold fathoms of water!

And their reasons made no more sense than they themselves did. They were doing this for power.

Power?

Power was what he had in his arm when he hurled his spear into the water and came up with a fish. Power was what a king wielded when he sat in judgment of his people, or made war or peace with the neighboring tribes.

And power was what the mighty Karimona possessed, with a current so strong that only the greatest of his people could swim against it. Power to make the crops grow, power to flood the landscape, power to take the breath from even a king's lungs and fill them with water.

Power was Gantamunu, and now these foolish Men had pitted themselves against him, against the most powerful god of all.

Well, let the Fani and the Fallani and Golomba do Man's bidding and move away from the source of all life. Their gods were evidently not strong enough to oppose the Men who dared to try to change the shape and course of the Karimona, but Gantamunu feared neither Man nor god. He might not protect the Polombi, for he was a harsh god, but he would protect his river.

Balator, who was Matunay's personal shaman, had suggested that instead of making the usual sacrifices of fish and fruit to Gantamunu, the Polombi would find favor in his eyes by destroying the Men's work. Of course, there were so many Men and so much work that they couldn't stop all progress, but they could cut a line here, break a support post there, overturn a supply raft, even throw mud in the delicate equipment the Men set such store by.

And so they did. For months they went unnoticed, or at least unhindered, but lately the Men had taken to posting guards up and down the river at all their work sites. Already twenty-nine Polombi had been killed, and sixty-seven more had been taken off to prison, which was worse than death for a being that had spent all its life under the brilliant sun of Karimon.

Matunay was of two minds concerning the sabotage. He approved of it, certainly, but he saw no reason for any Polombi to die when it was obvious that Gantamunu would not allow the completion of the project. After the first of his people were killed and incarcerated, he did not order his warriors to continue the practice, but on the other hand

he did not forbid it, and the boldest of his young warriors continued a campaign of harassment, while he waited patiently for Gantamunu to drive the aliens from his river.

On this particular evening, two of his warriors had staggered into camp, exhausted, to report that they had overturned yet another raft, but had lost three companions in the process. One had been shot, one had been captured, and the third had drowned. Upon receiving the news, Matunay walked in silence along the river bank, trying to sort matters out in his mind. Finally, unable to do so, he returned to his throne—a small tree stump covered with the hide of a Water Horse—and summoned Balator, his shaman.

Balator, whose skin was shedding, arrived a few minutes later, looking like some moldering corpse risen from the grave. He grunted a greeting to his king, then squatted down next to the throne to await Matunay's bidding.

"I am troubled, Balator," said Matunay.

"What troubles you, my king?"

"Tonight five of our warriors went down the river to overturn a raft that contained the Men's supplies," said Matunay.

"Did you send them, my king?" asked Balator.

"No, but I did not stop them," answered Matunay. "They were seen by the Men who guard. Two escaped, and three did not."

"I am sorry to hear that, my king."

"They are warriors; that is the chance they take."

"Then this is not why you summoned me?"

"Let me continue. One of the warriors was shot and killed, and one was captured."

"That is only two, my king," said Balator. "What became of the third?"

"He drowned."

"Ah," said Balator.

"That is why I must speak with you, Balator," said Matu-

nay. "They were acting on Gantamunu's behalf. Why would he drown one of his chosen people? Why does he not drown all the Men, and all the Fani and Tulabete and Golomba who work for them?"

"We shall see," said Balator. He reached into a pouch that hung about his neck and pulled out a number of bones and shining stones. He stared at them for a moment, muttered a brief chant, and rolled them on the ground, then repeated the process thrice more.

"What do the signs tell you?" asked Matunay.

"Gantamunu is pleased with you, my king," said Balator, "as he is pleased with all the Polombi."

"Then why did my warrior drown in Gantamunu's river?" persisted Matunay.

"Soon Gantamunu shall strike, and the Men shall know the full extent of his power and his fury," answered Balator. "But before he does this, he must feed deeply and build his strength, for though they are his enemies, the Men are themselves brave and strong. Every Polombi, every Man, every Fani, every Tulabete, every fish that dies in the Karimona lends its essence to Gantamunu. Every Brown-buck that dies beneath the jaws of a Rivertooth, every Fleet-jumper that is killed by a Wildfang while slaking its thirst, every bird that is pulled beneath the surface by a stingliz-ard, each of them adds to Gantamunu's strength."

"Then why doesn't he strike now?" demanded Matunay.

"He is Gantamunu," answered Balator serenely. "He will know when to strike."

"Ah!" said Matunay. "You are saying that he will wait until the day that the Men actually try to stop the flow of the river, for then they will truly understand how powerful he is?"

"I am saying only that he grows stronger by the day, and that he will know when to strike," answered Balator.

"Then shall I order my warriors not to act against the Men?"

Balator rolled the bones and stones again.

"You are to do precisely as you have done. You will order no one to act against the Men, but those who wish must be allowed to. And you will mourn no warrior who is lost, for his soul will simply hasten the moment of Gantamunu's fierce and terrible retribution against these beings who think that they can destroy Gantamunu's abode."

"So it shall be," said Matunay.

Balator arose and returned to his dwelling, which had been hollowed out on the riverbank.

Matunay sat on his throne for another few minutes, considering what his shaman had said. Finally he arose and once again began walking along the river, an enormous burden lifted from his shoulders. He need no longer feel guilty for not preventing his unarmed warriors from risking capture or death at the hands of the hated aliens; every one of them who died brought the day of Gantamunu's revenge closer.

Now, too, he understood why Gantamunu had not acted yet. To destroy a handful of Men when they had only half-completed their project would not have been decisive, and from what he knew of Men, they would return. But to wait until they erected their seven-hundred-foot wall of concrete and then to blow it down with a single mighty breath . . . *that* would show them whose god was the most powerful.

Yes, he thought, nodding his head grimly. Soon Gantamunu would show them the true meaning of power.

Thirty-four

"How the hell did this happen?" demanded Emily Peterson, staring out the window of her temporary office overlooking the dam.

"I don't know," said her foreman with a helpless shrug. "We put the pilings in deep enough, we gauged the flow of the river right, we built the damned thing seventy feet thick. There's no reason for it."

"Don't tell me there's no reason for it. We spent four years building a dam, and now the entire wall has a crack in it from top to bottom! I want to know why!"

"I don't know!" he yelled back at her. "Fire me if you want, but I did my job right. We used nothing but first-quality materials, we didn't just match the specs, we exceeded them. That goddamned thing was built to last a thousand years!"

"Could it have been sabotage?"

"You think a bunch of illiterate fishermen could put a crack eight hundred feet long and seventy feet wide in a concrete dam?" he said sardonically. "You think *anyone* could, without our knowing about it?"

Emily glared at him. "Then what went wrong?"

He shrugged again. "I don't have an answer."

"Well, *I'm* going to have to have an answer when the government asks me—and you can be sure they're going to ask me."

"I've run all the specifications through the computer again and again, and it can't come up with a reason. In fact, it says it can't have happened."

"John Blake is not going to accept that as an answer," replied Emily. "That man has his eye on the governorship of Rockgarden, and this is *his* project. He's going to find a scapegoat before he'll let it sink his career."

"You can hand him my head on a platter if you think it'll help," said her foreman earnestly. "But I'm telling you that there is no logical reason why the wall should have cracked. We've even checked for seismic activity, and we came up blank. Not so much as a tremor."

"If I need your head, rest assured I'll come after it," said Emily. "For the time being, I'll handle the political damage control. What are you doing about controlling the damage to the dam?"

"We're reinforcing the wall, of course, and I've got the computer working on another location for a new wall, about a quarter of a mile downstream."

"Why there? All our studies showed us that this was the optimum location."

"Because until I know what caused *this* wall to crack, I don't see any sense building another one abutting it."

"Won't that make it fifty feet wider?"

"Fifty-seven feet four inches."

She stared at him. "You're sure that's where we want to build it?"

"Mrs. Peterson," said the foreman, "at this point I'm not sure of a damned thing. But that's where the computer says we should put it, so unless you tell me otherwise, that's where I'm putting it."

"What will we do with the damaged wall?"

"I suppose we can use a molecular imploder on it after we finish work on the new one."

She lowered her head in thought for a long moment, then looked up.

"All right," she said. "Do what you can to reinforce the cracked wall, and then start putting in pilings for the new one. And I want security tripled."

"Yes, Mrs. Peterson."

"And I want our best engineers to work overtime with their computers until someone can tell me exactly what went wrong."

"Yes, Mrs. Peterson," he said, backing away toward the door to her office.

"All right," she said. "Get out of here."

He made a grateful escape, while Emily stared out her window at the enormous crack in the dam's wall and wondered, for the hundredth time, how it had happened.

Matunay, king of the Polombi, stood on the opposite bank of the river, hands on hips, and looked with satisfaction at the enormous crack in the aliens' wall. He knew, of course, that this was the revenge of Gantamunu, and would have been more than happy to explain it to the Men, but nobody thought to ask him.

Thirty-five

"What has happened?" asked Matunay. "Why does Gantamunu not strike again?"

"Possibly it took all his strength to destroy the first wall," answered Balator. "I do not know."

"You must roll the bones and ask him, for the Men have told us that we must leave tomorrow morning, that when the sun is at its highest they will begin flooding the land."

"I will roll the bones," said Balator with a shrug, "but Gantamunu has been silent since the last rains."

"And during that time the Men have built an even larger, thicker wall than the one he destroyed," said Matunay, frowning. "Why? We must know his answer."

Balator pulled the bones and shining stones from the pouch about his neck and cast them onto the ground. Then he gathered them up, cast them again, and repeated the process a third time, after which he leaned forward and studied their configuration.

"Well?" demanded Matunay. "What does he say?"

"Nothing," replied Balator. "Gantamunu does not respond to the bones."

"He *must!*" exclaimed Matunay. "You are reading the signs wrong, shaman."

"I am reading what the signs say."

"Cast the bones again," ordered Matunay.

Balator sighed, gathered up his little collection of bones and stones, and threw them onto the dirt once more.

"There is no answer," he said at last.

"He knows you are casting the bones?" queried Matunay.

"Is he not the all-powerful Gantamunu?" replied Balator testily.

"Then even his silence must be an answer. What, precisely, did you ask him?"

"I asked him if we should leave our homes."

"And since he didn't say yes, the answer is obvious: we must remain."

"There is no point to it, my king. The Men will turn our land into a lake, and if we remain we will drown."

"Gantamunu will not allow us to drown," said Matunay with absolute conviction. "We are his children. He saved us the last time, and he will save us again. You have misinterpreted his silence, shaman."

"Gantamunu will surely take his revenge upon the Men, but it is blasphemy to tell him that he must do so at a certain time or place," answered Balator. "We should climb to the safety of the hills in the morning, and wait for him to act."

"He may not act if he thinks we have lost our faith in him," said Matunay. He paused. "*You* climb the hills if you wish, but Matunay, king of the Polombi, will stay here where Gantamunu can see him."

All through the night they argued, neither changing his position, and when the sun came up Balator and the remaining Polombi ascended the hills to the point at which the human engineers had told them they would be safe, and Matunay remained on the riverbank.

Even when the floodgates opened and billions upon bil-

lions of gallons of water headed directly toward him, Matunay's faith never wavered. He stood facing the flood, arms folded resolutely across his chest, and calmly awaited Gantamunu's miracle.

Thirty-six

L ake Zantu was created in less than three days. It was 317 miles long and 82 wide, reached a depth of almost 4,500 feet, and was dotted with 73 islands, from which the surviving wildlife was being rescued and transported to the newly made lakeshore.

And a week later Lake Zantu was only 76 miles wide.

"Correct me if I'm wrong," said John Blake, who was on an inspection tour with Emily Peterson, "but this shoreline looks like it was recently underwater."

"It was."

"You can't lose three miles of shoreline through evaporation," he said. "What's going on here?"

"Every action has an equal and opposite reaction. I thought you learned that in school."

"They taught me lots of things in school. How does that apply to this particular situation?"

"We added trillions of tons of water to a limited section of land, and the end result was that we put a dent in the surface of the planet."

"A *dent?*"

"Our figures took it into consideration. Starting tomorrow we'll raise the lake to its original level."

"Will this do any lasting damage to the planet?" asked Blake.

"Not a bit," she assured him. "We'll have the generators operational in another month, you'll have a huge new fishing industry inside of three years, and if you can avoid a war with the Republic, you might very well draw more tourists to the lake than to the wildlife parks."

"Well, that's comforting, anyway." He looked up to the top of one of the hills. "Who are those snakes up there? Why aren't they working on the generators or moving animals or something?"

"They're the Polombi," replied Emily.

"Well, in a couple of years, they can go back to fishing," said Blake.

"We took away more than their livelihood," said Emily. "We took away their entire way of life."

"It wasn't much of a way of life from what I could see," said Blake.

"No," agreed Emily. "But it was theirs."

"Maybe I'll pay their king a visit and explain the facts of life to him."

"He was drowned when we created the lake."

"I thought we moved everyone to safety," said Blake, frowning.

"Everyone who was *willing* to move. He insisted on staying. He thought Gantamunu would protect him."

"Their water god?" said Blake contemptuously. "Well, I guess they know whose god is stronger now." He turned to Emily. "Take my word for it: in another year, they'll be working side by side with the rest of your snakes."

She shook her head. "In another year they'll be begging for handouts and waiting for Gantamunu to become strong enough to destroy the dam."

"Nonsense," said Blake. "We landed on the planet, and the Tulabete adjusted. We built Athens, and the Fani ad-

justed. We unearthed Castle Karimon, and the Rakko adjusted. The Polombi will adjust too."

"You didn't deprive the Fani and Tulabete and Rakko of their homeland and their culture." She looked at the mournful figures up on the hill. "Those poor bastards have nothing left. We've taken away everything they had, and we've replaced it with nothing."

"In three years they'll all be fishermen again."

"In three years Men are going to be cruising Lake Zantu with huge boats and pulling in thousands of fish every few minutes in their nets. You don't really expect the Polombi to go out with their canoes and their fishing spears and compete, do you?"

"Then they'll do something else."

"They can't farm the hills," she answered. "First, they don't know how, and second, it's Fani land. By the same token, they can't become hunters: they've never hunted before, and they're living in a national park where they can be arrested for hunting. What do you think they're going to do?"

"We *had* to have the dam," said Blake irritably. "You know that."

"Yes," she agreed with a sigh. "I know that."

Blake looked at the Polombi one last time. "What do you suppose will become of them?"

"Seriously?" said Emily. "I think every last one of them will be dead within a quarter of a century."

She was wrong: Balator, the last Polombi, lived for twenty-seven more years.

VI

BLAKE'S MILLENNIUM

Thirty-seven

A nother day, another delegation.

John Blake sighed, then got to his feet to greet the three men and five women who entered his office. They exchanged formal greetings, sat down around the conference table that had been set up next to a window overlooking Gardener Square, and then the self-appointed leader of the delegation got down to business.

"Mr. Blake, I'll come straight to the point of our visit," he said, pouring himself a glass of water from the pitcher that had been provided for that purpose. "We have spent the past six days studying the economic and political condition of the native populace of Rockgarden, and frankly, we find it appalling."

"The wheels of change grind slowly," answered Blake, lighting up one of his smokeless Denebian cigars. "But rest assured, Mr. Heinrich, they *are* grinding."

"I'm afraid that answer is unacceptable to us," said Heinrich. "You are running for the office of Governor of Rockgarden. It is incumbent upon both you and your opponents to address the problem confronting this planet, and none of you seems willing to do so."

Blake stared at him for a long moment. "As I see it, the major problem confronting me at the moment is that outsiders who have no stake in the future of Rockgarden are trying to influence our planetary election. You may tell the Republic that Rockgarden is fully capable of determining its own future without your interference."

"We are not here to exchange threats, sir, but merely to apprise you of the gravity of the situation," said Heinrich. "If you choose to become a pariah among human worlds, you must be aware of the consequences."

"That certainly sounds like a threat to *me*," said Blake. He paused, looking at each of his visitors in turn. "Who are you to tell us how to run our world? Did you clear the trees and the scrub and turn a wilderness into the most productive farmland in the Spiral Arm? Did you pull precious ores, ores that the Republic desperately needs, out of our land? Did you change the entire topography of this world by creating Lake Zantu?" He glared at them again. "No, you sat in your glass towers on Deluros VIII and let us tame a world and pacify its natives in a savage war, and now you're telling us to turn the planet over to the race that tried to hinder us at every step."

"It is *their* planet," one of the women pointed out.

"Rubbish," said Blake. "If we left Rockgarden, they'd be back to living in burrows and eating bugs for a living inside two weeks."

"I rather doubt it," said Heinrich, finishing his water and pouring himself a second glass. "More than two thousand of them have attended schools within the Republic. A number of them have even written books." He paused, then added accusingly: "The most brilliant of them is currently incarcerated, without charge or bail, in an Athens jail."

"Have you *read* Thomas Paka's book?" demanded Blake. "It's an outline for revolution."

"It is a cry for social justice," interjected another of the women.

"You tell me what disrupting communications and destroying the generators at Lake Zantu have to do with social justice!" said Blake heatedly.

"You have kept his people in servitude since colonizing Rockgarden," said Heinrich. "Surely he has a right to oppose your policies."

"If I were him, I might have written the same book," agreed Blake. "But I'm not. I'm a Man, and like every other Man on this planet, I'm outnumbered almost two hundred to one by the snakes. We've achieved a very uneasy equilibrium here, and we don't need members of the Republic coming in and threatening to upset it. If you want to walk away from Lodin XI and Peponi and five thousand other worlds that you opened up and tamed through human sweat and sacrifice, that's your business—but Rockgarden isn't bound by the Republic's rules, and we're not about to turn this world over to a race that is demonstrably not capable of running it."

"We are your last best hope, Mr. Blake," said Heinrich. "You are sitting on a powder keg here. If social justice is not achieved, and quickly, the inhabitants will not have to read Thomas Paka's book to know that they have no choice but to join in an armed rebellion."

"They tried it once before, and we put it down," said Blake. "If it happens again, we'll defeat them again."

"I am afraid we are making no more progress with you than with your rivals for office," said Heinrich sadly. "I think we shall have to return to Deluros VIII and recommend that all trade with Rockgarden be cut off until major changes are made in the fabric of your society."

"Last month it was Admiral McAffee of the Second Fleet, and three weeks ago it was the Assistant Comptroller of the Treasury," said Blake contemptuously. "And earlier this

week it was the Commerce Division of the Department of Alien Affairs."

"I don't quite understand you, Mr. Blake."

"What I'm saying is that we've been threatened by experts, Mr. Heinrich."

"You are making a serious mistake."

"The Republic made a serious mistake when it tried to tell an independent world how to run its internal affairs. We know we have problems, but we'll address them in our own way and in our own good time. We will not be coerced, threatened, frightened, or bribed into doing the Republic's bidding."

"What you are doing to these natives is patently, blatantly *wrong*," said Heinrich severely.

"What we are doing," answered Blake, "is precisely what the Republic did all over the galaxy for close to two thousand years, until you were so overextended that you lost a couple of wars and found out that you couldn't afford fifty thousand colony worlds. You didn't grant Peponi and the others their independence for noble motives; it was economics, plain and simple." He glared at Heinrich. "So don't give us your smug, superior attitude. This is Rockgarden, Mr. Heinrich; we know better."

"I see no sense continuing this discussion any further," said Heinrich. "Our minimum demand is universal suffrage: one being, one vote. If you will not address the problem, our business here is done."

"I have never said I wouldn't address that problem," replied Blake. "Only that our timetables are likely to differ."

"By how much?"

"I'm giving a speech tonight," said Blake. "If you're still on Rockgarden, you might try to catch the broadcast."

"You didn't answer my question, Mr. Blake."

"I'll answer it in my speech."

They got up from the conference table and filed out of

his office, and Blake looked out the window, past Gardener Square, at the clean, broad avenues of Athens, and tried not to think about how quickly they would turn into slums under snake rule. Rockgarden was no paradise, despite all the brochures the government sent out to prospective colonists—how could it be, when Men were outnumbered hundreds to one by an increasingly hostile native population?—but he was damned well not going to let it become the raging inferno that Thomas Paka and his followers sought to make it. At least, he thought with satisfaction, all the candidates agreed on the major issue; the election for the governorship of Rockgarden would be decided on minor points, and if he lost he could live with that.

After a few minutes he sat down at his desk, activated his computer, pulled up the speech that his staff had written for this evening's rally, and began making notes and minor changes. This word was too difficult to pronounce and would break the flow of the speech, that concept had to be made less complex or it would be lost on his audience, this joke had been used too often and was due to be retired, that position would play better in Mastaboni than Athens and needn't be covered tonight.

Finally, by lunchtime, he had whipped the speech into its final shape, and he spent the rest of the afternoon out in the streets, pressing flesh, posing for pictures, soliciting votes, and providing sound bites for the evening news.

Then, at seven o'clock, amidst thunderous applause, he stepped onto the stage of the Athens Playhouse and addressed his select thousand-credit-a-seat audience.

The speech touched on all the partisan economic and political issues that his audience wanted to hear, poked gentle fun at his opponents, and carefully delineated the minimal differences between himself and the other candidates. Finally, when it was through, he raised his hands for silence and stared intently into the holo cameras that were transmitting his image throughout the continent.

"There is one final subject that I have promised to address," he said, "and that is the matter of universal suffrage."

The members of the press sat up alertly, as this was not in the prepared text that had been handed out.

"I have said throughout my political career that when the snakes have proven that they are ready to share power, we Men will have no compunction at welcoming them into the government, and passing laws that guarantee one being, one vote."

This was not what his audience had expected to hear, and suddenly the theater was completely silent.

"In my considered opinion," concluded Blake, "that day will not arrive for a thousand years."

If he had more to say, it couldn't be heard amid the impassioned cheering.

The next morning, the *Athens Times* enthusiastically endorsed "Blake's Millennium," and the *Mastaboni News* followed suit a day later.

And two weeks later, John Blake became governor of Rockgarden in the greatest electoral landslide in the planet's brief history.

Thirty-eight

I t began neither with a bang nor a whimper, but with a boycott. The Republic responded to Blake's election by cutting off all trade with Rockgarden. Of all the human-controlled planets in the galaxy, only Goldstone refused to honor the boycott and continued to supply John Blake's world.

Blake turned the boycott into both a political and an economic asset: political, because the citizenry was outraged that an off-world body was trying to involve itself in their internal affairs, and economic, because it forced Rockgarden to diversify its industries in order to become self-sufficient. Within six months there were factories lining the outskirts of Athens and Mastaboni producing everything from soap to groundcars, and within a year Rockgarden, while it was still undergoing some hardships, was able to supply all of its own most vital necessities.

The Republic summoned Blake's government to come to Deluros VIII and discuss the situation. Blake ignored the first two invitations and responded to the third with a curt negative.

Unrest continued to grow almost daily among the

snakes, and soon the jails couldn't hold all the dissenters, so Blake's government created large prison camps surrounded by lethally charged electric fences out in the bush.

Then, early one morning, while most of the human population was still in bed, a group of some three hundred Tulabete, under the leadership of a schoolteacher named Moses Selabali, attacked and destroyed the entire human town of New Oxford, which was on the road halfway between Mastaboni and Athens. Fourteen Men were killed and sixty-seven were taken prisoner, to be released in exchange for the freedom of Thomas Paka, the jailed author.

"My government does not deal with outlaws and criminals," answered Blake, when the proposal was made public.

Selabali executed ten hostages the next day, and ten every day thereafter, until all sixty-seven were dead.

The government responded by marching into Selabali's village—he himself wasn't there—and slaughtering all four hundred snakes that they found there.

A month later the Fani, demanding freedom for Paka, blew up a train that was traveling from Athens to Mastaboni. Seventeen Men were killed and more than one hundred hospitalized.

The government, not knowing which Fani village was responsible, took a scattershot approach, destroying ten Fani villages at random.

The next morning a bomb went off in the Athens Art Museum, destroying most of the collection that Violet Gardner had willed to Rockgarden.

Blake ordered his troops to burn down the most sacred shrine the Fani possessed.

All was quiet for another month. Then ten human farms were burned just outside Mastaboni.

Blake again ordered instant retaliation, and waited for news from his army.

And waited.

And waited.

When the officer in charge finally reported back, it was to inform him that they had met fierce, well-armed resistance. The Tulabete were supplied with both sonic and laser weapons, none of them made on Rockgarden.

And when the Fani took credit for attacking the outpost town of Fuentes, the troops who had been directed to quell the disturbance reported the same thing: they were up against a large, well-organized force armed with off-world weaponry.

Blake called a meeting of his cabinet, to lay out the situation to them.

"Well," said his Minister of Defense, "it's obvious that someone has been arming them. I just wish I knew *who*."

"It's got to be the Republic," said another minister.

Blake shook his head. "No. The Republic has never armed an alien race and turned them loose on Men before."

"Then who could it be?"

"There's five thousand bleeding-heart organizations out there, each of them prepared to take the aliens' side in any dispute they have with Men. Most of these groups are well financed, and they have excellent intelligence capabilities. I'm sure that half a dozen of them have been supplying arms to the snakes."

"How?"

"We can't patrol the whole damned planet," answered Blake. "They could be using almost anyone as a contact: a Republic reporter, anyone who represents himself as a trader from Goldstone, an alien tourist, anyone."

"So do we close up the whole planet and not allow anyone in or out?" asked the Minister of Trade. "I suppose we could make do, though losing our commerce with Goldstone will be quite a hardship."

"We can't deny the whole galaxy access to Rockgarden," said Blake. "The Republic is temporarily content to give moral support to the snakes, but if we shut them out com-

pletely, and don't let them know what's going on here, the day will come when they decide to take us over by force." He paused. "Besides, our own citizens come and go every day. I can't very well imprison them on their own planet." He shook his head again. "No, we'll just have to tighten our security and try to pinpoint and then stop the flow of weapons."

"My reports say that the snakes have stockpiled an awful lot of weaponry already," remarked the Minister of Defense. "Evidently they've been planning this for years, perhaps ever since Paka and Selabali visited the Republic. This is no spur of the moment uprising; it's just the tip of the iceberg. I think we'd better prepare ourselves for a long, hard military campaign."

"Well, we have one thing in our favor," said Blake.

"What is that?"

"The Tulabete and the Fani hate each other a hell of a lot more than they hate us. If they get their hands on enough guns, they're going to forget all about their recent enemies and go after their traditional ones. I can see them spending the next half century trying to wipe each other out." He paused, and allowed himself the luxury of a smile. "I, for one, wish them each the best of luck."

Thirty-nine

But the Fani and the Tulabete *didn't* forget their most recent enemy. The attacks grew bolder and more frequent, the requests became demands, and unlike their disastrous defeat against Fuentes some decades earlier, this time they used the terrain to their advantage and fought a hit-and-run guerrilla war. They knew they outnumbered the enemy hundreds to one, but they also knew that Men possessed better weapons and a trained, disciplined military force that they were not prepared to meet head-on in battle.

The pattern was repeated over and over again. A human outpost or farm would be destroyed. When the army showed up, there were no snakes around. When they questioned the local snake villages, no one had seen or heard anything. But if a Man lingered too long behind his fellows in one of those villages, or on a forest trail, or in the foothills of the Tenya Mountains, as often as not he would simply disappear, never to be seen again.

The retributions were swift and terrible. Entire villages were razed to the ground, crops were burned, herds of Tallgrazers were confiscated or, more often, killed.

Finally Blake gave his permission to the army to hire human mercenaries from other worlds, mercenaries who had had experience fighting guerrilla wars. Within a month three hundred of them were under contract. Known informally as the Bush Brigade, they combed the forests and savannahs and engaged in a number of pitched battles with the snakes. For the most part they killed the enemy; but they also needed information, and they were not above using both drugs and torture to obtain it.

The snakes responded in kind. They needed no information, but they also began torturing their victims.

Then one day Thomas Paka, who had spent the past two years languishing in the Athens jail, sent a message that he would like to meet with John Blake.

Blake agreed, and had him brought to one of the interrogation rooms on the main floor of the jail. He waited until Paka's handcuffs were secured to the metal chair on which he was seated, then entered the room and ordered the guards to leave. Paka was just starting to shed his skin, and it was loose and starting to peel in half a hundred places; Blake thought it gave him the appearance of a revived corpse, but he had seen the condition thousands of time and made no mention of it.

"Good afternoon, Mr. Blake," said Paka in excellent Terran. "I thank you for agreeing to meet with me." He paused. "I have not seen you in some time."

"Good afternoon, Mr. Paka," replied Blake coldly. "I am not inclined to visit traitors in their cells."

"Whether one is a traitor or a patriot depends entirely upon one's point of view," said Paka. "And upon who is holding the weapon."

"It depends upon a simple reading of the law," answered Blake. "You have tried to overthrow the legally elected government of Rockgarden."

"From a prison cell?" replied Paka sardonically. "I was

imprisoned without being charged of any crime more than a year before the revolution began."

"A bunch of savages chopping up isolated farmers and settlers can hardly be called a revolution," answered Blake.

"I have never advocated such methods," said Paka. "Though I have been given to understand that your own army has been equally brutal."

"I thought you asked for this meeting because you wanted to deal," said Blake. "If you just wanted to talk about which side is more brutal, I have better things to do with my time."

"No," said Paka. "I have a personal favor to ask of you."

"A favor?" repeated Blake suspiciously.

Paka nodded. "Word has reached me that my wife is dying. I wish to go to her side."

"Just like that?"

"I give you my pledge that if you will release me, I will return as soon as she has died."

"I can't do that. You're much too dangerous to be released." Blake paused. "Besides, if you're like the rest of the snakes, you've probably got three or four more wives stashed away."

"I have only one wife, and I love her deeply."

"Snakes are incapable of love," said Blake.

"Snakes are capable of every emotion that Men feel," replied Paka. "Except, perhaps, contempt for other species."

"I doubt it," said Blake. "But even if that were true, I still can't let you go."

"I am not a military threat, Mr. Blake," said Paka. "I am a theorist and a writer. I have never led an army or participated in a battle in my life. I have never raised a hand against any Man or snake." He looked directly into Blake's eyes. "I give you my solemn word that I will not do so now."

"It doesn't matter," said Blake. "All over the planet, Men are being gutted like fish, frequently in your name. I don't

care whether you know military tactics or not—the Fani aren't using them anyway. This isn't a war or a revolution; it's a legal government fighting a bunch of terrorists—and you and this Tulabete, Moses Selabali, are their leaders."

"How can I be a leader when I have been in jail for more than two years?" demanded Paka in frustration.

"You're not their *leader*; you're their *hero*. That makes you even *more* dangerous."

"Mr. Blake, I have never asked a favor of a Man before," said Paka. "But I am asking you—I am *begging* you—to let me visit my wife before she dies."

Blake shook his head. "I'm not without sympathy for you, Mr. Paka," he said, "but I can't take the chance. I've got three million Men depending on me to defend their lives and their property, and I can do that a lot more efficiently if you're in jail than if you're not."

"Your Christ would disapprove of you," said Paka bitterly.

"What does a snake know about Christ?" replied Blake contemptuously.

"I am a Christian," said Paka. "And Christians do not do this to one another."

"*You?*" snorted Blake. "Don't make me laugh."

"It is true."

"You think Jesus died for *your* sins?"

"I do not accept his divinity, only his wisdom," answered Paka.

"Then you're *not* a Christian."

"I am a believer in the doctrine of Jesus Christ, not that of his disciples."

"Did Jesus tell his followers to torture and mutilate innocent men and women?"

"No," said Paka. "And neither did I."

"This blasphemy has gone far enough," said Blake irritably.

"It is not blasphemy, but the simple truth."

"All right—you want to prove you're a Christian?" said Blake suddenly. "Then renounce the violence your people have committed. Make a speech telling them to lay down their weapons and surrender. I can have cameras in here in five minutes."

Paka shook his head. "Jesus lived in a world populated by Men. They crucified him. I will not have you crucify my people."

"I'll grant a general amnesty."

"I do not trust you, Mr. Blake."

"And I do not trust you, Mr. Paka," said Blake. "Therefore, I think we have nothing further to say."

"I have one thing," said Paka.

"Oh?"

"I want you to remember that I volunteered to return to prison if you allowed me to visit my wife, and you refused."

"That sounds suspiciously like a threat, Mr. Paka," said Blake.

"It is merely a statement." Paka paused. "I will make another one. Prior to this moment, I have fought for social justice, but I have never hated you or any Man. That is no longer true."

"I think I've wasted enough time with you," said Blake, walking to the door and summoning the guards. Three burly men entered the room, released Paka from his chair, cuffed his hands behind his back, and hurried him back to his cell.

Blake returned to the executive mansion and spent the rest of the afternoon reviewing some legislation that was awaiting his signature. Then he stopped by his private club for a workout, ate dinner in the club's restaurant, and spent a pleasant evening playing cards and talking politics. He returned to the mansion at about midnight, pleasantly tired and ready for bed, only to find an urgent message waiting for him.

A team of twenty Fani, under cover of night, had broken into the jail, killed the warden and seven guards, and had released more than two hundred prisoners.

Included among the escapees was Thomas Paka.

Forty

Within a month Blake realized that he wasn't going to be able to stop the flow of arms. A Republic ship, loaded with laser rifles, crashed on the Desert Continent, and once he knew that the Republic itself was supplying the snakes he knew there was no way to stop it.

Within two months, he realized that he should have allowed Thomas Paka to visit his wife; for if Paka was a writer and a theorist up to that fateful day, he was now a hate-filled leader capable of arousing enormous passions among his followers.

Within three months he realized that the Fani and the Tulabete were not going to fight each other until they had settled their business with the colonists. Paka and Moses Selabali had been seen together on five separate occasions, and the attacks from the Fani and Tulabete armies had become much better coordinated.

Within six months he realized that this was going to be a long, brutal war of attrition. Though more snakes joined Paka's and Selabali's armies every day, though they now outnumbered the human soldiers five-to-one, though the Republic kept opening up new channels through which to

supply them with arms, they continued to fight a guerrilla war. The attacking parties were a little larger than before, and a lot better armed, but never did they congregate in large enough numbers for Blake's generals to join anything remotely resembling a definitive battle.

Within a year the Fani had actually secured the northern quarter of Faniland—mostly hills and mountains—to the point that Paka could address huge rallies there in relative safety.

Within eighteen months, Selabali was able to do the same in southern Tulabete Country. Athens and Mastaboni were still totally secure, as were the mines and most of the prime farmland, but Blake's forces were spread as thinly as he dared along the perimeters of what now became Human Territory.

Within two years sixteen thousand Men had been killed, and while it was true that more than one hundred thousand snakes had been killed, there were a lot more snakes left than Men.

Within four years Paka and Selabali had felt secure enough to leave their generals in charge and go off to nearby Flowergarden for a covert meeting with various politicians from the Republic. When they returned, it was to announce the creation of the Karimon government-in-exile, of which Paka and Selabali were co-chairmen.

The Republic immediately recognized the Karimon government, and at Paka's request, put a military blockade around the planet, thus halting the already-decreasing flow of goods from Goldstone. The Republic still wouldn't openly participate in the war, but it was doing everything within its power to support the natives against the colonists.

Two nights later John Blake spent the entire evening huddled with his advisors. The war was not going well, and it was certain to get worse in the coming months and years. The economy was still healthy, but it could only sustain an

all-out war for so long before it began crumbling, especially given the naval blockade. Paka and Selabali were heroes in the Republic, visionary leaders who dared to stand firm against human oppression, and funds were pouring into the accounts they had set up on friendly worlds.

It was time, announced Blake, for action, for the kind of bold political stroke that would stymie the Republic, neutralize the ferocious Paka and the wily Selabali, and turn the tide of events in favor of Man once more.

It was time to turn Rockgarden over to the snakes.

Forty-one

John Blake sat in the lounge of the presidential suite of the Grand Athens Hotel, smoking a Denebian cigar and sipping an Antarrean brandy. He had entered the building through the kitchen entrance, ascended to the penthouse via the service elevator, and had his security guards cordon off the entire floor. It was essential to his plans that no one—and especially no snakes—know that the Governor of Rockgarden was holding a secret meeting here. As far as the rest of the world knew, he was spending a quiet evening at the executive mansion.

Tomorrow they would have some inkling that he had spent the night doing more than reading and sleeping, but if this meeting went as he hoped it would, tomorrow would be too late for his enemies to do anything but adjust to the new reality he planned to impose on the situation.

He had been sitting there in a high-backed chair long enough to smoke his cigar halfway down when the door to the suite slid open and two of his most trusted assistants ushered his guest into the room.

"Will there be anything else, Governor?" asked one of them.

Blake shook his head. "Just wait outside. I'll let you know when we're through."

The men nodded and left, and the visitor who had accompanied them stood where he was, staring at Blake.

"I'm sorry for the manner in which you were brought here," said Blake, "but the need for secrecy was absolute. Won't you please sit down?"

The visitor, a snake in late middle age, walked cautiously into the middle of the lounge and looked around.

"Anywhere will do," said Blake, gesturing to a number of chairs and couches. "Wherever you'll be most comfortable."

The snake sat down on a leather chair and stared at Blake.

"Can I offer you some brandy?"

"I do not drink," replied the snake.

"A cigar, perhaps?"

"No, thank you."

"Pity," said Blake. He picked up his brandy snifter, took a sip, and stared at his guest.

"Why am I here, Governor?" asked the snake at last.

"We have some business to discuss, Father Janna," said Blake. "I'm an enormous admirer of yours, you know."

The snake named Father Janna stared at him with distrustful orange cat's-eyes.

"It's true," continued Blake. "You are the first ordained Christian minister of your race. I think that's quite an accomplishment." He paused. "You're not Catholic. I would have thought you would be called Reverend Janna rather than Father."

"You brought me all the way here just to ask why I am called Father Janna?"

Blake chuckled. "No, of course not. But I *am* curious."

"It's no mystery. I prefer the term Father, and so I gave it to myself."

"Why not?" replied Blake. "I'm told on the Inner Fron-

tier men change names as often as you and I change clothes. I think every man should have a name that satisfies him."

"It satisfies me," answered Father Janna. "And I should point out that I am not a Man."

"Every *being*, then," amended Blake. He noted that his cigar had gone out, and he relit it. "And you are quite an accomplished being, Father Janna. I have followed your career with great interest."

"I wasn't aware of that."

"Oh, but I have," said Blake. "You have led an exemplary life. You have fed the hungry and cared for the sick, you have converted huge numbers of your own people to Christianity, and, above all, you have been a voice of moderation in this damnable conflict that seems to just go on and on."

"I do not believe that killing ever solved anything, Governor Blake," said Father Janna.

"Nor do I." Blake sighed. "I wish Moses Selabali and that maniac Paka felt as you did."

"Please do not misunderstand me, Governor Blake," said Father Janna. "I disapprove of Thomas Paka's methods, not his goals. This is our planet, and I think one day even you will see that denying my race the right to govern itself is immoral."

"What would you say if I told you that day had arrived?" asked Blake, staring intently at the snake and trying to read his reaction.

"I would praise God and thank Him for bringing you to your senses."

"What if I further told you that I was prepared, as of this moment, to allow your people to share equally in the governing of Rockgarden?"

"I would tell you that my prayers had been answered."

"What I am *not* prepared to do," continued Blake, "is share power with either Thomas Paka or Moses Selabali.

They have committed too many atrocities against my people."

"They have not acted, but reacted," answered Father Janna. "They have responded to almost a century of repression, and whatever you think of their methods, you will have to involve them in the new government for it to have any legitimacy."

"They are unacceptable to my race," answered Blake. "The moment calls for moderation, not extremism. The transition must proceed by slow, careful steps. We are willing to *share* power, not *relinquish* it."

"That is an acceptable first step," said Father Janna, "but eventually you must relinquish it. Three million Men cannot govern half a billion snakes."

"Once we have secured our rights and our safety, once we know there will be no retribution against us and that we have created a society that is fair to both the majority and the minority races, then we will happily step aside. But I cannot put a timetable on it. To be perfectly frank, we will have to train an entire generation of snakes to take over the reins of government and to replace the human bureaucracy that now administers Rockgarden."

"That is a reasonable position," said Father Janna. "I feel certain that both sides can reach an accommodation on those grounds."

"The key to it," said Blake, "is turning over power to the right snake. It must be one who is willing to let the overzealous actions of both sides be forgotten, who understands that his people must be trained and prepared for self-government before my people turn over the reins of power, and one who disdains all violent solutions to the disagreements that will always occur when different sentient species share the same planet."

"I think you underestimate Thomas Paka," replied Father Janna. "He—"

"He would execute every Man who had ever opposed

him, and probably their families as well. He is bitter and hate-filled, and totally unacceptable to my people." Blake paused. "And in truth, Selabali isn't much better. If it came down to a choice between the two, we'd take him ahead of Paka . . . but there are almost a billion snakes on Rockgarden, so there is no reason to choose between those two evils."

"Then who did you have in mind, Governor Blake?"

Blake smiled. "I'm looking at him."

"You must be joking!" exclaimed Father Janna. "I have no political experience whatsoever!"

"You have something more important than experience, Father," said Blake. "You have intelligence and you have compassion, and that is what is required in the dangerous days ahead."

"But—"

"As for the rest of it, I'll teach you everything you have to know about running a government. We're going to be working together very closely, virtually side by side. If there's anything you don't understand, I'll always be there to explain it."

"This is insane!" replied Father Janna.

"Actually, it is a stroke of genius," replied Blake. "You haven't an enemy in the world, and there aren't too many on either side who can say that today. You are just the co-leader we need to pull this planet together."

"Are you quite sure you've given this sufficient thought?" asked Father Janna.

"There is no question in my mind that you are the perfect candidate for the job, the one member of your race best able to unify Rockgarden after this terrible ordeal we've all been through." He paused. "I would like to be able to announce this to the press tomorrow morning."

"May I have tonight to think about it?" asked Father Janna, getting to his feet.

"Certainly. I've arranged a room for you at a hotel in

Talimi"—the Grand Athens would not accept snakes—"and I'll contact you just after sunrise."

"I pray that I will make the proper decision," said Father Janna.

"I'm sure you will," replied Blake, standing up and escorting him to the door. "Especially when you consider that the alternative is the continuation of a war that has already left too many dead on both sides."

The door slid open, the security men escorted Father Janna back to the street, and Blake contacted his waiting staff via vidphone.

"How did it go?" asked his senior advisor anxiously.

"He'll sign up," answered Blake confidently.

"You're sure?"

"Relax," said Blake. "Tomorrow morning we announce the end of the war, the sharing of political power with the snakes, a desire to reestablish trade with the Republic, and, most importantly, the appointment of Father Janna to the highest office on the planet."

"And then?"

"Then we pull our puppet's strings and go back to running Rockgarden just as we always have," he said, "albeit with a somewhat lower profile."

Forty-two

At noon the next day John Blake called a press conference, and with holo cameras sending his image to all points of the Rockgarden compass, he announced that Men had reached an accommodation with snakes, and that henceforth he would be sharing his position as Governor with Father Janna.

He then stepped aside and watched respectfully as Father Janna walked up to the microphone and faced the press and the cameras.

"I am quite overwhelmed by the speed with which this has taken place," said Father Janna, "but I will do everything within my power to govern fairly and impartially. Movement toward majority rule will be slow and occasionally painful, and we will undoubtedly take some wrong steps, but the government of John Blake has shown its willingness to redress our grievances after years of war, and I think I speak on behalf of all my people when I thank Mr. Blake for taking this enormous first step."

He paused, and consulted some notes he carried with him. "To those of you who are still in the field, I say: lay down your arms. The day of peace is at hand, and the day

of full participation in our government is not far off. Mr. Blake has agreed to grant amnesty to all snakes who have taken up arms against his government; *I* hereby agree to grant amnesty to all Men who followed the dictates of their elected government and fought to curb the uprising. A new day has dawned on Rockgarden, a new era of understanding, and I urge every member of both races to move forward into the sunshine together."

Blake then stepped forward and shook Father Janna's hand, posed for an appropriate number of holographs, and then dismissed the press.

"That was an excellent speech," he said when he and his advisors were alone with Father Janna.

"The reaction among the reporters seemed . . . well . . . *subdued*," replied Father Janna unhappily.

"They'll get over it," replied Blake.

"I hope so." Father Janna paused. "What do I do now?"

Blake chuckled. "Now you go to your office, which is just down the hall from my own, and for the next two weeks my advisors will brief you on all the problems confronting Rockgarden. The war may be over, but we've got a lot of other problems. We've got a thirty-percent inflation rate, industrial productivity has fallen off, we've got to find a way to bring all the returning soldiers back into the economy. We will have to rebuild everything that the war has destroyed, we must decide what our response to the Republic's forthcoming overtures will be, we have farm policy to consider. . . . We'll keep you busy, Governor Janna, never fear."

"Please call me Father Janna; it's going to take time to get used to Governor Janna."

"Whatever you say, Father Janna," replied Blake. "And now, if you're ready to go to work . . ."

"Absolutely," replied Father Janna. "The one thing I don't want to be is a figurehead. The people must see that I am actually exercising power."

"They will," Blake assured him. "But you can't exercise it until you understand the issues. From this day forth, my advisors are your advisors."

"Shouldn't I also have advisors of my own species?"

"Of course," said Blake smoothly. "We'll begin assimilating them into the government almost immediately . . . but for the first few weeks, I think it makes more sense for you to be briefed by Men of unquestioned expertise in their various fields."

Father Janna nodded his head. "Yes, that seems reasonable. But I *will* be allowed to bring my own people in?"

"You're the Governor," said Blake. "You can do anything you want that isn't against the constitution."

Satisfied, Father Janna went off to his office.

"All right," said Blake when he was alone with his advisors. "You know the order in which you are to brief him. You are each to make our case as strongly as possible. You are never to show contempt or disdain for snakes. You are to lead him to the conclusions we want him to reach. You are, to the best of your abilities, to make him feel he has reached the conclusions on his own. You are never to overrule him. And if you feel there are certain areas where he will not mirror our views, you are to let me know immediately. Are there any questions?"

"Does he really have all the powers of the governorship?" asked the Minister of Defense.

"Absolutely," said Blake. Then he smiled. "Until he tries to exercise them."

He went to his office, poured himself an Antarrean brandy, even though it was a bit early in the day, leaned back on his chair, and looked out across Gardener Square.

It wasn't a bad gamble, he reflected. There was no doubt in his mind that he could control Father Janna; the snake was as much a bleeding heart as those idiots sitting in their glass offices on Deluros VIII. And it ought to satisfy the

Republic, too: he'd done everything they wanted, if not in the manner they wanted him to do it.

Of course, there was always a chance that Janna would start exercising his power, would issue some edicts that were not in the best interests of Men—but before that occurred, the snake armies would have disbanded and given up their arms, and no human military was going to enforce a snake's orders. No, as long as Men controlled the army, the treasury, the mines and the farms, they could live with a snake governor, especially one as powerless as Janna would be.

It was truly a bold solution, one that even Violet Gardener would have approved. When faced with an intolerable situation, you deal with your weakest enemy and you retain control of everything that will keep him weak. Textbook politics, actually.

He ordered his lunch in his office, then contacted the commander of his northern army. There had been no fighting since the announcement, but the snakes hadn't started coming in yet.

Well, that was to be expected. It had only been a couple of hours. Probably it would take a day or two for word to filter down from Thomas Paka and Moses Selabali and their generals.

The Bush Brigade reported the same thing: no contact, no action, no surrender.

He took a nap after lunch, stopped by Janna's office to give him encouragement, then spent the rest of the afternoon going over paperwork and signing a number of minor bills into law.

At dusk, accompanied by his bodyguards, he walked three blocks to his favorite restaurant and went directly to the table that was always reserved for him. He had toyed with inviting Janna to dinner, but the restaurant didn't allow snakes, and while he planned to give lip service to desegregation, it wasn't a policy he was in a hurry to imple-

ment, and so he sat alone, waving to some of the diners he knew at other tables, smiling at an editor from the local newstape.

He had been there for perhaps twenty minutes when one of his aides entered the restaurant and walked straight to his table.

"Yes? What is it?" he asked between mouthfuls.

"Problems."

"Paka?"

"And Selabali," said the aide, nodding.

"Let's have it."

"At five o'clock tonight, Paka's snakes launched a major offensive in the north, attacking the town of Tentamp. Early reports list more than eighty Men dead and four hundred wounded."

"And Selabali?"

"His Tulabete attacked a factory on the outskirts of Mastaboni and burned it to the ground. At least fifty Men were killed."

"Shit!" muttered Blake. "I *knew* things were going too smoothly." He looked at the aide. "Have we had any communication with them?"

"I wouldn't call it *communication*," said the aide wryly. "Paka radioed a message to General Tomlinson less than a minute before the attack. All it said was: *Death to Man Janna.* Selabali sent the same thing to the mayor of Mastaboni."

Blake sighed. "Well, they're smarter than *he* is, I'll give them that," he said grimly.

Forty-three

The attacks became more frequent.

A farm here, an outpost there, a safari bus in the Baski Plains—and just when it seemed that they were merely sporadic acts of small groups of terrorists, Paka's army, some thirty thousand strong, would meet a column of Blake's army head-on, or Selabali's forces would attack and destroy an entire town, leaving nothing—man or animal—alive.

Blake put Father Janna on video every night and had him plead with his people to lay down their arms and trust him to make a lasting peace. After a month, the snake army started jamming the signals, and within three months they were able to broadcast Paka's calls to arms on any channel they chose.

It was on a peaceful spring evening, just after the long rains had ended, that Blake turned on the news and found himself staring first at a blank holographic screen and then at Thomas Paka's image.

"This message is addressed to the government of John Blake and the traitor, Man Janna," he announced. "You think you can win a war of attrition; I tell you that you

cannot. You think you can stop the flow of arms to my troops; I tell you that you cannot. You think you can keep my race in a state of perpetual servitude, even as the traitor Janna does your bidding; I tell you that you cannot."

Paka paused for a moment, glaring into the camera from his hidden location.

"In a meeting of historic importance this morning, Moses Selabali, Robert Pelinori, James Laki, Wilson Grebna, and myself have formed the United Karimon Front. From this day forth, we will be acting in concert, under a central command. All of our actions will be coordinated, and they will not cease until John Blake—not the false man, Janna—publicly agrees to the principle of one being, one vote."

He paused again for the full magnitude of his statement to hit his audience, and then continued:

"No longer are you fighting against Rakko and Fani and Tulabete and Pangi and Meskitan. From this moment, you are fighting Karimonis, united in our desire to take back control of the planet of our birth."

"And where the hell do you think *I* was born, you goddamned snake?" Blake muttered at Paka's image.

"We will not lay down our arms until we have attained our goal," concluded Paka. "And I promise you this, John Blake: what has gone before will seem like a mild breeze compared to the storm that is coming."

The screen went blank again, and Blake, checking all the other channels, found that they, too, were jammed.

The next morning three hundred farms were destroyed and four mines exploded, killing hundreds of human and snake workers.

The emigration started that afternoon. Men who had fought the elements, fought the weeds and rocks, fought the droughts, and fought the snakes, decided that there was simply no sense to continue fighting. More than fifty who owned their own ships left by the end of the day, and

some eight hundred more applied for exit visas before the government offices closed that night.

By week's end, close to twenty thousand Men had decided to leave the planet, and Blake realized for the first time that he was on the losing end of the battle. He'd fought the snakes to a standstill thus far, but if their numbers increased every day while the number of Men left to fight decreased, it was only a matter of time before Athens itself would be overrun by Paka's and Selabali's armies.

Still, he hadn't been elected to preside over the loss of Man's primacy on Rockgarden, and he was the kind of man who fought best and most creatively when cornered. He spent the week in the executive mansion, coming up with hundreds of political, economic, and military plans, discarding each in turn as he was able to find flaws in it, then proceeding to the next. Finally, when he was down to just a handful of vague notions and ideas, he decided to pay a visit to Father Janna.

"Good evening, Mr. Blake," said Janna as he walked into the snake's office.

"Good evening, Father Janna," he said. "Do you mind if I sit down?"

"Please do."

Blake looked around, disdained the furniture that had been created for Men, and sat in a chair that was made for snakes. It was uncomfortable, but he wanted to put Janna at his ease.

"How's it going?" he asked.

"Not well, Mr. Blake," replied Janna. "I'm told I have received more than two hundred death threats since Paka's speech, all from members of my own tribe."

"From the Fani?" said Blake. "That's curious. I'd have thought the Tulabete would be the ones to threaten you, since you *are* a Fani."

"If Moses Selabali calls for my death, they'll respond,"

answered Janna. "But they're not about to take orders from Thomas Paka."

"I thought all that tribalism went out with the creation of this utopian Karimon Front."

Janna shook his head. "It will be many generations before tribalism ceases to be a major fact of life—if indeed it ever does."

Blake filed the fact away for future use. "Other than the threats, how are you progressing?"

"I feel totally useless," admitted Janna. "I am doing my best to understand the intricacies of our economic policy, but to what purpose? We've gone to a wartime economy, our farms have become battlegrounds, and even Goldstone has been prevented from trading with us. What is the good of knowing these things?"

"The war can't go on forever," said Blake. "Eventually we'll win, and those are precisely the things a good administrator has to know."

"Do you really foresee an end to the war?" asked Janna.

"Don't you?"

Janna sighed and shook his head. "They are *fanatics*, Mr. Blake."

"You want the same thing they do, and I'd hardly call *you* a fanatic," said Blake, lighting a cigar.

"I think it is a sin to kill any sentient being, no matter how much I may disapprove of his actions. Thomas Paka would say that a snake who is not willing to fight for his freedom after a century of subjugation is not a snake at all. You have heard and read his statements, Mr. Blake. From the moment I took the oath of office, he has called me Man Janna."

"A politician learns to turn a deaf ear to insults," said Blake.

"I don't think you understand the depth of this particular insult," replied Janna. "My understanding is that one of

the worst things a Man can be called is a bastard. This is infinitely more hateful in the eyes of my people."

"I'm sorry I got you into this," said Blake, who found, to his surprise, that he *was* mildly sorry that he had used this being of such obvious naïveté and good will, and that he had every intention of using him again.

"It was a gesture of trust on your part," said Father Janna. "You could not have foreseen the consequences. Though," he added bitterly, "*I* should have."

"Well, we can't worry about that now," said Blake. "We're losing thousands of Men every day, and Paka and Selabali are slaughtering those that are left, while the Republic cordons off the whole damned world and keeps supplying the rebels with more weapons and ammunition. We *must* come up with some kind of gesture before they destroy everything we've built."

"I have a question, Mr. Blake," said Janna.

"Oh? What is it?"

"I don't know if you can answer it, but it has been troubling me for quite some time." Janna paused, frowning, as if trying to figure out how to word what came next. "I have known Thomas Paka most of my life. We were students together both here and on Lodin XI, and I spoke to him many times after he returned from Deluros and began writing his books."

"What's the question?" asked Blake.

"This Paka I see and hear now is not the same one I knew. Something must have happened to radicalize him. My guess is that it happened in prison." He looked at Blake. "I was thinking, if perhaps he was subjected to torture, if he was physically abused, possibly the public punishment of the guilty parties might . . ." He searched for the words, and then shrugged. "I don't know. He will never share my views, but he might hate your race a little less. Can it be done?"

"He was never tortured," said Blake. "I gave orders that

he was to be treated with all the dignity befitting a leader of his people."

"Many jailors feel that a leader of *my* people has no dignity."

"He wasn't mistreated," said Blake firmly.

"Then I cannot imagine what radicalized him."

There was an uncomfortable pause.

"*I* did," said Blake at last.

"You?" repeated Janna. "How?"

"That is a matter between Paka and myself. I made the right decision. He disagrees."

"Is there any way you can change it?"

"Not at this point."

"Then I see no way out. Eventually the United Karimon Front will overthrow the government, and you and I will hang side by side."

"I'm not ready to give up just yet," said Blake.

They spoke for another hour without resolving anything, and then Blake returned to his mansion, to find that Paka had wiped out another small town on the northern border of Faniland.

Every morning Blake would meet with his cabinet and his advisors and state his resolve not to yield to Paka's demands—and every morning another five thousand Men had left Rockgarden or another snake attack had killed those Men who were least expecting to be attacked.

It was on the seventy-fourth day after the creation of the United Karimon Front that Blake walked into his cabinet room and found letters of resignation from two advisors and a cabinet member awaiting him.

"If the situation doesn't change, I'll be leaving next month," added his Minister of Transportation when Blake had finished reading the letters. "Face it, John—we did our best, but the battle is lost. Whether we lose the war to them or make an accommodation with them, the end result is going to be the same: in two or three years' time the snakes

are going to be running this planet. If I were you, I'd stop fighting a losing battle for our primacy, and start fighting to keep such money and land as we've managed to accumulate."

"I agree," added one of his advisors. "The war is lost. Some of us were born here, John; we've got every bit as much right to call ourselves citizens of Karimon as the snakes do. I think the battle now must be to keep what we've got."

"Is that the sense of this meeting?" asked Blake.

Every head nodded an affirmative.

"How about you?" he asked of his Defense Minister. "We've always acted on the assumption that the war can be won. Now I am asking you for your honest assessment of the situation: *can* we win?"

"We can hold them off for a few months or possibly even a few years," was the answer. "But they're gaining thousands of recruits every day, and of course the Republic is constantly resupplying them with weapons." He shook his head. "No, I can prolong the war, but under the current circumstances, there's no way we can win it."

"I'll take your opinions under advisement," said Blake. He turned on his heel and walked out of the meeting.

And, because he was a realist, a week later he decided to sue for peace and make the best deal he could get for those Men who remained on Rockgarden.

Forty-four

I t took the United Karimon Front, which Blake decided was a little less united than its name implied, almost a month to agree to peace talks.

Paka insisted that the talks be held on some other world; he had no intention of showing up in Athens to talk and being arrested.

Blake insisted that representatives of the Republic be present. He was absolutely certain that Deluros VIII, having finally gotten what it wanted, wasn't about to leave two million Men to the mercy of the snakes once the reins of power changed hands.

Then Paka and Selabali issued a joint statement that they would not attend the meeting if Father Janna was present.

Blake balked at that. He had no loyalty to Janna at all, but having made him the co-governor, he felt that ordering him to stay behind would be a public admission of what everyone except Janna privately knew: that Janna was simply a figurehead who had been brought in so that Blake's government could continue to rule the planet.

It was Janna himself who provided the solution: with Blake and his advisors gone, *someone* had to be in charge of

Rockgarden; after all, there were still millions of troops out there. Therefore, he would stay behind in case this was not the display of good faith that he hoped it was.

Blake suggested half a dozen planets, all of them inhabited solely by Men. The United Karimon Front rejected them all.

Paka suggested three planets that Blake turned down simply because he felt it was required of him, having had his own suggested venues rejected.

At last Selabali suggested that the meeting take place on their sister world of Flowergarden, and Blake agreed. So, to his surprise, did Paka.

Then came the debate over the participants. The United Karimon Front submitted a list of thirty-four freedom fighters. Blake knew that this was just for show, that all the decisions would be made by Paka and Selabali, the leaders of the two major tribes. He accepted Paka, Selabali, Robert Pelinori and three other Tulabete, and turned down twenty-eight names. Selabali agreed, Paka didn't, and the conference was held up another week before Selabali finally convinced Paka to accept Blake's list.

Blake, aware that the conference would be covered by hundreds of members of the Republic's press, elected to attend it alone. Let the trillions of Men throughout the galaxy dwell upon the image of a lone, beleaguered Man standing against a table full of snakes. (He hoped a few of them would be shedding their skins during the conference; the more hideous they appeared, the more public sympathy he could stockpile.)

The last point to be settled was which members of the huge Republic bureaucracy would act as go-betweens and moderators. Paka wanted the Chairman of the Bureau of Alien Affairs, but Blake found that branch of the Republic too sympathetic to his enemy's cause. He responded by suggesting first the Department of Cartography, which he knew was anathema to the snakes, and once they had

turned it down, he followed with the Division of Constitutional Law, a branch of the Department of Justice that had drawn up constitutions for more than a thousand planets that had been incorporated into the Republic. Since it showed a willingness to scrap the current Rockgarden constitution, the United Karimon Front finally agreed to it.

Blake agreed to any seating arrangement that the snakes wanted, and finally, after almost ten weeks of preparation and maneuvering, the peace talks took place.

Blake, well aware of the dozens of cameras trained on him, sat across a broad table from the snakes and made his opening statement:

"There has been too much killing, too much violence, too much misunderstanding between the races on Rockgarden. I have come here, of my own volition, representing the race of Men who inhabit Rockgarden, to seek an accommodation with our former enemies and to reach an agreement that is fair to both sides. I acknowledge that there have been injustices in the past, that innocent members of *both* species have suffered, but I have not come here to trade accusations. I am here to help build a future in which my race and yours can live in harmony, in which one side is not made to suffer for the gain or benefit of the other. As far as I am concerned, everything, every point of dispute, is negotiable."

"You could have saved many lives by saying these words five, or even two years ago," said Moses Selabali in his sibilant voice.

"Everything is negotiable," replied Blake. "I do not regard acts of wanton terrorism as legitimate negotiating."

Selabali seemed about to reply, when Herbert Willis, the Director of the Division of Constitutional Law, intervened.

"Excuse me," he said, "but before we begin with a series of recriminations, perhaps I can be of some use here in sorting out the issues."

"I have no objections," said Blake promptly.

Selabali said nothing, but nodded his acquiescence.

"Mr. Blake, for some years now both the natives of the planet and the Republic have been pressing for the government to accept the principle of one being, one vote. It seems to me that that principle is basic to any cessation of hostilities and any constitution that may come out of this conference. Is your government prepared to accept it?"

"First," said Blake, "I must point out that I, and well over ninety percent of the Men of Rockgarden, are also natives of the planet. We were born there, we grew up there, we have worked to develop it into a modern, functioning world, and I resent the implication that we are any less Rockgardeners than the gentlemen sitting across the table from me." He paused. "In answer to your question, on the day that I asked Father Janna to share power with me, the government of Rockgarden has been totally committed to the principle of one being, one vote."

Paka uttered a snort of derision, but made no comment.

"Have any members of the—you call yourselves Karimonis, do you?—have any members of the Karimonis exercised that franchise?"

"No," said Paka.

"Mr. Blake?" said Willis.

"It's not that simple," replied Blake. "You make it sound like everyone could simply go out and vote tomorrow."

"You claim to support that very principle. Therefore, I feel I must ask why they cannot?"

"First," said Blake, "there happens to be a war going on. Second, we must take a planetary census to establish a voter roll. Third, since we are dealing with a population that has a literacy rate of about fourteen percent, we must agree upon a form of balloting that will not instantly disenfranchise five out of every six Karimonis. Fourth, we must call a general election, and we have been unable to do so when the very people who will benefit from such an election are

out in the bush shooting any human that wanders into their line of fire."

"Your first and fourth reservations will vanish with the cessation of the war," said Willis. "Let us see if we can address the other two. Mr. Paka, what suggestions have you for a ballot that will be comprehensible to your people?"

"Let them vote by voice," answered Paka, "in front of members of all competing parties who will then tabulate that vote."

"Mr. Blake?"

"That's not a very good idea," answered Blake. "It undermines the concept of the secret ballot."

"Why must a ballot be secret?" asked Paka.

"So that the voter cannot be intimidated," replied Blake.

"Men may intimidate other men," said Paka. "Karimonis do not intimidate Karimonis."

"The Fani and the Tulabete have been butchering each other for thousands of years," shot back Blake. "Why should they stop now?"

"Please, Mr. Blake," said Willis. He turned to Moses Selabali. "Would this be acceptable as a temporary measure that could be replaced by written ballot at such time as your race achieves a literacy rate of, shall we say, fifty percent?"

"Yes," said Selabali.

"You're making a big mistake," said Blake, staring directly at Selabali. "The Tulabete took huge losses in the last war, and you're bearing the brunt of the fighting in this one. The Fani have got you outnumbered, three to one."

"Do not listen to him, Moses," said Paka. "He is trying to divide us. The alternative is not to vote at all until we have raised our literacy rate to *his* standard."

"I will accept balloting by voice," said Selabali after a moment's consideration.

"Fine," said Willis. "We are making excellent progress. Now, what about a planetary census?"

"That is impossible," replied Paka. "Many of our people live in isolated areas under very primitive conditions. It is entirely conceivable that ten percent of my race has never even seen a Man."

"What has that got to do with anything?" asked Blake.

"It would take years to complete such a census, and those who would take the longest to find and count are those with the least interest in voting."

"What about a census of the more populated areas?" continued Willis. "How quickly could it be done?"

"Within a year," said Paka.

"If the Republic's Departments of Census and Cartography were to help, it could be done within four months," offered Selabali.

"An excellent suggestion, Mr. Selabali," said Willis. "I shall certainly suggest it to them, and I see no reason why they should refuse." He paused and smiled. "We are truly making excellent progress, gentlemen. I had no idea we would solve the major questions so quickly."

"You have not come to the major questions yet," said Paka, staring fiercely at Blake.

"Oh? I am afraid I don't understand."

"He gives us the vote because he knows we will win it in battle, and because in his heart he knows it is ours to begin with," said Paka. "Soon we must come to those things that he does *not* believe are ours, and then we shall see how earnest he is to live in peace and harmony with the enemies of his blood."

"What do you mean, Mr. Paka?" asked Willis.

"Let us begin with the land," said Paka. "Two million human farmers own ninety percent of the farmland on Karimon, while almost a billion Karimonis must scrape at their meager two- and three-acre plots for their subsistence. Tell me, Mr. Blake, are Men willing to turn over their farms to us?"

Blake looked into the video cameras and spoke.

"You must understand," he said, "that less than two percent of the land on Rockgarden was under cultivation when Violet Gardener received the Republic's permission to open the planet up to human habitation and development. Neither Mr. Paka nor Mr. Selabali can point to any instance where a cultivated farm was appropriated by a human being. This is an industry that Men developed—and we developed it to the point, in less than half a century, where we not only are able to feed a billion Karimonis, but our greatest source of hard currency comes from the export of food to neighboring worlds. We bring in more from food production than from our mining industries." He paused. "That land was cleared by Men, cultivated by Men, worked by Men—and now Mr. Paka, who has already received the thing he says he has been fighting for, the vote, wants two million Men to walk away from the land their families have farmed for generations. I say that this is unfair. If the Karimonis have suddenly developed a desire to take up farming, let them pay a fair market price to those Men who are willing to sell them their farms, and let them leave the rest of us alone."

"How can we pay for farms or anything else when you have spent the last century exploiting us?" demanded Paka.

"Are you implying that you had a stockpile of money when we arrived on your planet, and that we appropriated it?" asked Blake with a smile.

"We had a *planet* and you appropriated it!"

"Please, gentlemen," said Willis. "This is obviously an extremely sensitive point. We are not going to solve it today, and there is no sense arguing about who is most at fault. We are here to negotiate a peace and a constitution; this is one of the points that will require long and serious negotiation."

"There is another point that goes hand in glove with it," said Blake.

"And what is that?"

"Proportional representation," replied Blake. "We can't allow it."

"You see?" said Paka angrily. "I told you this meeting was a farce."

"Let me finish," said Blake. "Men currently control ninety-five percent of the wealth on Rockgarden. We own all the mines and, as Mr. Paka pointed out, most of the farmland. These were industries that didn't even exist until we landed on the planet, and they have benefited both races. The mines have offered employment for Karimonis since the day they were opened, and no Karimoni has ever had to go hungry since our farming industry was created." He paused. "Yet there are a billion Karimoni and less than three million Men on Rockgarden—and the total will probably be under two million Men before this current situation has been resolved. If they are given proportional representation, no man will ever again hold elective office, and we will have no recourse against any abuses perpetrated by a Karimoni government. Mr. Paka could rule that a single credit constituted fair market value for a ten-thousand-acre farm, and we would have no way to protest or to fight against that ruling."

"So you give us one being, one vote with one hand, and with the other you wish to sign into law a constitution that gives you ninety percent of the power of our government?" demanded Paka.

"I'm not demanding any particular percent," replied Blake. "I am simply saying that proportional representation is unfair and unacceptable. Like many other Men, I consider Rockgarden my home, and I have no intention of leaving it. Therefore, I wish to secure my rights now, rather than have to fight for them later."

"No matter what arguments you use," said Paka, "what you are really saying is one Man, one vote, and one Karimoni, one one-millionth of a vote."

"Are you proposing that?" asked Blake.

Paka stood up, glared at Blake, and left the conference room without another word.

"Oh dear, oh dear," muttered Willis. He turned to an aide. "Somebody must stop him."

"He'll be back," said Blake.

"What makes you think so?" asked Selabali.

"Because any minute now he'll realize that you're still here, and he doesn't want a government run by the Tulabete any more than he wants one run by Men."

"You are mistaken, John Blake," said Selabali. "We are Tulabete and Fani and Rakko no longer. Now we are all just Karimoni."

"We'll see," said Blake confidently.

Five minutes later word reached the conference room that Thomas Paka had returned to his quarters at the hotel, and would join the afternoon session.

Forty-five

The first peace conference didn't settle much of anything, except to prove that John Blake was truly willing to negotiate and that the United Karimon Front was willing not to pursue the war until the last Man was dead.

But there was a second conference five weeks later, one that was *not* broadcast back to the Republic. It was attended by Paka, Selabali, Blake, Willis, and some two dozen legal scholars from the Division of Constitutional Law, and from that conference came a permanent ceasefire and a new constitution.

The constitution rambled on for some forty-seven written pages, but the gist of it was this:

The name of the world was once again officially Karimon.

Every sentient being now residing on Karimon was automatically a citizen and possessed the right to vote.

The government would have a single legislative body, composed of two hundred fifty members. For a period of twelve years, thirty of those seats were reserved for Men, and they could veto any legislation they felt was inimical to their race; after the twelve years had elapsed, proportional

representation would be the rule. (As much as Paka hated that provision, Blake hated it even more, but it was the best deal he could get, and at least it bought his people another dozen years.)

There would be a judiciary, all members to be appointed by the Governor.

And there would be a single Governor for the entire planet.

The day the constitution was ratified, three citizens of Karimon announced their candidacies for Governor: Moses Selabali, Thomas Paka, and John Blake.

Forty-six

"Mr. Blake?"

Blake looked up from his desk and saw Father Janna standing in the doorway.

"Come on in," he said, deactivating his computer and leaning back on his chair.

"Thank you," said Father Janna. "Are you sure I'm not disturbing you?"

"Not at all," said Blake. "Hell, I'm just going through the motions anyway. Another three months and I'm out of here."

"Yes," said Janna. "I have seen the polls."

"Well, there's nothing I can do about it. I may have a secure seat in the Parliament, but there's no way a Man is going to beat a snake in a general election for Governor."

"That is what I came to speak to you about."

"About my running for Governor?"

"About *my* running," said Janna.

"You?"

Janna nodded. "I do not trust Thomas Paka, Mr. Blake," he said. "Each time I hear him speak, he is less and less recognizable as the Paka I used to know." He paused. "He

is a Fani, and as such he must be favored to win, since there are more Fani than Tulabete. I do not want this to happen. Thomas Paka is a dangerous demagogue, and he must be defeated."

"And you think *you* can beat him?" asked Blake, unable to keep the amusement out of his voice.

"No, I am not that far removed from reality," replied Janna. "But I, too, am a Fani. If I announce my candidacy, perhaps I can take enough votes away from him so that Moses Selabali can win."

"I don't want to hurt your feelings, Father Janna," said Blake bluntly, "but you couldn't draw two percent of the Fani vote. Paka's their hero; they still think you're a traitor."

"I know I am unpopular," admitted Janna with no display of defensiveness. "But if there is even a chance of defeating him, I am willing to undergo the public abuse and humiliation that will certainly pour down upon me."

"It's a noble thought, and I appreciate it, but that's not the way to beat him," said Blake.

"*Is* there a way?"

"Possibly."

"How?" asked Janna.

"We are dealing with a basically illiterate society here," said Blake. "Forget about the war and the fine ideals. I don't expect ten percent of any tribe to vote. With one exception."

"Which is that?"

"*My* tribe," answered Blake. "We'll turn out one hundred percent of our people at the polls."

"Surely you don't expect to win?"

Blake smiled. "I'm no more out of touch with reality than you are, Father Janna. No, I don't expect to win." He paused and lit one of his ever-present cigars. "But if I throw my support to Selabali, it just might be enough for *him* to win."

"Have you mentioned this to him?"

"Not yet," said Blake. "I've set up a meeting with him next month. That will be plenty of time to work out a deal. He's going to need a cabinet and advisors and judges; I think I can recommend some very good people, in exchange for my support." He chuckled. "He'll never figure out that I'd give it to him anyway, just to keep Paka from destroying this planet."

Forty-seven

The meeting between John Blake and Moses Selabali was held in secret, promises and assurances were given, agreements were made, and two days later John Blake publicly withdrew from the race and urged all his supporters to give their votes to Moses Selabali. There wasn't a Man on the planet who didn't understand exactly what had happened.

The next poll, a week later, showed that Selabali had edged almost two points ahead of Thomas Paka, and Karimon's human population breathed a collective sigh of relief.

Then Paka announced that he was carrying his campaign to Mastaboni, the heart of Tulabete Country, and that he would be giving a major address that would be carried by all the video networks.

Nice try, you clever snake, thought Blake. *But you're still a Fani. They might forget they're supposed to be civilized and tear you to pieces before you get ten words out.*

At eight o'clock that evening, Blake turned on the holo. Instantly there was an image of a huge sporting stadium, filled with Tulabete and a handful of Men. If there was a Fani anywhere in the crowd, Blake couldn't spot him.

There were a few brief speeches by minor candidates for minor offices, and then Thomas Paka walked onto the stage to polite but unenthusiastic applause.

Dumb, thought Blake. *You don't want your own people to see you get booed off a stage. Unless,* he thought suddenly, *you want them to humiliate you so badly that your own people are inspired to go to the polls in even greater numbers to make sure you win. Maybe you're not as dumb as I thought.*

"Fellow Karimonis!" said Paka, raising his hands. "Five months ago I went to the planet of Flowergarden to battle for your rights against John Blake, the Man who represents everything we have fought against during this long and bitter conflict. Now I address you not as Fani to Tulabete, but as Karimoni to Karimoni, and I bring you glad tidings."

He paused and waited for silence, then pointed into the darkness to a spot some three miles distant, a spot he himself had never seen.

"Jalanopi's tree still stands!" he shouted.

The cheer from the crowd was so loud that it shorted out the sound system. They screamed, they laughed, they began dancing in the aisles, and Paka finally had to leave before they could fix the microphones. But it made no difference: nothing he could have said would have made a difference after that. Blake could even hear cries of *"Jalanopi's tree still stands!"* coming through the closed windows of his executive mansion.

Damn! thought Blake. *It's all over. You're going to take Rockgarden straight to hell, just because you came up with a slogan the Tulabete love.*

Two months later, Thomas Paka won the governorship of Karimon with eighty-one percent of the vote.

John Blake's thousand years had lasted less than a decade.

VII

PAKA'S TIGHTROPE

Forty-eight

I t was Thomas Paka's fourth day in office, and he was starting to wonder if he was ever going to get any work done. So far he had attended two inaugural celebrations, held a press conference, and played host to a seemingly endless stream of diplomats, human and alien alike, who had come to congratulate him or wish him good luck.

He glanced at his computer, and saw, thankfully, that he only had one more appointment for the day, this one with Mordecai Kiichana, the President of Alpha Bednares II. He walked over to the wetbar in the corner of his office, a leftover from Blake's days as Governor, poured himself a glass of water, and returned to his desk. He stared out at Independence Park—the new official name for Gardener Square—for a few minutes, watching the Karimonis and Men walking through it as if they were all in a hurry to get to important meetings, and then, finally, he drank his water and informed his receptionist that he was ready to see his visitor.

The door slid back and Mordecai Kiichana stepped into the office. He was tall, taller even than Paka, humanoid in shape, though his purple eyes were very wideset on his head

and his nostrils were mere slits in his face. His ears were pointed and mobile, constantly twitching. His body was covered with a tawny fur, over which he wore what seemed to pass for a military uniform. His weaponry was abundant, but so polished and shining that Paka was sure none had ever been drawn in anger or fired anywhere, even on a practice range, and he wore so many medals that a smaller frame might have been weighted down with them.

"Good afternoon, Mordecai," said Paka, getting to his feet and greeting Kiichana warmly. "I am so glad you could come."

"It is my pleasure to be here," replied Kiichana.

"I have met too many strangers this week; it is very nice to see an old friend once again," said Paka. "Not only a friend," he amended, "but one of my heroes."

"Please, Thomas," said Kiichana. "You embarrass me."

"Won't you sit down?"

"Thank you, but I prefer to stand," said Kiichana. "I have never become used to human furniture."

"I haven't had a chance to refurnish the office since I became Governor," said Paka apologetically. "Things will be different on your next visit."

"I am sure they will." Kiichana cleared his throat. "I have come here to wish you success as Karimon embarks upon its bold new course as an independent world."

"For which I thank you," said Paka.

"And I have also come to tell you how to assure that success."

"I reject no one's counsel," said Paka, "and certainly not the hero of Alpha Bednares II. I will be happy to listen to you."

"I hope so," said Kiichana, "for they did not listen to me on Greenvalley or Laginappe II or Scheinwald V, and they have all suffered for it."

"May I offer you something to drink before we speak?" asked Paka.

"Just water," said Kiichana. "My metabolism rebels at both your drinks and those of Men."

"So be it," said Paka. He considered getting up and pouring the water himself, decided that such an act was too servile for a newly elected planetary leader, and summoned his receptionist to do it for him. After Kiichana had been given his water and the receptionist had returned to the outer office, Paka looked at him expectantly.

"How much do you know of the history of my world, Thomas?" asked Kiichana.

"I know what I've read and what you have told me over the years: that you fought the Republic for eight long years and finally obtained your independence, and that you yourself were a great warrior who was proclaimed President for Life."

"Not unlike yourself," noted Kiichana.

"I'm no warrior," replied Paka, shaking his head. "I'm a simple scholar and schoolteacher who got caught up in momentous events. Until an incident occurred a few years ago that changed my outlook, I even leaned toward pacifism."

"Be that as it may," replied Kiichana, "our careers parallel each other, much as the history of our worlds parallel each other. Alpha Bednares II had been under the yoke of human tyranny for almost two centuries, and our slogan was identical to yours: *One being, one vote.*"

"And eventually you got it."

"Eventually." Kiichana paused. "And, as you noted, I was elected President for Life. I had wonderful plans, Thomas. I was going to turn my world into a paradise for my people. There would be farmland for everyone, jobs for everyone, equality for everyone. Never again would we be under the thumb of Man. I planned to redress all our grievances and give us a fresh new start. I could see Utopia just around the corner, just as I am certain you yourself can see it." He smiled sadly. "I was very idealistic, but I was a

fool. I am here to advise you not to become a fool as well."

"But I know that you instituted your reforms," said Paka, confused.

"Certainly I did. I fulfilled every promise I made."

"Well, then?"

"Alpha Bednares II has been independent for seventeen years," said Kiichana. "During that time we have changed from an exporter to an importer of food and raw materials, our per capita income has dropped by almost eighty percent, most of our factories have fallen into disrepair, and we are now on the Republic's list of the one hundred most impoverished worlds. Even as I speak to you, my military forces are bracing themselves for a fifth attempt at a coup."

"What went wrong?" asked Paka.

"I made one foolish, emotional decision," answered Kiichana, "and I set my world back more than a century because of it." He paused. "It is a decision I hope to prevent you from making as well."

"I'm listening," said Paka.

"I banished all Men from my world," said Kiichana. "I repossessed their farms and divided them up among my people. My government took over ownership of their factories. We set up segregated townships where Men could live, as they had done to us for two centuries. It was very satisfying—but it spelled disaster for my world." He leaned forward and stared into Paka's eyes. "I urge you, Thomas, no matter how much you hate them, no matter how badly you wish to redress your grievances, no matter what moral imperatives you think apply to the situation, think of Karimon first and vengeance second. You may hate the sight of Men, but I've toured your world this week, and it cannot function without them any more than mine can. You need their technical expertise, their ability to produce high yields from their farms, their ability to attract human investment."

"And what of the suffering they have caused, of the

injustices they have perpetrated since they day they arrived?"

"You live with it, and you never give them an opportunity to dominate you again—but you don't kick them off your planet," answered Kiichana. "You need only compare my world with Peponi, a planet whose president literally begged its human population to remain after independence. They have a thriving economy, they still manage to feed themselves, their factories still function." He paused. "My people are deserting the cities and going back to subsistence farming. There is no employment for them, no safety net of social programs, not even any food for sale. I made a mistake, and I will live with it—but I have traveled to other newly independent worlds urging them not to make the same mistake, as I am now urging you."

"My people expect me to take some action against the Men who remain," said Paka. "We were coerced into accepting a constitution that gives them a disproportionate amount of political power."

"Use it to your advantage," said Kiichana promptly.

"To my advantage?" said Paka, startled. "How?"

"Your people will be land-hungry," said Kiichana. "You can leave the productive farms in the hands of the Men who developed them, and blame the constitution for your inability to repossess the land. Give them a few minor victories, but leave the economic power in the hands of the Men who remain until you can train a generation of your own people to take over and run the planet as efficiently. You're an accomplished politician or you wouldn't be sitting in this office. Use that political skill to walk a tightrope between what your people want and what is best for Karimon."

There was another, longer silence, as Paka considered what his visitor had said.

"This has been a most unusual conversation, Mordecai," he said. "I will think long and hard upon it."

"When you do, you will see that I'm right," replied Kii-chana. "I *hate* them," he added passionately, "but I'd give half my planet to have them back."

"Have you considered asking them back?" suggested Paka. "Surely there are ways to entice them."

Kiichana shook his head. "Don't you think I've tried? There are a million worlds out there. Once you've kicked them off your planet, you've proven that it can be done— and what has been done once can be done again. Once they leave, they don't come back—and they make sure that you suffer the full consequences of your decision." He paused. "They are no more forgiving than I would be if the circumstances were reversed."

"No," agreed Paka. "Compassion for others was never one of their virtues."

"Nor, in truth, is it mine," added Kiichana. "But practi-cality and pragmatism are essential virtues for a leader. As much as you may hate them, you need them even more. You have taken the weapons from their hands; settle for that until your people have the expertise to take everything else from them as well. If you move prematurely, what happened to my world will surely happen to yours."

"I thank you for your thoughts, my old friend," said Paka. "I shall consider my next actions very carefully."

"That is all I ask," said Kiichana, getting to his feet. "I will be sending a permanent ambassador next week, and I hope that Alpha Bednares II can obtain a favored trading status with Karimon." He smiled wryly. "Against the day that we once again have something to trade."

"I would welcome a close relationship with your world," answered Paka, "as I cherish my close relationship with its President." He paused. "I would like to consult with you on a regular basis during the weeks to come."

"I am at your disposal," said Kiichana. "I will have one of my aides give you the code that will route your messages through to me."

"Before you leave, I wonder if you would do me the honor of joining me for dinner?"

"It would be my pleasure," replied Kiichana.

"I plan to invite some of my most trusted associates as well," said Paka. "I would like them to hear what you have to say."

Forty-nine

P aka, sitting in his office, activated his holo screen and watched Moses Selabali rise from his seat in the Parliament to address the assembled members.

"It is time," said Selabali in his deep, stentorian voice, "for this august body to address the issue that has been facing us since independence—the equitable redistribution of land. There can be no greater injustice than for two hundred thousand Men to control ninety percent of Karimon's arable farmland, while more than a billion Karimonis must eke out a meager living on their pitiful one- and two-acre tracts of overused land. I have here"—he held up a thick document—"a report from the Ministry of Agriculture suggesting three different methods of land apportionment, any of which the government will support. No Man currently owning farmland will be deprived of it in its entirety, but the current situation is intolerable, and I say that the time for action is now."

John Blake raised his hand for recognition.

"Speaking on behalf of my constituents," he said, "I say to Mr. Selabali that we have absolutely no objection to any reapportioning of farmland anywhere on the planet." He

paused. "Providing, of course, that fair market value is paid for the land, and that no farm owner is forced to sell against his will."

"That is ridiculous!" snapped Selabali.

"Is it?" replied Blake. "Is it ridiculous to point out that once you turn the land over to a billion snakes, it will *still* be apportioned in two-acre sections, but that with no large, efficient farms left, you will have destroyed our ability to feed our cities, you will have left us without our primary source of foreign exchange, and you will have condemned Karimon to an aeon of subsistence farming? Once the land is divided, every family will own two or three acres—but families grow, while the land doesn't. Within two generations, those two-acre plots will become quarter-acre plots, and even the owners will not be able to live on what they produce. We have a system that works now; it would be catastrophic to change it."

"We have a system under which less than one percent of Karimon's population controls ninety percent of the planet's farmland," retorted Selabali. "Simple justice cries out for land reform."

"Does simple justice tell you how you're going to feed three billion Karimonis twenty years from now when the biggest farm in existence is three acres?" shot back Blake.

He's right, thought Paka, watching the debate in the comfort of his office. *I hate to admit it, but he's right. Mordecai Kiichana knew whereof he spoke.*

The debate continued for three days, with neither Blake nor Selabali yielding an inch.

Finally Paka announced that he himself would address the legislature, and the next morning, right after it was called into session, he walked over from the executive mansion and stood before the members.

"I have listened to the arguments in this chamber for the past three days," he began. "I do not doubt the sincerity of either side. One argues for justice, one for pragmatism."

He paused and looked into the holo cameras that were focused upon him. "We have had a century of pragmatism, and it has spawned nothing but hatred, mistrust, and revolution. It is time for justice!"

The snakes rose to their feet and applauded, and Paka left the podium and returned to his office.

That afternoon the vote was taken. Each of the three reapportionment plans received the votes of an overwhelming majority of the snakes. Each was vetoed by John Blake's party, and no action was taken.

"And to think," mused Paka in the privacy of his office as he watched the vote on his holo screen, "that I fought tooth and nail against this constitution."

That night there were riots in Athens, Mastaboni, Tentamp, and half a dozen smaller cities. Paka waited until noon the next day, then addressed his people and explained that while he was as outraged as they were, Karimon was a world of laws and that the laws must be obeyed.

"We have not given up," he told them. "As long as I am the Governor of Karimon, we will never cease our effort to make land available to all our people. We have lost only one battle; the war goes on."

He then went back to his private quarters at the executive mansion, sat down on a customized chair with a satisfied smile on his face, and thanked the god of his ancestors for the enemy of his blood, John Blake.

Fifty

During the next seven years, Paka's government was a whirlwind of activity.

Many of the changes were symbolic: Athens was renamed Talami, for the native village that had existed there before Violet Gardener built her city. Peterson Dam became Paka Dam, Fuentes National Park was rechristened Baski National Park, the Gardener Spaceport outside Mastaboni became the Moses Selabali Spaceport.

Some of the changes were cosmetic: the shantytowns that existed on the outskirts of every formerly human settlement were razed to the ground, all hotels and restaurants and public meeting places were required by law to have furniture fitted for snakes as well as men, and the major newstapes now issued editions in the Fani and Tulabete dialects as well as Terran.

A few of the changes were meaningful: Paka decreed mandatory free schooling for every Karimoni, upgraded the roads to the more remote villages in Faniland and promised to do the same in Tulabete Country as soon as the budget could accommodate it, and mandated free hospitals for any citizen who could not afford medical care.

The changes he *didn't* make were perhaps the most meaningful of all: Men continued to control most of the farmland, all of the mines, the tourist and travel industries, and constituted almost ninety percent of the merchant class. And while the people complained—and none complained more vociferously and publicly than Paka himself—Karimon was a world that worked. He had inherited a world that had been forced to become totally self-sufficient during the war and the embargo, and as long as he didn't dismantle the apparatus, it continued to function.

Still, there were problems. As the calendar edged toward the twelve-year deadline for the current constitution, more and more Men began emigrating to Goldstone and other nearby worlds. With very few exceptions the land was sold from one Man to another . . . and on those few occasions that the government was able to purchase one of the large farms, Paka made enormous political capital by turning it over to hundreds of land-starved snakes from the locality.

Finding enough teachers and doctors to run his schools and hospitals proved another problem. Men were uninterested in teaching or curing Karimonis, and there were not enough qualified Karimonis to supply even a fiftieth of Karimon's needs. So Paka depleted his tiny treasury still further by financing the education of the best and the brightest of his race on the worlds of the Republic. The return on his investment was less than he had anticipated, as fully half of them elected to remain off-planet, where they found greater economic opportunities.

The biggest problem of all, strangely enough, came not from Men, but from Moses Selabali. The Tulabete leader had taken to criticizing Paka at every opportunity for dragging his feet on the true reforms that were needed: land distribution and government ownership of the mining and manufacturing sectors.

Paka ignored him for as long as he could, and when even some Fani began calling for more action, he called an

executive session of the legislature, created the office of Associate Governor, and offered it to Selabali, who accepted.

If he thought that becoming a member of the executive branch would put an end to Selabali's sniping, he was mistaken, for now Selabali stated his case not only publicly but in every cabinet meeting, every state dinner, every function at which he served as Paka's stand-in.

When the polls showed that Selabali was picking up support, Paka took to the airwaves and publicly accused Selabali of trying to undermine the government. Stopping just short of accusing him of treason, he removed him from office and then, by a bare majority of two votes—Blake and the rest of the Men abstained, since this was strictly a Karimoni affair, and Blake had long since figured out who his real ally was—he abolished the office of Associate Governor a mere seven months after creating it.

Selabali, who now held no government position, having resigned from the legislature when he joined the executive branch, went back home to Tulabete Country, where, in Mastaboni and elsewhere, he continued condemning Paka for refusing to take action and began calling for his removal from office.

Paka responded by issuing an order for Selabali's arrest and marched his army into Mastaboni to search for him. The Tulabete refused to give him up, and an overeager officer ordered his men to fire into the crowd.

The result was seventy-three dead Tulabete and riots in every city in Tulabete Country. Paka sent in more soldiers to quell the riots, and ordered them to fire only in self-defense. They defended themselves 3,241 times in the first week, and suddenly guns that had been secreted away after the war were brought out, oiled, polished, and used against the Karimon army.

When the dust had cleared some two months later, more than sixty thousand Tulabete were dead, three villages had

been razed to the ground, and rumors abounded that Moses Selabali had fled the planet. Some reports had him hiding on Flowergarden, others on Goldstone, a few had him arguing for Paka's removal in the highest chambers of Deluros VIII.

Shortly thereafter, Blake requested a meeting with Paka, who granted it.

"Things have changed," noted Blake upon being ushered into Paka's office.

"This office is no longer occupied by a Man," replied Paka. "Therefore it no longer requires human furnishings. I can send for a human chair if you wish."

"No, I'll make do on one of these things," said Blake, sitting on the edge of a chair that had been created expressly for Karimonis.

"Well, Mr. Blake?" said Paka.

"I'll get right to the point," said Blake. "You've made a bloody mess of things, and if you're not careful, you're going to have a civil war on your hands."

"My government will not allow armed disturbances by Men *or* Karimonis," said Paka firmly. "The Tulabete must be—" he searched for the proper word "—*pacified.*"

"If that's your official story, fine," said Blake. "But you know and I know and most of Selabali's followers know that the Tulabete weren't armed until after your army started using them for target practice."

"They are armed now, and that is all that matters."

"And if you wipe out another fifty thousand Selabali voters before they are disarmed, you won't weep bitter tears over it, will you?" said Blake with a grin.

"You may not say such things to the Governor of Karimon!" exploded Paka.

"Even if they're true?"

"I could have you thrown into jail for your conduct!"

"True," agreed Blake. "But then you'd still be facing a civil war. I'm here to give you a way out, but if I can't speak

frankly, I might as well leave and let your government go straight to hell."

He made as if to stand up, and Paka held up a hand.

"Speak," he said.

"That's more like it," said Blake. He lit a cigar and leaned forward on his chair. "You need two things, Mr. Paka," he continued. "You need support from someone other than the Fani, and you need a meaningful gesture of conciliation for the Tulabete. I am prepared to supply you with both."

"Just like that?"

"Just like that."

"There is a price, I assume."

Blake smiled. "There is always a price, Mr. Paka."

"Let me hear your proposal and your fee, and I will give you my decision," said Paka.

"Fair enough," agreed Blake. He took a long puff on his cigar and was delighted to see Paka's nostrils wrinkle in distaste. "As I said, you need support from someone other than your own tribe. My party will support your actions against the Tulabete and will endorse your candidacy for reelection next year." Blake paused to see Paka's reaction, but the Fani's face was an emotionless mask. "You also need to make a major gesture to the Tulabete. We will cede the government ten square miles of farmland south of Mastaboni at fifty percent of market price, which you can then turn over to however many million Tulabete want it as a gesture of good will."

"And the price?" asked Paka.

"As I said, fifty percent of market value."

"Do not be obtuse, Mr. Blake," said Paka. "The price?"

"The current constitution has only five years to go before it's replaced by one of your own devising," replied Blake. "At that time, I expect that not a single Man will ever again sit in your legislature." He stared into Paka's orange cat's-eyes. "You must promise me never to enforce a program of

land redistribution for as long as you hold office. That's my price."

"And if I refuse?"

"You won't refuse, because you know that it's in the best interests of Karimon."

Paka lowered his head in thought, his long tongue flicking out absently. Finally he looked up at his visitor.

"I agree to your proposition," he said. "But I must add a condition of my own."

"What is it?"

"News of this agreement could come back to haunt me politically," said Paka. "It must remain secret. If I find out that you have told anyone else, I will feel free to disregard it."

"How can I enforce it if only you and I know about it?"

"Because, as you say, I know that land redistribution is not in the best interests of Karimon," replied Paka.

It was Blake's turn to consider the offer. Finally he nodded his head.

"Governor Paka," he said, "you've got yourself a deal."

He extended his hand. Paka stared at it for a moment, then forced himself to reach out and take it.

Fifty-one

Thomas Paka won reelection easily, though not by the overwhelming majority he achieved in the first election. The Tulabete supported Moses Selabali, whose name appeared on the ballot although he himself was still in exile deep within the Republic, but the election went peacefully.

A good politician rewards his supporters, and Paka, over the years, had become an excellent politician. As the damage from the war had been repaired and the manufacturing and mining sectors had regained their former strength, more money poured into the treasury. It was never quite enough, but Paka spent what there was on the Fani. Those hospitals and schools that could be staffed were placed in Faniland, the newly paved roads led to Fani villages, the government was staffed by Fani appointees. Men could take care of themselves, and Paka took care of the rest of his followers.

Within a year Tulabete Country was once again seething with unrest. A series of dams on the Punda River had cut their water supply, their requests for public works were denied, their schools were inadequate, their medical facili-

ties almost nonexistent. The Moses Selabali Spaceport was not upgraded, and the newer, heavier ships that were now in operation landed at the Paka Spaceport in Talami, which meant that their passengers tended to spend their money in Faniland rather than Tulabete Country.

Still, Paka knew just how far he could push the Tulabete before they required another gesture, and when the time came he declared amnesty for Moses Selabali and publicly invited him to rejoin the government, offering him any position he wanted short of Minister of Defense or the Governorship itself. Selabali, who felt he could do more for his people by making peace with Paka and working within the government than by continuing to oppose it from light-years away, agreed, and accepted the post of Minister of Public Works, and Paka allowed him to siphon just enough public monies away from Faniland to keep the Tulabete, if not satisfied, then at least hopeful.

As for the Men, they continued to emigrate, though at a lesser rate, as John Blake constantly stated his faith in the fairness of Paka's government and his willingness to live out his life on Karimon. And, since he was every bit as skilled a politician as Paka, and he was fighting a holding action, he urged his fellow Men to begin placing qualified Karimonis in positions of authority in their various enterprises.

"If we don't do it ourselves," he explained to various associates, "sooner or later Tom Paka is going to be forced to make us do it. He's walking a narrow enough tightrope as it is, and if he gives in to one demand, they're going to figure out that eventually he'll have to give in to all of them."

Within a year Karimonis had been assimilated into middle-management positions in the mining industry, the manufacturing sector, the huge farms, even the tourist and safari industries. More schools were built, and for the first time there was widespread optimism that Thomas Paka's

government might well turn Karimon into the planet its populace hoped it might become.

It was one of the very few times John Blake had misread the political climate on his world, for with the problems of employment and education on the road to resolution, the inhabitants turned once again to their major grievance: the land itself.

Fifty-two

Thomas Paka sat, alone and isolated, in his huge office. He had ordered the computer to turn the windows opaque, for he had no desire to see the protesters and picketers marching across the street in Independence Park.

He had ordered the army to disperse them last week, but after six Fani were killed, he recanted and allowed the marchers to congregate as long as they didn't precipitate any violence.

Sitting on his broad chrome desk was a printout of the private poll he had commissioned. His approval rating was twelve percent in Tulabete Country, eighteen percent in Rakko Country, and only thirty percent in his own Faniland. There was no mechanism for a recall election, but Moses Selabali, who had resigned from his position ten months ago and had once again been elected to the legislature, was proposing a constitutional amendment that would make such a recall possible.

All because of that damned farmland.

The old constitution had expired last month, a vote to extend it had been overwhelmingly defeated—not a single Karimoni had voted for it—and now that John Blake and

his fellow Men had lost their power, there was no legal reason why a land-reform bill should not pass unanimously.

How could he address his people and tell them that they would destroy the land, that once it was divided into a billion tiny plots it could never be put back again, that within two decades of such a redistribution famine would be the order of the day? He would be impeached before he was finished explaining his position.

He wished that there was somebody he could talk to. His wife, perhaps, or his old friend Mordecai Kiichana. But his wife had died during the war, and Kiichana had been deposed and killed some eight years ago.

John Blake? Blake would listen, might even sympathize, but could offer no advice. All he would do was remind Paka of the deal they had made so many years ago—and Paka didn't need reminding. He needed someone to tell him how to honor the agreement without losing his job.

He called up his library on the computer and began trying to find legal reasons to stall, to put off the one thing everyone wanted him to do and the one thing that he knew would bring his planet back to the primitive conditions that had existed in the days of the fabled Jalanopi. He could ask Cartography to survey the entire world and recommend the most practical way of subdividing it . . . but Karimon was an independent world, and Cartography had no legal rights there. And even if he invited them, he was postponing the reapportionment by no more than half a year.

He could announce that land reform would begin in Rakko Country. There were very few human farmers there, and the government could afford to buy them out at market value. But the Fani and the Tulabete would never be willing to wait in line for their land, and the debate over where to begin could take months.

Months. As opposed to centuries of famine and poverty.

He could put the planet under martial law, but he'd need some pretext, some exterior threat. If it was the Canphorites, the Republic would be there to protect their interests within a day. If it was the Republic, there would be a pogrom directed at the Men whose farms and expertise he was trying to save for Karimon. If he claimed that the enemy lay within, sooner or later he would have to produce it, and then he'd be back to where he was now.

It was getting very precarious, this tightrope of his. Finally he closed his eyes, leaned back on his chair, and found himself longing for the days of his youth, when he lived and fished beside the broad Karimona River, when he wanted nothing more than the feel of the sun on his back and soft grass beneath his feet, and when all problems seemed capable of solution.

Fifty-three

Thomas Paka was still wrestling with his conscience, his doubts, and his devils three days later when word reached him that John Blake had suffered a massive stroke and died before he could be taken to a hospital.

Paka attended the funeral, the only Karimoni, other than his bodyguards, to do so.

As he was driven back to the executive mansion, he felt more alone than he ever had in his life. As long as Blake was alive, he had a personal as well as a moral reason not to allow a land-redistribution bill. With Blake gone, there was no one to release the details of their secret agreement should he break it.

The next week Moses Selabali introduced legislation to purchase eighty percent of the existing farmland for the purpose of breaking it up into three-acre tracts for "the dispossessed Karimonis who have waited patiently for their elected government to redress the imbalance and give them what is rightfully theirs."

A Fani politician suggested that the purchase be enlarged to ninety percent of the farmland under cultivation. The remaining ten percent, not surprisingly, was owned by

Fani and Tulabete politicians. The amendment passed overwhelmingly.

Paka sent word from the executive mansion that he could not sign the bill into law when the treasury was unable to pay for the land, that passing a bill the government could not possibly enforce would cause a constitutional crisis.

Selabali took the floor and proposed that the government set the price for the land—that whatever they chose to pay would perforce constitute fair market value.

Paka waited another day, and then sent the question to the legislature: what if a human farmer was offered more money by someone else—for example, an off-world conglomerate? How could the government refuse to allow a landowner to accept the highest offer?

The legislature wrestled with the problem for another day and concluded that they would condemn all the land in question, thereby taking it off the market, and then pay whatever price they chose.

Fools, thought Paka, when he had received their answer. *Have they never looked at Alpha Bednares II, or any of the other worlds that followed this course of action? I hate Men as much as any of them, and with more cause—but can't anyone but me see that we* need *them?*

He activated his holoscreen and watched the various newstapes. Tulabete and Fani, Rakko and Pangi were shown dancing in the streets of their cities and villages at the news that the land they so hungered for would finally be theirs.

The scene changed to a statue of Paka himself, not a quarter mile distant in the center of Independence Park. Some fifteen or twenty Fani were camped out in front of it. When asked why, their leader responded that they planned to tear it down should Thomas Paka reject the land-reform bill.

"Ah, Karimon, Karimon," whispered Paka in the silence

of his office. "I have done so much for you, and I can do so much more, if you would just let me. Is that so much to ask—that you let me continue doing what I do best, rather than turn the planet over to Selabali and his group of Tulabete incompetents? They're going to send this world straight to hell whether I remain Governor or not; at least as Governor I can slow its descent."

The next morning he walked into his office and signed the bill into law.

Epilogue

Thomas Paka was elected to a third term.

Within five years only four hundred Men remained on Karimon; more than three hundred of them were missionaries.

Within seven years the Baski and Pundi Pools National Parks were subdivided into two-acre farm plots to satisfy the land-starved populace, and the tourist and safari businesses sought out other worlds.

Within eight years Karimon was importing more than half its food.

Within ten years Karimon's per capita income had decreased by forty percent.

Within twelve years most of the mines had been shut down due to obsolete and malfunctioning equipment.

Within thirteen years, famine had decimated the Rakko.

The government did what little it could, and promised that better times were coming.

Fifteen years after Paka signed the Land Reform Act, the generators that supplied power to Mastaboni broke down. No one on the planet was capable of repairing them.

That winter they chopped down Jalanopi's tree for firewood.